Strategic Management Theory

An Integrated Approach

Charles W. L. Hill
University of Washington

Gareth R. Jones
Texas A&M University

Houghton Mifflin Company

Boston   **New York**

D1449918

DR Pluenh
4450

To my wife, Alexandra Hill, for her ever increasing support and affection
Charles W. L. Hill

For Nicholas and Julia and Morgan and Nia
Gareth R. Jones

Editor-in-Chief: George T. Hoffman
Associate Sponsoring Editor: Susan M. Kahn
Senior Project Editor: Rachel D'Angelo Wimberly
Editorial Assistant: May Jawdat
Senior Production/Design Coordinator: Jennifer Meyer Dare
Senior Manufacturing Coordinator: Marie Barnes
Marketing Manager: Steven W. Mikels
Marketing Associate: Lisa Boden

Cover image and design: © Ron Chapple/Getty Images

Printed in the U.S.A.

Library of Congress Control Number: 2002109474

ISBN: 0-618-31819-4

2 3 4 5 6 7 8 9 — DOW — 07 06 05 04 03

Contents

PART II   The Nature of Competitive Advantage

3   Internal Analysis: Distinctive Competencies, Competitive Advantage, and Profitability   74

4   Building Competitive Advantage Through Functional-Level Strategy   109

PART III   **Strategies**

5   Building Competitive Advantage Through Business-Level Strategy   149

6 Competitive Strategy and the Industry Environment   188

7 Strategy in High-Technology Industries   224

8 Strategy in the Global Environment

PART IV   Implementing Strategy

11 Corporate Performance, Governance, and Business Ethics   365

12 Implementing Strategy in Companies That Compete in a Single Industry   402

13 Implementing Strategy in Companies That Compete Across Industries and Countries   446

Appendix: Analyzing a Case Study and Writing a Case Study Analysis　　C1

Preface

In its fifth edition, *Strategic Management: An Integrated Approach* was the most widely used strategic management textbook on the market. In every edition we have attracted new users who share with us the concern for currency in text and examples to ensure that cutting edge issues and theories in strategic management are addressed. This revision of *Strategic Management Theory* was fairly significant. The first edition of this book was written in the late 1980s. Although we have always endeavored to keep the book as up-to-date as possible, we felt that the structure of the book, and some of the key themes, still reflected strategic thinking as it was then and not as it is today. To make sure that the book was absolutely current in its content and coverage of material, we decided to embark upon a significant rewrite. The objective of the rewrite was to maintain all that was good about prior editions, while adding new material to the text when appropriate, and deleting materials that most professors now ignore. We believe that the result is a book that is much more focused on the realities of strategy and competitive advantage in the 2000s than any other textbook on the market, and is closely aligned with the needs of today's professors and students.

Comprehensive and Up-To-Date Coverage

The overall organization of this edition, as noted in Figure 1.3 on page 9, reflects that of previous editions and is designed so that the concepts build upon one another, with early chapters providing a strong foundation for later ones. Though the overall organization remains familiar, there have been significant changes in some of the chapters, and new chapters have been added to reflect current thinking in the field of strategic management.

Changes in Organization of the Book

- Chapter 7, **"Strategy in High-Technology Industries"** is new. This chapter was added to strengthen the book's coverage of strategy in markets driven by rapid technological change.

- Chapter 11, **"Corporate Performance, Governance, and Business Ethics"** is new. This chapter was added to strengthen coverage of material on business ethics and corporate governance in light of numerous examples of unethical behavior by corporate managers, the failure of corporate governance mechanisms such as the board of directors to check unethical behavior, and the negative impact of such failures on corporate performance. For example, unethical behavior at WorldCom and Enron was unchecked by the boards of those companies, and contributed to the poor performance and bankruptcy of both enterprises in 2002.

- The material that appeared in Chapter 2 of the fifth edition, "Stakeholders and the Corporate Mission" has been merged into other chapters where appropriate. Material on mission and goals has been moved into Chapter 1, "The Strategic Management Process." Material on stakeholders, business ethics, and corporate governance has been moved to the new Chapter 11 where it has received expanded treatment.

- Chapters 11–14 in the fifth edition have been compressed into two chapters in the sixth edition, Chapters 12 and 13. Chapter 12 covers implementation issues that are relevant for firms that compete in a single industry including organizational structure, strategic control, and culture. It also addresses implementation issues of functional and generic business-level strategies, along with restructuring and reengineering. Chapter 13 provides information about implementation issues for firms competing in multiple businesses, and it specifically focuses on implementing global strategies and the impact of information technology on strategy implementation.

Major Content Changes Within Chapters

■ In Chapter 1 there is a new section added on **performance and competitive advantage** to drive home the point that strategy is about attaining a sustainable competitive advantage.

■ In Chapter 3 there is a new section on **analyzing sources of competitive advantage and profitability.** This section explains in detail how strategic choice impacts the profitability of a company as measured by the return on invested capital. This section shows how an analysis of financial statements can reveal the financial impact of major differences in strategic choices. It also explains how strategic managers must think through the impact of their decisions on the financial position of the company.

■ In Chapter 5 a new section has been added on **business strategy and game theory.** This section shows how managers can make better strategic choices by drawing on principles derived from game theory.

■ In Chapter 6 the section on **strategy in embryonic and growth industries** has been substantially revised to add more material, particularly on how the nature of competition changes as industries pass through different growth stages and how this impacts the choice of strategy. This section looks at why many companies that are successful in embryonic industries fail to cross the chasm that separates an embryonic industry from a growth industry.

■ Chapter 7 is new to this edition. The chapter looks at the importance of technological standards in industries, the nature of "network economics," and strategies for winning "format wars" between companies that are promoting different, and incompatible, technical standards. Also discussed are the cost structure of high-technology firms and its strategic implications, strategies for managing intellectual property rights, and strategies for capturing a first-mover advantage. The chapter closes with a review of the strategic implications of technological paradigm shifts for both new entrants and incumbent firms in an industry.

■ Chapter 9 contains a new section on **horizontal integration.** This section looks at why companies in the same industry acquire or merge with each other and the strategic implications of this. The chapter also contains an expanded treatment of strategic outsourcing and looks at how companies can outsource activities to attain a competitive advantage.

■ Chapter 11 is a new chapter that looks at **corporate performance, governance, and business ethics.** The chapter explains how poor corporate performance can be caused by a combination of poor corporate governance systems and unethical behavior. The chapter reviews the strategic importance of managing stakeholders, putting strong corporate governance mechanisms in place, and making ethical decisions. Agency theory is used to explain failures of corporate governance and poor managerial ethics. The chapter draws heavily on recent examples of corporate fraud to illustrate the main points. The opening case features Enron, and discussions of recently discovered fraud/unethical behavior at WorldCom, Tyco, and Computer Associates are contained within the chapter.

Throughout the revision, we have been careful to preserve the *balanced and integrated* nature of our account of the strategic management process. Moreover, as we added new material, we deleted less current or less important concepts and information to ensure that students would concentrate on the core concepts and issues in the field. We have also paid close attention to retaining the book's readability.

Practicing Strategic Management: An Interactive Approach

We hope you are excited by the hands-on learning possibilities provided by the exercises/assignments in the end-of-chapter *Practicing Strategic Management* sections. Following the Chapter Summary and Discussion Questions, each chapter contains the following assignments/exercises:

■ *Small Group Exercise.* This short (20 minute) experiential exercise asks students to divide into groups and discuss a scenario concerning some aspect of strategic management. For example, the scenario in Chapter 11 asks students to identify the stakeholders of their educational institution and evaluate how stakeholders' claims are being and should be met.

■ *Exploring the Web.* The Internet exercise requires students to explore a particular web site and answer chapter-related questions. For example, the Chapter 8 assignment is to go to the web site of IBM and analyze its strategy for competing in the global marketplace. This section also asks students to explore the Web for relevant sites of their own choosing and answer questions.

■ *Article File.* As in the last edition, this exercise requires students to search business magazines to identify a company that is facing a particular strategic management problem. For instance, students are asked to locate and research a company pursuing a low-cost or a differentiation strategy, and to describe this company's strategy, its advantages and disadvantages, and the core competencies required to pursue it. Students' presentations of their findings lead to lively class discussions.

■ *Strategic Management Project.* Students, in small groups, choose a company to study for the whole semester and then analyze the company using the series of questions provided at the end of every chapter. For example, students might select Ford Motor Co. and, using the series of chapter questions, collect information on Ford's top managers, mission, ethical position, domestic and global strategy and structure, and so on. Eventually, students would write a case study of their company and present it to the class at the end of the semester. We treat the students' own projects as the major class assignment and their case presentations as the climax of the semester's learning experience.

■ *Closing case study.* A short closing case provides an opportunity for a short class discussion of a chapter-related theme.

In creating these exercises it is not our intention to suggest that they should *all* be used for *every* chapter. For example, over a semester an instructor might combine a group Strategic Management Project with five to six Article File assignments and five to six Exploring the Web exercises, while doing eight to ten Small Group Exercises in class.

We have found that our interactive approach to teaching strategic management appeals to students. It also greatly improves the quality of their learning experience. Our approach is more fully discussed in the *Instructor's Resource Manual.*

Teaching and Learning Aids

Taken together, the teaching and learning features of *Strategic Management* provide a package that is unsurpassed in its coverage and that supports the integrated approach that we have taken throughout the book.

For the Instructor

■ The **Instructor's Resource Manual** has been completely revised. For each chapter we provide a clearly focused *synopsis*, a list of *teaching objectives*, a *comprehensive lecture outline* including references to the transparencies, and *answers to discussion questions*. Each chapter opening case also has a corresponding *teaching note* to help guide class discussion. Also, the lecture outlines include summaries and teaching notes for the *Strategy in Action* boxes. Finally, the manual includes comments on the Practicing Strategic Management sections and suggested answers to the Closing Case Discussion Questions.

■ The **Test Bank** (in the *Instructor's Resource Manual*) has been revised and offers a set of comprehensive true/false and multiple-choice questions, and new essay questions for each chapter in the book. The mix of questions has been adjusted to provide fewer fact-based or simple memorization items and to provide more items that rely on synthesis or application. Also, more items now reflect real or hypothetical situations in organizations. Every question is keyed to the teaching objectives in the *Instructor's Resource Manual* and includes an answer and page reference to the textbook.

■ New for this edition is the **HM ClassPrep with HMTesting CD**. This instructor CD provides a variety of teaching resources in electronic format allowing for easy customization to meet specific instructional needs. Included in ClassPrep are **PowerPoint slides** for classroom presentation and Word files from the *Instructor's Resource Manual* that can be easily edited.

  HMTesting, the computerized version of the *Test Bank*, allows instructors to select, edit, and add questions, or generate randomly selected questions to produce a test master for easy duplication. Online Testing and Gradebook functions allow instructors to administer tests via their local area network or the World Wide Web, set up classes, record grades from tests or assignments, analyze grades, and produce class and individual statistics.

■ A package of **color transparencies** is available for adopters. These include nearly all the figures found in the chapters.

■ New **Videos** from CNN's award-winning "CEO Exchange" series are available to adopters. This series uses in-depth interviews with internationally recognized and respected CEOs to shed light on those managerial, organizational, and technological issues that are shaping the marketplace of ideas. In addition, this series explores the personal side of commerce, as industry icons discuss the values and experiences that shape and influence their business philosophies, strategies, and decisions. The programs that accompany this book are "Jack Welch: Icon of Leadership," "Creating New Categories, Businesses, and Markets" (featuring Thomas Stemberg, chairman and CEO of Staples, and Carl Yankowski, former CEO of Palm, a market leader in hand-held computers), "The Built to Order Revolution" (featuring Michael Dell, chairman and CEO of Dell Computer Corporation, and Frederick Smith, chairman, president, and CEO of FedEx Corporation), and "Innovators of Silicon Valley" (featuring Scott McNealy, chairman and CEO of Sun Microsystems, and Marc Andreessen, chairman of Loudcloud and co-founder of Netscape). Each program includes business students and faculty asking questions of the discussants. We are confident this video series will help highlight many issues of interest and can be used to spark class discussion.

■ An extensive **web site** contains many features to aid instructors including downloadable files from the *Instructor's Resource Manual*, the downloadable PowerPoint slides, the Video Guide, and sample syllabi. Additional materials on the student web site may also be of use to instructors.

For the Student

■ A student **web site** provides help for students as they make their way through the course. The web site features links to the companies highlighted in each chapter's boxes and opening and closing cases, links to other sites of general interest while studying strategic management, the Exploring the Web exercises with any updates as necessary to account for the inevitable changes that occur to the relevant sites, ACE self-tests related to each chapter, and a glossary and flashcards of key terms.

■ The **Real Deal UpGrade CD-ROM** includes a glossary of key terms, chapter learning objectives, brief chapter outlines, chapter summaries, and quizzes to test understanding of the major concepts.

Acknowledgments

This book is the product of far more than two authors. We are grateful to George Hoffman, our editor-in-chief, and Steve Mikels, our marketing manager, for their help in promoting and developing the book and for providing us with timely feedback and information from professors and reviewers that have allowed us to shape the book to meet the needs of its intended market. We are also grateful to Susan Kahn, associate sponsoring editor, for ably coordinating the planning of our book and for managing the creation of the ancillary materials; and grateful to Rachel D'Angelo Wimberly, senior project editor, and May Jawdat, editorial assistant, for their adept handling of production. We also thank the departments of management at the University of Washington and Texas A&M University for providing the setting and atmosphere in which the book could be written, and the students of these universities who reacted to and provided input for many of our ideas. In addition, the following reviewers of this and earlier editions gave us valuable suggestions for improving the manuscript from its original version to its current form:

Ken Armstrong, *Anderson University*
Kunal Banerji, *West Virginia University*
Glenn Bassett, *University of Bridgeport*
Thomas H. Berliner, *The University of Texas at Dallas*
Richard G. Brandenburg, *University of Vermont*
Steven Braund, *University of Hull*
Philip Bromiley, *University of Minnesota*
Geoffrey Brooks, *Western Oregon State College*
Lowell Busenitz, *University of Houston*
Gene R. Conaster, *Golden State University*
Steven W. Congden, *University of Hartford*
Catherine M. Daily, *Ohio State University*
Robert DeFillippi, *Suffolk University Sawyer School of Management*
Helen Deresky, *SUNY–Plattsburgh*
Gerald E. Evans, *The University of Montana*
John Fahy, *Trinity College, Dublin*
Patricia Feltes, *Southwest Missouri State University*
Mark Fiegener, *Oregon State University*
Isaac Fox, *Washington State University*
Craig Galbraith, *University of North Carolina at Wilmington*
Scott R. Gallagher, *Rutgers University*

Eliezer Geisler, *Northeastern Illinois University*
Gretchen Gemeinhardt, *University of Houston*
Lynn Godkin, *Lamar University*
Robert L. Goldberg, *Northeastern University*
Graham L. Hubbard, *University of Minnesota*
Tammy G. Hunt, *University of North Carolina at Wilmington*
James Gaius Ibe, *Morris College*
W. Grahm Irwin, *Miami University*
Jonathan L. Johnson, *University of Arkansas Walton College of Business Administration*
Marios Katsioloudes, *St. Joseph's University*
Robert Keating, *University of North Carolina at Wilmington*
Geoffrey King, *California State University–Fullerton*
Rico Lam, *University of Oregon*
Robert J. Litschert, *Virginia Polytechnic Institute and State University*
Franz T. Lohrke, *Louisiana State University*
Lance A. Masters, *California State University–San Bernardino*
Robert N. McGrath, *Embry-Riddle Aeronautical University*

Charles Mercer, *Drury College*
Van Miller, *University of Dayton*
Joanna Mulholland, *West Chester University of Pennsylvania*
Francine Newth, *Providence College*
Paul R. Reed, *Sam Houston State University*
Rhonda K. Reger, *Arizona State University*
Malika Richards, *Indiana University*
Ronald Sanchez, *University of Illinois*
Joseph A. Schenk, *University of Dayton*
Brian Shaffer, *University of Kentucky*
Pradip K. Shukla, *Chapman University*
Dennis L. Smart, *University of Nebraska at Omaha*
Barbara Spencer, *Clemson University*
Lawrence Steenberg, *University of Evansville*
Kim A. Stewart, *University of Denver*
Ted Takamura, *Warner Pacific College*
Bobby Vaught, *Southwest Missouri State*
Robert P. Vichas, *Florida Atlantic University*
Daniel L. White, *Drexel University*
Edgar L. Williams, Jr., *Norfolk State University*

Charles W. L. Hill
Gareth R. Jones

The Strategic Management Process

Opening Case

Dell Computer

Dell Computer is one of the most extraordinary success stories in business history. Started in 1984 by Michael Dell in his dorm room when he was an undergraduate student at the University of Texas in Austin, Dell has become the world's largest producer of computer systems. The company sells notebook and desktop computers, network servers, storage products, workstations, and peripheral hardware. In 2002, its sales are projected to exceed $30 billion. Dell is a highly profitable company and is the highest performer in its industry. The figure shows that its profit rate has exceeded that of all its competitors in every year since 1995. This superior performance persisted through 2001, a difficult and dismal year for the computer industry: slumping demand from corporate customers led to excess productive capacity and substantial price competition. In 2001, Dell's return on invested capital was 26 percent compared to 1.5 percent at Compaq, and zero at Apple and Gateway. How did Dell achieve its high performance? What explains the company's persistently high profitability?

The answer can be found in Dell's business model: selling directly to customers. Michael Dell reasoned that by cutting out wholesalers and retailers, he would obtain the profit they

Profitability in the Personal Computer Industry, 1995–2001

Data Source: Value Line Investment Survey

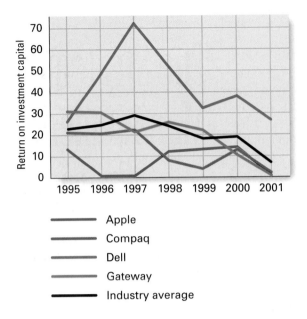

would otherwise receive and could give part of the profit back to customers in the form of lower prices. Initially, Dell did its direct selling through mailings and telephone contacts, but since the mid-1990s, most of its sales have been made through its web site. By 2001, 85 percent of Dell's sales were made through the Internet. Dell's sophisticated interactive web site allows customers to mix and match product features such as microprocessors, memory, monitors, internal hard drives, CD and DVD drives, keyboard and mouse format, and so on to customize their own computer system.

Another major reason for Dell's high performance is the way it manages its supply chain to minimize its cost structure, in particular, the costs of holding inventory yet with the ability build a computer to individual customer specifications within three days. Dell has about 200 suppliers, over half of them located outside the United States. Dell uses the Internet to feed real-time information about order flow to its suppliers so they have up-to-the-minute information about demand trends for the components they produce, along with volume expectations for the upcoming four to twelve weeks. Dell's suppliers use this information to adjust their own production schedules, manufacturing just enough components for Dell's needs and shipping them by the most appropriate mode so that they arrive just in time for production. This tight coordination is pushed back even further down the supply chain because Dell shares this information with its suppliers'

biggest suppliers. For example, Selectron builds motherboards for Dell that incorporate digital signal processing chips from Texas Instruments. To coordinate the supply chain, Dell passes information to both Texas Instruments and Selectron. Texas Instruments then adjusts its schedules to Selectron's needs, and Selectron adjusts its schedule to fit the order data it receives from Dell. All of this coordination results in lower costs along the supply chain.

Dell's ultimate goal is to drive all inventories out of the supply chain apart from those actually in transit between suppliers and Dell, effectively replacing inventory with information. Although it has not yet achieved this goal, it has succeeded in driving down inventory to the lowest level in the industry. Dell has about five days of inventory on hand, compared to thirty, forty-five, or even ninety days at competitors such as Compaq Computer and Gateway. This is a major source of competitive advantage in the computer industry, where component costs account for 75 percent of revenues and typically fall by 1 percent per week due to rapid obsolescence. Thus, lowering its cost structure by streamlining its inventory management systems is a critical reason for Dell's high profitability.

Sources: D. Hunter, "How Dell Keeps from Stumbling," *Business Week,* May 14, 2001, pp. 38–40; "Enter the Eco-System: From Supply Chain to Network," *Economist,* November 11, 2000; "Dell's Direct Initiative," *Country Monitor,* June 7, 2000, p. 5; Dell Computer Corporation 10K, 2001.

Overview

Why do some organizations succeed while others fail? Why has Dell Computer been able to do so well in the fiercely competitive personal computer industry, while others like Compaq, Gateway, and Apple have not had the same success in recent years? In the retail industry, what distinguishes successes such as Wal-Mart and Target from struggling rivals Sears and Kmart? In the market for database software, why have Oracle and Microsoft managed to build and retain strong market positions, while rivals such as Informix and Sybase have lost significant market share? In the airline industry, how is it that Southwest Airlines has managed to keep increasing its revenues and profits through both good times and bad, while rivals such as Delta and US Airways have struggled to avoid bankruptcy? How did Sony come to dominate the market for video games with its highly successful PlayStation, while former industry leader Sega saw its market share slump from 60 percent in the early 1990s to the low single digits by 2000, and finally pulled out of the market in 2001?

In this book, we argue that the strategies that an organization's managers pursue have a major impact on its performance relative to its peers. A **strategy** is an action that managers take to attain one or more of the organization's goals. For most, if not all organizations, an overriding goal is to achieve superior performance relative to rivals. If a company's strategy results in superior performance, it is said to have a *competitive advantage.* Dell's strategies produced superior performance from 1996 to 2001; Dell thus has had a competitive advantage over its rivals.

How did Dell attain this competitive advantage? In the early 1990s, Michael Dell hired a number of highly experienced managers from established companies such as IBM. Then Dell and these managers developed and pursued strategies that enabled the company to satisfy customers better than its competitors did while simultaneously giving it a cost structure that was the lowest in the industry. In 2001, Dell took advantage of its low cost structure to launch a price war in the personal computer industry. It took significant market share from its competitors while remaining profitable. In contrast, Dell's competitors saw their profitability slump, and some, like Gateway, had losses. (We will return to the example of Dell several times throughout this book in a *Running Case* that examines various aspects of Dell's strategy and performance.)

Much of strategic management is about identifying and describing the strategies that managers can pursue to attain superior performance and a competitive advantage for their organization. Many of these strategies are generic—that is, they apply to all organizations, large and small, manufacturing and service, and profit seeking and nonprofit. A central aim of this book is to give you a thorough understanding of the analytical techniques and skills necessary to identify and exploit strategies successfully. The first step toward achieving this objective is to explain in more detail what *superior performance* and *competitive advantage* mean. Then the nature of the **strategic management process**—the process by which managers choose a set of strategies for a company that will allow it to achieve superior performance—is described. By the end of this chapter, you will understand the processes managers use to choose strategies for their organization and have an appreciation for the strengths and weaknesses of these processes.

Superior Performance and Competitive Advantage

In the business world, superior performance is typically thought of in terms of one company's profitability relative to that of other companies in the same or a similar kind of business or industry. The **profitability** of a company can be measured by the return that it makes on the capital invested in the enterprise.[1] The return on invested capital that a company earns is defined as its profit over the capital invested in the firm (profit/capital invested). By *profit,* we mean before-tax profits. By *capital,* we mean the sum of money invested in the company, that is, stockholders' equity plus debt owed to creditors. This capital is used to buy the resources a company needs to produce and sell goods and services. A company that uses its resources efficiently makes a positive return on invested capital. The more efficient a company is, the higher are its profitability and return on invested capital.

Firm-Specific Performance and Profitability

A company's profitability—its return on invested capital—is determined by the strategies its managers adopt. For example, in the *Opening Case,* we saw that Michael Dell's direct selling strategy enabled his company to lower prices and increase its revenues over time. In addition, Dell's strategy for using the Web to manage its supply chain allowed it to lower costs by taking inventory out of its system. As a result, Dell has been more profitable than its competitors.

A company is said to have a **competitive advantage** over its rivals when its profitability is greater than the average profitability for all firms in its industry. The greater the extent to which a company's profitability exceeds the average profitability for its industry, the greater is its competitive advantage. A company is said to have a **sustained competitive advantage** when it is able to maintain above-average profitability for a number of years. Clearly, Dell Computer had a significant and sustained competitive advantage between 1996 and 2001.

Much of this book is devoted to examining the strategies that managers can use to gain and maintain a competitive advantage for their company, thereby enabling it to achieve above-average profitability over a sustained period of time. At the most basic level, strategy is concerned with understanding the relationship between *prices, customer demand, and cost structure* and manipulating these variables in a way that lead to higher profitability. It follows that to *think strategically* is to think about which actions to take to optimize prices, increase customer demand, and/or lower costs, and to do so in a manner that is consistent with boosting the *profitability* of the company. A company's **business model** is management's model of how the strategies they pursue will allow the company to gain a competitive advantage and achieve superior profitability. Business models are usually based on financial projections of the pricing structure, unit sales volume, revenues, cost structure, profit levels, and profitability that the company can attain if it successfully implements its strategies and meets its goals. Strategies are the actions that managers take to execute a business model. Dell's direct distribution business model, for example, is based on the central idea that prices for PCs can be lowered through bypassing distributors and selling directly to consumers. The business model also assumes that at lower prices, Dell will gain market share, increasing its revenues and allowing it to realize substantial scale economies and unit cost reductions that will make the company very profitable, even at lower price points. Dell's success in the PC industry is a testament to the fact that its business model is superior to the business model of rivals such as Gateway and Compaq.

Managers do not make strategic decisions in a vacuum. Strategic thinking and strategy making take place in a competitive arena where managers think not only about the strategies *their* firm is pursuing, but also about the strategies their *competitors* are pursuing and about how competitors might respond to any strategic initiative they decide to take. Firm performance and profitability are determined by the success of the strategies that its managers pursue relative to the strategies pursued by the managers of rival firms. The best-made plans and strategy will not be successful if they do not take into account what competitors are doing now and what they will do in the future.

Industry Structure and Profitability

A company's profitability is also determined by the characteristics of its industry. Different industries are characterized by different competitive conditions. In some, demand is growing rapidly, and in others it is contracting. Some might be beset by excess capacity and persistent price wars, and others by excess demand and rising prices. In some, technological change might be revolutionizing competition, and others might be characterized by a lack of technological change. In some industries, high profitability among incumbent firms might induce new firms to enter the industry, and these new entrants might depress prices and profits in the industry. In other industries, new entry might be difficult, and periods of high profitability might persist for a considerable time. Thus, the different competitive conditions prevailing in different industries might lead to different average profitability. The average profit rate might be higher in some industries and lower in other industries because competitive conditions vary from industry to industry.

Figure 1.1 shows the average return on invested capital earned by firms in several different industries between 1997 and 2001. The drug industry had a favorable competitive environment to operate in: demand for drugs was high, and competition was generally not based on price. Just the opposite was the case in the steel and air transport industries: both are extremely price competitive. In addition, the steel industry was characterized by declining demand, excess capacity, and price wars. Exactly how industries differ is discussed in detail in Chapter 2. For now, the important point to remember is that the profitability of a firm is determined by two main factors: its relative success in its industry and the overall performance of its industry relative to other industries.[2]

Performance in Nonprofit Enterprises

A final point concerns the concept of superior performance in the nonprofit sector. By definition, nonprofit enterprises such as government agencies, universities, and charities are not in "business" to make profits. Nevertheless, they are expected to use their resources efficiently and operate effectively, and their managers set goals to measure their performance. The performance goal for a business school might be to get its programs ranked among the best in the nation. The performance goal for a charity might be to prevent childhood illnesses in poor countries. The performance goal

FIGURE 1.1

Return on Invested Capital in Selected Industries, 1997–2001

Data Source: Value Line Investment Survey

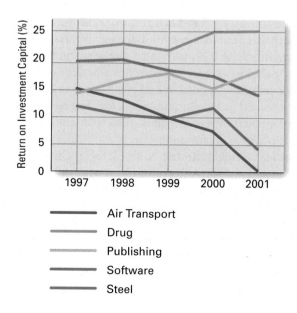

Air Transport

Drug

Publishing

Software

Steel

for a government agency might be to improve its services while not exceeding its budget. The managers of nonprofits need to map out strategies to attain these goals. They also need to understand that nonprofits compete with each other for scarce resources just as businesses do. For example, charities compete for scarce donations, and their managers must plan and develop strategies that lead to high performance and demonstrate a track record of meeting performance goals. A successful strategy gives potential donors a compelling message as to why they should contribute additional donations. Thus, planning and thinking strategically is as important for managers in the nonprofit sector as it is for managers in profit-seeking firms.

Strategic Managers

In most companies, there are two main types of managers: **general managers,** who bear responsibility for the overall performance of the company or for one of its major self-contained subunits or divisions, and **functional managers,** who are responsible for supervising a particular function, that is, a task, activity, or operation, like accounting, marketing, R&D, information technology, or materials management.

A company is a collection of functions or departments that work together to bring a particular product or service to the market. If a company provides several different kinds of products or services, it often duplicates these functions and creates a series of self-contained divisions (each of which contains its own set of functions) to manage each different product or service. The general managers of these divisions then become responsible for their particular product line. The overriding concern of general managers is for the health of the whole company or division under their direction; they are responsible for deciding how to create a competitive advantage and achieve high profitability with the resources and capital they have at their disposal. Figure 1.2 shows the organization of a **multidivisional company,** that is, a company that competes in several different businesses and has created a separate self-contained division to manage each of these. As you can see, there are three main levels of management: corporate, business, and functional. General managers are found at the first two of these levels, but their strategic roles differ depending on their sphere of responsibility.

Corporate-Level Managers

The corporate level of management consists of the chief executive officer (CEO), other senior executives, the board of directors, and corporate staff. These individuals occupy the apex of decision making within the organization. The CEO is the principal general manager. In consultation with other senior executives, the role of *corporate-level managers* is to oversee the development of strategies for the whole organization. This role includes defining the mission and goals of the organization, determining what businesses it should be in, allocating resources among the different businesses, formulating and implementing strategies that span individual businesses, and providing leadership for the organization.

Consider General Electric as an example. GE is active in a wide range of businesses, including lighting equipment, major appliances, motor and transportation equipment, turbine generators, construction and engineering services, industrial electronics, medical systems, aerospace, aircraft engines, and financial services. The main strategic responsibilities of its CEO, Jeffrey Immelt, are setting overall strategic objectives, allocating resources among the different business areas, deciding whether the firm should divest itself of any of its businesses, and determining whether it should acquire any new ones. In other words, it is up to Immelt to develop strategies

FIGURE 1.2

Levels of Strategic
Management

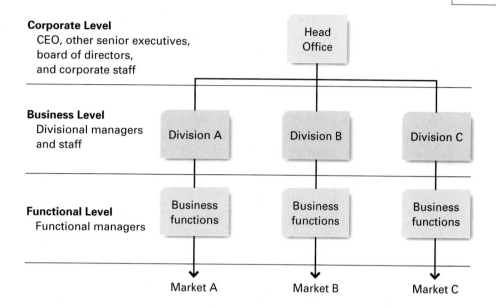

Corporate Level
CEO, other senior executives,
board of directors,
and corporate staff

Head Office

Business Level
Divisional managers
and staff

Division A   Division B   Division C

Functional Level
Functional managers

Business functions   Business functions   Business functions

Market A   Market B   Market C

that span individual businesses; his concern is with building and managing the corporate portfolio of businesses to maximize corporate profitability.

It is *not* his specific responsibility to develop strategies for competing in the individual business areas, such as financial services. The development of such strategies is the responsibility of the general managers in these different businesses or *business-level managers.* However, it is Immelt's responsibility to probe the strategic thinking of business-level managers to make sure that they are pursuing robust strategies that will contribute toward the maximization of GE's long-run profitability and to hold them into account for their performance.

Besides overseeing resource allocation and managing the divestment and acquisition processes, corporate-level managers provide a link between the people who oversee the strategic development of a firm and those who own it (the shareholders). Corporate-level managers, and particularly the CEO, can be viewed as the guardians of shareholder welfare. It is their responsibility to ensure that the corporate and business strategies that the company pursues are consistent with maximizing shareholder wealth. If they are not, then ultimately the CEO is likely to be called to account by the shareholders.

Business-Level Managers

A business unit is a self-contained division (with its own functions—for example, finance, purchasing, production, and marketing departments) that provides a product or service for a particular market. The principal general manager at the business level, or the business-level manager, is the head of the division. The strategic role of these managers is to translate the general statements of direction and intent that come from the corporate level into concrete strategies for individual businesses. Thus, whereas corporate-level general managers are concerned with strategies that span individual businesses, business-level general managers are concerned with strategies that are specific to a particular business. At GE, a major corporate goal is to be first or second in every business in which the corporation competes. Then the general managers in each division work out for their business the details of a strategy that is consistent with this objective.

Functional-Level Managers

Functional-level managers are responsible for the specific business functions or operations (human resources, purchasing, product development, customer service, and so on) that constitute a company or one of its divisions. Thus, a functional manager's sphere of responsibility is generally confined to *one* organizational activity, whereas general managers oversee the operation of a *whole* company or division. Although they are not responsible for the overall performance of the organization, functional managers nevertheless have a major strategic role: to develop functional strategies in their area that help fulfill the strategic objectives set by business- and corporate-level general managers.

In GE's aerospace business, for instance, manufacturing managers are responsible for developing manufacturing strategies consistent with the corporate objective of being first or second in that industry. Moreover, functional managers provide most of the information that makes it possible for business- and corporate-level general managers to formulate realistic and attainable strategies. Indeed, because they are closer to the customer than the typical general manager is, functional managers themselves may generate important ideas that subsequently may become major strategies for the company. Thus, it is important for general managers to listen closely to the ideas of their functional managers. An equally great responsibility for managers at the operational level is strategy implementation: the execution of corporate- and business-level plans.

Strategic Planning

A number of business writers have emphasized that strategy is the outcome of a formal planning process and that top management plays the most important role in this process.[3] Although this view has some basis in reality, it is not the whole story. As we shall see later in the chapter, valuable strategies often emerge from deep within the organization without prior planning. Nevertheless, a consideration of formal, rational planning is a useful starting point for our journey into the world of strategy. Accordingly, we consider what might be described as a typical formal strategic planning model.

A Model of the Strategic Planning Process

The formal strategic planning process has five main steps:

1. Select the corporate mission and major corporate goals.

2. Analyze the organization's external competitive environment to identify *opportunities* and *threats*.

3. Analyze the organization's internal operating environment to identify the organization's *strengths* and *weaknesses*.

4. Select strategies that build on the organization's strengths and correct its weaknesses in order to take advantage of external opportunities and counter external threats.

5. Implement the strategy.

The task of analyzing the organization's external and internal environment and then selecting an appropriate strategy is normally referred to as **strategy formulation.** In contrast, **strategy implementation** typically involves designing appropriate organizational structures and control systems to put the organization's chosen strategy into action.

These steps are illustrated in Figure 1.3 as the plan of this book. Each step illustrated in the figure constitutes a *sequential* step in the strategic planning process. At

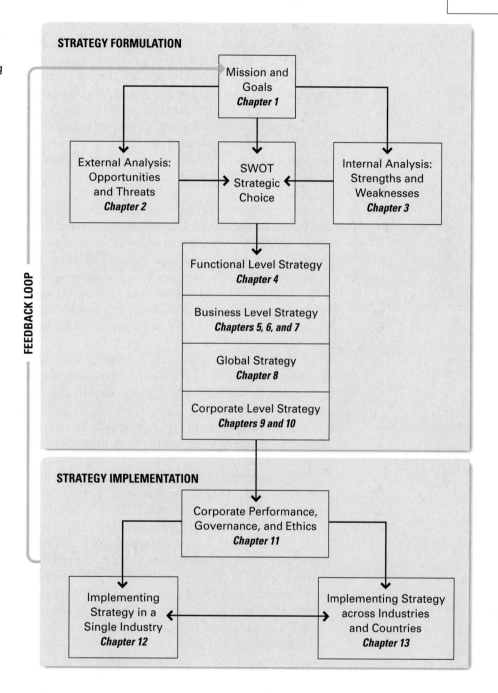

FIGURE 1.3

Main Components of
the Strategic Planning
Process

step 1, each round or cycle of the planning process begins with a statement of the corporate mission and major corporate goals. The mission statement is followed by the foundation of strategic thinking: external analysis, internal analysis, and strategic choice, that is, the analysis and choice of which strategies to pursue. The strategy-making process ends with the design of the organizational structure and control systems necessary to implement the organization's chosen strategy. In this chapter the issue of how to select a corporate mission and choose major goals is discussed in detail. Detailed discussion of the other parts of strategic planning is reserved for later chapters.

Some organizations go through a new cycle of the strategic planning process every year. This does not necessarily mean that managers choose a new strategy each year. In many instances, the result is simply to modify and reaffirm a strategy and structure already in place. The strategic plans generated by the planning process generally look out over a period of one to five years, with the plan being updated, or *rolled forward,* every year. In many organizations, the results of the annual strategic planning process are used as input into the budgetary process for the coming year so that strategic planning is used to shape resource allocation within the organization. Strategy in Action 1.1 looks at how Microsoft uses strategic planning to drive its resource allocation decisions.

Mission Statement

The first component of the strategic management process is crafting the organization's **mission statement:** a description or declaration of *why* a company is in operation, which provides the framework or context within which strategies are formulated. A mission statement typically has three main components: a statement of the *raison d'être* of a company or organization—its reason for existence—which is normally referred to as the *mission* or *vision* of the company; a statement of the key *values* or *guiding standards* that will drive and shape the actions and behavior of employees; and a statement of *major goals* or *objectives.*

The Mission or Vision.

The mission or vision is a formal declaration of what the company is trying to achieve over the medium to long term. (The terms *vision* and *mission* are often used interchangeably.) Its purpose is to provide a platform for thinking strategically. The Boeing Company states that its vision for Boeing in 2016 is "people working together as a global enterprise for aerospace leadership."[4] Microsoft's vision is "to empower people through great software, any time, any place, on any device."[5]

These statements declare some desired future state that a company's managers are striving to attain. Boeing wants to be a "global enterprise" in which people "work together" for "aerospace leadership." The statement is significant because Boeing currently does not see itself as a global enterprise (the vast majority of Boeing's assets are in the United States). Rather, it is striving to become one. Similarly, Microsoft wants its software to run on "any device," not just personal computers or servers, and at "any time, any place." This statement emphasizes the company's ambitions to have its software running on *all* computing devices, including videogame terminals, hand-held computers, smart phones, embedded processors, and set-top boxes. This vision statement, which has grown broader over time as new uses for software are being developed, has guided Microsoft's product diversification efforts because mission and vision statements *help set the context within which strategies are formulated.*

Formulating the Mission.

An important first step in the process of formulating a mission statement is to come up with a definition of the organization's business. Essentially, the definition answers these questions: "What is our business? What will it be? What should it be?"[6] The responses guide the formulation of a mission statement.

To answer the question, "What is our business?" Derek Abell, a prominent business scholar, has suggested that a company should define its business in terms of three dimensions: who is being satisfied (what customer groups), what is being satisfied (what customer needs), and how customers' needs are being satisfied (by what skills, knowledge, or distinctive competencies).[7] Figure 1.4 (on p. 12) illustrates these dimensions. Abell's approach stresses the need for a *customer-oriented* rather than

Strategy in Action   1.1

Strategic Planning at Microsoft

There is a widespread belief that strategic planning does not apply to high-tech industries. "You can't plan for the unpredictable," the argument goes, "and technology markets are characterized by rapid and unpredictable change, so why bother with planning?" Nevertheless, the world's most successful high-tech company, Microsoft, has had a formal strategic planning process in place for many years. The genesis of Microsoft's planning process goes back to 1994 when the rapidly growing company hired Bob Herbold from Procter & Gamble as Microsoft's chief operations officer. Herbold was hired to bring some operating discipline to Microsoft's fluid, freewheeling culture, but without undermining the entrepreneurial values and passion for innovation that had made Microsoft so successful. Microsoft's top managers, Bill Gates and Steve Balmer, had been growing increasingly frustrated with the lack of operating efficiency and coherence at Microsoft, and they wanted to do something about it.

One area that Herbold focused on was strategic planning, almost nonexistent when he arrived. What did exist was "a rat's nest of incompatible planning approaches used by the different units and divisions. . . . Bill [Gates] wanted a more formal planning process because, as he said, 'We have no sense of where we will be in two years except for the product guys saying they have great new products coming along.'" At the very least, Gates felt that Microsoft needed some sense of its financial outlook for the next year or two that it could communicate to investors.

Herbold, Gates, and Balmer understood that any assumptions underlying a plan could be made invalid by unforeseen changes in the business environment, and such changes were commonplace in the software industry. At the same time, they acknowledged that Microsoft had some fairly traditional businesses with established revenue streams, such as Microsoft Office and Windows, and the company needed a plan for the future to craft a strategy for these businesses, focus product development efforts, and allocate resources to these businesses. Moreover, the company needed to plan for the future of its newer businesses, such as MSN, the video game business (X-Box), and its hand-held computer business.

What has emerged at Microsoft is a three-year planning process that compares the subsequent performance of divisions and units against the strategies and goals outlined in the plan to determine future resource alloca-

tion. The planning process is built on a standard format that makes it easy to compare the performance data obtained from each of Microsoft's different businesses or divisions. Planning data include projections for market share, revenues, and profits three years into the future, as well as a statement of major strategies and goals. These projections are updated every year in a rolling plan because the industry changes so much.

Unit strategies are hashed out over the year in strategic planning review meetings between top managers (Gates and Balmer) and division managers. Typically, the unit managers develop strategies, and the top managers probe the strategic thinking of unit managers, asking them to justify their assumptions and ultimately approving, amending, or not approving the unit strategy. Unit strategies are also debated at regular strategy conferences, which Gates and Balmer normally attend.

The strategies that result from these processes are the product of an intense dialogue between top management and unit managers. Unit managers are held accountable for any commitments made in the plan. Thus, the plan not only drives resource allocation, it is also used as a control mechanism. Gates and Balmer determine the overall strategy of Microsoft in consultation with the board of directors, although many of the ideas for new businesses, new products, and acquisitions do not come from the top. Instead, they are proposed by employees within the units and approved if they survive scrutiny.

The planning process is formal, decentralized, and flexible. It is formal insofar as it is a regular process that uses standard information to help drive resource allocation for the coming year and holds managers accountable for their performance. It is decentralized insofar as unit managers propose many of the strategies that make up the plan, and those plans are accepted only after scrutiny by the top managers. It is flexible in that top managers do not see the plan as a straitjacket, but as a document that helps to map out where Microsoft may be going over the next few years. All managers recognize that the assumptions contained in the plan may be invalidated by unforeseen events, and they are committed to rapidly changing strategies if the need arises, as it has often in the past.

Sources: Interviews by Charles Hill. R. J. Herbold, "Inside Microsoft: Balancing Creativity and Discipline," *Harvard Business Review* (January 2002): 72–79.

FIGURE 1.4

Abell's Framework for
Defining the Business

Source: D. F. Abell, *Defining
the Business: The Starting
Point of Strategic Planning*
(Englewood Cliffs, Prentice-
Hall, 1980, page 7.

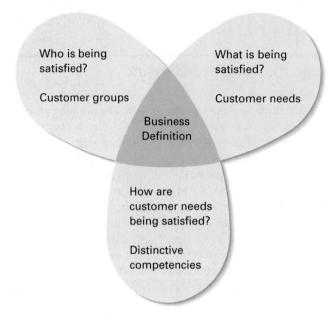

a *product-oriented* business definition. A product-oriented business definition focuses on the characteristics of the products sold and markets served, not on which kinds of customer needs the products are satisfying. Abell maintains that such an approach obscures the company's true mission because a product is only the physical manifestation of applying a particular skill to satisfy a particular need for a particular customer group. In practice, that need may be served in many different ways, and a broad customer-oriented business definition that identifies these ways can safeguard companies from being caught unaware by major shifts in demand. Indeed, by helping anticipate demand shifts, Abell's framework can assist companies in capitalizing on the changes in their environment. It can help answer the question, "What will our business be?" Recall that Microsoft's managers quickly realized they were not just offering software to satisfy only consumers' desktop computing needs; their mission was to offer software that would satisfy any form of customers' needs for complex information processing software for any kind of device.

The need to take a customer-oriented view of a company's business has often been ignored. History is littered with the wreckage of once-great corporations that did not define their business or defined it incorrectly so that ultimately they declined. Back in the 1950s and 1960s, there were many office equipment companies such as Smith Corona and Underwood that defined their businesses as being the production of typewriters. This product-oriented definition ignored the fact that they were really in the business of satisfying customers' information processing needs. Unfortunately for those companies, when a new technology came along that better served customer needs for information processing (computers), demand for typewriters plummeted. The last great typewriter company, Smith Corona, went bankrupt in 1996, a victim of the success of computer-based word processing technology.

In contrast, IBM correctly foresaw what its business would be. In the 1950s, IBM was a leader in the manufacture of typewriters and mechanical tabulating equipment using punch-card technology. However, unlike many of its competitors, IBM defined its business as *providing a means for information processing and storage,* rather than just supplying mechanical tabulating equipment and typewriters.[8] Given this definition, the company's subsequent moves into computers, software systems, office systems, and printers seem logical.

Values. The values of a company state how managers and employees should conduct themselves, how they should do business, and what kind of organization they should build to help a company achieve its mission. Insofar as they help drive and shape behavior within a company, values are commonly seen as the bedrock of a company's **organizational culture:** the set of values, norms, and standards that control how employees work to achieve an organization's mission and goals. An organization's culture is commonly seen as an important source of its competitive advantage.[9] (We discuss the issue of organization culture in depth in Chapter 12.) For example, Nucor Steel is one of the most productive and profitable steel firms in the world. Its competitive advantage is based in part on the extremely high productivity of its workforce, something, the company maintains, that is a direct result of its cultural values, which determine how it treats its employees. These values are as follow:

- "Management is obligated to manage Nucor in such a way that employees will have the opportunity to earn according to their productivity."
- "Employees should be able to feel confident that if they do their jobs properly, they will have a job tomorrow."
- "Employees have the right to be treated fairly and must believe that they will be."
- "Employees must have an avenue of appeal when they believe they are being treated unfairly."[10]

At Nucor, values emphasizing pay for performance, job security, and fair treatment for employees help to create an atmosphere within the company that leads to high employee productivity. In turn, this has helped to give Nucor one of the lowest cost structures in its industry, which helps to explain the company's profitability in a very price-competitive business.

Another example of how strong cultural values can help a company pursue its mission and create a competitive advantage is given in Table 1.1, which sets out the values emphasized at Texas Instruments. Note the explicit commitment to

TABLE 1.1

Values at Texas Instruments

Values	
TI has established shared values and beliefs that unite us as a company and guide our actions and decisions:	
Integrity	We respect and value people by treating others as we want to be treated. We are honest by representing ourselves and our intentions truthfully.
Innovation	We learn and create by understanding that impatience with the status quo drives business and personal growth. We act boldly by pioneering new business directions and opportunities.
Commitment	We take responsibility by being at our competitive best for TI. We commit to win by being personally dedicated to making TI a winner.

innovation, integrity and commitment. These value statements send a strong message to employees about the kind of company that Texas Instruments wants to become. If reinforced by top managers through rewards and exemplary behavior, such values help to shape behavior within the company and thus the culture of the organization. Organizational culture is an important source of competitive advantage, so statements such as these should be seen as more than just public relations exercises.

In one study of organizational values, researchers identified a set of values associated with high-performing organizations that help companies achieve superior financial performance through their impact on employee behavior.[11] These values included respect for the interests of key organizational **stakeholders**: individuals or groups that have an interest, claim, or stake in the company, in what it does, and in how well it performs.[12] They include stockholders, bondholders, employees, customers, the communities in which the company does business, and the general public. The study found that deep respect for the interests of customers, employees, suppliers, and shareholders was associated with high performance. The study also noted that the encouragement of leadership and entrepreneurial behavior by mid- and lower-level managers and a willingness to support change efforts within the organization contributed to high performance. Companies found to emphasize such values consistently throughout their organization include Hewlett-Packard, Wal-Mart, and PepsiCo. The same study identified the values of poorly performing companies—values that, as might be expected, are *not* articulated in company mission statements: (1) arrogance, particularly to ideas from outside the company; (2) a lack of respect for key stakeholders; and (3) a history of resisting change efforts and "punishing" mid- and lower-level managers who showed "too much leadership." General Motors was held up as an example of one such organization. According to the authors, a mid- or lower-level manager who showed too much leadership and initiative there was not promoted!

Major Goals and Objectives. Having stated a **mission** or vision that is founded on a customer-oriented definition of the company's business, and having articulated some key values, strategic managers can take the next step in the formulation of a mission statement: establishing major goals and objectives. A **goal** is a desired future state or objective that a company attempts to realize. In this context, the purpose of goals is to specify with precision what must be done if the company is to attain its mission or vision.

Well-constructed goals have four main characteristics:[13]

1. They are *precise and measurable*. Measurable goals give managers a yardstick or standard against which they can judge their performance.

2. They *address crucial issues*. To maintain focus, managers should select a limited number of major goals to assess the performance of the company. The goals that are selected should be crucial or important ones.

3. They are *challenging but realistic*. They give all employees an incentive to look for ways of improving the operations of an organization. If a goal is unrealistic in the challenges it poses, employees may give up; a goal that is too easy may fail to motivate managers and other employees.[14]

4. They *specify a time period* in which they should be achieved when that is appropriate. Time constraints tell employees that success requires a goal to be attained

by a given date, not after that date. Deadlines can inject a sense of urgency into goal attainment and act as a motivator. However, not all goals require time constraints.

Well-constructed goals also provide a means by which the performance of managers can be evaluated.

Profitability: Maximizing Returns to Shareholders. Although most profit-seeking organizations operate with a variety of goals, a central goal of most corporations is to maximize shareholder returns, which means increasing the long-run returns earned by shareholders from owning shares in the corporation. A company's shareholders are its legal owners and the providers of risk capital—the source of the capital resources that allows it to pursue its mission and business. Shareholders receive their rewards or returns from assuming this risk in two ways: from dividend payments and from capital appreciation in the market value of a share (that is, by increases in stock market prices). *A company can best maximize shareholder returns by pursuing strategies that maximize its own profitability.* In general, the more efficient a company is, the higher its profitability will be, and the better its future prospects look to shareholders, and the greater is its ability to pay dividends in the future. Thus, higher profitability leads to greater demand for a company's shares. Demand bids up the share price and leads to capital appreciation.

It is important that top managers do not make the mistake of overemphasizing current profitability to the detriment of long-term profitability, however.[15] The overzealous pursuit of current profitability to maximize short-term returns can encourage such misguided managerial actions as cutting expenditures judged to be nonessential in the short run—for instance, expenditures for research and development, marketing, and new capital investments. Although cutting current expenditure increases current profitability, the resulting underinvestment, lack of innovation, and diminished marketing can jeopardize long-run profitability. These expenditures are vital if a company is to pursue its long-term mission and sustain its competitive advantage and profitability over time. Despite these negative consequences, managers may make such decisions because the adverse effects of a short-run orientation may not materialize and become apparent to shareholders for several years or because they are under extreme pressure to hit short-term profitability goals.[16] It is also worth noting that pressures to maximize short-term profitability may result in managers' acting in an unethical manner. This apparently occurred at Enron Corporation, where profits were systematically inflated by managers who manipulated the firm's financial accounts in a manner that misrepresented the true performance of the firm to shareholders. (Chapter 11 provides a detailed discussion of the issues.)

To guard against short-run behavior, managers need to ensure that they adopt goals whose attainment will increase the long-run performance and competitiveness of their enterprise. Long-term goals are related to such issues as product development, customer satisfaction, and employee productivity, and they emphasize specific objectives or targets concerning such things as efficiency, product quality, and innovation. Recall from the opening case how Dell's managers are continually striving to reduce inventory costs on an ongoing basis. The thinking here is that to achieve long-run goals, companies like Dell have to make continual investments in plant, equipment, R&D, information technology, and people. Only by paying constant attention to their processes and operations can companies improve their customer satisfaction, productivity, product quality, and innovation over the long run. Managers' ability to make the right decisions gives their companies a competitive advantage and boosts *long-term* profitability. Both analysts and shareholders watch how well a company makes these decisions and attains its goals, and its stock price fluctuates according to the perception of how well a company has succeeded. Positive shareholder perceptions boost stock price and help maximize the returns to be had from holding a company's stock.

External Analysis
The second component of the strategic management process is an analysis of the organization's external operating environment. The essential purpose of the external analysis is to identify strategic *opportunities* and *threats* in the organization's operating environment that will affect how it pursues its mission. Three interrelated environments should be examined at this stage: the immediate or *industry environment* in which the organization operates, the country or *national environment*, and the wider socioeconomic or *macroenvironment*.

Analyzing the industry environment requires an assessment of the competitive structure of the organization's industry, including the competitive position of the specific or focal organization and its major rivals. It also requires analysis of the nature, stage, dynamics, and history of the industry. Because many markets are now global markets, analyzing the industry environment also means assessing the impact of globalization on competition within an industry. Analyzing the national environment requires an assessment of whether the national context, that is, the particular configuration of country-specific forces within which a company operates, facilitates the attainment of a competitive advantage in the *global* marketplace. If it does not, then the company might have to consider shifting a significant part of its operations to countries where the national context does facilitate the attainment of a competitive advantage. Analyzing the macroenvironment consists of examining macroeconomic, social, government, legal, international, and technological factors that may affect the organization.

Internal Analysis
Internal analysis, the third component of the strategic management process, serves to pinpoint the *strengths* and *weaknesses* of the organization. Such issues as identifying the quantity and quality of a company's resources and capabilities and ways of building unique skills and company-specific or distinctive competencies are considered here when we probe the sources of competitive advantage. Building and sustaining a competitive advantage requires a company to achieve superior efficiency, quality, innovation, and responsiveness to its customers. Company strengths lead to superior performance in these areas, whereas company weaknesses translate into inferior performance.

SWOT Analysis and the Business Model
The next component of strategic thinking requires the generation of a series of strategic alternatives, or choices of future strategies to pursue, given the company's internal strengths and weaknesses and its external opportunities and threats. The comparison of **s**trengths, **w**eaknesses, **o**pportunities, and **t**hreats is normally referred to as a **SWOT analysis**.[17] Its central purpose is to identify the strategies that will create a firm-specific business model that will best *align, fit,* or *match* a company's resources and capabilities to the demands of the environment in which it operates. Strategic managers compare and contrast the various alternative possible strategies against each other with respect to their ability to achieve major goals and superior profitability. Thinking strategically requires managers to identify the set of *strategies* that will create and sustain a competitive advantage:

- *Functional-level strategy,* directed at improving the effectiveness of operations within a company, such as manufacturing, marketing, materials management, product development, and customer service

- *Business-level strategy,* which encompasses the business's overall competitive theme, the way it positions itself in the marketplace to gain a competitive advantage, and the different positioning strategies that can be used in different industry settings—for example, *cost leadership, differentiation, focusing on a particular niche or segment of the industry,* or some *combination* of these

- *Global strategy,* addressing how to expand operations outside the home country to grow and prosper in a world where competitive advantage is determined at a global level

- *Corporate-level strategy,* which answers the primary questions: What business or businesses should we be in to maximize the long-run profitability of the organization, and how should we enter and increase our presence in these businesses to gain a competitive advantage?

SWOT analysis helps managers to craft a business model (or models) that will allow a company to gain a competitive advantage in its industry (or industries). Competitive advantage leads to increased profitability, and this maximizes a company's chances of surviving in the fast-changing, global competitive environment that characterizes most industries today.

Strategy Implementation

Having chosen a set of strategies to achieve a competitive advantage and increase performance, managers must put that strategy into action: strategy has to be implemented. In this book, the subject of strategy implementation is broken down into three main components: (1) corporate performance, governance, and ethics; (2) implementing strategy in a single industry; and (3) implementing strategy across industries and across countries.

The Feedback Loop

The feedback loop in Figure 1.3 indicates that strategic planning is ongoing; it *never* ends. Once a strategy has been implemented, its execution must be monitored to determine the extent to which strategic goals and objectives are actually being achieved and to what degree competitive advantage is being created and sustained. This information and knowledge pass back up to the corporate level through feedback loops and become the input for the next round of strategy formulation and implementation. Top managers can then decide whether to reaffirm existing corporate goals and strategies or suggest changes for the future. For example, a strategic objective may prove to be too optimistic, and so the next time more conservative objectives are set. Or feedback may reveal that strategic objectives were attainable but implementation was poor. In that case, the next round in strategic planning may concentrate more on implementation.

Strategy as an Emergent Process

The basic planning model suggests that an organization's strategies are the result of a plan, that the strategic planning process itself is rational and highly structured, and that the process is orchestrated by top management. But recently, several scholars have criticized the formal planning model for three main reasons: the unpredictability of the real world, the role that lower-level managers can play in the strategic management process, and the fact that many successful strategies are often the result of serendipity, not rational strategizing. They have advocated an alternative view of strategy making.[18]

Strategy Making in an Unpredictable World

Critics of formal planning systems argue that we live in a world in which uncertainty, complexity, and ambiguity dominate, and in which small chance events can have a large and unpredictable impact on outcomes.[19] In such circumstances, they claim, even the most carefully thought-out strategic plans are prone to being rendered useless by rapid and unforeseen change. In an unpredictable world, there is a premium on being able to respond quickly to changing circumstances, altering the strategies of the organization accordingly.

A dramatic example of this occurred in 1994 and 1995 when Microsoft CEO Bill Gates shifted the company strategy after the unanticipated emergence of the World Wide Web (see Strategy in Action 1.2). According to critics of formal systems, such a flexible approach to strategy making is not possible within the framework of a traditional strategic planning process, with its implicit assumption that an organization's strategies need to be reviewed only during the annual strategic planning exercise.

Strategy Making by Lower-Level Managers

Another criticism leveled at the rational planning model of strategy is that too much importance is attached to the role of top management.[20] An alternative view now gaining wide acceptance is that individual managers deep within an organization can and often do exert a profound influence over the evolution of strategy.[21] Writing with Robert Burgelman of Stanford University, Andy Grove, the former CEO of Intel, noted that many important strategic decisions at Intel were initiated not by top managers but by the autonomous action of midlevel managers deep within Intel.[22] These strategic decisions included the decision to exit an important market (the DRAM memory chip market) and develop a certain class of microprocessors (RISC-based microprocessors) in direct contrast to the stated strategy of Intel's top managers. We saw in Strategy in Action 1.2 how autonomous action by two young employees drove the evolution of Microsoft's strategy toward the Internet. Another famous example of autonomous action example is given in Strategy in Action 1.3.

Serendipity and Strategy

Business history is replete with examples of accidental events that help to push companies in new and profitable directions. What these examples suggest is that many successful strategies are not the result of well-thought-out plans but of serendipity, that is, stumbling across good things unexpectedly. One such example occurred at 3M during the 1960s. At that time, 3M was producing fluorocarbons for sale as coolant liquid in air-conditioning equipment. One day, a researcher working with fluorocarbons in a 3M lab spilled some of the liquid on her shoes. Later that day when she spilled coffee over her shoes, she watched with interest as the coffee formed into little beads of liquid and then ran off her shoes without leaving a stain. Reflecting on this phenomenon, she realized that a fluorocarbon-based liquid might turn out to be useful for protecting fabrics from liquid stains, and so the idea for Scotch Guard was born. Subsequently, Scotch Guard became one of 3M's most profitable products and took the company into the fabric protection business, an area it had never planned to participate in.[23]

Serendipitous discoveries are often the unintended consequence of scientific endeavor, but this is not always the case. In the mid-1980s, an employee at a small software company, WRQ, wanted to access the company's Hewlett Packard computer from home by turning his personal computer into an HP terminal. No software existed to perform this task, so he wrote a program for his personal use that enabled his personal computer to emulate a Hewlett Packard terminal. Some of his colleagues thought that other companies might want to buy this software, so WRQ tried to sell

Strategy in Action   1.2

A Strategic Shift at Microsoft

The Internet has been around since the 1970s, but prior to the early 1990s, it was a drab place, lacking the color, content, and richness of today's environment. What changed the Internet from a scientific tool to a consumer-driven media environment was the invention of hypertext markup language (HTML) and the related invention of a browser for displaying graphics-rich web pages based on HTML. The combination of HTML and browsers effectively created the World Wide Web (WWW). This was a development that was unforeseen.

A young programmer at the University of Illinois in 1993, Mark Andreesen, had developed the first browser, known as Mosaic. In 1994, he left Illinois and joined a start-up company, Netscape, which produced an improved browser, the Netscape Navigator, along with software that enabled organizations to create web pages and host them on computer servers. These developments led to a dramatic and unexpected growth in the number of people connecting to the Internet. In 1990, the Internet had 1 million users. By early 1995, the number had exceeded 80 million and was growing exponentially.

Prior to the emergence of the Web, Microsoft did have a strategy for exploiting the Internet, but it was one that emphasized set-top boxes, video on demand, interactive TV, and an online service, MSN, modeled after AOL and based on proprietary standards. In early 1994, Gates received emails from two young employees, Jay Allard and Steve Sinofsky, who argued that Microsoft's current strategy was misguided and ignored the rapidly emerging Web. In companies with a more hierarchical culture, such

action might have been ignored, but in Microsoft, which operates as a meritocracy in which good ideas trump hierarchical position, it produced a very different response. Gates convened a meeting of senior executives in April 1994, then wrote a memo to senior executives arguing that the Internet represented a sea change in computing and that Microsoft had to respond.

What ultimately emerged was a 180 degree shift in Microsoft's strategy. Interactive TV was placed on the backburner, and MSN was relaunched as a Web service based on HTML. Microsoft committed to developing its own browser technology and within a few months had issued Internet Explorer to compete with Netscape's Navigator (the underlying technology was gained by an acquisition). Microsoft licensed Java, a computer language designed to run programs on the Web, from a major competitor, Sun Microsystems. Internet protocols were built into Windows 95 and Windows NT, and Gates insisted that henceforth Microsoft's applications, such as the ubiquitous Office, embrace the WWW and have the ability to convert documents into an HTML format. The new strategy was given its final stamp on December 7, 1995, Pearl Harbor Day, when Gates gave a speech arguing that the Internet was now pervasive in everything Microsoft was doing. By then, Microsoft had been pursuing the new strategy for a year. In short, Microsoft quickly went from a proprietary standards approach to one that embraced the public standards on the WWW.

Source: Interviews by Charles Hill.

---

it as a product. To their surprise, they found that the demand was strong. Personal computers were starting to make their way onto the desks of many people in business, but these people still wanted to access data stored on mainframe computers and therefore needed software that would transform their personal computers into mainframe terminals. For the next fifteen years, the company generated sales of over $100 million from terminal emulation software.

The point is that serendipitous discoveries and events can open up all sorts of profitable avenues for a company. But some companies have missed out on profitable opportunities because serendipitous discoveries or events were inconsistent with their prior (planned) conception of what their strategy should be. In one of the classic examples of such myopia, a century ago the telegraph company Western Union turned down an opportunity to purchase the rights to an invention made by

Strategy in Action 1.3

The Genesis of Autonomous Action at 3M

In the 1920s, the Minnesota Mining and Manufacturing Company (3M) was a small manufacturer of sandpaper. Its best-selling product, wet-and-dry sandpaper, was introduced in 1921 and was sold primarily to automobile companies, which used it to sand auto bodies between paint coats and was valued for producing a smooth finish. A problem with wet and dry, however, was that the grit did not always stay bound to the sandpaper, and bits of grit that had detached from the paper could ruin an otherwise perfect paint job. To deal with this problem in the early 1920s, the CEO, a young William McKnight, hired 3M's first research scientist, Richard Drew. Drew himself was straight out of college; this was his first job. McKnight charged Drew with developing a stronger adhesive to bind the grit to paper backing better.

While experimenting with adhesives, Drew developed a weak adhesive that had an interesting quality: if placed on the back of a strip of paper and stuck to a surface, the strip of paper could be peeled off the surface it was adhered to without leaving any adhesive residue on that surface. This serendipitous discovery gave Drew an epiphany. He had been visiting auto body paint shops to see how 3M's sandpaper was used and noticed a problem with paint running. His epiphany was to cover the back of a strip of paper with his weak adhesive and use it as "masking tape" to cover parts of the auto body that were not to be painted. An excited Drew took his idea to McKnight and explained how masking tape might create an entirely new business for 3M. McKnight reminded Drew that he had been hired to fix a specific problem and pointedly suggested that he concentrate on doing that and not on dreaming up other business ideas.

Chastised, Drew went back to his lab but could not get the idea out of his mind, so he continued to work on it at night, long after everyone else had gone home. He

succeeded in perfecting the masking tape product and then went to visit several auto body shops to show them his innovation. He quickly received several commitments for orders. Drew then went to McKnight again. He told him that he had continued to work on the masking tape idea on his own time, had perfected the product, and got several customers interested in purchasing it. This time it was McKnight's turn to be chastised. Realizing that he had almost killed a good business idea, McKnight reversed his original position and gave Drew the go-ahead to pursue the idea.

Sticky tape subsequently became a huge business for 3M. Moreover, McKnight went on to become a long-serving CEO and then chairman of 3M's board until 1966. Drew became the chief science officer and also served until the 1960s. Together they helped build 3M and shaped its organization culture. One of the main principles of that culture came out of the original incident between Drew and McKnight: top management should "delegate responsibility and encourage men and women to exercise their initiative." According to McKnight, as business grows, "It becomes increasingly necessary to delegate responsibility and to encourage men and women to exercise their initiative. . . . Mistakes will be made. But if a person is essentially right, the mistakes he or she makes are not as serious in the long run as the mistakes management will make if it undertakes to tell those in authority exactly how they must do their jobs. . . . Management that is destructively critical when mistakes are made kills initiative. And it's essential that we have many people with initiative if we are to continue to grow." Based on their own experience, McKnight and Drew established a culture at 3M that encourages autonomous action.

Source: M. Dickson, "Back to the Future," *Financial Times,* 1994, May 30, 1994, p. 7. http://www.3m.com/profile/looking/mcknight.jhtml.

Alexander Graham Bell. The invention was the telephone, a technology that subsequently made the telegraph obsolete.

Intended and Emergent Strategies

Henry Mintzberg's model of strategy development provides a more encompassing view of what strategy actually is. According to this model, illustrated in Figure 1.5, a company's *realized strategy* is the product of whatever planned, **intended strategies,** are actually put into action *and* of any unplanned, or **emergent, strategies.** In

FIGURE 1.5

Emergent and
Deliberate Strategies

Source: Adapted from H.
Mintzberg and A. McGugh,
Administrative Science
Quarterly, Vol. 30. No 2, June
1985.

Mintzberg's view, emergent strategies are the unplanned responses to unforeseen circumstances. They often arise from autonomous action by individual managers deep within the organization or from serendipitous discoveries or events. They are *not* the product of formal top-down planning mechanisms.

Mintzberg maintains that emergent strategies are often successful and may be more appropriate than intended strategies. Richard Pascale has described how this was the case for the entry of Honda Motor Co. into the U.S. motorcycle market.[24] When a number of Honda executives arrived in Los Angeles from Japan in 1959 to establish a U.S. operation, their original aim (intended strategy) was to focus on selling 250-cc and 350-cc machines to confirmed motorcycle enthusiasts rather than 50-cc Honda Cubs, which were a big hit in Japan. Their instinct told them that the Honda 50s were not suitable for the U.S. market, where everything was bigger and more luxurious than in Japan.

However, sales of the 250-cc and 350-cc bikes were sluggish, and the bikes themselves were plagued by mechanical failure. It looked as if Honda's strategy was going to fail. At the same time, the Japanese executives who were using the Honda 50s to run errands around Los Angeles were attracting a lot of attention. One day they got a call from a Sears, Roebuck buyer who wanted to sell the 50-cc bikes to a broad market of Americans who were not necessarily already motorcycle enthusiasts. The Honda executives were hesitant to sell the small bikes for fear of alienating serious bikers, who might then associate Honda with "wimpy" machines. In the end, they were pushed into doing so by the failure of the 250-cc and 350-cc models.

Honda had stumbled onto a previously untouched market segment that was to prove huge: the average American who had never owned a motorbike. Honda had also found an untried channel of distribution: general retailers rather than specialty motorbike stores. By 1964, nearly one out of every two motorcycles sold in the United States was a Honda.

The conventional explanation of Honda's success is that the company redefined the U.S. motorcycle industry with a brilliantly conceived *intended* strategy. The fact was that Honda's intended strategy was a near disaster. The strategy that *emerged* did so not through planning but through unplanned action in response to unforeseen circumstances. Nevertheless, credit should be given to the Japanese management for recognizing the strength of the emergent strategy and for pursuing it with vigor.

The critical point demonstrated by the Honda example is that successful strategies can emerge within an organization without prior planning often in response to unforeseen circumstances. As Mintzberg has noted, strategies can take root virtually wherever people have the capacity to learn and the resources to support that capacity.

In practice, the strategies of most organizations are probably a combination of the intended (planned) and the emergent. The message for management is that it needs to recognize the process of emergence and to intervene when appropriate, killing off bad emergent strategies but nurturing potentially good ones.[25] To make such decisions, managers must be able to judge the worth of emergent strategies. *They must be able to think strategically.* Although emergent strategies arise from within the organization without prior planning—that is, without going through the steps illustrated in Figure 1.3 in a *sequential* fashion—top management still has to evaluate emergent strategies. Such evaluation involves comparing each emergent strategy with the organization's goals, external environmental opportunities and threats, and internal strengths and weaknesses. The objective is to assess whether the emergent strategy fits the organization's needs and capabilities. In addition, Mintzberg stresses that an organization's capability to produce emergent strategies is a function of the kind of corporate culture that the organization's structure and control systems foster. In other words, the different components of the strategic management process are just as important from the perspective of emergent strategies as they are from the perspective of intended strategies.

Strategic Planning in Practice

Despite these criticisms, research suggests that formal planning systems do help managers make better strategic decisions. A study that analyzed the results of twenty-six previously published studies came to the conclusion that on average, strategic planning has a positive impact on company performance.[26] For strategic planning to work, it is important that top-level managers plan not just in the context of the *current* competitive environment but also try to find the strategy that will best allow them to achieve a competitive advantage in the *future* competitive environment. To try to forecast what that future will look like, managers can use scenario planning techniques to plan for different possible futures. They can also involve operating managers in the planning process and seek to shape the future competitive environment by emphasizing strategic intent.

Scenario Planning

One reason that strategic planning may fail over the long run is that strategic managers, in their initial enthusiasm for planning techniques, may forget that the future is inherently unpredictable. Even the best-laid plans can fall apart if unforeseen contingencies occur, and that happens all the time in the real world. The recognition that uncertainty makes it difficult to forecast the future accurately led planners at Royal Dutch Shell to pioneer the *scenario approach* to planning.

In the scenario approach, managers are given a set of possible future scenarios for the development of competition in their industry. Some scenarios are optimistic and some pessimistic, and then teams of managers are asked to develop specific strategies to cope with each different scenario. A set of industry-specific indicators is chosen and used as signposts to track the development of their industry and identify the probability that any particular scenario is coming to pass. The idea is to get managers to understand the dynamic and complex nature of their environment, think through problems in a strategic fashion, and generate a range of strategic options that might be pursued under different circumstances.[27]

The scenario approach to planning has spread rapidly among large companies. According to one survey, over 50 percent of the Fortune 500 companies use some form of scenario planning methods.[28] Strategy in Action 1.4 examines how managers at one of these companies, Duke Energy, use a scenario approach.

Involving Functional Managers

A serious mistake that some companies have made in constructing their strategic planning process has been to treat planning as an exclusively top management responsibility. This *ivory tower* approach can result in strategic plans formulated in a

Strategy in Action   1.4

Scenario Planning at Duke Energy

Duke Energy in 2002 was one of the top ten energy generators in the United States, the second largest marketer of natural gas in the country, and the third largest marketer of power. It operates in an industry that has become significantly more complex and unpredictable over the last decade. Substantial deregulation has changed the competitive landscape. The rise of the Internet is changing the way in which power is bought and sold in the United States. New electronic markets for energy contracts have been created, and major producers and customers now routinely buy and sell power on a daily basis on a spot market. These changes are increasing the level of competition and potentially depressing prices for power. The rate of growth in energy consumption is also highly sensitive to underlying economic growth. Errors in predicting future growth rates can result in over- or underinvestment in future production capacity, leaving a generator such as Duke with too much capacity or too little. Moreover, the lead times for bringing new capacity on stream are long, and Duke has to make investment decisions now based on its projection of what demand and supply conditions will look like in five years.

To deal with these uncertainties, Duke Energy has adopted a scenario planning methodology for testing strategy. In 2000, managers were working with three future scenarios for the next five years: Economic Treadmill, which imagines U.S. economic growth slipping to 1 percent per year; Market.com, in which the Internet revolutionizes the buying and selling of electricity and natural gas; and Flawed Competition, which assumes continuing, uneven deregulation of the energy industry and a U.S. economic growth rate of over 3 percent.

Duke has generated twenty to twenty-three signposts for each scenario to indicate that a scenario might be coming to pass. In mid-2000, three of twenty signposts of the Economic Treadmill were flashing, eleven of twenty for Flawed Competition, and three of twenty-three for Market.com. Duke assumed from this analysis that Flawed Competition was the most likely scenario and that the United States would grow at about 3 percent per annum. Based on this scenario, Duke has begun to invest in additional production capacity, building thousands of megawatts of new-generation capacity and hundreds of miles of natural gas pipeline, connecting supply from the Rockies, Gulf Coast, and eastern Canada to markets in the West, Midwest, Florida, and New England. By 2004, Duke Energy will have added more than 26,000 megawatts of new-generation capacity, enough electricity to light 26 million homes. In addition, it is planning to build more than 1,300 miles of natural gas pipeline that can deliver nearly 3.5 billion cubic feet per day.

Managers at Duke have also considered what they would do strategically if the other scenarios emerged. This exercise has led them to take some strategic steps—hedging their bets—in case another scenario should emerge. For example, if the Market.com scenario emerges, it becomes very important to be able to acquire customers over the Internet. Recognizing this, Duke created an e-commerce unit to explore the business possibilities. If the Economic Treadmill scenario starts to emerge, Duke is prepared to scale back on its capacity expansion plans midstream so that it does not have too much capacity, a situation that would depress prices and profits.

Source: B. Wysocki, "Power Grid: Soft Landing or Hard," *Wall Street Journal,* July 7, 2000, p. A1 (http://www.duke-energy.com/decorp/content/AboutUs/deip9.asp?RBU=1).

vacuum by top managers who have little understanding or appreciation of current operating realities. Consequently, top managers may formulate strategies that do more harm than good. For example, when demographic data indicated that houses and families were shrinking, planners at GE's appliance group concluded that smaller appliances were the wave of the future. Because they had little contact with homebuilders and retailers, they did not realize that kitchens and bathrooms were the two rooms that were *not* shrinking. Nor did they appreciate that working women wanted big refrigerators to cut down on trips to the supermarket. GE ended up wasting a lot of time designing small appliances with limited demand.

The ivory tower concept of planning can also lead to tensions between corporate-, business-, and functional-level managers. The experience of GE's appliance group is again illuminating. Many of the corporate managers in the planning group were recruited from consulting firms or top-flight business schools. Many of the functional managers took this pattern of recruitment to mean that corporate managers did not think they were smart enough to think through strategic problems for themselves. They felt shut out of the decision-making process, which they believed to be unfairly constituted. Out of this perceived lack of procedural justice grew an us-versus-them mindset that quickly escalated into hostility. As a result, even when the planners were right, operating managers would not listen to them. For example, the planners correctly recognized the importance of the globalization of the appliance market and the emerging Japanese threat. However, operating managers, who then saw Sears Roebuck as the competition, paid them little heed.

Correcting the ivory tower approach to planning requires recognizing that successful strategic planning encompasses managers at *all* levels of the corporation. Much of the best planning can and should be done by functional managers who are closest to the facts. The role of corporate-level planners should be that of *facilitators* who help functional managers do the planning by setting the broad strategic goals of the organization and providing the resources required to identify the strategies that might be required to attain those goals.

It is not enough to involve lower-level managers in the strategic planning process, however; they also need to perceive that the decision-making process is fair, a concept that Chan Kim and Renee Mauborgne refer to as **procedural justice.**[29] If people perceive the decision-making process to be unjust, they are less likely to be committed to any resulting decisions and to cooperate voluntarily in activities designed to implement those decisions. Consequently, the strategy chosen might fail for lack of support among those who must implement it at the operating level.

Strategic Intent

The formal strategic planning model has been characterized as the *fit model* of strategy making. This is because it attempts to achieve a fit between the internal resources and capabilities of an organization and external opportunities and threats in the industry environment. Gary Hamel and C. K. Prahalad have criticized the fit model because it can lead to a mindset in which management focuses too much on the degree of fit between the *existing* resources of a company and *current* environmental opportunities, and not enough on building *new* resources and capabilities to create and exploit *future* opportunities.[30] Strategies formulated with only the present in mind, argue Prahalad and Hamel, tend to be more concerned with today's problems than with tomorrow's opportunities. As a result, companies that rely exclusively on the fit approach to strategy formulation are unlikely to be able to build and maintain a competitive advantage. This is particularly true in a dynamic competitive environment, where new competitors are continually arising and new ways of doing business are constantly being invented.

As Prahalad and Hamel note, again and again, companies using the fit approach have been surprised by the ascent of competitors that initially seemed to lack the resources and capabilities needed to make them a real threat. This happened to Xerox, which ignored the rise of Canon and Ricoh in the photocopier market until they had become serious global competitors; to General Motors, which initially overlooked the threat posed by Toyota and Honda in the 1970s; and to Caterpillar, which ignored the danger Komatsu posed to its heavy earthmoving business until it was almost too late to respond.

The secret of the success of companies like Toyota, Canon, and Komatsu, according to Prahalad and Hamel, is that they all had bold ambitions that outstripped their existing resources and capabilities. All wanted to achieve global leadership, and they set out to build the resources and capabilities that would enable them to attain this goal. Consequently, top management created an obsession with winning at all levels of the organization that they sustained over a ten- to twenty-year quest for global leadership. It is this obsession that Prahalad and Hamel refer to as **strategic intent.** They stress that strategic intent is more than simply unfettered ambition. It encompasses an active management process, which includes "focusing the organization's attention on the essence of winning; motivating people by communicating the value of the target; leaving room for individual and team contributions; sustaining enthusiasm by providing new operational definitions as circumstances change; and using intent consistently to guide resource allocations."[31]

Thus, underlying the concept of strategic intent is the notion that strategic planning should be based on setting ambitious goals that stretch a company and then finding ways to build the resources and capabilities necessary to attain those goals. As Prahalad and Hamel note, in practice the two approaches to strategy formulation are not mutually exclusive. All the components of the strategic planning process that we discussed earlier (see Figure 1.3) are important.

In addition, say Prahalad and Hamel, the strategic management process should begin with challenging goals, such as attaining global leadership, that stretch the organization. And throughout the process, the emphasis should be on finding ways (strategies) to develop the resources and capabilities necessary to achieve these goals rather than on exploiting *existing* strengths to take advantage of *existing* opportunities. The difference between strategic fit and strategic intent, therefore, may just be one of emphasis. Strategic intent is more internally focused and is concerned with building new resources and capabilities. Strategic fit focuses more on matching existing resources and capabilities to the external environment.

Strategic Leadership and Decision Making

Even the best-designed strategic planning systems will fail to produce the desired results if managers do not use the information at their disposal effectively. Consequently, it is important that strategic managers learn to make better use of the information they have and understand the reasons that sometimes they make poor decisions. One important way in which managers can make better use of their knowledge and information is to understand how to become an effective or strategic leader and to learn how to understand and manage their emotions during the course of decision making.[32]

Strategic Leadership and Emotional Intelligence

One of the key strategic roles of both general and functional managers is to use all their knowledge, energy, and enthusiasm to provide strategic leadership for their subordinates and develop a high-performing organization. **Strategic leadership** refers to a manager's ability to articulate a strategic vision for the company, or a part of the company, and to motivate others to buy into that vision. Several authors have identified a few key characteristics of good strategic leaders that do lead to high performance: (1) vision, eloquence, and consistency, (2) commitment, (3) being well informed, (4) willingness to delegate and empower, (5) astute use of power, and (6) emotional intelligence.[33]

Vision, Eloquence, and Consistency. One of the key tasks of leadership is to give an organization a sense of direction. Strong leaders seem to have a vision of where the organization should go, are eloquent enough to communicate this vision to others within the organization in terms that energize people, and consistently articulate their vision until it becomes part of the culture of the organization.[34] John F. Kennedy, Martin Luther King, Jr., and Margaret Thatcher have all been held up as examples of visionary leaders. Think of the impact of Kennedy's phrase, "Ask not what your country can do for you, ask what you can do for your country," and of King's "I have a dream" speech. Kennedy and Thatcher were also able to use their political office to push for governmental actions that were consistent with their vision, and King was able to pressure the government from outside to make changes in society. Strong business leaders include rivals Microsoft's Bill Gates and Sun Microsystems's Scott McNeally, Avon's Andrea Jung, and Jack Welch and Herb Kelleher, the former CEOs of General Electric and Southwest Airlines, respectively.

Commitment. Strong leaders demonstrate their commitment to their vision by actions and words, and they often lead by example. Consider Nucor's former CEO, Ken Iverson. Nucor is a very efficient steelmaker with perhaps the lowest cost structure in the steel industry. It has turned in thirty years of profitable performance in an industry where most other companies have lost money because of its relentless focus on cost minimization. In his tenure as CEO, Iverson set the example: he answered his own phone, employed only one secretary, drove an old car, flew coach class, and was proud of the fact that his base salary was the lowest in the Fortune 500 (Iverson made most of his money from performance-based pay bonuses). This commitment was a powerful signal to employees that Iverson was serious about doing everything possible to minimize costs. It earned him the respect of Nucor employees, which made them more willing to work hard. Although Iverson has retired, his legacy lives on in the cost-conscious organization culture that has been built at Nucor, and like all other great leaders, his impact will go beyond his tenure as a leader.

Being Well Informed. Effective strategic leaders develop a network of formal and informal sources who keep them well informed about what is going on within their company. Herb Kelleher at Southwest Airlines, for example, was able to find out a lot about the health of his company by dropping in unannounced on aircraft maintenance facilities and helping workers there to perform their tasks; McDonald's Ray Kroc and Wal-Mart's Sam Walton routinely dropped in unannounced to visit their restaurants and stores. Using informal and unconventional ways to gather information is wise because formal channels can be captured by special interests within the organization or by gatekeepers, managers who may misrepresent the true state of affairs within the company to the leader, such as may have happened at Enron (see Chapter 11). People like Kelleher who constantly interact with employees at all levels are better able to build informal information networks than leaders who closet themselves and never interact with lower-level employees.

Willingness to Delegate and Empower. High-performance leaders are skilled at delegation. They recognize that unless they learn how to delegate effectively, they can quickly become overloaded with responsibilities. They also recognize that empowering subordinates to make decisions is a good motivation tool. Delegating also makes sense when it results in decisions being made by those who must implement them. At the same time, astute leaders recognize that they need to maintain control over certain key decisions. Thus, although they will delegate many *important* decisions to lower-level employees, they will not delegate those that they judge to be of *critical importance* to the future success of the organization under their leadership.

The Astute Use of Power. In a now classic article on leadership, Edward Wrapp noted that effective leaders tend to be very astute in their use of power.[35] By this he meant three things. First, strategic leaders must play the power game with skill and attempt to build consensus for their ideas rather than use their authority to force ideas through; they act as members or democratic leaders of a coalition rather than as dictators. Second, good leaders often hesitate to commit themselves publicly to detailed strategic plans or precise objectives, since in all probability the emergence of unexpected contingencies will require adaptation. Thus, a successful leader might commit the organization to a particular vision, such as minimizing costs or boosting product quality, without stating precisely how or when this will be achieved. Good leaders often have precise private objectives and strategies that they would like to see the organization pursue. However, they recognize the futility of public commitment given the likelihood of change and the difficulties of implementation.

Third, Wrapp claimed that effective leaders possess the ability to push through programs in a piecemeal fashion. They recognize that on occasion, it may be futile to try to push total packages or strategic programs through an organization, since significant objections to at least part of such programs are likely to arise. Instead, the successful leader may be willing to take less than total acceptance in order to achieve modest progress toward a goal. The successful leader tries to push through ideas one piece at a time, so that they appear incidental to other ideas, though in fact they are part of a larger program or hidden agenda that moves the organization in the direction of the manager's objectives.

Jeffery Pfeffer has articulated a similar vision of the politically astute manager who gets things done in organizations by the intelligent use of power.[36] In Pfeffer's view, power comes from control over resources: budgets, capital, positions, information, and knowledge that is important to the organization. Politically astute managers use these resources to acquire another critical resource: critically placed allies who can help a manager attain preferred strategic objectives. Pfeffer stresses that one does not need to be a CEO to assemble power in an organization. Sometimes quite junior functional managers can build a surprisingly effective power base and use it to influence organizational outcomes.

Emotional Intelligence. Emotional intelligence is a term that Daniel Goldman coined to describe a bundle of psychological attributes that many strong and effective leaders exhibit:[37]

- Self-awareness—the ability to understand one's own moods, emotions, and drives, as well as their effect on others
- Self-regulation—the ability to control or redirect disruptive impulses or moods, that is, to think before acting
- Motivation—a passion for work that goes beyond money or status and a propensity to pursue goals with energy and persistence
- Empathy—understanding the feelings and viewpoints of subordinates, and taking those into account when making decisions
- Social skills—friendliness with a purpose

According to Goldman, leaders who possess these attributes—who exhibit a high degree of emotional intelligence—tend to be more effective than those who lack these attributes. Their self-awareness and self-regulation help to elicit the trust and confidence of subordinates. In Goldman's view, people respect leaders who, because they are self-aware, recognize their own limitations and because they are self-regulating consider decisions carefully. Goldman also argues that self-aware and self-regulating individuals tend to be more self-confident and therefore better able to cope with ambiguity and more open to change. A strong motivation exhibited in a passion for work can also be infectious, helping to persuade others to join together in pursuit of a common goal or organizational mission. Finally, strong empathy and social skills can help leaders earn the loyalty of subordinates. Empathetic and socially adept individuals tend to be skilled at managing disputes between managers, better able to find common ground and purpose among diverse constituencies, and better able to move people in a desired direction than leaders who lack these skills. In short, Goldman's arguments are that the psychological makeup of a leader matters.

Cognitive Biases and Strategic Decision Making

The rationality of human decision makers is bounded by our own cognitive capabilities.[38] We are not supercomputers, and it is difficult for us absorb and process large amounts of information effectively. As a result, when making decisions, we tend to fall back on certain rules of thumb, or heuristics, that help us to make sense out of a complex and uncertain world. However, sometimes they lead to severe and systematic errors in the decision-making process.[39] Systematic errors are those that appear time and time again. They seem to arise from a series of **cognitive biases** in the way that human decision makers process information and reach decisions. Because of cognitive biases, many managers end up making poor strategic decisions.

A number of biases have been verified repeatedly in laboratory settings, so we can be reasonably sure that they exist and that we are all prone to them.[40] The **prior hypothesis bias** refers to the fact that decision makers who have strong prior beliefs about the relationship between two variables tend to make decisions on the basis of these beliefs, even when presented with evidence that their beliefs are wrong. Moreover, they tend to seek and use information that is consistent with their prior beliefs, while ignoring information that contradicts these beliefs. To put this bias in a strategic context, it suggests that a CEO who has a strong prior belief that a certain strategy makes sense might continue to pursue that strategy, despite evidence that it is inappropriate or failing.

Another well-known cognitive bias, **escalating commitment,** occurs when decision makers, having already committed significant resources to a project, commit even more resources if they receive feedback that the project is failing.[41] This may be an irrational response; a more logical response would be to abandon the project and move on (that is, to cut your losses and run), rather than escalate commitment. Feelings of personal responsibility for a project apparently induce decision makers to stick with a project despite evidence that it is failing.

A third bias, **reasoning by analogy,** involves the use of simple analogies to make sense out of complex problems. The problem with this heuristic is that the analogy may not be valid. A fourth bias, **representativeness,** is rooted in the tendency to generalize from a small sample or even a single vivid anecdote. This bias violates the statistical law of large numbers, which says that it is inappropriate to generalize from a small sample, let alone from a single case. In many respects, the dot-com boom of the late 1990s was based on reasoning by analogy and representativeness. Prospective entrepreneurs saw some of the early dot-com companies such Amazon and Yahoo achieve rapid success, at least judged by some metrics. Reasoning by analogy from a very small sample, they assumed that any dot-com could achieve similar success. Many investors reached similar conclusions. The result was a massive wave of start-ups that jumped into the Internet space in an attempt to capitalize on the perceived opportunities. That the vast majority of these companies subsequently went bankrupt is testament to the fact that the analogy was wrong and the success of the small sample of early entrants was no guarantee that all dot-coms would succeed.

The final cognitive bias is referred to as the **illusion of control:** the tendency to overestimate one's ability to control events. General or top managers seem to be particularly prone to this bias: having risen to the top of an organization, they tend to be overconfident about their ability to succeed. According to Richard Roll, such overconfidence leads to what he has termed the **hubris hypothesis** of takeovers.[42] Roll argues that top managers are typically overconfident about their abilities to create value by acquiring another company. Hence, they end up making poor acquisition decisions, often paying far too much for the companies they acquire. Subsequently, servicing the debt taken on to finance such an acquisition makes it all but impossible to make money from the acquisition.

Groupthink and Strategic Decisions

Because most strategic decisions are made by groups, the group context within which decisions are made is clearly an important variable in determining whether cognitive biases will operate to adversely affect the strategic decision-making processes.

The psychologist Irvin Janis has argued that many groups are characterized by a process known as groupthink and as a result make poor strategic decisions.[43] **Groupthink** occurs when a group of decision makers embarks on a course of action without questioning underlying assumptions. Typically, a group coalesces around a person or policy. It ignores or filters out information that can be used to question the policy and develops after-the-fact rationalizations for its decision. Commitment to mission or goals becomes based on an emotional rather than an objective assessment of the "correct" course of action. The consequences can be poor decisions.

This phenomenon may explain, at least in part, why companies often make poor strategic decisions in spite of sophisticated strategic management. Janis traced many historical fiascoes to defective policymaking by government leaders who received social support from their in-group of advisers. For example, he suggested that President John F. Kennedy's inner circle suffered from groupthink when the members of this group supported the decision to launch the Bay of Pigs invasion of Cuba in 1961, even though available information showed that it would be an unsuccessful venture and would damage U.S. relations with other countries. Janis has observed that groupthink-dominated groups are characterized by strong pressures toward uniformity, which make their members avoid raising controversial issues, questioning weak arguments, or calling a halt to soft-headed thinking.

Techniques for Improving Decision Making

The existence of cognitive biases and groupthink raises the issue of how to bring critical information to bear on the decision mechanism so that a company's strategic decisions are realistic and based on thorough evaluation. Two techniques known to enhance strategic thinking and counteract groupthink and cognitive biases are devil's advocacy and dialectic inquiry (see Figure 1.6).[44] **Devil's advocacy** requires the generation of both a plan and a critical analysis of the plan. One member of the decision-making group acts as the devil's advocate, bringing out all the reasons that might make the proposal unacceptable. In this way, decision makers can become aware of the possible perils of recommended courses of action.

FIGURE 1.6

Processes for Improving Decision Making

Devil's Advocacy

Expert plan

↓

Devil's advocate criticizes

↓

Final plan

Dialectic Inquiry

Expert plan 1 (thesis)   Expert plan 2 (antithesis)

↓

Debate (synthesis)

↓

Final plan

Dialectic inquiry is more complex, for it requires the generation of a plan (a thesis) and a counter-plan (an antithesis) that reflect *plausible but conflicting* courses of action.[45] Strategic managers listen to a debate between advocates of the plan and counter-plan and then make a judgment of which plan will lead to the higher performance. The purpose of the debate is to reveal problems with definitions, recommended courses of action, and assumptions of both plans. As a result of this exercise, strategic managers are able to form a new and more encompassing conceptualization of the problem, which becomes the final plan (a synthesis). Dialectic inquiry can promote thinking strategically.

Summary of Chapter

1. A strategy is an action that a company takes to attain one or more of its goals.
2. The profitability of a company can be measured by the return that it makes on the capital invested in the enterprise. Profitability is determined by the strategies the company adopts.
3. A company has a competitive advantage over its rivals when it is more profitable than the average for all firms in its industry. It has a sustained competitive advantage when it is able to maintain an above-average profitability over a number of years.
4. General managers are responsible for the overall performance of the organization or for one of its major self-contained divisions. Their overriding strategic concern is for the health of the total organization under their direction.

5. Functional managers are responsible for a particular business function or operation. Although they lack general management responsibilities, they play a very important strategic role.
6. Formal strategic planning models stress that an organization's strategy is the outcome of a rational planning process.
7. The major components of the strategic management process are defining the mission and major goals of the organization; analyzing the external and internal environments of the organization; choosing a business model and strategies that align or fit an organization's strengths and weaknesses with external environmental opportunities and threats; and adopting organizational structures and control systems to implement the organization's chosen strategy.
8. A revision of the concept suggests that strategy can emerge from deep within an organization in the

absence of formal plans as lower-level managers respond to unpredicted situations.

9. Strategic planning often fails because executives do not plan for uncertainty and because ivory tower planners lose touch with operating realities.

10. The fit approach to strategic planning has been criticized for focusing too much on the degree of fit between existing resources and current opportunities, and not enough on building new resources and capabilities to create and exploit future opportunities.

11. Strategic intent refers to an obsession with achieving an objective that stretches the company and requires it to build new resources and capabilities.

12. Good leaders of the strategy-making process have a number of key attributes: vision, eloquence, and consistency; commitment; being well informed; a willingness to delegate and empower; political astuteness; and emotional intelligence.

13. In spite of systematic planning, companies may adopt poor strategies if their decision-making processes are vulnerable to groupthink and if individual cognitive biases are allowed to intrude into the decision-making process.

14. Devil's advocacy and dialectic inquiry are techniques for enhancing the effectiveness of strategic decision making.

Discussion Questions

1. What do we mean by *strategy?*

2. What do you think are the sources of sustained superior profitability?

3. What are the strengths of formal strategic planning? What are its weaknesses?

4. **Discuss the accuracy of this statement:** Formal strategic planning systems are irrelevant for firms competing in high-technology industries where the pace of change is so rapid that plans are routinely made obsolete by unforeseen events.

5. Evaluate President George W. Bush against the leadership characteristics discussed in the text. On the basis of this comparison, do you think that President Bush is a good strategic leader?

Practicing Strategic Management

SMALL-GROUP EXERCISE: DESIGNING A PLANNING SYSTEM

Break up into groups of three to five people each. Appoint one group member as a spokesperson for the group, who will communicate your findings to the class when called on to do so by the instructor.

You are a group of senior managers working for a fast-growing computer software company. Your product allows users to play interactive role-playing games over the Internet. In the past three years, your company has gone from being a start-up enterprise with 10 employees and no revenues to a company with 250 employees and revenues of $60 million. It has been growing so rapidly that you have not had time to create a strategic plan, but now your board of directors is telling you that they want to see a plan, and they want it to drive decision making and resource allocation at the company. They want you to design a planning process that will have the following attributes:

1. It will be democratic, involving as many key employees as possible in the process.

2. It will help to build a sense of shared vision within the company about how to continue to grow rapidly.

3. It will lead to the generation of three to five key strategies for the company.

4. It will drive the formulation of detailed action plans, and these plans will be subsequently linked to the company's annual operating budget.

Design a planning process to present to your board of directors. Think carefully about who should be included in this process. Be sure to outline the strengths and weaknesses of the approach you choose, and be prepared to justify why your approach might be superior to alternative approaches.

ARTICLE FILE 1

At the end of every chapter in this book is an article file task. The task requires you to search newspapers or magazines in the library for an example of a real company that satisfies the task question or issue.

Your first article file task is to find an example of a company that has recently changed its strategy. Identify whether this change was the outcome of a formal planning process or whether it was an emergent response to unforeseen events occurring in the company's environment.

STRATEGIC MANAGEMENT PROJECT: MODULE 1

To give you practical insight into the strategic management process, we provide a series of strategic modules; one is at the end of every chapter in this book. Each module asks you to collect and analyze information relating to the material discussed in that chapter. By completing these strategic modules, you will gain a clearer idea of the overall strategic management process.

The first step in this project is to pick a company to study. We recommend that you focus on the same company throughout the book. Remember also that we will be asking you for information about the corporate and international strategy of your company, as well as its structure. We strongly recommend that you pick a company for which such information is likely to be available.

There are two approaches that can be used to select a company to study, and your instructor will tell you which one to follow. The first approach is to pick a well-known company that has a lot of information written about it. For example, large publicly held companies such as IBM, Microsoft, and Southwest Airlines are routinely covered in the business and financial press. By going to the library at your university, you should be able to track down a great deal of information on such companies. Many libraries now have comprehensive web-based electronic data search facilities such as *ABI/Inform, The Wall Street Journal Index,* the *F&S Index,* and the *Nexis-Lexis* databases. These enable you to identify any article that has been written in the business press on the company of your choice within the past few years. A number of nonelectronic data sources are also available and useful. For example, *F&S Predicasts* publishes an annual list of articles relating to major companies that appeared in the national and international business press. *S&P Industry Surveys* is also a great source for basic industry data, and *Value Line Ratings and Reports* contain good summaries of a firm's financial position and future prospects. Collect full financial information on the company that you pick. This can be accessed from web-based electronic databases such as the Edgar database, which archives all forms that publicly quoted companies have to file with the Securities and Exchange Commission (SEC); for example, 10-K filings can be accessed from the SEC's Edgar database. Most SEC forms for public companies can now be accessed from Internet-based financial sites, such as Yahoo's finance site (**http://finance.yahoo.com/**).

A second approach is to pick a smaller company in your city or town to study. Although small companies are not routinely covered in the national business press, they may be covered in the local press. More important, this approach can work well if the management of the company will agree to talk to you at length about the strategy and structure of the company. If you happen to know somebody in such a company or if you have worked there at some point, this approach can be very worthwhile. However, we *do not* recommend this approach unless you can get a *substantial* amount of guaranteed access to the company of your choice. If in doubt, ask your instructor before making a decision. The key issue is to make sure that you have access to enough interesting information to complete a detailed and comprehensive analysis.

Your assignment for Module 1 is to choose a company to study and to obtain enough information about it to carry out the following instructions and answer the questions:

1. Give a short account of the history of the company, and trace the evolution of its strategy. Try to determine whether the strategic evolution of your company is the product of intended strategies, emergent strategies, or some combination of the two.

2. Identify the mission and major goals of the company.

3. Do a preliminary analysis of the internal strengths and weaknesses of the company and the opportunities and threats that it faces in its environment. On the basis of this analysis, identify the strategies that you think the company should pursue. (You will need to perform a much more detailed analysis later in the book.)

4. Who is the CEO of the company? Evaluate the CEO's leadership capabilities.

EXPLORING THE WEB
Visiting 3M

Go to the web site of 3M (**http://www.3m.com**) and visit the section that describes its history (**http://www.3m.com/profile/looking/index.jhtml**). Using the information contained here, map out the evolution of strategy at 3M from its establishment to the present day. To what degree do you think that this evolution was the result of detailed long-term strategic planning, and to what degree was it the result of unplanned actions taken in response to unpredictable circumstances?

General Task: Search the Web for a company site with sufficient information to map out the evolution of that company's strategy over a significant period of time. What drove this evolution? To what degree was it the result of detailed long-term strategic planning, and to what degree the result of unplanned actions taken in response to unpredictable circumstances?

Closing Case

The Evolution of Strategy at Yahoo

In 1993, Jerry Yang and David Filo were two graduate engineering students at Stanford University. Instead of writing their dissertations (which they probably should have been), the two were spending a lot of time surfing the Web and building lists of their favorite sites. On a whim, they decided to post their list on the Web, which they dubbed "Jerry's Guide to the World Wide Web." Almost by accident, they had created one of the first web directories and in the process had solved a pressing need: how to find things on the Web. In 1994, they changed the name of the directory to Yahoo (**http://www.yahoo.com**), which is supposed to stand for "Yet Another Hierarchical Officious Oracle," although Filo and Yang insist they selected the name because they considered themselves yahoos.

By late 1994, Yahoo was drawing over 100,000 people a day. The directory had outgrown the limited capacity of the Stanford site, and Yahoo was borrowing server space from nearby Netscape. Yang and Filo had decided to put their graduate studies on hold while they turned their attention to building Yahoo into a business. One of their first employees, Srinija Srinivasan, or "ontological yahoo" as she became known within the company, refined and developed the classification scheme that has become the hallmark of Yahoo's web directory. Yang and Filo's business model was to derive revenues from renting advertising space on the pages of the fast-growing directory.

To develop the business, they needed capital to fund investments in servers, software development, and classification personnel. A solution came in the form of an investment from Sequoia Capital, a Silicon Valley venture capital firm. As part of the investment package, Sequoia required Yang and Filo to hire an experienced CEO. The man chosen for the job was Andrew Koogle, a forty-five-year-old engineer with fifteen years of experience in the management of high-technology firms, including a stint as president of InterMec, a Seattle-based manufacturer of bar code scanning equipment.

By mid-1996, Koogle was heading a publicly traded company that listed 200,000 web sites under 20,000 different categories and was being used by 800,000 people daily. This was just the beginning. In conjunction with Yang, Filo, and another "gray-haired" hire, chief operating officer Jeffrey Mallett, Koogle crafted a vision of Yahoo as a global media company whose principal asset would be a major Internet gateway, or portal, that would enable any-one to connect with anything or anybody. Koogle's ambition was to transform Yahoo's simple directory service into a conduit for bringing together buyers and sellers, thereby facilitating commercial transactions over the Web (e-commerce). In this vision, Yahoo would continue to generate revenues from the sale of advertising space on its directory pages, and it would also garner significant revenues from e-commerce transactions by taking a small slice of each transaction executed over its service. The service, Yahoo! Store (**http://store.yahoo.com**), enables businesses to quickly create, publish, and manage secure online stores to market and sell goods and services. After launching their store, merchants are included in searches on Yahoo! Shopping (**http://shopping.yahoo.com**), Yahoo's Internet shopping service.

To make this vision a reality, Yahoo had to become one of the most useful and well-known locations on the Web—in short, it had to become a mega-brand. A directory alone would not suffice, no matter how useful. In order to increase traffic, Yahoo began to add features that increased its appeal to users. One was to supplement the directory with compelling content. Another was to allow registered users to customize Yahoo pages to match their needs. For example, registered Yahoo users can customize a page in Yahoo's financial area so that they can track the value of their personal stock portfolio. The page provides links to message boards, where individual investors can discuss a company's prospects. Other links connect investors to valuable content pertaining to the companies in their stock portfolio, including news reports and commentary, research reports, detailed financial data, and each company's web site.

To build brand awareness, Yahoo spent heavily on advertising, using radio and television ads targeted at mainstream America. To expand the reach of the service, Yahoo embarked on a strategy of opening up Yahoo services around the world. It also began to work with content providers and merchants to build their online presence and, by extension, to increase the value of Yahoo's site to users who could access the content and merchants through Yahoo. Yahoo increased its value to advertisers by enabling them to target their advertising message to certain demographics better. For example, the online broker E*Trade advertises heavily on Yahoo's financial pages. Such targeted advertising increases the conversion rate or yield associated with advertisements.

By many measures, the results of this strategy were spectacular. In 2000, the company generated revenues of almost $900 million. By September 2001, Yahoo had more than 210 million unique users worldwide, up from 166 million in September 2000 and just 50 million in 1998. Traffic increased to a record 1.25 billion page views per day on average during September 2001, up from 167 million page views per day in December 1998. According to Nielsen//NetRatings, worldwide consumers spent an average of 147 minutes on the Yahoo network, up from 119 minutes in the previous quarter. Some 80 million active registered users logged onto one or more personalized Yahoo services during September 2001, up from 55 million in September 2000.

However, in the first nine months of 2001, sales slumped by 34 percent and the company registered a loss of $84 million versus a profit of $169 million in the previous period. The revenue and profit declines reflected slumping advertising revenues, which accounted for close to 80 percent of Yahoo's revenues in 2000. The problem, in the wake of a slowdown in business activity in the United States, had resulted in declining advertising revenues across the board. Moreover, many of the best advertisers on Yahoo had been other dot-com companies, and a large number of these had gone bankrupt in 2001.

In the wake of slumping revenues, CEO Koogle resigned and was replaced by Terry Semel, a former Warner Brothers executive. Semel's strategic goal for Yahoo was twofold: to reduce the company's dependence on advertising revenues and to increase the quality of advertising revenues by targeting well-established companies as opposed to dot-com enterprises. Semel's strategy for boosting nonadvertising revenues was to introduce a range of subscription-based value-added or premium services, such as online music that would be broadcast by the Net to a subscriber's computer or digital device. In addition, Semel wanted the company to push more aggressively into the co-marketing business, helping established companies to sell their merchandise on the Web, and taking a cut of their revenues.

Discussion Questions

1. To what extent was the evolution of strategy at Yahoo planned? To what extent was it an emergent response to unforeseen events?

2. Could Yahoo have done a better job of anticipating the slowdown in advertising revenue that occurred in 2000–2001 and positioning itself for that slowdown? How? What might it have done differently from a strategic planning perspective?

3. Does Yahoo have a source of potential long-term competitive advantage? Where does this come from?

4. What does Koogle's resignation in May 2001 tell you about the role of a CEO in a public company?

Sources: S. G. Steinberg, "Seek and Ye Shall Find (Maybe)," *Wired* (May 1996). L. Himelstein, H. Green, and R. Siklos, "Yahoo! The Company, the Strategy, the Stock," *Business Week,* September 7, 1998, p. 66. S. Moran, "For Yahoo, GeoCities May Only Be the Start," *Internet World,* March 15, 1999. Yahoo 1998 and 2000 Annual Reports and www.yahoo.com. K. Swisher, "Time Runs Short for Terry Semel to Save Yahoo," *Wall Street Journal,* October 15, 2001, p. B1. N. Wingfield, "Yahoo Restructuring to Slash 400 Jobs," *Wall Street Journal,* November 16, 2001, p. B10.

External Analysis: The Identification of Industry Opportunities and Threats

2

Opening Case

Boom and Bust in Telecommunications

In the mid-1990s, the telecommunications services industry was beset by three significant changes. The first of these was the arrival of the World Wide Web as a prime-time phenomenon. As the volume of Web traffic grew at an exponential pace, so too did demand for the capacity to transmit the digital data on which the Web was based. In 1996, in an effort to foster greater competition among telecommunications service providers, the U.S. government deregulated the U.S. telecommunication service industry. Local and long-distance phone companies and cable TV companies were allowed to enter each other's markets. In addition, deregulation made it much easier for new entrants to get into the telecommunications service business. Similar moves to deregulate telecommunications services took place in other countries. Finally, wireless services made inroads in many developed nations, with market penetration rates for wireless phones reaching as high as 70 percent in Finland and 30 percent in the United States, where demand was growing rapidly. By decade's end, the wireless industry was beginning to embrace the Web, with wireless companies planning to offer their customers Internet access through wireless phones.

Many analysts believed that demand for telecommunications services would expand exponentially for years to come. In the near future, some argued, vast amounts of data will flow around the world through fiber-optic cable as ever more companies, individuals, and organizations connect to the Internet by high-speed wire line and wireless networks, and as they used the Internet for a vast array of high-bandwidth services, including videoconferencing and the transmitting of music files. The possibilities seemed limitless. A host of companies were established to compete with incumbent telecommunications service providers and to exploit the expected bandwidth boom. They included PSINet, 360 Networks, Covad Communications, Global Crossing, Level 3 Communications, ICG Communications, RCN Corporation, XO Communications, and WinStar.

Driven by a desire to share in the coming boom for telecommunications services, these new entrants raised billions of dollars in equity and some $650 billion in debt from the capital markets. They used the funds to build out fiber-optic networks within cities, between cities, and between countries. They invested in optical technology that increased by a hundred-fold the amount of data that could be sent down a single strand of glass fiber. And they built out wireless networks. Telecom service providers in the United States alone boosted their capital spending by 25 percent each year from 1996 to 2000, when they invested $124 billion. Worldwide, a staggering $1.2 trillion was spent on telecommunications equipment in 2000.

Producers of telecommunications equipment such as switches, routers, fiber-optic cables, and optical gear were beneficiaries of this boom. Lucent, Cisco, Nortel Networks, JDS Uniphase, Corning, and other companies saw their sales and profits surge. Cisco, founded only in the mid-1980s, made an after-tax profit of $2.7 billion in 2000 on sales of $19 billion. To grab even more sales, these equipment companies started making loans to the telecom service start-ups to help them buy the equipment. It seemed like a sure thing, a perfect bet on a glittering future. But the glittering future didn't arrive as expected.

By 2000, it became clear that although the volume of data traffic was doubling every year, the capacity to transmit data along fiber-optic networks was increasing much faster than that as dozens of service providers rushed to grab a share of the projected boom in demand. The result was huge excess capacity and plummeting prices for data transmission services using fiber-optic networks. By 2001, it was estimated that there was ten times more fiber-optic capacity than needed. Suddenly the telecommunications service providers were in trouble, particularly the new ones that had borrowed heavily to finance their growth. They could not generate enough revenues to cover the interest payments on their debt. As 2000 turned into 2001, many started to go bankrupt. PSINet, 360 Networks, Covad Communications, ICG Communications, and WinStar are among the many that filed for bankruptcy protection. By early 2002, others such as Level 3 and Global Crossing were teetering on the brink. In the space of a year, shares in Level 3 fell from $132 a share to under $3. Global Crossing saw its shares fall from a high of $64 a share in 1999 to $0.50 by the end of 2001. And in 2002, it too went bankrupt.

As telecommunications service providers started to go bankrupt, demand for telecommunications equipment imploded. Lucent saw its sales drop by 30 percent and was forced to take some $15 billion in charges to write off the value of loans given to service providers that no longer existed and to close down excess capacity. Lucent's stock price fell from a high of $70 a share in May 2000 to under $2 a share by mid-2002. Cisco, long the darling of the industry, lost over $1 billion on falling sales, and its share price slumped from a high of $80 in May 2000 to around $16 by early 2002. JDS Uniphase took a record $50 billion charge against earnings in 2001 to write down the value of companies it had acquired during the boom.

In retrospect, what happened can be analyzed quite easily. Although demand for telecommunications capacity did increase markedly, demand projections got way ahead of reality. Moreover, each service company raised capital and made investments on the assumption that they would be the ones to capture a significant proportion of those inflated demand projections, while failing to appreciate that given the number of other competitors making similar investments, there would not be enough demand to go around. The result of this myopic behavior was excess capacity in the services business. This triggered a price war and ruined any hope that many new service providers had of becoming profitable. As the service providers started to lose money, they slashed their capital investment budgets, which caused the slump in the equipment market. What had been an extraordinary profitable sector turned into an economic disaster zone; an unprecedented boom and been replaced by an unprecedented bust.

Sources: J. Shinal, "Dead Dot.Coms Can Still Cause Havoc," *Business Week,* March 12, 2001, p. 50; S. Rosenbush and P. Elstrom, "Eight Lessons from the Telecom Mess," *Business Week,* August 13, 2001, pp. 60–67; S. Rosenbush and B. Einhorn, "Those Wires Sure Are Cold," *Business Week,* September 17, 2001, pp. 104–105; "Drowning in Glass," *Economist,* March 24, 2001, p. 76.

Overview

The process of thinking strategically requires that managers understand how the structure and competitive dynamics of their industry affect the performance and profitability of their companies. Armed with an appreciation of the forces in their industry that give rise to opportunities and threats, managers should be able to make better strategic decisions. One interpretation of what happened in the telecommunication markets during the 1990s is that the opportunities were exaggerated and the threats were ignored because managers viewed demand conditions through rose-colored lenses. Managers systematically misread the realities of the situation because their decision making was colored and distorted by the kinds of cognitive biases and errors discussed in Chapter 1 (and no scenario planning was taking place). The result was excessive investment in telecommunications equipment, excess network capacity, plunging prices for telecommunications services, the failure of significant service revenues to materialize, and a wave of disastrous bankruptcies that helped plunge the economy into recession.

This chapter examines the conceptual models that can prevent mistakes in strategic thinking. It discusses several models that provide managers with a rational or objective means to analyze the dynamics of the industries in which their companies compete and help to identify the opportunities and threats that are inherent in them. **Opportunities** arise when a company can take advantage of conditions in its environment to formulate and implement strategies that enable it to become more profitable. Surging demand for telecommunications services, when coupled with deregulation, was seen as an enormous opportunity for new companies to enter the telecom service industry and compete with existing companies for industry revenues. **Threats** arise when conditions in the external environment endanger the integrity and profitability of the company's business. The irony in the telecommunications industry was that the rapid entry of new companies to take advantage of growing demand and profits led to the excess industry capacity that created the threat that led to the price war and falling industry profits.

This chapter begins with an analysis of the industry environment. First, it examines concepts and tools for analyzing the competitive structure of an industry and identifying industry opportunities and threats. Second, it analyzes the competitive implications that arise when groups of companies *within* an industry pursue similar and different kinds of competitive strategies. Third, it explores the way an industry evolves over time and the accompanying changes in competitive conditions is examined. Fourth, it looks at the way in which forces in the macroenvironment affect industry structure and creates and shapes opportunities and threats. Finally, it discusses the way in which the national and global environment shapes the competitive forces at work both within and across industries is discussed.

By the end of the chapter, you will understand that to succeed, a company must either fit its strategy to the external environment in which it operates or must be able to reshape the environment to its advantage through its chosen strategy.

Defining an Industry

An **industry** can be defined as a group of companies offering products or services that are close substitutes for each other—that is, products or services that satisfy the same basic customer needs. A company's closest **competitors,** its rivals, are those that serve the same basic customer needs. For example, carbonated drinks, fruit punches, and bottled water can be viewed as close substitutes for each other because they serve the same basic customer needs for refreshing and cold nonalcoholic beverages. Thus, we can talk about the soft drink industry, whose major players are Coca-Cola, PepsiCo, and Cadbury Schweppes. Similarly, desktop computers and notebook computers satisfy the same basic need that customers have for computer hardware on which to run personal productivity software, browse the Internet, send email, play games, and store, display, and manipulate digital images. Thus, we can talk about the personal computer industry, whose major players are Dell, Compaq, Hewlett Packard, IBM, Gateway, and Apple Computer.

The starting point of external analysis is to identify the industry that a company competes in. To do this, managers must begin by looking at the basic customer needs their company is serving—that is, they must take a customer-oriented view of their business as opposed to a product-oriented view (see Chapter 1). An industry is the *supply side* of a market, and companies in the industry are the suppliers. Customers are the *demand side* of a market and are the buyers of the industry's products. *The basic customer needs that are served by a market define an industry's boundary.* It is very important for managers to realize this, for if they define industry boundaries incorrectly, they may be caught flat-footed by the rise of competitors that serve the same basic customer needs with different product offerings. For example, for a long time, Coca-Cola saw itself as being in the soda industry—meaning carbonated soft drinks—whereas in fact it was in the soft drink industry, which includes noncarbonated soft drinks. In the mid-1990s, Coca-Cola was caught by surprise by the rise of customer demand for bottled water and fruit drinks, which began to cut into the demand for sodas. Coca-Cola moved quickly to respond to these threats, introducing its own brand of water, Dasani, and acquiring orange juice maker Minute Maid. By defining its industry boundaries too narrowly, Coke almost missed the rapid rise of the noncarbonated soft drinks segment of the soft drinks market.

Industry and Sector

An important distinction that needs to be made is between an *industry* and the **sector,** that is, the group of closely related industries of which it is a part. For example, the telecommunications sector encompasses two industries: the telecommunications equipment industry and the telecommunications services industry. Similarly, as illustrated in Figure 2.1, the computer sector comprises several related industries: the computer component industries (e.g., the disk drive industry, the semiconductor industry, and the modem industry), the computer hardware industries (e.g., the personal computer industry, the handheld computer industry, and the mainframe computer industry), and the computer software industry. Industries within a sector may be involved with each other in many different ways. For example, companies in the telecommunications equipment industry are the *suppliers* of the telecommunications services industry, and companies in the computer component industries *supply* inputs to companies in the computer hardware industries. Companies in the computer software industry provide important *complements* to computer hardware: the software programs that customers purchase to run on their hardware. And companies in the personal, hand-held, and mainframe industries are in indirect *competition* with each other because all provide products that are *substitutes* for each other.

Industry and Market Segments

It is also important to recognize the difference between an *industry* and the *market segments* within that industry. **Market segments** are distinct groups of customers within a market that can be differentiated from each other on the basis of their distinct attributes and specific demands. In the soft drink industry, for example, although all customers demand refreshing and cold nonalcoholic beverages, there is a group within this market who in addition demand (need) sodas that do not contain caffeine. Coca-Cola has recognized the existence of this caffeine-free market segment and sought to satisfy the needs of customers within it by producing and

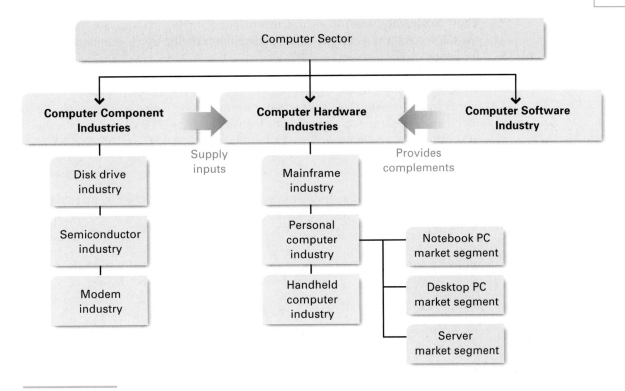

FIGURE 2.1

The Computer Sector: Industries and Segments

marketing noncaffeinated colas. Similarly, in the personal computer industry, there are different segments where customers desire desktop machines, lightweight portable machines, and servers that sit at the center of a network of personal computers (see Figure 2.1). Personal computer makers recognize the existence of these different segments by producing a range of product offerings that appeal to customers in different segments. Customers in all of these different segments, however, share a common need for PCs on which to run personal software applications.

Changing Industry Boundaries

Industry boundaries may change over time as customer needs evolve or new technologies emerge that enable companies in hitherto unrelated industries to satisfy established customer needs in new ways. We have noted that during the 1990s, as consumers of soft drinks began to develop a taste for bottled water and noncarbonated fruit-based drinks, Coca-Cola found itself in direct competition with the manufacturers of bottled water and fruit-based soft drinks: all were in the same industry.

For an example of how technological change can alter industry boundaries, consider the convergence that is currently taking place between the computer and telecommunications industries. Historically, the telecommunications equipment industry has been considered a distinct entity from the computer hardware industry. However, as telecommunications equipment has moved from traditional analogue technology to digital technology, so telecommunications equipment has increasingly come to resemble computers. The result is that the boundaries between these different industries is blurring. A digital wireless phone, for example, is nothing more than a small hand-held computer with a wireless connection, and small hand-held computers often now come with wireless capabilities, transforming them into phones.

Thus, Nokia and Motorola, which manufacture wireless phones, are now finding themselves competing directly with Handspring and Palm, which manufacture hand-held computers.

Industry competitive analysis begins by focusing on the overall industry in which a firm competes before market segments or sector-level issues are considered. Tools that managers can use to perform such industry analysis are discussed in the following sections: Porter's five forces model, strategic group analysis, and industry life cycle analysis.

Porter's Five Forces Model

Once the boundaries of an industry have been identified, the task facing managers is to analyze competitive forces in the industry environment to identify opportunities and threats. Michael E. Porter's well-known framework, known as the five forces model, helps managers with this analysis.[1] His model, shown in Figure 2.2, focuses on five forces that shape competition within an industry: (1) the risk of entry by potential competitors, (2) the intensity of rivalry among established companies within an industry, (3) the bargaining power of buyers, (4) the bargaining power of suppliers, and (5) the closeness of substitutes to an industry's products.

Porter argues that the stronger each of these forces is, the more limited is the ability of established companies to raise prices and earn greater profits. Within Porter's framework, a *strong* competitive force can be regarded as a *threat* because it depresses profits. A *weak* competitive force can be viewed as an *opportunity* because it allows a company to earn greater profits. The strength of the five forces may change through time as industry conditions change, as illustrated by the opening telecommunications case. The task facing managers is to recognize how changes in the five forces give rise to new opportunities and threats and to formulate appropriate strategic responses. In addition, it is possible for a company, *through its choice of strategy,* to alter the strength of one or more of the five forces to its advantage. This is discussed in the following chapters.

Risk of Entry by Potential Competitors

Potential competitors are companies that are not currently competing in an industry but have the capability to do so if they choose. For example, electric utilities are potential competitors to telecommunications companies in the markets for phone

FIGURE 2.2

Porter's Five Forces Model

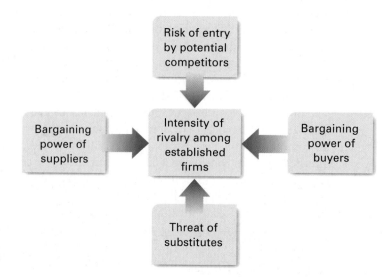

service and Internet access. In order to be able to deliver electricity to residential and commercial property, many electric utilities have been granted rights of way by state and local governments for their electric cable. There is nothing to stop electric utilities from laying fiber-optic along these rights of way and offering high-bandwidth communications services to residential and commercial customers. In fact, a number of utilities have started to do this. For example, Tacoma City Light in Washington State used its rights of way to run fiber-optic lines to several commercial buildings in the city of Tacoma and has taken business away from the dominant telecommunications provider in the region, Verizon. Tacoma City Light is also laying coaxial cable to homes in its service region and offering cable TV service in direct competition to the local cable provider, AT&T Broadband.[2]

Established companies already operating in an industry often attempt to discourage potential competitors from entering the industry because the more companies that enter, the more difficult it becomes for established companies to protect their share of the market and generate profits. AT&T Broadband's response to Tacoma City Light was to threaten intense competition on price and service for cable TV. A high risk of entry by potential competitors represents a threat to the profitability of established companies. But if the risk of new entry is low, established companies can take advantage of this opportunity to raise prices and earn greater returns.

The risk of entry by potential competitors is in part a function of the height of **barriers to entry,** that is, factors that make it costly for companies to enter an industry. The greater the costs are that potential competitors must bear to enter an industry, the greater are the barriers to entry and the *weaker* is this competitive force. High entry barriers may keep potential competitors out of an industry even when industry profits are high. Economist Joe Bain, who did the classic work on barriers to entry, identified three main sources of barriers to new entry: brand loyalty, absolute cost advantages, and economies of scale.[3] Two more that are important in many situations can be added to Bain's list of entry barriers: customer switching costs and government regulation.

Brand Loyalty. **Brand loyalty** is buyers' preference for the products of any established company. A company can create brand loyalty through continuous advertising of its brand-name products and company name, patent protection of products, product innovation achieved through company research and development programs, an emphasis on high product quality, and good after-sales service. Significant brand loyalty makes it difficult for new entrants to take market share away from established companies. Thus, it reduces the threat of entry by potential competitors since they may see the task of breaking down well-established customer preferences as too costly.

Absolute Cost Advantages. Sometimes established companies have an **absolute cost advantage** relative to potential entrants, meaning that entrants cannot expect to match the established companies' lower cost structure. Absolute cost advantages arise from three main sources (1) superior production operations and processes due to experience, patents, or secret processes; (2) control of particular inputs required for production, such as labor, materials, equipment, or management skills; and (3) access to cheaper funds because existing companies represent lower risks than new entrants. If established companies have an absolute cost advantage, the threat of entry as a competitive force is weaker.

Economies of Scale. **Economies of scale** are the relative cost advantages associated with large volumes of production that lower a company's cost structure. Sources of scale economies include (1) cost reductions gained through mass producing a standardized output, (2) discounts on bulk purchases of raw material inputs and component parts, (3) the advantages gained by spreading fixed production costs over a large production volume, and (4) the cost savings associated with spreading marketing and advertising costs over a large as compared to a small volume of output. If these cost advantages are significant, a new company that enters the industry and produces on a small scale suffers a significant cost disadvantage relative to established companies. If the new company decides to enter on a large scale to obtain these economies of scale, it has to bear the high risks associated with a large investment. A further risk of large-scale entry is that the increased supply of products will depress prices and result in vigorous retaliation by established companies. For these reasons, the threat of entry is reduced when established companies have economies of scale.

Customer Switching Costs. **Switching costs** arise when it costs a customer time, energy, and money to switch from the products offered by one established company to the products offered by a new entrant. When switching costs are high, customers can be *locked in* to the product offerings of established companies, even if new entrants offer better products.[4] A familiar example of switching costs concerns the costs associated with switching from one computer operating system to another. If a person currently uses Microsoft's Windows operating system and has a library of related software applications (e.g., word processing software, spreadsheet, games) and document files, it is expensive for that person to switch to another computer operating system. To effect the change, this person would have to buy a new set of software applications and convert all existing document files to run with the new system. Faced with such an expense of money and time, most people are unwilling to make the switch *unless* the competing operating system offers a *substantial* leap forward in performance. Thus, the higher the switching costs are, the higher is the barrier to entry for a company attempting to promote a new computer operating system.

Government Regulation. Historically, government regulation has constituted a major entry barrier into many industries. For example, until the mid-1990s, U.S. government regulation prohibited providers of long-distance telephone service from competing for local telephone service and vice versa. Other potential providers of telephone service, including cable television service companies such as AOL Time Warner and Viacom (which could in theory use their cables to carry telephone traffic as well as TV signals), were prohibited from entering the market altogether. These regulatory barriers to entry significantly reduced the level of competition in both the local and long-distance telephone markets, enabling telephone companies to earn higher profits than might otherwise have been the case. As noted in the *Opening Case,* all this changed in 1996 when the government deregulated the industry significantly. In the months that followed this announcement, local, long-distance, and cable TV companies all announced their intention to enter each other's markets, and a host of new players entered the market. The five forces model predicts that falling entry barrier due to government deregulation would result in significant new entry, an increase in the intensity of industry competition, and lower industry profit rates.

In summary, if established companies have built brand loyalty for their products, have an absolute cost advantage with respect to potential competitors, have significant scale economies, are the beneficiaries of high switching costs, or enjoy regulatory protection, the risk of entry by potential competitors is greatly diminished; it is a weak competitive force. Consequently, established companies can charge higher prices, and industry profits are higher. Indeed, empirical evidence suggests that the height of barriers to entry is one of the most important determinants of profit rates in an industry.[5] Clearly, it is in the interest of established companies to pursue strategies consistent with raising entry barriers to secure these profits. A detailed example of entry barriers is given in Strategy in Action 2.1, which looks at the Japanese brewing industry.

Even when entry barriers are very high, new firms may still enter an industry if they perceive that the benefits outweigh the substantial costs of entry. This is what appears to have occurred in the telecommunications industry following deregulation in 1996. The new entrants had to undertake huge capital expenditure to build out their networks and match the scale advantages of established companies. However, they were able to raise the capital to do so from investors who shared management's euphoric vision of future demand in the industry. In time, this euphoric vision proved to be false, and many of the new entrants went bankrupt, but not before their investments had created excess capacity in the industry and sparked intense price competition that depressed the returns for all players, new entrants and established companies alike.

Rivalry Among Established Companies

The second of Porter's five competitive forces is the intensity of rivalry among established companies within an industry. **Rivalry** refers to the competitive struggle between companies in an industry to gain market share from each other. The competitive struggle can be fought using price, product design, advertising and promotion spending, direct selling efforts, and after-sales service and support. More intense rivalry implies lower prices or more spending on non-price-competitive weapons, or both. Because intense rivalry lowers prices and raises costs, it squeezes profits out of an industry. Thus, intense rivalry among established companies constitutes a strong threat to profitability. Alternatively, if rivalry is less intense, companies may have the opportunity to raise prices or reduce spending on non-price-competitive weapons, which leads to a higher level of industry profits. The intensity of rivalry among established companies within an industry is largely a function of three factors: (1) industry competitive structure, (2) demand conditions, and (3) the height of exit barriers in the industry.

Industry Competitive Structure. The *competitive structure* of an industry refers to the number and size distribution of companies in it, something that strategic managers determine at the beginning of an industry analysis. Industry structures vary, and different structures have different implications for the intensity of rivalry. A **fragmented industry** consists of a large number of small or medium-sized companies, none of which is in a position to determine industry price. A **consolidated industry** is dominated by a small number of large companies (an **oligopoly**), or in extreme cases, by just one company (a **monopoly**) and companies often are in a position to determine industry prices. Examples of fragmented industries are agriculture, dry cleaning, video rental, health clubs, real estate brokerage, and sun tanning parlors. Consolidated industries include the aerospace, automobile, pharmaceutical, and stockbrokerage industries.

Many fragmented industries are characterized by low entry barriers and commodity-type products that are hard to differentiate. The combination of these traits tends to result in boom-and-bust cycles as industry profits rise and fall. Low entry

Strategy in Action

Entry Barriers into the Japanese Brewing Industry

In 1565, an English visitor to Japan noted that the Japanese "feed moderately but drink largely." This is still the case today: the Japanese have one of the highest levels of beer consumption per capita in the world. In 1998, for example, 50 liters of beer were sold for every man, woman, and child in the country, making Japan's level of beer consumption per capita similar to that of big beer drinking nations such as Australia, Britain, and Germany.

The Japanese market is dominated by Kirin, Asahi, Sapporo, and Suntory, which have a combined market share of around 97 percent. Collectively, these companies enjoy one of the highest profit rates of any industry in Japan. Despite this high level of profitability, there has been very little entry into this industry over the last three decades. Suntory is the only successful new entrant in the past thirty years, and its market share stands at no more than 6 percent.

Normally, a lack of new entry into a profitable industry indicates the presence of high entry barriers, and that is certainly the case here. Like other large brewing companies all over the world, Japan's big four spend heavily on advertising and promotions. Moreover, Japan's big brewers have been aggressive in the area of product development. During the 1990s, Asahi gained significant share from its competitors by pushing its "Super Dry" beer. The resulting brand identification certainly helped to limit the potential for new entry. But some argue that there is more to it than this, and in fact Japan's brewing companies have also been the beneficiaries of significant regulatory barriers to entry. Brewers in Japan must have a license from the Ministry of Finance (MOF), and until 1994 the MOF would not issue a license to any brewer producing less than 2 million liters annually. This restriction represented an imposing hurdle to any potential new entrant: because a new company could not enter at a small scale of output, it would have to invest in very expensive brewing facilities. Why this regulation? Bureaucratic convenience. It is easier to collect tax from 4 companies than from 400.

Another significant barrier to entry has been Japan's distribution system. Roughly half the beer consumed in Japan is distributed and sold in bars and restaurants whose owners are loyal to the big brewers and are often reluctant to distribute competing brands that might alienate their main supplier. Small liquor stores are another main distribution outlet for beer, and they too were unwilling to sell the products of new entrants for fear that the big brewers might "punish" them by denying them access to adequate supplies.

It appears that some of the barriers to entering Japan's brewing industry are declining, however. As part of an economic liberalization plan, in 1994 the MOF reduced the production threshold required to gain a license from 2 million liters to 60,000 liters, low enough to allow for the entry of microbreweries using the same technology that is now found in many brew pubs in the United States and Britain. Moreover, regulatory changes also allowed for the establishment of large new discount stores in Japan. (Until 1994, small retailers could effectively block the opening of a large discount store in their region by appealing to the local authorities.) Unlike traditional small retailers, large discount retailers are motivated more by price and profit than by loyalties to an established supplier and are eager to sell the beer of foreign companies and microbreweries, in addition to that of Japan's big four.

Given the decline in barriers to entry associated with regulation and distribution channels, many observers thought that Japan's big four brewers would have to face up to new competitors after 1994. So far, however, this has not been the case. Japan's big four brewing companies continue to dominate the domestic market, a testament perhaps to the significance of advertising, promotions, and product differentiation as barriers to entry. However, Japan's brewers are facing indirect competition from an alternative alcoholic beverage, wine, which is starting to become fashionable among younger people.

Sources: "Only Here for the Biru," *Economist,* May 14, 1994, pp. 69–71; T. Craig, "The Japanese Beer Industry," in C. W. L. Hill and G. R. Jones, *Strategic Management: An Integrated Approach* (Boston: Houghton Mifflin, 1995); "Japan's Beer Wars," *Economist,* February 28, 1998, p. 68; A. Harney, "Japan's Favorite Beer Could Face Losing Its Sparkle," *Financial Times,* March 24, 1999, p. 27.

barriers imply that whenever demand is strong and profits are high, new entrants will flood the market, hoping to profit from the boom. The explosion in the number of video stores, health clubs, and sun tanning parlors during the 1980s and 1990s exemplifies this situation.

Often the flood of new entrants into a booming fragmented industry creates excess capacity, so companies start to cut prices in order to use their spare capacity. The difficulty companies face when trying to differentiate their products from those of competitors can exacerbate this tendency. The result is a price war, which depresses industry profits, forces some companies out of business, and deters potential new entrants. For example, after a decade of expansion and booming profits, many health clubs are now finding that they have to offer large discounts in order to hold onto their membership. In general, the more commodity-like an industry's product is, the more vicious will be the price war. This bust part of the cycle continues until overall industry capacity is brought into line with demand (through bankruptcies), at which point prices may stabilize again.

A fragmented industry structure, then, constitutes a threat rather than an opportunity. Most booms are relatively short-lived because of the ease of new entry and will be followed by price wars and bankruptcies. Because it is often difficult to differentiate products in these industries, the best strategy for a company is to try to minimize its costs so it will be profitable in a boom and survive any subsequent bust. Alternatively, companies might try to adopt strategies that change the underlying structure of fragmented industries and lead to a consolidated industry structure in which the level of industry profitability is increased. Exactly how companies can do this is something we shall consider in later chapters.

In consolidated industries, companies are interdependent, because one company's competitive actions or moves (with regard to price, quality, and so on) directly affect the market share of its rivals, and thus their profitability. When one company makes a move, this generally "forces" a response from its rivals, and the consequence of such competitive interdependence can be a dangerous competitive spiral. Rivalry increases as companies attempt to undercut each other's prices or offer customers more value in their products, pushing industry profits down in the process. The fare wars that have periodically created havoc in the airline industry provide a good illustration of this process.

When demand for airline travel fell during the recession of 2001, and particularly after the terrorist attacks of September 11, airlines started cutting prices to try to maintain their passenger loads in the face of declining demand. When one airline serving a particular route cut its prices, its competitors would follow. The result was a downward price spiral. In the fourth quarter of 2001, prices fell by 15 percent as airlines tried to induce people to fly. Despite this, passenger traffic fell by 19 percent, and revenue at major airlines fell by over 30 percent. U.S. Airlines alone lost some $4.2 billion in the last three months of 2001 and $6.4 billion for the entire year.[6] Clearly, high rivalry between companies in consolidated industries and the possibility of a price war constitute a major threat.

Companies in consolidated industries sometimes seek to reduce this threat by following the prices set by the dominant company in the industry.[7] However, companies must be careful, for explicit face-to-face price-fixing agreements are illegal. (Tacit, indirect agreements, arrived at without direct or intentional communication, are legal.) Instead, companies set prices by watching, interpreting, anticipating, and responding to each other's behavior (something discussed in detail in Chapter 5 when the competitive dynamics of game theory is examined). However, tacit price leadership agreements often break down under adverse economic conditions, as has occurred in the breakfast cereal industry, profiled in Strategy in Action 2.2.

Industry Demand. The level of industry demand is a second determinant of the intensity of rivalry among established companies. Growing demand from new customers or additional purchases by existing customers tend to moderate competition by providing greater scope for companies to compete for customers. Growing demand tends to reduce rivalry because all companies can sell more without taking market share away from other companies. High industry profits are often the result. Conversely, declining demand results in more rivalry as companies fight to maintain market share and revenues (as in the breakfast cereal industry). Demand declines when customers are leaving the marketplace or each customer is buying less. Now a company can grow only by taking market share away from other companies. Thus, declining demand constitutes a major threat, for it increases the extent of rivalry between established companies.

Exit Barriers. Exit barriers are economic, strategic, and emotional factors that prevent companies from leaving an industry. If exit barriers are high, companies become locked into an unprofitable industry where overall demand is static or declining. The result is often excess productive capacity, which leads to even more intense rivalry and price competition as companies cut prices in the attempt to obtain the customer orders needed to use their idle capacity and cover their costs.[8] Common exit barriers include the following:

- Investments in assets such as specific machines, equipment, and operating facilities that are of little or no value in alternative uses or cannot be sold off. If the company wishes to leave the industry, it has to write off the book value of these assets.

- High fixed costs of exit, such as the severance pay, health benefits, and pensions that have to be paid to workers who are being made redundant when a company ceases to operate.

- Emotional attachments to an industry, as when a company's owners or employees are unwilling to exit from an industry for sentimental reasons or because of pride.

- Economic dependence on the industry because a company relies on a single industry for its revenue and profit.

- The need to maintain an expensive collection of assets at or above some minimum level in order to participate effectively in the industry.

As an example of the effect of exit barriers in practice, consider the express mail and parcel delivery industry. The key players in this industry such as Federal Express and UPS rely on the delivery business entirely for their revenues and profits. They have to be able to guarantee their customers that they will deliver packages to all major localities in the United States, and much of their investment is specific to this purpose. To meet this guarantee, they need a nationwide network of air routes and ground routes, an asset that is required in order to participate in the industry. If excess capacity develops in this industry, as it does from time to time, Federal Express cannot incrementally reduce or minimize its excess capacity by deciding not to fly to and deliver packages in, say, Miami because that proportion of its network is underused. If it did that, it would no longer be able to guarantee to its customers that it would be able to deliver packages to all major locations in the United States, and its customers would switch to some other carrier. Thus, the need to maintain a nation-

Strategy in Action   2.2

Price Wars in the Breakfast Cereal Industry

For decades, the breakfast cereal industry was one of the most profitable in the United States. The industry has a consolidated structure dominated by Kellogg, General Mills, and Kraft Foods with its Post brand. Strong brand loyalty, coupled with control over the allocation of supermarket shelf space, helped to limit the potential for new entry. Meanwhile, steady demand growth of around 3 percent per annum kept industry revenues expanding. For years, Kellogg, which accounted for over 40 percent of the market share, acted as the price leader in the industry. Every year Kellogg increased cereal prices, its rivals followed, and industry profits remained high.

This favorable industry structure started to change in the early 1990s when growth in demand slowed and then stagnated as a latte and bagel or muffin replaced cereal as the morning fare for many American adults. Then came the rise of powerful discounters such as Wal-Mart, which entered the grocery industry in the early 1990s and began to promote aggressively its own brand of cereal, priced significantly below the brand-name cereals. As the decade progressed, other grocery chains such as Kroger's started to follow suit, and brand loyalty in the industry began to decline as customers realized that a $2.50 bag of wheat flakes from Wal-Mart tasted about the same as a $3.50 box of Cornflakes from Kellogg. As sales of cheaper store brand cereals began to take off, supermarkets, no longer as dependent on brand names to bring traffic into their stores, began to demand lower prices from the branded cereal manufacturers.

For several years, the manufacturers of brand cereals tried to hold out against these adverse trends, but in the mid-1990s the dam broke. In 1996, Kraft (then owned by Philip Morris) aggressively cut prices by 20 percent for its

Post brand in an attempt to gain market share. Kellogg soon followed with a 19 percent price cut on two-thirds of its brands, and General Mills quickly did the same. The decades of tacit price collusion were officially over.

If the breakfast cereal companies were hoping that the price cuts would stimulate demand, they were wrong. Instead, demand remained flat while revenues and margins followed prices down and Kellogg's operating margins dropped from 18 percent in 1995 to 10.2 percent in 1996, a trend experienced by the other brand cereal manufacturers.

By 2000, conditions had only worsened. Private label sales continued to make inroads, gaining over 10 percent of the market. Moreover, sales of breakfast cereals started to contract at 1 percent per annum. To cap it off, an aggressive General Mills continued to launch expensive price and promotion campaigns in an attempt to take share away from the market leader. Kellogg saw its market share slip to just over 30 percent in 2001, *behind* the 31 percent now held by General Mills. For the first time since 1906, Kellogg no longer led the market. Moreover, profits at all three major producers remained weak in the face of continued price discounting.

In mid-2001, General Mills finally blinked and raised prices a modest 2 percent in response to its own rising costs. Competitors followed, signaling perhaps that after a decade of costly price warfare, pricing discipline might once more emerge in the industry, only this time General Mills, not Kellogg, would be the price leader.

Sources: G. Morgenson, "Denial in Battle Creek," *Forbes,* October 7, 1996, p. 44; J. Muller, "Thinking out of the Cereal Box," *Business Week,* January 15, 2001, p. 54; A. Merrill, "General Mills Increases Prices," *Star Tribune,* June 5, 2001, p. 1D.

---

wide network is an exit barrier that can result in persistent excess capacity in the air express industry during periods of weak demand. Finally, both UPS and Federal Express managers and employees are emotionally tied to this industry because they both were first movers, in the ground and air segments of the industry, respectively, and because their employees are also major owners of their companies' stock and they are dependent financially on the fortunes of the delivery business.

The Bargaining Power of Buyers   The third of Porter's five competitive forces is the bargaining power of buyers. An industry's buyers may be the individual customers who ultimately consume its products (its end users) or the companies that distribute an industry's products to end users, such as retailers and wholesalers. For example, while soap powder made by Procter & Gamble and Unilever is consumed by end users, the principal buyers of soap powder are supermarket chains and discount stores, which resell the product to end users. The **bargaining power of buyers** refers to the ability of buyers to bargain down prices charged by companies in the industry or to raise the costs of companies in the industry by demanding better product quality and service. By lowering prices and raising costs, powerful buyers can squeeze profits out of an industry. Thus, powerful buyers should be viewed as a threat. Alternatively, when buyers are in a weak bargaining position, companies in an industry can raise prices, and perhaps reduce their costs by lowering product quality and service, and increase the level of industry profits. According to Porter, buyers are most powerful in the following circumstances:

- When the industry that is supplying a particular product or service is composed of many small companies and the buyers are large and few in number. These circumstances allow the buyers to dominate supplying companies.

- When the buyers purchase in large quantities. In such circumstances, buyers can use their purchasing power as leverage to bargain for price reductions.

- When the supply industry depends on the buyers for a large percentage of its total orders.

- When switching costs are low so that buyers can play off the supplying companies against each other to force down prices.

- When it is economically feasible for buyers to purchase an input from several companies at once so that buyers can play off one company in the industry against another.

- When buyers can threaten to enter the industry and produce the product themselves and thus supply their own needs, also a tactic for forcing down industry prices.

The auto component supply industry, whose buyers are large automobile manufacturers such as GM, Ford, and DaimlerChrysler, is a good example of an industry in which buyers have strong bargaining power and thus a strong competitive threat. Why? The suppliers of auto component are numerous and typically small in scale; their buyers, the auto manufacturers, are large in size and few in number. Daimler-Chrysler, for example, does business with nearly 2,000 different component suppliers in the United States and normally contracts with a number of different companies to supply the same part. Additionally, to keep component prices down, both Ford and GM have used the threat of manufacturing a component themselves rather than buying it from auto component suppliers. The automakers have used their powerful position to play off suppliers against each other, forcing down the price they have to pay for component parts and demanding better quality. If a component supplier objects, the automaker uses the threat of switching to another supplier as a bargaining tool.

Another issue is that the relative power of buyers and suppliers tends to change in response to changing industry conditions. For example, due to changes now taking place in the pharmaceutical and health care industries, major buyers of pharmaceuticals (hospitals and health maintenance organizations) are gaining power over the suppliers of pharmaceuticals and have been able to demand lower prices.

The Bargaining Power of Suppliers

The fourth of Porter's five competitive forces is the bargaining power of suppliers—the organizations that provide inputs into the industry, such as materials, services, and labor (which may be individuals, organizations such as labor unions, or companies that supply contract labor). The **bargaining power of suppliers** refers to the ability of suppliers to raise input prices, or to raise the costs of the industry in other ways—for example, by providing poor-quality inputs or poor service. Powerful suppliers squeeze profits out of an industry by raising the costs of companies in the industry. Thus, powerful suppliers are a threat. Alternatively, if suppliers are weak, companies in the industry have the opportunity to force down input prices and demand higher-quality inputs (e.g., more productive labor). As with buyers, the ability of suppliers to make demands on a company depends on their power relative to that of the company. According to Porter, suppliers are most powerful in these situations:

- The product that suppliers sell has few substitutes and is vital to the companies in an industry.

- The profitability of suppliers is not significantly affected by the purchases of companies in a particular industry, in other words, when the industry is not an important customer to the suppliers.

- Companies in an industry would experience significant switching costs if they moved to the product of a different supplier because a particular supplier's products are unique or different. In such cases, the company depends on a particular supplier and cannot play suppliers off against each other to reduce price.

- Suppliers can threaten to enter their customers' industry and use their inputs to produce products that would compete directly with those of companies already in the industry.

- Companies in the industry cannot threaten to enter their suppliers' industry and make their own inputs as a tactic for lowering the price of inputs.

An example of an industry in which companies are dependent on a powerful supplier is the personal computer industry. They are heavily dependent on Intel, the world's largest supplier of microprocessors for PCs. The industry standard for personal computers runs on Intel's X86 microprocessor chips, such as its Pentium series. Intel's competitors, such as Advanced Micro Devices (AMD), must develop and supply chips that are compatible with Intel's standard. Although AMD has developed competing chips, Pentium still supplies about 85 percent of the chips used in PCs primarily because only Intel has the manufacturing capacity required to serve a large share of the market. It is beyond the financial resources of Intel's competitors, such as AMD, to match the scale and efficiency of Intel's manufacturing systems. This means that while PC manufacturers can buy some microprocessors from Intel's rivals, most notably AMD, they still have to turn to Intel for the bulk of their supply. Because Intel is in a powerful bargaining position, it can charge higher prices for its microprocessors than would be the case if its competitors were more numerous and stronger (i.e., if the microprocessor industry were fragmented).

Substitute Products   The final force in Porter's model is the threat of **substitute products**: the products of different businesses or industries that can satisfy similar customer needs. For example, companies in the coffee industry compete indirectly with those in the tea and soft drink industries because all three serve customer needs for nonalcoholic drinks. The existence of close substitutes is a strong competitive threat because this limits the price that companies in one industry can charge for their product, and thus industry profitability. If the price of coffee rises too much relative to that of tea or soft drinks, coffee drinkers may switch to those substitutes.

If an industry's products have few close substitutes, so that substitutes are a weak competitive force, then, other things being equal, companies in the industry have the opportunity to raise prices and earn additional profits. Thus, there is no close substitute for microprocessors, which gives companies like Intel and AMD the ability to charge higher prices than would be the case if there were a substitute for microprocessors.

A Sixth Force: Complementors

Andrew Grove, the former CEO of Intel, has argued that Porter's five forces model ignores a sixth force: the power, vigor, and competence of complementors.[9] **Complementors** are companies that sell products that add value to (complement) the products of companies in an industry because when used *together,* the products better satisfy customer demands. For example, the complementors to the personal computer industry are the companies that make software applications to run on those machines. The greater the supply of high-quality software applications to run on personal computers, the greater is the value of personal computers to customers, the greater the demand for PCs, and the greater the profitability of the personal computer industry.

Grove's argument has a strong foundation in economic theory, which has long argued that *both* substitutes and complements influence demand in an industry.[10] Moreover, recent research has emphasized the importance of complementary products in determining demand and profitability in many high-technology industries, such as the computer industry in which Grove made his mark.[11] The issue, therefore, is that when complements are an important determinant of demand for an industry's products, industry profits depend critically on there being an adequate supply of complementary products. When the number of complementors is increasing and they produce attractive complementary products, this boosts demand and profits in the industry and can open up many new opportunities for creating value. Conversely, if complementors are weak and are not producing attractive complementary products, this can be a threat that slows industry growth and limits profitability.

The systematic analysis of forces in the industry environment using the Porter framework is a powerful tool that helps managers to think strategically. It is important to recognize that one competitive force often affects the others, so that all forces need to be considered and thought about when performing industry analysis. Indeed, industry analysis leads managers to think systematically about the way their strategic choices will both be affected by the forces of industry competition and how their choices will affect the five forces and change conditions in the industry. Had managers or investors in the telecommunications service industry stopped to consider what would happen to the industry when new and existing companies simultaneously expanded capacity—intense rivalry and price competition—perhaps the huge boom and bust cycle could have been avoided. For an illustration of how important industry analysis is in driving strategy, consider the *Running Case* on Dell Computer, which looks at how the nature of rivalry in the personal computer industry has changed in recent years.

Strategic Groups Within Industries

Companies in an industry often differ significantly from each other with respect to the way they strategically position their products in the market in terms of such factors as the distribution channels they use, the market segments they serve, the quality of their products, technological leadership, customer service, pricing policy, advertising policy, and promotions. As a result of these differences, within most

Running Case

Dell—Changing Rivalry in the Personal Computer Industry

Throughout the 1990s, the personal computer industry was a good one to be in. New entry was limited by the brand loyalty and scale economies enjoyed by the established companies in the business. The most significant new entrant during the decade, Hewlett Packard, was able to enter because it already competed in the computer sector (it made midrange computers) and could leverage its brand loyalty and existing scale economies to reduce the costs of entry (something companies outside the computer sector could not do) into the personal computer market. Also, a robust supply of complementary products, including Microsoft's Office productivity suite, online service providers such as AOL and MSN, Internet browsers, email programs, personal finance software such as Quicken, digital imaging hardware and software, and PC games, helped to keep customer demand growing at 15 percent per annum compounded, giving all PC makers a chance to increase their revenues and profits. Nor were there any potential substitutes that might limit demand growth. In this growing industry, rivalry between companies, while vigorous, did not lead to major price wars, and this helped to keep industry profitability high.

The industry did have two strong suppliers that enjoyed substantial bargaining power: Intel, which provided the microprocessor for the majority of personal computers, and Microsoft, which provided the operating system. To sell their machines, personal computer companies had to include an Intel or Intel-compatible microprocessor and a Microsoft operating system. This enabled Intel and Microsoft to charge higher prices than would otherwise have been the case and thus reduced the profitability of the personal computer industry somewhat. However, this negative was not enough to offset the positive growth fundamentals, which were strong. Moreover, the buyers in the industry—individual customers, corporations, and distributors such as CompUSA—did not exercise significant bargaining power.

All of this changed in 2000 as the industry became consolidated. Dell now had a 14 percent share of worldwide PC shipments, Compaq 11 percent, Hewlett Packard 8 percent, IBM 6 percent, Fujitsu 5 percent, and Gateway 4 percent. With almost half of the world market in the hands of just six companies, there was now a substantial level of interdependence among industry companies. Moreover, these companies offered such similar products that analysts worried that PCs were fast becoming mere

"commodities" like corn or wheat and that price would become be the main competitive weapon. Since differentiating products on nonprice factors was becoming increasingly difficult, analysts postulated that it would be only a matter of time before one player cut prices, and the others would be forced to respond in kind in order to try to hold onto their market share, plunging the entire industry into a price war.

This scenario became more likely in 2001 when the growth rate in the industry began to slow to single digits. There were two reasons for the slowing growth. First, after two decades of robust growth, the market had become mature. By 2001, almost all businesses and 65 percent of homes in the United States had personal computers. Second, demand for personal computers was hurt by a lack of compelling complementary products that might persuade businesses and household customers to replace their existing equipment with more powerful machines. For the first time in two decades, worldwide unit shipments of personal computers fell to 130 million, down from 132 million in 2000. In the large U.S. market, demand fell by 13 percent in 2001.

The combination of a consolidated industry, a product that was increasingly difficult to differentiate, and slowing demand set the scene for a marked change in the intensity of rivalry in the industry. Dell, which had the lowest cost structure in the industry, launched a price war. Its rivals were forced to respond in kind in order to try to maintain their market share, and prices and profits in the industry plunged. During 2001, the average selling price in the industry fell from $1,850 a machine to $1,460. By late 2001, Dell was the only major personal computer company making money, and it was also gaining market share and increasing revenues. Industry observers believed that Dell's strategic goal was to drive some of its weaker competitors out of the market altogether, leading to a more consolidated industry in which Dell would be the dominant player.

By early 2002 it looked as if Dell might be getting closer to achieving this goal. Compaq and Hewlett Packard, the number two and three companies, had announced their intention to merge, partly in an attempt to rationalize their PC manufacturing operations, closing down some of their plants to take surplus capacity out of the industry. IBM announced its intention to exit the business of making PCs, selling its facilities to a contract manufacturer. Gateway was still hanging on, but its sales revenues had slumped by 35 percent during 2001 as prices plunged, and it was losing money. To many, it seemed as if Dell had analyzed the structure of its industry in late 2000 and decided that the time was ripe to launch a price war in which it would be the major beneficiary.

Sources: G. McWilliams, "Dell Boosts Estimates for Profits and Sales," *Wall Street Journal,* January 21, 2002, p. B4. W. M. Bulkeley, "As PC Industry Slumps, IBM Hands Off Manufacturing of Desktops," *Wall Street Journal,* January 9, 2002, p. B1. G. McWilliams, "Computer Trouble: As More Buyers Suffer from Upgrade Fatigue, PC Sales Are Falling," *Wall Street Journal,* August 24, 2001, p. A1. J. Pellet, "Who's Afraid of Michael Dell?" *Chief Executive* (July 2001): 28–35.

industries, it is possible to observe groups of companies in which each company follows the same basic product positioning strategy as the other companies in the group, but a strategy that is *different* from that followed by companies in other groups. These different groups of companies are known as **strategic groups.**[12]

Normally, the basic differences between the positioning strategies that companies in different strategic groups use can be captured by a relatively small number of strategic factors. For example, in the pharmaceutical industry, two main strategic groups stand out (see Figure 2.3).[13] One group, which includes such companies as Merck, Eli Lilly, and Pfizer, is characterized by competitive positioning based on heavy R&D spending and a focus on developing new, proprietary, blockbuster drugs. The companies in this *proprietary* strategic group are pursuing a high-risk, high-return strategy. It is a high-risk strategy because basic drug research is difficult and expensive. Bringing a new drug to market can cost up to $500 million in R&D money and a decade of research and clinical trials. The risks are high because the failure rate in new drug development is very high: only one out of every ten drugs entering clinical trials is ultimately approved by the U.S. Food and Drug Administration. However, the strategy is also a high-return one because a single successful drug can be patented, giving the innovator a twenty-year monopoly on its production and sale. This lets these proprietary companies charge a high price for the patented drug, allowing them to earn millions, if not billions, of dollars over the lifetime of the patent.

FIGURE 2.3

Strategic Groups in the Pharmaceutical Industry

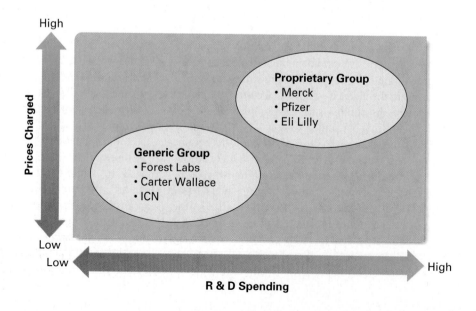

The second strategic group might be characterized as the *generic drug* strategic group. This group of companies, which includes Forest Labs, ICN, and Carter Wallace, focuses on the manufacture of generic drugs: low-cost copies of drugs that were developed by companies in the proprietary group whose patents have now expired. Low R&D spending and an emphasis on low prices characterize the competitive positioning of companies in this strategic group. They are pursuing a low-risk, low-return strategy. It is low risk because they are not investing millions of dollars in R&D. It is low return because they cannot charge high prices.

Implications of Strategic Groups

The concept of strategic groups has a number of implications for the identification of opportunities and threats within an industry. First, because all the companies in a strategic group are pursuing a similar positioning strategy, customers tend to view the products of such enterprises as *direct substitutes* for each other. Thus, a company's *closest* competitors are those in its strategic group, not those in other strategic groups in the industry. The most immediate threat to a company's profitability comes from rivals within its own strategic group. For example, in the retail industry, there is a group of companies that might be characterized as discounters. Included in this group are Wal-Mart, Kmart, Target, and Fred Meyer. These companies compete most vigorously with each other, as opposed to with other retailers in different groups, such as Nordstrom or The Gap. Kmart, for example, was driven into bankruptcy in late 2001, not because Nordstrom or The Gap took business from it, but because Wal-Mart and Target gained share in the discounting group by virtue of their superior strategies.

A second competitive implication is that different strategic groups can have a different standing with respect to each of the competitive forces; thus, *each strategic group may face a different set of opportunities and threats.* The risk of new entry by potential competitors, the degree of rivalry among companies within a group, the bargaining power of buyers, the bargaining power of suppliers, and the competitive force of substitute and complementary products can each be a relatively strong or weak competitive force depending on the competitive positioning approach adopted by each strategic group in the industry. For example, in the pharmaceutical industry, companies in the proprietary group have historically been in a very powerful position in relation to buyers because their products are patented and there are no substitutes. Also, rivalry within this group has been low because competition in the industry revolves around being the first to patent a new drug (so-called patent races), not around drug prices. Thus, companies in this group have been able to charge high prices and earn high profits. In contrast, companies in the generic group have been in a much weaker position because many companies are able to produce different versions of the same generic drug after patents expire. Thus, in this strategic group, products are close substitutes, rivalry has been high, and price competition has led to lower profits for this group as compared to companies in the proprietary group.

The Role of Mobility Barriers

It follows from these two issues that some strategic groups are more desirable than others because Porter's five forces open up greater opportunities and present fewer threats for those groups. Managers, after having analyzed their industry, might identify a strategic group where the five forces are weaker and higher profits can be made. Sensing an opportunity, they might contemplate changing their positioning approach and move to compete in that strategic group. However, taking advantage of this opportunity may be difficult because of mobility barriers between strategic groups.

Mobility barriers are within-industry factors that inhibit the movement of companies between strategic groups. They include the barriers to entry into a group and the barriers to exit from a company's existing group. For example, Forest Labs would encounter mobility barriers if it attempted to enter the proprietary group in the pharmaceutical industry because it lacks R&D skills, and building these skills would be an expensive proposition. Essentially, over time, companies in different groups develop different cost structures and skills and competencies that give them different pricing options and choices. A company contemplating entry into another strategic group must evaluate whether it has the ability to imitate, and indeed outperform, its potential competitors in that strategic group. Managers must determine if it is cost-effective to overcome mobility barriers before deciding whether the move is worthwhile.

In summary, an important task of industry analysis is to determine the sources of the similarities and differences among companies in an industry and to work out the broad themes that underlie competition in an industry. This analysis often reveals new opportunities to compete in an industry by developing new kinds of products to meet the needs of customers better. It can also reveal emerging threats that can be countered effectively by changing competitive strategy. This issue is taken up in Chapters 5, 6, and 7, which examine crafting competitive strategy in different kinds of markets to build a competitive advantage over rivals and best satisfy customer needs.

Industry Life Cycle Analysis

An important determinant of the strength of the competitive forces in an industry (and thus of the nature of opportunities and threats) is the changes that take place in it over time. The similarities and differences between companies in an industry often become more pronounced over time, and its strategic group structure frequently changes. The strength and nature of each of Porter's five competitive forces also change as an industry evolves, particularly the two forces of risk of entry by potential competitors and rivalry among existing firms.[14]

A useful tool for analyzing the effects of industry evolution on competitive forces is the **industry life cycle** model, which identifies five sequential stages in the evolution of an industry that lead to five distinct kinds of industry environment: embryonic, growth, shakeout, mature, and decline (see Figure 2.4). The task facing managers is to *anticipate* how the strength of competitive forces will change as the industry environment evolves and to formulate strategies that take advantage of opportunities as they arise and that counter emerging threats.

Embryonic Industries

An *embryonic* industry is just beginning to develop (for example, personal computers in 1976). Growth at this stage is slow because of such factors as buyers' unfamiliarity with the industry's product, high prices due to the inability of companies to reap any significant scale economies, and poorly developed distribution channels. Barriers to entry tend to be based on access to key technological know-how rather than cost economies or brand loyalty. If the core know-how required to compete in the industry is complex and difficult to grasp, barriers to entry can be quite high, and established companies will be protected from potential competitors. Rivalry in embryonic industries is based not so much on price as on educating customers, opening up distribution channels, and perfecting the design of the product. Such rivalry can be intense, and the company that is the first to solve design problems often

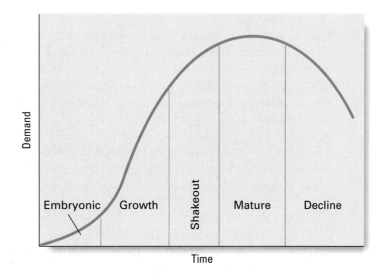

has the opportunity to develop a significant market position. An embryonic industry may also be the creation of one company's innovative efforts, as happened with personal computers (Apple), vacuum cleaners (Hoover), and photocopiers (Xerox). In such circumstances, the company has a major opportunity to capitalize on the lack of rivalry and build a strong hold on the market.

**Growth
Industries**
Once demand for the industry's product begins to take off, the industry develops the characteristics of a growth industry. In a *growth* industry, first-time demand is expanding rapidly as many new customers enter the market. Typically, an industry grows when customers become familiar with the product, prices fall because experience and scale economies have been attained, and distribution channels develop. The U.S. cellular telephone industry was in the growth stage for most of the 1990s. In 1990, there were only 5 million cellular subscribers in the nation. By 2002, this figure had increased to 88 million, and overall demand was still growing at a rate in excess of 25 percent per year.

Normally, the importance of control over technological knowledge as a barrier to entry has diminished by the time an industry enters its growth stage. Because few companies have yet achieved significant scale economies or built brand loyalty, other entry barriers tend to be relatively low as well, particularly early in the growth stage. Thus, the threat from potential competitors generally is highest at this point. Paradoxically, however, high growth usually means that new entrants can be absorbed into an industry without a marked increase in the intensity of rivalry. Thus, rivalry tends to be relatively low. Rapid growth in demand enables companies to expand their revenues and profits without taking market share away from competitors. A strategically aware company takes advantage of the relatively benign environment of the growth stage to prepare itself for the intense competition of the coming industry shakeout.

**Industry
Shakeout**
Explosive growth cannot be maintained indefinitely. Sooner or later, the rate of growth slows, and the industry enters the shakeout stage. This is now occurring in the personal computer industry (see the *Running Case* in this chapter). In the *shakeout* stage, demand approaches saturation levels: most of the demand is limited to replacement because there are few potential first-time buyers left.

As an industry enters the shakeout stage, rivalry between companies becomes intense. Typically, companies that have become accustomed to rapid growth continue to add capacity at rates consistent with past growth. However, demand is no longer growing at historic rates, and the consequence is the emergence of excess productive capacity. This condition is illustrated in Figure 2.5, where the solid curve indicates the growth in demand over time and the broken curve indicates the growth in productive capacity over time. As you can see, past point t_1, demand growth becomes slower as the industry becomes mature. However, capacity continues to grow until time t_2. The gap between the solid and the broken lines signifies excess capacity. In an attempt to use this capacity, companies often cut prices. The result can be a price war, which drives many of the most inefficient companies into bankruptcy, which is enough to deter any new entry.

Mature Industries
The shakeout stage ends when the industry enters its *mature* stage: the market is totally saturated, demand is limited to replacement demand, and growth is low or zero. What growth there is comes from population expansion that brings new customers into the market or an increase in replacement demand.

As an industry enters maturity, barriers to entry increase, and the threat of entry from potential competitors decreases. As growth slows during the shakeout, companies can no longer maintain historic growth rates merely by holding on to their market share. Competition for market share develops, driving down prices. Often the result is a price war, as happened in the airline and personal computer industries. To survive the shakeout, companies begin to focus on cost minimization and building brand loyalty. The airlines, for example, tried to cut operating costs by hiring nonunion labor and to build brand loyalty by introducing frequent-flyer programs. Personal computer companies have sought to build brand loyalty by providing excellent after-sales service and working to lower their cost structures. By the time an industry matures, the surviving companies are those that have brand loyalty and low-cost operations. Because both these factors constitute a significant barrier to entry, the threat of entry by potential competitors is greatly diminished. High entry barriers in mature industries give companies the opportunity to increase prices and profits.

As a result of the shakeout, most industries in the maturity stage have consolidated and become oligopolies. As you can see from the *Running Case* in this chapter, this process now seems to be unfolding in the personal computer industry, with the

FIGURE 2.5

Growth in Demand and Capacity

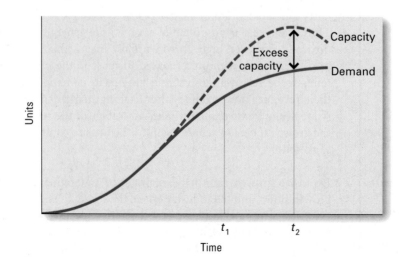

price war that Dell started leading some companies to exit the industry (IBM) or merge their operations (Compaq and Gateway). The end result will be a more consolidated industry structure. In mature industries, companies tend to recognize their interdependence and try to avoid price wars. Stable demand gives them the opportunity to enter into price leadership agreements. The net effect is to reduce the threat of intense rivalry among established companies, thereby allowing greater profitability. Nevertheless, the stability of a mature industry is always threatened by further price wars. A general slump in economic activity can depress industry demand. As companies fight to maintain their revenues in the face of declining demand, price leadership agreements break down, rivalry increases, and prices and profits fall. The periodic price wars that occur in the airline industry seem to follow this pattern.

Declining Industries

Eventually, most industries enter a *decline stage:* growth becomes negative for a variety of reasons, including technological substitution (for example, air travel for rail travel), social changes (greater health consciousness hitting tobacco sales), demographics (the declining birthrate hurting the market for baby and child products), and international competition (low-cost foreign competition pushing the U.S. steel industry into decline). Within a declining industry, the degree of rivalry among established companies usually increases. Depending on the speed of the decline and the height of exit barriers, competitive pressures can become as fierce as in the shakeout stage.[15] The main problem in a declining industry is that falling demand leads to the emergence of excess capacity. In trying to use this capacity, companies begin to cut prices, thus sparking a price war. The U.S. steel industry experienced these problems because steel companies tried to use their excess capacity despite falling demand. The same problem occurred in the airline industry in the 1990–1992 period and again in 2001–2002, as companies cut prices to ensure that they would not be flying with half-empty planes (that is, that they would not be operating with substantial excess capacity). Exit barriers play a part in adjusting excess capacity. The greater the exit barriers, the harder it is for companies to reduce capacity and the greater is the threat of severe price competition.

In summary, a third task of industry analysis is to identify the opportunities and threats that are characteristic of different kinds of industry environments in order to develop an effective business model and competitive strategy. Strategic managers have to tailor their strategies to changing industry conditions. And they have to learn to recognize the crucial points in an industry's development so that they can forecast when the shakeout stage of an industry might begin or when an industry might be moving into decline. This is also true at the level of strategic groups, for new embryonic groups may emerge because of shifts in customer needs and tastes or some groups may grow rapidly because of changes in technology and others will decline as their customers defect. Thus, for example, companies in the upscale retail group such as Macy's, Dillard's, and Nordstrom are facing declining sales as customers defect to discount retailers like Target and Wal-Mart and online companies like amazon.com and landsend.com.

Limitations of Models for Industry Analysis

The five forces, strategic groups, and life cycle models provide useful ways of thinking about and analyzing the nature of competition within an industry to identify opportunities and threats. However, each has its limitations, and managers need to be aware of their shortcomings.

Life Cycle Issues

It is important to remember that the industry life cycle model is a generalization. In practice, industry life cycles do not always follow the pattern illustrated in Figure 2.4. In some cases, growth is so rapid that the embryonic stage is skipped altogether. In others, industries fail to get past the embryonic stage. Industry growth can be revitalized after long periods of decline through innovation or social change. For example, the health boom brought the bicycle industry back to life after a long period of decline.

The time span of the stages can also vary significantly from industry to industry. Some industries can stay in maturity almost indefinitely if their products become basic necessities of life, as is the case for the car industry. Other industries skip the mature stage and go straight into decline, as in the case of the vacuum tube industry. Transistors replaced vacuum tubes as a major component in electronic products even though the vacuum tube industry was still in its growth stage. Still other industries may go through several shakeouts before they enter full maturity, as appears to be happening in the telecommunications industry.

Innovation and Change

Over any reasonable length of time, in many industries competition can be viewed as a process driven by innovation.[16] Indeed, innovation is frequently the major factor in industry evolution and causes the movement through the industry life cycle. Innovation is attractive because companies that pioneer new products, processes, or strategies can often earn enormous profits. Consider the explosive growth of Apple Computer, Toys "R" Us, Dell Computer, and Wal-Mart. In a variety of different ways, all of these companies were innovators. Apple pioneered the personal computer, Toys "R" Us pioneered a new way of selling toys (through large discount warehouse-type stores), Dell pioneered a whole new way of selling personal computers (by mail order), and Wal-Mart pioneered the low-price discount superstore concept.

Successful innovation can transform the nature of industry competition. In recent decades, one frequent consequence of innovation has been to lower the fixed costs of production, thereby reducing barriers to entry and allowing new, and smaller, enterprises to compete with large established organizations. For example, two decades ago, large integrated steel companies such as US Steel, LTV, and Bethlehem Steel dominated the steel industry. The industry was a typical oligopoly, dominated by a small number of large producers, in which tacit price collusion was practiced. Then along came a series of efficient mini-mill producers such as Nucor and Chaparral Steel, which used a new technology: electric arc furnaces. Over the past twenty years, they have revolutionized the structure of the industry. What was once a consolidated industry is now much more fragmented and price competitive. The successor company to US Steel, USX, now has only a 15 percent market share, down from 55 percent in the mid-1960s, and both Bethlehem and LTV have been through Chapter 11 bankruptcy proceedings. In contrast, the mini-mills as a group now hold over 40 percent of the market, up from 5 percent twenty years ago.[17] Thus, the mini-mill innovation has reshaped the nature of competition in the steel industry.[18] A five forces model applied to the industry in 1970 would look very different from a five forces model applied in 2002.

In his more recent work, Michael Porter, the originator of the five forces and strategic group concepts, has explicitly recognized the role of innovation in revolutionizing industry structure. Porter now talks of innovations as "unfreezing" and "reshaping" industry structure. He argues that after a period of turbulence triggered by innovation, the structure of an industry once more settles down into a fairly stable pattern, and the five forces and strategic group concepts can once more be applied.[19] This view of the evolution of industry structure is often referred to as *punctuated equilibrium.*[20] The punctuated equilibrium view holds that long periods of equilibrium, when an industry's structure is stable, are punctuated by periods of rapid change when industry structure is revolutionized by innovation; there is an unfreezing and refreezing process.

Figure 2.6 shows what punctuated equilibrium might look like for one key dimension of industry structure: competitive structure. From time t_0 to t_1, the competitive structure of the industry is a stable oligopoly, with a few companies sharing the market. At time t_1, a major new innovation is pioneered by either an existing company or a new entrant. The result is a period of turbulence between t_1 and t_2. After a while, the industry settles down into a new state of equilibrium, but now the competitive structure is far more fragmented. Note that the opposite could have happened: the industry could have become more consolidated, although this seems to be less common. In general, innovations seem to lower barriers to entry, allow more companies into the industry, and as a result lead to fragmentation rather than consolidation.

During a period of rapid change when industry structure is being revolutionized by innovation, value typically migrates to business models based on new positioning strategies.[21] In the stock brokerage industry, value has migrated away from the full-service broker model to the online trading model. In the steel industry, the introduction of electric arc technology led to a migration of value away from large, integrated enterprises and toward small mini-mills. In the book-selling industry, value has migrated away from small boutique "bricks and mortar" booksellers toward large bookstore chains like Barnes & Noble and online bookstores such as amazon.com.

Because the five forces and strategic group models are static, they cannot adequately capture what occurs during periods of rapid change in the industry environment when value is migrating. Similarly, a simple view of the industry life cycle does not allow for an industry to repeat a stage or even jump stages that technological upheavals can lead to. Nevertheless, they are useful tools for analyzing industry structure during periods of stability.

Some scholars question the validity of the punctuated equilibrium approach. Richard D'Avani has argued that many industries are **hypercompetitive,** meaning

FIGURE 2.6

Punctuated
Equilibrium and
Competitive Structure

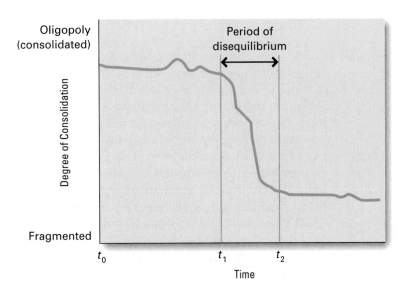

that they are characterized by permanent and ongoing innovation (the computer industry is often cited as an example of a hypercompetitive industry).[22] The structure of such industries is constantly being revolutionized by innovation, so there are no periods of equilibrium. When this is the case, some might argue that the five forces and strategic group models are of limited value because they represent no more than snapshots of a moving picture. Thus, managers must constantly repeat industry analysis and pay attention to changes in the forces of competition.

Company Differences

Another criticism of industry models is that they overemphasize the importance of industry structure as a determinant of company performance and underemphasize the importance of variations or differences among companies within an industry or a strategic group.[23] As we discuss in the next chapter, there can be enormous variance in the profit rates of individual companies within an industry. Research by Richard Rumelt and his associates, for example, suggests that industry structure explains only about 10 percent of the variance in profit rates across companies.[24] The implication is that individual company differences explain much of the remainder. Other studies have put the explained variance closer to 20 percent, which is still not a large figure.[25] Similarly, a growing number of studies have found only weak evidence of a link between strategic group membership and company profit rates, despite the fact that the strategic group model predicts a strong link.[26] Collectively, these studies suggest that the individual resources and capabilities of a company are far more important determinants of its profitability than is the industry or strategic group of which the company is a member. Although these findings do not make the five forces and strategic group models irrelevant, they do mean that the models have limited usefulness. A company will not be profitable just because it is based in an attractive industry or strategic group. As we discuss in Chapters 3 and 4, more is required.

The Macroenvironment

Just as the decisions and actions of strategic managers can often change an industry's competitive structure, so too can changing conditions or forces in the wider **macroenvironment**, that is, the broader economic, technological, demographic, social, and political context in which companies and industries are embedded (see Figure 2.7). Changes in the forces in the macroenvironment can have a direct impact on any or all of the forces in Porter's model, thereby altering the relative strength of these forces and, with it, the attractiveness of an industry.

Economic Forces

Economic forces affect the general health and well-being of a nation or the regional economy of an organization, which in turn affect companies' and industries' ability to earn an adequate rate of return. The four most important factors in the macroenvironment are the growth rate of the economy, interest rates, currency exchange rates, and inflation (or deflation) rates. Economic growth, because it leads to an expansion in customer expenditures, tends to produce a general easing of competitive pressures within an industry. This gives companies the opportunity to expand their operations and earn higher profits. Because economic decline (a recession) leads to a reduction in customer expenditures, it increases competitive pressures. Economic decline frequently causes price wars in mature industries.

The level of interest rates can determine the demand for a company's products. Interest rates are important whenever customers routinely borrow money to finance their purchase of these products. The most obvious example is the housing market, where mortgage rates directly affect demand. Interest rates also have an impact on

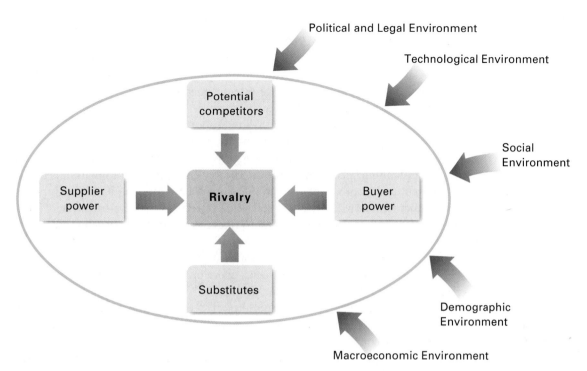

FIGURE 2.7

The Role of the Macroenvironment

the sale of autos, appliances, and capital equipment, to give just a few examples. For companies in such industries, rising interest rates are a threat and falling rates an opportunity.

Interest rates are also important insofar as they influence a company's cost of capital, and therefore its ability to raise funds and invest in new assets. The lower that interest rates are, the lower the cost of capital for companies will be, and the more investment there will be. This is not always a good thing. In the late 1990s, the very low cost of capital allowed dot-com and telecommunications companies with questionable business plans to raise large amounts of money and invest those funds in computers and telecommunications gear (the low cost of capital lowered barriers to entry by enabling start-ups to raise the capital required to circumvent entry barriers). This was initially good for the manufacturers of telecommunications equipment and computers, but the demand signal that was being sent was not sustainable: many of the dot-com and telecommunications start-ups of the 1990s went bankrupt between 2000 and 2002. Second-hand computers and telecommunications equipment from these bankrupt companies flooded the market, depressing first-time demand for that equipment and helping to plunge the computer and telecommunications equipment businesses into a deep slowdown. (For example, in January 2002, Internet auction house eBay listed more than 3,000 Cisco products that were being auctioned for much less than their initial prices.)

Currency exchange rates define the value of different national currencies against each other. Movement in currency exchange rates has a direct impact on the competitiveness of a company's products in the global marketplace. For example, when the value of the dollar is low compared with the value of other currencies, products made in the United States are relatively inexpensive and products made overseas are relatively expensive. A low or declining dollar reduces the threat from foreign competitors while creating opportunities for increased sales overseas. For example, the fall in the value of the dollar against the Japanese yen that occurred between 1985 and 1995, when the dollar-to-yen exchange rate declined from 240 yen per dollar to 85 yen per dollar, sharply increased the price of imported Japanese cars, giving U.S. car manufacturers some protection against those imports.

Price inflation can destabilize the economy, producing slower economic growth, higher interest rates, and volatile currency movements. If inflation keeps increasing, investment planning becomes hazardous. The key characteristic of inflation is that it makes the future less predictable. In an inflationary environment, it may be impossible to predict with any accuracy the real value of returns that can be earned from a project five years hence. Such uncertainty makes companies less willing to invest. Their holding back in turn depresses economic activity and ultimately pushes the economy into a slump. Thus, high inflation is a threat to companies.

Price deflation also has a destabilizing effect on economic activity. If prices are deflating, the real price of fixed payments goes up. This is particularly damaging for companies and individuals with a high level of debt who must make regular fixed payments on that debt. In a deflationary environment, the increase in the real value of debt consumes more of household and corporate cash flows, leaving less for other purchases and depressing the overall level of economic activity. Although significant deflation has not been seen since the 1930s, in the 1990s it started to take hold in Japan.

Technological Forces

Since World War II, the pace of technological change has accelerated.[27] This has unleashed a process that has been called a "perennial gale of creative destruction."[28] Technological change can make established products obsolete overnight and simultaneously create a host of new product possibilities. Thus, technological change is both creative and destructive—both an opportunity and a threat.

One of the most important impacts of technological change is that it can affect the height of barriers to entry and therefore radically reshape industry structure. The Internet, because it is so pervasive, has the potential for changing the competitive structure of many industries. It often lowers barriers to entry and reduces customer switching costs, changes that tend to increase the intensity of rivalry in an industry and lower both prices and profits.[29] For example, the Internet has lowered barriers to entry into the news industry. Providers of financial news now have to compete for advertising dollars and customer attention with new Internet-based media organizations that sprung up during the 1990s such as TheStreet.com, the Motley Fool, and Yahoo's financial section. The resulting increase in rivalry has given advertisers more choices, enabling them to bargain down the prices that they must pay to media companies. Similarly, in the automobile industry, the ability of customers to comparison-shop for cars online and purchase cars online from a number of distributors such as Auto Nation has increased the ability of customers to find the best value for money. Customers' increased bargaining power enables them to put downward pressure on car prices and squeeze profits out of the automobile industry.

Another example of how technology change is reshaping an established industry can be found by looking at the impact of biotechnology on the pharmaceutical industry. Although Merck, Pfizer, and Eli Lilly have long dominated the industry, a significant number of small biotechnology companies using recombinant DNA technology are threatening to change the competitive landscape. Between 1945 and 1990, only one new firm became a major player in the pharmaceutical industry: Syntex. Since 1990, a number of biotechnology companies have started to generate significant sales, including Amgen, Biogen, Genetech, and Chiron. Moreover, there are now over 300 publicly traded companies in the United States developing novel medicines using biotechnology. The chance is that some of these will develop into significant companies in their own right, illustrating once again that technological change lowers entry barriers and allows new players to challenge the dominance of established companies.

Demographic Forces

Demographic forces are outcomes of changes in the characteristics of a population, such as age, gender, ethnic origin, race, sexual orientation, and social class. Like the other forces in the general environment, demographic forces present managers with opportunities and threats and can have major implications for organizations. Over the past thirty years, for example, women have entered the work force in increasing numbers. Between 1973 and 2002, the percentage of women in the work force increased from 44 to 60 percent in the United States, 48 to 68 percent in Canada, and 51 to 68 percent in Britain.[30] This dramatic increase has brought issues such as equal pay for equal work and sexual harassment at work to the forefront of issues that managers must address if they are to attract and make full use of the talents of female workers.

Changes in the age distribution of a population are another example of a demographic force that affects managers and organizations. Currently, most industrialized nations are experiencing the aging of their populations as a consequence of falling birth and death rates and the aging of the baby boom generation. In Germany, for example, the percentage of the population over age sixty-five is expected to rise from 15.4 percent in 1990 to 20.7 percent in 2010. Comparable figures for Canada are 11.4 and 14.4 percent; for Japan, 11.7 and 19.5 percent; and for the United States, 12.6 and 13.5 percent.[31]

The aging of the population is increasing opportunities for organizations that cater to older people; the home health care and recreation industries, for example, are seeing an upswing in demand for their services. As the baby boom generation from the late 1950s to the early 1960s has aged, it has created a host of opportunities and threats. During the 1980s, many baby boomers were getting married and creating an upsurge in demand for the customer appliances normally bought by couples marrying for the first time. Companies such as Whirlpool Corporation and General Electric capitalized on the resulting upsurge in demand for washing machines, dishwashers, dryers, and the like. In the 1990s, many of these same baby boomers were starting to save for retirement, creating an inflow of money into mutual funds and creating a boom in the mutual fund industry. In the next twenty years, many of these same baby boomers will retire, creating a boom in retirement communities.

Social Forces

Social forces refer to the way in which changing social mores and values affect an industry. Like the other macroenvironmental forces discussed here, social change creates opportunities and threats. One of the major social movements of recent decades has been the trend toward greater health consciousness. Its impact has been immense, and companies that recognized the opportunities early have often reaped significant gains. Philip Morris, for example, capitalized on the growing health consciousness trend when it acquired Miller Brewing Company and then redefined competition in the beer industry with its introduction of low-calorie beer (Miller Lite). Similarly, PepsiCo was able to gain market share from its rival, Coca-Cola, by being the first to introduce diet colas and fruit-based soft drinks. At the same time, the health trend has created a threat for many industries. The tobacco industry, for example, is in decline as a direct result of greater customer awareness of the health implications of smoking.

Political and Legal Forces

Political and legal forces are outcomes of changes in laws and regulations. They result from political and legal developments within society and significantly affect managers and companies.

Political processes shape a society's laws, which constrain the operations of organizations and managers and thus create both opportunities and threats.[32] For example, throughout much of the industrialized world, there has been a strong trend toward deregulation of industries previously controlled by the state and privatization of organizations once owned by the state. In the United States, deregulation of the airline industry in 1979 allowed twenty-nine new airlines to enter the industry between 1979 and 1993. The increase in passenger carrying capacity after deregulation led to excess capacity on many routes, intense competition, and fare wars. To respond to this more competitive task environment, airlines have had to look for ways to reduce operating costs. The development of hub-and-spoke systems, the rise of nonunion airlines, and the introduction of no-frills discount service are all responses to increased competition in the airlines' task environment. Despite these innovations, the airline industry still experiences intense fare wars, which have lowered profits and caused numerous airline company bankruptcies. The global telecommunications service industry is now experiencing the same kind of turmoil following the deregulation of that industry in the United States and elsewhere (see the *Opening Case*).

In most countries, the interplay between political and legal forces, on the one hand, and industry competitive structure, on the other, is a two-way process in which the government sets regulations that influence competitive structure, and firms in an industry often seek to influence the regulations that governments enact by a number of means. First, when permitted, they may provide financial support to politicians or political parties that espouse views favorable to the industry and lobby government legislators directly to shape government regulations. For example, during the 1990s and early 2000s, the now-bankrupt energy trading company Enron lobbied government legislators to persuade them to deregulate energy markets in the United States, an action that Enron would benefit from. Second, companies and industries may lobby the government through industry associations. In 2002, the United States Steel Industry Association was a prime mover in persuading President Bush to enact a 30 percent tariff on imports of foreign steel into the United States. The purpose of the tariff was to protect American steel makers from foreign competitors, thereby reducing the intensity of rivalry in the United States steel markets.

The Global and National Environments

Many important processes operating at the level of the global and national environments directly and indirectly affect the competitive structure of an industry (Chapter 8 is devoted to describing strategy at the global level). Here we look at two of these: the globalization of production and markets and the effect of national or country-specific factors on home industries' competitive advantage.

The Globalization of Production and Markets

The past fifty years have seen a dramatic lowering of barriers to cross-border trade and investment. For example, the average tariff rate on manufactured goods traded between advanced nations has fallen from around 40 percent to under 4 percent. Similarly, in nation after nation, regulations prohibiting foreign companies from entering domestic markets and establishing production facilities, or acquiring domestic companies, have been removed. As a result of these two developments, there has been a surge in both the volume of international trade and the value of foreign direct investment. Between 1950 and 2000, the volume of world trade increased more than twenty-fold, while the inflation-adjusted value of world gross domestic product (GDP) increased a little over sixfold. Foreign direct investment increased from $60 billion in 1980, to $210 billion in 1990, and $1.4 trillion in 2001.[33] These two trends have led to the globalization of production and the globalization of markets.[34]

The globalization of production has been increasing as companies take advantage of lower barriers to cross-border trade and investment to disperse important parts of their production process around the globe. Doing so enables them to take advantage of national differences in the cost and quality of factors of production such as labor, energy, land, and capital, which allow them to lower their cost structures and boost profits. For example, the Boeing Company's commercial jet aircraft, the 777, uses 132,500 engineered parts that are produced around the world by 545 suppliers. Eight Japanese suppliers make parts of the fuselage, doors, and wings; a supplier in Singapore makes the doors for the nose landing gear; three suppliers in Italy manufacture wing flaps; and so on. Part of Boeing's rationale for outsourcing so much production to foreign suppliers is that these suppliers are the best in the world at performing their particular activity. Therefore, the result of having foreign suppliers build specific parts is a better final product.[35]

As for the globalization of markets, it has been argued that the world's economic system is moving from one in which national markets are distinct entities, isolated from each other by trade barriers and barriers of distance, time, and culture, toward a system in which national markets are merging into one huge global marketplace. Increasingly, customers around the world demand and use the same basic product offerings. Consequently, in many industries, it is no longer meaningful to talk about the German market, the U.S. market, or the Japanese market; there is only the global market. The global acceptance of Coca-Cola, Citigroup credit cards, blue jeans, the Sony PlayStation, McDonald's hamburgers, the Nokia wireless phone, and Microsoft's Windows operating system are examples of this trend.[36]

The trend toward the globalization of production and markets has several important implications for competition within an industry. First, industry boundaries do not stop at national borders. Because many industries are becoming global in scope, actual and potential competitors exist not only in a company's home market but also in other national markets. Managers who analyze only their home market can be caught unprepared by the entry of efficient foreign competitors. The globalization of markets and production implies that companies around the globe are finding their home markets under attack from foreign competitors. For example, in Japan, Merrill Lynch and Citicorp are making inroads against Japanese financial service institutions. In the United States, Fuji has been taking market share from Kodak, and Finland's Nokia has taken the lead from Motorola in the market for wireless phone handsets (see Strategy in Action 2.3). In the European Union, the once dominant Dutch company Philips has seen its market share in the customer electronics industry taken by Japan's JVC, Matsushita, and Sony.

Second, the shift from national to global markets during the past twenty years has intensified competitive rivalry in industry after industry. National markets that once were consolidated oligopolies, dominated by three or four companies and subjected to relatively little foreign competition, have been transformed into segments of fragmented global industries, where a large number of companies battle each

Strategy in Action

2.3

Finland's Nokia

The wireless phone market is one of the great growth stories of the last decade. Starting from a very low base in 1990, annual global sales of wireless phones surged to reach 400 million units in 2001. Two companies currently dominate the global market for wireless handsets: Motorola and Nokia. In 2001, the global market leader was Nokia, which had a 35 percent share, three times that of its nearest competitor, Motorola, which had around 13 percent, and way ahead of Ericsson and Siemens, each with around 6 to 8 percent.

Nokia's roots are in Finland, not normally a country that jumps to mind when we talk about leading-edge technology companies. In the 1980s, Nokia was a rambling Finnish conglomerate with activities that embraced tire manufacturing, paper production, customer electronics, and telecommunications equipment. Much of the answer to how this former conglomerate emerged to take a global leadership position in wireless handsets lies in the history, geography, and political economy of Finland and its Nordic neighbors.

The story starts in 1981 when the Nordic nations got together to create the world's first international wireless telephone network. Sparsely populated and inhospitably cold, they had good reason to become pioneers: it cost far too much to lay down a traditional wire line telephone service. Yet the same features that made it difficult make telecommunications all the more valuable there: people driving through the Arctic winter and owners of remote northern houses needed a telephone to summon help if things go wrong. As a result, Sweden, Norway, and Finland became the first nations in the world to take wireless telecommunications seriously. They found, for example, that although it cost up to $800 per subscriber to bring a traditional wireline service to remote locations, the same locations could be linked by wireless cellular for only $500 per person. As a consequence, 12 percent of people in Scandinavia owned cellular phones by 1994, compared with less than 6 percent in the United States, the world's second most developed market. This lead continued during the decade. By 2001, over 70 percent of Finland's phone users had a wireless phone, compared to 33 percent in the United States, and the figure for Finland may reach 100 percent by 2010.

Nokia, a long-time telecommunications equipment supplier, was well positioned to take advantage of this development from the start, but there were also other forces at work that helped Nokia develop its competitive edge. Unlike virtually every other developed nation, Finland has never had a national telephone monopoly. Instead, the country's telephone services have long been provided by about fifty or so autonomous local telephone companies whose elected boards set prices by referendum (which naturally means low prices). This army of independent and cost-conscious telephone service providers prevented Nokia from taking anything for granted in its home country. With typical Finnish pragmatism, its customers were willing to buy from the lowest-cost supplier, whether that was Nokia, Ericsson, Motorola, or some other company. This situation contrasted sharply with that prevailing in most developed nations until the late 1980s and early 1990s, where domestic telephone monopolies typically purchased equipment from a dominant local supplier or made it themselves. Nokia responded to this competitive pressure by doing everything possible to drive down its manufacturing costs while staying at the leading edge of wireless technology.

The consequences of these forces are clear: the once obscure Finnish firm is now a global leader in the wireless market. In no small part, Nokia has the lead because Scandinavia started switching over to digital technology five years before the rest of the world. In addition, spurred on by its cost-conscious customers, Nokia now has the lowest cost structure of any wireless handset equipment manufacturer in the world and is a more profitable enterprise than its global competitors.

Sources: "Lessons from the Frozen North," *Economist,* October 8, 1994, pp. 76–77. G. Edmondson, "Grabbing Markets from the Giants," *Business Week,* Special Issue: 21st Century Capitalism, 1995, p. 156. Q. Hardy, "Bypassing the Bells—A Wireless World," *Wall Street Journal,* September 21, 1998, p. R16. Q. Hardy and G. Naik, "Nokia Takes the Lead as Wireless Makers Sell 162.9 Million Phones in 1998," *Wall Street Journal,* February 8, 1999, p. A1. "A Finnish Fable," *Economist,* October 14, 2000. "Nokia Succumbs," *Economist,* June 16, 2001.

other for market share in country after country. This rivalry has driven down profit rates and made it all the more critical for companies to maximize their efficiency, quality, customer responsiveness, and innovative ability. The painful restructuring and downsizing that has been going on at companies such as Motorola and Kodak is as much a response to the increased intensity of global competition as it is to anything else. However, not all global industries are fragmented. Many remain consolidated oligopolies, except that now they are consolidated global, rather than national, oligopolies.

Third, as competitive intensity has increased, so has the rate of innovation. Companies strive to gain an advantage over their competitors by pioneering new products, processes, and ways of doing business. The result has been to compress product life cycles and make it vital for companies to stay on the leading edge of technology. In regard to highly competitive global industries, where the rate of innovation is accelerating, the criticism that Porter's five forces model is too static may be particularly relevant.

Finally, although globalization has increased both the threat of entry and the intensity of rivalry within many formerly protected national markets, it has also created enormous opportunities for companies based in those markets. The steady decline in barriers to cross-border trade and investment has opened up many once protected markets to companies based outside them. Thus, for example, in recent years, Western European, Japanese, and U.S. companies have accelerated their investments in the nations of Eastern Europe, Latin America, and Southeast Asia as they try to take advantage of growth opportunities in those areas.

National Competitive Advantage

Despite the globalization of production and markets, many of the most successful companies in certain industries are still clustered in a small number of countries. For example, many of the world's most successful biotechnology and computer companies are based in the United States, many of the world's most successful customer electronics companies are based in Japan, and many of the world's most successful chemical and engineering companies are based in Germany. This suggests that the nation-state within which a company is based may have an important bearing on the competitive position of that company in the global marketplace.

Companies need to understand how national factors can affect competitive advantage, for then they will be able to identify (1) where their most significant competitors are likely to come from and (2) where they might want to locate certain productive activities. Thus, seeking to take advantage of U.S. expertise in biotechnology, many foreign companies have set up research facilities in San Diego, Boston, and Seattle, where U.S. biotechnology companies tend to be clustered. Similarly, in an attempt to take advantage of Japanese success in customer electronics, many U.S. electronics companies have set up research and production facilities in Japan, often in conjunction with Japanese partners.

In a study of national competitive advantage, Michael Porter identified four attributes of a national or country-specific environment that have an important impact on the global competitiveness of companies located within that nation:[37]

- ■ *Factor endowments:* A nation's position in factors of production such as skilled labor or the infrastructure necessary to compete in a given industry

- ■ *Demand conditions:* The nature of home demand for the industry's product or service

- ■ *Relating and supporting industries:* The presence or absence in a nation of supplier industries and related industries that are internationally competitive

■ *Firm strategy, structure, and rivalry:* The conditions in the nation governing how companies are created, organized, and managed and the nature of domestic rivalry

Porter speaks of these four attributes as constituting the *diamond,* arguing that companies are most likely to succeed in industries or strategic groups where the four attributes are favorable (see Figure 2.8). He also argues that the diamond's attributes form a mutually reinforcing system in which the effect of one attribute is dependent on the state of others.

Factor Endowments.   **Factor endowments**—the cost and quality of factors of production—are a prime determinant of the competitive advantage that certain countries might have in certain industries. Factors of production include **basic factors,** such as land, labor, capital, and raw materials, and **advanced factors,** such as technological know-how, managerial sophistication, and physical infrastructure (roads, railways, and ports). The competitive advantage that the United States enjoys in biotechnology might be explained by the presence of certain advanced factors of production—for example, technological know-how—in combination with some basic factors, which might be a pool of relatively low-cost venture capital that can be used to fund risky start-ups in industries such as biotechnology.

Local Demand Conditions.   Home demand plays an important role in providing the impetus for "upgrading" competitive advantage. Companies are typically most sensitive to the needs of their closest customers. Thus, the characteristics of home demand are particularly important in shaping the attributes of domestically made products and creating pressures for innovation and quality. A nation's companies gain competitive advantage if their domestic customers are sophisticated and

FIGURE 2.8

National Competitive Advantage

Source: Adapted from M. E. Porter. The Competitive Advantage of Nations. *Harvard Business Review,* March–April, 1990, page 77.

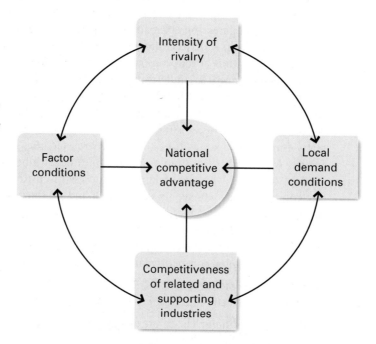

demanding and pressure local companies to meet high standards of product quality and produce innovative products. Japan's sophisticated and knowledgeable buyers of cameras helped stimulate the Japanese camera industry to improve product quality and introduce innovative models. A similar example can be found in the cellular phone equipment industry, where sophisticated and demanding local customers in Scandinavia helped push Nokia of Finland and Ericsson of Sweden to invest in cellular phone technology long before demand for cellular phones took off in other developed nations. As a result, Nokia and Ericsson, together with Motorola, are significant players in the global cellular telephone equipment industry. The case of Nokia is reviewed in more depth in Strategy in Action 2.3.

Competitiveness of Related and Supporting Industries. The third broad attribute of national advantage in an industry is the presence of internationally competitive suppliers or related industries. The benefits of investments in advanced factors of production by related and supporting industries can spill over into an industry, thereby helping it achieve a strong competitive position internationally. Swedish strength in fabricated steel products (such as ball bearings and cutting tools) has drawn on strengths in Sweden's specialty steel industry. Switzerland's success in pharmaceuticals is closely related to its previous international success in the technologically related dye industry. One consequence of this process is that successful industries within a country tend to be grouped into clusters of related industries. Indeed, this was one of the most pervasive findings of Porter's study. One such cluster is the German textile and apparel sector, which includes high-quality cotton, wool, synthetic fibers, sewing machine needles, and a wide range of textile machinery.

Intensity of Rivalry. The fourth broad attribute of national competitive advantage in Porter's model is the strategy, structure, and rivalry of companies within a nation. Different nations are characterized by different management ideologies that either help or do not help them to build national competitive advantage. For example, the predominance of engineers on the top management teams of German and Japanese companies can be attributed to an emphasis in these countries on improving manufacturing processes and product design. In contrast, people with finance backgrounds dominate the top management teams of many U.S. companies. This might lead to a lack of attention in U.S. companies to improving manufacturing processes and product design. Conversely, the dominance of finance may have led to a corresponding overemphasis on maximizing short-term financial returns. One consequence of these different management ideologies has been a relative loss of U.S. competitiveness in many engineering-based industries where manufacturing processes and product design issues are all important, such as automobiles. A second issue is a strong association between vigorous domestic rivalry and the creation and persistence of competitive advantage in an industry. Rivalry induces companies to look for ways to improve efficiency, which makes them better international competitors. Domestic rivalry creates pressures to innovate, improve quality, reduce costs, and invest in upgrading advanced factors. All this helps to create world-class competitors. The stimulating effects of strong domestic competition are clear in the story of the rise of Nokia of Finland in the market for wireless handsets and telephone equipment (see Strategy in Action 2.3).

Summary of Chapter

1. An industry can be defined as a group of companies offering products or services that are close substitutes for each other. Close substitutes are products or services that satisfy the same basic customer needs.

2. The main technique used to analyze competition in the industry environment is the five forces model. The five forces are (1) the risk of new entry by potential competitors, (2) the extent of rivalry among established firms, (3) the bargaining power of buyers, (4) the bargaining power of suppliers, and (5) the threat of substitute products. The stronger each force is, the more competitive the industry and the lower the rate of return that can be earned.

3. The risk of entry by potential competitors is a function of the height of barriers to entry. The higher the barriers to entry are, the lower is the risk of entry and the greater are the profits that can be earned in the industry.

4. The extent of rivalry among established companies is a function of an industry's competitive structure, demand conditions, and barriers to exit. Strong demand conditions moderate the competition among established companies and create opportunities for expansion. When demand is weak, intensive competition can develop, particularly in consolidated industries with high exit barriers.

5. Buyers are most powerful when a company depends on them for business but they themselves are not dependent on the company. In such circumstances, buyers are a threat.

6. Suppliers are most powerful when a company depends on them for business but they themselves are not dependent on the company. In such circumstances, suppliers are a threat.

7. Substitute products are the products of companies serving customer needs similar to the needs served by the industry being analyzed. The more similar the substitute products are to each other, the lower is the price that companies can charge without losing customers to the substitutes.

8. Some argue for a sixth competitive force of some significance: the power, vigor, and competence of complementors. Powerful and vigorous complementors may have a strong positive impact on demand in an industry.

9. Most industries are composed of strategic groups: groups of companies pursuing the same or a similar strategy. Companies in different strategic groups pursue different strategies.

10. The members of a company's strategic group constitute its immediate competitors. Because different strategic groups are characterized by different opportunities and threats, it may pay a company to switch strategic groups. The feasibility of doing so is a function of the height of mobility barriers.

11. Industries go through a well-defined life cycle: from an embryonic stage, through growth, shakeout, and maturity, and eventually decline. Each stage has different implications for the competitive structure of the industry, and each gives rise to its own set of opportunities and threats.

12. The five forces, strategic group, and industry life cycles models all have limitations. The five forces and strategic group models present a static picture of competition that deemphasizes the role of innovation. Yet innovation can revolutionize industry structure and completely change the strength of different competitive forces. The five forces and strategic group models have been criticized for deemphasizing the importance of individual company differences. A company will not be profitable just because it is based in an attractive industry or strategic group; much more is required. The industry life cycle model is a generalization that is not always followed, particularly when innovations revolutionize an industry.

13. The macroenvironment affects the intensity of rivalry within an industry. Included in the macroenvironment are the macroeconomic environment, the technological environment, the demographic and social environment, and the political and legal environment.

14. The global environment has been changing rapidly in recent years. A fundamental change is occurring in the world economy: the globalization of production and of markets. The consequences of this change include more intense rivalry, more rapid innovation, and shorter product life cycles.

15. There is a link between the national environment and the competitive advantage of a company in the global economy.

Discussion Questions

1. Under what environmental conditions are price wars most likely to occur in an industry? What are the implications of price wars for a company? How should a company try to deal with the threat of a price war?

2. Discuss Porter's five forces model with reference to what you know about the U.S. airline industry. What does the model tell you about the level of competition in this industry?

3. Identify a growth industry, a mature industry, and a declining industry. For each industry, identify the following: (a) the number and size distribution of companies, (b) the nature of barriers to entry, (c) the height of barriers to entry, and (d) the extent of product differentiation. What do these factors tell you about the nature of competition in each industry?

What are the implications for the company in terms of opportunities and threats?

4. Assess the impact of macroenvironmental factors on the likely level of enrollment at your university over the next decade. What are the implications of these factors for the job security and salary level of your professors?

Practicing Strategic Management

SMALL-GROUP EXERCISE: COMPETING WITH MICROSOFT

Break up into groups of three to five people, and appoint one group member as a spokesperson who will communicate your findings to the class.

You are a group of managers and software engineers at a small start-up. You have developed a revolutionary new operating system for personal computers that offers distinct advantages over Microsoft's Windows operating system: it takes up less memory space on the hard drive of a personal computer; it takes full advantage of the power of the personal computer's microprocessor, and in theory can run software applications much faster than Windows; it is much easier to install and use than Windows; and it responds to voice instructions with an accuracy of 99.9 percent, in addition to input from a keyboard or mouse. The operating system is the only product offering that your company has produced.

Complete the following exercises:

1. Analyze the competitive structure of the market for personal computer operating systems. On the basis of this analysis, identify what factors might inhibit adoption of your operating system by customers.

2. Can you think of a strategy that your company might pursue, either alone or in conjunction with other enterprises, in order to "beat Microsoft"? What will it take to execute that strategy successfully?

ARTICLE FILE 2

Find an example of an industry that has become more competitive in recent years. Identify the reasons for the increase in competitive pressure.

STRATEGIC MANAGEMENT PROJECT: MODULE 2

This module requires you to analyze the industry environment in which your company is based using the information you have already gathered:

1. Apply the five forces model to the industry in which your company is based. What does this model tell you about the nature of competition in the industry?

2. Are any changes taking place in the macroenvironment that might have an impact, positive or negative, on the industry in which your company is based? If so, what are these changes, and how might they affect the industry?

3. Identify any strategic groups that might exist in the industry. How does the intensity of competition differ across these strategic groups?

4. How dynamic is the industry in which your company is based? Is there any evidence that innovation is reshaping competition or has done so in the recent past?

5. In what stage of its life cycle is the industry in which your company is based? What are the implications of this for the intensity of competition both now and in the future?

6. Is your company based in an industry that is becoming more global? If so, what are the implications of this change for competitive intensity?

7. Analyze the impact of national context as it pertains to the industry in which your company is based. Does national context help or hinder your company in achieving a competitive advantage in the global marketplace?

EXPLORING THE WEB
Visiting Boeing and Airbus

Visit the web sites of the Boeing Corporation (**http://www .boeing.com**) and Airbus Industrie (**http://www.airbus .com**). Go to the news features of both sites, and read through the press releases issued by both companies. Also look at the annual reports and company profile (or history features) contained on both sites. With this material as your guide:

1. Use Porter's five forces model to analyze the nature of competition in the global commercial jet aircraft market.

2. Assess the likely outlook for competition over the next ten years in this market. Try to establish whether new entry into this industry is likely, whether demand will grow or shrink, how powerful buyers are likely to become, and what the implications of all this are for the nature of competition ten years out.

General Task: Search the Web for information that allows you to assess the current state of competition in the market for personal computers. Use that information to perform an analysis of the structure of the market in the United States. (Hint: Try visiting the web sites of personal computer companies. Also visit Electronic Business Today at **http://www.ebtmag.com**).

Closing Case

How the Internet Revolutionized the Stockbrokerage Industry

For years, only professional stockbrokers with expensive computer hardware could trade online. An individual investor who wanted to buy or sell a stock had to call a stockbroker and place an order, for which the stockbroker would charge a commission. At full-service stockbrokers such as Merrill Lynch, which offer clients detailed research reports, stock recommendations, and financial planning services, these commissions could run to 2.5 percent of the value of the order. Thus, an order worth $10,000 could generate $250 in commissions.

The situation began to change in 1994 when a small discount broker, K. Aufhauser & Co., took advantage of new technology to become the first to offer its clients the ability to trade online over the Internet, effectively bypassing stockbrokers. The offering allowed Aufhauser to operate with fewer personnel, and the cost saving was passed on to customers in the form of lower commissions. At first, online trading was nothing more than a curiosity, but several things changed this. First, the Internet started to make rapid inroads into the homes of individual Americans. Second, within a short space of time, a vast amount of investment information was being offered on the Internet. Individual investors soon found that they could go to sites such as the Motley Fool at America Online or Yahoo's finance site and get much of the information that they needed to make informed investment decisions. No longer did they have to call their stockbrokers to ask for information. Third, a number of small companies quickly followed Aufhauser's lead and took advantage of the Internet to offer their clients online trading for commissions that were significantly below those offered by full-service stockbrokers in the physical world. Finally, America's long bull market drew ever more individuals into the stock market, particularly among America's large baby boom generation, who were drawn to

investing in order to build up funds for retirement. Increasingly, these newcomers set up online trading accounts.

The effects of these trends were dramatic. By mid-2000, 150 firms were offering online trading over the Internet. Many of these companies did not even exist six years before. The arrival of the Internet had lowered barriers to entry and allowed these companies to enter the stockbrokerage industry and compete against established brokers. As the competition for the business of online investors started to heat up, commissions started to fall. By early 1999, online brokerages such as E*Trade were charging deep discount fees of $14.95 per market order for trades of up to 5,000 shares. Thus, whereas an order for 1,000 shares of a stock trading at $20 a share could cost the client of a full-service broker as much as $500 in commission, the same trade could be executed over E*Trade for $14.95! Attracted by such low prices, from little more than a trickle in 1994, the volume of online trades grew to account for 40 percent of all stock trades by individuals as of mid-2000. Discount broker Charles Schwab emerged as the leader of this new segment, with eight out of ten online trades in 2000 being executed by Schwab.

At first, full-service brokers derided online trading as dangerous and justified their high commissions by claiming that they offered their clients sound financial advice and proprietary research reports. However, with as many as 40 percent of all stockbrokers lacking much in the way of experience and with the rapid increase in the amount of investment information that could be accessed online, such arguments sounded increasingly shrill and self-serving. By early 1999, it was becoming apparent that full-service brokers needed to adapt to the new technology or risk seeing their client base evaporate.

The landmark event occurred in June 1999 when Merrill Lynch, the world's largest full-service broker, bowed to the inevitable and announced that it too would soon offer its clients the ability to trade online for a fee of $29.95 for trades of up to 1,000 shares. In addition, Merrill Lynch changed its pricing structure for many individual clients, replacing a fee structure that was based on the number of trades with a new flat fee that allowed unlimited numbers of trades. An internal Merrill report estimated that as a result, its army of 14,800 well-paid stockbrokers, who were paid chiefly in commissions, might initially see their incomes decline by 18 percent as a result of this move. Merrill knew that it faced a potential rebellion from its stockbrokers, but it also knew that it had no choice: forecasts suggested that more than 50 percent of stock trades by individuals would be online by 2001. The early results suggest that Merrill did the right thing. Soon after the introduction of Merrill's online trading service, account transfers to rival firms dried. Many of Merrill's clients realized that the combination of its research and online trading made it a better value proposition than discount online trading houses, such as E*Trade, which could not offer the same depth and breadth of research.

In late 2000, the online trading revolution appeared to stall when the NASDAQ stock market began what would prove to be a 60 percent decline in value over the next twelve months. As the stock market imploded, the volume of online trading dried up. Schwab saw online trading volumes drop over 50 percent in the first six months of 2001, which decimated the company's bottom line, leading to a 60 percent fall in net income. The same happened at other former high-flying Internet stockbro-

kers, including E*Trade, which lost money in 2001 on a 40 percent decline in online trading volume and declining revenues. It remains to be seen whether this represents nothing more than a temporary setback in the rise of online trading, or the end of the boom.

Sources: C. Gasparino and R. Buckman, "Horning In: Facing Internet Threat Merrill to Offer Trading Online for Low Fee," *Wall Street Journal*, June 1, 1999, p. A1. "Bears or Bulls, More and More People Are Trading Shares Online," *Economist*, October 17, 1998. L. N. Spiro and E. C. Baig, "Who Needs a Broker?" *Business Week*, February 22, 1999, p. 113. "A Reluctant Success," *Economist*, June 9, 2001, pp. 79–80. M. J. Ybarra, "The Brokerage Blues," *Upside* (August 2001): 46–51.

Discussion Questions

1. How did the rise of the Internet alter competitive forces in the brokerage industry?

2. How does the rise of online brokers change the likely long-term profitability of the stockbrokerage industry?

3. How did the change in competitive forces in the brokerage industry change the strategies required for success in that industry?

4. Do you think the decline in online trading volumes observed in 2001 represents the highwater market for the rise of online trading, or is it simply a temporary setback?

5. What was Merrill Lynch's strategy for gaining the business of individual investors in the pre-Internet era? What is the strategy today? What should be the strategy in the future?

Internal Analysis: Distinctive Competencies, Competitive Advantage, and Profitability

Opening Case

BJ'S Wholesale-Competitive Advantage

BJ's Wholesale is a membership-based warehouse club that, like its main competitors, Costco and Wal-Mart's Sam's Club, offers fee-paying members a limited selection of low-priced products across a wide range of merchandise categories. The typical warehouse club carries 4,000 items compared to 40,000 to 60,000 items at discount retailers and supermarkets. The warehouse club business model is aimed at driving down operating costs to enable the club to charge lower prices than those found at other retail establishments and still be profitable. Warehouse clubs lower their cost structure by purchasing in large volumes, maximizing inventory turnover, achieving efficient distribution, and reduced handling of merchandise in no-frills, self-service warehouse facilities.

BJ's is currently the best performer in the highly competitive warehouse club segment of the U.S. retail industry. Founded in 1984, it has grown to over 120 stores, most of them concentrated in the northeastern United States (Costco and Sam's Club both have over 400 stores). In 2001, BJ's generated $5.3 billion in sales, an increase of 15 percent over 2000. Not only has the company grown rapidly, it has also done so profitably. In 2001, its return on invested capital (ROIC) was 19 percent compared to 13.5 percent for Wal-Mart, 11 percent for Costco, and an average for the retail industry of 10 percent. Moreover, this performance was not a one-time event: BJ's ROIC has outperformed that of the industry and its closest competitors every year since 1996.

How does BJ's achieve its superior profitability? By buying in bulk, BJ's is able to get deep price discounts from merchandise vendors, lowering its cost of goods sold. Moreover, because it also sells its own label products, it is able to use this as a lever to bargain down the prices it pays for branded merchandise. BJ's eliminates many of the merchandise handling costs associated with traditional multiple-step distribution channels by purchasing full truckloads of merchandise directly from manufacturers and storing merchandise on the sales floor rather than in central warehouses. In essence, BJ's devotes far less space to storing inventory than traditional retailers do, thereby driving down its investments in property, plant, and equipment relative to its sales base and driving up its ROIC. BJ's warehouses have minimal fixtures, which also reduces investments in property plant and equipment relative to sales and increases the company's return on capital. Moreover, because its high sales volume leads to rapid inventory turnover, it generates cash from the sale of a large portion of inventory before it is required to pay its merchandise vendors, thereby reducing its working capital and boosting its ROIC.

Although these strategies help explain its superior performance, Costco and Sam's Club operate with a similar business model. So what does BJ's do differently from competitors that explain its superior profitability? First, unlike Costco, BJ's pursues a clustering strategy and places its stores close to each other so that they *cannibalize* sales from each other. By doing this, BJ's can maximize the efficiency of its distribution system, and this increases profitability. BJ's strong presence in a locality also maximizes opportunities for word-of-mouth advertising, which reduces the need for costly advertising, which also increases profitability. Finally, it combines purchases for nearby clubs and ships them on a same-day basis, which results in higher volume discounts, reduced freight expenses, and lower receiving costs.

Second, BJ's focuses on only smaller towns and suburban locations outside cities, which tend to be less expensive than the larger urban locations favored by its competitors, thereby reducing BJ's investment in stores and increasing its profitability. The average BJ's location is 111,000 square feet, 20 percent less than Costco and 10 percent less than Sam's Club. Although the average Costco store racks up twice the sales of the average BJ's store ($100 million versus $43 million), due to differences in location and store size costs, the average breakeven sales figure for a Costco store is $45 million, or 45 percent of average sales, compared to $17 million at BJ's, or 39 percent of average sales. Lower breakeven sales figures translate into higher profitability.

Third, BJ's has tried to differentiate itself by focusing on and catering to the needs of individual retail customers. In contrast, its competitors focus on both small business and individuals. To do this, BJ's carries more merchandise items than its competitors do: 6,000 on average versus 4,000 each at Costco and Sam's Club. Thus, BJ's might carry four or five styles of TVs compared to one or two at Costco. BJ's believes that its wider selection appeals more to retail customers and allows it to charge slightly higher prices than Costco and Sam's Club. Whereas Costco operates with markups on goods in the 8 to 12 percent range, BJ's places markups as high as 15 percent of goods. This retail customer orientation also led BJ's to be the first warehouse store to accept credit cards and debit cards (to keep costs down, Costco and Sam's Club were long a cash- or check-only operation). The suburban location strategy also ties into BJ's focus on retail customers.

Finally, BJ's has been a leader in investments in information technology. It was the first warehouse club to introduce scanning devices that work in conjunction with electronic point of sale (EPOS) terminals, which have enabled it to streamline its reordering and payments systems. BJ's analyzes sales data daily for stock replenishment purposes. The efficiencies gained have allowed it to employ fewer people. The company has lowered its payroll as a percentage of sales in each of the past three years, which has translated into lower sales expenses and greater profitability. BJ's has also used its information systems to collect detailed purchasing data on individual members. This permits buying staff and store managers to track changes in members' buying behavior, altering stocking accordingly to meet customer needs better.

Thus, through its distinctive approach to doing business—its focus on providing a broader range of products for individual retail customers in suburban locations and its aggressive use of information systems—BJ's has been able to achieve higher profitability than its competitors in the sector.

Sources: BJ's Wholesale, 2000 10K Report. Costco Wholesale 2001 10K Report. K. Clark, "Two Strategies, One Popular Segment," *Chain Store Age* (November 2001): 56–58. M. Prior, "The Super Growth Leaders," *DSN Retailing*, December 10, 2001, pp. 29–30.

Why, within a particular industry or market, do some companies outperform others? What is the basis of their (sustained) competitive advantage?

The *Opening Case* provides some clues to the sources of competitive advantage. The conclusion from its description of how BJ's operates is that BJ's competitive advantage derives from the *distinctive way its managers have pursued the warehouse club business model and the way they have combined specific strategies to give BJ's superior efficiency, responsiveness to customers, and innovation.* As you will see in this chapter, three of the four main building blocks of competitive advantage are *efficiency, innovation,* and *responsiveness to customers;* the fourth is the *quality of product or service offering.*

This chapter focuses on internal analysis, which is concerned with identifying the *strengths* and *weaknesses* of the company. Together with an analysis of the company's external environment, internal analysis gives managers the information they need to choose the strategies and business model that will enable their company to attain a sustained competitive advantage. Internal analysis is a three-step process. First, managers must understand the process by which companies create value for customers and profit for themselves, and they need to understand the role of *resources, capabilities,* and *distinctive competencies* in this process. Second, they need to understand how important superior *efficiency, innovation, quality,* and *responsiveness to customers* are in creating value and generating high profitability. Third, they must be able to analyze the sources of their company's competitive advantage to identify what is driving the profitability of their enterprise and where opportunities for improvement might lie. In other words, they must be able to identify how the *strengths* of the enterprise boost its profitability and how any *weaknesses* lead to lower profitability.

Three more critical issues in internal analysis are addressed in this chapter. First, what factors influence the *durability* of competitive advantage? Second, why do successful companies often lose their competitive advantage? Third, how can companies avoid competitive failure and sustain their competitive advantage over time?

After reading this chapter, you will understand the nature of competitive advantage and why managers need to perform internal analysis, just as they must conduct industry analysis, to achieve superior performance and profitability.

Distinctive Competencies and Competitive Advantage

A company has a *competitive advantage* over its rivals when its profitability is greater than the average profitability for all companies in its industry. It has a *sustained competitive advantage* when it is able to maintain above-average profitability over a number of years. Figure 3.1 compares BJ's profitability (measured by return on invested capital, ROIC) against that of several other well-known retailers for the period 1996–2001. BJ's outperformed all of them, including Wal-Mart, the world's largest retailer, which also enjoys superior profitability. BJ's profitability was 50 percent higher than the average for the U.S. retail industry during this period: it had a competitive advantage. What are the sources of BJ's competitive advantage and superior profitability, or that of any other company? Moreover, what is the link between strategy, competitive advantage, and profitability?

Strategy, Distinctive Competencies, and Competitive Advantage

The primary objective of strategy is to achieve a competitive advantage because then superior profitability will follow. Thus, strategy is the driver of competitive advantage and profitability. All the levels of strategy identified in Chapter 1—functional, business, global, and corporate—are involved in creating a competitive advantage, and they are discussed in detail in the next chapters. No matter what the level, however,

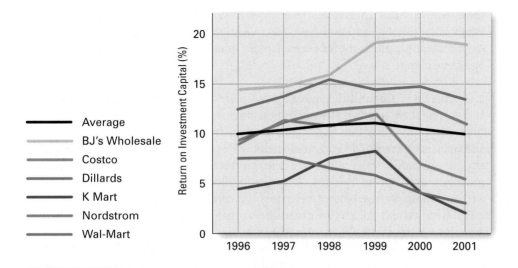

FIGURE 3.1

Profitability in the U. S. Retail Industry, 1996–2001

to use strategy to achieve a competitive advantage, a company must create distinctive competencies.

Distinctive competencies are firm-specific strengths that allow a company to *differentiate* its products and/or achieve substantially *lower costs* than its rivals and thus gain a competitive advantage. It can be argued, for example, that Toyota has distinctive competencies in the development and operation of manufacturing processes. Toyota pioneered a whole range of manufacturing techniques, such as just-in-time inventory systems, self-managing teams, and reduced setup times for complex equipment. These competencies, collectively known as the Toyota *lean production* system, helped it attain superior efficiency and product quality, which are the basis of its competitive advantage in the global automobile industry.[1] Distinctive competencies arise from two complementary sources: *resources* and *capabilities*.[2]

Resources. **Resources** are the capital or financial, physical, social or human, technological, and organizational factor endowments that allow a company to create value for its customers. Company resources can be divided into two types: tangible and intangible resources. **Tangible resources** are something physical, such as land, buildings, plant, equipment, inventory, and money. **Intangible resources** are nonphysical entities that are the creation of the company and its employees, such as brand names, the reputation of the company, the knowledge that employees have gained through experience, and the intellectual property of the company, including patents, copyrights, and trademarks.

The more *firm specific* and *difficult to imitate* is a resource, the more likely a company is to have a distinctive competency. For example, Polaroid's distinctive competency in instant photography was based on a firm-specific and valuable intangible resource: technological know-how in instant film processing that was protected from imitation by a thicket of patents. Once a process can be imitated, as when patents expire, or a superior technology, such as digital photography, comes along, the distinctive competency disappears, as has happened to Polaroid. Another important quality of a resource that leads to a distinctive competency is that it is *valuable:* in some way, it helps to create strong *demand* for the company's products. Thus, Polaroid's technological know-how was valuable while it created strong demand for its photographic products; it became far less valuable when superior digital technology came along.

Capabilities. **Capabilities** refer to a company's skills at coordinating its resources and putting them to productive use. These skills reside in an organization's rules, routines, and procedures, that is, the style or manner through which it makes decisions and manages its internal processes to achieve organizational objectives. More generally, a company's capabilities are the product of its organizational structure, processes, and control systems. They specify how and where decisions are made within a company, the kind of behaviors the company rewards, and the company's cultural norms and values. (We discuss how organizational structure and control systems help a company obtain capabilities in Chapters 12 and 13.) Capabilities are intangible. They reside not so much in individuals as in the way individuals interact, cooperate, and make decisions within the context of an organization.[3]

A Critical Distinction. The distinction between resources and capabilities is critical to understanding what generates a distinctive competency. A company may have firm-specific and valuable resources, but unless it has the capability to use those resources effectively, it may not be able to create a distinctive competency. It is also important to recognize that a company may not need firm-specific and valuable resources to establish a distinctive competency so long as it *does have* capabilities that no competitor possesses. For example, the steel mini-mill operator Nucor is widely acknowledged to be the most cost-efficient steel maker in the United States. Its distinctive competency in low-cost steel making does not come from any firm-specific and valuable resources. Nucor has the same resources (plant, equipment, skilled employees, know-how) as many other mini-mill operators. What distinguishes Nucor is its unique capability to manage its resources in a highly productive way. Specifically, Nucor's structure, control systems, and culture promote efficiency at all levels within the company.

In sum, for a company to have a distinctive competency it must at a minimum have either (1) a firm-specific and valuable resource and the capabilities (skills) necessary to take advantage of that resource (as illustrated by Polaroid) or (2) a firm-specific capability to manage resources (as exemplified by Nucor). A company's distinctive competency is strongest when it possesses *both* firm-specific and valuable resources and firm-specific capabilities to manage those resources.

Figure 3.2 illustrates the relationship of a company's strategies, distinctive competencies, and competitive advantage. Distinctive competencies shape the strategies that the company pursues, which lead to competitive advantage and superior profitability. However, it is also very important to realize that the strategies a company adopts can build new resources and capabilities or strengthen the existing resources and capabilities of the company, thereby enhancing the distinctive competencies of the enterprise. Thus, the relationship between distinctive competencies and strategies is not a linear one; rather, it is a reciprocal one in which distinctive competencies shape strategies, and strategies help to build and create distinctive competencies.[4] The history of The Walt Disney Company since the 1980s illustrates the way this process works.

In the early 1980s, Disney suffered a string of poor financial years that culminated in a 1984 management shakeup when Michael Eisner was appointed CEO. Four years

FIGURE 3.2

Strategy, Resources, Capabilities, and Competencies

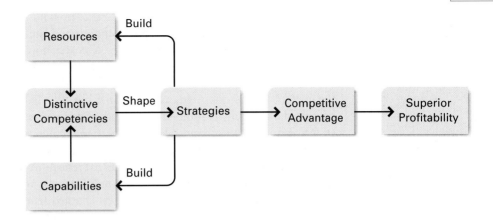

later, Disney's sales had increased from $1.66 billion to $3.75 billion, its net profits from $98 million to $570 million, and its stock market valuation from $1.8 billion to $10.3 billion. What brought about this transformation was the company's deliberate attempt to use its resources and capabilities more aggressively: Disney's enormous film library, its brand name, and its filmmaking skills, particularly in animation. Under Eisner, many old Disney classics were re-released, first in movie theaters and then on video, earning the company millions in the process. Then Eisner reintroduced the product that had originally made Disney famous: the full-length animated feature. Putting together its brand name and in-house animation capabilities, Disney produced a stream of major box office hits, including *The Little Mermaid, Beauty and the Beast, Aladdin, Pocahontas,* and *The Lion King.* Disney also started a cable television channel, the Disney Channel, to use this library and capitalize on the company's brand name. In other words, Disney's existing resources and capabilities shaped its strategies.

Through his choice of strategies, Eisner also developed new competencies in different parts of the business. In the filmmaking arm of Disney, for example, Eisner created a new low-cost film division under the Touchstone label, and the company had a string of low-budget box office hits. It entered into a long-term agreement with the computer animation company Pixar to develop a competency in computer-generated animated films. This strategic collaboration has produced several hits, including *Toy Story* and *Monsters Incorporated.* In sum, Disney's transformation was based not only on strategies that took advantage of the company's existing resources and capabilities, but also on strategies that built new resources and capabilities, such as those that underlie the company's competency in computer-generated animated films.

Competitive Advantage, Value Creation, and Profitability

Competitive advantage leads to superior profitability. At the most basic level, how profitable a company becomes depends on three factors: (1) the amount of *value* customers place on the company's products, (2) the *price* that a company charges for its products, and (3) the *costs* of creating that value. Note the important distinction between *value* and *price. Value* is something that customers assign to a product. It is a function of the attributes of the product, such as its performance, design, quality, and point-of-sale and after-sale service. For example, most customers would place a much higher value on a top-end Lexus car from Toyota than on a low-end basic economy car from General Motors, precisely because they perceive the Lexus to have better performance and superior design, quality, and service. A company that strengthens the value of its products in the eyes of customers gives it more *pricing options:* it can raise prices to reflect that value or hold prices lower, which induces more customers to purchase its product and expand unit sales volume.

Whatever pricing option a company chooses, however, the price a company charges for a good or service is typically less than the value placed on that good or service by the customer. This is so because the customer captures some of that value in the form of what economists call a *consumer surplus.*[5] The customer is able to do this because the company is competing with other companies for the customer's business, so the company must charge a lower price than it could were it a monopoly supplier. Moreover, it is normally impossible to segment the market to such a degree that the company can charge each customer a price that reflects that individual's unique assessment of the value of a product—what economists refer to as a customer's *reservation price.* For these reasons, the price that gets charged tends to be less than the value placed on the product by many customers. Nevertheless, remember the basic principle here: *the more value a company creates, the more pricing options it has.*

These concepts are illustrated in Figure 3.3: *V* is the average value per unit of a product to a customer, *P* is the average price per unit that the company decides to charge for that product, and *C* is the average unit costs of producing that product (including actual production costs and the cost of capital investments in production systems). The company's average profit per unit is equal to $P - C$, and the consumer surplus is equal to $V - P$. The company makes a profit so long as *P* is more than *C*, and its profitability will be greater the lower *C* is *relative* to *P*. Bear in mind that the difference between *V* and *P* is in part determined by the intensity of competitive pressure in the market place; the lower the intensity of competitive pressure is, the higher the price that can be charged relative to *V* is, but it is also determined by the company's pricing choice.[6] As we shall see, a company may choose to keep prices low relative to volume because lower prices enable the company to sell more products, attain scale economies, and boost its profit margin by lowering *C* relative to *P*.

Note also that the *value created* by a company is measured by the difference between perceived value (*V*) and costs of production (*C*), that is $V - C$. A company creates value by converting factors of production that cost *C* into a product on which customers place a value of *V*. A company can create more value for its customers by lowering *C* or making the product more attractive through superior design, performance, quality, service and the like. When customers place a greater value on the product (*V* increases), they are willing to pay a higher price (*P* increases). This discussion suggests that a company has a competitive advantage and high profitability when it creates more value for its customers than do rivals.[7]

FIGURE 3.3

Value Creation per Unit

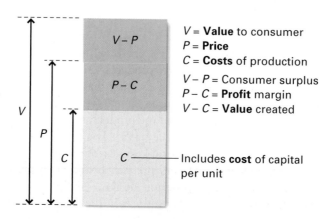

$V =$ **Value** to consumer
$P =$ **Price**
$C =$ **Costs** of production

$V - P =$ Consumer surplus
$P - C =$ **Profit** margin
$V - C =$ **Value** created

Includes **cost** of capital per unit

The company's pricing options are captured in Figure 3.4. Suppose a company's current pricing option is the one pictured in the middle column of Figure 3.4. Imagine that the company decides to pursue strategies to increase the perceived value of its product offering from V to V^* in order to boost its profitability. Increasing value initially raises production costs because the company has to spend money to increase product performance, quality, service, and other factors. Now there are two different pricing options that the company can pursue. Option 1 is to raise prices to reflect the higher value: the company raises prices more than its costs increase, and profit margins $(P - C)$ increase. Option 2 involves a very different set of choices: the company *lowers* prices in order to expand unit volume. Basically, what is happening here is that customers recognize that they are getting a great bargain because price is now much lower than value (the *consumer surplus* has increased) so they rush out to buy more (*demand* had increased). As unit volume expands due to increased demand, the company is able to realize scale economies and reduce its average unit costs. The net result is although prices are lowered and creating the extra value initially cost more, the average unit costs of production fall as volume increases and scale economies are attained, so profit margins widen.

Of course, there are more pricing options than those illustrated in Figure 3.4. For example, the company could have held prices constant, raised prices by less than illustrated in Option 1, or expanded profit margins by simultaneously raising prices and realizing some cost scale economies from a higher unit volume. What a company does depends on its industry environment and its business model, issues considered in the following chapters.

For now, the important point is that managers must understand the dynamic relationships among *value, pricing, demand,* and *costs* and make decisions on the basis of that understanding to maximize competitive advantage and profitability. Option 2 in Figure 3.4, for example, might not be a viable strategy if demand did not increase rapidly with lower prices or if there are few economies of scale to be had by increasing volume. Managers must understand the impact of value creation and pricing decisions on demand and how unit costs change with increases in volume. In other words, they must have a good grasp of the demand for the company's product and its

FIGURE 3.4

Value Creation and Pricing Options

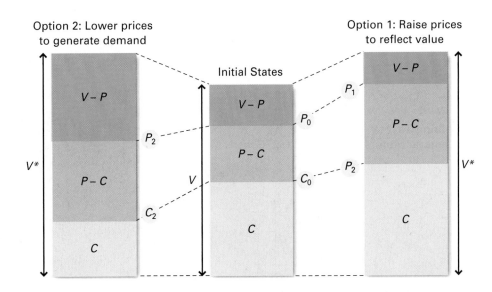

cost structure at different levels of output if they are to make decisions that maximize profitability.

Consider the automobile industry. According to a study by Harbour & Associates, in 2001 Toyota made $900 profit on every vehicle it manufactured in North America. General Motors, in contrast, made only $176 profit per vehicle. What accounts for the difference? First, Toyota has the best reputation for quality in the industry. According to annual surveys issued by J. D. Power, Toyota consistently tops the list in terms of quality, while GM cars are at best in the middle of the pack. The higher quality translates into a higher value and allows Toyota to charge 5 to 10 percent higher prices than General Motors for equivalent cars. Second, Toyota has a lower cost per vehicle than General Motors, due in part to superior labor productivity. For example, in Toyota's North American plants, it took an average of 31.06 employee hours to build a car in 2001, compared to 40.52 at GM plants in North America. That 9.5 hour productivity advantage translates into much lower labor costs for Toyota and, hence, a lower overall cost structure. Hence, as summarized in Figure 3.5, Toyota's advantage over GM derives from greater perceived value (V), which has allowed the company to charge a higher price (P) for its cars, and from a lower cost structure (C), which taken together implies significantly greater profitability per vehicle ($P - C$).

Toyota's decisions with regard to pricing are guided by its managers' understanding of the relationship of value, prices, demand, and costs. Given its ability to create more value, Toyota could have charged even higher prices than illustrated in Figure 3.5, but that might have led to lower sales volume, fewer scale economies, higher unit costs, and lower profit margins. Toyota's managers have sought to find the pricing option that enables the company to maximize its profitability given their assessment of demand for its products and its cost function. Thus, superior value creation does not necessarily require a company to have the lowest cost structure in an industry or to create the most valuable product in the eyes of customers. Rather, it requires that the gap between perceived value (V) and costs of production (C) be greater than the gap attained by competitors.

Differentiation and Cost Structure

Note that Toyota has *differentiated* itself from General Motors by its superior quality, which allows it to charge higher prices, and its *lower cost structure*. Thus, its competitive advantage over General Motors is the result of strategies that have led to distinctive competencies, resulting in greater *differentiation* and a lower *cost structure*.[8]

Indeed, at the heart of any company's business model is the combination of strategies aimed at creating distinctive competencies that (1) *differentiate* its products in some way so it creates more *value* for customers, which gives it more pricing

FIGURE 3.5

Comparing Toyota and General Motors

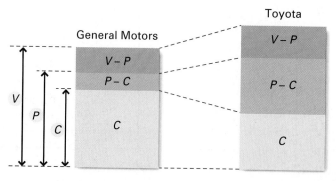

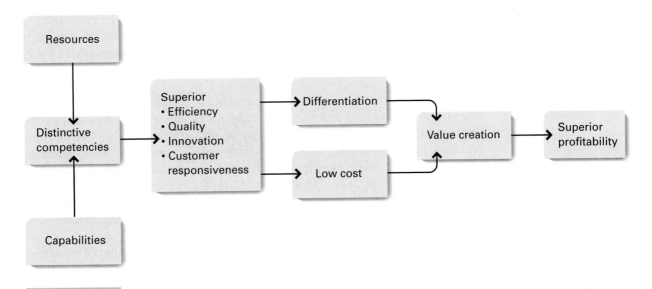

FIGURE 3.6

The Roots of Competitive Advantage

options, and (2) result in a *lower cost structure,* which also gives it a broader range of pricing choices.[9] Achieving a sustained competitive advantage and superior profitability requires the right choices with regard to value creation through differentiation and pricing given the demand conditions in the company's market, and the company's cost structure at different levels of output. This issue is addressed in detail in the following chapters and captured in Figure 3.6.

The Value Chain

All of the functions of a company—such as production, marketing, R&D, service, information systems, materials management, and human resources—have a role in lowering the cost structure and increasing the perceived value of the products through differentiation. As the first step in examining this concept, consider the value chain, which is illustrated in Figure 3.7.[10] The term **value chain** refers to the idea that a company is a chain of activities for transforming inputs into outputs that customers value. The process of transformation is composed of a number of primary activities and support activities that add value to the product.

FIGURE 3.7

The Value Chain

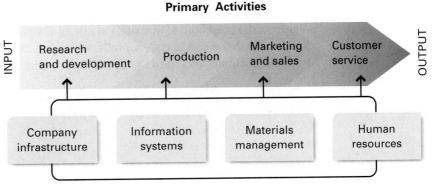

Primary activities have to do with the design, creation, and delivery of the product, its marketing, and its support and after-sales service. In the value chain illustrated in Figure 3.7, the primary activities are broken down into four functions: research and development, production, marketing and sales, and customer service.

Research and Development. **Research and development** (R&D) is concerned with the design of products and production processes. Although we think of R&D as being associated with the design of physical products and production processes in manufacturing enterprises, many service companies also undertake R&D. For example, banks compete with each other by developing new financial products and new ways of delivering those products to customers. Online banking and smart debit cards are two recent examples of the fruits of new product development in the banking industry. Earlier examples of innovation in the banking industry were ATM machines, credit cards, and debit cards.

By superior product design, R&D can increase the functionality of products, which makes them more attractive to customers by raising value. Alternatively, the work of R&D may result in more efficient production processes, thereby lowering production costs. Either way, the R&D function can help to lower costs or permit a company to charge higher prices. At Intel, for example, R&D creates value by developing ever more powerful microprocessors and helping to pioneer ever more efficient manufacturing processes (in conjunction with equipment suppliers).

Production. **Production** is concerned with the creation of a good or service. For physical products, when we talk about production, we generally mean manufacturing. For services such as banking or retail operations, "production" typically takes place when the service is delivered to the customer, as when a bank makes a loan to a customer. By performing its activities efficiently, the production function of a company helps to lower its cost structure. For example, the efficient production operations of Honda and Toyota help those automobile companies achieve higher profitability relative to competitors such as General Motors. The production function can also perform its activities in a way that is consistent with high product quality, which leads to differentiation (and higher value) and lower costs.

Marketing and Sales. There are several ways in which the **marketing and sales** functions of a company can help to create value. Through brand positioning and advertising, the marketing function can increase the value that customers perceive to be contained in a company's product. Insofar as these help to create a favorable impression of the company's product in the minds of customers, they increase value. For example, in the 1980s, the French company Perrier persuaded U.S. customers that slightly carbonated bottled water was worth $1.50 per bottle rather than a price closer to the $0.50 that it cost to collect, bottle, and distribute the water. Perrier's marketing function essentially increased the perception of value that customers ascribed to the product.

Marketing and sales can also create value by discovering customer needs and communicating them back to the R&D function of the company, which can then design products that better match those needs. For another example of value creation by the marketing function of an enterprise, see Strategy in Action 3.1, which looks at how Pfizer's sales force increased the perception of the value associated with one of its main pharmaceuticals, Zoloft.

Strategy in Action   3.1

Value Creation at Pfizer

The antidepressant drug Prozac, introduced by Eli Lilly & Co. in 1988, was one of the most lucrative mental health drugs in history. In 1995, U.S. customers alone filled almost 19 million prescriptions for Prozac, used to mitigate the effects of a wide range of mental disorders, including chronic depression, bulimia, and obsessive disorders. Worldwide sales of the drug topped $2 billion in 1995, making it a gold mine for Lilly.

During the 1990s, Prozac's market position came under attack from an aggressive marketing and sales campaign by rival pharmaceutical company Pfizer. In 1992, Pfizer introduced its own antidepressant, Zoloft. According to medical experts, the differences between Prozac and Zoloft are slight at best. Both drugs function in the same basic manner, by boosting serotonin, a brain chemical believed to be in short supply in many depressed people. Both drugs also have a similar list of possible side effects. Prozac's label cites nausea, nervousness, anxiety, insomnia, and drowsiness as possible side effects. Zoloft's label lists nausea and other stomach problems, diarrhea, sexual dysfunction, and sleepiness. As one expert noted, "These drugs are so similar that you have to be kidding yourself if you think one drug is going to be consistently superior to the other in treating patients."

Despite the similarity between the two products, Pfizer gained share from Lilly in the antidepressant market. By 1998, Zoloft accounted for 40 percent of the market, up from little more than zero in 1992. The main reason for this success seems to have been Pfizer's aggressive marketing and sales campaign, which created an impression in the eyes of physicians that Zoloft is a safer drug. Pfizer sales representatives bill their product as just as effective as Prozac but without its occasional downside, anxiety. The reference to anxiety seems carefully designed to remind doctors of a spate of failed lawsuits alleging that Prozac caused suicides and other violent acts. Pfizer's sales force also logged more "face time" with physicians than Lilly's. According to Scott-Levin and Associates, in 1995 Zoloft sales representatives made 660,000 sales visits to doctors, 70,000 more than the Prozac sales force logged. About three-quarters of these were not to psychiatrists but to basic primary care physicians, who increasingly prescribe antidepressants but presumably are less familiar with their more subtle properties than psychiatrists are. Doctors also claim that Pfizer salespeople play up Prozac's clinical reputation for being more agitating than Zoloft. They also emphasize that unlike Zoloft, Prozac remains in the bloodstream for weeks after a patient stops taking it, raising the possibility of adverse drug interaction if a patient switches to other medications.

The important point here is that Pfizer's marketing and sales force altered physicians' perceptions of the relative value of Prozac and Zoloft. For Pfizer, the payoff came in terms of rapidly increasing revenues and market share and, of course, a greater return on the company's investment in developing Zoloft.

Source: R. Langreth, "High Anxiety: Rivals Threaten Prozac's Reign," *Wall Street Journal,* May 9, 1996, pp. B1–B2.

Customer Service. The role of the **service** function of an enterprise is to provide after-sales service and support. This function can create a perception of superior value in the minds of customers by solving customer problems and supporting customers after they have purchased the product. For example, Caterpillar, the U.S.-based manufacturer of heavy earthmoving equipment, can get spare parts to any point in the world within twenty-four hours, thereby minimizing the amount of downtime its customers have to face if their Caterpillar equipment malfunctions. This is an extremely valuable support capability in an industry where downtime is very expensive. It has helped to increase the value that customers associate with Caterpillar products, and thus the price that Caterpillar can charge for its products.

Support Activities

The **support activities** of the value chain provide inputs that allow the primary activities to take place. These activities are broken down into four functions: materials management, human resources, information systems, and company infrastructure (see Figure 3.7).

Materials Management. The **materials management** (or logistics) function controls the transmission of physical materials through the value chain, from procurement through production and into distribution. The efficiency with which this is carried out can significantly lower cost, thereby creating more value. Wal-Mart, the U.S. retailing giant, reportedly has the most efficient materials management setup in the retail industry. By tightly controlling the flow of goods from its suppliers through its stores and into the hands of customers, Wal-Mart has eliminated the need to hold large inventories of goods. Lower inventories mean lower costs, and hence greater value creation.

Human Resources. There are a number of ways in which the **human resource** function can help an enterprise to create more value. This function ensures that the company has the right mix of skilled people to perform its value-creation activities effectively. It is also the job of the human resource function to ensure that people are adequately trained, motivated, and compensated to perform their value-creation tasks. If the human resources are functioning well, employee productivity rises (which lowers costs) and customer service improves (which raises perceived value), thereby enabling the company to create more value.

Information Systems. **Information systems** refer to the largely electronic systems for managing inventory, tracking sales, pricing products, selling products, dealing with customer service inquiries, and so on. Information systems, when coupled with the communications features of the Internet, are holding out the promise of being able to improve the efficiency and effectiveness with which a company manages its other value-creation activities. For example, Wal-Mart uses information systems to alter the way it does business. By tracking the sale of individual items very closely, its materials management function has enabled it to optimize its product mix and pricing strategy. Wal-Mart is rarely left with unwanted merchandise on its hands, which saves on costs, and the company is able to provide the right mix of goods to customers, which increases the perception of value that customers associate with Wal-Mart.

Company Infrastructure. **Company infrastructure** is the companywide context within which all the other value creation activities take place: the organizational structure, control systems, and company culture. Because top management can exert considerable influence in shaping these aspects of a company, top management should also be viewed as part of the infrastructure of a company. Indeed, through strong leadership, top management can shape the infrastructure of a company and, through that, the performance of all other value-creation activities that take place within it.

The Generic Building Blocks of Competitive Advantage

The four factors that build and sustain competitive advantage—superior efficiency, quality, innovation, and customer responsiveness—are the product of the company's distinctive competencies. In turn, they allow a company to (1) differentiate its product offering, and hence create greater perceived customer value, and (2) lower its cost structure (see Figure 3.8). These factors are *generic* building blocks of competitive advantage: any company, regardless of its industry or the products or services it pro-

FIGURE 3.8

Generic Building
Blocks of Competitive
Advantage

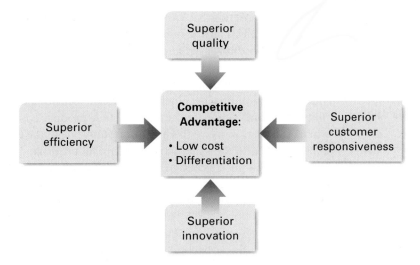

duces, can pursue them. Although they are discussed sequentially below, they are highly interrelated, and the important ways they affect each other should be noted. For example, superior quality can lead to superior efficiency, and innovation can enhance efficiency, quality, and responsiveness to customers.

Efficiency   In one sense, a business is simply a device for transforming inputs into outputs. Inputs are basic factors of production such as labor, land, capital, management, and technological know-how. Outputs are the goods and services that the business produces. The simplest measure of efficiency is the quantity of inputs that it takes to produce a given output, that is, efficiency = outputs/inputs. The more efficient a company is, the fewer the inputs required to produce a given output. For example, if it takes General Motors thirty hours of employee time to assemble a car and it takes Ford twenty-five hours, we can say that Ford is more efficient than GM. And as long as other things are equal, such as wage rates, we can assume from this information that Ford will have a lower cost structure than GM. Thus, efficiency helps a company attain a competitive advantage through a lower cost structure. Similarly, an analysis of financial statements suggests that in 2000, BJ's Wholesale generated $7.47 of sales for every dollar of capital it invested in its business, whereas Costco generated $6.29 of sales for every dollar of capital it invested in its business. Clearly BJ's is more efficient in its use of capital: it needs less capital (the input) to generate a dollar of sales (the output) than Costco.

As these examples suggest, two of the most important components of efficiency for many companies are employee productivity and capital productivity. *Employee productivity* is usually measured by output per employee and *capital productivity* by output per unit of invested capital (this is discussed in depth in the next section). Holding all else constant, the company with the highest labor and capital productivity in an industry will typically have the lowest cost structure and therefore a cost-based competitive advantage. The concept of productivity is not limited to employee and capital productivity. Pharmaceutical companies, for example, often talk about the productivity of their R&D spending, by which they mean how many new drugs they develop from their investment in R&D. Other companies talk about their sales force productivity, which means how many sales they generate from every sales call, and so on. The important point to remember is that high productivity leads to greater efficiency and lower costs.

Strategy in Action 3.2 looks at how Southwest Airlines has attained its low-cost position in the U.S. airline industry. As you will see, its competitive advantage derives from its superior labor productivity.

Quality:
Reliability and
Other Attributes
A product can be thought of as a bundle of attributes.[11] For example, the attributes of many physical products include the form, features, performance, durability, reliability, style, and design of the product.[12] A product is said to have *superior quality* when customers perceive there to be greater value in the attributes of a specific product, compared to the same attributes in rival products. For example, a Rolex watch has attributes—such as design, styling, performance, and reliability—that customers perceive as being superior to the same attributes in many other watches. Thus, we can refer to a Rolex as a high-quality product: Rolex has *differentiated* its watches by these attributes.

Among the various attributes of products, one in particular has taken on special significance in the last two decades: *reliability*. A product can be said to be *reliable* when it consistently does the job it was designed for, does it well, and rarely, if ever, breaks down. As we shall see, increasing product reliability has been the central goal of an influential management philosophy that came out of Japan in the 1980s and is commonly referred to as **total quality management.** Because of its unique role in the overall perception of quality, in this book we separate out *reliability* from other attributes of a product when discussing product quality. Thus, we define **quality products** as goods and services that are *reliable* in the sense that they do the job they were designed for and do it well, which increases perceived value, but they are also differentiated by various *attributes* that customers perceive to have a higher value.

The position of a product against these two dimensions, reliability and other attributes, can be plotted on a figure similar to Figure 3.9. For example, a Lexus has attributes—such as design, styling, performance, and safety features—that customers perceive as being superior to those of most other cars. Lexus is also a very reliable car. Thus, the overall level of quality of the Lexus is very high, which creates an impression of value in the minds of customers and gives Toyota the option of charging a premium price for the Lexus. Toyota also produces another very reliable vehicle, the Toyota Corolla, but this is aimed at less wealthy customers and it lacks many of the superior attributes of the Lexus. Thus, although this is also a high-quality car in the sense of being reliable, it is not as high quality as a Lexus. At the other end of the spectrum, we can find poor-quality products that have both low reliability and inferior attributes, such as poor design, performance, and styling. An example is the Yugo, a car that was made in the former Yugoslavia in the 1980s. The Yugo was a boxy, low-powered vehicle aimed at the budget segment of the market, and it had a dismal reputation for styling, reliability, and safety. Thus, its overall quality was very low. A car (or any other product, for that matter) might also have a collection of superior attributes but nevertheless suffer from very poor reliability, which would damage its overall quality.

The concept of quality applies whether we are talking about Toyota automobiles, clothes designed and sold by the Gap, the customer service department of Citibank, or the ability of airlines to arrive on time. Quality is just as relevant to services as it is to goods.[13] The impact of high product quality on competitive advantage is twofold.[14] First, providing high-quality products increases the value of those products in the eyes of customers. This enhanced perception of value gives the company the option of charging a higher price for its products. In the automobile industry, for example, Toyota can charge a higher price for its cars because of the higher quality of

Strategy in Action

Southwest Airlines' Low Cost Structure

3.2

Southwest Airlines has long been one of the standout performers in the U.S. airline industry. It is famous for its low fares, generally some 30 percent below those of its rivals, which are balanced by an even lower cost structure, which has enabled it to record superior profitability even in bad years such as 2001, when the industry faced slumping demand. Southwest was the only airline among the top eight in the United States to show a profit for the quarter immediately following the September 11 terrorist attacks on the World Trade Center and the Pentagon.

A major source of Southwest's low cost structure seems to be its very high employee productivity. One way the airlines measure employee productivity is by the ratio of employees to passengers carried. According to figures from the Air Transport Association, in 2000 Southwest had an employee-to-passenger ratio of 1 to 2,424, followed by Alaska Airlines at 1,518 and Delta Airlines at 1,493. The worst performer among the major U.S. airlines, United, had an employee-to-passenger ratio of 1 to 938 in 2000. These figures suggest that holding size constant, Southwest runs its operation with far fewer people than any of its competitors. How does it do this?

First, Southwest devotes enormous attention to whom it hires. On average, the company hired only 3 percent of those interviewed in a year. When hiring, it places a big emphasis on teamwork and a positive attitude. Southwest rationalizes that skills can be taught, but a positive attitude and a willingness to pitch in cannot. Southwest also creates incentives for its employees to work hard. All employees are covered by a profit-sharing plan, and at least 25 percent of an employee's share of the profit-sharing plan has to be invested in Southwest Airlines stock. This gives rise to a simple formula: the harder employees work, the more profitable Southwest becomes, and the richer the employees get. The results are clear. At other airlines, one would never see a pilot helping to check passengers onto the plane. At Southwest, pilots and flight attendants have been known to help clean the aircraft and check in passengers at the gate. They do this to turn around an aircraft as quickly as possible and get it into the air again because an aircraft doesn't make money when it is sitting on the ground.

Southwest also reduces its costs by striving to keep its operations as simple as possible. By operating only one type of plane, the Boeing 737, it reduces training costs, maintenance costs, and inventory costs while increasing efficiency in crew and flight scheduling. The operation is nearly ticketless, which reduces cost and back-office accounting functions. There is no seat assignment, which again reduces costs. There are no meals or movies in flight, and the airline will not transfer baggage to other airlines, reducing the need for baggage handlers. Another major difference between Southwest and most other airlines is that Southwest flies point to point rather than operating from congested airport hubs. As a result, its costs are lower because there is no need for dozens of gates and thousands of employees needed to handle banks of flights that come in and then disperse within a two-hour window, leaving the hub empty until the next flights a few hours later.

Source: M. Brelis, "Simple Strategy Makes Southwest a Model for Success," *Boston Globe,* November 5, 2000, p. F1. Southwest Airlines 10K 2001.

its products. Thus, compared with General Motors, Toyota has had both lower costs and the ability to charge higher prices. As a result, historically it has operated with a bigger profit margin than GM.

The second impact of high quality on competitive advantage comes from the greater efficiency and the lower unit costs associated with *reliable* products. When products are reliable, less employee time is wasted making defective products or providing substandard services and less time has to be spent fixing mistakes, which translates into higher employee productivity and lower unit costs. Thus, high product quality not only enables a company to differentiate its product from that of rivals, but if the product is reliable, it also lowers costs.

FIGURE 3.9

A Quality Map for
Automobiles

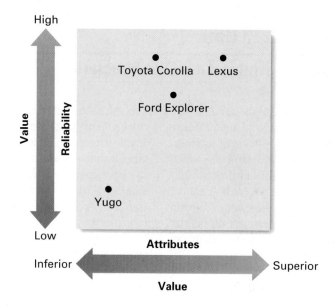

The importance of reliability in building competitive advantage has increased dramatically over the past decade. Indeed, so crucial is the emphasis placed on reliability by many companies that achieving high product reliability can no longer be viewed as just one way of gaining a competitive advantage. In many industries, it has become an absolute imperative for survival. Strategy in Action 3.3, which looks at the turnaround of Continental Airlines, illustrates the importance of quality in a service environment.

Innovation   **Innovation** refers to the act of creating new products or processes. There are two main types of innovation: product innovation and process innovation. **Product innovation** is the development of products that are new to the world or have superior attributes to existing products. Examples are Intel's invention of the microprocessor in the early 1970s, Cisco's development of the router for routing data over the Internet in the mid-1980s, and Palm's development of the PalmPilot, the first commercially successful hand-held computer, in the mid-1990s. **Process innovation** is the development of a new process for producing products and delivering them to customers. Examples include Toyota, which developed a range of new techniques collectively known as the Toyota *lean production system* for making automobiles: just-in-time inventory systems, self-managing teams, and reduced setup times for complex equipment. Wal-Mart pioneered efforts to use information systems to manage its logistics, product mix, and product pricing, and Staples applied the supermarket business model to the retail office supplies business.

Product innovation creates value by creating new products, or enhanced versions of existing products, that customers perceive as more desirable, thus increasing the company's pricing options. Process innovation often allows a company to create more value by lowering production costs. Toyota's lean production system, for example, helped to boost employee productivity, thus giving Toyota a cost-based competitive advantage.[15] Similarly, Staples' application of the supermarket business model to retail office supplies dramatically lowered the cost of selling office supplies. Staples passed on some of this cost saving to customers in the form of lower prices, which enabled the company to increase its market share rapidly.

Strategy in Action   3.3

Continental Airlines Goes from Worst to First

When Gordon Bethune left Boeing to become the CEO of Continental Airlines in 1994, the company was the worst performing and least profitable of all major U.S. airlines. One of its major problems was the lack of reliability. In 1994, Continental planes arrived on time only 61 percent of the time, placing it dead last in the influential Air Customer Satisfaction Study produced by J. D. Power & Associates. Worse, airline travelers ranked on-time performance the most important factor when deciding which airline to fly on. Reliability was the primary metric passengers used to determine an airline's quality.

Bethune soon came to the conclusion that the prior management had cut costs so far that service had suffered. In his words, "Our service was lousy and nobody knew when a plane might land. We were unpredictable and unreliable, and when you are an airline, where does that leave you? It leaves you with a lot of empty planes. We had a lousy product, and nobody particularly wanted to buy it." Bethune's solution? He told Continental employees that if the airline's on-time performance improved, every employee would receive a $65 bonus. The total cost to the airline was $2.6 million. Bethune was proposing to improve performance by spending more money, and it worked. When the program was launched in January 1995, 71 percent of the planes landed on time. By year end, the figure was up to 80 percent, and Continental had risen to fifth place in its on-time performance. For 1996,

Bethune announced that the airline had to finish third or higher for employees to get the bonus, which he increased to $100. The airline finished second. It has not dropped out of the top three since.

To support the drive to increase reliability, Bethune reorganized the way employees were managed. Out went the employee manual, to be replaced by a new set of guidelines for employees. Under these guidelines, front-line employees were given significant decision-making power to fix customer problems. For example, if a flight is canceled, a customer service agent might have to decide which passengers should receive priority to get on the next flight. Under the old system, the employee would have had to refer to the rule book, and if that did not provide an answer, ask a higher-level manager. This inflexible approach led to significant frustration among both passengers and employees. Under the new system, the customer service agent has been given the power to fix the problem as she sees fit. According to Bethune, concentrating decision-making power in the hands of employees has given them the ability to solve customer problems in creative ways, which has had a dramatic impact on customers' perception of the quality of service they get at Continental.

Source: G. Bethune, "From Worst to First," *Fortune,* May 25, 1998, pp. 185–190.

In the long run, innovation of products and processes is perhaps the most important building block of competitive advantage.[16] Competition can be viewed as a process driven by innovations. Although not all innovations succeed, those that do can be a major source of competitive advantage because, by definition, they give a company something **unique**—something its competitors lack (at least until they imitate the innovation). Uniqueness can allow a company to differentiate itself from its rivals and charge a premium price for its product or, in the case of many process innovations, reduce its unit costs far below those of competitors.

Responsiveness to Customers   To achieve superior responsiveness to customers, a company must be able to do a better job than competitors of identifying and satisfying its customers' needs. Customers will then place more value on its products, creating a differentiation based on competitive advantage. Improving the quality of a company's product offering is consistent with achieving responsiveness, as is developing new products with features that existing products lack. In other words, achieving superior quality and innovation is integral to achieving superior responsiveness to customers.

Another factor that stands out in any discussion of responsiveness to customers is the need to customize goods and services to the unique demands of individual customers or customer groups. For example, the proliferation of soft drinks and beers can be viewed partly as a response to this trend. Automobile companies have become more adept at customizing cars to the demands of individual customers. For instance, following the lead of Toyota, the Saturn division of General Motors builds cars to order for individual customers, letting them choose from a wide range of colors and options.

An aspect of responsiveness to customers that has drawn increasing attention is **customer response time:** the time that it takes for a good to be delivered or a service to be performed.[17] For a manufacturer of machinery, response time is the time it takes to fill customer orders. For a bank, it is the time it takes to process a loan or that a customer must stand in line to wait for a free teller. For a supermarket, it is the time that customers must stand in checkout lines. Customer survey after customer survey has shown slow response time to be a major source of customer dissatisfaction.[18]

Other sources of enhanced responsiveness to customers are superior design, superior service, and superior after-sales service and support. All of these factors enhance responsiveness to customers and allow a company to differentiate itself from its less responsive competitors. In turn, differentiation enables a company to build brand loyalty and charge a premium price for its products. Consider how much more people are prepared to pay for next-day delivery of express mail, as opposed to delivery in three to four days. In 1996, a two-page letter sent by overnight Express Mail within the United States cost about $10, compared with 32 cents for regular mail. Thus, the price premium for express delivery (reduced response time) was $9.68, or a premium of 3,025 percent over the regular price.

Analyzing Competitive Advantage and Profitability

If a company's managers are to perform a good internal analysis, they need to be able to analyze the financial performance of their company, identifying how its strategies contribute (or not) to profitability. To perform this crucial step of identifying strengths and weaknesses effectively, they need to be able to compare, or *benchmark,* the performance of their company against that of competitors and the historic performance of the company itself. This will help them to determine whether they are more or less profitable than competitors and whether the performance of the company has been improving or deteriorating through time; whether their strategies of the company are maximizing the value being created; whether their cost structure is out of line with those of competitors; and whether they are using the resources of the company to the greatest effect.

As we noted in Chapter 1, the key measure of a company's financial performance is its profitability, which captures the return that a company is generating on its investments. Although several different measures of profitability exist, such as return on assets and return on equity, many authorities on the measurement of profitability argue that return on invested capital (ROIC) is the best measure because "it focuses on the true operating performance of the company."[19] ROIC is defined as net profit over invested capital, or ROIC = Net profit/invested capital.

Net profit is calculated by subtracting the total costs of operating the company away from its total revenues (total revenues − total costs). *Net profit* is what is left over before the government takes its share in taxes. *Invested capital* is the amount that is invested in the operations of a company: property, plant, equipment, inventories, and other assets. Invested capital comes from two main sources: interest-bearing debt and shareholders' equity. Interest-bearing debt is money the company borrows from banks and those who purchase its bonds. Shareholders' equity is the money raised from selling shares to the public, *plus* earnings that the company has retained in prior years and are available to fund current investments. ROIC measures the effectiveness with which a company is using the capital funds that it has available for investment. As such, it is recognized to be an excellent measure of the value a company is creating.[20]

A company's ROIC can be algebraically decomposed into two major components: *return on sales* and *capital turnover*:[21] Specifically:

$$\text{ROIC} = \text{Net profits/invested capital}$$
$$= \text{Net profits/revenues} \times \text{revenues/invested capital,}$$

where net profits/revenues is the return on sales, and revenues/invested capital is capital turnover. Return on sales measures how effectively the company converts revenues into profits. Capital turnover measures how effectively the company employs its invested capital to generate revenues. These two ratios can be further decomposed into some basic accounting ratios, as shown in Figure 3.10 (these ratios are defined in Table 3.1).[22]

Figure 3.10 says that a company's managers can increase ROIC by pursuing strategies that increase the company's return on sales. To increase the company's return on sales, they can pursue strategies that reduce the cost of goods sold (COGS) for a given level of sales revenues (COGS/sales); reduce the level of spending on sales force, marketing, general, and administrative expenses (SG&A) for a given level of sales revenues (SG&A/sales); and reduce R&D spending for a given level of sales revenues

TABLE 3.1

Definitions of Basic Accounting Terms

Term	Definition	Source
Cost of goods sold (COGS)	Total costs of manufacturing products	Income statement
Sales, general, and administrative expenses (SG&A)	Costs associated with selling products and administering the company	Income statement
R&D expenses (R&D)	Research and development expenditure	Income statement
Working capital	The amount of money the company has to work with in the short term	Balance sheet
Property, plant, and equipment (PPE)	The value of investments in the property, plant, and equipment that the company uses to manufacture and sell its products; also known as *fixed capital*	Balance sheet
Return on sales (ROS)	Net profit expressed as a percentage of sales; measures how effectively the company converts revenues into profits	Ratio
Capital turnover	Revenues divided by invested capital; measures how effectively the company uses its capital to generate revenues	Ratio
Return on invested capital (ROIC)	Net profit divided by invested capital	Ratio
Net profit	Total revenues minus total costs before tax	Income statement
Invested capital	Interest-bearing debt plus shareholders' equity	Balance sheet

FIGURE 3.10

Drivers of Profitability
(ROIC)

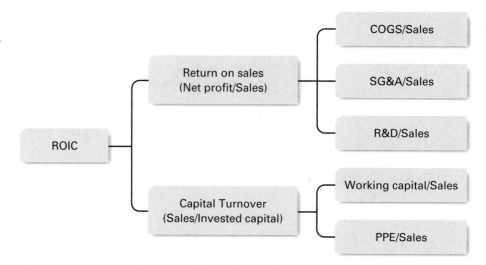

(R&D/sales). Alternatively, they can increase return on sales by pursuing strategies that increase sales revenues more than they increase the costs of the business, as measured by COGS, SG&A, and R&D expenses. That is, they can increase the return on sales by pursuing strategies that *lower costs* or increase value through *differentiation,* and allow the company to increase its prices more than its costs.

Figure 3.10 also tells us that a company's managers can boost the profitability of their company by getting greater sales revenues from their invested capital, thereby increasing capital turnover). They do this by pursuing strategies that reduce the amount of *working capital,* such as the amount of capital invested in inventories, needed to generate a given level of sales (working capital/sales) and then pursuing strategies that reduce the amount of *fixed capital* that they have to invest in plant, property, and equipment (PPE) to generate a given level of sales (PPE/sales). That is, they pursue strategies that reduce the amount of capital that they need to generate every dollar of sales, and thus their cost of capital. Now recall that cost of capital is part of the cost structure of a company (see Figure 3.2), so strategies designed to increase capital turnover also *lower the cost structure.*

To see how these basic drivers of profitability help us to understand what is going on in a company and to identify its strengths and weaknesses, let us return to the *Opening Case* and the example of BJ's Wholesale. BJ's superior profitability can be understood in terms of the impact of its strategies on the various ratios identified in Figure 3.10. Recall first that BJ's is more profitable not only than many other retail establishments, but also than Costco, which has a similar business model and is a direct competitor. In 2000, BJ's ROIC was 19.7 percent, and Costco's was 12.9 percent. The first point to make is that BJ's superior profitability came in part from higher return on sales: 4.34 percent in 2000 versus 3.27 percent for Costco. But where did the higher return on sales come from? BJ's ratio of COGS/sales at 88.7 percent was actually not quite as good as Costco's, which stood at 88.1 percent, so it certainly was not from prices relative to the costs of goods sold. However, BJ's SG&A expenses as a percentage of sales were 6.9 percent, compared to 8.7 percent for Costco, suggesting that BJ's had higher return on sales, and thus higher ROIC, in part because it spent less on sales, marketing, general, and administrative expenses.

To understand why BJ's was spending significantly less than Costco on SG&A/sales, we have to we have to go back to BJ's strategy. Recall that BJ's was an innovator in using information systems to automate its point of sale terminals, inventory reordering systems, and payment systems. This enabled it to reduce its dependence on people to perform these functions, thereby reducing its payroll and SG&A expenses for a given level of sales. Moreover, BJ's strategy of entering small towns or basing stores close to each other in suburban areas means that the company has a visible presence in these areas, which reduces its need to advertise and also brings down its SG&A expenses. So in part, BJ's superior profitability relative to its closest competitor, Costco, comes from lower SG&A expenses, which are a direct result of the strategies its managers pursue with regard to information systems and location.

Superior profitability can also come from more efficient use of capital. A comparative analysis of BJ's and Costco shows that in 2000, Costco's capital turnover ratio (sales/invested capital) was 6.29 compared to 7.41 at BJ's. BJ's was getting significantly more sales from its capital investment than Costco. Costco generates $6.29 in revenues from every dollar invested and BJ's generates $7.41. The big difference is in the ratio of property plant and equipment to sales (PPE/sales). For Costco, this ratio was 0.16, and for BJ's it was 0.11. BJ's was getting more sales from its investment in property, plant, and equipment than Costco was. Again, the difference is the result of strategy. BJ's strategy of entering small towns or suburban areas has enabled it to buy or rent less expensive real estate than Costco. In sum, BJ's superior profitability relative to its close competitor, Costco, seems to derive from lower SG&A expenses and PPE expenses relative to sales, which are the result of the strategies that BJ's pursues.

For another example of the impact of strategy on profitability, see the *Running Case* for this chapter, which compares Dell Computer to Compaq Computer.

In sum, the methodology described in this section can be a very useful tool to analyze why and how well a company is achieving and sustaining a competitive advantage. It highlights a company's strengths and weaknesses, showing where there is room for improvement and where a company is excelling. As such, it can drive strategy formulation, as it apparently has at Dell Computer (see the *Running Case*).

The analysis can be taken a lot further than we have here. For example, consider just one element in Figure 3.10 and the figure in the *Running Case:* ratio of costs of goods sold to sales (COGS/sales). This ratio is an indicator of the production efficiency of an enterprise: the lower the value of the ratio is, the more efficient the company is in manufacturing products, other things being equal. However, the ratio hides a lot of detail. For example, it does not reveal whether the efficiency comes from high production employee productivity, low costs of raw material inputs, or some other source. Working this out would further decomposition of the ROIC tree shown in Figure 3.10 into more basic elements. Although such detailed analysis is generally beyond the scope of this book, you should bear in mind how important such work can be in identifying a company's strengths and weaknesses.[23]

The Durability of Competitive Advantage

The next question we must address is how long a competitive advantage will last once it has been created. In other words, what is the *durability* of competitive advantage given that other companies are also seeking to develop distinctive competencies that will give them a competitive advantage? The answer depends on three factors: barriers to imitation, the capability of competitors, and the general dynamism of the industry environment.

Running Case

Drivers of Profitability for Dell Computer and Compaq

In the *Opening Case* to Chapter 1, we noted that Dell has had a persistently higher profit rate than its competitors, such as Compaq (see Figure). And we suggested that Dell's superior profitability came from the pursuit of a different strategy that enabled it to attain a very low-cost structure relative to that of its rivals. The figure shown here compares the drivers of profitability, as measured by ROIC, for Dell and Compaq in 2000. The figures are given in percentages to aid comparison. What we see is that in 2000, Dell, with an ROIC of 38.1 percent, was significantly more profitable than Compaq, which had an ROIC of 13.3 percent.

The figure helps us to identify the source of Dell's superior profitability by detailing some of the drivers of profitability at Dell and Compaq. Dell's cost structure is lower not because its COGS is lower; in fact, it is higher than Compaq's as a percentage of revenues. However, Dell spends only 10 percent of revenues on SG&A compared to Compaq's 14 percent. The reason is that Dell sells

direct via the Web, while Compaq sells through distributors and has a much bigger sales force as a result—hence the higher SG&A. Moreover, Dell spends less on R&D than Compaq (1.5 percent of sales as against 3.5 percent). In part, this difference reflects the fact that Dell has positioned itself as a low-cost producer of personal computers and servers, whereas Compaq tries to differentiate its product offering by producing leading-edge machines that incorporate proprietary technology developed in-house. In other words, different strategies lead to different cost structures.

What is also striking, and a major source of Dell's superior profitability, is that its capital turnover ratio is far superior to that of Compaq. This suggests that Dell is using its capital much more efficiently than Compaq. Dell's lower working capital to sales ratio reflects the more efficient management of inventory, which reduces the need to working capital to finance that inventory. What is particularly striking is Dell's PPE/sales ratio,

Comparing Dell
and Compaq

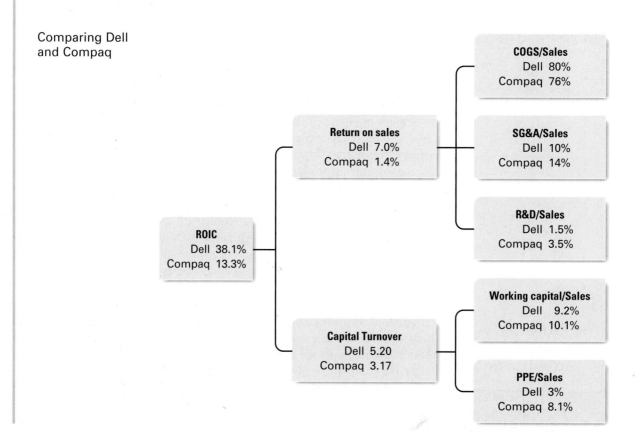

which is only 3 percent compared to 8.1 percent at Compaq. This means that Dell is using far less property, plant, and equipment to generate its sales than Compaq is. This is the direct consequence of Dell's business model in which a substantial proportion of the work that goes into making Dell computers is outsourced to suppliers. Dell adds value by using its web-based information systems to coordinate the entire supply chain in a very efficient manner. As a result of this strategy, it does not have to invest as much capital in factories to make computers. Thus, Dell's superior profitability comes from a low-cost operating structure and the efficient use of its capital, both of which are the consequences of Dell's basic strategy of direct marketing and managing the supply chain via web-based information systems.

Interestingly, Dell measures its own performance by ROIC. According to Michael Dell, ROIC "is a focusing device. We introduced it in 1995 with a companywide push to educate everyone about the benefits of a positive ROIC. . . . We explained specifically how everyone could contribute by reducing cycle times, eliminating scrap and waste, selling more, forecasting accurately, scaling operations effectively, increasing inventory turns, collecting accounts receivables efficiently, and doing things right the first time. And we made it the core of our incentive compensation program for all employees."

Source: Data taken from 2000 10K reports filed with the Securities and Exchange Commission by Dell and Compaq. Dell quote from Michael Dell, *Direct from Dell: Strategies That Revolutionized an Industry* (New York: HarperBusiness, 1999), p. 135.

Barriers to Imitation

A company with a competitive advantage will earn higher-than-average profits. These profits send a signal to rivals that the company has some valuable distinctive competency that allows it to create superior value. Naturally, its competitors will try to identify and imitate that competency, and insofar as they are successful, ultimately their increased success may whittle away the company's superior profits.[24]

How quickly rivals will imitate a company's distinctive competencies is an important issue, because the speed of imitation has a bearing on the durability of a company's competitive advantage. Other things being equal, the more rapidly competitors imitate a company's distinctive competencies, the less durable its competitive advantage will be, and the more important it is that the company endeavor to improve its competencies to stay one step ahead of the imitators. It is important to stress at the outset that ultimately almost any distinctive competency can be imitated by a competitor. The critical issue is *time:* the longer it takes competitors to imitate a distinctive competency, the greater the opportunity the company has to build a strong market position and reputation with customers, which is then more difficult for competitors to attack. Moreover, the longer it takes to achieve an imitation, the greater is the opportunity for the imitated company to improve on its competency or build other competencies, thereby staying one step ahead of the competition.

Barriers to imitation are a primary determinant of the speed of imitation. **Barriers to imitation** are factors that make it difficult for a competitor to copy a company's distinctive competencies; the greater the barriers to imitation, the more sustainable are a company's competitive advantage.[25] Barriers to imitation differ depending on whether a competitor is trying to imitate resources or capabilities.

Imitating Resources. In general, the easiest distinctive competencies for prospective rivals to imitate tend to be those based on possession of firm-specific and valuable tangible resources, such as buildings, plant, and equipment. Such resources are visible to competitors and can often be purchased on the open market. For example, if a company's competitive advantage is based on sole possession of efficient-scale manufacturing facilities, competitors may move fairly quickly to establish similar facilities. Although Ford gained a competitive advantage over General Motors in the 1920s by being the first to adopt an assembly line manufacturing technology to produce automobiles, General Motors quickly imitated that innovation, competing away Ford's distinctive competence in the process. A similar process is occurring in the auto industry now, as companies try to imitate Toyota's famous production system.

Intangible resources can be more difficult to imitate. This is particularly true of brand names, which are important because they symbolize a company's reputation. In the heavy earthmoving equipment industry, for example, the Caterpillar brand name is synonymous with high quality and superior after-sales service and support. Similarly, the St. Michael's brand name used by Marks & Spencer, Britain's largest retailer, symbolizes high-quality but reasonably priced clothing. Customers often display a preference for the products of such companies because the brand name is an important guarantee of high quality. Although competitors might like to imitate well-established brand names, the law prohibits them from doing so.

Marketing and technological know-how are also important intangible resources and can be relatively easy to imitate. The movement of skilled marketing personnel between companies may facilitate the general dissemination of marketing know-how. For example, in the 1970s, Ford was acknowledged as the best marketer among the big three U.S. auto companies. In 1979, it lost a lot of its marketing know-how to Chrysler when its most successful marketer, Lee Iacocca, joined Chrysler and subsequently hired many of Ford's top marketing people to work with him at Chrysler. More generally, successful marketing strategies are relatively easy to imitate because they are so visible to competitors. Thus, Coca-Cola quickly imitated PepsiCo's Diet Pepsi brand with the introduction of its own brand, Diet Coke.

With regard to technological know-how, the patent system in theory should make technological know-how relatively immune to imitation. Patents give the inventor of a new product a twenty-year exclusive production agreement. For example, the biotechnology company Immunex discovered and patented Enbrel, which is capable of halting the disease-causing mechanism that leads to rheumatoid arthritis. All prior treatments simply provided patients with some relief from the symptoms of rheumatoid arthritis. Approved by the Food and Drug Administration in 1998, Enbrel racked up sales of over $400 million in its first year on the market and may ultimately generate annual revenues of $2 billion for Immunex. (In 2002, Immunex was acquired by Amgen.) Despite the large market potential, Immunex's patent stops potential competitors from introducing their own version of Enbrel. However, whereas it is relatively easy to use the patent system to protect a biological product from imitation, this is not true of many other inventions. In electrical and computer engineering, for example, it is often possible to invent around patents. That is, produce a product that is functionally equivalent, but does not rely upon the patented technology. One study found that 60 percent of patented innovations were successfully invented around in four years.[26] This suggests that in general, distinctive competencies based on technological know-how can be relatively short-lived.

Imitating Capabilities. Imitating a company's capabilities tends to be more difficult than imitating its tangible and intangible resources, chiefly because capabilities are based on the way in which decisions are made and processes managed deep within a company. It is hard for outsiders to discern them.

On its own, the invisible nature of capabilities would not be enough to halt imitation; competitors could still gain insights into how a company operates by hiring people away from that company. However, a company's capabilities rarely reside in a single individual. Rather, they are the product of how numerous individuals interact within a unique organizational setting.[27] It is possible that no one individual within a company may be familiar with the totality of a company's internal operating routines and procedures. In such cases, hiring people away from a successful company in order to imitate its key capabilities may not be helpful.

Capability of Competitors

According to work by Pankaj Ghemawat, a major determinant of the capability of competitors to imitate a company's competitive advantage rapidly is the nature of the competitors' prior strategic commitments.[28] By **strategic commitment,** Ghemawat means a company's commitment to a particular way of doing business—that is, to developing a particular set of resources and capabilities. Ghemawat's point is that once a company has made a strategic commitment, it will have difficulty responding to new competition if doing so requires a break with this commitment. Therefore, when competitors have long-established commitments to a particular way of doing business, they may be slow to imitate an innovating company's competitive advantage. Its competitive advantage will thus be relatively durable.

The U.S. automobile industry again offers an example. From 1945 to 1975, the industry was dominated by the stable oligopoly of General Motors, Ford, and Chrysler, all of which geared their operations to the production of large cars, which American customers demanded at the time. When the market shifted from large cars to small, fuel-efficient ones during the late 1970s, U.S. companies lacked the resources and capabilities required to produce these cars. Their prior commitments had built the wrong kind of skills for this new environment. As a result, foreign producers, and particularly the Japanese, stepped into the market breach by providing compact, fuel-efficient, high-quality, and low-cost cars. The failure of U.S. auto manufacturers to react quickly to the distinctive competency of Japanese auto companies gave the latter time to build a strong market position and brand loyalty, which subsequently has proved difficult to attack.

Another determinant of the ability of competitors to respond to a company's competitive advantage is the absorptive capacity of competitors.[29] **Absorptive capacity** refers to the ability of an enterprise to identify, value, assimilate, and use new knowledge. For example, in the 1960s and 1970s, Toyota developed a competitive advantage based on its innovation of lean production systems. Competitors such as General Motors were slow to imitate this innovation, primarily because they lacked the necessary absorptive capacity. General Motors was such a bureaucratic and inward-looking organization that it was very difficult for the company to identify, value, assimilate, and use the knowledge that underlay lean production systems. Indeed, long after General Motors had identified and understood the importance of lean production systems, it was still struggling to assimilate and use that new knowledge. Put differently, internal inertia forces can make it difficult for established competitors to respond to a rival whose competitive advantage is based on new products or internal processes—that is, on innovation.

Taken together, factors such as existing strategic commitments and low absorptive capacity limit the ability of established competitors to imitate the competitive advantage of a rival, particularly when that competitive advantage is based on innovative products or processes. This is why when innovations reshape the rules of competition in an industry, value often migrates away from established competitors and toward new enterprises that are operating with new business models.

Industry Dynamism

A dynamic industry environment is one that is changing rapidly. We examined the factors that determine the dynamism and intensity of competition in an industry in

Chapter 2 when we discussed the external environment. The most dynamic industries tend to be those with a very high rate of product innovation—for instance, the customer electronics industry and the personal computer industry. In dynamic industries, the rapid rate of innovation means that product life cycles are shortening and that competitive advantage can be fleeting. A company that has a competitive advantage today may find its market position outflanked tomorrow by a rival's innovation.

In the personal computer industry, the rapid increase in computing power during the past two decades has contributed to a high degree of innovation and a turbulent environment. Reflecting the persistence of innovation, Apple Computer in the late 1970s and early 1980s had an industrywide competitive advantage due to its innovation. In 1981, IBM seized the advantage with its introduction of its first personal computer. By the mid-1980s, IBM had lost its competitive advantage to high-power "clone" manufacturers such as Compaq that had beaten IBM in the race to introduce a computer based on Intel's 386 chip. In turn, in the 1990s, Compaq subsequently lost its competitive advantage to Dell, which pioneered new low-cost ways of delivering computers to customers using the Internet as a direct selling device.

The durability of a company's competitive advantage depends on the height of barriers to imitation, the capability of competitors to imitate its innovation, and the general level of dynamism in the industry environment. When barriers to imitation are low, capable competitors abound, and the environment is dynamic, with innovations being developed all the time, then competitive advantage is likely to be transitory. But even within such industries, companies can build a more enduring competitive advantage if they are able to make investments that build barriers to imitation.

During the 1980s, Apple Computer built a competitive advantage based on the combination of a proprietary disk operating system and an intangible product image. The resulting brand loyalty enabled Apple to carve out a fairly secure niche in an industry where competitive advantage has otherwise proven to be very fleeting. However, by the mid-1990s, its strategy had been imitated, primarily due to the introduction of Microsoft's Windows operating system, which imitated most of the features that had enabled Apple to build brand loyalty. By 1996, Apple was in financial trouble, providing yet another example that no competitive advantage lasts forever. Ultimately, anything can be imitated. Interestingly enough though, Apple has shown remarkable resilience; in the late 1990s, it clawed its way back from the brink of bankruptcy to establish a viable position within its niche once again.

Avoiding Failure and Sustaining Competitive Advantage

How can a company avoid failure and escape the traps that have snared so many once successful companies? How can managers build a sustainable competitive advantage? Much of the remainder of this book deals with these issues. Here, we make a number of key points that set the scene for the coming discussion.

Why Companies Fail

When a company loses its competitive advantage, its profitability falls. The company does not necessarily fail; it may just have average or below-average profitability and can remain in this mode for a considerable time, although its resource and capital base is shrinking. Failure implies something more drastic. A failing company is one whose profitability is now substantially lower than the average profitability of its competitors; it has lost the ability to attract and generate resources so that its profit margins and invested capital are shrinking rapidly.

Why does a company lose its competitive advantage and fail? The question is particularly pertinent since some of the most successful companies of the twentieth century have seen their competitive position deteriorate at one time or another. IBM, General Motors, American Express, Digital Equipment, and Compaq Computer, among many others, all at one time held up as examples of managerial excellence, have gone through periods where their financial performance was poor and they clearly lacked any competitive advantage. We explore three related reasons for failure: inertia, prior strategic commitments, and the Icarus paradox.

Inertia. The inertia argument says that companies find it difficult to change their strategies and structures in order to adapt to changing competitive conditions.[30] IBM is a classic example of this problem. For thirty years, it was viewed as the world's most successful computer company. Then in the space of a few years, its success turned into a disaster: it lost $5 billion in 1992, leading to layoffs of more than 100,000 employees. IBM's troubles were caused by a dramatic decline in the cost of computing power as a result of innovations in microprocessors. With the advent of powerful low-cost microprocessors, the locus of the computer market shifted from mainframes to small, low-priced personal computers, leaving IBM's huge mainframe operations with a diminished market. Although IBM had, and still has, a significant presence in the personal computer market, it had failed to shift the focus of its efforts away from mainframes and toward personal computers. This failure meant deep trouble for one of the most successful companies of the twentieth century (although IBM has now executed a successful turnaround with a repositioning as a provider of e-commerce infrastructure and solutions).

One reason that companies find it so difficult to adapt to new environmental conditions seems to be the role of capabilities in causing inertia. Organizational capabilities—the way a company makes decisions and manages its processes—can be a source of competitive advantage, but they are difficult to change. IBM always emphasized close coordination among operating units and favored decision processes that stressed consensus among interdependent operating units as a prerequisite for a decision to go forward.[31] This capability was a source of advantage for IBM during the 1970s, when coordination among its worldwide operating units was necessary to develop, manufacture, and sell complex mainframes. But the slow-moving bureaucracy that it had spawned was a source of failure in the 1990s, when organizations had to adapt readily to rapid environmental change.

Capabilities are difficult to change because a certain distribution of power and influence is embedded within the established decision-making and management processes of an organization. Those who play key roles in a decision-making process clearly have more power. It follows that changing the established capabilities of an organization means changing its existing distribution of power and influence, and those whose power and influence would diminish resist such change. Proposals for change trigger turf battles. This power struggle and the political resistance associated with trying to alter the way in which an organization makes decisions and manages its process—that is, trying to change its capabilities—bring on inertia. This is not to say that companies cannot change. However, because change is so often resisted by those who feel threatened by it, change in most cases has to be induced by a crisis. By then, the company may already be failing, as happened at IBM.

Prior Strategic Commitments. Ghemawat has argued that a company's prior strategic commitments not only limit its ability to imitate rivals but may also cause competitive disadvantage.[32] IBM, for instance, had major investments in the mainframe computer business, so when the market shifted, it was stuck with significant resources specialized to that particular business: its manufacturing facilities were geared to the production of mainframes, its research organization was similarly specialized, and so was its sales force. Because these resources were not well suited to the newly emerging personal computer business, IBM's difficulties in the early 1990s were in a sense inevitable. Its prior strategic commitments locked it into a business that was shrinking. Shedding these resources was bound to cause hardship for all organization stakeholders.

The Icarus Paradox. Danny Miller has postulated that the roots of competitive failure can be found in what he termed the *Icarus paradox*.[33] Icarus is a figure in Greek mythology who used a pair of wings, made for him by his father, to escape from an island where he was being held prisoner. He flew so well that he went higher and higher, ever closer to the sun, until the heat of the sun melted the wax that held his wings together and he plunged to his death in the Aegean Sea. The paradox is that his greatest asset, his ability to fly, caused his demise. Miller argues that the same paradox applies to many once successful companies. According to Miller, many companies become so dazzled by their early success that they believe more of the same type of effort is the way to future success. As a result, they can become so specialized and inner directed that they lose sight of market realities and the fundamental requirements for achieving a competitive advantage. Sooner or later, this leads to failure.

Miller identifies four major categories among the rising and falling companies, which he labels "craftsmen," "builders," "pioneers," and "salesmen." The "craftsmen," such as Texas Instruments and Digital Equipment Corp. (DEC), achieved early success through engineering excellence. But then they became so obsessed with engineering details that they lost sight of market realities. (The story of DEC's demise is summarized in Strategy in Action 3.4.) Among the "builders" are Gulf & Western and ITT. Having built successful, moderately diversified companies, they then became so enchanted with diversification for its own sake that they continued to diversify far beyond the point at which it was profitable to do so. Miller's third group are the "pioneers" like Wang Labs. Enamored of their own originally brilliant innovations, they continued to search for additional brilliant innovations and ended up producing novel but completely useless products. The final category comprises the "salesmen," exemplified by Procter & Gamble and Chrysler. They became so convinced of their ability to sell anything that they paid scant attention to product development and manufacturing excellence and as a result spawned a proliferation of bland, inferior products.

Steps to Avoid Failure   Given that so many traps wait for companies, the question arises as to how strategic managers can use internal analysis to find them and escape them. We now look at several tactics that managers can use.

Focus on the Building Blocks of Competitive Advantage. Maintaining a competitive advantage requires a company to continue focusing on all four generic building blocks of competitive advantage—efficiency, quality, innovation, and responsiveness to customers—and to develop distinctive competencies that con-

Strategy in Action   3.4

The Road to Ruin at DEC

DEC's original success was founded on the minicomputer, a cheaper, more flexible version of its mainframe cousins that Ken Olson and his brilliant team of engineers invented in the 1960s. They then improved on their original minicomputers until they could not be beat for quality and reliability. In the 1970s, their VAX series of minicomputers was widely regarded as the most reliable computers ever produced, and DEC was rewarded by high profit rates and rapid growth. By 1990, it was number 27 on the Fortune 500 list of the largest corporations in America.

Buoyed by its success, DEC turned into an engineering monoculture: its engineers became idols; its marketing and accounting staff, however, were barely tolerated. Component specs and design standards were all that senior managers understood. Technological fine tuning became such an obsession that the needs of customers for smaller, more economical, user-friendly computers were ignored. DEC's personal computers, for example, bombed because they were out of touch with the needs of customers, and the company failed to respond to the threat to its core market presented by the rise of computer workstations and client-server architecture. Indeed, Ken Olson was known for dismissing such new products. He once said, "We always say that customers are right, but they are not always right." Perhaps. But DEC, blinded by its early success, failed to remain responsive to its customers and changing market conditions.

By the early 1990s, DEC was in deep trouble. Olson was forced out in July 1992, and the company lost billions of dollars between 1992 and 1995. It returned to profitability in 1996, primarily because of the success of a turnaround strategy aimed at reorientating the company to serve precisely those areas that Olson had dismissed. In 1998, the company was acquired by Compaq Computer.

Sources: D. Miller, *The Icarus Paradox* (New York: HarperBusiness, 1990). P. D. Llosa, "We Must Know What We Are Doing," *Fortune*, November 14, 1994, p. 68.

---

tribute to superior performance in these areas. One of the messages of Miller's Icarus paradox is that many successful companies become unbalanced in their pursuit of distinctive competencies. DEC, for example, focused on engineering quality at the expense of almost everything else including, most important, responsiveness to customers. Other companies forget to focus on any distinctive competency at all.

Institute Continuous Improvement and Learning. The only constant in the world is change. Today's source of competitive advantage may soon be rapidly imitated by capable competitors or made obsolete by the innovations of a rival. In such a dynamic and fast-paced environment, the only way that a company can maintain a competitive advantage over time is to continually improve its efficiency, quality, innovation, and responsiveness to customers. The way to do this is to recognize the importance of learning within the organization.[34] The most successful companies are not those that stand still, resting on their laurels. They are those that are always seeking out ways of improving their operations and in the process are constantly upgrading the value of their distinctive competencies or creating new competencies. Companies such as General Electric and Toyota have a reputation for being learning organizations. This means that they are continually analyzing the processes that underlie their efficiency, quality, innovation, and responsiveness to customers. Their objective is to learn from prior mistakes and to seek out ways to improve their processes over time. This has enabled Toyota, for example, to continually upgrade its employee productivity and product quality, allowing it to stay ahead of imitators.

Track Best Industrial Practice and Use Benchmarking. One of the best ways to develop distinctive competencies that contribute to superior efficiency, quality, innovation, and responsiveness to customers is to identify and adopt best industrial practice. Only in this way will a company be able to build and maintain the resources and capabilities that underpin excellence in efficiency, quality, innovation, and responsiveness to customers. (What constitutes best industrial practice is an issue we discuss in some depth in Chapter 4.) It requires tracking the practice of other companies, and perhaps the best way to do so is through **benchmarking:** the process of measuring the company against the products, practices, and services of some of its most efficient global competitors. For example, when Xerox was in trouble in the early 1980s, it decided to institute a policy of benchmarking as a means of identifying ways to improve the efficiency of its operations. Xerox benchmarked L. L. Bean for distribution procedures, Deere & Company for central computer operations, Procter & Gamble for marketing, and Florida Power & Light for total quality management processes. By the early 1990s, Xerox was benchmarking 240 functions against comparable areas in other companies. This process has been credited with helping it dramatically improve the efficiency of its operations.[35]

Overcome Inertia. Overcoming the internal forces that are a barrier to change within an organization is one of the key requirements for maintaining a competitive advantage, and an entire chapter, Chapter 14, is spent discussing this issue. Suffice it to say here that identifying barriers to change is an important first step. Once this step has been taken, implementing change requires good leadership, the judicious use of power, and appropriate changes in organizational structure and control systems.

The Role of Luck

A number of scholars have argued that luck plays a critical role in determining competitive success and failure.[36] In its most extreme version, the luck argument devalues the importance of strategy altogether. Instead, it states that in the face of uncertainty, some companies just happen to pick the correct strategy.

Although luck may be the reason for a company's success in particular cases, it is an unconvincing explanation for the persistent success of a company. Recall our argument that the generic building blocks of competitive advantage are superior efficiency, quality, innovation, and responsiveness to customers. Keep in mind also that competition is a process in which companies are continually trying to outdo each other in their ability to achieve high efficiency, superior quality, outstanding innovation, and quick responsiveness to customers. It is possible to imagine a company getting lucky and coming into possession of resources that allow it to achieve excellence on one or more of these dimensions. However, it is difficult to imagine how *sustained* excellence on any of these four dimensions could be produced by anything other than conscious effort, that is, by strategy. Luck may indeed play a role in success, and managers must always exploit a lucky break (Strategy in Action 3.5 discusses the role of luck in the early history of Microsoft and how Bill Gates exploited that luck). However, to argue that success is entirely a matter of luck is to strain credibility. As the great banker of the early twentieth century, J. P. Morgan, once said, "The harder I work, the luckier I seem to get." Managers who strive to formulate and implement strategies that lead to a competitive advantage are more likely to be lucky.

Strategy in Action

3.5

Bill Gates's Lucky Break

The product that launched Microsoft into its leadership position in the software industry was MS-DOS, the operating system for IBM and IBM-compatible PCs. The original DOS program, however, was developed not by Microsoft but by Seattle Computer, where it was known as Q-DOS (which stood for "quick and dirty operating system"). When IBM was looking for an operating system to run its original PC, it talked to a number of software companies, including Microsoft, asking whether they could develop such a system. Seattle Computer was not one of those companies. Bill Gates, already a player in the emerging Seattle computer community, knew that Seattle Computer had developed a disk operating system and took action: he borrowed $50,000 from his father, a senior partner in a prominent Seattle law firm, and then went to see the CEO of Seattle Computer and offered to purchase the rights to the company's Q-DOS system. He did not, of course, reveal that IBM was looking for a disk operating system. Seattle Computer, short of cash, quickly agreed. Gates then renamed the system MS-DOS, upgraded it somewhat, and licensed it to IBM. The rest, as they say, is history.

So was Gates lucky? Of course he was. It was lucky that Seattle Computer had not heard about IBM's request. It was lucky that IBM approached Microsoft. It was lucky that Gates knew about Seattle Computer's operating system. And it was lucky that Gates had a father wealthy enough to lend him $50,000 on short notice. Nevertheless, to attribute all of Microsoft's subsequent success to luck would be wrong. Although MS-DOS gave Microsoft a tremendous head start in the industry, it did not guarantee that Microsoft would continue to enjoy the kind of worldwide success that it has. To do that, Microsoft had to build the appropriate set of resources and capabilities required to produce a continual stream of innovative software, which is precisely what the company did with the cash generated from MS-DOS.

Source: Stephen Manes and Paul Andrews, *Gates* (New York: Simon & Schuster 1993).

Summary of Chapter

1. Distinctive competencies are the firm-specific strengths of a company. Valuable distinctive competencies enable a company to earn a profit rate that is above the industry average.

2. The distinctive competencies of an organization arise from its resources (its financial, physical, human, technological, and organizational assets) and capabilities (its skills at coordinating resources and putting them to productive use).

3. In order to achieve a competitive advantage, a company needs to pursue strategies that build on its existing resources and capabilities and formulate strategies that build additional resources and capabilities (develop new competencies).

4. The source of a competitive advantage is superior value creation.

5. To create superior value, a company must lower its costs or differentiate its product so that it creates more value and can charge a higher price, or do both simultaneously.

6. Managers must understand how value creation and pricing decisions affect demand and how costs change with increases in volume. They must have a good grasp of the demand conditions in the company's market and the cost structure of the company at different levels of output if they are to make decisions that maximize the profitability of their enterprise.

7. The four generic building blocks of competitive advantage are efficiency, quality, innovation, and responsiveness to customers. Superior efficiency enables a company to lower its costs; superior quality allows it to charge a higher price and lower its costs; and superior customer service lets it charge a higher price. Superior innovation can lead to higher prices, particularly in the case of product innovations, or lower unit costs, particularly in the case of process innovations.

8. If a company's managers are to perform a good internal analysis, they need to be able to analyze the financial performance of their company, identifying how

the strategies of the company relate to its profitability, as measured by the return on invested capital.

9. The durability of a company's competitive advantage depends on the height of barriers to imitation, the capability of competitors, and environmental dynamism.

10. Failing companies typically earn low or negative profits. Three factors seem to contribute to failure: organizational inertia in the face of environmental change, the nature of a company's prior strategic commitments, and the Icarus paradox.

11. Avoiding failure requires a constant focus on the basic building blocks of competitive advantage, continuous improvement, identification and adoption of best industrial practice, and victory over inertia.

Discussion Questions

1. What are the main implications of the material discussed in this chapter for strategy formulation?

2. When is a company's competitive advantage most likely to endure over time?

3. It is possible for a company to be the lowest-cost producer in its industry and simultaneously have an output that is the most valued by customers. Discuss this statement.

4. Why is it important to understand the drivers of profitability, as measured by the return on invested capital?

5. Which is more important in explaining the success and failure of companies: strategizing or luck?

Practicing Strategic Management

SMALL-GROUP EXERCISE: ANALYZING COMPETITIVE ADVANTAGE

Break into a group of three to five people. Drawing on the concepts introduced in this chapter, analyze the competitive position of your business school in the market for business education. Then answer the following questions:

1. Does your business school have a competitive advantage?

2. If so, on what is this advantage based, and is this advantage sustainable?

3. If your school does not have a competitive advantage in the market for business education, identify the inhibiting factors that are holding it back.

4. How might the Internet change the way in which business education is delivered?

5. Does the Internet pose a threat to the competitive position of your school in the market for business education, or is it an opportunity for your school to enhance its competitive position? (Note that it can be both.)

ARTICLE FILE 3

Find a company that has sustained its competitive advantage for more than ten years. Identify the source of the competitive advantage, and explain why it has lasted so long.

STRATEGIC MANAGEMENT PROJECT: MODULE 3

This module deals with the competitive position of your company. With the information you have at your disposal, perform the tasks and answer the questions listed:

1. Identify whether your company has a competitive advantage or disadvantage in its primary industry. (Its primary industry is the one in which it has the most sales.)

2. Evaluate your company against the four generic building blocks of competitive advantage: efficiency, quality, innovation, and responsiveness to customers. How does this exercise help you understand the performance of your company relative to its competitors?

3. What are the distinctive competencies of your company?

4. What role have prior strategies played in shaping the distinctive competencies of your company? What has been the role of luck?

5. Do the strategies your company is pursuing now build on its distinctive competencies? Are they an attempt to build new competencies?

6. What are the barriers to imitating the distinctive competencies of your company?

7. Is there any evidence that your company finds it difficult to adapt to changing industry conditions? If so, why do you think this is the case?

EXPLORING THE WEB
Visiting Johnson & Johnson

Visit the web site of Johnson and Johnson (**http://www.jnj.com**). Read through the material contained on the site, paying particular attention to the features on company history, Johnson & Johnson's credo, innovations, and company news. On the basis of the information contained here, answer the following questions:

1. Do you think that Johnson & Johnson has a distinctive competence?
2. What is the nature of this competence? How does it help the company to attain a competitive advantage?
3. What are the resources and capabilities that underlie this competence? Where do these resources and capabilities come from?
4. How imitable is Johnson & Johnson's distinctive competence?

General Task: Search the Web for a company site that goes into depth about the history, products, and competitive position of that company. On the basis of the information you collect, answer the following questions:

1. Does the company have a distinctive competence?
2. What is the nature of this competence? How does it help the company to attain a competitive advantage?
3. What are the resources and capabilities that underlie this competence? Where do these resources and capabilities come from?
4. How imitable is the company's distinctive competence?

Closing Case

Cisco Systems

Cisco Systems is one of the great recent success stories. Two Stanford University computer scientists, Leonard Bosack and Sandra Lerner, founded the company in 1984. In the early 1980s, Stanford University had accumulated many separate computer networks, each using different machines and different electronic languages to communicate among themselves. The problem was that these networks could not talk to each other. Bosack and Lerner, who were married at the time, were the managers of separate networks and worked on the problem of hooking these networks together, partly, so legend has it, in order to be able to send each other email messages. Their solution was a specialized computer known as a router that was able to connect different computer systems. Realizing that this device might have commercial value, they established Cisco and shipped their first product in 1987. The company went public in 1990 with annual sales of around $70 million. Soon after, Cisco's sales started to increase exponentially as routers became a critical component of the rapidly expanding Internet. By 1999, Cisco had evolved into the dominant supplier of network equipment for the Internet—including routers, switches, and hubs—with annual sales in excess of $19 billion, no debt, and a return on invested capital of around 22 percent.

Cisco's rapid sales growth and high profitability owe much to its product innovation, which has continued at a rapid pace since the company went public, but it is also due to the company's aggressive adoption of an e-business infrastructure. Here too Cisco has been an innovator. This infrastructure has enabled the company to reap major efficiency gains, while providing its customers with superior point-of-sales service and after-sales service and support. Cisco was one of the first companies to move much of its sales effort onto the Internet. The process began in 1996 when it realized that its traditional sales infrastructure could not keep up with increasing demand. Rather than hire additional personnel to manage customer accounts, the company began to experiment with online sales. It developed a computer program to walk customers through the process of ordering equipment online. A critical feature of this program helps customers to order exactly the right mix of equipment, thereby avoiding any ordering mistakes, such as ordering incompatible equipment. In 1997, the company sold $500 million worth of equipment online. By 1999, this figure had ballooned to $10 billion, or 80 percent of its total sales, making the company one of the most aggressive adopters of an online sales approach in the world.

Customers seem to love the automated order processing system, primarily because it minimizes ordering mistakes and allows for quicker execution of orders. For example, at Sprint, a major customer, it used to take sixty days from the signing of a contract to complete a networking project. Now it takes thirty-five to forty-five days, primarily due to the efficiency of Cisco's online ordering system. Moreover, Sprint has been able to cut its order processing staff from twenty-one to six, significantly saving costs. As for Cisco, the company has just 300 service agents handling all of its customer accounts, compared to the 900 it would need if sales were not handled online. The difference represents an annual saving of $20 million.

Cisco has also placed its customer support functions online. All routine customer service functions are now handled online by a computer program that can translate a customer's fuzzy inquiry into a standard description of a familiar problem; then it provides the four most likely explanations onscreen, allowing the customer to avoid blind alleys and time wasted. Since implementing the system in 1996, Cisco's sales have quadrupled, while its engineering support staff has merely doubled to 800. Without automated sales support, Cisco calculates that it would need at least 1,000 additional service engineers, which would cost around $75 million. Cisco has also moved to distributing all support software over the Internet rather than transferring it to disks and mailing it to customers. This has saved it another $250 million per year in annual operating costs.

Discussion Questions

1. What are the sources of competitive advantage at Cisco?

2. How does the implementation of an e-business infrastructure at Cisco help the company to create value?

3. How secure do you think Cisco's competitive advantage is?

4. In 2000–2002, the telecommunications equipment industry suffered a sharp contraction in demand. Although Cisco's sales continued to expand, hitting $22 billion in 2001, its return on invested capital fell to just 6.7 percent. In 2002, revenues fell to under $18.5 billion and profitability shrank to under 6 percent. On the basis of the case, do you think that Cisco did worse or better than its rivals? How successful do you think Cisco will be once demand revives? Why?

Sources: "Cisco@speed," *Economist,* June 26, 1999, p. 12. S. Tully, "How Cisco Mastered the Net," *Fortune,* August 17, 1997, pp. 207–210. C. Kano, "The Real King of the Internet," *Fortune,* September 7, 1998, pp. 82–93.

Building Competitive Advantage Through Functional-Level Strategy

4

Opening Case

CSX—Getting the Trains to Run on Time

CSX Corporation, whose business is the transportation of freight, is one of the largest U.S. railroads as the result of a 1996 merger with Conrail. The merger took place because managers expected to reap huge savings in costs from operating an expanded freight rail network: a 23,000-mile network in twenty-three states in the eastern half of the United States. However, these cost savings did not result, and a host of postmerger problems associated with trying to join together two previously independent networks emerged.

Following the merger, the operating efficiency of the railroad fell. Trains were often late or delayed because of poor track and congested terminals. The Federal Railroad Administration told CSX that a government audit of 4,000 miles of its track had found serious defects, including excessive space between rails that could lead to train derailments. Employee morale was poor in the merged company, and customers, who relied on CSX Corporation to deliver products on time, were dissatisfied with its service and defecting to other railroads. As a result of these problems, earnings took a hit. CSX's operating margins fell from 21.4 percent in 1997 to 15.2 percent in 1999, primarily due to rising costs. Its stock price tumbled from a 1998 high of $62 to just $19.50 by mid-2000.

In 2000, the company launched an efficiency campaign to try to correct the problems. First, management recognized that if they were to improve operations, they needed to focus on some key measures of operating efficiency. They picked fourteen critical operating metrics—including safety standards (train derailments and accidents), train velocity (average speed), cars on line (a measure of inventory), terminal dwell time (how much time a locomotive is sitting idle at a terminal), and on-time departures and arrivals—each of which was given a clear ninety-day target for improvement. Performance against each of these targets was measured daily and communicated immediately throughout the organization.

By the end of 2001, it was clear that CSX had made substantial improvement against these targets. Train derailments had fallen by 39 percent, from 10.6 per week in 2000 to 6.5 per week in 2001. Train velocity for merchandise improved from 18.7 miles per hour in 2000 to 21.7 miles per hour in 2001. Over the same period, terminal dwell time fell from 30.8 hours to 24.5 hours, on-time originations rose from 69.2 percent to 88.1 percent, on-time arrivals increased from 51.3 percent to 75.6 percent, and the number of cars on line fell from 258,000 to 240,000. All of these measures implied increased operating efficiency and reliability.

How did CSX achieve this? The company's managers refer to their new business model as "Railroad 101." First, CSX management focused on congested terminals in its troubled southern region, where trains often got backed up for days. CSX put in extra resources—people and locomotives—and gave them the authority to do whatever was necessary to solve the congestion. Among other things, they changed several long-standard practices, such as holding up locomotives from departure in order to maximize the number of freight cars and train length. Although this practice was meant to boost productivity by realizing scale economies, paradoxically it hurt productivity and raised costs because of its unintended consequences: poor on-time performance, which alienated customers, and poor on time performance of the locomotive and crew time. Second, CSX focused resources on fixing defective track, which reduced derailments and also reduced unproductive locomotive and crew downtime, while increasing on-time performance.

Simultaneously, CSX launched a major initiative to build a web-based customer interface as a way of improving customer service. This interface allows customers to perform several important functions online. For example, a new shipment tracking function enables customers to obtain train and car information, including origination, current location, and destination. Customers can create and send bills of lading online, order empty railcars for the coming week, change the status of orders, or retrieve the history of previous orders.

CSX soon found that as a result of its initiatives, its reputation with customers was improving. The increased reliability of service not only boosted productivity and lowered costs but also created more value for customers. In turn, CSX found that its customers were willing to pay more for its services, and the company pushed through modest price increases in 2001 and 2002, which its customers accepted.

Sources: W. C. Vantuono, "Turnaround Time at CSXT," *Railway Age* (August 2001): 29–30. D. Machalaba, "CSX Corp.'s Railroad Unit Gets Business Back on Track," *Wall Street Journal,* January 29, 2002, p. B4. CSX Corporation, earnings and productivity information www.csx.com.

Overview

In this chapter, we take a close look at **functional-level strategies:** those aimed at improving the effectiveness of a company's operations and thus its ability to attain superior efficiency, quality, innovation, and customer responsiveness.

It is important to keep in mind the relationships of functional strategies, distinctive competencies, differentiation, low cost, value creation, and profitability (see Figure 4.1). Note that distinctive competencies shape the functional-level strategies that a company can pursue and that through their choices with regard to functional-level strategies, managers can build resources and capabilities that enhance a company's distinctive competencies. Note also that the ability of a company to attain superior efficiency, quality, innovation, and customer responsiveness will determine if its product offering is *differentiated* from that of rivals and if it has a *low cost structure.* Recall that companies that increase value through differentiation, while simultane-

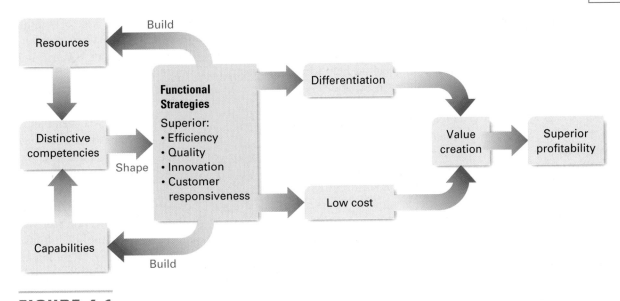

FIGURE 4.1

The Roots of Competitive Advantage

ously lowering their cost structure, create more value than their rivals, and this leads to a competitive advantage and superior profitability.

The *Opening Case* illustrates some of these relationships. CSX, a large railroad operator, pursued functional-level strategies to improve the efficiency, reliability (quality), and customer responsiveness of its service. By improving safety and removing congestion at terminals, CSX was able to get its trains to run on time. With more of its assets carrying goods, rather than sitting in terminals or on sidings waiting for track to be repaired, productivity went up, costs went down, and service reliability improved. As reliability improved, the railroad was able to differentiate itself better, which allowed it to raise prices and capture more business from customers, particularly in the area of time-sensitive and perishable goods where on-time arrival is critical. As a result of better differentiation and lower costs, CSX's profitability improved in 2001 over the prior two years, despite the fact that the U.S. economy was in recession. The case shows just how important operating efficiency and reliability can be. CSX described its approach as "Railroad 101" by which it meant doing the basics as efficiently as possible. Much of this chapter is devoted to looking at the basic changes that can be made at the operating level to improve competitive position. By the end of this chapter, you will understand how functional level strategies can be used to build a sustainable competitive advantage.

Achieving Superior Efficiency

A company is a device for transforming inputs (labor, land, capital, management, and technological know-how) into outputs (the goods and services produced). The simplest measure of efficiency is the quantity of inputs that it takes to produce a given output; that is, efficiency = outputs/inputs. The more efficient a company is, the fewer the inputs required to produce a given output and therefore the lower its cost structure will be. Put another way, an efficient company has higher productivity, and therefore lower costs, than its rivals. Here we review the steps that companies can take at the functional level to increase their efficiency and thereby lower their cost structure.

Efficiency and Economies of Scale

Economies of scale are unit cost reductions associated with a large scale of output. You will recall from the last chapter that it is very important for managers to understand how the cost structure of their enterprise varies with output because this understanding should help to drive strategy. For example, if unit costs fall significantly as output is expanded—that is, if there are significant economies of scale—a company may benefit by keeping prices down and increasing volume.

One source of economies of scale is the ability to spread fixed costs over a large production volume. *Fixed costs* are costs that must be incurred to produce a product whatever the level of output; examples are the costs of purchasing machinery, setting up machinery for individual production runs, building facilities, and advertising and R&D. For example, in 2001, Anheuser-Busch spent $500 million on advertising, about twice as much as Coors, the number three brewer in the United States. Because of its much larger output, Anheuser-Busch's advertising cost per barrel of beer was only $5 compared to $10 at Coors, and thus it enjoyed significant economies of scale in advertising. For another example, Microsoft spent approximately $1 billion to develop the latest version of its Windows operating system, Windows XP. It can realize substantial scale economies by spreading the fixed costs associated with developing the new operating system over the enormous unit sales volume it expects for this system (95 percent of the world's personal computers use a Microsoft operating system). These scale economies are significant because of the trivial incremental (or marginal) cost of producing additional copies of Windows XP: once the master copy has been produced, additional CDs containing the operating system can be produced for a few cents. The key to Microsoft's efficiency and profitability (and that of other companies with high fixed costs and trivial incremental or marginal costs) is to increase sales rapidly enough that fixed costs can be spread out over a large unit volume and substantial scale economies can be realized.

Another source of scale economies is the ability of companies producing in large volumes to achieve a greater division of labor and specialization. Specialization is said to have a favorable impact on productivity, mainly because it enables employees to become very skilled at performing a particular task. The classic example of such economies is Ford's Model T car. The world's first mass-produced car, the Model T Ford was introduced in 1923. Until then, Ford had made cars using an expensive hand-built craft production method. By introducing mass-production techniques, the company achieved greater division of labor (it split assembly into small, repeatable tasks) and specialization, which boosted employee productivity. Ford was also able to spread the fixed costs of developing a car and setting up production machinery over a large volume of output. As a result of these economies, the cost of manufacturing a car at Ford fell from $3,000 to less than $900 (in 1958 dollars).

Service companies also benefit from the realization of scale economies. In 1996 two of the world's largest banks, Chemical Banking and Chase Manhattan, both of New York, merged their operations, primarily to achieve cost savings, anticipated to be more than $1.7 billion per year, primarily through economies of scale. Economies of scale would come from combining the 600 retail branches of the original banks. By closing excess branches and consolidating its retail business into a smaller number of branches, the bank was able to increase the capacity utilization of its retail banking network significantly. The combined bank was able to generate the same volume of retail business from fewer branches. The fixed costs associated with retail branches—including rents, personnel, equipment, and utility costs—fell, which translated into a substantial reduction in the costs required to serve the average customer and the bank's cost structure.

These examples illustrate that economies of scale can boost profitability, as measured by return on invested capital (ROIC), in a number of ways. Economies of scale exist in production, sales and marketing, and R&D, and the overall effect of realizing scale economies is to reduce spending as a percentage of revenues on costs of goods sold (COGS), sales, general, and administrative expenses (SG&A), and R&D expenses, thereby boosting return on sales and, by extension, ROIC (see Figure 3.10). Moreover, by making more intensive use of existing capacity, a company can increase the amount of sales generated from its property, plant, and equipment (PPE), thereby reducing the amount of capital it needs to generate a dollar of sales, increasing its capital turnover and its ROIC.

The concept of scale economies is illustrated in Figure 4.2, which shows that as a company increases its output, unit costs fall. This process comes to an end at an output of Q^1, where all scale economies are exhausted. Indeed, at outputs of greater than Q^1, the company may encounter **diseconomies of scale,** which are the unit cost increases associated with a large scale of output. Diseconomies of scale occur primarily due to the increasing bureaucracy associated with large-scale enterprises and the managerial inefficiencies that can result.[1] Larger enterprises have a tendency to develop extensive managerial hierarchies in which dysfunctional political behavior is commonplace, information about operating matters is accidentally and deliberately distorted by the number of managerial layers through which it has to travel to reach top decision makers, and poor decisions are the result. As a result, past some point (such as Q1 in Figure 4.2), the inefficiencies that result from such developments outweigh any additional gains from economies of scale, and unit costs start to rise as output expands.

Managers must know not only the extent of economies of scale, but also where diseconomies of scale begin to occur. At Nucor Steel, for example, the realization that diseconomies of scale exist has led to a decision not to build plants that employ more than 300 individuals. The belief is that it is more efficient to build two plants, each employing 300 people, than one plant employing 600 people. Although the larger plant might theoretically be able to reap greater scale economies, Nucor's management believes that these would be swamped by the diseconomies of scale that come with larger organizational units.

FIGURE 4.2

Economies and Diseconomies of Scale

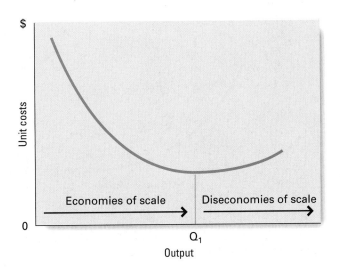

Efficiency and Learning Effects

Learning effects are cost savings that come from learning by doing. Labor, for example, learns by repetition how best to carry out a task. Therefore, labor productivity increases over time, and unit costs fall as individuals learn the most efficient way to perform a particular task. Equally important, management in new manufacturing facilities typically learns over time how best to run the new operation. Hence, production costs decline because of increasing labor productivity and management efficiency. Japanese companies like Toyota are noted for making learning a central part of their operating philosophy.

Learning effects tend to be more significant when a technologically complex task is repeated because there is more to learn. Thus, learning effects will be more significant in an assembly process that has 1,000 complex steps than in one with 100 simple steps. Although learning effects are normally associated with the manufacturing process, there is reason to believe that they are just as important in service industries. For example, one famous study of learning in the context of the health care industry found that more experienced medical providers posted significantly lower mortality rates for a number of common surgical procedures, suggesting that learning effects are at work in surgery.[2] The authors of this study used the evidence to argue for establishing regional referral centers for the provision of highly specialized medical care. These centers would perform many specific surgical procedures (such as heart surgery), replacing local facilities with lower volumes and presumably higher mortality rates.

In terms of the unit cost curve of a company, although economies of scale imply a movement along the curve (say, from A to B in Figure 4.3), the realization of learning effects implies a downward shift of the *entire* curve (B to C in Figure 4.3) as both labor and management become more efficient over time at performing their tasks at every level of output. In accounting terms, learning effects in a production setting will reduce the cost of goods sold as a percentage of revenues, enabling the company to earn a higher return on sales and return on invested capital.

No matter how complex the task is, however, learning effects typically die out after a limited period of time. Indeed, it has been suggested that they are really important only during the start-up period of a new process and cease after two or three years.[3] When changes occur to a company's production system—as a result of merger or the use of new information technology, for example—the learning process has to begin again.

FIGURE 4.3

The Impact of Learning and Scale Economies on Unit Costs

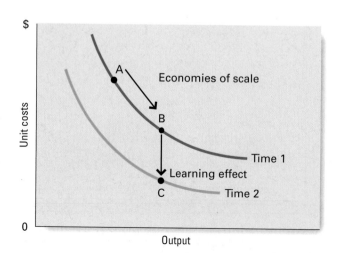

Efficiency and the Experience Curve

The experience curve refers to the systematic lowering of the cost structure, and consequent unit cost reductions, that have been observed to occur over the life of a product.[4] According to the experience curve concept, unit manufacturing costs for a product typically decline by some characteristic amount each time *accumulated* output of the product is doubled (accumulated output is the total output of a product since its introduction). This relationship was first observed in the aircraft industry, where it was found that each time accumulated output of airframes was doubled, unit costs declined to 80 percent of their previous level.[5] Thus, the fourth airframe typically cost only 80 percent of the second airframe to produce, the eighth airframe only 80 percent of the fourth, the sixteenth only 80 percent of the eighth, and so on. The outcome of this process is a relationship between unit manufacturing costs and accumulated output similar to that illustrated in Figure 4.4. Economies of scale and learning effects underlie the experience curve phenomenon. Put simply, as a company increases the accumulated volume of its output over time, it is able to realize both economies of scale (as volume increases) and learning effects. Consequently, unit costs and cost structure fall with increases in accumulated output.

The strategic significance of the experience curve is clear: increasing a company's product volume and market share will lower its cost structure relative to its rivals. Thus, company A in Figure 4.4, because it is farther down the experience curve, has a cost advantage over company B because of its lower cost structure. The concept is perhaps most important in industries that mass-produce a standardized output (for example, the manufacture of semiconductor chips). A company that wishes to become more efficient and lower its cost structure must try to ride down the experience curve as quickly as possible. This means constructing efficient scale manufacturing facilities even before it has generated demand for the product and aggressively pursuing cost reductions from learning effects. It might also need to adopt an aggressive marketing strategy, cutting prices to the bone and stressing heavy sales promotions and extensive advertising in order to build up demand, and hence accumulated volume, as quickly as possible. The need to be aware of the relationship of demand, price options, and costs noted in Chapter 4 is clear.

Once down the experience curve because of its superior efficiency, the company is likely to have a significant cost advantage over its competitors. For example, it has been argued that Intel uses such tactics to ride down the experience curve and gain a competitive advantage over its rivals in the market for microprocessors. Similarly, one

FIGURE 4.4

The Experience Curve

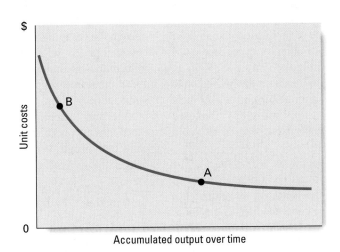

reason Matsushita came to dominate the global market for VHS videotape recorders is that it based its strategy on the experience curve.[6] The early success of Texas Instruments was also based on exploiting the experience curve, as Strategy in Action 4.1 details.

The company farthest down the experience curve cannot become complacent about its cost advantage. Strategy in Action 4.1 explains how obsession with the experience curve at Texas Instruments harmed the company. More generally, there are three reasons that managers should not become complacent about their efficiency-based cost advantages derived from experience effects. First, since neither learning effects nor economies of scale go on forever, the experience curve is likely to bottom out at some point; indeed, it must do so by definition. When this occurs, further unit cost reductions from learning effects and economies of scale will be hard to come by. Thus, in time, other companies can lower their cost structures and match the cost leader. Once this happens, a number of low-cost companies can have cost parity with each other. In such circumstances, a sustainable competitive advantage must rely on strategic factors besides the minimization of production costs by using existing technologies—factors such as better responsiveness to customers, product quality, or innovation.

Second, as noted in Chapter 2, changes that are always taking place in the external environment disrupt a company's business model, so cost advantages gained from experience effects can be made obsolete by the development of new technologies. The price of television picture tubes followed the experience curve pattern from the intro-

Strategy in Action   4.1

Too Much Experience at Texas Instruments

Texas Instruments (TI) was an early user of the experience curve concept. TI was a technological innovator, first in silicon transistors and then in semiconductors. The company discovered that with every doubling of accumulated production volume of a transistor or semiconductor, unit costs declined to 73 percent of their previous level. Building on this insight, when TI first produced a new transistor or semiconductor, it would slash the price of the product to stimulate demand. The goal was to drive up the accumulated volume of production and so drive down costs through the realization of experience curve economies. As a result, during the 1960s and 1970s, TI hammered its competitors in transistors and moved on to prevail in semiconductors and, ultimately, in hand-held calculators and digital watches. Until 1982, TI enjoyed rapid growth, with sales quadrupling between 1977 and 1981 alone.

After 1982, things began to go wrong for TI. The company's single-minded focus on cost reductions, an outgrowth of its strategic reliance on the experience curve, left it with a poor understanding of customer

needs and market trends. Competitors such as Casio and Hewlett-Packard began to make major inroads into TI's hand-held calculator business by focusing on features in addition to cost and price that customers demanded. TI was slow to react to this trend and lost substantial market share as a result. In the late 1970s, it also decided to focus on semiconductors for watches and calculators, where it had gained substantial experience-curve-based cost economies, rather than developing metal oxide semiconductors for computer memories and advanced semiconductors. As it turned out, with the growth in minicomputers and personal computers in the early 1980s, the market shifted toward high-power metal oxide semiconductors. Consequently, TI found itself outflanked by Intel and Motorola. In sum, TI's focus on realizing experience curve economies initially benefited the company, but then it seems to have contributed toward a myopia that cost the company dearly.

Sources: G. Stalk and T. M. Hout, *Competing Against Time* (New York: Free Press, 1990). D. Miller, *The Icarus Paradox* (New York: HarperBusiness, 1990).

duction of television in the late 1940s until 1963. The average unit price dropped from $34 to $8 (in 1958 dollars) in that time. However, the advent of color TV interrupted the experience curve. To make picture tubes for color TVs, a new manufacturing technology was required, and the price of color TV tubes shot up to $51 by 1966. Then the experience curve reasserted itself. The price dropped to $48 in 1968, $37 in 1970, and $36 in 1972.[7] In short, technological change can alter the rules of the game, requiring that former low-cost companies take steps to reestablish their competitive edge.

A further reason for avoiding complacency is that producing a high volume of output does not necessarily give a company a lower cost structure. Different technologies have different cost structures. For example, the steel industry has two alternative manufacturing technologies: an integrated technology, which relies on the basic oxygen furnace, and a mini-mill technology, which depends on the electric arc furnace. As illustrated in Figure 4.5, mini-mills are cost efficient at relative low volume (Q^m), whereas the basic oxygen furnace requires high volumes to attain maximum efficiency (Q^i: $Q^i > Q^m$). Moreover, even when both technologies are producing at their most efficient output levels, steel companies with basic oxygen furnaces do not have a cost advantage over mini-mills.

Consequently, the pursuit of experience economies by an integrated company using basic oxygen technology may not bring the kind of cost advantages that a naive reading of the experience curve phenomenon would lead the company to expect. Indeed, there have been significant periods of time when integrated companies have not been able to get enough orders to run at optimum capacity (they have been producing at Q^i). Hence, their production costs have been considerably higher than those of minimills.[8] More generally, as we discuss next, in many industries, new flexible manufacturing technologies hold out the promise of allowing small manufacturers to produce at unit costs comparable to those of large assembly-line operations.

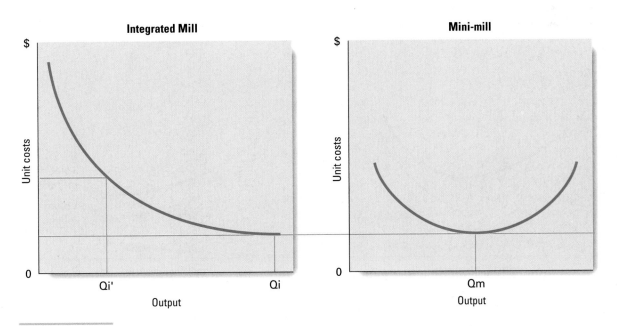

FIGURE 4.5

Unit Production Costs in an Integrated Mill and Mini-Mill

Efficiency, Flexible Manufacturing, and Mass Customization

Central to the concept of economies of scale is the idea that the best way to achieve high efficiency and a lower cost structure is through the mass production of a standardized output. The trade-off implicit in this idea is between unit costs and product variety. Producing greater product variety from a factory implies shorter production runs, which implies an inability to realize economies of scale and higher costs. That is, a wide product variety makes it difficult for a company to increase its production efficiency and thus reduce its unit costs. According to this logic, the way to increase efficiency and achieve a lower cost structure is to limit product variety and produce a standardized product in large volumes (see Figure 4.6a).

This view of production efficiency has been challenged by the rise of flexible manufacturing technologies. The term **flexible manufacturing technology**—or **lean production,** as it is often called—covers a range of manufacturing technologies designed to reduce setup times for complex equipment, increase the use of individual machines through better scheduling, and improve quality control at all stages of the manufacturing process.[9] Flexible manufacturing technologies allow the company to produce a wider variety of end products at a unit cost that at one time could be achieved only through the mass production of a standardized output (see Figure 4.6b). Indeed, research suggests that the adoption of flexible manufacturing technologies may increase efficiency and lower unit costs relative to what can be achieved by the mass production of a standardized output, while at the same time enabling the company to customize its product offering to a much greater extent than was once thought possible. The term **mass customization** has been coined to describe the ability of companies to use flexible manufacturing technology to reconcile two goals that were once thought to be incompatible: *low cost* and *differentiation through product customization*.[10]

Flexible manufacturing technologies vary in their sophistication and complexity. One of the most famous examples, Toyota's production system, is relatively unso-

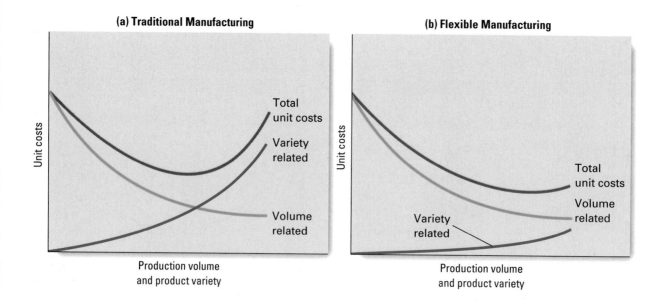

FIGURE 4.6

Tradeoff Between Costs and Product Variety

phisticated, but it has been credited with making Toyota the most efficient auto company in the global industry. Toyota's flexible manufacturing system is profiled in Strategy in Action 4.2. **Flexible machine cells** are another common flexible manufacturing technology. A flexible machine cell is a grouping of various types of machinery, a common materials handler, and a centralized cell controller (a computer). Each cell normally contains four to six machines capable of performing a variety of operations but dedicated to producing a family of parts or products. The settings on machines are computer controlled, which allows each cell to switch quickly between the production of different parts or products.

Improved capacity utilization and reductions in work-in-progress (that is, stockpiles of partly finished products) and waste are major efficiency benefits of flexible machine cells. Improved capacity utilization arises from the reduction in setup times and from the computer-controlled coordination of production flow between machines, which eliminate bottlenecks. The tight coordination between machines also reduces work-in-progress. Reductions in waste are due to the ability of computer-controlled machinery to identify ways to transform inputs into outputs while producing a minimum of unusable waste material. Free-standing machines might be in use 50 percent of the time; the same machines when grouped into a cell can be used more than 80 percent of the time and produce the same end product with half the waste, thereby increasing efficiency and resulting in lower costs.

The effects of installing flexible manufacturing technology on a company's cost structure can be dramatic. W. L. Gore, a privately owned company that manufactures

Strategy in Action   4.2

Toyota's Lean Production System

Toyota's flexible manufacturing system was developed by one of the company's engineers, Ohno Taiichi. After working at Toyota for five years and visiting Ford's U.S. plants, Ohno became convinced that the mass production philosophy for making cars was flawed. He saw numerous problems, including three major drawbacks. First, long production runs created massive inventories, which had to be stored in large warehouses. This was expensive because of the cost of warehousing and because inventories tied up capital in unproductive uses. Second, if the initial machine settings were wrong, long production runs resulted in the production of a large number of defects (that is, waste). And third, the mass production system was unable to accommodate consumer preferences for product diversity.

In looking for ways to make shorter production runs economical, Ohno developed a number of techniques designed to reduce setup times for production equipment, a major source of fixed costs. By using a system of levers and pulleys, he was able to reduce the time required

to change dies on stamping equipment from a full day in 1950 to three minutes by 1971. This advance made small production runs economical, which allowed Toyota to respond better to consumer demands for product diversity. Small production runs also eliminated the need to hold large inventories, thereby reducing warehousing costs. Furthermore, small product runs and the lack of inventory meant that defective parts were produced only in small numbers and entered the assembly process immediately. This reduced waste and made it easier to trace defects to their source and fix the problem. In sum, Ohno's innovations enabled Toyota to produce a more diverse product range at a lower unit cost than was possible with conventional mass production.

Sources: M. A. Cusumano, *The Japanese Automobile Industry* (Cambridge, Mass.: Harvard University Press, 1989). Ohno Taiichi, *Toyota Production System* (Cambridge, Mass.: Productivity Press, (1990). J. P. Womack, D. T. Jones, and D. Roos, *The Machine That Changed the World* (New York: Rawson Associates, 1990).

a wide range of products, from high-tech computer cables to its famous Gore-Tex fabric, has adopted flexible cells in several of its forty-six factories. In its cable-making facilities, the effect has been to cut the time taken to make computer cables by 50 percent, reduce stock by 33 percent, and shrink the space taken up by the plant by 25 percent.[11] More generally, in terms of the profitability framework developed in Chapter 3, flexible manufacturing technology should boost profitability (measured by ROIC) by reducing the cost of goods sold as a percentage of revenues, reducing the working capital needed to finance work in progress (because there is less of it), and reducing the amount of capital that needs to be invested in property plant and equipment to generate a dollar of sales (because less space is needed to store inventory).

Marketing and Efficiency

The marketing strategy that a company adopts can have a major impact on efficiency and cost structure. **Marketing strategy** refers to the position that a company takes with regard to pricing, promotion, advertising, product design, and distribution. Some of the steps leading to greater efficiency are fairly obvious. For example, riding down the experience curve to achieve a lower cost structure can be facilitated by aggressive pricing, promotions, and advertising, all of which are the task of the marketing function. Other aspects of marketing strategy have a less obvious but no less important impact on efficiency. One important aspect is the relationship of customer defection rates, cost structure, and unit costs.[12]

Customer defection rates are the percentage of a company's customers who defect every year to competitors. Defection rates are determined by customer loyalty, which in turn is a function of the ability of a company to satisfy its customers. Because acquiring a new customer entails certain one-time fixed costs for advertising, promotions, and the like, there is a direct relationship between defection rates and costs. The longer a company holds on to a customer, the greater is the volume of customer-generated unit sales that can be set against these fixed costs and the lower the average unit cost of each sale. Thus, lowering customer defection rates allows a company to achieve a lower cost structure.

One consequence of the defection-cost relationship depicted is illustrated in Figure 4.7. Because of the relatively high fixed costs of acquiring new customers, serving customers who stay with the company only for a short time before switching to competitors often leads to a loss on the investment made to acquire that customer. The longer a customer stays with the company, the more the fixed costs of acquiring that customer can be spread out over repeat purchases, boosting the profit per customer.

FIGURE 4.7

The Relationship Between Customer Loyalty and Profit per Customer

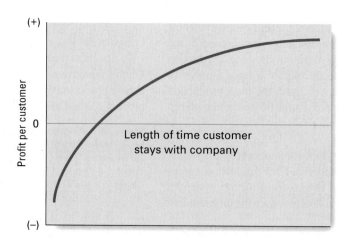

Thus, there is a positive relationship between the length of time that a customer stays with a company and profit per customer. So if a company can reduce customer defection rates, it can make a much better return on its investment in acquiring customers and thereby boost its profitability. In terms of the profitability framework developed in Chapter 3, reduced customer defection rates means that the company needs to spend less on sales, general, and administrative expenses to generate a dollar of sales revenue, which increases both return on sales and return on invested capital.

For an example, consider the credit card business.[13] Most credit card companies spend an average of $50 to recruit a customer and set up a new account. These costs come from the advertising required to attract new customers, credit checks required for each customer, and the mechanics of setting up an account and issuing a card. These one-time fixed costs can be recouped only if a customer stays with the company for at least two years. Moreover, when customers stay a second year, they tend to increase their use of the credit card, which raises the volume of revenues generated by each customer over time. As a result, although the credit card business loses $50 per customer in Year 1, it makes a profit of $44 in Year 3 and $55 in Year 6.

Another economic benefit of long-time customer loyalty is the free advertising that customers provide for a company. Loyal customers can dramatically increase the volume of business through referrals. A striking example is Britain's largest retailer, the clothing and food company Marks & Spencer, whose success is built on a well-earned reputation for providing its customers with high-quality goods at reasonable prices. The company has generated such customer loyalty that it does not need to advertise in Britain, a major source of cost saving.

The key message, then, is that reducing customer defection rates and building customer loyalty can be major sources of a lower cost structure. A 5 percent reduction in customer defection rates leads to the following increases in profits per customer over average customer life: 75 percent in the credit card business, 50 percent in the insurance brokerage industry, 45 percent in the industrial laundry business, and 35 percent in the computer software industry.[14]

A central component of developing a strategy to reduce defection rates is to identify customers who do defect, find out why they defected, and act on that information so that other customers do not defect for similar reasons in the future. To take these measures, the marketing function must have information systems capable of tracking customer defections.

Materials Management, Just-in-Time, and Efficiency

The contribution of materials management to boosting the efficiency of a company can be just as dramatic as the contribution of production and marketing. **Materials management** encompasses the activities necessary to get inputs and components to a production facility (including the costs of purchasing inputs), through the production process, and out through a distribution system to the end user.[15] Because there are so many sources of cost in this process, the potential for reducing costs through more efficient materials management strategies is enormous. For a typical manufacturing company, materials and transportation costs account for 50 to 70 percent of its revenues, so even a small reduction in these costs can have a substantial impact on profitability. According to one estimate, for a company with revenues of $1 million, a return on invested capital of 5 percent, and materials management costs that amount to 50 percent of sales revenues (including purchasing costs), increasing total profits by $15,000 would require either a 30 percent increase in sales revenues or a 3 percent reduction in materials costs.[16] In a typical competitive market, reducing materials costs by 3 percent is usually much easier than increasing sales revenues by 30 percent.

Improving the efficiency of the materials management function typically requires the adoption of a just-in-time (JIT) inventory system, designed to economize on inventory holding costs by having components arrive at a manufacturing plant just in time to enter the production process or goods at a retail store only when stock is depleted. The major cost saving comes from increasing inventory turnover, which reduces inventory holding costs, such as warehousing and storage costs, and the company's need for working capital. For example, Wal-Mart uses JIT systems to replenish the stock in its stores at least twice a week; many stores receive daily deliveries if they are needed. The typical competitor replenishes its stock every two weeks so that they have to carry a much higher inventory and need more working capital per dollar of sales. Compared to its competitors, Wal-Mart can maintain the same service levels with one-fourth the inventory investment, a major source of its lower cost structure. Thus, faster inventory turnover has helped Wal-Mart achieve an efficiency-based competitive advantage in the retailing industry.[17] More generally, in terms of the profitability model developed in Chapter 3, JIT inventory systems reduce the need for working capital (since there is less inventory to finance) and fixed capital to finance storage space (since there is less to store), which reduces capital needs, increases capital turnover, and, by extension, boosts the return on invested capital.

The drawback of JIT systems is that they leave a company without a buffer stock of inventory. Although buffer stocks are expensive to store, they can help tide a company over shortages on inputs brought about by disruption among suppliers (for instance, a labor dispute at a key supplier) and help a company respond quickly to increases in demand. However, there are ways around these limitations. For example, to reduce the risks linked to dependence on just one supplier for an important input, a company might decide to source inputs from multiple suppliers.

Recently, the efficient management of materials and inventory has been recast in terms of **supply chain management:** the task of managing the flow of inputs and components from suppliers into the company's production processes to minimize inventory holding and maximize inventory turnover. One of the exemplary companies in terms of supply chain management is Dell, whose goal is to streamline its supply chain to such an extent that it "replaces inventory with information" (See the *Running Case* in this section for details.) Strategy in Action 4.3 looks at how the three major office superstores—Office Depot, Staples, and Office Max—are competing against each other by trying to manage their supply chains more efficiently.

R&D Strategy and Efficiency

The role of superior research and development (R&D) in helping a company achieve a greater efficiency and a lower cost structure is twofold. First, the R&D function can boost efficiency by designing products that are easy to manufacture. By cutting down on the number of parts that make up a product, R&D can dramatically decrease the required assembly time, which translates into higher employee productivity, lower costs, and higher profitability. For example, after Texas Instruments redesigned an infrared sighting mechanism that it supplies to the Pentagon, it found that it had reduced the number of parts from 47 to 12, the number of assembly steps from 56 to 13, the time spent fabricating metal from 757 minutes per unit to 219 minutes per unit, and unit assembly time from 129 minutes to 20 minutes. The result was a substantial decline in production costs. Design for manufacturing requires close coordination between the production and R&D functions of the company, of course. Cross-functional teams that contain production and R&D personnel who work jointly on the problem best achieve this.

Strategy in Action

4.3

Supply Chain Management at Office Superstores

Over the past decade, Office Depot, Staples, and Office Max have been engaged in an intense race to dominate the office superstore business. Office superstores have adopted a supermarket approach to selling office supplies and equipment, which includes everything from paper and printer ink to computers and office furniture. Like all other supermarket-type retailers, their margins are razor thin. So to boost their profitability, all three have been looking at ways of managing their supply chains more efficiently. The goal is to coordinate the flow of materials from vendors to such a degree that inventory turns over more rapidly and so less store space needs to be devoted to storing inventory, which allows for smaller, less expensive stores. To the extent that they are successful, this strategy should produce higher sales per square foot, require less investment in store real estate, and tie up less working capital in inventory. All of this will boost profitability as measured by the return on invested capital.

Using inventory turnover as a metric, Office Depot is the clear leader, with a 7.1 inventory turn rate for 2001; its inventory turns over (i.e., is replaced) 7.1 times per year. Staples is next, with 4.2 inventory turns, followed by Office Max, with 3.2 inventory turns. Office Depot attributes its high inventory turnover to an early investment in information systems, which allow it to track the sales of individual items closely and link them to an optimal reordering cycle. In addition, these systems have helped it to identify slow-moving, low-margin items. Over the past few years, Office Depot has scaled back the number of products it keeps in stock—its stock keeping units (SKUs)—by about 20 percent by removing slow-moving, low-margin items from its stores. As a result, it can operate with slightly smaller stores and still generate comparable sales levels; its new stores are 25,000 square feet, compared to 30,000 square feet in older stores. As it has grown larger, Office Depot has also been able to use its

buying power to persuade vendors to drop-ship supplies at Office Depot warehouses on a just-in-time basis, thereby removing the need to hold expensive inventory.

For its part, Staples announced in 2001 that more efficient supply chain management was one of its top priorities. Staples has put some thirty initiatives in place in recent years in an attempt to manage its inventory better. Among them is working closely with its top thirty suppliers to develop joint processes for streamlining the supply process. Regular meetings with Hewlett Packard, for example, has prompted the retailer to move ink cartridges, one of its major categories, to the front of the store to yield faster inventory turns. Staples credits this action with a $6 million to $8 million reduction in inventory. More generally, Staples maintains that between 1998, when it started work on these initiatives, and 2001, the average inventory per store has fallen by some 30 percent. One of the most dramatic steps Staples has taken has been to eliminate the in-store stock of personal computers from some 200 stores, replacing the product displays and on-floor inventory with a web-based display that allows Staples customers to enter a customized order for a PC, which a Staples vendor then builds.

Office Max too is investing aggressively in supply chain management initiatives in an attempt to take inventory out of its system. Like its competitors, it has invested in information systems to track the sale of individual items and link that to reordering cycles. It is in the process of rationalizing its SKUs, removing slow-selling, low-margin items from stores, and downscaling the size of its stores while planning to boost sales per square foot. As a result, the average size of a new Office Max store has fallen by 15 percent over the last few years.

Source: M. Prior, "Major Office Suppliers Hone Supply Chain Efficiencies," *DSN Retailing*, November 5, 2001, pp. 27–31.

The second way in which the R&D function can help a company achieve a lower cost structure is by pioneering process innovations. A *process innovation* is an innovation in the way production processes operate that improves their efficiency. Process innovations have often been a major source of competitive advantage. Toyota's competitive advantage is based partly on the company's invention of new flexible manufacturing processes that dramatically reduced setup times. This process innovation enabled it to obtain efficiency gains associated with flexible manufacturing systems years ahead of its competitors.

Human Resource Strategy and Efficiency

Employee productivity is one of the key determinants of an enterprise's efficiency, cost structure, and profitability.[18] Productive manufacturing employees can lower the cost of goods sold as a percentage of revenues, a productive sales force can increase sales revenues for a given level of expenses, and productive employees in the company's R&D function can boost the percentage of revenues generated from new products for a given level of R&D expenses. Thus, productive employees lower the costs of generating revenues, increase the return on sales, and by extension boost the company's return on invested capital. The challenge for a company's human resource function is to devise ways to increase employee productivity. Among the choices it has are hiring strategies, training employees, organizing the work force into self-managing teams, and linking pay to performance.

Hiring Strategy. Many companies well known for their productive employees devote considerable attention to hiring. Wal-Mart, for example, seeks employees who share the values that are central to the Wal-Mart culture, including frugality, a belief in good customer service, and an appreciation for the value of money. Southwest Airlines hires people who have a positive attitude and work well in teams because it believe that people who have a positive attitude will work hard and interact well with customers, therefore helping to create customer loyalty. Nucor hires people who are self-reliant and goal oriented, because its employees work in self-managing teams where they have to be self-reliant and goal oriented to perform well. As these examples suggest, it is important to make sure that the hiring strategy of the company is consistent with its own internal organization, culture, and strategic priorities. The people a company hires should have attributes that match the strategic objectives of the company.

Employee Training. Employees are a major input into the production process. Those who are highly skilled can perform tasks faster and more accurately and are more likely to learn the complex tasks associated with many modern production methods than individuals with lesser skills. Training upgrades employee skill levels, bringing the company productivity-related efficiency gains from learning and experimentation.[19]

Self-Managing Teams. The use of **self-managing teams,** whose members coordinate their own activities, including making their own hiring, training, work, and reward decisions, has been spreading rapidly. The typical team comprises five to fifteen employees who produce an entire product or undertake an entire task. Team members learn all team tasks and rotate from job to job. Because a more flexible work force is one result, team members can fill in for absent coworkers and take over managerial duties such as work and vacation scheduling, ordering materials, and hiring new members. The greater responsibility thrust on team members and the empowerment it implies are seen as motivators. (Empowerment is the process of giving lower-level employees decision-making power.) People often respond well to being given greater autonomy and responsibility. Performance bonuses linked to team production and quality targets work as an additional motivator.

The effect of introducing self-managing teams is reportedly an increase in productivity of 30 percent or more and a substantial increase in product quality. Further cost savings arise from eliminating supervisors and creating a flatter organizational hierarchy, which also lowers the cost structure of the company. In manufacturing companies, perhaps the most potent way to lower the cost structure is to combine self-managing teams with flexible manufacturing cells. For example, after the introduction of flexible manufacturing technology and work practices based on self-managing teams, a General Electric plant in Salisbury, North Carolina, increased productivity by 250 percent compared with GE plants that produced the same products four years earlier.[20]

Still, teams are no panacea; in manufacturing companies, self-managing teams may fail to live up to their potential unless they are integrated with flexible manufacturing technology. Also, teams put a lot of management responsibilities on team members, and helping team members to cope with these responsibilities often requires substantial training—a fact that many companies often forget in their rush to drive down costs, with the result that the teams don't work out as well as planned.[21]

Pay for Performance. It is hardly surprising that linking pay to performance can help increase employee productivity, but the issue is not quite so simple as just introducing incentive pay systems. It is also important to define what kind of job performance is to be rewarded and how. Some of the most efficient companies in the world, mindful that cooperation among employees is necessary to realize productivity gains, link pay to group or team (rather than individual) performance. Nucor divides its work force into teams of thirty or so, with bonus pay, which can amount to 30 percent of base pay, linked to the ability of the team to meet productivity and quality goals. This link creates a strong incentive for individuals to cooperate with each other in pursuit of team goals; that is, it facilitates teamwork.

Information Systems, the Internet, and Efficiency

With the rapid spread of computers, the explosive growth of the Internet and corporate intranets (internal corporate computer networks based on Internet standards), and the spread of high-bandwidth fiber optics and digital wireless technology, the information systems function is moving to center stage in the quest for operating efficiencies and a lower cost structure.[22] The impact of information systems on productivity is wide ranging and potentially affects all other activities of a company. For example, in the *Closing Case* to Chapter 3, we saw how Cisco Systems has been able to realize significant cost savings by moving its ordering and customer service functions online. The company has just 300 service agents handling all of its customer accounts, compared to the 900 it would need if sales were not handled online. The difference represents an annual saving of $20 million a year. Moreover, without automated customer service functions, Cisco calculates that it would need at least 1,000 additional service engineers, which would cost around $75 million.[23] Dell Computer also makes extensive use of the Internet to lower its cost structure and differentiate itself from rivals (see the *Running Case*).

More generally, companies like Cisco and Dell are using web-based information systems to reduce the costs of coordination between the company and its customers and the company and its suppliers. By using web-based programs to automate customer and supplier interactions, the number of people required to manage these interfaces can be substantially reduced, thereby reducing costs. This trend extends beyond high-tech companies. Banks and financial service companies are finding that they can substantially reduce costs by moving customer accounts and support functions online. Such a move reduces the need for customer service representatives, bank tellers, stockbrokers, insurance agents, and others. For example, it costs an average of about $1.07 to execute a transaction at a bank, such as shifting money from one account to another; executing the same transaction over the Internet costs $0.01.[24]

Running Case

Dell's Utilization of the Internet

By 2001, more than 85 percent of Dell's computers were sold online. According to Michael Dell, "As I saw it, the Internet offered a logical extension of the direct (selling) model, creating even stronger relationships with our customers. The Internet would augment conventional telephone, fax, and face-to-face encounters, and give our customers the information they wanted faster, cheaper, and more efficiently." Dell's web site allows customers to customize their orders to get the system that best suits their particular requirements. By allowing customers to configure their order, Dell increases its customer responsiveness, thereby differentiating itself from rivals. Dell has also put much of its customer service functions online, reducing the need for telephone calls to customer service representatives and saving costs in the process. Each week, some 200,000 people access Dell's troubleshooting tips online. Each of these visits to Dell's web site saves the company a potential $15, which is the average cost of a technical support call. If just 10 percent of these online visitors were to call Dell by telephone instead, it would cost the company $15.6 million per year.

Dell uses the Internet to manage its supply chain, feeding real-time information about order flow to its suppliers, which use this information to schedule their own production, providing components to Dell on a just-in-time basis, thereby taking inventory out of the system and reducing Dell's need for working capital and space to store the inventory. Dell's ultimate goal is to drive all inventories out of the supply chain apart from that in transit between suppliers and Dell, effectively replacing inventory with information. In that way, Dell can drive significant costs out of its system.

Internet-based customer ordering and procurement systems have also allowed the company to synchronize demand and supply to an extent that few other companies can. For example, if Dell sees that it is running out of a particular component, say 17-inch monitors from Sony, it can manipulate demand by offering a 19-inch model at a lower price until Sony delivers more 17-inch monitors. By taking such steps to fine-tune the balance between demand and supply, Dell can meet customers' expectations and maintain its differential advantage. Moreover, balancing supply and demand allows the company to minimize excess and obsolete inventory. Dell writes off between 0.05 percent and 0.1 percent of total materials costs in excess or obsolete inventory. Its competitors write off between 2 and 3 percent, which again gives Dell a significant cost advantage.

Sources: B. Gates, *Business @ the Speed of Thought* (New York: Warner Books, 1999). "Enter the Eco-System: From Supply Chain to Network," *Economist,* November 11, 2000. "Dell's Direct Initiative," *Country Monitor,* June 7, 2000, p. 5. Michael Dell, *Direct from Dell: Strategies That Revolutionized an Industry* (New York: Harper-Business, 1999). (The Dell quote is from p. 91.)

Similarly, the theory behind Internet-based retailers such as Amazon.com is that by replacing physical stores and their supporting personnel with an online virtual store and automated ordering and checkout processes, significant costs can be taken out of the retailing system. Cost savings can also be realized by using web-based information systems to automate many internal company activities, from managing expense reimbursements to benefits planning and hiring processes, thereby reducing the need for internal support personnel.

For many years, skeptics questioned the impact that computer-based information systems were having on productivity, but recent data suggest that the gains are starting to appear. For the period 1996–2000, U.S. nonfarm productivity growth accelerated from a historic average of 1 percent per year to 2.8 percent per year. The productivity growth was greatest in the computer industry, which is not surprising given the efforts by companies like Cisco and Dell to implement web-based sales and service functions. Moreover, careful analysis has shown that productivity growth was greater in sectors of the economy that invested more in information technology during this period.[25]

Infrastructure and Efficiency

A company's infrastructure—that is, its structure, culture, style of strategic leadership, and control system—determines the context within which all other value creation activities take place. It follows that improving infrastructure can help a company increase efficiency and lower its cost structure. Above all, an appropriate infrastructure can help foster a companywide commitment to efficiency and promote cooperation among different functions in pursuit of efficiency goals. These issues are addressed at length in later chapters.

For now, it is important to note that strategic leadership is especially important in building a companywide commitment to efficiency. The leadership task is to articulate a vision that recognizes the need for *all* functions of a company to focus on improving efficiency. It is not enough to improve the efficiency of production, or of marketing, or of R&D in a piecemeal fashion. Achieving superior efficiency requires a companywide commitment to this goal that must be articulated by general and functional managers. A further leadership task is to facilitate cross-functional cooperation needed to achieve superior efficiency. For example, designing products that are easy to manufacture requires that production and R&D personnel communicate; integrating JIT systems with production scheduling requires close communication between material management and production; designing self-managing teams to perform production tasks requires close cooperation between human resources and production; and so on.

Table 4.1 summarizes the primary roles that various functions must take in order to achieve superior efficiency. Bear in mind that achieving superior efficiency is not something that can be tackled on a function-by-function basis. It requires an organization-wide commitment and an ability to ensure close cooperation among functions. Top management, by exercising leadership and influencing the infrastructure, plays a major role in this process.

TABLE 4.1

Primary Roles of Value Creation Functions in Achieving Superior Efficiency

Value Creation Function	Primary Roles
Infrastructure (leadership)	1. Provide companywide commitment to efficiency. 2. Facilitate cooperation among functions.
Production	1. Where appropriate, pursue economies of scale and learning economics. 2. Implement flexible manufacturing systems.
Marketing	1. Where appropriate, adopt aggressive marketing to ride down the experience curve. 2. Limit customer defection rates by building brand loyalty.
Materials management	1. Implement JIT systems.
R&D	1. Design products for ease of manufacture. 2. Seek process innovations.
Information systems	1. Use information systems to automate processes. 2. Use information systems to reduce costs of coordination.
Human resources	1. Institute training programs to build skills. 2. Implement self-managing teams. 3. Implement pay for performance.

Achieving Superior Quality

In Chapter 3, we noted that quality can be thought of in terms of two dimensions: product *reliability* and other product *attributes*. High-quality products are both reliable, in the sense that they do the job they were designed for and do it well, and are also perceived by consumers to have superior attributes. We also noted that superior quality gives a company two advantages. First, a strong reputation for quality allows a company to *differentiate* itself from rivals by creating more value in the eyes of customers, and this gives it the option of charging a premium price for its products. Second, eliminating defects or errors from the production process reduces waste, increases efficiency, and lowers the cost structure of the company and increases its profitability. For example, reducing the number of defects in a company's manufacturing process will lower the cost of goods sold as a percentage of revenues, thereby raising the company's return on sales and return on invested capital. In this section, we look in more depth at what managers can do to enhance the reliability and other attributes of the company's product offering.

Attaining Superior Reliability

The principal tool that managers use to increase the reliability of their product offering is total quality management, or some variation of that tool, such as the Six Sigma quality improvement methodology made famous by General Electric. **Total quality management** (TQM) stresses that all company operations should be oriented toward improving the reliability of a company's product offerings.[26] The TQM concept was developed by a number of American consultants, including W. Edwards Deming, Joseph Juran, and A. V. Feigenbaum.[27] Originally, these consultants won few converts in the United States. However, managers in Japan embraced their ideas enthusiastically and even named their premier annual prize for manufacturing excellence after Deming. The philosophy underlying TQM, as articulated by Deming, is based on the following five-step chain reaction:

1. Improved quality means that costs decrease because of less rework, fewer mistakes, fewer delays, and better use of time and materials.

2. As a result, productivity improves.

3. Better quality leads to higher market share and allows the company to raise prices.

4. This increases the company's profitability and allows it to stay in business.

5. Thus the company creates more jobs.[28]

Deming identified a number of steps that should be part of any TQM program:

- A company should have a clear business model to specify where it is going and how it is going to get there.

- Management should embrace the philosophy that mistakes, defects, and poor-quality materials are not acceptable and should be eliminated.

- Quality of supervision should be improved by allowing more time for supervisors to work with employees and giving them appropriate skills for the job.

- Management should create an environment in which employees will not fear reporting problems or recommending improvements.

- Work standards should be defined not only as numbers or quotas but should also include some notion of quality to promote the production of defect-free output.

- Management is responsible for training employees in new skills to keep pace with changes in the workplace.

- Achieving better quality requires the commitment of everyone in the company.

It took the rise of Japan to the top rank of economic powers in the 1980s to alert Western business to the importance of the TQM concept. Since then, TQM practices have spread rapidly throughout Western industry. Strategy in Action 4.4 describes one of the most successful implementations of a quality improvement process, General Electric's Six Sigma program.

Despite such instances of spectacular success, TQM practices are not universally accepted. A study by the American Quality Foundation found that only 20 percent of

Strategy in Action   4.4

General Electric's Six Sigma Quality Improvement Process

Six Sigma, a quality and efficiency program adopted by several major corporations, including Motorola, General Electric, and Allied Signal, aims to reduce defects, boost productivity, eliminate waste, and cut costs throughout a company. "Sigma" comes from the Greek letter that statisticians use to represent a standard deviation from a mean: the higher the number of sigmas, the smaller the number of errors. At 6 sigma, a production process would be 99.99966 percent accurate, creating just 3.4 defects per million units. Although it is almost impossible for a company to achieve such perfection, several companies strive toward that goal.

General Electric is perhaps the most fervent adopter of Six Sigma programs. Under the direction of long-serving CEO Jack Welch, GE spent nearly $1 billion between 1994 and 1998 to convert all of its divisions to the Six Sigma faith. Welch credits the program with raising GE's operating profit margins to 16.6 percent in 1998, up from 14.4 percent three years earlier.

One of the first products that was designed from start to finish using Six Sigma processes was a $1.25 million diagnostic computer tomography (CT) scanner, the Lightspeed, which produces rapid three-dimensional imagines of the human body. The new scanner captures multiple images simultaneously, requiring only twenty seconds to do full body scans that once took three minutes—important because patients must remain perfectly still during the scan. GE spent $50 million to run 250 separate Six Sigma analyses designed to improve the reliability and lower the manufacturing cost of the new scanner. Its efforts were rewarded when the Lightspeed's first customers soon noticed that it ran without downtime from the start, a testament to the reliability of the product.

Achieving that reliability took a lot of work. GE's engineers deconstructed the scanner into its basic components and tried to improve the reliability of each component through a detailed step-by-step analysis. For example, the most important part of CT scanners is vacuum tubes that focus X-ray waves. The tubes that GE used in previous scanners, which cost $60,000 each, suffered from low reliability. Hospitals and clinics wanted the tubes to operate for twelve hours a day for at least six months, but typically they lasted only half that long. Moreover, GE was scrapping some $20 million in tubes each year because they failed preshipping performance tests, and a disturbing number of faulty tubes were slipping past inspection, only to be pronounced dead on arrival.

To try to solve the reliability problem, the Six Sigma team took the tubes apart. They knew that one problem was a petroleum-based oil used in the tube to prevent short circuits by isolating the anode, which has a positive charge, from the negatively charged cathode. The oil often deteriorated after a few months, leading to short circuits, but the team did not know why. By using statistical "what-if" scenarios on all parts of the tube, the researchers learned that the lead-based paint on the inside of the tube was adulterating the oil. Acting on this information, the team developed a paint that would preserve the tube and protect the oil.

By pursuing this and other improvements, the Six Sigma team was able to extend the average life of a vacuum tube in the CT scanner from three months to over a year. Although the improvements increased the cost of the tube from $60,000 to $85,000, the increased cost was outweighed by the reduction in replacement costs, making it an attractive proposition for customers.

Sources: C. H. Deutsch, "Six-Sigma Enlightenment," *New York Times,* December 7, 1998, p. 1. J. J. Barshay, "The Six-Sigma Story," *Star Tribune,* June 14, 1999, p. 1. D. D. Bak, "Rethinking Industrial Drives," *Electrical/Electronics Technology,* November 30, 1998, p. 58.

U.S. companies regularly review the consequences of quality performance, compared with 70 percent of Japanese companies.[29] Another study, this one by Arthur D. Little, of 500 American companies using TQM found that only 36 percent believed that TQM was increasing their competitiveness.[30] A prime reason for this, according to the study, was that many companies had not fully understood or embraced the TQM concept. They were looking for a quick fix, whereas implementing a quality improvement program is a long-term commitment.

Implementing Reliability Improvement Methodologies

Among companies that have successfully adopted quality improvement methodologies, certain imperatives stand out. These are discussed below in the order in which they are usually tackled in companies implementing quality improvement programs. What needs to be stressed first, however, is that TQM is a cross-functional process. Its implementation requires close cooperation among all functions in the pursuit of the common goal of improving quality; it is a process that cuts across functions. The role played by the different functions in implementing TQM is summarized in Table 4.2.

Build Organizational Commitment to Quality. There is evidence that TQM will do little to improve the performance of a company unless everyone in the organization embraces it.[31] When Xerox launched its quality program, its first step was to educate the entire work force, from top management down, in the importance and operation of the TQM concept. It did so by forming groups, beginning with a group at the top of the organization that included the CEO. The top group was the first to receive basic TQM training. Each member of this group was then given the task of training a group at the next level in the hierarchy, and so on down throughout the organization until all 100,000 employees had received basic TQM training. Both top management and the human resource function of the company can play a major role in this process. Top management has the responsibility of exercising the

TABLE 4.2

The Role Played by Different Functions in Implementing TQM

Value Creation Function	Primary Roles
Infrastructure (leadership)	1. Provide leadership and commitment to quality. 2. Find ways to measure quality. 3. Set goals, and create incentives. 4. Solicit input from employees. 5. Encourage cooperation among functions.
Production	1. Shorten production runs. 2. Trace defects back to source.
Marketing	1. Focus on the customer. 2. Provide customers' feedback on quality.
Materials management	1. Rationalize suppliers. 2. Help suppliers implement TQM. 3. Trace defects back to suppliers.
R&D	1. Design products that are easy to manufacture.
Information systems	1. Use information systems to monitor defect rates.
Human resources	1. Institute TQM training programs. 2. Organize employees into quality teams.

leadership required to make a commitment to quality an organization-wide goal. The human resource function must take on responsibility for companywide training in TQM techniques.

Focus on the Customer. TQM practitioners see a focus on the customer as the starting point, and indeed, the raison d'être, of the whole quality philosophy.[32] The marketing function, because it provides the primary point of contact with the customer, should play a major role here. It needs to identify what customers want from the good or service that the company provides, what the company actually provides to customers, and the gap between what customers want and what they get, which could be called the quality gap. Then, together with the other functions of the company, it needs to formulate a plan for closing the quality gap.

Find Ways to Measure Quality. Another imperative of any TQM program is to create a metric that can be used to measure quality. This is relatively easy in manufacturing companies, where quality can be measured by criteria such as defects per million parts. It tends to be more difficult in service companies, but with a little creativity, suitable metrics can be devised. For example, one of the metrics Florida Power & Light uses to measure quality is meter-reading errors per month. Another is the frequency and duration of power outages. L. L. Bean, the Freeport, Maine, mail-order retailer of outdoor gear, uses the percentage of orders that are correctly filled as one of its quality measures. For some banks, the key measures are the number of customer defections per year and the number of statement errors per thousand customers. The common theme that runs through all these examples is identifying what quality means from a customer's perspective and devising a method to gauge this. Top management should take primary responsibility for formulating metrics to measure quality, but to succeed in this effort, it must receive input from the various functions of the company.

Set Goals and Create Incentives. Once a metric has been devised, the next step is to set a challenging quality goal and create incentives for reaching it. Xerox again provides an example. When it introduced its TQM program, its initial goal was to reduce defective parts from 25,000 per million to 1,000 per million. One way of creating incentives to attain such a goal is to link rewards, like bonus pay and promotional opportunities, to the goal. Thus, within many companies that have adopted self-managing teams, the bonus pay of team members is determined in part by their ability to attain quality goals. The task of setting goals and creating incentives is one of the key tasks of top management.

Solicit Input from Employees. Employees can be a vital source of information regarding the sources of poor quality. Therefore, a framework must be established for soliciting employee suggestions for improvements. Quality circles, which are meetings of groups of employees, have often been used to achieve this goal. Other companies have used self-managing teams as forums for discussing quality improvement ideas. Whatever forum is used, soliciting input from lower-level employees requires that management be open to receiving, and acting on, bad news and criticism from employees. According to Deming, one problem with U.S. management is that it has grown used to "killing the bearer of bad tidings." But, he argues, managers who are committed to the quality concept must recognize that bad news is a gold mine of information.[33]

Identify Defects and Trace Them to Source. TQM preaches the need to identify defects during the work process, trace them to their source, find out what caused them, and make corrections so that they do not recur. Production and materials management typically have primary responsibility for this task.

To uncover defects, Deming advocates the use of statistical procedures to pinpoint variations in the quality of goods or services. Deming views variation as the enemy of quality.[34] Once variations have been identified, they must be traced to their source and eliminated. One technique that helps greatly in tracing defects to their source is reducing lot sizes for manufactured products. With short production runs, defects show up immediately. Consequently, they can be quickly traced to the source, and the problem can be addressed. Reducing lot sizes also means that when defective products are produced, their number will not be large, thus decreasing waste. Flexible manufacturing techniques, discussed earlier, can be used to reduce lot sizes without raising costs. Consequently, adopting flexible manufacturing techniques is an important aspect of a TQM program.

JIT inventory systems also play a part. Under a JIT system, defective parts enter the manufacturing process immediately; they are not warehoused for several months before use. Hence, defective inputs can be quickly spotted. The problem can then be traced to the supply source and corrected before more defective parts are produced. Under a more traditional system, the practice of warehousing parts for months before they are used may mean that large numbers of defects are produced by a supplier before they enter the production process.

Supplier Relations. A major source of poor-quality finished goods is poor-quality component parts. To decrease product defects, a company has to work with its suppliers to improve the quality of the parts they supply. The primary responsibility in this area falls on the materials management function, which interacts with suppliers.

To implement JIT systems with suppliers and to get suppliers to adopt their own TQM programs, two steps are necessary. First, the number of suppliers has to be reduced to manageable proportions. Second, the company must commit to building a cooperative long-term relationship with the suppliers that remain. Asking suppliers to invest in JIT and TQM systems is asking them to make major investments that tie them to the company. For example, in order to implement a JIT system fully, the company may ask a supplier to relocate its manufacturing plant so that it is next door to the company's assembly plant. Suppliers are likely to be hesitant about making such investments unless they feel that the company is committed to an enduring, long-term relationship with them.

Design for Ease of Manufacture. The more assembly steps a product requires, the more opportunities there are for making mistakes. Designing products with fewer parts should make assembly easier and result in fewer defects. Both R&D and manufacturing need to be involved in designing products that are easy to manufacture.

Break Down Barriers Among Functions. Implementing TQM requires organization-wide commitment and substantial cooperation among functions. R&D has to cooperate with production to design products that are easy to manufacture, marketing has to cooperate with production and R&D so that customer problems identified by marketing can be acted on, human resource management has to cooperate with all the other functions of the company in order to devise suitable quality-training programs, and so on. The issue of achieving cooperation among subunits within a company is explored in Chapter 11. What needs stressing at this point is that ultimately it is the responsibility of top management to ensure that such cooperation occurs. Strategy in Action 4.5 describes the efforts of a service company to put TQM into practice and the benefits it has gained as a result.

Developing Superior Attributes

As we stated in Chapter 3, a product is a bundle of different attributes, and reliability is just one of them, albeit an important one. Products can also be *differentiated* by attributes such as their form, features, performance, durability, and styling. In addition, a company can differentiate itself by emphasizing attributes of the service

Strategy in Action   4.5

Improving Quality in Health Care

Following the lead of General Electric, a number of health care organizations have adopted the Six Sigma approach or similar quality improvement tools as a way of trying to improve the quality of their service offerings. One of them is Mount Carmel Health, a health care provider in Ohio. Mount Carmel Health implemented a Six Sigma program after suffering from poor financial performance in 2000. By early 2002, some fifty employees had been trained in Six Sigma principles, and they were leading some sixty projects in different phases of implementation.

One of the first projects focused on a simple and common problem among health care providers: timely and accurate reimbursement of costs. Mount Carmel discovered that it was writing off large amounts of potential revenues from the government-run Medicare programs as uncollectible because the charges were denied by Medicare administrators. Mount Carmel had low expectations for this business anyway so had never analyzed why the write-offs were so high. After careful analysis as part of a Six Sigma project, it discovered that a significant portion of the denials were due to the incorrect coding of reports submitted to Medicare. If the reports were coded correctly—that is, if fewer errors were made in the "production" of forms—the Six Sigma team estimated that annual income would be some $300,000 higher, so they devised improved processes for coding the forms to reduce the error rate. The result was that net income rose by over $800,000. It appeared that improving the coding process for this one parameter improved the reporting of many other parameters and led to a reimbursement rate much higher than anticipated.

In another case, Intermountain Health Care, a nonprofit chain of twenty-four hospitals operating in Idaho, Utah, and Wyoming, adopted a quality improvement methodology to find and eliminate inappropriate variations in medical care—that is, to provide the patient with better health care and in the process reduce costs. The starting point was to identify variations in practice across physicians, particularly with regard to the cost and success rate of treatments. These data were then shared among physicians within the Intermountain system. The next step was for the physicians to use these data to eliminate poor practices and generally upgrade the quality of medical care. The results were quite striking. One early improvement was an attempt by Intermountain's hospital in Salt Lake City to lower the rate of postoperative wound infections. Before the effort began, the hospital's post-op infection rate was 1.8 percent, 0.2 point below the national average but still unacceptably high from a quality care perspective. By using a bedside computer system to make sure that antibiotics were given to patients two hours before surgery, the hospital dropped the infection rate in half, to 0.9 percent, within a year. Since then the post-op infection rate has dropped further still, to 0.4 percent compared to the current national average of 2 percent. Given that the average post-op infection adds $14,000 to a hospital bill, this constitutes not only a big improvement in patient outcomes but also a big cost saving.

Sources: I. R. Lazarus and K. Butler, "The Promise of Six-Sigma," *Managed Healthcare Executive* (October 2001): 22–26. D. Scalise, "Six-Sigma, the Quest for Quality," *Hospitals and Health Networks* (December 2001): 41–44. J. F. Siler and S. Atchison, "The Rx at Work in Utah," *Business Week*, October 25, 1991, p. 113.

associated with the product, such as ordering ease, prompt delivery, easy installation, the availability of customer training and consulting, and maintenance services. Dell Computer, for example, differentiates itself on ease of ordering (via the Web), prompt delivery, easy installation, and the ready availability of customer support and maintenance services. Differentiation can also be based on the attributes of the people in the company whom customers interact with when making a product purchase, such as their competence, courtesy, credibility, responsiveness, and communication. Singapore Airlines, for example, enjoys an excellent reputation for quality service, largely because passengers perceive their flight attendants as competent, courteous, and responsive to their needs. Thus, we can talk about the product attributes, service attributes, and personnel attributes associated with a company's product offering (see Table 4.3).

For a product to be regarded as high quality, a company's product offering must be seen as superior to that of rivals. Achieving a perception of high quality on any of these attributes requires specific actions by managers. First, it is important for managers to collect marketing intelligence indicating which of these attributes are most important to customers. For example, consumers of personal computers may place a low weight on durability because they expect their PC to be made obsolete by technological advances within three years, but they may place a high weight on features and performance. Similarly, ease of ordering and timely delivery may be very important attributes for customers of online booksellers (as they indeed are for customers of Amazon.com), whereas customer training and consulting may be very important attributes for customers who purchase complex business-to-business software to manage their relationships with suppliers.

Second, once the company has identified the attributes that are important to customers, it needs to design its products, and the associated services, so that those attributes are embodied in the product, and it needs to make sure that personnel in the company are appropriately trained so that the correct attributes are emphasized. This requires close coordination between marketing and product development (the topic of the next section), and the involvement of the human resource management function in employee selection and training.

Third, the company must decide which of the significant attributes to promote and how best to position those attributes in the minds of consumers, that is, how to tailor the marketing message so that it creates a consistent image in the minds of customers.[35] At this point, it is important to recognize that although a product might be

---

TABLE 4.3

Attributes Associated with a Product Offering

Product Attributes	Service Attributes	Associated Personnel Attributes
Form	Ordering ease	Competence
Features	Delivery	Courtesy
Performance	Installation	Credibility
Durability	Customer training	Reliability
Reliability	Customer consulting	Responsiveness
Style	Maintenance and repair	Communication

differentiated on the basis of six attributes, covering all of those attributes in the company's communication messages may lead to an unfocused message. Many marketing experts advocate promoting only one or two central attributes to customers. For example, Volvo consistently emphasizes the safety and durability of its vehicles in all marketing messages, creating the perception in the minds of consumers (backed by product design) that Volvo cars are safe and durable. Volvo cars are also very reliable and have high performance, but the company does not emphasize these attributes in its marketing messages. In contrast, Porsche emphasizes performance and styling in all of its marketing messages; thus, a Porsche is positioned differently in the minds of consumers than a Volvo is. Both are regarded as high-quality products because both have superior attributes, but the attributes that the two companies have chosen to emphasize are very different. They are differentiated from the average car in different ways.

Finally, it must be recognized that competition does not stand still, but instead produces continual improvement in product attributes and often the development of new product attributes. This is obvious in fast-moving high-tech industries where product features that were considered leading edge just a few years ago are now obsolete, but the same process is also at work in more stable industries. For example, the rapid diffusion of microwave ovens during the 1980s required food companies to build new attributes into their frozen food products: they had to maintain their texture and consistency while being microwaved. A product could not be considered high quality unless it could do that. This speaks to the importance of having a strong R&D function in the company that can work with marketing and manufacturing to continually upgrade the quality of the attributes that are designed into the company's product offerings. Exactly how to achieve this is covered in the next section.

Achieving Superior Innovation

In many ways, building distinctive competencies that result in innovation is the most important source of competitive advantage. This is because innovation can result in new products that better satisfy customer needs, can improve the quality (attributes) of existing products, or can reduce the costs of making products that customers want. Thus, the ability to develop innovative new products or processes gives a company a major competitive advantage that allows it to (1) *differentiate* its products and charge a premium price and/or (2) *lower its cost structure* below that of its rivals. Competitors, however, attempt to imitate successful innovations and often succeed. Therefore, maintaining a competitive advantage requires a continuing commitment to innovation.

Robert Cooper found that successful new product launches are major drivers of superior profitability. Cooper looked at more than 200 new product introductions and found that of those classified as successes, some 50 percent achieve a return on investment in excess of 33 percent, half have a payback period of two years or less, and half achieve a market share in excess of 35 percent.[36] Many companies have established a track record for successful innovation. Among them are Du Pont, which has produced a steady stream of successful innovations, such as cellophane, Nylon, Freon, and Teflon; Sony, whose successes include the Walkman, the Compact Disc, and the PlayStation; Nokia, which has been a leader in the development of wireless phones; Pfizer, a drug company that during the 1990s and early 2000s produced eight blockbuster new drugs; 3M, which has applied its core competency in tapes and adhesives to developing a wide range of new products; Intel, which has consistently managed to lead in the development of innovative new microprocessors to run personal computers; and Cisco Systems, whose innovations helped to pave the way for the rapid growth of the Internet.

The High Failure Rate of Innovation

Although promoting innovation can be a source of competitive advantage, the failure rate of innovative new products is high. One study of product development in the chemical, drug, petroleum, and electronics industries suggested that only about 20 percent of R&D projects ultimately result in a commercially successful products or process.[37] An in-depth case study of product development in three companies (one in chemicals and two in drugs) reported that about 60 percent of R&D projects reached technical completion, 30 percent were commercialized, and only 12 percent earned a profit that exceeded the company's cost of capital.[38] A famous study by the consulting division of Booz, Allen & Hamilton found that over one-third of 13,000 new customer and industrial products failed to meet company-specific financial and strategic performance criteria.[39] Another study found that 45 percent of new products introduced into the marketplace did not meet their profitability goals.[40]

This evidence suggests that many R&D projects do not result in a commercial product and that between 33 percent and 60 percent of all new products that do reach the marketplace fail to generate an adequate economic return. Two well-publicized product failures are Apple Computer's Newton, a personal digital assistant, and Sony's Betamax format in the video player and recorder market. While many reasons have been advanced to explain why so many new products fail to generate an economic return, five explanations for failure appear on most lists: uncertainty, poor commercialization, poor positioning strategy, technological myopia, and being slow to market.[41]

Uncertainty. New-product development is an inherently risky process. It requires testing a hypothesis whose answer is impossible to know prior to market introduction: Have we tapped an unmet customer need? Is there sufficient market demand for this new technology? Although good market research can reduce the uncertainty about likely future demand for a new technology, uncertainty cannot be eradicated, so a certain failure rate is to be expected.

The failure rate is higher for quantum product innovations than for incremental innovations. A **quantum innovation** represents a radical departure from existing technology—the introduction of something that is new to the world. The development of the World Wide Web can be considered a quantum innovation in communications technology. Other quantum innovations include the development of the first photocopier by Xerox, the first videocassette recorder by AMPEX, and the first contact lenses by Bausch and Lomb. **Incremental innovation** refers to an extension of existing technology. For example, Intel's Pentium Pro microprocessor is an incremental product innovation because it builds on the existing microprocessor architecture of Intel's X86 series. The uncertainty of future demand for a new product is much greater if that product represents a quantum innovation that is new to the world than if it is an incremental innovation designed to replace an established product whose demand profile is already well known. Consequently, the failure rate tends to be higher for quantum innovations.

Poor Commercialization. A second reason frequently cited to explain the high failure rate of new product introductions is **poor commercialization**—something that occurs when there is definite customer demand for a new product, but the product is not well adapted to customer needs because of factors such as poor design and poor quality. For instance, many of the early personal computers failed to sell because customers needed to understand computer programming to use them. Steve Jobs at Apple Computer understood that if the technology could be made user friendly (if it could be *commercialized*), there would be an enormous market for it. Hence, the original personal computers that Apple marketed incorporated little in the way of radically new technology, but they made existing technology accessible to the average person. Paradoxically, the failure of Apple Computer to establish a market for the Newton, the hand-held personal digital system that Apple introduced in the summer of 1993, can be traced to poor commercialization of a potentially attractive technology. Apple predicted a $1 billion market for the Newton, but sales failed to materialize when it became clear that the Newton's handwriting software, an attribute that Apple chose to emphasize in its marketing promotions, could not adequately recognize messages written on the Newton's message pad.

Poor Positioning Strategy. Poor positioning strategy arises when a company introduces a potentially attractive new product, but sales fail to materialize because it is poorly positioned in the marketplace. **Positioning strategy** is the specific set of options a company adopts for a product on four main dimensions of marketing: price, distribution, promotion and advertising, and product features. Apart from poor product quality, another reason for the failure of the Apple Newton was poor positioning strategy. The Newton was introduced at such a high initial price (close to $1,000) that there would probably have been few buyers even if the technology had been adequately commercialized.

Technological Myopia. Another reason that many new product introductions fail is that companies often make the mistake of marketing a technology for which there is not enough customer demand. **Technological myopia** occurs when a company gets blinded by the wizardry of a new technology and fails to examine whether there is customer demand for the product. This problem may have been a factor in the failure of the desktop computer introduced by NeXT in the late 1980s (NeXT was founded by Steve Jobs, the founder of Apple Computer). Technologically, the NeXT machines were clearly ahead of their time with advanced software and hardware features that would not be incorporated into most PCs for another decade. However, customer acceptance was very slow, primarily because of the complete lack of applications software such as spreadsheet and word processing programs to run on the machines. Management at NeXT was so enthused by the technology incorporated in their new computer that they ignored this basic market reality. After several years of slow sales, NeXT eventually withdrew the machines from the marketplace.

Slow to Market. Finally, companies fail when they are slow to get their products to market. The more time that elapses between initial development and final marketing—that is, the slower the "cycle time"—the more likely it is that someone else will beat the company to market and gain a first-mover advantage.[42] By and large, slow innovators update their products less frequently than fast innovators do. Consequently, they can be perceived as technical laggards relative to the fast innovators. In the car industry, General Motors has suffered from being a slow innovator. Its product development cycle has been about five years, compared with two to three years at Honda, Toyota, and Mazda and three to four years at Ford. Because they are based on five-year-old technology and design concepts, GM cars are already out of date when they reach the market.

Building Competencies in Innovation

Companies can take a number of steps to build a competency in innovation and avoid failure. Five of the most important steps seem to be (1) building skills in basic and applied scientific research, (2) developing a good process for project selection and project management, (3) cross-functional integration, (4) product development teams, and (5) partly parallel development processes.[43]

Building Skills in Basic and Applied Research. Building skills in basic and applied research requires the employment of research scientists and engineers and the establishment of a work environment that fosters creativity. A number of top companies try to achieve this by setting up university-style research facilities, where scientists and engineers are given time to work on their own research projects, in addition to projects that are linked directly to ongoing company research. At Hewlett-Packard, for example, company labs are open to engineers around the clock. Hewlett-Packard even encourages its corporate researchers to devote 10 percent of company time to exploring their own ideas and does not penalize them if they fail. 3M allows researchers to spend 15 percent of the workweek researching any topic that intrigues them, as long as there is the potential of a payoff for the company. The most famous outcome of this policy is the ubiquitous Post-its. The idea for them evolved from a researcher's desire to find a way to keep the bookmark from falling out of his hymnal. Post-its are now a major 3M business, with annual revenues of around $300 million.

Project Selection and Management. Project management is the overall management of the innovation process, from generation of the original concept, through development, and into final production and shipping. Project management requires three important skills: the ability to generate as many good ideas as possible, the ability to select among competing projects at an early stage of development so that the most promising receive funding and potential costly failures are killed off, and the ability to minimize time to market. The concept of the development funnel, divided into three phases, summarizes what is required to build these skills (see Figure 4.8).[44]

The objective in Phase I is to widen the mouth of the tunnel to encourage as much idea generation as possible. To this end, a company should solicit input from all its functions, as well as from customers, competitors, and suppliers. At Gate 1, the funnel narrows. Here ideas are reviewed by a cross-functional team of managers who

FIGURE 4.8

The Development Funnel

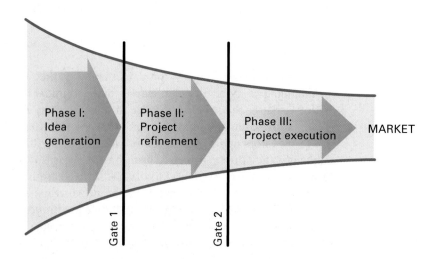

did not participate in the original concept development. Concepts that are ready to proceed then move to Phase II, where the details of the project proposal are worked out. Note that Gate 1 is not a go/no-go evaluation point. At this screen, ideas may be sent back for further concept development and then resubmitted for evaluation.

During Phase II, which typically lasts only one or two months, the data and information from Phase I are put into a form that will enable senior management to evaluate proposed projects against competing projects. Normally, this requires the development of a careful project plan, complete with details of the proposed target market, attainable market share, likely revenues, development costs, production costs, key milestones, and the like. The next big selection point, Gate 2, is a go/no-go evaluation point. Senior managers review the projects under consideration and select those that seem likely winners and make most sense from a strategic perspective given the long-term goals of the company. The overriding objective is to select projects whose successful completion will help to maintain or build a competitive advantage for the company. A related objective is to ensure that the company does not spread its scarce capital and human resources too thinly over too many projects and instead concentrates resources on projects where the probability of success and potential returns are most attractive. Any project selected to go forward at this stage will be funded and staffed, the expectation being that it will be carried through to market introduction. In Phase III, the project development proposal is executed by a cross-functional product development team.

Cross-Functional Integration. Tight cross-functional integration between R&D, production, and marketing can help a company to ensure that:

1. Product development projects are driven by customer needs.

2. New products are designed for ease of manufacture.

3. Development costs are kept in check.

4. Time to market is minimized.

5. Close integration between R&D and marketing is achieved to ensure that product development projects are driven by the needs of customers.

A company's customers can be one of its primary sources of new product ideas. The identification of customer needs, and particularly unmet needs, can set the context within which successful product innovation takes place. As the point of contact with customers, the marketing function can provide valuable information. Moreover, integrating R&D and marketing is crucial if a new product is to be properly commercialized. Otherwise, a company runs the risk of developing products for which there is little or no demand.

The case of Techsonic Industries illustrates the benefits of integrating R&D and marketing. This company manufactures depth finders—electronic devices that fishermen use to measure the depth of water beneath a boat and to track their prey. Techsonic had weathered nine new-product failures in a row when the company decided to interview sportspeople across the country to identify what it was they needed. They discovered an unmet need for a depth finder with a gauge that could be read in bright sunlight, so that is what Techsonic developed. In the year after the $250 depth finder hit the market, Techsonic's sales tripled to $80 million, and its market share surged to 40 percent.[45]

Integration between R&D and production can help a company to ensure that products are designed with manufacturing requirements in mind. Design for manufacturing lowers manufacturing costs and leaves less room for mistakes and thus can lower costs and increase product quality. Integrating R&D and production can help lower development costs and speed products to market. If a new product is not designed with manufacturing capabilities in mind, it may prove too difficult to build, given existing manufacturing technology. In that case, the product will have to be redesigned, and both overall development costs and time to market may increase significantly. For example, making design changes during product planning could increase overall development costs by 50 percent and add 25 percent to the time it takes to bring the product to market.[46] Moreover, many quantum product innovations require new processes to manufacture them, which makes it all the more important to achieve close integration between R&D and production, since minimizing time to market and development costs may require the simultaneous development of new products and new processes.[47]

Product Development Teams. One of the best ways to achieve cross-functional integration is to establish cross-functional product development teams, composed of representatives from R&D, marketing, and production. The objective of a team should be to take a product development project from the initial concept development to market introduction. A number of attributes seem to be important in order for a product development team to function effectively and meet all its development milestones.[48]

First, a heavyweight project manager—one who has high status within the organization and the power and authority required to get the financial and human resources that the team needs to succeed—should lead the team and be dedicated primarily, if not entirely, to the project. The leader should believe in the project (a champion) and be skilled at integrating the perspectives of different functions and helping personnel from different functions work together for a common goal. The leader should also be able to act as an advocate of the team to senior management.

Second, the team should be composed of at least one member from each key function. The team members should have a number of attributes, including an ability to contribute functional expertise, high standing within their function, a willingness to share responsibility for team results, and an ability to put functional advocacy aside. It is generally preferable if core team members are 100 percent dedicated to the project for its duration. This makes sure that their focus is on the project, not on the ongoing work of their function.

Third, the team members should be physically co-located to create a sense of camaraderie and facilitate communication. Fourth, the team should have a clear plan and clear goals, particularly with regard to critical development milestones and development budgets. The team should have incentives to attain those goals; for example, pay bonuses when major development milestones are hit. Fifth, each team needs to develop its own processes for communication and conflict resolution. For example, one product development team at Quantum Corporation, a California-based manufacturer of disk drives for personal computers, instituted a rule that all major decisions would be made and conflicts resolved at meetings that were held every Monday afternoon. This simple rule helped the team to meet its development goals.[49]

Partly Parallel Development Processes. One way in which a product development team can compress the time it takes to develop a product and bring it to market is to use a partly parallel development process. Traditionally, product development processes have been organized on a sequential basis, as illustrated in Figure 4.9a. A problem with this kind of process is that product development proceeds without manufacturing issues in mind. Most significant, because the basic design of a product is completed prior to the design of a manufacturing process and full-scale commercial production, there is no early warning system to indicate manufacturability. As a consequence, the company may find that it cannot cost-efficiently manufacture the product and have to send it back to the design stage for redesign. The cycle time lengthens as the product bounces back and forth between stages.

To solve this problem, companies typically use a process similar to that illustrated in Figure 4.9b. In the partly parallel development process, development stages overlap so that, for example, work starts on the development of the production process before the product design is finalized. By reducing the need for expensive and time-consuming product redesigns, such a process can significantly reduce the time it takes to develop a new product and bring it to market.

For an example, consider what occurred after Intel Corporation introduced its 386 microprocessor in 1986. A number of companies, including IBM and Compaq, were racing to be the first to introduce a 386-based personal computer. Compaq beat IBM by six months and gained a major share of the high-power market mainly because it used a cross-functional team and a partly parallel process to develop the product. The team included engineers (R&D) and marketing, production, and finance people. Each function worked in parallel rather than sequentially. While engineers were designing the product, production people were setting up the manufacturing facilities, marketing people were working on distribution and planning marketing campaigns, and the finance people were working on project funding.

The primary role that the various functions play in achieving superior innovation is summarized in Table 4.4. The table makes two matters clear. First, top management must bear primary responsibility for overseeing the whole development process. This entails both managing the development funnel and facilitating cooperation among

FIGURE 4.9

Sequential and Partly Parallel Development Processes

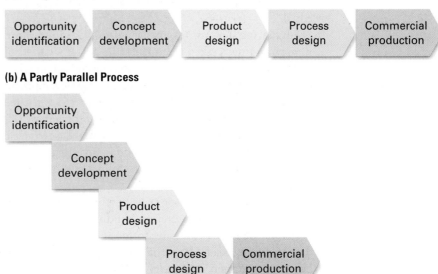

(a) A Sequential Process

Opportunity identification → Concept development → Product design → Process design → Commercial production

(b) A Partly Parallel Process

Opportunity identification

Concept development

Product design

Process design → Commercial production

TABLE 4.4

Function Roles for Achieving Superior Innovation

Value Creation Function	Primary Roles
Infrastructure (leadership)	1. Manage overall project (i.e., manage the development function). 2. Facilitate cross-functional cooperation.
Production	1. Cooperate with R&D on designing products that are easy to manufacture. 2. Work with R&D to develop process innovations.
Marketing	1. Provide market information to R&D. 2. Work with R&D to develop new products.
Materials management	No primary responsibility.
R&D	1. Develop new products and processes. 2. Cooperate with other functions, particularly marketing and manufacturing, in the development process.
Information Systems	1. Use information systems to coordinate cross-functional and cross-company product development work.
Human resources	1. Hire talented scientists and engineers.

the functions. Second, the effectiveness of R&D in developing new products and processes depends on its ability to cooperate with marketing and production.

Achieving Superior Responsiveness to Customers

To achieve superior responsiveness to customers, a company must give customers what they want, when they want it, and at a price they are willing to pay—so long as the company's long-term profitability is not compromised in the process. Customer responsiveness is an important *differentiating* attribute that can help to build brand loyalty. Strong product differentiation and brand loyalty give a company more pricing options; it can charge a premium price for its products or keep prices low to sell more goods and services to customers. Either way, the company that is more responsive to its customers' needs than rivals will have a competitive advantage, all else being equal.

Achieving superior responsiveness to customers means giving customers value for money, and steps taken to improve the efficiency of a company's production process and the quality of its products should be consistent with this aim. In addition, giving customers what they want may require the development of new products with new features. *In other words, achieving superior efficiency, quality, and innovation are all part of achieving superior responsiveness to customers.* There are two other prerequisites for attaining this goal. First, a company has to develop a competency in listening to and focusing on its customers and in investigating and identifying their needs. Second, it constantly needs to seek better ways to satisfy those needs.

Customer Focus

A company cannot be responsive to its customers' needs unless it knows what those needs are. Thus, the first step to building superior responsiveness to customers is to motivate the whole company to focus on the customer. The means to this end are demonstrating leadership, shaping employee attitudes, and using mechanisms for bringing customers into the company.

Leadership. Customer focus must start at the top of the organization. A commitment to superior responsiveness to customers brings attitudinal changes throughout a company that ultimately can be built only through strong leadership. A mission statement that puts customers first is one way to send a clear message to employees about the desired focus. Another avenue is top management's own actions. For example, Tom Monaghan, the founder of Domino's Pizza, stayed close to the customer by visiting as many stores as possible every week, running some deliveries himself, insisting that other top managers do the same, and eating Domino's pizza regularly.[50]

Employee Attitudes. Leadership alone is not enough to attain a superior customer focus. All employees must see the customer as the focus of their activity and be trained to focus on the customer, whether their function is marketing, manufacturing, R&D, or accounting. The objective should be to make employees think of themselves as customers—to put themselves in customers' shoes. At that point, employees will be better able to identify ways to improve the quality of a customer's experience with the company.

To reinforce this mindset, incentive systems within the company should reward employees for satisfying customers. For example, senior managers at the Four Seasons hotel chain, who pride themselves on their customer focus, like to tell the story of Roy Dyment, a doorman in Toronto who neglected to load a departing guest's briefcase into his taxi. The doorman called the guest, a lawyer, in Washington D.C., and found that he desperately needed the briefcase for a morning meeting. Dyment hopped on a plane to Washington and returned it—without first securing approval from his boss. Far from punishing Dyment for making a mistake and for not checking with management before going to Washington, the Four Seasons responded by naming Dyment Employee of the Year.[51] This action sent a powerful message to Four Seasons employees about the importance of satisfying customer needs.

Bringing Customers into the Company. "Know thy customer" is one of the keys to achieving superior responsiveness to customers. Knowing the customer not only requires that employees think like customers themselves; it also demands that they listen to what their customers have to say and, as much as possible, bring them into the company. Although this may not involve physically bringing customers into the company, it does mean bringing in customers' opinions by soliciting feedback from customers on the company's goods and services and by building information systems that communicate the feedback to the relevant people.

For an example, consider direct selling clothing retailer Lands' End. Through its catalog, the Internet, and customer service telephone operators, Lands' End actively solicits comments from its customers about the quality of its clothing and the kind of merchandise they want it to supply. Indeed, it was customers' insistence that initially prompted the company to move into the clothing segment. Lands' End used to supply equipment for sailboats through mail-order catalogs. However, it received so many requests from customers to include outdoor clothing in its offering that it responded by expanding the catalog to fill this need. Soon clothing became the main business, and Lands' End dropped the sailboat equipment. Today, the company still pays close attention to customer requests. Every month, a computer printout of customer requests and comments is given to managers. This feedback helps the company to fine-tune the merchandise it sells. Indeed, frequently new lines of merchandise are introduced in response to customer requests.[52]

**Satisfying
Customer Needs**

Once a focus on the customer is an integral part of the company, the next requirement is to satisfy customer needs that have been identified. As already noted, efficiency, quality, and innovation are crucial competencies that help a company satisfy customer needs. Beyond that, companies can provide a higher level of satisfaction if they differentiate their products by (1) customizing them, where possible, to the requirements of individual customers and (2) reducing the time it takes to respond to or satisfy customer needs.

Customization. **Customization** is varying the features of a good or service to tailor it to the unique needs or tastes of groups of customers or, in the extreme case, individual customers. Although extensive customization can raise costs, the development of flexible manufacturing technologies has made it possible to customize products to a much greater extent than was feasible ten to fifteen years ago without experiencing a prohibitive rise in cost structure (particularly when flexible manufacturing technologies are linked with web-based information systems). For example, online retailers such as Amazon.com have used web-based technologies to develop a home page customized for each individual user. When a customer accesses Amazon.com, he or she is offered a list of recommendations for books or music to purchase based on an analysis of prior buying history, a powerful competency that gives Amazon.com a competitive advantage.

The trend toward customization has fragmented many markets, particularly customer markets, into ever smaller niches. An example of this fragmentation occurred in Japan in the early 1980s when Honda dominated the motorcycle market there. Second-place Yamaha decided to go after Honda's lead. It announced the opening of a new factory that, when operating at full capacity, would make Yamaha the world's largest manufacturer of motorcycles. Honda responded by proliferating its product line and stepping up its rate of new-product introduction. At the start of what became known as the "motorcycle wars," Honda had 60 motorcycles in its product line. Over the next eighteen months, it rapidly increased its range to 113 models, customizing them to ever smaller niches. Honda was able to accomplish this without bearing a prohibitive cost penalty because it has a competency in flexible manufacturing. The flood of Honda's customized models pushed Yamaha out of much of the market, effectively stalling its bid to overtake Honda.[53]

Response Time. Giving customers what they want when they want it requires speed of response to customer demands. To gain a competitive advantage, a company must often respond to customer demands very quickly, whether the transaction is a furniture manufacturer's delivery of a product once it has been ordered, a bank's processing of a loan application, an automobile manufacturer's delivery of a spare part for a car that broke down, or the wait in a supermarket checkout line. We live in a fast-paced society, where time is a valuable commodity. Companies that can satisfy customer demands for rapid response build brand loyalty, differentiate their products, and can charge higher prices for them.

Increased speed often lets a company choose a premium pricing option, as the mail delivery industry illustrates. The air express niche of the mail delivery industry is based on the notion that customers are often willing to pay considerably more for overnight express mail as opposed to regular mail. Another example of the value of rapid response is Caterpillar, the manufacturer of heavy earth-moving equipment, which can get a spare part to any point in the world within twenty-four hours. Downtime for heavy construction equipment is very costly, so Caterpillar's ability to

TABLE 4.5

The Primary Role of Different Functions in Achieving Superior Responsiveness to Customers

Value Creation Function	Primary Roles
Infrastructure (leadership)	1. Through leadership by example, build a companywide commitment to responsiveness to customers.
Production	1. Achieve customization through implementation of flexible manufacturing. 2. Achieve rapid response through flexible manufacturing.
Marketing	1. Know the customer. 2. Communicate customer feedback to appropriate functions.
Materials management	1. Develop logistics systems capable of responding quickly to unanticipated customer demands (JIT).
R&D	1. Bring customers into the product development process.
Information systems	1. Use web-based information systems to increase responsiveness to customers.
Human resources	1. Develop training programs that get employees to think like customers themselves.

respond quickly in the event of equipment malfunction is of prime importance to its customers. As a result, many of them have remained loyal to Caterpillar despite the aggressive low-price competition from Komatsu of Japan.

In general, reducing response time requires (1) a marketing function that can quickly communicate customer requests to production, (2) production and materials management functions that can quickly adjust production schedules in response to unanticipated customer demands, and (3) information systems that can help production and marketing in this process.

Table 4.5 summarizes the steps different functions must take if a company is to achieve superior responsiveness to customers. Although marketing plays the critical role in helping a company attain this goal, primarily because it represents the point of contact with the customer, Table 4.5 shows that the other functions also have major roles. Moreover, like achieving superior efficiency, quality, and innovation, achieving superior responsiveness to customers requires top management to lead in building a customer orientation within the company.

Summary of Chapter

1. A company can increase efficiency through a number of steps: exploiting economies of scale and learning effects, adopting flexible manufacturing technologies, reducing customer defection rates, implementing just-in-time systems, getting the R&D function to design products that are easy to manufacture, upgrading the skills of employees through training, introducing self-managing teams, linking pay to performance, building a companywide commitment to efficiency through strong leadership, and designing structures that facilitate cooperation among different functions in pursuit of efficiency goals.

2. Superior quality can help a company lower its costs and differentiate its product and charge a premium price.

3. Achieving superior quality demands an organization-wide commitment to quality and a clear focus on the customer. It also requires metrics to measure quality goals and incentives that emphasize quality, input from employees regarding ways in which quality can be improved, a methodology for tracing defects to their source and correcting the problems that produce

them, rationalization of the company's supply base, cooperation with the suppliers that remain to implement total quality management programs, products that are designed for ease of manufacturing, and substantial cooperation among functions.

4. The failure rate of new-product introductions is high due to factors such as uncertainty, poor commercialization, poor positioning strategy, slow cycle time, and technological myopia.

5. To achieve superior innovation, a company must build skills in basic and applied research; design good processes for managing development projects; and achieve close integration between the different functions of the company, primarily through the adoption of cross-functional product development teams and partly parallel development processes.

6. To achieve superior responsiveness to customers often requires that the company achieve superior efficiency, quality, and innovation.

7. To achieve superior responsiveness to customers, a company needs to give customers what they want when they want it. It must ensure a strong customer focus, which can be attained through leadership; train employees to think like customers and bring customers into the company through superior market research; customize the product to the unique needs of individual customers or customer groups; and respond quickly to customer demands.

Discussion Questions

1. How are the four generic building blocks of competitive advantage related to each other?

2. What role can top management play in helping a company achieve superior efficiency, quality, innovation, and responsiveness to customers?

3. In the long run, will adoption of Six Sigma quality improvement processes give a company a competitive advantage, or will it be required just to achieve parity with competitors?

4. In what sense might innovation be called the single most important building block of competitive advantage?

Practicing Strategic Management

SMALL-GROUP EXERCISE: IDENTIFYING EXCELLENCE

Break up into groups of three to five people, and appoint one group member as a spokesperson who will communicate your findings to the class.

You are the management team of a start-up company that will produce disk drives for the personal computer industry. You will sell your product to manufacturers of personal computers (original equipment manufacturers). The disk drive market is characterized by rapid technological change, product life cycles of only six to nine months, intense price competition, high fixed costs for manufacturing equipment, and substantial manufacturing economies of scale. Your customers, the original equipment manufacturers, issue very demanding technological specification that your product has to comply with. They also pressure you to deliver your product on time so that it fits in with their own product introduction schedule.

1. In this industry, what functional competencies are the most important for you to build?

2. How will you design your internal processes to ensure that those competencies are built within the company?

ARTICLE FILE 4

Choose a company that is widely regarded as excellent. Identify the source of its excellence, and relate it to the material discussed in this chapter. Pay particular attention to the role played by the various functions in building excellence.

STRATEGIC MANAGEMENT PROJECT: MODULE 4

This module deals with the ability of your company to achieve superior efficiency, quality, innovation, and responsiveness to customers. With the information you have at your disposal, answer the questions and perform the tasks listed:

1. Is your company pursuing any of the efficiency-enhancing practices discussed in this chapter?

2. Is your company pursuing any of the quality-enhancing practices discussed in this chapter?

3. Is your company pursuing any of the practices designed to enhance innovation discussed in this chapter?

4. Is your company pursuing any of the practices designed to increase responsiveness to customers discussed in this chapter?

5. Evaluate the competitive position of your company in the light of your answers to questions 1–4. Explain what, if anything, the company needs to do to improve its competitive position.

EXPLORING THE WEB
Visiting Applied Materials

Visit the web site of Applied Materials, the world's largest manufacturer of semiconductor fabrication equipment (**http://www.appliedmaterials.com**). Go to the section titled "About" Applied Materials, and read the company's mission statement. What does this mission statement tell you about the kind of competitive advantage that Applied Materials is trying to build? How important are efficiency, quality, innovation, and responsiveness to customers to this company?

Now go to the sections of Applied's web site that detail the company's financial results, products, and press releases. Read through these sections and try to establish how successful Applied has been at meeting the objectives set down in its mission statement. What do you think the company has done at the functional level to increase its efficiency, responsiveness to customers, innovative ability, and product quality?

General Task: Search the Web for a company whose home page describes in some detail its approach to achieving one of the following: superior productivity, product quality, customer service, or innovation. Using this information, document the company's functional-level strategy and assess whether the strategy makes sense given what you have learned so far in this book?

Closing Case

Reinventing Levi's

Levi Strauss is an American icon. For two generations, it has dressed the world in its fabled blue jeans. In recent years, however, Levi's luster has begun to fade even more rapidly than the blue dye on an old pair of 501s. The fast-moving fashion world seems to be leaving it behind. After peaking in 1996 with sales of $7.1 billion, Levi's sales fell for the next five years, dropping to $4.1 billion in 2001. Levi's problems have several sources.

First, a combination of good design and savvy marketing has helped competitors such as The Gap take share from Levi's. The company badly missed the urban-inspired wide-legged jean trend. Levi's Dockers brand, which is suitable for casual dress, also seems to have become tired. Moreover, traditionally Levi has focused on jeans for men, where sales have been falling industry-wide, as opposed to women's jeans, where industry sales are at least stable. Second, some retailers say the company has had a take-it-or-leave-it sales attitude. "They were arrogant. They thought they were selling couture merchandise," complained the director of general merchandising for Fred Meyer, the Portland-based superstore unit of Kroger. Third, Levi's jeans were just too expensive. Unlike most of its competitors, which moved the bulk of their manufacturing to Asia or Central America long ago, Levi continued to have a significant manufacturing presence in the United States. But the high cost of labor in the United States means that it has to charge higher prices to recoup its costs, and customers didn't seem to be willing to pay a premium price for Levi jeans anymore.

Levi's solution to this problem has been threefold. First, the company closed all but eight of the twenty-two U.S. plants it operated in 1996, laying off 6,500 domestic employees, and moved manufacturing to low-cost foreign locations. Second, it is attempting to get ahead of fashion trends rather than follow them. Levi is now paying much more attention to women. It has recognized that women in junior, petite, and plus sizes call for special attention. New designs such as the Superlow line of jeans are meant to be feminine and sexy rather than retrofits of menswear.

Unlike prior designs that have mostly bubbled up in-house, the idea for the Superlows was adapted from the phenomenon of celebrities such as Mariah Carey cutting off the waistbands of Levi's mainstay 501s. After briefly testing the jeans in boutiques and mainstream stores such as J.C. Penney, the company began mass marketing of the Superlows for women within three months rather than the typical twelve months for past launches. The new look seems to have hit the spot. By late 2001, weekly sell-through rates (the fraction of an order that a retailer can move out the door) of Superlow jeans were ranging between 15 and 22 percent, well above the 5 percent typical for Levi's. Superlows now make up the largest portion of junior sales.

Third, the company announced that it would step up its Original Spin program to supply jeans that are custom made for individual customers. Levi's thinking is that if it can customize its jeans for each individual's body shape (no two people are identical), it will be able to charge a premium price and therefore cover the costs of continuing to have a substantial manufacturing presence in the United States. At the core of the Original Spin program is an attempt to use web-based technology and computer-controlled production equipment to implement a strategy of mass customization that has as its goal a desire to give each customer a better-fitting pair of jeans in their preferred style. The idea is that with the help of a sales associate, customers will create the jeans they want by picking from six colors, three basic models, five different leg openings, and two types of fly. Then their waist, rear, and inseam will be measured. The customer will try on a pair of plain "test-drive" jeans to make sure that they like the fit. If they do, the order will be punched into a web-based computer terminal linked to the stitching machines in a Levi Strauss factory. Customers can even give the jeans a name—for example, "Rebel" for a pair of black jeans. At the factory, computer-controlled tools precision-cut the jeans and stitch an individual bar code inside. The jeans are then sewn and washed, identified by the code, and shipped to the customer's home. The whole process takes no more than two to three weeks. The bar code tag stores the measurements for simple reordering.

Today, a fully stocked Levi's store carries approximately 130 pairs of ready-to-wear jeans. With the Original Spin program, the number of choices available will leap to 750. Sanjay Choudhuri, Levi's director of mass customization, feels that 750 is about the right number of choices. An unlimited amount of choice will create inefficiencies at the manufacturing plant. Levi's strategy is to offer a healthy number of choices that give the customer the illusion of infinite variety and can be produced with little or no additional cost penalty. Levi does hope to charge a premium price for this service of about 20 percent. However, in the company's view, the real benefit of the program is that it changes the nature of the relationship between Levi Strauss and its customers. Instead of an anonymous relationship in which the customer walks out of the store with a pair of off-the-shelf jeans, Levi Strauss aims to become each customer's personal "jeans adviser." If the program works, Levi might well extend it to embrace several other apparel offerings, such as its Dockers line of pants for men, in addition to rolling out the program in international markets.

Further down the road, Levi might use a device that will scan the entire body. The machine, which has been developed by an independent company, projects 300,000 pinpoints of light from head to toe, then photographs the body from six angles to produce a kind of three-dimensional portrait. Those data result in a custom pattern that can be transmitted to a production plant to manufacture jeans, shirts, or any other item of clothing. Within five years, body-scanning equipment may be found in Levi stores.

Case Discussion Questions

1. From a value creation perspective, what exactly is Levi trying to achieve by (a) moving manufacturing out of the United States, (b) refocusing its design efforts on women, and (c) introducing the Original Spin program?

2. How exactly might the Original Spin program change the nature of the relationship between Levi Strauss and its customers?

3. Do you think that the strategic actions Levi is taking will allow it to reverse its six-year decline and build a sustainable competitive advantage?

Sources: Erick Schonfeld, "The Customized, Digitized, Have It Your Way Economy," *Fortune,* September 28, 1998, p. 117. Molly Knight, "Levi's to Close 11 plants in Shift to Offshore Manufacturing," *Business and Industry,* February 24, 1999, p. 6. "The View from the Outside, Levi's Needs More Than a Patch," *New York Times,* February 28, 1999, p. 4. K. Barron, "Getting a Rise out of Levi's," *Fortune,* November 26, 2001, pp. 156–158.

Building Competitive Advantage Through Business-Level Strategy

5

Opening Case

Toyota's Goal? A High-Value Vehicle to Match Every Customer Need

The car industry has always been one of the most competitive in the world because of the huge revenues and profits that are at stake, with annual global car sales at over $250 billion. It is small wonder, then, that industry rivalry has been increasing as carmakers have been fighting to develop new kinds of car models that better satisfy the needs of particular groups of buyers. One company at the forefront of these endeavors is Toyota.

As the pioneer of lean production, Toyota has used its low-cost structure to produce efficiently an ever-increasing range of vehicles tailored to different segments of the car market. Its ability to go from the initial design stage to production stage in two to three years gives it the ability to bring out new models faster than its competitors and capitalize on the development of new market segments or niches. Low costs and fast time to market also allow it to correct mistakes quickly when it designs a car that subsequently proves to have little market appeal—and Toyota has made mistakes.

In 1999, for example, Toyota brought out the Echo, a subcompact car that featured state-of-the-art engineering to deliver exceptional fuel economy: around 50 to 60 miles per gallon.

Designed to be inexpensive to run and buy, Toyota targeted this vehicle at buyers in their twenties, expecting them to appreciate these qualities. Its designers were disappointed when they displayed little enthusiasm for the car; its styling did not appeal to this age group even if its performance did fit their budget. The Echo's buyers turned out to be individuals in their forties who appreciated its economy and found it a useful second car to get around in.

Recognizing their failure to position their product to hit the important market segment of young adults, the main car buyers of the future, Toyota's designers went back to the drawing board. Analyzing changing market trends and demographics, they sought to find the styling and features that would offer a car that was good looking, fun to drive for this market segment, and could be sold for $16,000 to $18,000. Toyota (and several other carmakers) realized that perhaps the time was right for the return to the hatchback, but an updated version of it. Hatchbacks had been very popular in the early 1980s; however, the cars then were small and often had an ungainly appearance. Sales of hatchbacks had dropped off quickly when carmakers began to offer new sports utility vehicles and updated small sedans; by 1995, relatively few were available.

Drawing on its design and manufacturing competencies, Toyota's engineers updated and shaped the hatchback to suit the needs of the young adults in their twenties: the result was the Toyota Matrix, introduced in 2002 at a price starting at $17,000. The Matrix features revolutionary body styling reflective of much more expensive, sporty cars. It is spacious inside and geared to the needs of its intended young buyers; for example, seats fold back to allow for carrying a large cargo volume, and many storage bins and two-prong plugs for power outlets allow for the use of VCRs, MP3 players, and other devices. The message is that the Matrix is designed to be functional, fun, and a sporty ride. To launch the car, Toyota partnered with Island Records and MP3.com to sponsor an eight-week Toyota Matrix "Fuel the Music" rock and roll tour featuring Island artists Sum41, Hoobastank, and American HiFi.

Toyota has also been a leader in positioning its whole range of vehicles to take advantage of emerging market segments. In the sports utility segment, its first offering was the expensive Toyota Land Cruiser, priced at over $35,000. Realizing the need for sports utility vehicles in other price ranges, it next introduced the 4Runner, priced at $20,000 and designed for the average sports utility customer; the RAV4, a small sports utility vehicle in the low $20,000 range followed; and then came the Sequoia, a bigger, more powerful version of the 4Runner in the upper $20,000 range. Finally, taking the technology from its Lexus R3000 vehicle, in 2001 it introduced the luxury Highlander sports utility in the low $30,000 range. It now offers six models of sports utility vehicles, each offering a combination of price, size, performance, styling, and luxury that appeals to different customer groups within the sports utility segment of the car market. Toyota also positions its sedans to appeal to different sets of buyers. For example, the Camry, one of the best-selling cars in the United States, is targeted toward the middle of the market, to customers who can afford to pay about $25,000 and want a balance of luxury, performance, safety, and reliability.

Toyota's strategy and business model on the demand side is to produce that range of vehicles that optimizes the amount of value it can create for different groups of customers. On the supply side, the number of models it makes is constrained by the need to keep its cost structure efficient and to choose the car pricing options that allows it to generate the sales revenue that result in the best return on invested capital.

The decision about how many kinds of vehicles to produce is also affected by the strategies of its rivals, for they are also trying to determine the optimum range of cars to produce. Toyota was not alone in its decision to produce a hatchback in 2002; other noticeable competitors included BMW, which introduced the redesigned Mini Cooper; Honda's new Civic hatchbacks; the already well-received PT Cruiser from DaimlerChrysler; and Ford's Focus. In fact, the number of hatchback models doubled between 2000 and 2002, as did the expected number of sales (to 650,000 vehicles). Competition in this market segment is now intense. Each car company needs to anticipate the actions of its rivals, and each hopes, like Toyota, that it has made the right choices to obtain a large share of customers in this important market segment.

Source: www.toyota.com, 2002.

Overview

As the *Opening Case* suggests, this chapter examines how companies can compete effectively in a market or industry and scrutinizes the potential strategies for maximizing competitive advantage and profitability. Its focus is on the most important level of strategy making that goes to make a company's business model: the choice of business-level strategies that a company can use to compete effectively in an industry and achieve superior performance.

By the end of this chapter, you will be able to identify and distinguish among the principal kinds of business-level strategies and tactics that managers can choose from to achieve a competitive advantage over their rivals. You will also understand why, and under what circumstances, strategic managers choose to pursue one rather than another of these strategies as the approach to create value and profit through their business model.

What Is Business-Level Strategy?

At the heart of **business-level strategy** is the objective of developing a firm-specific business model that will allow a company to gain a competitive advantage over its rivals in a market or industry. As we noted in Chapter 1, the way that strategic managers define their company's business is the first step in crafting business-level strategy. According to Abell, the process of business definition entails decisions about (1) customers' needs, or what is to be satisfied, (2) customer groups, or who is to be satisfied, and (3) distinctive competencies, or how customer needs are to be satisfied.[1] These three decisions are the basis of the choice of a business-level strategy because they determine where and how a company seeks to compete in a business or industry—essentially, how a company proposes to create *value* for customers. Consequently, the ways in which a company makes these three decisions to gain a competitive advantage over its rivals need to be considered.

Customer Needs and Product Differentiation

Customer needs are desires, wants, or cravings that can be satisfied by means of the attributes or characteristics of a product—a good or service. For example, a person's craving for something sweet can be satisfied by a box of Godiva chocolates, a carton of Ben & Jerry's ice cream, a Snickers bar, or a spoonful of sugar. Two factors determine which product a customer chooses to satisfy these needs: (1) the price of the product and (2) the way a product is differentiated from other products of its type.

Product differentiation is the process of designing products to satisfy customers' needs. A company obtains a competitive advantage when it creates, designs, and supplies a product in a way that better satisfies customer needs than its rivals do and chooses the correct pricing option—the one that results in the level of demand that optimizes profitability. Consider the luxury segment of the car market, where customers pay more than $35,000 to satisfy their needs for personal transportation. In this segment, Cadillac, Mercedes-Benz, Infiniti, BMW, Jaguar, Lexus, Lincoln, Audi, Volvo, Acura, and others are engaged in a continuing battle to design the "perfect" luxury car—the one that best meets the needs of those who have decided to purchase a personal luxury vehicle. Over time, the companies that attract the most luxury car buyers—because they have the distinctive competencies that allow them to produce the cars that possess the features or qualities these customers desire the most—are the ones that achieve a sustained competitive advantage over rivals.

There are many different luxury carmakers because even within this car market segment, customers have widely different kinds of needs. As a result, luxury carmakers can differentiate their product in a number of ways to satisfy a particular group of customers, just as Toyota did in the *Opening Case* in the sports utility segment. For example, some customers highly value a sporty ride and performance handling; Mercedes-Benz and BMW are on the cutting edge of technical design, which allows them to be able to offer this driving experience that no other maker has been able to match.

Toyota's Lexus division is well known for the smoothness and quietness of its cars and their exceptional reliability. Lexus cars consistently outrank all other cars in published reliability rankings, and this appeals to a large group of customers who appreciate these qualities. Volvo has a reputation for producing safe cars and Rolls Royce for the prestige that possessing such a car confers on its owner. Other luxury carmakers have not fared so well. Cadillac, Lincoln, Audi, Acura, and Infinity have found it more difficult to differentiate their cars, which sometimes compare unfavorably in terms of ride, comfort, safety, or reliability to their rivals. Although these less successful companies still sell many cars, customers often find their needs better satisfied by the attributes and qualities of their rivals' cars.

At every price range in the car market—cars under $15,000, from $15,000 to $25,000, $25,000 to $35,000, and the luxury segment above $35,000—many models of cars compete to attract customers. For each price range, a carmaker has to make a choice concerning how much to differentiate a particular car model. Typically, the more differentiated a product is, the more it will cost to design and produce, and differentiation leads to a higher cost structure. Thus, if a carmaker is to stay within the $15,000 to $25,000 price range, and yet design and produce a differentiated car that will give it a competitive advantage and allow it to outperform its competitors in the price range, strategic managers have to make crucial and difficult decisions. For example, they have to forecast what kind of features customers will most value: car styling, safety, performance, or something else; what size engine will be acceptable; and how much should be spent on air bags to make a car safe while making sure the car will not cost too much to produce—ensuring that they can make a good profit and still sell the car for less than $25,000.

Thus, the way that companies in a business or industry differentiate their products in order to attract customers is not a free choice. Strategic managers are constrained by the need to balance differentiation against cost, which is always reflected in the price of a product. In the under-$15,000 segment, carmakers compete by producing a car with a level of differentiation that offers customers the most value for their money in its price range while still allowing them to make an acceptable level of profit. If they succeed and the car sells well, then the higher perceived value translates into high demand and generates high sales revenues and profitability, even though the profit per vehicle sold might not be very high.

Differentiation has another important aspect. Companies that can create something distinct or different about their products and can satisfy customers' needs in ways that other products cannot can often charge a higher, or premium, price for their product. For example, superb design or technical sophistication allows companies to charge more for their products, and customers are often willing to pay those higher prices. For example, Mercedes-Benz buyers pay a high premium price to enjoy their vehicles, as do customers of Godiva chocolates, which retail for about $26 a pound—much more than, say, a Hershey bar.

Distinctness or distinctiveness can be achieved in countless different ways, which also explains why there may be so many companies competing in an industry. Distinctness may relate to the physical characteristics of the product, such as quality, reliability, or performance. Or it may lie in the product's appeal to customers' psychological needs, such as the body styling of a Porsche, Jaguar, or Corvette or a personal need for prestige or status.[2] Thus, a Lexus may be differentiated by its reputation for reliability and a Mercedes-Benz by its ability to satisfy customers' needs for power and status. Similarly, in the luxury segment, carmakers compete to offer customers a car with the ride, performance, and features that provide them with the most value (satisfies their needs) given the price of the car. Thus, Lexus cars are always several thousand dollars less than comparable cars from its rivals. For example, the Lexus ES300 introduced in 2001, at around $35,000, is $7,000 less than the BMW 5 series and $10,000 less than the Mercedes E Class, its nearest rivals. Most customers are discriminating and match price to differentiation even in the luxury car segment of the market. Of course, some customers simply want to purchase the absolute best technology there is and think nothing of spending $120,000 on the elegant Mercedes CL600 coupe because, among other qualities it possesses, it has an unmatched V12 engine.

In sum, product differentiation is a powerful competitive weapon. Companies that can differentiate their products more successfully than their rivals can increase the perceived value of those products. This gives them the opportunity to choose a higher price option and charge a premium price, and still generate the demand necessary to achieve above-average profitability. Successful differentiators obtain a competitive advantage, outperform their competitors, and can dominate the market or the market segment in which they compete.

Customer Groups and Market Segmentation

Market segmentation is the way a company decides to group customers, based on important differences in their needs or preferences, in order to gain a competitive advantage.[3] One principal way of grouping customers and segmenting the market is by what customers are able and willing to pay for a particular product. Once price has been taken into consideration, the other principal method of segmenting customers is according to the specific kinds of need that is being satisfied by a particular product. Managers, such as designers and engineers, have to think strategically about which segments they are going to compete in and then how they will differentiate their products for each segment. The result of this choice process determines a particular company's product range.

Market segmentation is an evolving, ongoing process that presents considerable opportunities for strategic managers. For example, in the car industry, savvy strategists often recognize opportunities to create a product for a new market segment that will attract a specific group of car buyers who before had to "satisfice," and buy a model that did not meet their needs exactly but was a reasonable compromise. This was the origin of the sports utility market segment. Many people wanted a more rugged and powerful vehicle capable of holding many people or towing heavy loads. They liked the comfort of a car but also the qualities of a pickup; by combining these two, carmakers created the SUV market segment. This process continues in the sports utility and other segments. Obviously, differentiation increases as new models are introduced and costs increase. However, if the right products are being made, the extra demand the new products generate results in sales revenues that more than make up for increasing costs and profitability increases. If managers make mistakes, however, and design products that have little appeal or price them too high, then the opposite occurs, and profitability will fall. In 2002, for example, Ford announced that it was ending production of its $52,000 luxury Lincoln truck after announcing that sales had been only in the hundreds, and not the 10,000 a year it had projected.

In general, a company can adopt three alternative strategies toward market segmentation.[4] First, it can choose not to recognize that different groups of customers have different needs and instead adopt the approach of serving the average customer. Second, it can choose to segment its market into different constituencies and develop a product to suit the needs of each. For example, Sony offers twenty-four different nineteen-inch color television sets, each targeted at a different market segment.

Third, a company can choose to recognize that the market is segmented but concentrate on serving only one of a few market segments or niches, such as the luxury car segment pursued by BMW.

The decision to provide many products for many market niches allows a company to satisfy a wider range of customer needs better. As a result, when it prices the product correctly, customer demand for the company's products rises and generates more revenue than would be the case if the company offered just one product for the whole market.[5]

Sometimes the nature of the product or the nature of the industry does not allow much differentiation, which is the case, for example, with bulk chemicals and cement.[6] In these industries, there may be little opportunity for obtaining a competitive advantage through product differentiation and market segmentation because there is little opportunity for serving customers' needs and customer groups in different ways. Instead, price is the main criterion that customers use to evaluate the product, and the competitive advantage lies with the company that has superior efficiency and the lowest cost structure, which allows it to charge the lowest prices.

Distinctive Competencies

The third issue in business-level strategy is to decide which distinctive competencies to create and build to achieve a competitive advantage in satisfying particular customers' needs and customer groups.[7] As Chapter 4 describes, there are four main ways companies can pursue a competitive advantage: superior efficiency, quality, innovation, and responsiveness to customers. In choosing a business-level strategy, strategic managers must decide which business model to follow that will best allow them to organize and combine their company's distinctive competencies to gain a competitive advantage.

The Dynamics of Business-Level Strategy

Companies pursue a business-level strategy to gain a competitive advantage that allows them to outperform rivals and achieve above-average profitability. In determining how to achieve a competitive advantage, strategic managers have to make a consistent or compatible set of choices concerning (1) how to differentiate and price their product, (2) when and how much to segment their market to maximize demand, and (3) and where and how to invest their capital to develop distinctive competencies that will create the most value while keeping their cost structures viable (because of the need to be price competitive). These three decisions determine which business-level strategy a company is pursuing. They also set in motion the specific set of functional-level strategies needed to create the differentiation and value and cost structure positions needed to pursue such a strategy. Business-level strategy is therefore the main determinant of a company's business model.

Figure 5.1 presents a way of thinking about the relationships of these variables in a company's business model.[8] The decision to differentiate a product increases the perceived value to the customer, so that market demand for the product increases. In turn, increased demand leads to economies of scale, which lowers the cost structure and unit costs. Thus, from this point of view, differentiation can lower unit costs.[9] Differentiation also requires additional expenditures on resources, for example, to improve product quality or support a higher level of service so that an increase in differentiation will also raise a company's cost structure and result in a higher unit cost.

To maximize profitability, managers must choose the pricing option that compensates for the extra costs of product differentiation but does not choke off an increase in expected demand. They must also search for other ways to reduce costs and therefore lower the company's cost structure but will not harm its level of differ-

FIGURE 5.1

The Dynamics of
Business-Level
Strategy

Source: Copyright © C. W. L.
Hill and G. R. Jones, "The
Dynamics of Business-Level
Strategy," (unpublished
manuscript, 2002).

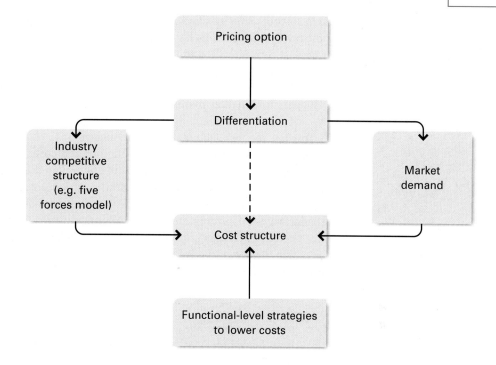

entiation. There are many specific functional strategies a company can adopt to achieve this. For example, Nordstrom, the luxury department store retailer, differentiates itself in the retail clothing industry by providing a high-quality shopping experience with elegant store operations and a high level of customer service, all of which raise Nordstrom's cost structure. However, Nordstrom can still lower its cost structure by, for example, managing its inventories efficiently and increasing inventory turnover. Also, its strategy of being highly responsive to customers results in more customers and higher demand, which means that sales per square foot increase, and this enables it to make more intensive use of its facilities and salespeople, which leads to scale economies and lower costs. Thus, no matter what the level of differentiation is that a company chooses to pursue in its business model, it always has to recognize the way its cost structure will vary as a result of its choice of differentiation and the other specific strategies it adopts to lower its cost structure; differentiation and cost structure decisions affect one another.

The last main dynamic shown in Figure 5.1 concerns the impact of the industry's competitive structure on a company's differentiation, cost structure, and pricing choices. Recall that strategic thinking takes place in an environment where watchful and agile competitors and potential competitors exist, so one company's choices are always made with reference to those of its major competitors. Often, therefore, a company may be forced to increase its level of differentiation because its competitors start to offer products with new or improved features. If competitors also decide to develop products for new market segments, this will also force it to follow suit.

On the cost side of the equation, industry competition drives a company's cost structure because differentiation increases costs and competitors' pricing decisions affect a company's pricing options. For example, a company's ability to charge a high premium price depends on the other choices customers have and its competitors' pricing choices. Companies need to consider carefully whether they can recoup the extra costs of differentiation given the pricing choices of the other companies in the industry. For example, Dell's decision not to choose a high-price option for its state-of-the-art computers led to problems for its competitors because they lacked Dell's low cost structure. Because they were forced to match Dell's low prices to compete effectively, many started to see losses because they had higher costs and this helped Dell gain more market share.

In sum, the task facing strategic managers at the business level is to position a company with respect to both differentiation and cost structure. That is, the choice of business-level strategy revolves around (1) how to differentiate products to create more value for customers, which permits a broader range of pricing options and (2) how to invest in functional activities to achieve a cost structure that also gives it a broader range of pricing choices.[10] Maximizing profitability is about making the right choices with regard to value creation through differentiation, costs, and pricing given both the demand conditions in the company's market and the competitive conditions in the company's industry.

Choosing a Generic Business-Level Strategy

In developing a business-level strategy and business model, usually strategic managers emphasize one of five generic competitive strategies: cost leadership, differentiation, cost leadership *and* differentiation, focus differentiation, and focus cost leadership.[11] These strategies are called *generic* because all companies or businesses can pursue them regardless of whether they are manufacturing, service, or nonprofit enterprises. These strategies are also generic because they can be pursued in different kinds of industry environments. Each of the generic strategies results from a company's consistent choices on product, market, and distinctive competencies—choices that reinforce each other and result in a competitive business model (see Table 5.1).

Cost-Leadership Strategy

A company's business model in pursuing a cost-leadership strategy is based on the intent to outperform competitors by doing everything it can to establish a cost structure that allows it to produce or provide goods or services at a lower unit cost than they can. It is also about finding ways to lower the cost structure given its choice of differentiation because differentiation typically raises costs. In essence, a company pursuing a cost-leadership strategy seeks to achieve a competitive advantage and above-average profitability by developing a business model primarily aimed at lowering its cost structure.

Two advantages accrue from a cost-leadership strategy. First, if its closest rivals in an industry, for example, those that compete in the same price range or market seg-

TABLE 5.1
Product/Market/Distinctive-Competency Choices and Generic Competitive Strategies

	Cost Leadership	Differentiation	Focus
Product Differentiation	Low (principally by price)	High (principally by uniqueness)	Low to high (price or uniqueness)
Market Segmentation	Low (mass market)	High (many market segments)	Low (one or a few segments)
Distinctive Competency	Manufacturing and materials management	Research and development, sales and marketing	Any kind of distinctive competency

ment, charge similar prices for their products, the cost leader achieves superior profitability than its competitors because of its lower costs. Second, and more common, because of its lower cost structure, the cost leader is able to charge a lower price than its competitors, and this gives it a competitive advantage. As discussed earlier, offering customers the same kind of value from a product but at a lower price attracts many more customers, so that even though it has chosen the lower price option, the increased volume of its sales causes the company's profits to surge. If its competitors try to get lost customers back by reducing their prices and companies start to compete on price, the cost leader will still be able to withstand competition better than the other companies because of its lower costs. It is likely to win any competitive struggle. For these reasons, cost leaders are likely to earn above-average profits. How does a company become the cost leader? It achieves this position by means of the way strategic managers make compatible product, market, and distinctive competency choices to gain a low-cost competitive advantage (see Table 5.1).

Strategic Choices. The cost leader chooses a low to moderate level of product differentiation relative to its competitors. Differentiation is expensive; the more a company expends resources to make its products distinct, the more its costs rise.[12] The cost leader aims for a level of differentiation not markedly inferior to that of the differentiator (a company that competes by spending resources on product development), but a level obtainable at low cost.[13] The cost leader does not try to be the industry leader in differentiation; it waits until customers want a feature or service before providing it. For example, a cost leader does not introduce a theater-quality sound system in DVD sets; instead, it adds such sound quality only when it is obvious that customers want it. Wal-Mart, for example, does not spend hundreds of millions of dollars on store design to create an attractive shopping experience as chains like Macy's, Dillard's, or Saks Fifth Avenue have done. Nor does it follow Kmart's strategy and pay celebrities like Martha Stewart millions to promote the distinctness or quality of its products. As Wal-Mart puts it in its mission statement, "We think of ourselves as buyers for our customers and we apply our considerable strengths to get the best *value* for you."[14]

The cost leader also frequently ignores the many different market segments in an industry and positions its products to appeal to the "average" customer. The reason the cost leader makes this choice is that developing or selling many different products tailored to the needs of different market segments is an expensive proposition. A cost leader normally engages in only a limited amount of market segmentation. In targeting the average customer, strategic managers try to produce or provide the least or smallest number of products that will be desired by the highest number of customers, something at the heart of Wal-Mart's and BJ's approach discussed in Chapter 3. Thus, although a customer may not get exactly the product he or she wants, paying a lower price than at the cost leader's competitors attracts more customers to its products.

In developing distinctive competencies, the overriding goal of the cost leader must be to increase its efficiency and lower its cost structure compared with its rivals. The development of distinctive competencies in manufacturing, materials management, and information technology is central to achieving this goal. For example, manufacturing companies pursuing a low-cost strategy concentrate on doing all they can to ride down the experience curve so that they can keep lowering their costs. Achieving a low-cost position requires that the company develop skills in flexible manufacturing, adopt efficient materials management techniques, and do all it can to increase inventory turnover and reduce costs of good sold. (Table 4.1 outlined the ways in which a company's functions can be used to increase efficiency.) Consequently, the manufacturing and materials management functions are the center of attention for a company pursuing a cost-leadership strategy, and the other functions shape their distinctive competencies to meet the needs of manufacturing and materials management.[15]

The sales function, for example, may develop the competency of capturing large, stable sets of customers' orders. In turn, this allows manufacturing to make longer production runs and so achieve economies of scale and reduce costs. At Dell, for example, online customers are provided with a limited set of choices so that Dell can customize PCs to a customer's need at low cost. Finding ways to customize its products at low cost is an important task facing managers pursuing a cost-leadership strategy. The human resource function may focus on instituting training programs and compensation systems that lower costs by improving employees' productivity, and the research and development function may specialize in process improvements to lower the manufacturing costs. Wal-Mart has taken advantage of advances in information technology to lower the costs associated with getting goods from manufacturers to customers just as Dell, the cost leader in the personal computer industry, uses the Internet to lower the cost of selling its computers. Strategy implementation, another source of cost savings in pursuing cost leadership, is the design of the organizational structure to match this strategy, since structure is a major source of a company's costs. Thus, a low-cost strategy usually implies tight production or sales controls and rigorous use of budgets to control the production process.

Advantages and Disadvantages. The advantages of each generic strategy are best discussed in terms of Porter's five forces model, introduced in Chapter 2.[16] The five forces are threats from competitors, powerful suppliers, powerful buyers, substitute products, and new entrants. The cost leader is protected from industry competitors by its cost advantage. Its lower costs also mean that it will be less affected than its competitors by increases in the price of inputs if there are powerful suppliers and less affected by a fall in the price it can charge for its products if there are powerful buyers. Moreover, since cost leadership usually requires a big market share, the cost leader purchases in relatively large quantities, increasing its bargaining power over suppliers. If substitute products start to come onto the market, the cost leader can reduce its price to compete with them and retain its market share. Finally, the leader's cost advantage constitutes a barrier to entry, since other companies are unable to enter the industry and match the leader's costs or prices. The cost leader is therefore relatively safe as long as it can maintain its cost advantage, and price is the key for a significant number of buyers.

The principal dangers of the cost-leadership approach lurk in competitors' ability to find ways to lower *their* cost structures and beat the cost leader at its own game. For instance, if technological change makes experience curve economies obsolete, new companies may apply lower-cost technologies that give them a cost advantage over the cost leader. The steel mini-mills discussed in Chapter 4 gained this advantage. Competitors may also draw a cost advantage from labor-cost savings. Foreign competitors in the Third World have very low labor costs; for example, wage costs in the United States are roughly 600 percent more than they are in Malaysia, China, or Mexico. Most U.S. companies now assemble their products abroad as part of their low-cost strategy; many are forced to do so simply to compete and stay in business, as Strategy in Action 5.1 illustrates.

Strategy in Action   5.1

Levi Strauss's Big Challenge

Levi Strauss, the well-known jeans maker, was once a leading differentiator in the apparel industry. Its jeans commanded a premium price as customers the world over perceived the value or status of wearing Levi jeans was worth paying extra for. Indeed, in Europe and Asia, Levi jeans were often sold at double or triple their U.S. price. No more. Levi is now fighting to lower its costs to be able to pursue a cost-leadership strategy, which has become the principal way to compete in the fast changing jeans industry.

Levi's problems arose because of changes in the business models of other jeans makers and apparel companies. Early in the 1990s, other jeans makers such as VF Corp (which makes Wrangler jeans), Calvin Klein, and Polo moved most of their jeans production capacity abroad to countries where labor costs are lowest. With their lower cost structures, these companies then began to charge lower prices for their products so that customers began to consider carefully whether a pair of Levi's was worth a premium price. Then, in a significant move, apparel companies such as Wal-Mart and Sam's, J.C. Penney, Sears, and Dillard's began to wonder why they should pay Levi a premium price for selling its jeans when they could sell jeans under their own labels at a lower price and still make more profit than if they sold Levi's jeans. So they contracted with low-cost foreign producers to make jeans under their own in-house labels. The result was that sales of Levi jeans plummeted as many customers began to buy jeans on the basis of their price and not a particular product's differentiated appeal.

Levi, because it still produced most of its jeans in the United States, was burdened with a high cost structure and could not reduce prices to compete. It started to suffer billions of dollars of losses in the 1990s as its sales fell from a peak of $7.1 billion in 1996 to just $4.6 billion in 2000. To survive in a market now driven by both competitors and buyers pursuing a low-cost strategy, Levi had to respond in kind. Since 1997, it has closed twenty-nine U.S. manufacturing facilities and laid off 20,000 employees. In 2002, it announced it would close six more plants and lay off 3,300 more employees, which will leave it with just two sewing and finishing facilities in San Antonio, which it will use to experiment with new kinds of jeans before it contracts with foreign manufacturers to produce these products in volume overseas. As Phillip Marineau, CEO of Levi, commented, "Outsourcing production supports a variable cost structure, helps us maintain strong margins, and enables us to invest more resources in product, marketing, and retail initiatives." Sometimes pursuing a low-cost strategy is the only way to survive in a market.

Sources: www.levistrauss.com (2002). T. Agins, "Levi Will Cut 20% of Work Force, Shut Six Plants in Restructuring," *Wall Street Journal*, April 9, 2002, p. B10.

Competitors' ability to imitate the cost leader's methods easily is another threat to the cost-leadership strategy. For example, companies in China routinely take apart the electronic products of Japanese companies like Sony and Panasonic to see how they are designed and assembled. Then, using Chinese-made components and a huge pool of inexpensive domestic labor, they manufacture clones of these products and flood the U.S. market with inexpensive tape players, radios, phones, and DVD players.

Finally, the cost-leadership strategy carries a risk that strategic managers in their single-minded desire to reduce costs might make decisions that decrease costs but then drastically affect demand for the product. This happened to Gateway Computer in 2001, when, to reduce the costs of customer service, customer support people were instructed not to help customers who were experiencing problems with their new Gateway computers if they had installed their own new software on the machines. New buyers, most of whom install, and Gateway's sales began to fall as word spread. Within six months, managers had reversed their decision, and once again Gateway began offering full customer support.

Implications. To pursue a full-blown cost-leadership strategy, strategic managers need to devote enormous efforts to incorporate all the latest information, materials management, and manufacturing technology into their operations to find new ways to reduce costs. Often, as we saw in Chapter 4, using new technology will also raise quality and increase responsiveness to customers as well. Pursuing a business model based on a low-cost approach is an ongoing endeavor that requires ongoing strategic thinking to make sure the business model is aligned to changing environmental opportunities and threats.

Strategic managers in companies throughout the industry are watching the cost leader and will move quickly to imitate its innovations because they also want to reduce their costs. A differentiator cannot let a cost leader get too great a cost advantage because the leader might then be able to use its high profits to invest more in product differentiation and beat the differentiator at its own competitive game! For example, Toyota and Honda began as cost leaders, manufacturing simple low-priced cars. Their cars sold well, and they then invested their profits to design and make new models of cars that became increasingly differentiated in features and quality. Today, Toyota and Honda, with cars in every market segment, are essentially pursuing a differentiation strategy, although Toyota remains the global cost leader as well. Its managers' ability to sustain both a low cost and a differentiation strategy has made it the most profitable car company in the world by far.

A cost leader must also respond to the strategic moves of its differentiated competitors and increase the quality and features of its products if it is to prosper in the long run. Even low-priced products, such as Timex watches and Bic razors, cannot be too inferior to the more expensive Seiko watches or Gillette razors if the low-cost, low-price policy is to succeed. All business-level strategy plays out with all rivals closely watching each other's strategic moves. If Seiko brings out a novel kind of liquid-crystal-illuminated watch dial or Gillette a three-bladed razor, managers at Timex and Bic will respond within months by incorporating these innovations in their low-priced products. This situation is very common in the high-priced women's fashion industry as well. As soon as the famous designers like Gucci and Dior have shown their spring and fall collections, their designs are copied and the plans transmitted to factories in Malaysia, where workers are ready to manufacture low-priced imitations that within months will reach low-price clothing retail stores around the world.

A generic strategy like cost leadership should be thought of as a specific plan of action that helps strategic managers keep focused on how to compete most effectively over time. It is all too easy for strategic managers, flush with the success of their cost-leadership strategy, to become less vigilant and lose sight of changes in the five forces of competition, and in the macroenvironment, that change the rules of the competitive game. McDonald's, long the cost leader in the fast food industry, was surprised when rivals like Taco Bell began to offer 99-cent daily specials. McDonald's had to learn how to make fast food more cheaply to compete, and the need to do so drove its managers to adopt new cooking techniques and food management practices that have ratcheted it down the experience curve. Today, 99-cent meals are a permanent fixture on most fast food menus.

Differentiation Strategy

The objective of the generic differentiation strategy is to achieve a competitive advantage by creating a product (good or service) that customers perceive as different or distinct in some important way. The differentiated company's ability to satisfy customers' needs in a way that its competitors cannot means that it can charge a premium price (one higher than that charged by its closest rivals). The ability to increase revenues by charging premium prices (rather than by reducing costs, as the cost leader does) allows the differentiator to outperform its competitors and achieve superior profitability. As noted earlier, customers pay a premium price when they believe the product's differentiated qualities are worth the extra money. Consequently, differentiated products are often priced on the basis of what the market will bear.[17]

Thus, Mercedes-Benz cars are more expensive than the cars of its closest rivals because customers believe they offer more features and confer more status on their owners. Similarly, a BMW is not a lot more expensive to produce than a Honda, but customers who perceive that the distinct sporty ride and prestige of owning a BMW is something worth paying a lot more for determine its high price. (In fact, in Japan, BMW prices its entry cars quite modestly to attract young, well-heeled Japanese customers from Honda.) Similarly, Rolex watches do not cost much to produce, their design has not changed very much for years, and their gold content represents only a small fraction of the price. Customers, however, buy a Rolex because of the distinct qualities they perceive in it: its look and its ability to confer status on its wearer.

Strategic Choices. As Table 5.1 shows, a differentiator chooses a high level of product differentiation to gain a competitive advantage. Product differentiation can be achieved in three principal ways (see Chapter 4): quality, innovation, and responsiveness to customer needs. For example, Procter & Gamble claims that its product quality is high and that Ivory soap is 99.44 percent pure. Maytag stresses reliability and the best repair record of any other washer on the market. IBM promotes the quality service provided by its well-trained sales force. Innovation is commonly the source of differentiation for technologically complex products, and many people pay a premium price for new and innovative products, such as a state-of-the-art computer, DVD player, or car.

When differentiation is based on responsiveness to customers, a company offers comprehensive after-sales service and product repair. This is an especially important consideration for complex products such as cars and domestic appliances, which are likely to break down periodically. Maytag, Dell Computer, and BMW all excel in responsiveness to customers. In service organizations, quality-of-service attributes are also very important. Neiman Marcus, Nordstrom, and FedEx can charge premium prices because they offer an exceptionally high level of service. Firms of lawyers, accountants, and consultants stress the service aspects of their operations to clients: their knowledge, professionalism, and reputation.

Finally, a product's appeal to customers' psychological desires is a source of differentiation. The appeal can be to prestige or status, as it is with BMWs and Rolex watches; to safety of home and family, as with Aetna or Prudential Insurance; or simply providing a superior shopping experience, as with Target and Macy's. Differentiation can also be tailored to age groups and to socioeconomic groups. Indeed, the bases of differentiation are endless.

A company that pursues a differentiation strategy strives to differentiate itself along as many dimensions as possible. The less it resembles its rivals, the more it is protected from competition and the wider is its market appeal. Thus, BMWs offer more than prestige; they also offer technological sophistication, luxury, reliability, and good, although very expensive, repair service. All these bases of differentiation help increase sales.

Generally, a differentiator chooses to segment its market into many segments and niches, just as Toyota did. Strategic managers recognize the revenue-enhancing ability of being able to attract more customers willing to pay a premium price in each market segment. Now and then, a company offers a product designed for most market segments and decides to be a broad differentiator, but a company might choose to serve just those segments in which it has a specific differentiation advantage. For example, Sony produces twenty-four models of television sets, filling all the niches from mid-priced to high-priced sets. However, its lowest-priced model is always priced about $60 above that of its competitors, bringing into play the premium-price factor. Consumers have to pay extra for a Sony. Similarly, although Mercedes-Benz has filled niches below its high-priced models with its S and C series, recently it has produced a car for the low-priced market segment. It sells this car only in Europe because it fears introducing it in the United States would dilute its exclusive image and affect its differentiated appeal.

Finally, in choosing which distinctive competency to pursue, a differentiated company concentrates on the organizational functions that provide the source of its differentiation advantage. Differentiation on the basis of innovation and technological competency depends on the R&D function, as discussed in Chapter 4. Efforts to improve service to customers depend on the quality of the sales function. Because developing the distinctive competency needed to provide a differentiation advantage is often expensive, a differentiator normally has a higher cost structure than the cost leader does.

Building new competencies in the functions that sustain its differentiated appeal does not mean neglecting cost control. As noted earlier, the differentiator studies how the cost leader operates and attempts to copy cost-saving innovations that will reduce its costs while preserving the source of its competitive advantage. The differentiator must control all costs that do not contribute to its differentiation advantage so that the price of the product does not exceed what customers are willing to pay, as noted in Nordstrom's case. Otherwise, it risks letting the cost leader go upmarket and steal its customers. Also, since superior profitability is the result of controlling costs as well as maximizing value and revenues, it pays to watch costs closely. The issue is not to minimize them to the point of losing the source of differentiation.[18] The owners of the famous Savoy Hotel in London, England, face just this problem. The Savoy's reputation has always been based on the incredibly high level of service it offers its customers. Three hotel employees serve the needs of each guest, and in every room, a guest can summon a waiter, maid, or valet by pressing a button at bedside. The cost of offering this level of service has been so high that the hotel makes less than 1 percent net profit every year.[19] Its owners try to find ways to reduce costs to increase profits, but if they reduce the number of hotel staff (the main source of the Savoy's high costs), they may destroy the main source of its differentiated appeal.

Advantages and Disadvantages. The advantages of the differentiation strategy can also be discussed in the context of the five forces model. Differentiation safeguards a company against competitors to the degree that customers develop brand loyalty for its products, a valuable asset that protects the company on all fronts. Powerful suppliers are rarely a problem because the differentiated company's strategy is geared more toward the price it can charge than toward costs. Also, differentiators can often pass on price increases to customers because they are willing to pay the premium price. Thus, a differentiator can tolerate moderate increases in the prices of its inputs better than the cost leader can. Differentiators are unlikely to experience problems with powerful buyers because the differentiator offers a distinct product. Only it can supply the product, and it commands brand loyalty. Differentiation and brand loyalty also create a barrier to entry for other companies seeking to enter the industry. New companies are forced to develop their own distinctive competency to be able to compete, an expensive undertaking.

Finally, the threat of substitute products depends on the ability of competitors' products to meet the same customers' needs as the differentiator's products and to break customers' brand loyalty. This can happen; phone companies are suffering as alternative ways of making phone calls through digital fiber-optic cable, satellite, and the Internet are becoming increasingly available. The issue is how much of a premium price a company can charge for distinctness before customers switch products. In the phone industry, the answer is "not much"; the large carriers were forced to reduce prices drastically so that 7 cents a minute is a common rate, down from 37 cents just a decade ago.

The main problems with a differentiation strategy center on strategic managers' long-term ability to maintain a product's perceived difference or distinctness in customers' eyes. What has become increasingly apparent is how quickly agile competitors move to imitate and copy successful differentiators. This has happened across many industries, such as retailing, computers, autos, home electronics, telecommunications, and pharmaceuticals. Patents and first-mover advantages (the advantages of being the first to market a product or service) last only so long, and as the overall quality of products produced by all companies goes up, brand loyalty declines. The story of the way American Express lost its competitive advantage, told in Strategy in Action 5.2, highlights many of the threats that face a differentiator.

Strategy in Action   5.2

Why So Many American Express Cards?

American Express's (AmEx) green, gold, and platinum charge cards (cards whose balance had to be paid off each month in full) used to be closely linked with high status and prestige. Obtaining an AmEx card required a high income, and obtaining a gold or platinum card required an even higher one. AmEx carefully differentiated its product by using famous people to advertise the virtues—exclusivity and distinctness—of possessing its card. Customers were willing to pay the high yearly fee to use the card. AmEx's cards were a premium product that allowed the company to charge both customers and merchants more because it offered quality service and conferred status on the user. For many years, its charge card operation was the money-spinner of AmEx's Travel Related Services (TRS) Division, and the company's stock price soared as its profits reached over $200 million by 1990.

AmEx's differentiated strategy suffered in the 1990s, however. Rival companies like MasterCard and Visa

began to issue true credit cards whose balance did not have to be paid off monthly, although of course high interest is charged on the unpaid balance. They also advertised that their cards could be used at locations where AmEx's were not accepted (because of the high fees it charged). In addition, various companies banded together with MasterCard and Visa to offer customers many other benefits of using their particular credit cards. For example, airlines issued credit cards through MasterCard or Visa that allowed customers to accumulate miles toward the purchase of an airline's tickets. This strategy encourages high customer loyalty, and by 1995, thousands of other companies, such as AT&T, GM, Yahoo, and Dell, began issuing credit cards that offer customers savings on their products.

AmEx failed to respond to these developments. Its managers were so convinced that their card was the best and commanded the most loyalty that they spurned attempts to ally with airlines, hotels, or car companies to develop new kinds of cards. Moreover, they failed to see the potential of credit cards that allow customers to carry unpaid balances. This was a grave error. The emergence of all these new credit cards, which better satisfied the needs of millions of new customers, broke the loyalty of AmEx customers. Soon the AmEx card had lost its differentiated appeal; it was now just one more credit card in an overcrowded market. More than 2 million of its users deserted AmEx, which lost hundreds of millions of dollars by 1996.

Under new management, AmEx strove to fight back and develop a new business model to restore its profitability. Realizing its mistakes, it started its own airline mileage program to try to entice its previous cardholders back. It also decided to issue a true credit card, but its managers bungled the introduction, and it flopped. Desperate, AmEx lowered the fees it charged merchants to process card payments and tried to increase the number of outlets that accept the card. However, it found that MasterCard and Visa, anticipating such a move, had allied to develop a proprietary electronic system to process credit card payments and would not let AmEx participate so that merchants were reluctant to take its card since this increased their paperwork.

In 2001, AmEx was helped enormously in its efforts to capture back customers when the Monopolies and Exchange Commission ruled that MasterCard and Visa had unfairly locked AmEx out of the market with their electronic system. AmEx would be allowed to participate, and with this hurdle overcome, it launched new credit cards and began to issue new kinds of cards that targeted specific market segments. In 1999, for example, it announced a new electronic smart card intended to be the global standard for travel and entertainment transactions. Among other things, this card permits electronic ticketing and boarding passes, automated car rental check-in, Internet identification and access, and payment functions including an electronic purse. It also brought out cash-back AmEx cards that gave cardholders up to 2 percent back on their purchases, creating a product similar to the Discover Card, which offers a 1 percent rebate. And it allied with airlines and hotels and developed cards specifically for their users.

By 2002, it offered nine kinds of charge cards and fourteen kinds of credit cards in the attempt to expand its market reach. It also spent over $1 billion a year on marketing and promotion to rebuild its brand name. AmEx hopes these moves will restore its differentiated image so that once again it becomes the credit card of choice. However, the growing importance of the electronic marketplace has created new challenges for the company, and the success of its efforts is still uncertain.

Sources: www.americanexpress.com (2002). L. Nathans Spiro and M. Landler, "Less-Than-Fantastic Plastic," *Business Week,* November 9, 1992, pp. 100–101; Edward Baig, "Platinum Cards: Move Over, Amex," *Business Week,* August 19, 1996, p. 84; John N. Frank, "American Express's Attention Getter," *Credit Card Management* (August 1996): 36–37. L. Beyer, "Breaking Tradition," *Credit Card Management* (1999): 57–60. R. Rolfe, "The Smart Centurion." *Credit Card Management* 12:1 (1999): 132–136.

A strategy of differentiation, then, requires a company to develop a competitive advantage by making choices about its product, market, and distinctive competencies that reinforce each other and together increase the value of a good or service in the eyes of customers. When a product has distinctness in customers' eyes, differentiators can charge a premium price. The disadvantages of a differentiation strategy are the ease with which competitors can imitate a differentiator's product and the difficulty of maintaining a premium price. When differentiation stems from the design or physical features of the product, differentiators are at great risk because imitation is easy. The risk is that over time, products such as VCRs or stereos become commodity-like products, for which the importance of differentiation diminishes as customers become more price sensitive. When differentiation stems from quality of service or reliability or from any intangible source, such as FedEx's guarantee or the prestige of a Rolex, a company is much more secure. It is difficult to imitate intangibles, and the differentiator can reap the benefits of this strategy for a long time. Nevertheless, all differentiators must watch out for imitators and be careful that they do not charge a price higher than the market will bear.

Cost Leadership and Differentiation Strategy

Changes in technology—in particular, the development of flexible manufacturing technologies (discussed in Chapter 4) and new digital, electronic, and information technologies (examined in detail in Chapter 7)—have made the choice between cost-leadership and differentiation strategies less clear-cut. This is illustrated in Table 5.1, which shows that for many companies, the choice of how much to differentiate their products, segment their markets, and leverage their distinctive competencies is a matter of positioning relative to the cost leader or the leading differentiator. In essence, the goal is to find a way to pursue the business models of the cost leader and differentiator simultaneously.

New technologies provide many ways for companies pursuing a cost-leadership strategy to differentiate their goods and services increasingly while maintaining a low cost structure. Conversely, technological developments often provide many ways for a company that has traditionally pursued a differentiation strategy to find ways to do it at a significantly lower cost so that it can choose a lower pricing option and build demand. The result has been that companies pursuing the different strategies have been drawn into closer competition for customers; rivalry among competitors has increased as they jockey for position, and competitive advantage has become more fragile and short lived than ever before.

Companies like Dell, BMW, and Toyota are continuously experimenting with new ways to reduce costs and segment their markets. The use of robots and flexible manufacturing cells reduces the costs of retooling the production line, and the costs associated with small production runs make it much easier to produce a wide variety of vehicle models and maintain an efficient cost structure. Today, flexible manufacturing enables a company pursuing differentiation to manufacture a range of products at a cost comparable to that of the cost leader. BMW, for example, has taken advantage of flexible manufacturing technologies to reduce its costs, but it also chose to charge only a modest premium price to boost its sales revenues and obtain its profits that way. Its new strategy worked: its market share and profitability have increased in recent years. Indeed, a factor promoting the trend toward market fragmentation and niche marketing in many customer goods industries, such as mobile phones, computers, and appliances, is the substantial reduction of the costs of differentiation by flexible manufacturing.

Another way that a differentiated producer may be able to realize significant economies of scale is by standardizing many of the component parts used in its end products. Toyota's various models of sports utility vehicles are built on only three different car platforms. As a result, Toyota is able to realize significant economies of scale in the manufacture and bulk purchase of standardized component parts despite its high level of market segmentation. Indeed, Toyota is driving the simultaneous cost-leadership and differentiation strategy business model in the car industry, and companies like Ford and DaimlerChrysler are struggling to keep up.

A company can also reduce both production and marketing costs if it limits the number of options it allows customers to choose from for a particular model of car. Increasingly, carmakers, for example, offer a model with an economy, luxury, or sports package that appeal to the principal market segments. Package offerings substantially lower manufacturing costs because long production runs of the various packages are possible. Once again, the company is getting gains from differentiation and from low cost at the same time. Just-in-time inventory systems can also help reduce costs and improve the quality and reliability of a company's products. This benefit is important to differentiated companies, for which quality and reliability are essential ingredients of the product's appeal. Rolls Royces, for example, are never supposed to break down. Improved quality control enhances a company's reputation and thus allows it to charge a premium price.

The Internet and e-commerce also provide an inexpensive way of informing millions of potential customers about the nature and quality of a company's products. Similarly, when customers do their own work on the Internet, such as managing their own finances, stock trades, bill paying, travel booking, and purchasing, the company is no longer bearing these costs because they have been shifted to customers. Direct selling to the customer also avoids the need to use wholesalers and other intermediaries, which results in great cost savings. It has been estimated that 40 percent of the profit in a new car goes to the dealership that sells the car and for costs associated with marketing the car.

Finally, the costs of making low-cost and differentiated products are often not very different because both are produced in countries with low labor costs. For example, the work of sewing an inexpensive cotton shirt for Sears does not cost less than sewing an expensive silk designer shirt for Nordstrom. The raw materials may cost more, but here too companies in countries like Malaysia, India, and China are constantly experimenting with ways to reduce the costs of weaving and dying silk and linen and assembling the final product. Differentiators try to charge what the market will bear (the highest price they can get) so that the profits to be obtained from selling foreign-made differentiated products can be enormous. For example, a $100 pair of Nike shoes may cost less than $1 in labor costs.

Taking advantage of the many ways new technology allows them to manage their value chains more efficiently, many companies are reaping the gains that follow from positioning themselves competitively to obtain the benefits from both low-cost and differentiation strategies. Like Nike, these companies can charge a premium price for their products compared with the price charged by the cost leader—the sneaker sold in Wal-Mart, for example—and their attention to reducing costs probably means they have lower costs than the pure differentiator, which is still focused solely on providing distinct products with high perceived quality. As a result, they achieve at least an equal, and probably a higher, level of profitability than companies pursuing only one of the generic strategies. Hence, the combined strategy is the most profitable to pursue, which is why companies have moved rapidly to take advantage of the new manufacturing and information technologies.

Focus Strategies: Low Cost and Differentiation

The last generic competitive strategies, the *focus low-cost* and *focus differentiation* strategies, are directed toward serving the needs of a *particular or specific market segment or niche*. In general, focus strategies position a company to compete for customers in a particular market segment, which can be defined geographically, by type of customer, or by segment of the product line.[20] For example, a geographic niche can be defined by region or even by locality. Selecting a niche by type of customer might mean serving only the very rich, the very young, or the very adventurous. Concentrating on only a segment of the product line means focusing only on vegetarian foods or very fast automobiles or designer clothes or sunglasses. In following a focus strategy, a company is *specializing* in some way.

Once it has chosen its market segment, a focused company positions itself using either a differentiation or a low-cost approach. Figure 5.2 compares these with a pure cost-leadership or differentiation strategy.

In essence, a focused company is a specialized differentiator or a cost leader. If a company uses a focused low-cost approach, it competes against the cost leader in the

FIGURE 5.2

Why Focus Strategies Are Different

market segments in which it has no cost disadvantage. For example, in local lumber, cement, bookkeeping, or pizza delivery markets, the focuser may have lower materials or transportation costs than the low-cost national company. The focuser may also have a cost advantage because it is producing complex or custom-built products that do not lend themselves easily to economies of scale in production and therefore offer few experience curve advantages. With a focus strategy, a company concentrates on small-volume custom products, for which it has a cost advantage, and leaves the large-volume standardized market to the cost leader—low-priced Mexican food specials versus Big Macs, for example.

If a company uses a focused differentiation approach, then all the means of differentiation that are open to the differentiator are available to the focused company. The point is that the focused company positions itself to compete with the differentiator in just one or a few segments. For example, Porsche, a focused company, competes against GM only in the sports car segment of the car market. Focused companies are likely to develop differentiated product qualities successfully because of their knowledge of a small customer set (such as sports car buyers), knowledge of a region, or expertise in a particular field (such as corporate law, management consulting, or web site management for retail customers or restaurants).

Concentration on a small range of products sometimes allows a focuser to develop innovations faster than a large differentiator can. However, the focuser does not attempt to serve all market segments because that would bring it into direct competition with the differentiator. Instead, it concentrates on building market share in one market segment; if it is successful, it may begin to serve more and more market segments and chip away at the differentiator's competitive advantage. The way in which many small software companies have emerged to take advantage of specialized niches in the outsourcing market, discussed in Strategy in Action 5.3, illustrates how focused companies can obtain a competitive advantage.

Table 5.1 illustrates the specific product, market, and distinctive competency choices made by a focused company. Differentiation can be high or low because the company can pursue a low-cost or a differentiation approach. As for customer groups, a focused company chooses specific niches in which to compete rather than going for a whole market, as a cost leader does, or filling a large number of niches, as a broad differentiator does. The focused company can pursue any distinctive competency because it can seek any kind of differentiation or low-cost advantage. Thus, it might find a cost advantage and develop a superior efficiency in low-cost manufacturing or web site hosting within a particular region or industry. Alternatively, it might develop superior skills in responsiveness to customers, based on its ability to

Strategy in Action 5.3

Finding a Niche in the Outsourcing Market

Outsourcing occurs when one company contracts with another company to perform one of the value creation functions on its behalf. Increasingly, many companies are finding it very difficult to keep up with the pace of technological change in the computer software industry and are outsourcing their data-processing needs to specialized software companies. Others are also outsourcing their web site design and management needs. Electronic Data Systems (EDS), IBM, and Computer Associates are some of the industry giants that manage other companies' data-processing and web site operations using their own proprietary software.

Different kinds of organizations, such as universities, banks, insurance agencies, local governments, and utilities, have different kinds of data-processing and web site design needs and problems. Often, each kind of company requires a specialized kind of software system that can be customized to its specific needs. As a result, it is difficult for any one software company to service the needs of a wide range of different companies, and the outsourcing market in data processing and web site design is fragmented. Large companies such as EDS and IBM have only relatively small market shares; consequently, opportunities abound for new companies to position themselves to provide dedicated service to a particular kind of business or industry.

Increasingly, small, specialized software companies have been springing up to manage the needs of particular kinds of clients. An example is Systems & Computer Technology, based in Malvern, Pennsylvania, which went head-to-head with EDS to secure a seven-year $35 million outsourcing contract to service the data-processing needs

of Dallas County. The company has yearly revenues of only $200 million, compared with EDS's $15 billion, but it won the contract because it specializes in servicing the needs of local government and institutions of higher education. It could show Dallas County its twelve ongoing contracts with municipal clients, whereas EDS could offer its experience with only one, a hospital. The focused company won out over the differentiator.

Other focused companies are also springing up—for instance, the Bisys Group and Systematics Company, which serve the needs of banks and universities. It appears that in the data-processing industry, small, focused companies are strong competitors because of their ability to provide specialized, personal service to specific clients in a way that large differentiators cannot. Indeed, EDS ran into problems because of the emergence of agile, Internet-based competitors that can provide e-commerce solutions at a price much lower than EDS's. The collapse of the e-commerce environment in 2001 intensified competition between large and small rivals, and the small specialist companies have benefited from their lower cost structures and ability to respond quickly to the changing needs of their clients.

Sources: J. W. Verity, "They Make a Killing Minding Other People's Business," *Business Week,* November 30, 1992, p. 96. Mark Willis, "Outsourcing Benefits Administration: A Disciplined Process for Conducting a Thorough Cost-Benefit Analysis," *Compensation and Benefits Management* (Winter 1996): 45–53. Jane Gebhart, "Beyond the Information Systems Outsourcing Bandwagon: The Insourcing Response," *Sloan Business Review* (Winter 1996): 177. B. Caldwell and J. Mateyaschuk, "Reviving EDS," *Informationweek* 742 (1999): 18–19.

serve the particular needs of regional or industry customers in ways that a national differentiator would find very expensive.

The many avenues a focused company can take to develop a competitive advantage explain why there are so many small companies in relation to large ones. A focused company has enormous opportunity to develop its own niche and compete against companies pursuing low-cost and differentiated strategies. A focus strategy provides an opportunity for an entrepreneur to find and then exploit a gap in the market by developing an innovative product that customers cannot do without.[21] The steel mini-mills discussed in Chapter 4 are a good example of how focused companies specializing in one market can grow so efficient that they become the cost leaders. Many large companies started with a focus strategy, and, of course, one means by which companies can expand is to take over other focused companies. For example, Cisco Systems, the largest Internet router maker, grew by buying over fifty small specialist software and hardware companies. Its managers believed these companies possessed the products and knowledge that would allow it to become the leading differentiator in the industry, and despite the downturn in e-commerce Cisco remains the dominant industry competitor.

Advantages and Disadvantages. A focused company's competitive advantages stem from the source of its distinctive competency: efficiency, quality, innovation, or responsiveness to customers. The company is protected from rivals to the extent that it can provide a product or service they cannot. This ability also gives the focuser power over its buyers because they cannot get the same thing from anyone else. With regard to powerful suppliers, however, a focused company is at a disadvantage, because it buys in small volume and thus is in the suppliers' power. However, as long as it can pass on price increases to loyal customers, this disadvantage may not be a significant problem. Potential entrants have to overcome the loyalty from customers the focuser has generated, and the development of customer loyalty also lessens the threat from substitute products. This protection from the five forces allows the focuser to earn above-average returns on its investment. Another advantage of the focus strategy is that it permits a company to stay close to its customers and respond to their changing needs. The difficulty a large differentiator sometimes experiences in managing a large number of market segments is not an issue for a focuser.

Because a focuser produces a small volume, its cost structure may be higher than that of a low-cost company. Higher costs can reduce profitability if a focuser is forced to invest heavily in developing a distinctive competency, such as expensive product innovation, in order to compete with a differentiated company. However, once again, flexible manufacturing systems are opening up new opportunities for focused companies because small production runs become possible at a lower cost. Increasingly, small, specialized companies are competing with large companies in specific market segments in which their cost disadvantage is much reduced.

A second problem is that the focuser's niche can suddenly disappear because of technological change or changes in customers' tastes. Unlike the more generalist differentiator, a focuser cannot move easily to new niches, given its concentration of resources and competency in one or a few niches. For example, clothing store chain Brooks Brothers, whose focus was on providing formal business attire, ran into great difficulty in the 1990s when business casual became the clothing norm at most companies. It found it hard to adapt to the changing market and was bought out in 2001. Diners have become almost a thing of the past as they have become unable to compete with the low prices and speed of fast food chains like McDonald's and the upscale atmosphere of Starbuck's. The disappearance of niches is one reason that so many small companies fail.

Finally, there is the very real prospect that differentiators will compete for a focuser's niche by offering a product that can satisfy the demands of the focuser's customers; for example, GM's new midsize Cadillac and Ford's new midsized Jaguar are aimed at Lexus, BMW, and Mercedes-Benz buyers. A focuser is vulnerable and has to defend its niche constantly.

Stuck in the Middle   Successful competitive positioning requires that a company make consistent product, market, and distinctive competency choices. In other words, a company must achieve a fit among the three components of business-level strategy to create a business model that gives it a competitive advantage. Thus, a low-cost company cannot strive for a high level of market segmentation, as a differentiator does, and provide a wide range of products because those choices would raise its cost structure too much and the company would lose its low-cost advantage. Similarly, a differentiator with a competency in innovation that tries to reduce its expenditures on research and development or one with a competency in responsiveness to customers through after-sales service that seeks to economize on its sales force to decrease costs is asking for trouble because it will lose its competitive advantage as its distinctive competency disappears.

Pursuing a business-level strategy successfully means giving serious attention to all elements of the business model on an ongoing basis. Many companies, through ignorance or error, do not do the planning necessary for success in their chosen strategy. Such companies are said to be "stuck in the middle" because they have made product and market choices that they have been unable to obtain or sustain a competitive advantage.[22] As a result, they have no consistent business-level strategy, experience below-average profitability, and suffer when industry competition intensifies.

Some stuck-in-the-middle companies may have started out pursuing cost leadership or differentiation strategies but then made wrong resource allocation decisions or experienced a hostile, changing environment. It is very easy for strategic managers to lose control of a generic strategy unless they keep close track of the business and its environment, constantly adjusting product and market choices to suit changing conditions within the industry. This is why it is so important that managers think strategically. In Chapter 1, we defined *strategic intent* as the way managers think about where they want their organization to be in the future and what kinds of resources and capabilities they will need to achieve this vision. Strategic intent provides a company with a sense of direction and stretches managers at all levels to be more inventive or innovative and to think how to make better use of resources. Moreover, it "implies a competitive distinct point of view about the future; it holds out to employees the promise of exploring new competitive territory."[23] The experience of Holiday Inns described in Strategy in Action 5.4 shows how a company can become stuck in the middle but also how a company can change its business model to regain its competitive advantage.

As the experience of Holiday Inns suggests, there are many paths to being stuck in the middle. Quite commonly, a focuser can get stuck in the middle when it becomes overconfident and starts to act like a broad differentiator. People Express, the defunct airline, exemplified a company in this situation. It started out as a specialized air carrier serving a narrow market niche: low-priced travel on the eastern seaboard. In pursuing this focus strategy based on cost leadership, it was very successful, but when it tried to expand to other geographic regions and began taking over other airlines to gain a larger number of planes, it lost its niche. People Express became one more carrier in an increasingly competitive market in which it had no special competitive advantage against the other national carriers. The result was financial trouble. People Express was swallowed up by Texas Air and incorporated into Continental Airlines. By contrast, Southwest Airlines, the focused low-cost company, has continued to focus on this strategy and has grown successfully.

Differentiators too can fail in the market and end up stuck in the middle if competitors attack their markets with more specialized or low-cost products that blunt their competitive edge. This happened to IBM in the large-frame computer market as personal computers became more powerful and able to do the job of the much more expensive mainframes. The increasing movement toward flexible manufacturing systems aggravates the problems of cost leaders and differentiators. Many large

Strategy in Action   5.4

Holiday Inns on Six Continents

The history of the Holiday Inns motel chain is one of the great success stories in U.S. business. Its founder, Kemmons Wilson, vacationing in the early 1950s, found motels to be small, expensive, and of unpredictable quality. This discovery, along with the prospect of unprecedented highway travel that would come with the new interstate highway program, triggered a realization: there was an unmet customer need—a gap in the market for quality accommodations. Holiday Inns was founded to meet that need. From the beginning, Holiday Inns set the standard for offering motel features such as air-conditioning and icemakers while keeping room rates reasonable. These amenities enhanced the motels' popularity, and motel franchising, Wilson's invention, made rapid expansion possible. By 1960, Holiday Inns could be found in virtually every city and on every major highway. Before the 1960s ended, more than 1,000 of them were in full operation, and occupancy rates averaged 80 percent. The concept of mass accommodation had arrived.

The service it offered appealed to the average traveler, who wanted a standardized product (a room) at an average price—the middle of the hotel room market. But by the 1970s, travelers were beginning to make different demands on hotels and motels. Some wanted luxury and were willing to pay higher prices for better accommodations and service. Others sought low prices and accepted rock-bottom quality and service in exchange. As the market fragmented into different groups of customers with different needs, Holiday Inns was still offering an undifferentiated, average-cost, average-quality product.

Although Holiday Inns missed the change in the market and thus failed to respond appropriately to it, the competition did not. Companies such as Hyatt siphoned off the top end of the market, where quality and service sold rooms. Chains such as Motel 6 and Days Inns captured the basic-quality, low-price end of the market. In between were many specialty chains that appealed to business travelers, families, or self-caterers (people who want to be able to cook in their hotel rooms). Holiday Inns' position was attacked from all sides. As occupancy rates dropped drastically with increasing competition, profitability declined.

Wounded but not dead, Holiday Inns began a counterattack. The original chain was upgraded to suit quality-oriented travelers. Then to meet the needs of different kinds of travelers, Holiday Inns created new hotel and motel chains: the luxury Crowne Plazas; the Hampton Inns serving the low-priced end of the market; and the all-suite Embassy Suites. Holiday Inns attempted to meet the demands of the many niches, or segments, of the hotel market that have emerged as customers' needs have changed over time. These moves were successful in the early 1990s, and Holiday Inns grew to become one of the largest suppliers of hotel rooms in the industry. However, by the late 1990s, it became clear that with intense competition in the industry from other chains such as Marriott, Holiday Inns was once again losing its differentiated appeal as its revenues and profits fell.

In the fast-changing hotel and lodging market, positioning each hotel brand or chain to maximize customer demand is an ever-changing endeavor. In 2000, the pressure on all hotel chains to adapt to the challenges of global competition and become a globally differentiated brand led to the takeover of the company and its incorporation in the international Six Continents Hotel chain. Today, around the globe, more than 3,200 hotels flying the flags of Holiday Inn, Holiday Inn Express, Crowne Plaza, Staybridge Suites by Holiday Inn, and luxury Inter-Continental Hotels and Resorts are positioning themselves to offer the services, amenities, and lodging experiences that will cater to virtually every travel occasion and guest need. A massive modernization campaign is under way in the United States to take existing full-service Holiday Inns to their next evolution and the opening of the first "Holiday Inn of the Future" is planned for late 2002. Holiday Inns plans to have a room to meet the need of every segment of the lodging market.

Sources: "The Holiday Inns Trip; A Breeze for Decades, Bumpy Ride in the 1980s," *Wall Street Journal,* February 11, 1987, p. 1. Holiday Inns, *Annual Report* (1985). U.S. Bureau of Labor Statistics, *U.S. Industrial Output* (Washington, D.C.: U.S. Government Printing Office, 1986). Mark Gleason and Alan Salomon, "Fallon's Challenge: Make Holiday Inn More 'In,'" *Advertising Age,* September 2, 1996, p. 14. Julie Miller, "Amenities Range from Snacks to Technology," *Hotel and Motel Management,* July 3, 1996, pp. 38–40. www.sixcontinenthotels.com, 2002.

companies become stuck in the middle unless they make the investment needed to pursue both strategies simultaneously. No company is safe in the jungle of competition, and each must be constantly on the lookout to take advantage of competitive advantages as they arise and to defend the advantages it already has.

Successful management of a generic competitive strategy requires strategic managers to attend to two main matters. First, they need to ensure that the product, market, and distinctive competency decisions they make result in a business-level strategy that gives them a competitive advantage and a business model that results in superior profitability. Second, they need to monitor the environment and their competitors constantly so that they can keep the company's sources of competitive advantage in tune with changing opportunities and threats.

Competitive Positioning and Business-Level Strategy

Business-level strategy determines how a company will compete for customers in a particular market segment or industry. In every market segment or industry, typically several companies are competing for the same set of customers. This means that the actions of one company will have an impact on the others, and over time, companies competing for the same customers become rivals locked in a competitive struggle to be the ones that obtain a competitive advantage and achieve above-average profitability. How many companies might be expected to achieve above-average profitability in a particular market or industry? And how can managers increase their chances of being one of the fortunate few? Several tools are useful in helping managers to position their companies competitively with regard to both the customer and their competitors. Here, we examine three of these tools: strategic group analysis, investment analysis, and game theory.

Strategic Group Analysis

Strategic group analysis helps a company identify the strategies that its industry rivals are pursuing. Within most industries, strategic groups emerge, each composed of companies pursuing a similar generic strategy.[24] All the companies inside an industry pursuing a low-cost strategy form one strategic group, all those seeking to pursue a broad differentiation strategy constitute another strategic group, and all those pursuing a focus differentiation or low-cost strategy form yet other strategic groups.

The concept of strategic groups has a number of implications for business-level strategy. First, strategic managers can map their competitors according to their choice of generic strategy. They can identify the different ways rivals have decided what customers' needs to satisfy, which customer groups to serve, and which distinctive competencies to develop. They can then use this knowledge to position themselves closer to customers and differentiate themselves from their competitors. In other words, careful strategic group analysis allows managers to uncover the most important basis of competition in an industry and identify products and market segments where they can compete most successfully for customers. Such analysis also helps to reveal what competencies are likely to be most valuable in the future so that companies can make the right investment decision. For example, the need to develop new models of cars that can be sold across the world and are assembled reliably by low-cost labor has dominated competitive positioning in the global car industry. U.S. car companies have bought or formed alliances with almost every other foreign car manufacturer to obtain marketing, design, or manufacturing knowledge.

Second, a company's nearest competitors are those companies pursuing a similar strategy in its strategic group. Customers tend to view the products of such enterprises as being direct substitutes for each other. Thus, a major threat to a company's profitability may arise primarily from within its own strategic group, not necessarily from the other companies in the industry pursuing different generic business-level strategies. For example, the competition for Toyota comes from Honda, Ford, and Volkswagen, not from Hyundai or Rolls Royce.

Third, different strategic groups can have a different standing with respect to each of Porter's five competitive forces because these forces affect companies in different ways. In other words, the risk of new entry by potential competitors, the degree of rivalry among companies within a group, the bargaining power of buyers, the bargaining power of suppliers, and the competitive force of substitute products can all vary in intensity among different strategic groups within the same industry. In the global car industry, for example, the smaller, more focused companies pursuing both low-cost and differentiated luxury strategies were in big trouble in the 1990s. Their input costs were rising, and they could not afford billions of dollars to design new models and build new flexible manufacturing plants needed to produce them. Indeed, some European, Korean, and even Japanese companies started to lose billions of dollars, while the big differentiators such as Toyota, Volkswagen, and Ford were making record profits.

As discussed in Chapter 2, mobility barriers are factors that inhibit the movement of companies between groups in an industry. The relative height of mobility barriers determines how successfully companies in one group can compete with companies in another group. For example, can a company in the differentiation strategic group also pursue a low-cost strategy and thus achieve the low cost-differentiation strategy? To the degree that one or more companies in one group can develop or obtain the functional and financial resources they need to lower their costs or embark on a major R&D expansion, they may be able to compete successfully with companies in another strategic group. In effect, they have created yet another strategic group: a combined low-cost and differentiation strategic group, which has the strongest competitive advantage and the greatest ability to earn above-average profits. In fact, the need to pursue a simultaneous global low-cost and differentiation strategy has been the major driving force behind the wave of merger activities among the large car companies that has left just a handful of global giants to compete in the 2000s. For example, Daimler Benz took over Chrysler, GM took control of Isuzu, and Ford merged with Mazda to pursue a global low-cost/differentiation strategy. Thus, the strategic group map in the global car industry has changed dramatically as companies fight to survive in the rapidly consolidating global car industry. A few companies like BMW and Porsche still pursue a focus differentiated strategy. However, some analysts believe it is only a matter of time before they will be forced to join with one of the low-cost/differentiators.

Choosing an Investment Strategy at the Business Level

A second major choice to be made at the business level is which type of investment strategy to pursue in support of the competitive strategy. An investment strategy sets the amount and type of resources—human, functional, and financial—that must be invested to maximize a company's profitability over time.[25] Recall from Chapter 3 that a company's return on invested capital is a major indicator of its competitive advantage in an industry. Generic competitive strategies provide competitive advantages, but they are expensive to develop and maintain. For example, a simultaneous differentiation/cost-leadership strategy is the most expensive, because it requires that a company invest resources not only in functions such as R&D, sales, and marketing to develop distinctive competencies but also in functions such as manufacturing and materials management to find ways to reduce costs. A focus strategy is probably the least expensive because fewer resources are needed to serve one market segment than the whole market.

In deciding on an investment strategy, a company must evaluate the potential return (on invested capital) from investing in a generic competitive strategy against the cost. In this way, it can determine whether pursuing a certain strategy is likely to be profitable and how profitability will change as competition within the industry changes. Two factors are crucial in choosing an investment strategy: the strength of a company's position in an industry relative to its competitors and the stage of the industry's life cycle in which the company is competing.[26]

In determining the strength of a company's relative competitive position, market share and distinctive competencies become important. A large market share signals greater potential returns from future investment because it suggests a company has brand loyalty and is in a strong competitive position. Similarly, the more difficult it is to imitate a company's distinctive competencies, such as those in R&D or manufacturing and marketing, the stronger a company's relative competitive position becomes. These two attributes also reinforce one another; for example, a large market share may help a company to create and develop distinctive competencies because high demand allows it to ride down the experience curve and lower its cost structure. Also, a large market share can create a large cash flow, which may allow for more investment to develop competencies in R&D or elsewhere. In general, companies with the largest market share and the strongest distinctive competencies are in the best position to build and sustain their competitive advantage. Companies with a small market share and little potential for developing a distinctive competency are in a much weaker competitive position.[27]

The second main factor influencing the investment attractiveness of a generic strategy is the stage of the industry life cycle. A particular industry environment, presenting different opportunities and threats, accompanies each life cycle stage. Each stage therefore has different implications for the investment of resources needed to obtain a competitive advantage. Competition is strongest in the shakeout stage of the life cycle and least important in the embryonic stage, for example. The risks of pursuing a strategy change over time. The difference in risk explains why the potential returns from investing in a competitive strategy depend on the life cycle stage. Table 5.2 summarizes the relationship among the stage of the life cycle, the competitive position, and the investment strategy at the business level.

TABLE 5.2

Choosing an Investment Strategy at the Business Level

Stage of Industry Life Cycle	Strong Competitive Position	Weak Competitive Position
Embryonic	Share building	Share building
Growth	Growth	Market concentration
Shakeout	Share increasing	Market concentration or harvest/liquidation
Maturity	Hold-and-maintain or profit	Harvest or liquidation/divestiture
Decline	Market concentration or harvest (asset reduction)	Turnaround, liquidation, or divestiture

Embryonic Strategy. In the embryonic stage, all companies, weak and strong, emphasize the development of a distinctive competency and an associated business model. During this stage, investment needs are great because a company has to establish a competitive advantage. Many fledgling companies in the industry are seeking resources to develop a distinctive competency. Thus, the appropriate business-level investment strategy is a **share-building strategy.** The aim is to build market share by developing a stable and distinct competitive advantage to attract customers who have no knowledge of the company's products.

Companies require large amounts of capital to build research and development competencies or sales and service competencies. They cannot generate much of this capital internally. Thus, a company's success depends on its ability to demonstrate a distinct competency to attract outside investors, or venture capitalists. If a company gains the resources to develop a distinctive competency, it will be in a relatively stronger competitive position. If it fails, its only option may be to exit the industry. In fact, companies in weak competitive positions at all stages in the life cycle may choose to exit the industry to cut their losses.

Growth Strategies. At the growth stage, the task facing a company is to consolidate its position and provide the base it needs to survive the coming shakeout. Thus, the appropriate investment strategy is the **growth strategy.** The goal is to maintain its relative competitive position in a rapidly expanding market and, if possible, to increase it—in other words, to grow with the expanding market. However, other companies are entering the market and catching up with the industry's innovators. As a result, first movers—companies first into the market with a particular kind of good or service—often require successive waves of capital infusion to maintain the momentum generated by their success in the embryonic stage. For example, differentiators need to engage in extensive research and development to maintain their technological lead, and cost leaders need to invest in state-of-the-art machinery and computers to obtain new experience curve economies. All this investment is very expensive.

The growth stage is also the time when companies attempt to consolidate existing market niches and enter new ones so that they can increase their market share. Increasing the level of market segmentation to become a broad differentiator is expensive as well. A company has to invest resources to develop a new sales and marketing competency. Consequently, at the growth stage, companies fine-tune their competitive strategy (which we discuss at length in Chapter 7) and make business-level investment decisions about the relative advantages of a differentiation, low-cost, or focus strategy, given financial needs and relative competitive position. If one company has emerged as the cost leader, for example, some others may decide to compete head-to-head with it and enter this strategic group, but others will not and instead will pursue a growth strategy using a differentiation or focus approach and invest resources in developing other competencies. As a result, strategic groups start to develop in an industry as each company seeks the best way to invest its scarce resources to maximize its competitive advantage.

Companies must spend a lot of money just to keep up with growth in the market, and finding additional resources to develop new skills and competencies is a difficult task for strategic managers. Consequently, companies in a weak competitive position at this stage engage in a **market concentration** strategy to consolidate their position. They seek to specialize in some way and may adopt a focus strategy and move to a focused strategic group to reduce their investment needs. If they are very weak, they may also choose to exit the industry and sell out to a stronger competitor.

Shakeout Strategies. By the shakeout stage, demand is increasing slowly, and competition by price or product characteristics becomes intense. Companies in strong competitive positions need resources to invest in a **share-increasing strategy** to attract customers from weak companies exiting the market. In other words, companies attempt to maintain and increase market share despite fierce competition. The way companies invest their resources depends on their generic strategy.

For cost leaders, because of the price wars that can occur, investment in cost control is crucial if they are to survive the shakeout stage; they must do all they can to reduce costs. Differentiators in a strong competitive position choose to forge ahead and become broad differentiators. Their investment is likely to be oriented toward marketing, and they are likely to develop a sophisticated after-sales service network. They also widen the product range to match the range of customers' needs. Differentiators in a weak position reduce their investment burden by withdrawing to a focused strategy—the **market concentration strategy**—to specialize in a particular niche or product. Weak companies exiting the industry engage in a **harvest** or **liquidation** strategy, both of which are discussed later in this chapter.

Maturity Strategies. By the maturity stage, a relatively stable strategic group structure has emerged in the industry, and companies have learned how their competitors will probably react to their competitive moves. At this point, companies want to reap the rewards of their previous investments in developing a generic strategy. Until now, profits have been reinvested in the business, and dividends have been small. Investors in strong companies have obtained their rewards through the appreciation of the value of their stock, because the company has reinvested most of its capital to maintain and increase market share. As market growth slows in the maturity stage, a company's investment strategy depends on the level of competition in the industry and the source of the company's competitive advantage.

In environments in which competition is high because of technological change or low barriers to entry, companies need to defend their competitive position. Strategic managers need to continue to invest heavily in maintaining the company's competitive advantage. Both low-cost companies and differentiators adopt a **hold-and-maintain** strategy to support their generic strategies. They expend resources to develop their distinctive competency so as to remain the market leaders. For example, differentiated companies may invest in improved after-sales service, and low-cost companies may invest in the latest production technologies.

It is at this point, however, that companies realize they must begin to pursue both a low-cost and a differentiation strategy if they are to protect themselves from aggressive competitors (both at home and abroad) that are watching for any opportunity or perceived weakness to take the lead in the industry. Differentiators take advantage of their strong position to develop flexible manufacturing systems to reduce their production costs. Cost leaders move to start differentiating their products to expand their market share by serving more market segments. For example, Gallo moved from the bulk wine segment and began marketing premium wines and wine coolers to take advantage of its low production costs. Soon, Gallo's new premium brands, like Falling Leaf chardonnay, became the best-selling wines in the United States.

Historically, however, many companies have felt protected from competition within the industry in the maturity stage and decide to exploit their competitive advantage to the fullest by engaging in a **profit strategy:** they attempt to maximize their present returns, not their future profitability, from previous investments. Typically, they reinvest proportionally less in improving their functional resources and increased returns to shareholders. The profit strategy works well only as long as competitive forces remain relatively constant, so that a company can maintain the profit margins developed by its competitive strategy. However, it must be alert to threats from the environment and take care not to become complacent and unresponsive to changes. All too often, market leaders fail to exercise vigilance in managing the environment, imagining that they are impervious to competition. Kodak, which had profited for so long from its strengths in film processing, was slow to respond to the threat of electronic imaging techniques. Sears and Kmart woke up too late to the threat posed by Wal-Mart. Paradoxically, very successful companies often fail to sense changes in the market.

Decline Strategies. The decline stage of an industry's life cycle begins when demand for its product starts to fall. Among the many possible reasons for decline are foreign competition and the loss of a company's distinctive competency as its rivals enter with new or more efficient technologies. A company must now decide what investment strategy to adopt in order to deal with new circumstances within its industry.[28] The initial strategies that companies can adopt are market concentration and asset reduction.[29]

With a **market concentration strategy,** a company attempts to consolidate its product and market choices. It narrows its product range and exits marginal niches in an attempt to redeploy its resources more effectively and improve its competitive position. Reducing customer groups served may also allow it to pursue a focus strategy in order to survive the decline stage. An **asset reduction strategy** requires a company to limit or decrease its investment in a business and to extract, or milk, the investment as much as it can. This approach is sometimes called a **harvest strategy** because a company will exit the industry once it has "harvested" all the returns it can. It reduces to a minimum the assets it employs in the business and forgoes investment for the sake of immediate profits.[30] A market concentration strategy generally indicates that a company is trying to turn around its business so that it can survive in the long run. Low-cost companies are more likely to pursue a harvest strategy because a smaller market share means higher costs and they are unable to move to a focus strategy. Differentiators, in contrast, have a competitive advantage in this stage if they can move to a focus strategy.

At any stage of the life cycle, companies that are in weak competitive positions may apply **turnaround strategies.**[31] The questions that a company has to answer are whether it has the resources available to develop a viable business-level strategy to compete in the industry and how much it will cost. A company stuck in the middle, for example, must assess the investment costs of developing a low-cost or differentiation strategy. Perhaps a company pursuing a low-cost strategy has not made the right product or market choices, or perhaps a differentiation has been missing niche opportunities. In such cases, the company can redeploy resources and change its strategy.

If a company decides that turnaround is not possible for competitive or life cycle reasons, then the two remaining investment alternatives are liquidation and divestiture: exit the industry by liquidating assets or selling the whole business. Both are radical forms of harvesting strategy, because the company is seeking to get back as much as it can from its investment in the business. Often, however, it can exit only at a loss and take a tax write-off. Timing is important; the earlier a company senses that divestiture is necessary, the more it can get for its assets. There are many stories about companies that buy weak or declining companies, thinking they can turn them around, and as the new acquisitions become a drain on their resources they then real-ize their mistake.

Strategic managers must always consider the costs of pursuing a generic strategy when developing or refining their business models. The issue is how to invest a com-pany's capital in resources that will result in the greatest potential future returns. Achieving superior performance and profitability requires constant attention to the bottom line—to understanding how to increase a company's return on invested cap-ital through the investment strategy in its business model.

Business-Level Strategy and Game Theory

Companies are in a constant competitive struggle with rivals in their industry and strategic group to gain more business from customers. A useful way of viewing this struggle is as a competitive game between companies, where companies are continu-ally using competitive moves and tactics to compete effectively in an industry. Com-panies that understand the nature of the competitive game they are playing can often make better strategic moves that increase the profitability of their business-level strategies. For example, they can find a better way to pursue a cost leadership or a dif-ferentiation strategy. A branch of work in the social sciences known as *game theory* can be used to model competition between a company and its rivals and help man-agers improve their business models and strategies.[32]

From a game theory perspective, companies in an industry can be viewed as play-ers that are all simultaneously making choices about which generic strategies to pur-sue to maximize their profitability. The problem strategic managers face is that the potential profitability of each strategy is not some fixed amount; it varies depending on the strategy one company selects and also the strategies that its rivals select. There are two basic types of game: sequential move games and simultaneous move games. In a *sequential move game,* such as chess, players move in turn, and one player can select a strategy to pursue after considering its rival's choice of strategies. In a *simul-taneous move game,* the players act at the same time, in ignorance of their rival's cur-rent actions. The classic game of rock-paper-scissors is a simultaneous move game.

In the business world, both sequential and simultaneous move games are com-monplace as strategic managers jockey for competitive position in the industry. Indeed, game theory is particularly useful in analyzing situations where a company is competing against a limited number of rivals, and there is a considerable level of interdependence in the industry, as occurs in a consolidated industry. In such a set-ting, the profitability of a strategy depends critically on the strategy pursued by rival companies. Several of the basic principles that underlie game theory are examined below; these principles can be useful in determining which business-level strategies managers should pursue.

Look Forward and Reason Back. One of the most basic messages of game theory is that managers need to think strategically in two related ways: (1) look for-ward, think ahead, and anticipate how rivals will respond to whatever strategic moves they make, and (2) reason backward to determine which strategic moves to pursue today given their assessment of how the company's rivals will respond to various future strategic moves. Managers who do both of these things should be able to dis-cover the specific competitive strategy that will lead to the greatest potential returns. This cardinal principle of game theory is known as *look forward and reason back.* To understand its importance consider this scenario.

Two large companies, UPS and FedEx, which specialize in next-day delivery of packages, dominate the U.S. air express industry. They have a very high fixed cost structure because they need to invest in a capital-intensive nationwide network of aircraft, trucks, and package sorting facilities. The key to their profitability is to increase volume sufficiently so that these fixed costs can be spread out over a large number of packages, reducing the unit cost of transporting each package.

Imagine that a bright young manager at UPS calculates that if UPS cuts prices for next-day delivery service by 15 percent, the volume of packages the company ships will grow by over 30 percent, and so will UPS's total revenues and profitability. Is this a smart move? The answer depends on whether the bright young manager has remembered to look forward and reason back and think through how FedEx would respond to UPS's price cuts.

Because UPS and FedEx are competing directly against each other, their strategies are interdependent. If UPS cuts prices, FedEx will lose market share, its volume of shipments will decline, and its profitability will suffer. Because FedEx is unlikely to accept this result, if UPS cuts prices by 15 percent, FedEx is likely to follow and cut its prices by 15 percent in order to hold onto market share. The net result is that the average level of prices in the industry will fall by 15 percent, as will revenues, and both players will see their profitability decline—a lose-lose situation. By looking forward and reasoning back, the new manager discovers that the strategy of cutting prices is not a good one.

Decision trees can be used to help in the process of looking forward and reasoning back. Figure 5.3 maps out the decision tree for the simple game analyzed above from the perspective of UPS. (Note that this is a sequential move game.) UPS moves first, and then FedEx must decide how to respond. Here, you see that UPS has to choose between two strategies: cutting prices by 15 percent or leaving them unchanged. If it leaves prices unchanged, it will continue to earn its current level of profitability, which is $100 million. If it cuts prices by 15 percent, one of two things can happen: FedEx matches the price cut, or FedEx leaves its prices unchanged. If FedEx matches UPS's price cut (FedEx decides to fight a price war), profits are competed away and UPS's profit will be $0. If FedEx does not respond and leaves its prices unaltered, UPS will gain market share and its profits will rise to $180 million. So the best pricing strategy for UPS to pursue depends on its assessment of FedEx's likely response.

FIGURE 5.3

A Decision Tree for
UPS's Pricing Strategy

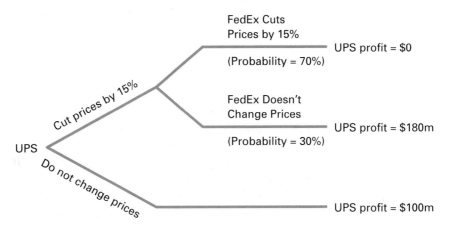

Figure 5.3 assigns probabilities to the different responses from FedEx: specifically there is a 70 percent chance that FedEx will match UPS's price cut and a 30 percent chance that it will do nothing. These probabilities come from an assessment of how UPS's price cut will affect FedEx's sales volume and profitability. The bigger the negative impact of UPS's price cut is on FedEx's sales volume and profitability, the more likely it is that FedEx will match UPS's price cuts. This is another example of the principle of looking forward and reasoning backward. Assigning a 70 percent probability to the top branch in Figure 5.3 assumes that the price cut from UPS will have a significant negative impact on FedEx's business and will force the company to respond with a price cut of its own. The probabilities can also come from looking at the history of FedEx's responses to UPS's price moves. If FedEx has a long history of matching UPS's price cuts, the probability that it will do so this time is high. If FedEx does not have a history of matching UPS's price cuts, the probability will be lower.

Now let us revisit the question of what strategy UPS should pursue. If UPS does not cut prices, its profits are $100 million. If it cuts prices, its expected profits are $(.70) \times \$0 + (.30) \times \$180 = \$60$ million. Since $60 million is less than $100 million, UPS should not pursue the price cutting strategy. If it did, FedEx would probably respond, and the net effect would be to depress UPS's profitability. Another way of looking at this scenario is to ask under what assumptions about the probability of FedEx's responding it would be worthwhile for UPS to cut prices by 15 percent. For UPS to move forward with its price cuts, the expected profits from doing so must be greater than $100 million, which is the profit from doing nothing. The way to work this out is to find the probability for which UPS is indifferent between leaving prices unaltered or changing them. Signifying probability by p, $\$100m = p \times \$180m$, and solving for p, $p = \$100m/\$180m = 0.556$. In other words, for UPS to go ahead with the proposed price cut, the probability that FedEx will do nothing must be greater than 55.6 percent.

Know Thy Rival. At this juncture, the question of whether this example is rather contrived might arise. After all, could UPS managers *really* anticipate how FedEx's profits could be affected if UPS cut its prices by 15 percent? And could UPS really assign a probability to FedEx's likely response? The answer is that although UPS's managers cannot calculate exactly what the profit impact and probabilities would be, they can make an informed decision by collecting competitive information and thinking strategically. For example, they could estimate FedEx's cost structure by looking at FedEx's published financial accounts. And because they are in the same business as FedEx and use the same basic business model, they can assess the effect of falling demand on FedEx's cost structure and bottom line. Moreover, by looking at the history of FedEx's competitive behavior, they can assess how FedEx will respond to a price cut.

This illustrates a second basic principle of game theory: know thy rivals. In other words, in thinking strategically, managers put themselves in the position of a rival to answer the question of how that rival is likely to act in a particular situation. If a company's managers are to be effective at looking forward and reasoning back, they must have a good understanding of what their rival is likely to do under different scenarios, and they need to be able to extrapolate their rival's future behavior based on this understanding.

Find the Most Profitable Dominant Strategy. A **dominant strategy** is one that makes you better off than you would be if you played any other strategy, *no matter what strategy your opponent uses*. To grasp this concept, consider a simultaneous move game based on a situation that developed in the U.S. car industry in the early 1990s (so far we have been considering a sequential move game). Two car companies, Ford and GM, both differentiators, have to decide whether to introduce cash-back rebate programs in November to move unsold inventory that is building up on the lots of car dealers nationwide. Each company can make one of two moves: offer rebates or do not offer rebates. Because the advanced planning associated with launching such a strategy is fairly extensive, both companies must make a decision about what to do by mid-October, which is before they have had a chance to see what their rival is doing.

In each of the previous four years, both companies have introduced just such programs on November 1 and kept them in place until December 31. Customers have become conditioned to expect these programs and increasingly have held back their new car purchases in anticipation of the cash rebate programs beginning in November. This learned behavior by customers has increased the strategic importance of the rebate programs and made the rebate programs themselves increasingly expensive for the automobile companies. Figure 5.4 lays out a payoff matrix associated with each strategy.

The four cells in this matrix represent the four possible outcomes of pursuing or not pursuing a cash rebate strategy. The numbers in parentheses in the center of each cell represent the profit that General Motors and Ford, respectively, will get in each case (in millions of dollars). If both General Motors and Ford decide not to introduce cash rebates (Cell 1), each will get $800 million in profit for the November 1–December 31 period. If GM introduces a cash rebate program but Ford doesn't, GM will gain market share at Ford's expense, and GM will get $1,000 million in profit, while Ford gets just $200 million (Cell 2). The converse holds if Ford introduces a rebate program but GM doesn't (Cell 3). If both companies introduce rebate programs, both get $400 million (remember, the rebates are expensive and essentially represent deep price discounting to move unsold inventory)(Cell 4). Finally, the figures in parentheses in the lower-left-hand corner of each cell represent the joint profit associated with each outcome.

If you look at this payoff matrix, you will see that GM's dominant strategy is to offer cash rebates because whatever strategy Ford pursues, GM does better if it offers cash rebates than if it doesn't. If Ford's strategy is to offer no cash rebates, GM's best strategy is to offer rebates and capture a profit of $1,000 million. If Ford's strategy is

FIGURE 5.4

A Payoff Matrix for
GM and Ford

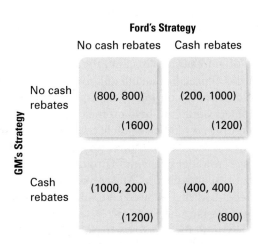

to offer cash rebates, GM's best strategy is again to offer cash rebates and get a profit of $400 million. So whatever Ford does, GM's best strategy is to offer cash rebates.

An interesting aspect of this game is that Ford also goes through the same reasoning process. Indeed, the payoff matrix shows that Ford's dominant strategy is also to offer cash rebates. The net result is that while both players get $400 million profit, the combined payoff of $800 million is the lowest of any combination! Clearly, both automakers could have done better if they had cooperated and jointly decided not to offer cash rebates. Why didn't they do this? There are two reasons. First, cooperation to set prices is illegal under U.S. antitrust law. Second, even though neither party will gain from offering rebates, *it cannot trust the other party not to offer cash rebates since then it would be even worse off.* As the payoff matrix shows, if Ford does not offer cash rebates, GM has a very big incentive to do so, and vice versa. So both companies assume that the other will offer rebates, both end up doing so, and customers receive the value and are the winners!

The payoff structure in this game is very famous. It is known as the *prisoner's dilemma game* because it was first explained using an example of two suspects, or "prisoners," who are being interrogated for possible involvement in a crime. In the original exposition, the prisoners could confess to the crime and also implicate their partner in the crime to get a reduced sentence, or not confess or implicate the other. If the other prisoner also either doesn't confess or implicate the other, they both end up going free. The problem is that neither prisoner can trust the other not to implicate the other in order to get a reduced sentence. So to reduce their losses (length of jail time), both end up confessing and implicate the other, and both go to jail.

The prisoner's dilemma is thought to capture the essence of many situations where two or more companies are competing against each other and their dominant strategy is to fight a price war, even if they would collectively be better off by *not* doing so. In other words, the prisoner's dilemma can be used to explain the mutually destructive price competition that breaks out in many industries from time to time. It also raises the question of whether companies can do anything to extricate themselves from such a situation. This brings us to the final principle of game theory explored here.

Strategy Shapes the Payoff Structure of the Game. An important lesson of game theory is that through its choice of strategy, a company can alter the payoff structure of the competitive game being played in the industry. To understand this, consider once more the cash rebate game played by Ford and GM where both companies are compelled to choose a dominant strategy that depresses total payoffs. How can they extricate themselves from this predicament? By changing the behavior of customers.

Recall that rebates were necessary only because customers had come to expect them and held off purchasing a car until the rebates were introduced. In a self-fulfilling prophecy, this depresses demand and forces the companies to introduce rebates to move unsold inventory on the lots of car dealers. If these expectations could be changed, customers would not hold off their purchases in anticipation of the rebates being introduced in November of each year. Companies would no longer have to introduce rebates to move unsold inventory on the lots of car dealers. So how can a company change customer behavior? Through its choice of strategy.

This is what GM actually did. After several years of rebate wars, GM decided to issue a new credit card that allowed cardholders to apply 5 percent of their charges toward buying or leasing a new GM car, up to $500 a year with a maximum of $3,500.

The credit card launch was one of the most successful in history: within two years, there were 9 million GM credit card holders, and the card had replaced the other incentives that GM offered, principally the end-of-year cash rebates. Because of the card, price-sensitive customers who typically waited for the rebates could purchase a reduced price car any time of the year. Moreover, once they had the card, they were much more likely to buy from GM than Ford. This strategy changed customer behavior. Customers no longer waited for rebates at the end of the year before buying, an inventory of unsold cars did not build up on the lots of dealers, and GM was not forced into fighting a rebate war to clear inventory.

If this strategy was so successful what was to stop Ford from imitating it? Nothing! Ford began to offer its own credit card soon after GM. In this case, however, imitation of the strategy led to increased profitability because both GM and Ford had found a clever way to differentiate themselves from each other: by issuing credit cards that created stronger brand loyalty. With the new cards, a GM cardholder was more likely to buy a GM car and a Ford cardholder was more likely to buy a Ford car. By reducing the tendency of customers to play GM and Ford dealers off against each other, the card also had the effect of enabling both GM and Ford to raise their prices. Figure 5.5 illustrates how strategy can change the payoff matrix.

By issuing credit cards and strengthening the differentiation component of their strategy, both Ford and GM reduced the value of cash rebates and made it less likely that customers would switch to the company that offers rebates. The payoff structure of the game changed and so did the dominant strategy. Now that GM's dominant strategy is to not offer cash rebates, for whatever Ford does, GM is better off by not offering rebates. The same is true for Ford. In other words, by their choice of strategy, General Motors and Ford have changed their dominant strategy in a way that boosts their profitability.

More generally, this example suggests that the way out of mutually destructive price competition associated with a prisoner's dilemma type of game is for the players to change their business models and differentiate their product offerings in the minds of customers, thereby reducing their sensitivity to price competition. In other words, by their choice of strategy and business model (one principally based on differentiation), companies can alter the payoff structure associated with the game, alter their dominant strategy, and move it away from a prisoner's dilemma type of game structure.

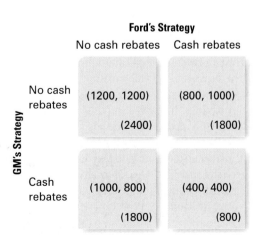

FIGURE 5.5

Altered Payoff Matrix for GM and Ford

This insight also points to the need for companies to think through how their choice of business strategy might change the structure of the competitive game they are playing. Although we have looked at how strategy can transform the payoff structure of the game in a way that is more favorable, the opposite can and does occur. Companies often unintentionally change their business models and pursue strategies that change the payoff structure of the game in a way that is much less favorable to them, and comes to resemble a prisoner's dilemma, as the competitive dynamics between Coca-Cola and PepsiCo in the soft drinks industry suggest in Strategy in Action 5.5.

In retrospect, what happened was that the Pepsi challenge changed the long-established competitive rules in the industry. As the basis of competition shifted from differentiation by abstract lifestyle advertising to direct product comparisons, and then to price competition, the payoff structure associated with their game changed and became more of a prisoner's dilemma type of structure. Had Pepsi's managers looked ahead and reasoned back, they might have realized that price competition would be the outcome of its new aggressive strategy and might not have launched the Pepsi challenge, especially because the company was gaining market share from Coke, albeit slowly. However, because Pepsi's strategy changed the nature of differentiation in the industry, it led to a lose-lose situation.

Strategy in Action   5.5

Coca-Cola and PepsiCo Go Head to Head

For thirty years, until the late 1970s, the cola segment of the soft drink industry went through a golden age in which the main players, Coca-Cola and PepsiCo, were very profitable. These two companies competed against each other on the basis of advertising their products, Coke and Pepsi, based on abstract lifestyle product attributes. PepsiCo would introduce advertisements showing that it was cool to drink Pepsi, and Coca-Cola would produce advertisements with catchy jingles such as "Things go better with Coke." Neither company competed on price. Coke led the market throughout the period, although by the mid-1970s, Pepsi was closing in.

It was at this juncture that Pepsi launched a new and innovative strategy: the Pepsi challenge. The Pepsi challenge was a taste test in which customers were blindfolded and asked which drink they preferred, Pepsi or Coke. In the test, about 55 percent of customers consistently said they preferred Pepsi, a significant result given that Pepsi trailed Coke in market share. Pepsi test-marketed the Pepsi challenge in Dallas, and it was so successful that in the late 1970s, it rolled out the challenge nationally, a situation that presented a real dilemma for Coke. It could

not respond with its own blind taste test, because in the tests, the majority of people preferred Pepsi. Moreover, the Pepsi challenge had changed the nature of competition in the industry. After thirty years of competition through product differentiation based on lifestyle product attributes with no direct (and aggressive) product comparisons, Pepsi had shifted to a direct product comparison based on a real attribute of the product: taste.

PepsiCo had altered its business model and changed how it chose to differentiate its product from Coke. As Pepsi was now gaining market share, Coca-Cola's managers decided to make an aggressive response: deep price discounts for Coke in local markets where they controlled the Coke bottler and the local Pepsi bottler was weak. This was a successful move; in markets where price discounting was used, Coke started to gain its share back. PepsiCo then decided to respond in kind and cut prices too. Before long, price discounting was widespread in the industry. Customers were coming to expect price discounting, brand loyalty had been eroded, and the value associated with differentiation had been reduced. Both Coke and Pepsi experienced declining profitability.

So how did the soft drink manufacturers try to extricate themselves from this situation? Over the course of a few years, they once more shifted the way in which they differentiated their products. They introduced new products, such as Diet Coke and Cherry Coke, to rebuild brand loyalty, and they reemphasized abstract advertising by using celebrities to help create a brand image for their soda, thus differentiating it from their competitors' offerings and reducing customer price sensitivity. They are still doing this today, advertising Pepsi, for example, using the gyrations and music of Brittney Spears as a device for building a brand image that differentiates its offering from Coke. However, it took several years for Pepsi and Coke to do this, and in the interim they had to grapple with a payoff structure that reduced profitability in the industry; moreover, price discounting is still common today.

Summary of Chapter

1. Business-level strategy refers to the way strategic managers devise a plan of action to use a company's resources and distinctive competencies to gain a competitive advantage over rivals in a market or industry.

2. At the heart of developing a generic business-level strategy are choices concerning product differentiation, market segmentation, and distinctive competency. The combination of those three choices results in the specific form of generic business-level strategy employed by a company.

3. Cost leadership, differentiation, cost leadership and differentiation, focused low cost, and focused differentiation are generic competitive strategies. Each has advantages and disadvantages. A company must constantly manage its strategy; otherwise, it risks being stuck in the middle.

4. Most industries are composed of strategic groups: groups of companies pursuing the same or a similar business-level strategy. The members of a strategic group constitute its immediate competitors. Because different strategic groups are characterized by different opportunities and threats, it may pay a company to switch strategic groups. The feasibility of doing so is a function of the height of mobility barriers.

5. The choice of investment strategy for supporting the competitive strategy depends on the strength of a company's competitive position in the industry and the stage of the industry's life cycle. The main types of investment strategy are share building, growth, share increasing, hold-and-maintain, profit, market concentration, asset reduction, harvest, turnaround, liquidation, and divestiture.

6. Game theory offers a number of interesting insights into the kinds of competitive moves and tactics that companies can adopt to increase the returns from pursuing their business-level strategies. Some principles of game theory are look forward and reason back, know thy rival, find the most profitable dominant strategy, remember that strategy can alter the payoff structure of the game, and use strategy to change the payoff structure of the game.

Discussion Questions

1. Why does each generic competitive strategy require a different set of product, market, and distinctive competency choices? Give examples of pairs of companies in (a) the computer industry and (b) the auto industry that pursue different competitive strategies.

2. How can companies pursuing a cost-leadership, differentiation, or focus strategy become stuck in the middle? In what ways can they regain their competitive advantage?

3. Over an industry's life cycle, what investment strategy choices should be made by (a) differentiators in a strong competitive position and (b) differentiators in a weak competitive position?

4. How do technical developments affect the generic strategies that companies in an industry pursue? How might they do so in the future?

5. Why is it difficult for a company in one strategic group to change to a different strategic group?

6. What insights would game theory offer (a) a small pizza place operating in a crowded college market and (b) a detergent manufacturer seeking to bring out new products in established markets?

Practicing Strategic Management

SMALL-GROUP EXERCISE: FINDING A STRATEGY FOR A RESTAURANT

Break up into groups of three to five people. You are a group of partners contemplating opening a new restaurant in your city and trying to decide what business-level strategy can provide your restaurant with the best competitive advantage to make it as profitable as possible.

1. Create a strategic group of the restaurants in your city, and define their generic strategies.
2. Identify which restaurants you think are the most profitable and why.
3. On the basis of this analysis, decide what kind of restaurant you want to open and why.

ARTICLE FILE 5

Find an example (or several examples) of a company pursuing one of the generic business-level strategies. Which strategy is it? What product, market, or distinctive competency choices is it based on? What are its advantages and disadvantages?

STRATEGIC MANAGEMENT PROJECT: MODULE 5

This part of the project focuses on the nature of your company's business-level strategy. If your company operates in more than one business, concentrate on either its core, or most central, business or on its most important businesses. Using all the information you have collected on your company so far, answer the following questions:

1. How differentiated are the products or services of your company? What is the basis of their differentiated appeal?
2. What is your company's strategy toward market segmentation? If it segments its market, on what basis does it do so?
3. What distinctive competencies does your company have? (Use the information from the module on func-

tional-level strategy in the last chapter to answer this question.) Is efficiency, quality, innovation, responsiveness to customers, or a combination of these factors the main driving force in your company?
4. Based on these product, market, or distinctive competency choices, what generic business-level strategy is your company pursuing?
5. What are the advantages and disadvantages associated with your company's choice of business-level strategy?
6. Is your company a member of a strategic group in an industry? If so, which one?
7. What investment strategy is your company pursuing to support its generic strategy? How does this match the strength of its competitive position and the stage of its industry's life cycle?
8. How could you improve its business-level strategy to strengthen its competitive advantage?

EXPLORING THE WEB
Visiting the Luxury Car Market

Enter the web sites of three luxury car makers such as Lexus (**www.lexususa.com**), BMW (**www.bmw.com**), and Cadillac (**www.cadillac.com, www.gm.com**), all of which compete in the same strategic group. Scan the sites to determine the key features of each company's business-level strategy. In what ways are their strategies similar and different? Which of these companies do you think has a competitive advantage over the others? How could these companies use game theory in deciding how to compete?

General Task: Search the Web for a company pursuing a low-cost strategy, a differentiation strategy, or both. What product, market, or distinctive competency choices has it made to pursue this strategy? How successful has it been in its industry using this strategy?

Closing Case

How E*Trade Uses the Internet to Gain a Low-Cost Advantage

In many industries, new entrants have taken advantage of the opportunities opened up by the Internet to overcome barriers to entry and compete successfully against market leaders. Consider the situation of E*Trade, the online brokerage company. For many years, large, established brokerages like Merrill Lynch had dominated the industry

and used their protected positions to charge high brokerage fees. E*Trade's managers bought and developed software and hardware that allowed their customers to make their own trades and to do so at a price as low as $19.95.

The low-cost competition story in the brokerage industry did not stop here. By 1999, E*Trade itself came under pressure from a new generation of online brokerage houses such as Suretrade, Ameritrade, and DLJ, which began offering customers trades for only $9.95 and even $7.95, undercutting E*Trade's prices by 100 percent. How could E*Trade, which had made its reputation by being the low-cost leader in the industry, compete against companies boasting that *they* were the new cost leaders?

The answer for E*Trade was to enhance its differentiated appeal to its customers by offering a higher quality of service and a broader product line. E*Trade introduced a new software package that made it even easier for customers to use the Internet to trade shares. Very importantly, the new software was more reliable in that customers were able to make their trades when they wanted. Previously, E*Trade, like other brokerage companies, had experienced many problems when too many customers made trades at once; often the overloaded system simply crashed, and customers were unable to buy or sell shares. In addition, E*Trade's new package offered customers more financial research tools and gave them access to more information about specific companies to aid in their investment decisions. E*Trade also offered customers increased access to real-time stock quotes so that they could take advantage of second-to-second changes in stock prices to make money. Finally, it offered customers the opportunity to invest in initial public offerings of shares from new companies, where both potential risks and returns are high.

In 1999, E*Trade decided to merge with an online bank, Telebank, in order to offer its customers a broad range of online banking services such as bill paying online and thus become a one-stop online shopping site for all of a customer's financial needs. It also took over a variety of other insurance and financial service companies to offer its customers a broad financial service product line.

The realization that it could not just be a low-cost company but also had to create a differentiation advantage in the quickly evolving online financial services industry has paid off for E*Trade. Its customers did not switch to the new low-cost leaders because customers perceived that for the $19.95 price, they were receiving extra value for money in terms of service and reliability. E*Trade's customer accounts have increased steadily and its stock price rose as investors perceive that the company's competitive advantage is sustainable and that the company is likely to remain a dominant player in the changed industry environment. Indeed, E*Trade has shown the other companies in the industry that to remain viable, they must all pursue a simultaneous low-cost and differentiation strategy—something that has become possible only because of the emergence of the Internet, which has created external economies that companies can exploit to increase their performance and competitive advantage.

Case Discussion Questions

1. How has E*Trade's business-level strategy changed over time?

2. What is happening in the stock brokerage industry today? How has E*Trade been altering its business-level strategy to compete?

Sources: www.E*trade.com (1999). www.E*trade.com, Press Releases (1999).

6

Competitive Strategy and the Industry Environment

Opening Case

Information Technology, the Internet, and Changing Strategies in the Fashion World

Well-known fashion houses like Channel, Dior, Gucci, and Armani charge thousands of dollars for the fashionable collections of suits and dresses that they introduce twice yearly in the fall and in the spring. Only the very rich can afford such differentiated and expensive clothing, however, so to expand demand for its luxury products, most luxury designers produce less expensive lines of clothing and accessories that are sold in upscale fashion retailers such as Neiman Marcus, Nordstrom, and Saks Fifth Avenue.

Both fashion clothes designers and retailers have experienced enormous problems in the past decade. New kinds of competitors have taken advantage of the opportunities opened by the Internet and advances in information technology (IT) to enter the high fashion market segment and compete head-to-head with them by offering high-quality clothes at significantly lower prices. Essentially, all of these new competitors have developed capabilities in using IT that allow them to pursue a focused differentiation strategy but at a much lower cost than the luxury fashion houses. This has allowed them to circumvent barriers to entry into the high fashion segment and develop well-received brand names.

First, upscale department stores and retail chains like Dillard's and Macy's, which target the middle of the fashion clothing market, have developed their own store-specific prestigious clothing labels. These well-made clothes are often sold at a significant price discount from luxury brands and thus attract customers away. Second, many small, agile fashion designers such as England's Jaeger and Laura Ashley and Spain's Zara now produce fashionable clothes at lower prices and sell them in their own chains of clothing stores. Zara, in particular, has achieved significant success, and its sales have soared. It has managed to position itself as the low price and cost leader in the fashion segment of the clothing market because it has created innovative information systems that lower costs and speed time to market.

Zara uses IT to manage the interface between its design and manufacturing operations efficiently. Major fashion houses like Dior and Gucci can take six or more months to design their collections and then three to six more before their moderately priced lines become available in upscale retailers. Zara's designers closely watch the trends in the high fashion industry and the kinds of innovations that the major houses are introducing. Then using their information systems, which are linked to their suppliers and the low-cost manufacturers it uses abroad, its designers can create a new collection in only five weeks, and these clothes can then be made in a week and in its stores soon after. This short time to market gives Zara great flexibility and has allowed it to compete effectively in the rapidly changing fashion market, where customer tastes evolve quickly.

IT also gives it instantaneous feedback on which of its clothes are selling well and in which countries, which gives it a competitive advantage because Zara can engage in constant product development and remain at the cutting edge of fashion, a major source of differentiation advantage. For example, Zara can manufacture more of a particular kind of dress or suit to meet high customer demand and constantly change the mix of clothes it offers customers in its rapidly expanding network of global stores to keep up with fashion. Moreover, it can do this at relatively small output levels, part of a specialized, focused strategy.

Indeed, another important aspect of Zara's competitive strategy is that its use of IT allows it to minimize the inventory it has to carry—the major cost of goods sold of a clothing maker/retailer—and thus is a major driver of profitability. Because of the quick manufacturing-to-sales cycle and just-in-time fashion, Zara has been able to offer its collections at comparatively low prices and still make profits that are the envy of the fashion clothing industry. Indeed, pricing has become the major competitive tool for managing competition in the fashion industry. When Zara offered its shares to the public for the first time in 2001, its shares soared in price due to its high return on invested capital. Investors believe that there will soon be a chain of Zara stores in most major cities across the world as its name becomes as common to customers as those of well-known designers.

The other clothing design and retail companies have woken up to the threat posed by companies like Zara. Many retailers have pioneered their own proprietary lines of clothes (Dillard's Daniel Cremeaux line is one) and use a similar strategy to Zara's. Clothing designers like Ralph Lauren and Tommy Hilfiger have been forced to adopt similar approaches, bringing out new clothes collections several times a year and instituting price markdowns to sell inventory quickly. Even the major fashion houses have taken note of what is happening. Gucci, for example, which began to experience problems in the 1990s, brought in Thomas Ford, an American, as its chief designer and invested its resources to produce a new Ford-designed clothes line for both men and women to attract back Gucci's customers. Using IT, Gucci has also been able to design, manufacture, and distribute its clothing at a faster rate too.

Increasingly, these companies are realizing that maintaining a competitive advantage and superior profitability cannot be achieved by brand image alone; all clothing companies must learn to use competitive moves and tactics to defend their differentiated appeal, something that can be quickly lost in today's fast-changing global marketplace.

Sources: www.zara.com (2002). www.gucci.com (2002). C. Vitzthum, "Just-in-Time-Fashion," *Wall Street Journal,* May 18, 2001, pp. B1, B4.

Overview

If strategic managers do succeed in developing a successful generic business-level strategy, they still face another crucial issue: positioning their company to sustain its competitive advantage over time in different kinds of industry environments. Different industry environments present particular kinds of opportunities and threats for companies, and a company's business model has to adapt and change to meet the changing environment. Various kinds of competitive maneuvers, gambits, and tactics become appropriate in different kinds of environment.

This chapter begins by examining the way in which companies in fragmented industries try to develop competitive strategies that support their generic strategies. It then considers the challenges of developing and sustaining a competitive advantage in embryonic, growth, mature, and declining industries.

By the end of this chapter, you will understand how the successful pursuit of a generic strategy depends on the selection of the right competitive strategy to manage the industry environment.

Strategies in Fragmented Industries

A *fragmented industry* is one composed of a large number of small and medium-sized companies—for example, the dry cleaning, restaurant, health club, and the legal services industries. There are several reasons that an industry may consist of many small companies rather than a few large ones.[1]

First, fragmented industries are characterized by low barriers to entry because of the lack of economies of scale. Many home buyers, for example, have a preference for dealing with local real estate agents, whom they perceive as having better local knowledge than national chains. Second, in some industries, there may even be diseconomies of scale. In the restaurant business, for example, customers often prefer the unique food and style of a popular local restaurant rather than the standardized offerings of some national chain. Third, low entry barriers that permit constant entry by new companies also serve to keep an industry fragmented. The restaurant industry exemplifies this situation. The costs of opening a restaurant are moderate and can be borne by a single entrepreneur. High transportation costs, too, can keep an industry fragmented, and local or regional production may be the only efficient way to satisfy customers' needs, as in the cement business. Finally, an industry may be fragmented because customers' needs are so specialized that only small job lots of products are required, and thus there is no room for a large mass-production operation to satisfy the market.

For some fragmented industries, these factors dictate the competitive strategy to pursue, and the *focus strategy* stands out as a principal choice. Companies may specialize by customer group, customer need, or geographic region, so that many small specialty companies operate in local or regional market segments. All kinds of custom-made products—furniture, clothing, hats, boots, and so on—fall into this category, as do all small service operations that cater to particular customers' needs, such as laundries, restaurants, health clubs, and furniture rental stores. Indeed, service companies make up a large proportion of the enterprises in fragmented industries because they provide personalized service to clients and therefore need to be responsive to their needs.

Strategic managers are eager to gain the cost advantages of pursuing a low-cost strategy or the sales-revenue-enhancing advantages of differentiation by circumventing the problems of a fragmented industry and finding a way to consolidate it. Consolidated industries offer much higher potential returns, and during the past thirty years, many companies have developed competitive strategies to consolidate fragmented industries and obtain these returns. These companies include large retailers such as Wal-Mart and Target, fast food chains such as McDonald's and Burger King, video rental chains such as Blockbuster Video and Hollywood Video, chains of health clubs such as Bally's and President and First Lady, repair shops like Midas Muffler, and even lawyers, consultants, and tax preparers. To grow, consolidate their industries, and become the industry leaders, these companies have pioneered new business models and used several specific strategies such as chaining, franchising, horizontal merger, and also using the Internet and IT.

Many of these pioneered a new business model in an industry that lowers costs or confers a differentiation advantage (or both). The way that a company can do this is by competing in a very different way from established rivals. Managers in a fragmented industry must seek out cost or differentiation advantages that others have not recognized. Once a company has a cost or differential advantage, it can increase its revenues at the expense of competitors and consolidate the industry in the process. Moreover, as the company pioneering the new business model grows larger, it may be able to capture additional scale economies and so increase its competitive advantage. The pioneering company can then use its growing cost-based advantage to choose a low-price option, price aggressively, generate high demand, and drive its established rivals out of the industry.

Chaining   Companies such as Wal-Mart and Midas International pursue a **chaining** strategy to obtain the advantages of cost leadership. They establish networks of linked merchandising outlets that are so interconnected that they function as one large business entity. The consolidated buying power that these companies possess through their nationwide store chains allows them to negotiate large price reductions with their suppliers, which promotes their competitive advantage. They overcome the barrier of high transportation costs by establishing sophisticated regional distribution centers, which can economize on inventory costs and maximize responsiveness to the needs of stores and customers. (This is Wal-Mart's specialty.) They also realize economies of scale from sharing managerial skills across the chain and from placing nationwide, rather than local, advertising.

The U.S. food retail business during the 1950s, when supermarkets revolutionized the business model behind the selling of food products, is a good example of the advantages of the chaining business model. Prior to the development of supermarkets, the food retail industry was fragmented with many small mom-and-pop retailers selling a limited range of products and providing full service to customers, including home delivery. Mostly regionally based at first, with fewer than a hundred stores, the first supermarkets differentiated themselves by offering a much larger selection of items in a big store layout. At the same time, they lowered their costs by moving from a full-service to a self-service model (they needed far fewer employees to run a store), and they passed on those cost savings to customers in the form of lower prices. In other words, the supermarkets competed in a very different way from established food retailers: they adopted a new business model.

As the supermarkets started to grow, opening hundreds of more stores, they were able to capture scale economies that were not available to smaller retailers. For example, by clustering their stores around central distribution warehouses in different cities and eventually regions, they were able to gain distribution efficiencies and reduce the amount of inventory they had to hold in a store. Also, by buying from vendors in large quantities, they were able to demand deep price discounts that they passed on to customers in the form of lower prices, enabling them to gain even more market share from smaller retailers. In the 1970s and 1980s, the supermarkets were also the first to introduce information systems based on point-of-sale terminals that tracked the sale of individual items. The information provided enabled the supermarkets to optimize their stocking of items, quickly cutting back on items that were not selling and devoting more shelf space to items that were selling faster. This reducing the need to hold inventory took even more costs out of the systems and ensured a good match between customer demands and items in the supermarket, which further differentiated the supermarkets from smaller retailers. Although these information systems were expensive to implement, the supermarkets could spread the costs over a large volume of sales. The small mom-and-pop retailers could not afford such systems because their sales base was too small. As a consequence of these developments, the food retail industry was becoming consolidated by the 1980s, a trend that is accelerating today. The small mom-and-pop food retailer is now almost extinct.

The new supermarket business model that provided a cost and differentiation advantage over the old established mom-and-pop model has been applied to a wide range of retail industries, consolidating one after the other. Barnes & Noble and Borders applied the supermarket business model to book retailing, Staples applied it to office supplies, Best Buy to electronic retailing, Home Depot to building supplies, and so on. In each case, the company that introduced the new business model helped to change the underlying competitive structure of the industry to its advantage, consolidating the industry and weakening the five forces of competition in the process.

Franchising

For differentiated companies in fragmented industries, such as McDonald's or Century 21 Real Estate, the competitive advantage comes from a business model that employs franchise agreements. In franchising, the franchisor (parent) grants to its franchisees the right to use the parent's name, reputation, and business skills at a particular location or area. When franchisees also manage the business, they are strongly motivated to make the business model work effectively and make sure that quality and standards are consistently high so that customers' needs are always satisfied. Such motivation is particularly critical in a strategy of differentiation, where it is important for a company to maintain its distinctive edge. One reason that industries are fragmented is the difficulty of maintaining control over the many small outlets that must be operated while at the same time retaining their differentiated appeal. The franchising model solves this problem.[2] In addition, franchising lessens the financial burden of swift expansion and so permits rapid growth of the company. Finally, a nationwide franchised company can reap the advantages of large-scale advertising, as well as economies in purchasing, management, and distribution, as McDonald's does very efficiently. Indeed, McDonald's is able to pursue cost leadership and differentiation simultaneously only because franchising allows costs to be controlled locally and differentiation to be achieved by marketing on a national level.

Horizontal Merger

Companies such as Anheuser-Busch, Dillard's Department Stores, and Blockbuster Entertainment have been choosing a strategy of *horizontal merger* to consolidate their respective industries. For example, Dillard's arranged the merger of regional store chains in order to form a national company. By pursuing horizontal merger, companies are able to obtain economies of scale or secure a national market for their product. As a result, they are able to pursue a cost-leadership or a differentiation strategy, or both. The many important strategic implications of horizontal merger are discussed in detail in Chapter 9.

Using IT and the Internet

The arrival of new technology often gives a company the opportunity to develop new business models that can consolidate a fragmented industry. eBay and Amazon.com, for example, used the Internet to develop a new business model—auctions and bookselling—that is consolidating a fragmented industry. Before eBay, the auction business was extremely fragmented, with local auctions in cities being the principal way in which people could dispose of their antiques and collectibles. By harnessing the Internet, eBay can now assure sellers that they are getting wide visibility for their collectibles and are likely to receive a higher price for their product. Similarly, Amazon.com's success in the book market has accelerated the consolidation of the book retail industry, with many small bookstores closing because they cannot compete by price or selection. Clear Channel Communications, profiled in Strategy in Action 6.1, has used many of these methods simultaneously to create a business model that has made it the biggest radio broadcaster in the United States.

The challenge in a fragmented industry is to figure out the best strategy to overcome a fragmented market so that the competitive advantages associated with different generic business-level strategies can be realized. It is difficult to think of any major service activities—from consulting and accounting firms to businesses satisfying the smallest customer need, such as beauty parlors and car repair shops—that have not been consolidated by companies that developed new business models or used franchising and horizontal mergers.

Strategy in Action   6.1

Clear Channel Creates a National Chain of Local Radio Stations

In 2002, Clear Channel Communications, based in San Antonio, Texas, operated over 1,200 U.S. radio stations compared with its largest competitors: Viacom with 186 and Citadel with 205. The company started out with only one station in San Antonio in 1995, something that used to be typical of the radio broadcasting industry. Historically, the industry was fragmented because a federal law prevented any company from owning more than 40 stations nationwide; as a result, a large proportion of the local radio stations were independently owned and operated.

Clear Channel took advantage of the repeal of this law in 1996 to start to buy up radio stations and, most important, find a business model that would allow it to obtain the gains from consolidating this fragmented industry. Its strategic managers recognized from the beginning that the major way to increase the profitability of city and small town radio stations was to obtain economies of scale from operating and marketing on a national level. The issue was to find ways to raise the quality of its programming to increase its value to listeners, increase the number of listeners, and thus increase advertising revenues (because advertising rates are based on the number of listeners). At the same time, it needed to find ways to reduce each station's high operating costs and lower its cost structure. How to do both simultaneously was the challenge.

On the value side of the equation, an important issue that had to be addressed was how to achieve the economies of scale from having a national reach while maintaining the local ties of a station to its community. Many listeners like to feel they are listening to a local station that understands who they are and what their needs are. Yet if all programming and service is handled on a local level, how can economies of scale from a national base be achieved? Most cost savings come from standardization of service across stations, from broadcasting uniform content. Similarly, local listeners often become used to the glitzy, slick productions put on by national cable television broadcasting companies such as MTV and the main TV networks. Because they are national, these companies can afford to pay large sums to stars and celebrities and invest heavily in developing quality products. Such large expenditures are beyond most radio stations' budgets and simply increase the cost of goods sold too much. Moreover, advertising rates had to be kept at a level that both large national companies and small local ones would find acceptable; they could not simply be raised to cover higher costs.

Clear Channel's managers began to experiment with IT and the Internet and took advantage of emerging digital technology that allowed for the easy and rapid manipulation and transfer of large volumes of data. By the late 1990s, music and programming could easily be recorded, stored in digital format, and edited. Its managers hit on a strategy called "voice tracking." To obtain economies of scale, Clear Channel employed popular regional or national DJs to record its daily programs, and these same DJs customize their productions to suit the needs of local markets. For example, one technology allows DJs to isolate and listen to the end of one track and the beginning of the next; then they can insert whatever talk, news, or information that is appropriate between tracks as and when they like. The local stations supply this local information; after they have customized their program, the DJs send it over the Internet, where the local operators handle it. This practice has enormous advantages. On the cost side, the programming costs of a limited number of popular DJs are much lower than the cost of employing an army of local DJs. On the differentiation side, the quality of programming is much higher because Clear Channel can invest more in its programming and because the appeal of some DJs is much higher than others. Over time, higher-quality programming increases the number of listeners, and this attracts more national advertisers, whose digital advertisements can be easily inserted in the programming by local operators.

In addition, Clear Channel is developing its own proprietary brand name, KISS, across its radio stations so that when people travel, they will be attracted to its local stations wherever they are. It also hopes this will stimulate word-of-mouth advertising. As its brand becomes national, this widened scope will attract larger advertisers and boost its sales revenues. To speed this process, it is also now in the process of linking its different businesses—for example, it is the largest billboard and concert operator in the United States—to its KISS label. Through these means, it hopes that increased customer demand will drive up advertising revenues, which will allow it to start or buy more radio stations and expand its reach and thereby lower its cost structure and so increase its future profitability.

Sources: www.clearchannel.com (2002). A. W. Mathews, "From a Distance: A Giant Chain Is Perfecting the Art of Seeming Local," *Wall Street Journal*, February 25, 2002, pp. A1, A4.

Strategies in Embryonic and Growth Industries

As Chapter 2 discusses, an embryonic industry is one that is just beginning to develop, and a growth industry is one in which first-time demand is expanding rapidly as many new customers enter the market. Embryonic and growth industries pose special challenges in choosing and pursuing a business-level strategy because the attributes of customers change as market demand expands and new groups of customers who have new and evolving needs emerge. Also, other factors affect the rate at which a market grows and expands. Strategic managers have to be aware of the way competitive dynamics in embryonic and growth industries change over time because they commonly have to build and develop new kinds of competencies and refine their business models to compete effectively over time.

Most embryonic industries emerge when a technological innovation creates new product or market opportunities that companies start to take advantage of. For example, a century ago, the car industry was born following the development of a new technology, the internal combustion engine, which gave rise to many new products, including the motorcar and motorbus. In 1975, the PC industry was born after new microprocessor technology was developed to build the world's first commercially available PC, the Altair 8800, sold by MITS. Shortly afterward, the PC software industry was born when a Harvard dropout, Bill Gates, and his old school friend, Paul Allen, wrote a version of a popular computer language, BASIC, that would run on the Altair 8800.[3] In 1986, the Internet protocol (IP) network equipment industry was born following the development of the router, an IP switch, by an obscure California start-up, Cisco Systems.

Customer demand for the products of an embryonic industry is frequently limited at first for a variety of reasons. Strategic managers who understand how markets develop are in a much better position to build a business model and strategy that will lead to a sustained competitive advantage. Reasons for slow growth in market demand include (1) the limited performance and poor quality of the first products, (2) customer unfamiliarity with what the new product can do for them, (3) poorly developed distribution channels to get the product to customers, (4) a lack of complementary products to increase the value of the product for customer, and (5) high production costs because of small volumes of production. For example, demand for the first cars was limited by their poor performance (they were no faster than a horse, far noisier, and frequently broke down), a lack of important complementary products such as a network of paved roads and gas stations, and high production costs, which made them a luxury item. Similarly, demand for the first PCs was limited because buyers had to be able to program a computer to use it, and there were no software application programs that could be purchased to run on the PCs. Because of such problems, early demand for the products of embryonic industries comes from a small set of technologically sophisticated customers who are willing to put up with, and may even enjoy, imperfections in the product. Computer hobbyists, who got great joy out of tinkering with their imperfect machines and finding ways to make them work, bought the first PCs.

An industry moves from an embryonic to a growth stage when a *mass market* starts to develop for the industry's product (a mass market is one in which large numbers of customers enter the market). Mass markets typically start to develop when three things occur: (1) ongoing technological progress makes a product easier to use and increases the value of the product to the average customer, (2) key complementary products are developed that do the same, and (3) companies in the industry strive to find ways to reduce production costs so they can lower their cost structure and choose a low price option, and this stimulates high demand.[4] For example, a mass market for cars emerged when (1) technological progress increased the performance of cars, (2) a network of paved roads and gas stations was established (which meant a car could go more places and thus had more value), and (3) Henry Ford began to mass-produce cars, which dramatically lowered production costs and allowed him to reduce prices, causing the demand for cars to surge. Similarly, the mass market for PCs started to emerge when technological advances made them easier to use, a supply of complementary software such as spreadsheets and word processing programs was developed that increased the value of owning a PC, and companies in the industry started to use mass production to build PCs at low cost.

Strategic managers with knowledge about changing market demand can focus on how they must change their business models to build competencies in low-cost manufacturing and product development. For example, they need to share their knowledge with companies that can supply complementary products so that customers will be convinced the new product is worth buying. Another important factor they must understand is how customer groups and needs change over time.

The Changing Nature of Market Demand

The development of most markets follows an S-shaped growth curve similar to that illustrated in Figure 6.1. As the stage of market development moves from embryonic to growth, customer demand first accelerates and then decelerates as a market approaches saturation. As noted in Chapter 2, in a saturated market, most customers have already bought the product, and demand is limited to replacement demand; the market is mature. Figure 6.1 shows that different groups of customers who have different needs enter the market over time.[5]

The first group of customers to enter the market are referred to as the *innovators*. Innovators are "technocrats" who get great delight from being the first to purchase and experiment with products based on a new technology, even though that

FIGURE 6.1

Market Development
and Customer Groups

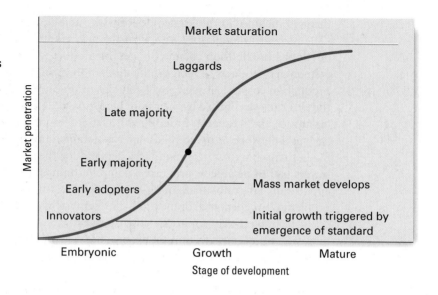

FIGURE 6.1

Market Development
and Customer Groups

technology is imperfect and expensive. They often have an engineering mindset and want to own the technology for its own sake. In the PC industry, the first customers were software engineers and computer hobbyists who wanted to write computer code at home.[6]

The *early adopters* are the second group of customers to enter the market. Early adopters understand that the technology might have important future applications and are willing to experiment with it to see if they can pioneer uses for it, often by finding new ways to satisfy customer needs. Early adopters are often visionaries who appreciate how the technology may be used in the future and try to be the first to profit from its use. Jeff Bezos, the founder of Amazon.com, was an early adopter of the Internet and web-based technology, who saw in 1994 that the Internet could be used in innovative ways to sell books. He saw this possibility before anyone else and was one of the first dot-com pioneers to purchase web servers and related software and use it to sell products over the Internet. Amazon was thus an early adopter.

Both innovators and early adopters enter the market while the industry is in its embryonic stage. The next group of customers, the *early majority,* represents the leading wave or edge of the mass market; their entry signifies the beginning of the growth stage. Customers in the early majority are comfortable with the new technology and products. However, they are pragmatists: they weigh the benefits of adopting new products against their costs and wait to enter the market until they are confident that products will offer them tangible benefits. Once they start to enter the market, however, they do so in large numbers. This is what happened in the PC market after IBM's introduction of the PC in 1981. For the early majority, IBM's entry into the market legitimized the technology and signaled that the benefits of adoption would be worth the costs of purchasing and learning to use the product. The growth of the PC market was then given further impetus by the development of important applications that added value to it, such as new spreadsheet and word processing programs. These applications transformed the PC from a hobbyist's toy into a business productivity tool.

Once the mass market attains a critical mass, with something like 30 percent of the potential market penetrated, the next wave of customers enters the market. This wave is characterized as the *late majority:* the customers who purchase a new technology or product only when it is clear it will be around for a long time. A typical late majority customer group is the customers who started to enter the PC market in the mid-1990s who were older and somewhat intimidated by computers. However, watching others similar to themselves buying PCs to send email and browse the Web, they overcame their hesitancy and started to purchase PCs. By 2002, some 65 percent of homes in the United States had at least one PC, suggesting that the product was well into the late majority group and thus the market was approaching saturation. Indeed, the entry of the late majority signals the end of the growth stage.

Laggards, the last group of customers to enter the market, are inherently conservative and technophobic. They often refuse to adopt a new technology even if its benefits are obvious or unless they are forced by circumstances—to reply to a colleague's email, for example—to do so. People who stick to using typewriters rather than computers to write letters and books could be considered laggards today.

Figure 6.2 looks at the differences among these groups of consumers in a somewhat different way. The bell-shaped curve represents the total market, and the divisions in the curve show the percentage of customers who on average fall into each customer group. The early adopters are a very small percentage of the total customers who will ultimately buy the product. Thus, it illustrates a vital competitive fact: *Most market demand and industry profits arise when the early and late majority enters the market.* And research has found that although many of the early pioneering companies do well in attracting innovators and early adopters, many of these companies often *fail* to attract a significant share of early and late majority customers and ultimately go out of business.

Strategic Implications: Crossing the Chasm

Why are pioneering companies often unable to develop a business model that allows them to become the market leaders? Once again, the issue revolves around understanding the basic issues in business-level strategy: identifying customer needs, identifying customer groups, and choosing distinctive competencies. *Innovators and early adopters have very different customer needs from the early majority.* In an influential book, Geoffrey Moore argued that as a consequence of the differences in customer needs between these groups, the distinctive competencies required for companies to succeed in the emerging mass market are quite different from the distinctive competencies required to succeed in the embryonic market.[7] Therefore,

FIGURE 6.2

Market Share of Different Customer Groups

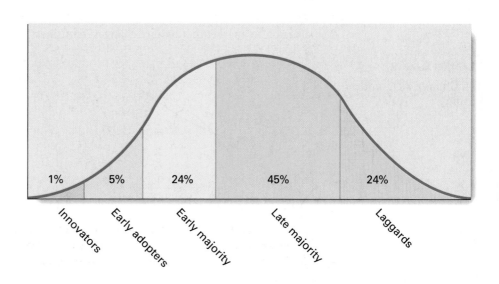

different strategies and business models are often required as a market develops over time for these reasons:

- Innovators and early adopters are technologically sophisticated individuals who are willing to tolerate engineering imperfections in the product. The early majority, however, value ease of use and reliability. Companies competing in an embryonic market typically pay more attention to increasing the performance of a product than to its ease of use and reliability. Those competing in a mass market need to make sure that the product is reliable and easy to use. Thus, the product development capabilities required for success are different as a market develops over time.

- Innovators and early adopters are typically reached through specialized distribution channels, and the products are often sold by word of mouth or focused promotion campaigns. Reaching the early majority requires mass-market distribution channels and mass media advertising campaigns, which require a different set of marketing and sales capabilities.

- Because innovators and the early majority are relatively few in number and are not particularly price sensitive, companies serving them do not need capabilities in mass production. To serve a rapidly growing mass market, large-scale manufacturing capabilities may be critical to ensure that a high-quality product can be produced reliably at a low price point.

In sum, the competencies (resources and capabilities) required to compete in an embryonic market populated by early adopters and innovators are very different from those required to compete in a high-growth mass market populated by the early majority. As a consequence, the transition between the embryonic market and the mass market is not a smooth, seamless one. Rather, it represents a *competitive chasm*, or gulf, that companies must cross. According to Moore, many companies do not or cannot develop the right business model; they fall into the chasm and go out of business. This insight is consistent with the observation that although embryonic markets are frequently populated by large numbers of small companies, once the mass market begins to develop, the number of companies in the marketplace drops off sharply.[8]

Figure 6.3 illustrates Moore's thesis by showing that a wide chasm exists between innovators and early majority, that is, between the embryonic market and the rapidly growing mass market. Note also that other smaller chasms exist between other sets of customers, and that these too represent important, although less dramatic, breaks in the nature of the market that require changes in business-level strategy (for example,

FIGURE 6.3

The Chasm: AOL and Prodigy

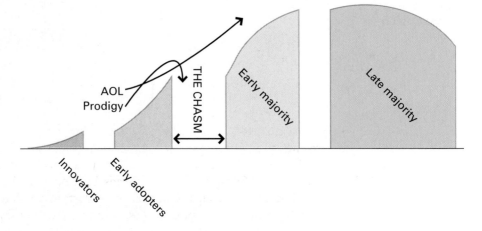

a different approach to market segmentation). The implication of Moore's thesis is that a company must often build new competencies if it is to cross the chasm: it must accumulate new resources and capabilities to build and sustain a competitive advantage. Strategy in Action 6.2 describes how the early leader in online services, Prodigy, fell into the chasm, while AOL successfully crossed it because AOL built competencies that were to be vital in the mass market and Prodigy did not.

To cross this chasm successfully, Moore argues, companies need to find a beachhead, a strategic opportunity, to compete for the mass market. By this, he means that managers must correctly identify the customer needs of the first wave of early majority users who are the leading edge of the mass market. Even in a market where the majority of customers are still innovators and early adopters, some members of the early majority will start to enter. Once companies have identified these customers' needs, they must alter their business model in response by developing new competencies and redesigning products. Strategic managers must also look to their company's value chains and develop distribution channels and marketing strategies for reaching the early majority. They must also design the product so that it matches the needs of the early majority, can be modified easily, and can be produced or provided at low cost. In this way, they will have ready a suitable product, at a reasonable price, that they can sell to the early majority as they start to enter the market in large numbers.

Equally important, industry pioneers must not become too focused on the needs of their early or initial customers because this may lead them to ignore the needs of the early majority, which can lead them to competitive disaster. In fact, anticipating the moves of their competitors by drawing on game theory principles is another useful tool they can use to help them choose the right business model, as the early history of Apple Computer illustrates. Apple stumbled across the leading edge of the early majority in 1979 when it noticed that business customers were beginning to purchase the Apple II in order to run VisiCalc, the first business spreadsheet program made for PCs. It soon became a best-seller and helped to drive sales of the Apple II. However, Apple failed to appreciate the real importance of this event—*that it revealed the needs of business customers*—and instead continued to focus its sales and marketing efforts on computer hobbyists and higher educational institutions, where many of its early adopters were to be found. In fact, Apple had a direct sales force that visited universities but no sales force visiting businesses! Although VisiCalc was helping to sell Apple computers, Apple made no effort to develop its own business applications or get other companies to do so.

Apple had found a beachhead—the developing needs of business customers—but squandered that advantage. It was left to IBM to recognize the importance of the business customer group and develop a business model to meet the needs of the early majority. It entered the market with its IBM PC in 1981, which was an instant success and the beginning of Apple's problems. IBM offered a version of VisiCalc for the IBM PC, along with an early word processing program, Easy Writer. This, together with IBM's established business-focused sales force, soon propelled IBM into a leadership position among the early majority of business and home office users.[9]

Strategic Implications of Market Growth Rates

A final important issue that strategic managers must understand in embryonic and growth industries is that different markets develop at different rates. The rate at which a market develops can be assessed by its growth rate, which measures the rate at which the industry's product spreads in the marketplace. Figure 6.4 charts the growth rates of a number of important products in the United States from their initial introduction to the present time. Although many of these products display the

Strategy in Action

6.2

How Prodigy Fell into the Chasm

Before America Online (AOL) became a household name, Prodigy was a market leader. Founded in 1984, Prodigy was a joint venture between Sears, IBM, and CBS. CBS soon dropped out, but IBM and Sears stuck with it, investing $500 million in developing the network and finally launching it in 1990. The goal was to build the largest proprietary online network whose focus was to be online shopping: the system would give its customers the ability to buy anything, even plane tickets, online. IBM knew about computers, and Sears knew about retail. It seemed like the perfect marriage.

Launched in the fall of 1990, the service quickly accumulated half a million users. There was little sense of competition at the time. The largest competitor, CompuServe, was conservatively managed, and its business model was focused on technical users and financial services (CompuServe was owned by H&R Block, America's largest tax return service). There was another small competitor, AOL, but in the words of one Prodigy executive, "It was just a little thing off to the side." Ten years later, the little thing had become the largest online service in the world, with 33 million members. Prodigy had exited the online business altogether after IBM and Sears had invested, and lost, some $1.2 billion on the venture.

Why did Prodigy fail? The company appeared to be focusing on the mass market. Its target customers were not computer-oriented early adopters but typical middle-class Americans. And its strategy to sell products online seemed correct; surely this ultimately had to become a major application of the Internet. The problem was that the long-term vision was right, but the business model was not. One of the surprise early drivers of customers signing up for online services and the creation of the mass market was email. AOL offered its members unlimited email, while Prodigy charged members a fee for sending more than thirty emails per month—a big difference in business models. Another important application of online service was chatrooms, a service that customers were increasingly embracing. AOL saw chatrooms as one of the unique possibilities of online service for satisfying customer needs and rushed to develop the software that would soon make chatrooms one of its most popular features.

The lawyers at Prodigy's corporate headquarters, however, feared that Prodigy might be held legally liable for comments made in chatrooms or events that arose from them and discouraged Prodigy from offering this service. The same problem hindered Prodigy's introduction of bulletin boards, also a popular feature at CompuServe and AOL. Prodigy introduced bulletin boards but censored them, removing the kind of posting that its lawyers thought might create legal problems. This censorship, lack of chatrooms, and charges for email rankled members, who soon started to switch in droves to AOL.

The nature of the software interface used to allow customers to connect to an online service also became a critical competitive issue as the market developed. When it was introduced, Prodigy's primitive graphical user interface was acceptable by the PC standards of the time, which were based on Microsoft's MS-DOS operating system. When Microsoft introduced its much more user-friendly Windows 3.0 systems in 1990, AOL moved quickly to redesign its software interface to be compatible with Windows, and this made AOL much easier to use. Prodigy, however, was part owned by IBM, which at that time was trying to promote its own new PC operating system—the ill-fated OS/2. So Prodigy dragged its feet. It waited to introduce a Windows version of its own interface until December 1993, by which time it had lost the majority of Windows users to AOL. Prodigy's software was also much more complicated for users to install and update. AOL could be installed on a computer in five minutes, and small updates were installed automatically when the user was online. Prodigy's users had to wait until there was a major revision of the service to obtain new features.

By 1996, it was effectively over. AOL was growing by leaps and bounds, and Prodigy was losing customers at a rapid pace. The combination of a clunky interface, failure to embrace two killer applications that drove online services into the mass market (chatrooms and email), censorship, and slow product development conspired to trip up Prodigy and send it tumbling into the chasm. Meanwhile, AOL, by correctly sensing the product attributes that mass-market customers desired in an online service, crossed the chasm with ease.

Sources: www.aoltimewarner.com (2002). Kara Swisher, *aol.com* (New York: Random House, 1998).

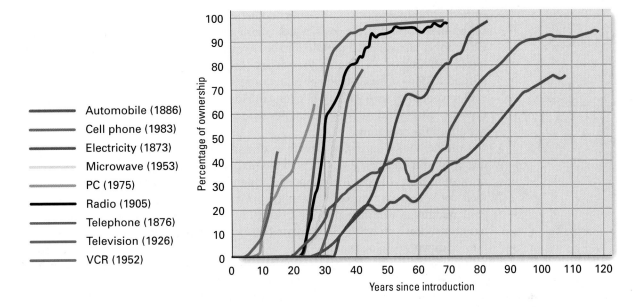

Automobile (1886)
Cell phone (1983)
Electricity (1873)
Microwave (1953)
PC (1975)
Radio (1905)
Telephone (1876)
Television (1926)
VCR (1952)

FIGURE 6.4

Differences in Diffusion Rates

Source: Peter Brimelow, "The Silent Boom," *Forbes,* July 7, 1997, pp. 170–171.
Reprinted by permission of Forbes Magazine © 2002 Forbes, Inc.

classic **S**-shaped growth curve, their markets have grown at different rates. For example, demand for TVs has grown more rapidly than demand for cars. The market growth rates for new kinds of products seem to have accelerated over time, probably because the increasing use of the mass media and low-cost mass production help to accelerate the demand for new products. However, there are also differences in the growth rate for new products introduced at around the same time. For example, the cell phone was introduced somewhat later than the PC, and yet market demand has grown more rapidly. Similarly, following the introduction of the PalmPilot in 1996, demand for hand-held computers has grown even more rapidly than demand for cell phones did.

Factors Affecting Market Growth Rates. A number of factors explain the variation in market growth rates for different products and thus the speed with which a particular industry develops. It is important for strategic managers to understand the source of these differences, for by their choice of strategy and business model, they can accelerate or retard the rate at which a particular market grows.[10] *In other words, business-level strategy is a major determinant of industry profitability.*

The first factor that accelerates customer demand is a new product's *relative advantage,* that is, the degree to which a new product is perceived as better at satisfying customer needs than the product it supersedes. The degree of relative advantage can be measured by the extra value it provides for customers, which can be economic or social in nature. For example, the early growth in demand for cell phones was partly driven by their economic benefits. Early studies showed that because business customers could always be reached by cell phone, they made better use of their time—for example, by not showing up at a meeting that had been canceled at the last minute—and saved two hours per week in time that would otherwise have been wasted. For busy executives, the early adopters, the productivity benefits of owning a cell phone outweighed the costs, which translated into a relative economic advantage. Cell phones also diffused rapidly for social reasons, in particular, because they conferred glamour or prestige on their users (something that also drives demand for advanced kinds of hand-held computers and smart phones). Indeed, it was considered so cool to be seen with a cell phone in Hong Kong in the 1980s that some entrepreneurs established thriving businesses selling fake cell phones to people who could not afford the real thing.

Another factor in driving growth in demand is *compatibility,* which refers to the degree to which a new product is perceived as being consistent with the current needs or existing values of potential adopters. Demand for cell phones grew rapidly because their operation was compatible with the prior experience of potential adopters who used traditional wire-line phones. In contrast, demand for contraceptive products has grown slowly in nations with strong Catholic and Muslim communities because they clash with religious values.

Complexity is a third factor. Complexity is the degree to which a new product is perceived as difficult to understand and use. Early PCs with their clunky operating system interfaces were complex to use, and this held back adoption. The first cell phones were very simple to use, and this accelerated adoption.

A fourth factor is *trialability,* which is the degree to which a new product can be experimented with on a hands-on trial basis. Many people first used cell phones by borrowing one from a colleague to make a call, and this positive experience helped to accelerate growth rates. In contrast, the original PCs were more difficult to obtain to experiment with and use because they were expensive and some training was involved, and this led to slower growth rates.

A fifth factor is *observability,* which refers to the degree to which the results of adopting a new product can be clearly seen and appreciated by other people. The PalmPilot diffused rapidly because it was easy to observe its users scheduling meetings, entering addresses, documenting expenses, and so on. The utility of the device was clear. The same was true of the cell phone and hence its rapid adoption. It was less easy to observe the benefits that many people got from using PCs because they were often used behind closed doors in a business setting.

A final factor that is very important in the growth of many new products is the *availability of complementary products.* Cell phone use grew rapidly because an important complement—a nationwide telecommunications network to route calls—was already in place; cell phone operators merely had to build out cell sites and connect them to that network.

Strategic Implications of Differences in Growth Rates. From a strategic perspective, companies can increase the demand for a new technology or product if they develop a business model that clearly shows its relative advantage, make it as compatible as possible with customers' prior needs and experiences, reduce its complexity, make it possible for customers to try and observe others using the technology or product, and make sure that the necessary complementary products are in place. These considerations must drive product development and a company's business-level strategy. Many companies that have paid attention to these factors have invested in developing the right kinds of distinctive competencies and gained a competitive advantage and market share as a result.

The early success of Apple was based on the fact that the less complex design of its Apple II PC made it easier to use than competing designs. The Apple II also had a relative economic advantage because some key complements (particularly VisiCalc, the first business spreadsheet) soon became available for the machine. As we noted earlier, however, Apple largely squandered its early advantage by not paying attention to the way customer needs were evolving. Similarly, the first Sony PlayStation was very popular because Sony pioneered the marketing strategy of setting up displays in retail stores where potential customers could try a PlayStation and others could observe them trying it.

Another important issue is that new products often spread in a way that is analogous to a viral model of infection. Lead adopters (the first customers who buy a product) in a community become "infected" with the product (enthused by it). Subsequently, they infect other people by telling them about its advantages, and after having observed the benefits of the product, these others also adopt it. A good example of this model of diffusion occurred with Hotmail, the free email service now owned by Microsoft. When it was established, its developers decided to add a tag line on the bottom of the email that read "get your free e-mail at Hotmail.com." This tag line proved remarkably efficient in recruiting new members. Someone would sign on at one institution, say the University of Washington, and send email via Hotmail to friends. Some of the recipients would also sign on. Within a few days, there would be ten members at the University of Washington, then one hundred, and within a month a thousand—all "infected" from the original user.

Companies promoting new products can take advantage of this viral diffusion phenomenon by identifying and aggressively courting potential opinion leaders—customers whose views command respect—in a community. For example, when the manufacturers of new high-tech medical equipment, such as an MRI scanner, start to sell a new product, they first try to get well-known doctors at major research and teaching hospitals to adopt the technology. They may give these opinion leaders free machines for their research purposes and work closely with them in developing the technology. Once these opinion leaders commit to the technology, and particularly if they give it their stamp of approval by using it for research and teaching purposes, doctors at many other hospitals often follow.

In sum, understanding competitive dynamics in embryonic and growth industries is an important strategic issue. The way in which different kinds of customer groups emerge and customer needs change are important determinants of business-level strategy. Similarly, understanding the factors that affect a market's growth rate allow managers to tailor their business model to a changing industry environment. (Much more is said about competition in dynamic, changing, high-tech industries in the next chapter.)

Strategy in Mature Industries

As a result of fierce competition in the shakeout stage, an industry becomes consolidated, and so a mature industry is often dominated by a small number of large companies. Although it may also contain many medium-sized companies and a host of small, specialized ones, the large companies determine the nature of competition in the industry because they can influence the five competitive forces. Indeed, these large companies owe their leading positions to the fact that they developed the most successful generic business-level strategies in the industry.

By the end of the shakeout stage, strategic groups of companies pursuing similar generic competitive strategies have normally emerged in an industry. As we discussed in Chapter 5, for example, companies pursuing a low-cost strategy can be viewed as composing one strategic group, all those pursuing differentiation constitute another, and other companies focusing on particular kinds of market niches form still other strategic groups. Finally, companies whose business models are responding to changing customer needs may be developing both low-cost and differentiation competencies, which will change strategic group structure and promote competition.

As Chapter 5 discusses, companies in an industry constantly analyze each other's business-level strategies, and they know that if they move to change their strategies, their actions are likely to stimulate a competitive response from rivals in their strategic group and other groups that may be threatened by the change in strategy. Industry companies are, in other words, playing a competitive game, and such games can be analyzed using game theory. For example, a differentiator that starts to lower its prices because it has adopted a more cost-efficient technology not only threatens other differentiators in its group, it also threatens low-cost companies, which see their competitive edge being eroded. These other companies may now change their strategies in response, most likely by reducing their prices, as is currently occurring in the PC industry.

Thus, the way one company changes its strategy and fine-tunes its business model over time affects the way the other companies in the industry pursue theirs. Hence, the high level of strategic interdependence that exists in mature, consolidated industries makes it very important for managers to look forward and reason back before launching a strategic initiative. They must think through how their rivals will respond to their actions and pursue a strategy that makes the most sense given this reasoning. In fact, the main issue facing a company in a mature industry is to adopt a competitive strategy that simultaneously enables it to maximize its profitability given the strategies that all other companies in the industry are likely to pursue. No generic strategy will generate above-average profits if competitive forces in an industry are so strong that companies are at the mercy of each other, potential entrants, powerful suppliers, powerful customers, and others. As a result, in mature industries, competitive strategy revolves around understanding how large companies *collectively* try to reduce the strength of industry competition to preserve both company and industry profitability.

Interdependent companies can help protect their competitive advantage and profitability by adopting competitive moves and tactics to reduce the threat of each competitive force. In the next sections, we examine the various price and nonprice competitive moves and tactics that companies use—first, to deter entry into an industry, and second, to reduce the level of rivalry within an industry. Many of these competitive moves and tactics were first understood by applying the principles of game theory to analyzing competitive interactions in a consolidated industry. We then discuss methods that companies can employ to gain more control over suppliers and buyers.

Strategies to Deter Entry: Product Proliferation, Pricing Games, and Maintaining Excess Capacity

Companies can use three main methods to deter entry by potential rivals and hence maintain and increase industry profitability: product proliferation, pricing games, and maintaining excess capacity (see Figure 6.5). Of course, *potential entrants* will try to circumvent such entry-deterring strategies by incumbent companies. Competition is rarely a one-way street.

Product Proliferation. Companies most commonly produce a range of products aimed at different market segments so that they have broad product lines. Sometimes, to reduce the threat of entry, they expand the range of products they make to

FIGURE 6.5

Strategies for
Deterring Entry of
Rivals

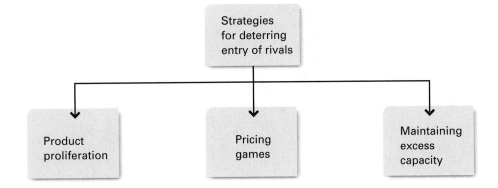

fill a wide variety of niches. This creates a barrier to entry because potential competitors now find it harder to break into an industry in which all the niches are
filled.[11] This strategy of pursuing a broad product line to deter entry is known as
product proliferation.

Because the large U.S. carmakers were so slow to fill the small-car niches (they did
not pursue a product proliferation strategy), they were vulnerable to the entry of the
Japanese into these market segments in the United States in the 1980s. Ford and GM
really had no excuse for this situation, for in their European operations, they had a
long history of small-car manufacturing. Managers should have seen the opening and
filled it ten years earlier, but the (mistaken) view was that "small cars mean small
profits." Better small profits than no profits! In the soap and detergent industry, on
the other hand, competition is based on the production of new kinds of soaps and
detergents to satisfy or create new desires by customers. Thus, the number of soaps
and detergents, and especially the way they are packaged (powder, liquid, or tablets),
proliferates, making it very difficult for prospective entrants to attack a new market
segment.

Figure 6.6 indicates how product proliferation can deter entry. It depicts product
space in the restaurant industry along two dimensions: atmosphere, which ranges
from fast food to candlelight dining, and quality of food, which ranges from average
to gourmet. The circles represent product spaces filled by restaurants located along
the two dimensions. Thus, McDonald's is situated in the average quality/fast food
area. A gap in the product space gives a potential entrant or an existing rival an
opportunity to enter the market and make inroads. The shaded unoccupied product
space represents areas where new restaurants can enter the market. When all the
product spaces are filled, this barrier to entry makes it much more difficult for a new
company to gain a foothold in the market and differentiate itself.

Pricing Games. In some situations, pricing strategies can be used to deter entry
by other companies, thus protecting the profit margins of companies already in an
industry. One entry-deterring strategy is to cut prices every time a new company
enters the industry or, even better, every time a potential entrant is *contemplating*
entry, and then raise prices once the new or potential entrant has withdrawn. The
goal here is to send a signal to potential entrants that new entry will be met with price
cuts. If incumbent companies in an industry consistently pursue such a strategy,
potential entrants will come to understand that their entry will spark off a price war,
the threat of new entry will be reduced, average prices will be higher, and industry
profitability will increase.

FIGURE 6.6

Product Proliferation
in the Restaurant
Industry

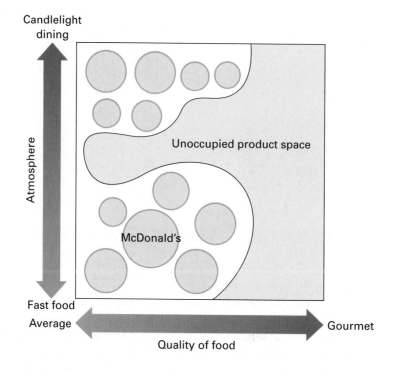

The pricing signal sent must be clear and credible. Put differently, it is important that established companies in the industry develop a reputation for responding to new entry by aggressively cutting prices. If they lack this reputation and do not always cut prices when a new firm enters their industry, the signal will lack credibility, and potential entrants will be more likely to try their luck and risk entry.[12]

Large airlines have been known to pursue such a selective price-cutting strategy to deter budget airlines from entering their most profitable markets. For example, if a budget airline were to try to enter a profitable market, say, flights from New York to Chicago, the response of the established airlines might be to increase the number of daily flights they run between those two cities. Increasing capacity in this manner has the effect of driving down prices and making the market less attractive for the new entrant, which subsequently withdraws from the market. Once the new entrant has gone, the airlines might reduce the number of flights they run per day, thereby raising prices. Companies must be very careful when they pursue such a pricing strategy, however, for it could be perceived as predatory pricing, that is, pricing to drive out competitors, which is illegal under U.S. antitrust law. **Predatory pricing** involves using revenue generated in one product market to support pricing below the company's costs of production in another to drive rivals out of the market.

A second entry deterring pricing strategy is known as limit pricing. **Limit pricing** is a strategy that can be used when the established companies in an industry enjoy scale economies, but those scale economies are not sufficient to deter entry. This is illustrated in Figure 6.7, where the average cost structure of potential new entrants is shown to be higher than the average cost structure of established companies.

The justification is that initially, new entrants will have a lower sales volume than established companies and will not enjoy the same scale economies. However, imagine that for established companies in the industry, the profit-maximizing output is Q_1 and the prevailing price for their product is P_1. This price is above the average cost

FIGURE 6.7

Limit Pricing Strategy

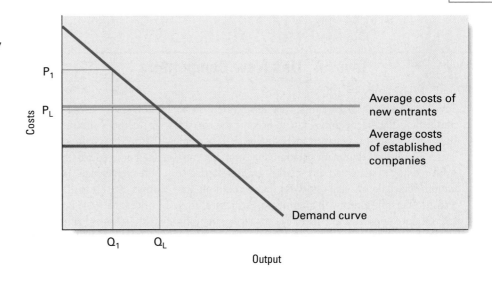

structure of potential new entrants, so although they will not be as profitable as established companies, the potential competitors still have an incentive to enter the market. Established companies can eliminate this incentive by charging a price that is *below* the average cost structure of new entrants, but still *above* their own average cost structure. In Figure 6.7, this price is P_L, which is known as the *limit price.* By adopting such a price, established companies can effectively deter entry and still be profitable. In fact, a limit-pricing strategy may well be consistent with maximizing the long-run profitability of an industry precisely because it reduces the incentive that potential entrants have to enter the market.

However, a limit-pricing strategy will not keep out an entrant that plans to adopt a new technology that will give it a cost advantage over established companies or that has pioneered a new business model that its managers expect will also give it a competitive advantage. In fact, many of the most successful entrants into mature industries are companies that have done just this. For example, the Japanese car companies were able to enter the U.S. market because they had pioneered new lean manufacturing technologies that gave them a cost and quality advantage over established U.S. companies. Today, Japanese car companies' share of the U.S. market is limited only by an informal trade agreement; it could easily double if they were allowed to import all the cars they wished and sell them at whatever price they chose, which might drive one or more U.S. car companies out of the market.

It is also important to note that selective price-cutting and limit-pricing strategies may not deter a strong potential competitor—for example, a leading company in another industry that is trying to find profitable investment opportunities in other industries. It is difficult, for example, to imagine 3M's being afraid to enter an industry because companies there threaten to drive down prices. 3M has the resources to withstand any short-term losses. Hewlett-Packard also had few worries about entering the highly competitive PC industry because of its powerful set of distinctive competencies. Hence, when faced with such a scenario, it may be in the interests of incumbent companies to accept new entry gracefully, giving up market share gradually to the new entrants to prevent price wars from developing and thus save their profits, if this is feasible. As Strategy in Action 6.3 details, Toys 'R' Us has been forced to give up market share in the toy market, and it has lost much of its prominence as a result.

Strategy in Action

6.3

Toys "R" Us's New Competitors

Toys "R" Us, based in Paramus, New Jersey, grew at an astonishing 25 percent annual rate to become the market leader in the retail toy market in 1990 with a 20 percent share. To reach its dominant position, the company consolidated the fragmented toy market by developing a nationwide chain of retail outlets so that it could pursue a cost-leadership strategy. To lower its cost structure, Toys "R" Us developed efficient materials management techniques for ordering and distributing toys to its stores, and it provided a low level of customer service compared to traditional small toy shops. This business model allowed it to achieve a low expense-to-sales ratio of 17 percent, and it then used this favorable cost structure to promote a philosophy of everyday low pricing. The company deliberately set out to undercut the prices of its rivals, and it succeeded: two of its largest competitors, Child World and Lionel went bankrupt.

With its dominant position in the industry established, Toys "R" Us continued to build its chain of toy stores, and it began stocking an ever larger and more complex array of products. This would raise its costs; nevertheless, its managers reasoned that they could afford to do so since they were in the driver's seat, and customers would find more value in a wider toy selection. Moreover, raising prices to customers could offset any cost increases, or perhaps the company could negotiate higher price discounts from toy makers like Mattel or Parker Bros.

The company received a shock in 1995 when its commanding position was threatened by the entry of a new set of rivals. Recognizing the high profits that Toys "R" Us was earning, rapidly expanding companies such as Wal-Mart, Kmart, and Target began to make toy selling a major part of their business model. What could Toys "R" do to stop them? Not much. Because of its failure to control costs, Toys "R" Us could not stop their entry into its business by reducing its prices; in other words, by failing to pursue its cost leadership strategy faithfully, it had lost its ability to play pricing games as it had done with its earlier rivals. The entry of these other companies also reduced its power over its suppliers, the toy makers, because they now had important new customers. Finally, some of the new entrants, Wal-Mart in particular, were

now the cost leaders in the retail industry, and their size gave them the resources to withstand any problems if Toys "R" Us attempted to start a price war. Toys "R" Us had no credible threat to use to threaten them or fend off their challenge. In fact, Wal-Mart simply imitated the Toys "R" Us earlier approach and began selling toys at prices that were below those of Toys "R" Us! Indeed, Toys "R" Us's sales fell from 25 percent in 1990 to 17 percent by 1999, when Wal-Mart became the market leader with 18 percent.

To survive, Toys "R" Us has had to return to its low-cost strategy in its core toy business. It installed new IT to increase the efficiency of its purchasing and distribution operations. It reduced the number of items its stores carry by over 30 percent to slash its cost structure. At the same time, recognizing that it might never be able to match Wal-Mart's low costs, it changed its business model to try to create customer value by developing other kinds of stores for related market segments, such as Kids "R" Us and Babies "R" Us. In 2000, it introduced a new kind of store, Imaginarium, a premier specialty upscale toy retailer, and in this business it pursues a focus differentiation strategy. Each Imaginarium employs a knowledgeable team of "toyologists," expert salespeople extensively trained to provide parents and children with the highest level of one-on-one customer service. It also went online and attempted to develop a major web presence. However, faced with the high costs of online selling today, it subsequently partnered with Amazon.com; toys bought in its shop on Amazon's web site can be picked up at any Toys "R" Us store.

To date, these moves have halted the decline in its market share, and in 2002 it announced a gain of a few points. Its profitability has not increased in any significant way, however, and its new CEO, John Eyles, is striving to work on both the value and cost sides of the equation to find the business model that will work best in the highly competitive toy business.

Sources: M. Maremont and G. Bowens, "Brawls in Toyland," *Business Week,* December 21, 1992, pp. 36–37. S. Eads, "The Toys 'R' Us Empire Strikes Back," *Business Week,* June 7, 1999, pp. 55–59. www.toysrus.co (2002); amazon.com (2002).

Maintaining Excess Capacity. A third competitive technique that allows companies to deter entry involves maintaining excess capacity, that is, maintaining the physical capability to produce more of a product than customers currently demand. Existing industry companies may deliberately develop some limited amount of excess capacity to warn potential entrants that if they enter the industry, existing firms can retaliate by increasing output and forcing down prices until entry would become unprofitable. However, as with selective price cutting, the threat to increase output has to be *credible,* that is, companies in an industry must collectively be able to raise the level of production quickly if entry appears likely.

Strategies to Manage Rivalry

Beyond seeking to deter entry, companies also wish to develop a competitive strategy to manage their competitive interdependence and decrease price rivalry. Unrestricted competition over prices reduces both company and industry profitability. Several competitive tactics and gambits are available to companies to manage industry relations. The most important are price signaling, price leadership, nonprice competition, and capacity control.

Price Signaling. A company's ability to choose the price option that leads to superior performance is a function of several factors, including the strength of demand for a product and the intensity of competition between rivals. Price signaling is a first means by which companies attempt to control rivalry among competitors so as to allow the industry to choose the most favorable pricing option.[13] **Price signaling** is the process by which companies increase or decrease product prices to convey their intentions to other companies and so influence the way they price their products.[14] Companies use price signaling to improve industry profitability.

Companies may use price signaling to announce that they will respond vigorously to hostile competitive moves that threaten them. For example, they may signal that if one company starts to cut prices aggressively, they will respond in kind, a common game theory outcome. A **tit-for-tat strategy** is a well-known price signaling strategy that involves a company's doing exactly what its rivals do: if its rivals cut prices, the company follows; if its rivals raise prices, the company follows. By pursuing this strategy consistently over time, a company sends a clear signal to its rivals that it will match any pricing moves they make, the idea being that, sooner or later, rivals will learn that the company will always pursue a tit-for-tat strategy. Because rivals now know that the company will match any price reductions and cutting prices will only reduce profits, price cutting becomes less common in the industry. Moreover, a tit-for-tat strategy also signals to rivals that price increases will be followed, increasing the probability that rivals will initiate price increases to raise profits. Thus, a tit-for-tat strategy can be a useful way of shaping pricing behavior in an industry.[15]

The airline industry is a good example of the power of price signaling, where prices typically rise and fall depending on the current state of customer demand. If one carrier signals the intention to lower prices, a price war frequently ensues as other carriers copy each other's signals. If one carrier feels demand is strong, it might test the waters by signaling an intention to increase prices, and price signaling thus becomes a competitive tool to obtain uniform price increases. Nonrefundable tickets, another way of obtaining a more favorable pricing option, originated as a market signal by one company that was quickly copied by all other companies in the industry. Carriers recognized that they could stabilize their revenues and earn interest on customers' money if they collectively acted to force customers to assume the risk of buying airline tickets in advance. In essence, price signaling allows companies to give one another information that enables them to understand each other's competitive product or market strategy and make coordinated, price competitive moves.

Price Leadership. **Price leadership**—one company's assuming the responsibility for choosing the most favorable industry pricing option—is a second tactic used to reduce price rivalry and thus enhance the profitability of companies in a mature industry.[16] Formal price leadership, or price setting by companies jointly, is illegal under antitrust laws, so the process of price leadership is often very subtle. In the car industry, for example, prices are set by imitation. The price set by the weakest company—that is, the one with the highest cost structure—is often used as the basis for competitors' pricing. Thus, U.S. carmakers set their prices, and Japanese carmakers then set theirs with reference to the U.S. prices. The Japanese are happy to do this because they have lower costs than U.S. companies, so they make higher profits than U.S. carmakers without competing with them by price. Pricing is done by market segment. The prices of different auto models in the model range indicate the customer segments that the companies are aiming for and the price range they believe the market segment can tolerate. Each manufacturer prices a model in the segment with reference to the prices charged by its competitors, not by reference to competitors' costs. Price leadership also allows differentiators to charge a premium price and helps low-cost companies like Toyota by increasing their margins.

Although price leadership can stabilize industry relationships by preventing head-to-head competition and thus raise the level of profitability within an industry, it has its dangers. It helps companies with high cost structures, allowing them to survive without becoming more productive or more efficient. Thus, it may foster complacency as companies may keep harvesting profits without reinvesting much to improve their productivity. In the long term, such behavior makes them vulnerable to new entrants that have lower costs because they have developed new low-cost production techniques. That is what happened in the U.S. car industry after the Japanese entered the market. After years of tacit price fixing, with GM as the price leader, the carmakers were subjected to growing low-cost Japanese competition, to which they were unable to respond. Indeed, most U.S. carmakers survived only because the Japanese carmakers were foreign firms. Had the foreign firms been new U.S. entrants, the government would probably not have taken steps to protect Chrysler, Ford, or GM.

Nonprice Competition. A third very important aspect of product and market strategy in mature industries is the use of **nonprice competition** to manage rivalry within an industry. Using various tactics and maneuvers to try to prevent costly price cutting and price wars does not preclude competition by product differentiation. Indeed, in many industries, product differentiation is the principal tactic used to prevent competitors from obtaining access to a company's customers and attacking its market share. In other words, companies rely on product differentiation to deter potential entrants and manage rivalry within their industry. Product differentiation allows industry rivals to compete for market share by offering products with different or superior features or by applying different marketing techniques. In Figure 6.8, product and market segment dimensions are used to identify four nonprice competitive strategies based on product differentiation: market penetration, market development, product development, and product proliferation. (Notice that this model applies to new market segments, not new markets.)[17]

FIGURE 6.8

Four Nonprice
Competitive
Strategies

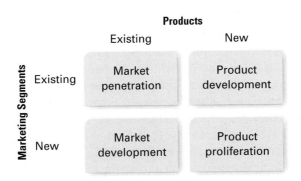

Market Penetration. When a company concentrates on expanding market share in its existing product markets, it is engaging in a strategy of **market penetration.**[18] Market penetration involves heavy advertising to promote and build product differentiation. In a mature industry, the thrust of advertising is to influence customers' brand choice and create a brand-name reputation for the company and its products. In this way, a company can increase its market share by attracting the customers of its rivals. Because brand-name products often command premium prices, building market share in this situation is very profitable.

In some mature industries—for example, soap and detergent, disposable diapers, and brewing—a market-penetration strategy becomes a way of life.[19] In these industries, all companies engage in intensive advertising and battle for market share. Each company fears that by not advertising, it will lose market share to rivals. Consequently, in the soap and detergent industry, Procter & Gamble spends more than 20 percent of sales revenues on advertising, with the aim of maintaining and perhaps building market share. These huge advertising outlays constitute a barrier to entry for prospective entrants.

Product Development. **Product development** is the creation of new or improved products to replace existing ones.[20] The wet-shaving industry depends on product replacement to create successive waves of customer demand, which then create new sources of revenue for companies in the industry. Gillette, for example, periodically comes out with a new and improved razor, such as the Sensor shaving system, which often gives a boost to its market share. Similarly, in the car industry, each major car company replaces its models every three to five years to encourage customers to trade in their old models and buy the new one.

Product development is crucial for maintaining product differentiation and building market share.[21] For instance, the laundry detergent Tide has gone through more than fifty changes in formulation during the past forty years to improve its performance. The product is always advertised as Tide, but it is a different product each year. Refining and improving products is an important competitive tactic in defending a company's generic competitive strategy in a mature industry, but this kind of competition can be as vicious as a price war because it is very expensive and raises costs dramatically.

Market signaling to competitors can also be an important part of a product development strategy. One company may let the others know that it is proceeding with product innovations that will provide a competitive advantage the others will be unable to imitate effectively because their entry into the market will be too late. For example, software companies such as Microsoft often announce new operating systems years in advance. The purpose of the announcement is to deter prospective competitors from making the huge investments needed to compete with the industry leaders and let its customers know that the company still has the competitive edge so important to retaining customers' loyalty. However, preemptive signaling can backfire, as IBM found out when it announced that its PS/2 operating system would not be compatible with the operating systems already standard in the industry. Other companies in the industry collectively signaled to IBM and IBM's customers that they would band together to protect the existing operation systems, thus preserving industry standards and preventing IBM from obtaining a competitive advantage from its new technology. IBM subsequently backed down. If a preemptive move is to succeed, competitors must believe that a company will act according to its signals and stick to its position. If the threat is not credible, the signaling company weakens its position.

Market Development. **Market development** finds new market segments for a company's products. A company pursuing this strategy wants to capitalize on the brand name it has developed in one market segment by locating new market segments in which to compete. In this way, it can exploit the product differentiation advantages of its brand name. The Japanese auto manufacturers provide an interesting example of the use of market development. When they entered the market, each Japanese manufacturer offered a car such as the Toyota Corolla and the Honda Accord aimed at the economy segment of the auto market. Then they upgraded each car over time, and now each is directed at a more expensive market segment. The Accord is a leading contender in the midsize car segment, and the Corolla fills the small-car segment that used to be occupied by the Celica, which is now aimed at a sportier market segment. By redefining their product offerings, Japanese manufacturers have profitably developed their market segments and successfully attacked their industry rivals, wresting market share from these companies. Although the Japanese used to compete primarily as low-cost producers, market development has allowed them to become differentiators as well. Toyota has used market development to pursue a simultaneous low-cost and differentiation strategy.

Product Proliferation. **Product proliferation** can be used to manage rivalry within an industry and to deter entry. The strategy of product proliferation generally means that large companies in an industry all have a product in each market segment or niche and compete head-to-head for customers. If a new niche develops, such as sports utility vehicles, designer sunglasses, or Internet web sites, then the leader gets a first-mover advantage, but soon all the other companies catch up. Once again, competition is stabilized, and rivalry within the industry is reduced. Product proliferation thus allows the development of stable industry competition based on product differentiation, not price—that is, nonprice competition based on the development of new products. The battle is over a product's perceived quality and uniqueness, not over its price.

The story of competition in the hamburger segment of the fast food industry told in Strategy in Action 6.4 illustrates how many of these strategies work in practice.

Capacity Control. Although nonprice competition helps mature industries avoid the cutthroat price cutting that reduces company and industry levels of profitability, price competition does periodically break out when excess capacity exists in an industry. Excess capacity arises when companies collectively produce too much output, and to dispose of it, they cut prices. When one company cuts prices, the

Strategy in Action

6.4

Fast Food Is a Ruthless Business

In the mature and saturated fast food industry, competition for customers by hamburger chains has been intense. McDonald's, the industry leader, has been under intense pressure to maintain its profit margins, because as the price of fast food has fallen, price wars have periodically broken out. Taco Bell started the first price war in the industry when it introduced its $.99 taco. Taken aback, McDonald's and other burger chains, such as Burger King and Wendy's, had to find ways to lower their costs and prices. As a result of price competition, all the burger chains were forced to learn how to lower their cost structures to make a cheaper hamburger. Today, constant innovation in food preparation is the name of the game, and companies have been able to lower their prices.

With most fast food restaurants now offering comparable prices, the focus of competition has shifted to other aspects of their products. First, the major chains competed by introducing bigger burger patties to increase market penetration. Burger King started the battle in an aggressive campaign to increase its market share at the expense of McDonald's. It added a full ounce of beef to its 1.8 ounce regular patty and followed this with an intense advertising campaign based on the slogan, "Get Your Burger's Worth," directed at McDonald's burger, which then was 40 percent lighter. The campaign worked for Burger King for a while, and its market share rose by 18 percent, but then in a nonprice tit-for-tat, McDonald's announced that it would enlarge its regular patty by 25 percent to beat back the challenge from Burger King and from Wendy's, which has always offered a larger burger (and whose "Where's the Beef?" slogan helped it gain market share).

Burger King and McDonald's have also pursued market penetration by opening up new kinds of restaurants to attract customers. Because all of the big chains have thousands of restaurants each, many analysts thought that the market was saturated, meaning that it would not be profitable to open more restaurants. However, McDonald's in particular has opened hundreds of restaurants in new locations, such as gas stations and large retail stores (for example, Wal-Mart), and new kinds of restaurants, such as small ones at airports and those that contain indoor playgrounds. These moves have helped it protect its market share and maintain its margins.

The main burger chains are also constantly experimenting with product development and introducing improved kinds of burgers to appeal to regular customers—burgers that add cheese, bacon, different kinds of vegetables, and exotic sauces, and new kinds of burgers, such as diet or low-fat burgers to attract new customers. They also all introduced whole-meal offerings, such as McDonald's "value meals," to provide a competitive package to attract customers. Individual restaurants are also allowed to customize their menus to suit the tastes of customers in the region in which they are located. For example, McDonald's restaurants in New England have lobster on the menu, and those in Japan serve sushi. Such product development is a major part of competitive strategy in the industry.

Recognizing the competition from other kinds of fast food chains such as those specializing in chicken or Mexican food, the burger chains have also moved to broaden their menus. McDonald's, for example, offers chicken dishes, pizza, and salads and increasingly tries to be a one-stop shop for all kinds of foods. This is a form of product proliferation designed to keep customers coming back. It makes it more difficult for a competitor or potential entrant to find a new food niche to take advantage of and attract away customers.

In the mature fast food industry, developing new competitive strategies to fend off attacks by other companies within the industry and to protect and enhance competitive advantage is a never-ending task for strategic managers. Indeed, recently, a franchisee in Orlando announced a new gourmet McDonald's restaurant. In a restaurant featuring gilded decor and sophisticated game and media rooms, they will serve white pizza, barbecue pizza, crème blur cheesecake with raspberry oculus, and cappuccino. Can this really be McDonald's?

Sources: R. Gibson, "Bigger Burger by McDonald's: A Two Ounce," *Wall Street Journal,* April 18 1996, p. B1. www.mcdonalds.com (2002). D. Leonhardt, "McDonald's: Can It Regain Its Golden Touch?" *Business Week,* February 28, 1998, pp. 22–27. D. Leonhardt and A. T. Palmer, "Getting off Their McButts," *Business Week,* February 22, 1999, pp. 65–66. "Gourmet McDonald's? Central Florida Has It," *Orlando Sentinel,* December 19, 2001, p. A4.

others quickly follow (a game theory prediction; see Chapter 5) because they fear that the price cutter will be able to sell its entire inventory while they will be left with unwanted goods. The result is that a price war develops.

Excess capacity may be caused by a shortfall in demand, as when a recession lowers the demand for cars and causes car companies to give customers price incentives to purchase a new car. In this situation, companies can do nothing except wait for better times. By and large, however, excess capacity results from companies within an industry simultaneously responding to favorable conditions: they all invest in new plants to be able to take advantage of the predicted upsurge in demand. Paradoxically, each individual company's effort to outperform the others means that collectively, the companies create industry overcapacity, which hurts them all, a game theory prediction. Although demand is rising, the consequence of each company's decision to increase capacity is a surge in industry capacity, which drives down prices. To prevent the accumulation of costly excess capacity, companies must devise strategies that let them control—or at least benefit from—capacity expansion programs. Before we examine these strategies, however, we need to consider in greater detail the factors that cause excess capacity.[22]

Factors Causing Excess Capacity. The problem of excess capacity often derives from technological developments. Sometimes new low-cost technology is the culprit because all companies invest in it simultaneously to prevent being left behind. Excess capacity occurs because the new technology can produce more than the old. In addition, new technology is often introduced in large increments, which generate overcapacity. For instance, an airline that needs more seats on a route must add another plane, thereby adding hundreds of seats even if only fifty are needed. To take another example, a new chemical process may operate efficiently only at the rate of a 1,000 gallons a day, whereas the previous process was efficient at 500 gallons a day. If all companies within an industry change technologies, industry capacity may double and enormous problems can result.

Overcapacity may also be caused by competitive factors within an industry. Entry into an industry is one such a factor. The entry of South Korean companies into the global semiconductor industry in the 1990s caused massive overcapacity and price declines. Similarly, the entry of steel producers from the former Soviet Union countries into the global steel market produced excess capacity and plunging prices in the world steel market in the late 1990s and early 2000s. Sometimes the age of a company's plant is the source of the problem. For example, in the hotel industry, given the rapidity with which the quality of hotel furnishings declines, customers are always attracted to new hotels. When new hotel chains are built alongside the old chains, excess capacity can result. Often companies are simply making simultaneous competitive moves based on industry trends, but those moves eventually lead to head-to-head competition. Most fast food chains, for instance, establish new outlets whenever demographic data show population increases. However, the companies seem to forget that all other chains use the same data (they are not fully anticipating their rivals' actions). Thus, a locality that has no fast food outlets may suddenly see several being built at the same time. Whether they can all survive depends on the growth rate of demand relative to the growth rate of the chains.

Choosing a Capacity-Control Strategy. Given the various ways in which capacity can expand, companies clearly need to find some means of controlling it. If they are always plagued by price cutting and price wars, they will be unable to recoup the investments in their generic strategies. Low profitability within an industry caused by overcapacity forces not just the weakest companies but also sometimes the major players as well to exit the industry. In general, companies have two strategic choices: either (1) each company individually must try to preempt its rivals and seize the initiative, or (2) the companies collectively must find indirect means of coordinating with each other so that they are all aware of the mutual effects of their actions.

To *preempt* rivals, a company must forecast a large increase in demand in the product market and then move rapidly to establish large-scale operations that will be able to satisfy the predicted demand. By achieving a first-mover advantage, the company may deter other firms from entering the market since the preemptor will usually be able to move down the experience curve, reduce its costs and therefore its prices as well, and threaten a price war if necessary.

This strategy, however, is extremely risky, for it involves investing resources in a generic strategy before the extent and profitability of the future market are clear. Wal-Mart, with its strategy of locating in small rural towns to tap an underexploited market for discount goods, preempted Sears and Kmart. Wal-Mart has been able to engage in market penetration and market expansion because of the secure base it established in its rural strongholds.

A preemptive strategy is also risky if it does not deter competitors and they decide to enter the market. If the competitors have a stronger generic strategy or more resources, such as Microsoft or Intel, they can make the preemptor suffer. Thus, for the strategy to succeed, the preemptor must generally be a credible company with enough resources to withstand a possible price war.

To *coordinate* with rivals as a capacity-control strategy, caution must be exercised since collusion on the timing of new investments is illegal under antitrust law. However, tacit coordination is practiced in many industries as companies attempt to understand and forecast the competitive moves of each other. Generally, companies use market signaling and engage in a kind of tit-for-tat strategy to secure coordination. They make announcements about their future investment decisions in trade journals and newspapers. In addition, they share information about their production levels and their forecasts of demand within an industry to bring supply and demand into equilibrium. Thus, a coordination strategy reduces the risks associated with investment in the industry. This is very common in the chemical refining and oil business, where new capacity investments frequently cost hundreds of millions of dollars.

Supply and Distribution Strategy

As you saw in Chapter 2, when an industry becomes consolidated and comprises a few large companies, it may gain strength over its suppliers and buyers. Suppliers can become dependent on the industry for buying their inputs, and buyers can become dependent on the industry as a source of important products. By the mature stage, to protect their market position, brand name, and product quality, many companies decide to take over more of the distribution of their products and control the source of inputs crucial to the production process. That is, sometimes strategic considerations move them to be more involved in the value chain. When they seek ownership of supply or distribution operations, they are pursuing a strategy of vertical integration. At the same time, to reduce costs, mature companies often outsource, or "deintegrate," their value chains if this will lead to competitive advantage. Both of these choices are considered in detail in Chapter 9.

There are many reasons that a mature company might decide to control its supplier and distributor relationships and protect its generic strategy. In this way, it can safeguard its ability to dispose of its outputs or acquire inputs in a timely, reliable manner, thereby reducing costs and improving product quality. One way to analyze the issues in choosing a distribution or supplier strategy is to contrast two kinds of relationship that can exist between a company and its suppliers and distributors.

The first relationship, which can be called the *anonymous approach,* is for a company and its suppliers and distributors to have an arms-length, short-term relationship in which each party simply tries to strike the best bargain to make the most profit, inputs are inspected as they arrive, and defective ones are sent back. Often purchasing and distribution personnel are routinely rotated to prevent kickbacks. In contrast, with a *relational approach,* a company and its suppliers and distributors cooperate and try to develop a long-term perspective and base their exchanges on trust. With a relational approach, suppliers are sensitive to the needs of the company, respond quickly to changes in the specification of inputs, and adjust supply to meet the requirements of a company's just-in-time inventory system. The results of this close relationship are lower costs and the ability to respond to unexpected changes in demand. Developing close supplier-distributor relationships supports both companies' generic strategies. Clearly, it pays a company to develop a long-term relationship with its suppliers and distributors, and more and more companies, such as Motorola, McDonald's, and Wal-Mart, have formed close linkages with their suppliers.

A company has many options to choose from in deciding on the appropriate way to distribute its products to gain a competitive advantage. It may distribute its products to an independent distributor, which in turn distributes them to retailers. Alternatively, it might distribute directly to retailers or even to the final customer. This option is being used more and more by companies as they use the Internet to market and sell their products, as the *Running Case* illustrates.

In general, the *complexity of a product and the amount of information* needed about its operation and maintenance determine the distribution strategy chosen. Car companies, for example, use franchisees rather than car supermarkets to control the distribution of their autos. The reason is the high level of after-sales service and support needed to satisfy customers. Carmakers are able to penalize franchisees by withholding cars from a dealership if customers' complaints rise, giving them effective control over franchisees' behavior.

Large electronics manufacturers and producers of customer durables such as appliances generally prefer to use a network of distributors to control distribution. To enhance market share and control the way products are sold and serviced, manufacturers choose five or six large distributors in each state to control distribution. The distributors are required to carry the full line of a company's products and invest in after-sales service facilities. The result is that the manufacturer receives good feedback on how its products are selling, and the distributor becomes knowledgeable about a company's products and thus helps the company maintain and increase its control over the market. The company is able to discipline its distributors if they start to discount prices or otherwise threaten the company's reputation or generic strategy.

Large manufacturers such as Johnson & Johnson, Procter & Gamble, and General Foods typically sell directly to a retailer and avoid giving profits to a distributor or wholesaler. They do so in part because they have lower profit margins than the makers of electronic equipment and customer durables. However, this strategy also allows them to influence a retailer's behavior directly. For example, they can refuse to supply a particular product that a retailer wants unless the retailer stocks the entire range of the company's products. In addition, the companies are assured of shelf space for new products. Coca-Cola and PepsiCo are able to influence retailers to reduce the

Running Case

Compaq and Dell Go Head-to-Head in Customer Service

As new developments in technology alter the nature of competition in the PC industry, the distribution strategies of its major players are also changing. These changes are evident in the struggle between Dell Computer and Compaq Computer for domination of the PC market.

Founded by a team of engineers, Compaq from the start emphasized the engineering and research side of the PC business. For example, it was the first company to bring out a computer using Intel's new 486 chip. Its differentiation strategy was to produce high-end PCs based on the newest technology, which would command a premium price. Compaq specialized in the business market, and it developed a sophisticated dealer network to distribute, sell, and service its expensive PCs. Dell, on the other hand, focused from the beginning on the marketing and distribution end of the PC business. Its low-cost strategy was to assemble a PC and then sell it directly to customers through mail order outlets, cutting out the dealer in order to offer a rock-bottom price. Its managers viewed the company primarily as a distribution or mail order company, not as an engineering one.

As computers increasingly became commodity products and prices fell drastically, Compaq realized that its strategy of selling only though high-priced dealers would mean disaster; it then changed its strategy to produce a low-cost computer and in the 1990s began its own mail order distribution, offering its machines directly to customers and, more recently, to businesses. However, Compaq has not been as successful as Dell in its online distribution strategy because Dell was first to do so and gained a first-mover advantage and because Dell established a more customer-friendly web site and until 2002 enjoyed the record for fewest customer complaints. Moreover, although each company offered next-day delivery and installation of computers, as well as extended warranties, Dell reached ahead in providing the best online customer service, and indeed made quality customer service, as well as price, a main focus of its competitive advantage.

In 2000, Compaq's new CEO, Michael Capellas, announced a bold new Internet distribution and sales strategy to catch up with Dell and make Compaq the leader in online selling to businesses and customers. He directed all of Compaq's business units to make the Internet a major focus of their business models. Apparently, Capellas's efforts have been rewarded: a report in April 2002 announced that Dell's customer service had slipped, with 40 percent more customer complaints, and it was now tied with Compaq for first place. Apparently, the combination of exceptionally strong Christmas sales in 2001 and an understaffed service department overtaxed Dell's service abilities. In 2002, Dell was scrambling to hire hundreds of new service reps to solve the problem. Compaq, because of its 2002 merger with Hewlett-Packard, will also have more resources and capabilities to upgrade its service capabilities. The battle between these companies is not over.

Sources: K. Pope, "Out for Blood: For Compaq and Dell Accent Is on Personal in the Computer Wars," *Wall Street Journal,* February 13, 1993, pp. A1, A6. M. Stepanek, "What Does No. 1 Do for an Encore?" *Business Week,* November 2, 1998, pp. 44–47. A. Taylor III, "Compaq Looks Inside for Salvation," *Fortune,* August 16, 1999, pp. 124–129. M. Kessler, "Dude, Dell's Service Has Slipped, But Company's Working on It," *USA Today,* April 29, 2002, p. B2. www.hp.com (2002).

shelf space given to competing products or even to exclude them because soft drinks have the highest profit margins of products sold in supermarkets. Gallo is one of the few winemakers that controls the distribution and retailing of its own products. This is one reason Gallo is so consistently profitable.

In sum, devising the appropriate strategy for acquiring inputs and disposing of outputs is a crucial part of competitive strategy in mature industries. Companies can gain a competitive advantage through the way they choose to control their relationships with distributors and suppliers. By choosing the right strategy, they are able to control their costs, their price and nonprice strategies, their reputation, and product quality. These critical issues are expanded on in Chapter 9.

Strategies in Declining Industries

Sooner or later, many industries enter into a decline stage, in which the size of the total market starts to shrink. Examples are the railroad industry, the tobacco industry, and the steel industry. Industries start declining for a number of reasons, including technological change, social trends, and demographic shifts. The railroad and steel industries began to decline when technological changes brought viable substitutes for their products. The advent of the internal combustion engine drove the railroad industry into decline, and the steel industry fell into decline with the rise of plastics and composite materials. As for the tobacco industry, changing social attitudes toward smoking, which are themselves a product of growing concerns about the health effects of smoking, have caused decline.

There are four main strategies that companies can adopt to deal with decline: (1) a **leadership strategy,** by which a company seeks to become the dominant player in a declining industry; (2) a **niche strategy,** which focuses on pockets of demand that are declining more slowly than the industry as a whole; (3) a **harvest strategy,** which optimizes cash flow; and (4) a **divestment strategy,** by which a company sells off the business to others. Before examining each of these strategies in detail, it is important to note that the choice of strategy depends in part on the *intensity* of the competition.

The Severity of Decline

When the size of the total market is shrinking, competition tends to intensify in a declining industry and profit rates tend to fall. The intensity of competition in a declining industry depends on four critical factors, which are indicated in Figure 6.9. First, the intensity of competition is greater in industries in which decline is rapid as opposed to industries, such as tobacco, in which decline is slow and gradual.

Second, the intensity of competition is greater in declining industries in which exit barriers are high. As you recall from Chapter 2, high exit barriers keep companies locked into an industry even when demand is falling. The result is the emergence of excess productive capacity and, hence, an increased probability of fierce price competition.

Third, and related to the previous point, the intensity of competition is greater in declining industries in which fixed costs are high (as in the steel industry). The reason is that the need to cover fixed costs, such as the costs of maintaining productive capacity, can make companies try to use any excess capacity they have by slashing prices, which can trigger a price war.

Finally, the intensity of competition is greater in declining industries in which the product is perceived as a commodity (as it is in the steel industry) in contrast to industries in which differentiation gives rise to significant brand loyalty, as was true until very recently of the declining tobacco industry.

FIGURE 6.9

Factors that Determine the Intensity of Competition in Declining Industries

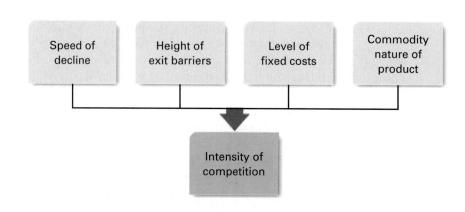

Not all segments of an industry typically decline at the same rate. In some segments, demand may remain reasonably strong despite decline elsewhere. The steel industry illustrates this situation. Although bulk steel products, such as sheet steel, have suffered a general decline, demand has actually risen for specialty steels, such as those used in high-speed machine tools. Vacuum tubes provide another example. Although demand for them collapsed when transistors replaced them as a key component in many electronics products, vacuum tubes still had some limited applications in radar equipment for years afterward. Consequently, demand in this vacuum tube segment remained strong despite the general decline in the demand for vacuum tubes. The point, then, is that there may be pockets of demand in an industry in which demand is declining more slowly than in the industry as a whole or not declining at all. Price competition thus may be far less intense among the companies serving such pockets of demand than within the industry as a whole.

Choosing a Strategy

Four main strategies are available to companies in a declining industry: a leadership strategy, a niche strategy, a harvest strategy, and a divestment strategy. Figure 6.10 provides a simple framework for guiding strategic choice. Note that the intensity of competition in the declining industry is measured on the vertical axis and that a company's strengths relative to remaining pockets of demand are measured on the horizontal axis.

Leadership Strategy. A leadership strategy aims at growing in a declining industry by picking up the market share of companies that are leaving the industry. A leadership strategy makes most sense (1) when the company has distinctive strengths that allow it to capture market share in a declining industry and (2) the speed of decline and the intensity of competition in the declining industry are moderate. Philip Morris has pursued such a strategy in the tobacco industry. By

FIGURE 6.10

Strategy Selection in a Declining Industry

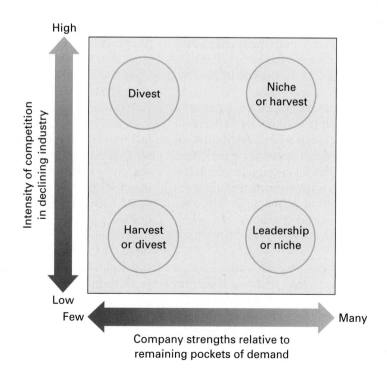

aggressive marketing, Philip Morris has increased its market share in a declining industry and earned enormous profits in the process.

The tactical steps companies might use to achieve a leadership position include aggressive pricing and marketing to build market share, acquiring established competitors to consolidate the industry, and raising the stakes for other competitors—for example, by making new investments in productive capacity. Such competitive tactics signal to other competitors that the company is willing and able to stay and compete in the declining industry. These signals may persuade other companies to exit the industry, which would further enhance the competitive position of the industry leader. Strategy in Action 6.5 offers an example of a company, Richardson Electronics, that has prospered by taking a leadership position in a declining industry. It is one of the last companies in the vacuum tube business.

Niche Strategy. A niche strategy focuses on pockets of demand in the industry in which demand is stable or declining less rapidly than the industry as a whole. The strategy makes sense when the company has some unique strengths relative to those niches where demand remains relatively strong. As an example, consider Naval, a company that manufactures whaling harpoons and small guns to fire them and makes money doing so. This might be considered rather odd, since the world com-

Strategy in Action   6.5

How to Make Money in the Vacuum Tube Business

At its peak in the early 1950s, the vacuum tube business was a major industry in which companies such as Westinghouse, General Electric, RCA, and Western Electric had a large stake. Then along came the transistor, making most vacuum tubes obsolete, and one by one all the big companies exited the industry. One company, however, Richardson Electronics, not only stayed in the business but also demonstrated that high returns are possible in a declining industry. Primarily a distributor (although it does have some manufacturing capabilities), Richardson bought the remains of a dozen companies in the United States and Europe as they exited the vacuum tube industry. Richardson now has a warehouse that stocks more than 10,000 different types of vacuum tubes. The company is the world's only supplier of many of them, which helps explain why its gross margin is in the 35 to 40 percent range.

Richardson survives and prospers because vacuum tubes are vital parts of some older electronic equipment that would be costly to replace with solid-state equipment. In addition, vacuum tubes still outperform semiconductors in some limited applications, including radar and welding machines. The U.S. government and General Motors are big customers of Richardson.

Speed is the essence of Richardson's business. The company's Illinois warehouse offers overnight delivery to some 40,000 customers, processing 650 orders a day, whose average price is $550. Customers such as GM do not really care whether a vacuum tube costs $250 or $350; what they care about is the $40,000 to $50,000 downtime loss that they face when a key piece of welding equipment isn't working. By responding quickly to the demands of such customers and being the only major supplier of many types of vacuum tubes, Richardson has placed itself in a position that many companies in growing industries would envy: a monopoly position. In 1997, however, a new company, Westrex, was formed to take advantage of the growing popularity of vacuum tubes in high-end stereo systems, and by 1999 was competing head to head with Richardson in some market segments. Clearly, competition can be found even in a declining industry.

Source: P. Haynes, "Western Electric Redux," *Forbes*, January 26, 1998, pp. 46–47.

munity has outlawed whaling. However, Naval survived the terminal decline of the harpoon industry by focusing on the one group of people who are still allowed to hunt whales, although only in very limited numbers: North American Eskimos. Eskimos are permitted to hunt bowhead whales, provided that they do so only for food and not for commercial purposes. Naval is the sole supplier of small harpoon whaling guns to Eskimo communities, and its monopoly position allows it to earn a healthy return in this small market.[23]

Harvest Strategy. As we noted in Chapter 5, a harvest strategy is the best choice when a company wishes to get out of a declining industry and perhaps optimize cash flow in the process. This strategy makes the most sense when the company foresees a steep decline and intense future competition or lacks strengths relative to remaining pockets of demand in the industry. A harvest strategy requires the company to cut all new investments in capital equipment, advertising, R&D, and the like. The inevitable result is that it will lose market share, but because it is no longer investing in this business, initially its positive cash flow will increase. Essentially, the company is taking cash flow in exchange for market share. Ultimately, cash flows will start to decline, and at this stage it makes sense for the company to liquidate the business. Although this strategy is very appealing in theory, it can be somewhat difficult to put into practice. Employee morale in a business that is being run down may suffer. Furthermore, if customers catch on to what the company is doing, they may defect rapidly. Then market share may decline much faster than the company expected.

Divestment Strategy. A divestment strategy rests on the idea that a company can maximize its net investment recovery from a business by selling it early, before the industry has entered into a steep decline. This strategy is appropriate when the company has few strengths relative to whatever pockets of demand are likely to remain in the industry and when the competition in the declining industry is likely to be intense. The best option may be to sell out to a company that is pursuing a leadership strategy in the industry. The drawback of the divestment strategy is that it depends for its success on the ability of the company to spot its industry's decline before it becomes serious and to sell out while the company's assets are still valued by others.

Summary of Chapter

1. In fragmented industries composed of a large number of small and medium-sized companies, the principal forms of competitive strategy are chaining, franchising, and horizontal merger.

2. In embryonic and growth industries, the way in which different kinds of customer groups emerge over time, and customer needs change, are important determinants of business-level strategy. Similarly, understanding the factors that affect a market's growth rate allow managers to tailor their business model to a changing industry environment.

3. Mature industries are composed of a few large companies whose actions are so highly interdependent

that the success of one company's strategy depends on the responses of its rivals.

4. The principal competitive tactics and moves used by companies in mature industries to deter entry are product proliferation, pricing games, and maintaining excess capacity.

5. The principal competitive tactics and maneuvers used by companies in mature industries to manage rivalry are price signaling, price leadership, nonprice competition, and capacity control.

6. Companies in mature industries need to develop a supply-and-distribution strategy to protect the source of their competitive advantage.

7. In declining industries in which market demand has leveled off or is falling, companies must tailor their

price and nonprice strategies to the new competitive environment. They also need to manage industry capacity to prevent the emergence of capacity expansion problems.

8. There are four main strategies a company can pursue when demand is falling: leadership, niche, harvest, and divestment. The choice is determined by the severity of industry decline and the company's strengths relative to the remaining pockets of demand.

Discussion Questions

1. Why are industries fragmented? What are the main ways in which companies can turn a fragmented industry into a consolidated one?
2. What are the key problems in maintaining a competitive advantage in embryonic and growth industry environments? What are the dangers associated with being the leader?
3. Discuss how companies can use (a) product differentiation and (b) capacity control to manage rivalry and increase an industry's profitability.

Practicing Strategic Management

SMALL-GROUP EXERCISE: HOW TO KEEP THE HOT SAUCE HOT

Break up into groups of three to five people, and appoint one group member as a spokesperson who will communicate your findings to the class. You are the managers of a company that has pioneered a new kind of hot sauce for chicken that has taken the market by storm. The hot sauce's differentiated appeal has been based on a unique combination of spices and packaging that has allowed you to charge a premium price. Over the past three years, your hot sauce has achieved a national reputation, and now major food companies such as Kraft and Nabisco, seeing the potential of this market segment, are beginning to introduce hot sauces of their own, imitating your product.

1. Describe the generic business-level strategy you are pursuing.
2. Describe the industry's environment in which you are competing.
3. What kinds of competitive tactics and maneuvers could you adopt to protect your generic strategy in this kind of environment?
4. What do you think is the best strategy for you to pursue in this situation?

ARTICLE FILE 6

Find an example of the ways in which a company or group of companies in a particular industry environment has adopted a competitive strategy to protect or enhance its business-level strategy.

STRATEGIC MANAGEMENT PROJECT: MODULE 6

This part of the project continues the analysis of your company's business-level strategy and considers how conditions in the industry's environment affect the company's competitive strategy. With the information you have at your disposal, perform the tasks and answer the questions listed:

1. In what kind of industry environment (for example, embryonic, mature) does your company operate? Use the information from Strategic Management Project: Module 2 to answer this question.
2. Discuss how your company has attempted to develop a competitive strategy to protect its business-level strategy. For example, if your company is operating in an embryonic industry, discuss the ways it has attempted to increase its competitive advantage over time. If it operates in a mature industry, discuss how it has tried to manage the five forces of industry competition.
3. What new strategies would you advise your company to pursue to increase its competitive advantage? For example, what kinds of strategy toward buyers or suppliers should it adopt? How should it attempt to differentiate its products in the future?
4. Based on this analysis, do you think your company will be able to maintain its competitive advantage in the future? Why or why not?

EXPLORING THE WEB
Visiting Wal-Mart

Enter the web site of retailer Wal-Mart (**www.walmartstores .com**). Click on "About Wal-Mart," and then click on "Timeline." Study the events in Wal-Mart's timeline, and from them outline the way Wal-Mart's competitive strategy in the retailing industry has developed over time.

General Task: Search the Web for a company that has recently changed its competitive strategy in some way. What precipitated the change in its strategy? What were the strategy changes the company made?

Closing Case

How eBay Revolutionized the Auction Business

In the 1990s, many entrepreneurs attempted to use new information technologies and particularly the Internet to provide new or improved services to customers. Their goal was to use the potential of the new technology to find ways to obtain a competitive advantage over existing firms in a particular industry environment. Nowhere has this been more evident than in the auction industry.

Traditionally, auctions have been places where buyers and sellers meet face-to-face to determine the fair market value of a product. Auction houses range from the most prestigious ones, like Sotheby's and Christie's, which sell fine art and antiques, to small local auction companies that sell the contents of someone's house.

In the early 1990s, Pierre Omidyar had an idea for a new kind of auction company, an online auction company, which he believed would revolutionize the selling of all kinds of products—not just fine arts and antiques but any kind of collectible, from cars to Beanie Babies—by bringing buyers and sellers together by using the Internet. He left his job at Microsoft and began to write the software that would provide the platform for an online auction service. The result was eBay, which was launched on Labor Day in 1995.

On the eBay web site, sellers describe their product electronically, post a photograph, and set an initial price, which buyers can then bid up: the highest bidder wins. eBay charges a modest fee to list the product plus a low percentage of the final sales price. Sellers have the advantage that their product appears before buyers in every part of the United States and abroad—anywhere where someone has a computer and can log on to eBay's online auction site. Buyers enjoy access to a huge array of merchandise that can be quickly scanned by using the appropriate keywords on eBay's search engine. eBay thus provides a low-cost forum in which buyers and sellers can meet to buy and sell products. It makes its money from the sheer volume of products that it sells. Every day, millions of items are listed, so that even with low fees, it generates high profits.

As you can imagine, eBay's low-cost approach has generated many imitators; after all, it is relatively easy to write a software program and develop an online auction site. However, eBay's early start has also given it another major competitive advantage: being the first in the online auction business, it has attracted a loyal audience of buyers and sellers who will not switch to other online auction companies, even when they provide the service for free. For example, by 1999, Yahoo and MSN, and hundreds of small, specialized companies had developed their own online auction businesses and decided to charge users nothing for their services. However, many of these, including Yahoo's auction site, have not attracted many buyers and sellers. The reason is that sellers know that eBay's site attracts many more buyers than does Yahoo's so that they are likely to obtain the highest price, and eBay buyers know that they will find the greatest selection on eBay and so focus their search there. Thus, eBay has not only developed a low-cost competency; it also has developed a substantial reputation that has given it a differentiation advantage as well.

Other online companies are not content to give away the lucrative online auction market to eBay, however, and are searching for ways to fight back. In June 1999, bookseller Amazon.com announced that it was forming an alliance with Sotheby's to create an upmarket online auction service, and other companies are also searching for partners. In October 1999, Yahoo, Amazon.com, and others announced that they were banding together to combine their auction businesses to offer a credible alternative to eBay.

After this announcement, eBay's price, which has soared several thousand percent because investors thought that its strategy had given it a sustainable competitive advantage over its rivals, fell back. Through his innovative use of new information technology, Omidyar has brought increased value for millions of buyers and sellers and in the meantime has created over a billion dollars of value for himself in his eBay stock. The question now is whether eBay can maintain the value it has created.

Case Discussion Questions

1. Describe the nature of competition and the industry environment of the online auction industry.

2. Go to eBay's web site, and analyze the strategies it has been pursuing to protect its competitive position (for example, different kinds of auction sites and services).

Sources: www.ebay.com (1999). www.amazon.com press releases (1999).

7

Strategy in High-Technology Industries

Opening Case

Extending the Wintel Monopoly to Wireless

Microsoft and Intel are co-owners of the dominant Wintel standard, based on the combination of a Microsoft operating system and an Intel microprocessor that is used in over 90 percent of the world's PCs. ("Wintel" was coined because Microsoft's Windows operating system is designed to run on an Intel microprocessor.) This fact has helped to make Microsoft and Intel the two most valuable companies in the global computer industry. Now the duo is trying to extend their standard and make it the dominant one in the wireless phone industry. The focus of their attention is next-generation wireless phones, or 3G phones, which will increasingly come to resemble computers. They will have color screens; a full range of personal information management applications such as address and date books; and the ability to browse the Internet, send and receive text-based email, and run a variety of applications, including pocket-sized versions of Microsoft's popular Office suite.

The strategy that Microsoft and Intel are pursuing is to create a reference design, or template, for making 3G wireless phones that they will license to electronics companies that wish to manufacture these devices. Microsoft will supply the operating system, which will be based on its Pocket PC operating system, a Windows-based operating system for small digital devices. Intel will supply key elements of the onboard microprocessor technology. Both companies will work together to produce the reference design, which is a set of standard specifications outlining how to build a handset using Microsoft and Intel technology. In creating this design, Microsoft and Intel claim that their main motive is to "demystify and democratize the wireless industry, so that more companies can break into the market. We want to enable one of them to become the next Nokia," said a Microsoft spokesman. (Nokia is the global leader in the market, with a 40 percent share of all wireless handset sales.) More generally, the idea is to try to accelerate the adoption of 3G wireless technology.

If all goes well, the Microsoft-Intel reference design will be licensed to a number of electronics companies that will use it to make wireless handsets. These companies will no longer have to invest in creating the design themselves, enabling them to cut R&D expenses and hence handset prices. As cheap handsets reach the market, probably in 2003–2004, demand will start to expand. As the installed base of Microsoft-Intel phones grows, more applications will be written to run on those phones. In addition, software companies will write web-based applications that reside on servers and can be accessed by consumers with a Microsoft-Intel phone over a wireless connection. These two developments will increase the value of owning a Microsoft-Intel phone, as opposed to a phone based on a different reference design. As the value increases, more consumers will buy phones based on the Microsoft-Intel design, as opposed to phones made by companies like Nokia, and the installed base of Microsoft-Intel phones will expand further, creating an incentive to develop more software for those phones, and so on. In other words, through the operation of a positive feedback loop, the reference design now being developed by Microsoft and Intel could become the de facto standard in the wireless handset market.

If this occurs, Microsoft and Intel will have extended their dominant position in PCs to the wireless handset market. They should be able to profit from this by charging a licensing fee for the reference design and by developing and selling complementary products, such as additional applications that run on a wireless handset or reside on servers that consumers with handsets can access via wireless connections to the Web.

The eventual outcome is less clear than the strategy. For one thing, several other companies are promoting alternative and potentially incompatible reference designs and operating systems for wireless handsets. These include Qualcomm, Nokia, Ericsson, and Motorola, all heavyweights in the wireless market. For another, it is still not clear that the wireless handset market has the same imperatives for standardization as the personal computer market does. If it does, however, the market will probably hone in on a single reference design. Whether that design is the one promoted by Microsoft and Intel or by another competitor depends in large part on the differential success of the strategies these different companies are pursuing as they try to win this emerging format war.

Sources: D. Pringle, "Wintel Duo Targets the Cellphone," *Wall Street Journal,* February 19, 2002, p. E2. A. Doland, "Looking Beyond the Basic Cell Phone," *Columbian,* February 19, 2002, p. E2. B. McDonough, "Microsoft Jostles for Mobile Market Position," Wireless.Newsfactor.com, February 19, 2002.

Overview

In this chapter, we look at the nature of competition and strategy in high-technology industries. **Technology** refers to the body of scientific knowledge used in the production of goods or services. **High-technology (high-tech) industries** are those in which the underlying scientific knowledge that companies in the industry use is advancing rapidly, and by implication so are the attributes of the products and services that result from its application. The computer industry is often thought of as the quintessential example of a high-technology industry. Other industries often considered high tech are telecommunications, where new technologies based on wireless and the Internet have proliferated in recent years; consumer electronics, where the digital technology underlying products from DVD players to video game terminals and digital cameras is advancing rapidly; pharmaceuticals, where new technologies based on cell biology, recombinant DNA, and genomics are revolutionizing the process of drug discovery; power generation, where new technologies based on fuel cells and cogeneration may change the economics of the industry; and aerospace, where the combination of new composite materials, electronics, and more efficient jet engines may give birth to a new era of near-supersonic commercial aircraft, such as Boeing's planned sonic cruiser.

This chapter focuses on high-technology industries for a number of reasons. First, technology is accounting for an ever larger share of economic activity. Estimates suggest that roughly 15 percent of total economic activity in the United States is accounted for by information technology industries.[1] This figure actually underestimates the true impact of technology on the economy, because it ignores the other high-technology areas we just mentioned. Moreover, as technology advances, many low-technology industries are becoming more high tech. For example, the development of biotechnology and genetic engineering transformed the production of seed corn, long considered a low-technology business, into a high-technology business. Moreover, high-technology products are making their way into a wide range of businesses; today a Ford Taurus contains more computing power than the multimillion dollar mainframe computers used in the Apollo space program, and the competitive advantage of physical stores, such as Wal-Mart, is based on their use of information technology.[2] The circle of high-technology industries is both large and expanding, and even in industries not thought of as high tech, technology is revolutionizing aspects of the product or production system.

Although high-tech industries may produce very different products, when it comes to developing a business model and strategies that will lead to a competitive advantage and superior profitability, they face a similar situation. This chapter examines the competitive features found in many high-tech industries and the kinds of strategies that companies must adopt to build business models that will allow them to achieve superior performance and profitability.

By the time you have completed this chapter, you will have an understanding of the nature of competition in high-tech industries and strategies that companies can pursue to succeed in those industries.

Technical Standards and Format Wars

Especially in high-tech industries, ownership of **technical standards**—a set of technical specifications that producers adhere to when making the product or a component of it—can be an important source of competitive advantage.[3] *Indeed, the source of product differentiation is based on the technical standard.* Often, only one standard will come to dominate a market, so many battles in high-tech industries revolve around companies competing to be the one that sets the standard.

Battles to set and control technical standards in a market are referred to as **format wars;** they are essentially battles to control the source of differentiation and thus the value that such differentiation can create for the customer. Because differentiated products often command premium prices and are often expensive to develop, the competitive stakes are enormous. The profitability and very survival of a company may depend on the outcome of the battle, for example, the outcome of the battle now being waged over the establishment and ownership of the reference design for next-generation wireless handsets will help to determine which companies will be the leaders in the decades to come.

Examples of Standards

A familiar example of a standard is the layout of a computer keyboard. No matter what keyboard you buy, the letters are all in the same pattern.[4] The reason is quite obvious. Imagine if each computer maker changed the ways the keys were laid out—

if some started with QWERTY on the top row of letters (which is indeed the format used and is known as the QWERTY format), some with YUHGFD, and some with ACFRDS. If you learned to type on one layout, it would be irritating and time-consuming to have to relearn on a YUHGFD layout. So we have this standard format (QWERTY) because it makes it easy for people to move from computer to computer because the input medium, the keyboard, is set out in a standard way.

Another example of a technical standard concerns the dimensions of containers used to ship goods on trucks, railcars, and ships: all have the same basic dimensions—the same height, length, and width—and all make use of the same locking mechanisms to hold them onto a surface or to bolt against each other. Having a standard ensures that containers can easily be moved from one mode of transportation to another—from trucks, to railcars, to ships, and back to railcars. If containers lacked standard dimensions and locking mechanisms, it would suddenly become much more difficult to ship containers around the world. Shippers would have to make sure that they had the right kind of container to go on the ships and trucks and railcars scheduled to carry a particular container around the world—very complicated indeed.

Consider, finally, the personal computer. Most share a common set of features: an Intel or Intel-compatible microprocessor, random access memory (RAM), a Microsoft operating system, an internal hard drive, a floppy disk drive, a CD drive, a keyboard, a monitor, a mouse, a modem, and so on. We call this set of features the dominant design for personal computers (a **dominant design** refers to a common set of features or design characteristics). Embedded in this design are several technical standards (see Figure 7.1). For example, there is the Wintel technical standard based on an Intel microprocessor and a Microsoft operating system. Microsoft and Intel own that standard, which is central to the personal computer. Developers of software applications, component parts, and peripherals such as printers adhere to this standard when developing their own products because this guarantees that their products will work well with a personal computer based on the Wintel standard. Another technical standard for connecting peripherals to the PC is the Universal Serial Bus (or USB), established by an industry standards-setting board. No one owns it; the standard is in the public domain. A third technical standard is for communication between a PC and the Internet via a modem. Known as TCP/IP, this standard was also

FIGURE 7.1

Technical Standards for Personal Computers

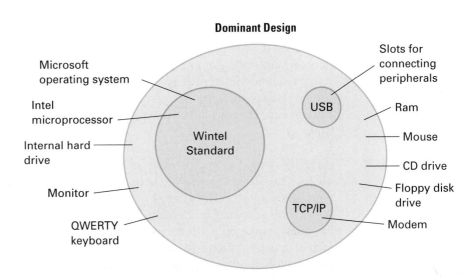

set by an industry association and is in the public domain. Thus, as with many other products, the PC is actually based on several technical standards. It is also important to note that when a company owns a standard, as Microsoft and Intel do with the Wintel standard, it may be a source of competitive advantage and high profitability.

Benefits of Standards

Standards emerge because there are economic benefits associated with them. First, having a technical standard helps to guarantee *compatibility* between products and their complements, other products used with them. For example, containers are used with railcars, trucks, and ships, and PCs are used with software applications. Compatibility has tangible economic benefits of reducing the costs associated with making sure that products work well with each other.

Second, having a standard can help to *reduce confusion* in the minds of consumers. A few years ago, several consumer electronics companies were vying with each other to produce and market the first DVD players, and they were championing different variants of the basic DVD technology—different standards—that were incompatible with each other; a DVD disc designed to run on a DVD player made by Toshiba would not run on a player made by Sony, and vice versa. The companies feared that selling these incompatible versions of the same technology would produce confusion in the minds of consumers, who would not know which version to purchase and might decide to wait and see which technology ultimately dominated the marketplace. With lack of demand, the technology might fail to gain traction in the marketplace and would not be successful. To avoid this possibility, the developers of DVD equipment established a standard-setting body for the industry, the DVD Forum, which established a common technical standard for DVD players and discs that all companies adhered to. The result was that when DVDs were introduced, there was a common standard and no confusion in consumers' minds. This helped to boost demand for DVD players, making this one of the fastest-selling technologies of the late 1990s and early 2000s. First introduced in 1997, by 2001 some 13 million DVD players were sold in the United States, and they are now in one in four homes in the country.[5] However, so far the DVD Forum has not been able to agree on a common standard for the next version of DVDs, DVD recorders., which is slowing diffusion and adoption of the technology (see Strategy in Action 7.1).

Third, the emergence of a standard can help to *reduce production costs*. Once a standard emerges, products based on that standard design can be mass-produced, enabling the manufacturers to realize substantial economies of scale and lower their cost structures. The fact that there is a central standard for PCs (the Wintel standard) means that the component parts for a PC can be mass-produced. A manufacturer of internal hard drives, for example, can mass-produce drives for Wintel PCs, enabling it to realize substantial scale economies. If there were several competing and incompatible standards, each of which required a unique type of hard drive, production runs for hard drives would be shorter, unit costs would be higher, and the cost of PCs would go up.

Fourth, the emergence of standards can help to reduce the *risks associated with supplying complementary products* and thus increase the supply for those complements. Consider the risks associated with writing software applications to run on personal computers. This is a risky proposition, requiring the investment of considerable sums of money for developing the software before a single unit is sold. Imagine what would occur if there were ten different operating systems in use for PCs, each with only 10 percent of the market, rather than the current situation, where 95 percent of the world's PCs adhere to the Wintel standard. Software developers would be faced with the need to write ten different versions of the same software applica-

Strategy in Action   7.1

Where Is the Standard for DVD Recorders?

A few years ago, the 200-member DVD Forum achieved something of a coup when it managed to broker an agreement among some of its most important members on a common set of standards for DVD players. This common standard reduced consumer confusion and helped to propel DVD players into a mass market phenomenon, now replacing analog VHS video players in many living rooms. Nevertheless, current technology lacks one attribute of VHS technology: it cannot record. It's not that a technology for making DVD recorders does not exist; in fact, several do, and therein lies the problem. The DVD Forum has been unable to get some of its most powerful members to agree on a common technical standard for DVD recorders, primarily because different companies want to see their variant of the technology become the industry standard.

There are at least three versions of DVD recorders now on offer: Hewlett Packard is pushing one format, Sony and Philips are sponsoring another, and Matsushita yet another. And most important, DVD discs recorded using one format may not play on widely used DVD players or on computers that use another recording format.

First introduced in 1999, by 2001 some 350,000 DVD recorders had sold, many of them incorporated into new personal computers. But industry observers feel that sales could have been much higher had there been harmonization of standards. By way of comparison, some 40 million CD recorders were sold in 2001, making CD recording technology solidly mainstream (DVDs can hold ten times

as many data as CDs and are thus better suited to recording video). One reason for the slow takeup of DVD recorders has been the confusion over standards, and it's not just consumers who are confused. Many retailers are hesitant about stocking the technology until the battle over standards is resolved.

Another reason for the slow market growth has been the high price of DVD recorders. As of mid-2002, a standalone DVD recorder still cost around $1,500, putting the technology out of the reach of most people. However, DVD-recordable drives built into personal computers had fallen to $400 per unit, bringing them close to the price point at which a mass market develops. For the price to fall lower, producers need to be able to manufacture in high volume and realize significant scale economies. But here lies the catch: to generate significant demand to support mass production and bring prices down, it may first be necessary to harmonize standards and reduce consumer confusion—and that is something that the producers currently seem unwilling to do. For the time being, the different companies are continuing to push their own proprietary standard in the hope that they establish it as the leading standard in the industry and reap the associated gains.

Sources: E. Ramstad, "DVD Makers Battle over Tech Standard," *Wall Street Journal,* November 9, 2000, p. B6. B. Dudley, "Dueling DVD-Recorder Formats Make Playing Discs a Challenge," *Seattle Times,* January 9, 2002, p. C3.

---

tion, each for a much smaller market segment. This would change the economics of software development, increase its risks, and reduce potential profitability. Moreover, because of their higher cost structure and fewer economies of scale, the price of software programs would increase.

Thus, although many people complain about the consequences of Microsoft's near monopoly of PC operating systems, that monopoly does have at least one good effect: it substantially reduces the risks facing the makers of complementary products and the costs of those products. In fact, standards lead to both low-cost and differentiation advantages for individual companies and can help raise the level of industry profitability.

Establishment of Standards   Standards emerge in an industry in three main ways. First, recognizing the benefits of establishing a standard, companies in an industry might lobby the government to mandate an industry standard. In the United States, for example, the Federal

Communication Commission (FCC), after detailed discussions with broadcasters and consumer electronics companies, has mandated a single technical standard for digital television broadcast (DTV) and is requiring broadcasters to have capabilities in place for broadcasting digital signals based on this standard by 2006. The FCC took this step because it believed that without government action to set the standard, the rollout of DTV would be very slow. With a standard set by the government, consumer electronics companies can have greater confidence that a market will emerge, and this should encourage them to develop DTV products.

Second, technical standards are often set by cooperation among businesses, without government help, often through the medium of an industry forum, such as the DVD Forum. Companies cooperate in this way when they decide that competition among them to create a standard might be harmful because of the uncertainty that it would create in the minds of consumers.

When standards are set by the government or an industry association, they fall into the **public domain,** meaning that anyone can freely incorporate the knowledge and technology on which the standard is based into their products. For example, no one owns the QWERTY format, and therefore no one company can profit from it directly. Similarly, the language that underlies the presentation of text and graphics on the Web, hypertext markup language (HTML), is in the public domain; it is free for all to use. The same is true for TCP/IP, the communications standard used for transmitting data on the Internet.

Often, however, the industry standard is selected competitively by the purchasing patterns of customers in the marketplace—that is, by *market demand*. In this case, the strategy and business model a company has developed for promoting its technological standard is of critical importance because ownership of an industry standard that is protected from imitation by patents and copyrights is a valuable asset—a source of sustained competitive advantage and superior profitability. Microsoft and Intel, for example, both owe their competitive advantage to their ownership of Format wars, which exist between two or more companies competing against each other to get their designs adopted as the industry standard, are common in high-tech industries because of the high stakes. The Wintel standard became the dominant standard for PCs only after Microsoft and Intel won format wars against Apple Computer's proprietary system and later against IBM's OS/2 operating system. Microsoft and Real Networks are currently competing head to head in a format war to establish rival technologies—Windows Media Player and RealPlayer—as the standard for streaming video and audio technology on the Web. The *Opening Case* tells how Microsoft and Intel are also engaged in a format war in the wireless business as they try to get their standard for 3G wireless phones established as the industry standard.

Network Effects, Positive Feedback, and Lockout

There has been a growing realization that when standards are set by competition between companies promoting different formats, network effects are a primary determinant of how standards are established.[6] **Network effects** arise in industries where the size of the "network" of *complementary* products is a primary determinant of demand for an industry's product. For example, the demand for automobiles early in the twentieth century was an increasing function of the *network* of paved roads and gas stations. Similarly, the demand for telephones is an increasing function of the number of other numbers that can be called with that phone; that is, of the size of the telephone network (i.e., the telephone network is the complementary product). When the first telephone service was introduced in New York City, only a hundred numbers could be called. The network was very small because of the limited number of wires and telephone switches, which made the telephone a relatively useless piece of equipment. As more and more people got telephones and as the network of wires and switches expanded, the value of a telephone connection increased. This led to an increase in demand for telephone lines, which further increased the value of owning a telephone, setting up a positive feedback loop. The same type of positive feedback loop is now at work in the Internet.

To understand why network effects are important in the establishment of standards, consider the classic example of a format war: the battle between Sony and Matsushita to establish their respective technology for videocassette recorders (VCRs) as the standard in the marketplace. Sony was first to market with its Betamax technology, followed by Matsushita with its VHS technology. Both companies sold VCR recorder-players, and movie studios issued films prerecorded on VCR tapes for rental to consumers. Initially, all tapes were issued in Betamax format to play on Sony's machine. Sony *did not* license its Betamax technology, preferring to make all of the player-recorders itself. When Matsushita entered the market, it realized that to make its VHS format players valuable to consumers, it would have to encourage movie studios to issue movies for rental on VHS tapes. The only way to do that, Matsushita's managers reasoned, was to increase the installed base of VHS players as rapidly as possible. They believed that the greater the installed base of VHS players, the greater the incentive would be for movie studios to issue movies for rental on VHS format tapes. The more prerecorded VHS tapes were available for rental, the greater the value of a VHS player became to consumers, and therefore, the greater the demand would be VHS players (see Figure 7.2). Matsushita wanted to exploit a positive feedback loop.

To do this, Matsushita chose a licensing strategy under which any consumer electronics company was allowed to manufacture VHS format players under license. The strategy worked. A large number of companies signed on to manufacture VHS players, and soon far more VHS players were available for purchase in stores than Betamax players. As sales of VHS players started to grow, movie studios issued more films for rental in VHS format, and this stoked demand. Before long, it was clear to anyone who walked into a video rental store that there were more and more VHS tapes available for rent and fewer and fewer Betamax tapes. This served to reinforce the positive feedback loop, and ultimately Sony's Betamax technology was shut out of the market. The pivotal difference between the two companies was strategy: Matsushita chose a licensing strategy, and Sony did not. As a result, Matsushita's VHS technology became the de facto standard for VCRs, while Sony's Betamax technology was locked out.

FIGURE 7.2

Positive Feedback in the Market for VCRs

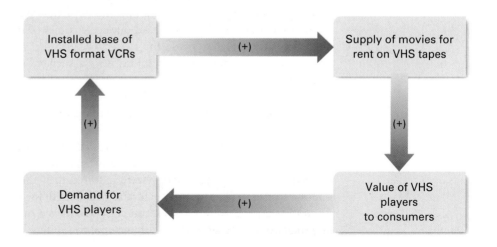

The general principle that emerges from this example is that when two or more companies are competing with each other to get their technology adopted as a standard in an industry, and when network effects and positive feedback loops are important, the company that wins the format war will be the one whose strategy best exploits positive feedback loops. It turns out that this is a very important strategic principle in many high-technology industries, particularly computer hardware, software, telecommunications, and consumer electronics. Microsoft is where it is today because it exploited a positive feedback loop. So did Dolby (see Strategy in Action 7.2).

An important implication of the positive feedback process is that as the market settles on a standard, companies promoting alternative standards can become **locked out** of the market when consumers are unwilling to bear the switching costs required for them to abandon the established standard and adopt the new standard. In this context, **switching costs** are the costs that consumers must bear to switch from a product based on one technological standard to a product based on another.

For illustration, imagine that a company developed an operating system for personal computers that was both faster and more stable (crashed less) than the current standard in the marketplace, Microsoft Windows. Would this company be able to gain significant market share from Microsoft? Only with great difficulty. Consumers buy personal computers not for their operating system but for the applications that run on that system. A new operating system would initially have a very small installed base, so few developers would be willing to take the risks in writing word processing programs, spreadsheets, games, and other applications for that operating system. Because there would be very few applications available, consumers who did make the switch would have to bear the switching costs associated with giving up some of their applications—something that they might be unwilling to do. Moreover, even if applications were available for the new operating system, consumers would have to bear the costs of purchasing those applications, another source of switching costs. In addition, they would have to bear the costs associated with learning to use the new operating system, yet another source of switching costs. Thus, many consumers would be unwilling to switch even if the new operating system performed better than Windows, and the company promoting the new operating system would be locked out of the market.

Consumers *will* bear switching costs if the benefits of adopting the new technology outweigh the costs of switching. For example, in the late 1980s and early 1990s, millions of people switched from analog record players to digital CD players even though the switching costs were significant: they had to purchase the new player technology, and many people purchased duplicate copies of their favorite music recordings. They nevertheless made the switch because for many people, the perceived benefit—the incredibly better sound quality associated with CDs—outweighed the costs of switching.

As this process started to get under way, a positive feedback started to develop, with the growing installed base of CD players leading to an increase in the number of music recordings issued on CDs, as opposed to or in addition to vinyl records. Past some point, the installed base of CD players got so big that music companies started to issue recordings only on CDs. Once this happened, even those who did not want to switch to the new technology were required to if they wished to purchase new music recordings. The industry standard had shifted: the new technology had locked in as the standard, and the old technology was locked out. It follows that despite its dominance, the Wintel standard for personal computers could one day be superseded

Strategy in Action   7.2

How Dolby Became the Standard in Sound Technology

Inventor Ray Dolby's name has become synonymous with superior sound in homes, movie theaters, and recording studios. The technology produced by his company, Dolby Laboratories, is part of nearly every music cassette and cassette recorder, prerecorded videotape, and, most recently, DVD movie disc and player. Since 1976, close to 1 billion audio products that use Dolby's technology have been sold worldwide. More than 29,000 movie theaters now show films in Dolby Digital Surround Sound, and some 10 million Dolby Digital home theater receivers have been sold since 1999. Dolby technology has become the industry standard for high-quality sound in the music and film industry. Any company that wants to promote its products as having superior technology licenses sound technology from Dolby. How did Dolby build this technology franchise?

The story goes back to 1965 when Dolby Laboratories was founded in London by Ray Dolby (the company's headquarters moved to San Francisco in 1976). Dolby, who had a Ph.D in physics from Cambridge University in England, had invented a technology for reducing the background hiss in professional tape recording without compromising the quality of the material being recorded. Dolby manufactured the sound systems incorporating his technology, but sales to professional recording studios were initially slow. Then in 1968 Dolby had a big break. He met Henry Kloss, whose company, KLH, was a highly regarded American producer of audio equipment (record players and tape decks) for the consumer market. Dolby reached an agreement to license his noise-reduction technology to KLH, and soon other manufacturers of consumer equipment started to approach Dolby to license the technology. Dolby briefly considered manufacturing record players and tape decks for the consumer market, but as he later commented, "I knew that if we entered that market and tried to make something like a cassette deck, we would be in competition with any licensee that we took on. . . . So we had to stay out of manufacturing in that area in order to license in that area."

Dolby adopted a licensing business model and then had to determine what licensing fee to charge. He knew his technology was valuable, but he also understood that charging a high licensing fee would encourage manufacturers to invest in developing their own noise-reduction technology. He decided to charge a modest fee to reduce the incentive that manufacturers would have to develop

their own technology. Then there was the question of which companies to license to. Dolby wanted the Dolby name associated with superior sound, so he needed to make sure that licensees adhered to quality standards. Therefore, the company set up a formal quality control program for its licensees' products. Licensees have to agree to have their products tested by Dolby, and the licensing agreement states that they cannot sell products that do not pass Dolby's quality tests. By preventing products with substandard performance from reaching the market, Dolby has maintained the quality image of products featuring Dolby technology and trademarks. Today, Dolby Laboratories tests samples of hundreds of licensed products every year under this program. By making sure that the Dolby name is associated with superior sound quality, Dolby's quality assurance strategy has increased the power of the Dolby brand, making it very valuable to license.

Another key aspect of Dolby's strategy was born in 1970 when Dolby began to promote the idea of releasing prerecorded cassettes encoded with Dolby noise-reduction technology so that they would have low noise when played on players equipped with Dolby noise-reduction technology. Dolby decided to license the technology on prerecorded tapes for free, instead collecting licensing fees just from the sales of tape players that used Dolby technology. This strategy was hugely successful and set up a positive feedback loop that helped to make Dolby technology ubiquitous. Growing sales of prerecorded tapes encoded with Dolby technology created a demand for players that contained Dolby technology, and as the installed base of players with Dolby technology grew, the proportion of prerecorded tapes that were encoded with Dolby technology surged, further boosting demand for players incorporating Dolby technology. By the mid-1970s, virtually all prerecorded tapes were encoded with Dolby noise-reduction technology. This strategy remains in effect today for all media recorded with Dolby technology and encompasses not only videocassettes but video games and DVD releases encoded with Dolby Surround or Dolby Digital.

As a result of its licensing and quality assurance strategies, Dolby has become the standard for high-quality sound in the music and film industries. Although the company is small—its revenues were around $125 million in 2001—its influence is large. It continues to push the boundaries of sound-reduction technology (it has been a leader in digital sound since the mid-1980s) and has successfully extended its noise-reduction franchise, first into films, then into DVD and video game technology, and most recently onto the Web, where it has licensed its digital technology to a wide range of media companies for digital music delivery and digital audio players, such as those built into personal computers and devices like Compaq's popular iPAQ hand-held computer.

Sources: M. Snider, "Ray Dolby, Audio Inventor," *USA Today,* December 28, 2000, p. D3. D. Dritas, "Dealerscope Hall of Fame: Ray Dolby," *Dealerscope* (January 2002): 74–76. J. Pinkerton, "At Dolby Laboratories: A Clean Audio Pipe," *Dealerscope* (December 2000): 33–34. Company history archived at www.dolby.com.

if a competitor finds a way of providing sufficient benefits that enough consumers are willing to bear the switching costs associated with moving to a new operating system.

Strategies for Winning a Format War

From the perspective of a company pioneering a new technological standard in a marketplace where network effects and positive feedback loops operate, the key question becomes, "What strategy should we pursue to establish our format as the dominant one?"

The various strategies that companies should adopt to win format wars revolve around *finding ways to make network effects work in their favor and against their competitors.* Winning a format war requires a company to build the installed base for its standard as rapidly as possible, thereby leveraging the positive feedback loop, inducing consumers to bear switching costs, and ultimately locking the market into its technology. It requires the company to jump-start and then accelerate demand for its technological standard or format such that it becomes established as quickly as possible as the industry standard, thereby locking out competing formats. There are a number of key strategies and tactics that can be adopted to try and achieve this.[7]

Ensure a Supply of Complements

It is important for the company to make sure that in addition to the product itself, there is an adequate supply of complements. For example, no one will buy the Sony PlayStation II unless there is an adequate supply of games to run on that machine. And no one will purchase a Palm hand-held computer unless there are enough software applications to run on it. Companies normally take two steps to ensure an adequate supply of complements.

First, they may diversify into the production of complements and seed the market with sufficient supply to help jump-start demand for their format. Before Sony produced the original PlayStation in the early 1990s, it established its own in-house unit to produce video games for the PlayStation. When it launched the PlayStation, Sony also simultaneously issued sixteen games to run on the machine, giving consumers a reason to purchase the format. Second, they may create incentives or make it easy for independent companies to produce complements. Sony also licensed the right to produce games to a number of independent game developers, charged the developers a lower royalty rate than they had to pay to competitors such as Nintendo and Sega, and provided them with software tools that made it easier for them to develop the games. Thus, the launch of the Sony PlayStation was accompanied by the simultaneous launch of thirty or so games, which quickly helped to stimulate demand for the machine.

Leverage Killer Applications

Killer applications are applications or uses of a new technology or product that are so compelling that they persuade customers to adopt the new format or technology in droves, thereby "killing" demand for competing formats. Killer applications often help to jump-start demand for the new standard. For example, in the late 1990s, hand-held computers based on the Palm operating system became the dominant format in the market for personal digital assistants (PDA). The killer applications that drove adoption of the Palm format were the personal information management functions and a pen-based input medium (based on **Graffiti**) that Palm bundled with its original PalmPilot, which it introduced in 1996. There had been PDAs before the PalmPilot, including Apple Computer's ill-fated Newton, but it was the applications and ease of use of the PalmPilot that persuaded many consumers to enter this market. Within eighteen months of its initial launch, more than 1 million PalmPilots had been launched, making for a faster demand ramp-up than the first cell phones and pagers. Similarly, the killer applications that induced consumers to sign up to online services such as AOL were email, chatroom, and the ability to browse the Web.

Ideally, the company promoting a technological standard will want to develop the killer applications itself—that is, develop the appropriate complementary products—as Palm did with the PalmPilot. However, it may also be able to leverage the applications that others develop. For example, the early sales of the IBM PC following its 1981 introduction were driven primarily by IBM's decision to license two important software programs for the PC, VisiCalc (a spreadsheet program) and Easy Writer (a word processing program), both developed by independent companies. IBM saw that they were driving rapid adoption of rival personal computers, such as the Apple II, so it quickly licensed them, produced versions that would run on the IBM PC, and sold them as complements to the IBM PC, a strategy that was to prove very successful.

Aggressively Price and Market

A common tactic to jump-start demand is to adopt a **razor and blade strategy:** pricing the product (razor) low in order to stimulate demand and increase the installed base, and then trying to make high profits on the sale of complements (razor blades), which are priced relatively high. This strategy owes its name to the fact that it was pioneered by Gillette to sell its razors and razor blades. Many other companies have followed this strategy—for example, Hewlett Packard typically sells its printers at cost but makes significant profits on the subsequent sale of its replacement cartridges. In this case, the printer is the "razor," and it is priced low to stimulate demand and induce consumers to switch from their existing printer, while the cartridges are the "blades," which are priced high to make profits. The inkjet printer represents a proprietary technological format because only Hewlett Packard cartridges can be used with the printers, and not cartridges designed for competing inkjet printers, such as those sold by Canon. A similar strategy is used in the video game industry: manufacturers price video game consoles at cost to induce consumers to adopt their technology, while making profits on the royalties they receive from the sales of games that run on their system.

Aggressive marketing is also a key factor in jump-starting demand to get an early lead in installed base. Substantial up-front marketing and point-of-sales promotion techniques are often used to try to get potential early adopters to bear the switching costs associated with adopting the format. If these efforts are successful, they can be the start of a positive feedback loop. Again, the Sony PlayStation provides a good example. Sony co-linked the introduction of the PlayStation with nationwide television advertising aimed at its primary demographic (eighteen to thirty-four-year-olds) and in-store displays that allowed potential buyers to play games on the machine before making a purchase. More recently, Microsoft earmarked $500 million for marketing its new X-Box in 2002. Successful marketing can set the ball rolling and create a positive feedback loop.

Cooperate with Competitors

Companies have been close to simultaneously introducing competing and incompatible technological standards a number of times. A good example is the compact disc. Initially four companies—Sony, Philips, JVC, and Telefunken—were developing CD players using different variations of the underlying laser technology. If this situation had persisted, they might have ultimately introduced incompatible technologies into the marketplace, so a CD made for a Philips CD player would not play on a Sony CD player. Understanding that the near-simultaneous introduction of such incompatible technologies can create significant confusion among consumers and often leads them to delay their purchases, Sony and Philips decided to join forces with each other and cooperate on developing the technology. Sony contributed its error correction technology, and Philips contributed its laser technology. The result of this cooperation was that momentum among other players in the industry shifted toward the Sony-Philips alliances; JVC and Telefunken were left with little support. Most important, recording labels announced that they would support the Sony-Philips format but not the Telefunken or JVC format. Telefunken and JVC subsequently decided to abandon their efforts to develop CD technology. The cooperation between Sony and Philips was important because it reduced confusion in the industry and allowed a single format to rise to the fore, which speeded up adoption of the technology. The cooperation was a win-win situation for both Philips and Sony, which eliminated the competitors and were able to share in the success of the format.

License the Format

Another strategy often adopted is to license the format to other enterprises so that they can produce products based on it. The company that pioneered the format gains from the licensing fees that flow back to it and from the enlarged supply of the product, which can stimulate demand and help accelerate market adoption. This was the strategy that Matsushita adopted with its VHS format for the videocassette recorder. In addition to producing VCRs at its own factory in Osaka, Matsushita let a number of other companies produce VHS format players under license (Sony decided not to license its competing Betamax format and produced all Betamax format players itself), and so VHS players were more widely available. More people purchased VHS players, which created an incentive for film companies to issue more films on VHS tapes (as opposed to Betamax tapes), which further increased demand for VHS players, and hence helped Matsushita to lock in VHS as the dominant format in the marketplace. Sony, ironically the first to market, saw its position marginalized by the reduced supply of the critical complement, prerecorded films, and ultimately withdrew Betamax players from the consumer marketplace.

Dolby, we saw in Strategy in Action 7.2, adopted a similar licensing strategy to get its noise-reduction technology adopted as the technological standard in the music and film industries. By charging a modest licensing fee for use of the technology in recording equipment and forgoing licensing fees on media recorded using Dolby technology, Dolby deliberately sought to reduce the financial incentive that potential competitors might have to develop their own, possibly superior, technology. Dolby calculated that its long-run profitability would be maximized by adopting a licensing strategy that limited the incentive of competitors to enter the market (this can be thought of as an example of limit pricing; see Chapter 6).

The correct strategy to pursue in a particular scenario requires that the company consider all of these different strategies and tactics and pursue those that seem most appropriate given the competitive circumstances prevailing in the industry and the likely strategy of rivals. Although there is no one best mix of strategies and tactics, of critical importance is keeping the goal of rapidly increasing the installed base of products based on its standard at the front of its mind. By helping to jump-start demand for its format, a company can induce consumers to bear the switching costs associated with adopting its technology and leverage any positive feedback process that might exist. Also important is not pursuing strategies that have the opposite effect. For example, pricing high to capture profits from early adopters, who tend not to be as price sensitive as later adopters, can have the unfortunate effect of slowing demand growth and letting a more aggressive competitor pick up share and establish its format as the industry standard.

Costs in High-Technology Industries

In many high-tech industries, the fixed costs of developing the product are very high, but the costs of producing one extra unit of the product are very low. This is most obvious in the case of software. For example, it reportedly cost Microsoft $1 billion to develop Windows XP, the latest version of its Windows operating system, but the costs of producing one more copy of Windows XP is virtually zero. Once Windows XP was completed, Microsoft produced master disks that it sent out to PC manufacturers, such as Dell Computer, which then loaded a copy of Windows XP onto every PC it sells. The cost to Microsoft was effectively zero, and yet it receives a significant licensing fee for each copy of Windows XP installed on a PC.[8] For Microsoft, the *marginal cost* of making one more copy of Windows XP is close to zero, although the *fixed costs* of developing the product are $1 billion.

Many other high-technology products have similar cost economics: very high fixed costs and very low marginal costs. Most software products share these features, although if the software is sold through stores, the costs of packaging and distribution will raise the marginal costs, and if it is sold by a sales force direct to end users, this too will raise the marginal costs. Many consumer electronics products have the same basic economics. The fixed costs of developing a DVD player or a video game console can be very expensive, but the costs of producing an incremental unit are very low. The costs of developing a new drug, such as Viagra, can run to over $500 million, but the marginal costs of producing each additional pill is at most a few cents.

Comparative Cost Economics

To grasp why this cost structure is strategically important, it must be understood that in many industries, marginal costs *rise* as a company tries to expand output (economist call this the *law of diminishing returns*). To produce more of a good, a company has to hire more labor and invest in more plant and machinery. At *the margin,* the additional resources used are not as productive, so this leads to increasing marginal costs. However, the law of diminishing returns often does not apply in many high-tech settings, such as the production of software or sending one more bit of data down a digital telecommunications network.

Consider two companies, α and β (see Figure 7.3). Company α is a conventional producer and faces diminishing returns, so as it tries to expand output, its marginal costs rise. Company β is a high-tech producer, and its marginal costs do not rise at all as output is increased. Note that in Figure 7.3, Company β's marginal cost curve is drawn as a straight line near to the horizontal axis, implying that marginal costs are close to zero and do not vary with output, whereas Company α's marginal costs rise as output is expanded, illustrating diminishing returns. Company β's flat and low marginal cost curve means that its average cost curve will fall continuously over all ranges of output as it spreads its fixed costs out over greater volume. In contrast, the

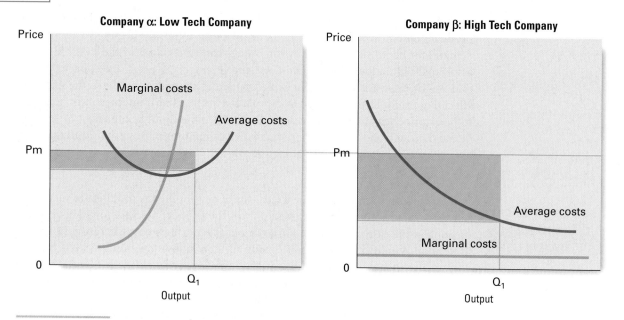

FIGURE 7.3

Cost Structures in High-Technology Industries

rising marginal costs encountered by Company α mean that its average cost curve is the **U**-shaped curve familiar from basic economics texts. For simplicity, assume that both companies sell their product at the same price, P_m, and both sell exactly the same quantity of output, $0 - Q_1$. You will see from Figure 7.3 that at an output of Q_1, Company β has much lower average costs than Company α and as a consequence is making far more profit (profit is the shaded area in Figure 7.3).

Strategic Significance

If a company can shift from a cost structure where it encounters increasing marginal costs to one where fixed costs may be high but marginal costs are much lower, its profitability may increase. In the consumer electronics industry, such a shift has been playing out for two decades. Music recordings used to be based on analog technology where marginal costs rose as output expanded due to diminishing returns (as in the case of Company α in Figure 7.3). Since the 1980s, digital systems such as CD players have replaced analog systems. Digital systems are software based, and this implies much lower marginal costs of producing one more copy of a recording. As a result, the music labels have been able to lower prices, expand demand, and see their profitability increase (their production system that has more in common with Company β in Figure 7.3).

This process is still unfolding. The latest technology for making copies of music recordings is based on distribution over the Internet (for example, by downloading onto an MP3 player). Here, the marginal costs of making one more copy of a recording are lower still. In fact, they are close to zero and do not increase with output. The only problem is that the low costs of copying and distributing music recordings have created a major copyright problem that the major music labels have yet to solve (we discuss this in more detail shortly when we consider intellectual property rights). The same shift is now beginning to affect other industries. Some companies are building their strategies around trying to exploit and profit from this shift. For an example, Strategy in Action 7.3 looks at SonoSite.

Strategy in Action 7.3

Lowering Costs Through Digitalization

The ultrasound unit has been an important piece of diagnostic equipment in hospitals for some time. Ultrasound units use the physics of sound to produce images of soft tissues in the human body. They can produce detailed three-dimensional color images of organs and, by using contrast agents, track the flow of fluids through an organ. A cardiologist, for example, can use an ultrasound in combination with contrast agents injected into the bloodstream to track the flow of blood through a beating heart. In additional to the visual diagnosis, ultrasound also produces an array of quantitative diagnostic information of great value to physicians.

Modern ultrasound units are sophisticated instruments that cost around $250,000 to $300,000 each for a top-line model. They are fairly bulky instruments, weighing some 300 pounds, and are wheeled around hospitals on carts.

A few years back, a group of researchers at ATL, one of the leading ultrasound companies, came up with an idea for reducing the size and cost of a basic unit. They theorized that it might be possible to replace up to 80 percent of the solid circuits in an ultrasound unit with software, in the process significantly shrinking the size and reducing the weight of machines and thereby producing portable ultrasound units. Moreover, by digitalizing much of the ultrasound, replacing hardware with software, they could considerably drive down the marginal costs of making additional units, allowing them to make a good profit at much lower price points.

They reasoned that a portable and inexpensive ultrasound unit would find market opportunities in totally new niches. For example, a small, inexpensive ultrasound unit could be placed in an ambulance or carried into battle by an army medic, or purchased by family physicians for use in their offices. Although they realized that it would be some time, perhaps decades, before such small, inexpensive machines could attain the image quality and diagnostic sophistication of top-of-the-line machines, they saw the opportunity in terms of creating market niches that previously could not be served by ultrasound companies due to the high costs and bulk of the product.

The researchers ultimately became a project team within ATL and were then spun out of ATL as an entirely new company, SonoSite. In late 1999, they introduced their first portable product, weighing just six pounds and costing around $25,000. SonoSite targeted niches that full-sized ultrasound products could not reach: ambulatory care and foreign markets that could not afford the more expensive equipment. In 2001, the company sold $46 million worth of its product. In the long run, SonoSite plans to build more features and greater image quality into the small hand-held machines, primarily by improving the software. This could allow the units to penetrate U.S. hospital markets that currently purchase the established technology, much as client-server systems based on PC technology came to replace mainframes for some functions in business corporations.

Sources: Interviews by Charles W. L. Hill. SonoSite 10K for 2001.

Another implication of its cost structure is that when a high-tech company faces high fixed costs and low marginal costs, its strategy should emphasize the low-cost option: deliberately drive prices down to drive volume up. Look again at Figure 7.3 and you will see that *the high-tech company's average costs fall rapidly as output expands.* This implies that prices can be reduced to stimulate demand, and so long as prices fall less rapidly than average costs, per unit profit margins will expand as prices fall. This is a consequence of the fact that the firm's marginal costs are low and do not rise with output. This strategy of pricing low to drive volume and reap wider profit margins is central to the business model of some very successful high-technology companies, including Microsoft. When Microsoft founder Bill Gates was called into a U.S. Senate hearing during the Microsoft antitrust investigation in 2000, he explained to the bemused senators that Microsoft did not behave like a classic monopolist, raising prices and restricting output to maximize profits. Rather, he said, Microsoft cut prices to stimulate sales and thus increase its profit margins. Gates claimed the strategy was good for consumers—they got cheaper software—and good for Microsoft's profit margins. It was clear from the questioning that the senators had trouble believing this explanation, but for Gates and his company, it has been a central aspect of their strategy since the early 1980s.

Managing Intellectual Property Rights

Ownership of a technology can be a source of sustained competitive advantage and superior profitability, particularly when the company owns a technology that is the standard in an industry, such as Microsoft and Intel's Wintel standard for personal computers and Dolby's ownership of the standard for noise-reduction technology in the music and film recording industries. Even if a technology is not standard but is valued by a sufficient numbers of consumers, ownership of that technology can still be very profitable. Apple's current personal computer technology is by no means the standard in the marketplace, much as Apple would like it to be. In fact, the company's iMac technology accounts for less than 10 percent of the personal computers sold every year. But that small slice of a very large market is still a valuable niche for Apple.

Intellectual Property Rights

Because new technology is the product of intellectual and creative effort, we call it intellectual property. The term **intellectual property** refers to the product of any intellectual and creative effort and includes not only new technology but also a wide range of intellectual creations, including music, films, books, and graphic art. As a society, we value the products of intellectual and creative activity. Intellectual property is seen as a very important driver of economic progress and social wealth.[9] But it is also often expensive, risky, and time-consuming to create intellectual property.

For example, a new drug to treat a dangerous medical condition such as cancer can take twelve to sixteen years to develop and cost $500 million. Moreover, only 20 percent of new drugs that are tested in humans actually make it to the market.[10] The remainder fail because they are found to be unsafe or ineffective. Given the costs, risks, and time involved in this activity, few companies would be willing to embark on the road required to develop a new drug and bring it to market unless they could be reasonably sure that if they were successful in developing the drug, their investment would be profitable. If the minute they introduced a successful cancer drug, their competitors produced imitations of that drug, no company would even consider making the initial investment.

To make sure that this does not happen, we grant the creators of intellectual property certain rights over their creation. These rights, which stop competitors from copying or imitating the creation for a number of years, take the legal forms of patents, copyrights, and trademarks, which all serve the same basic objective: to give individuals and companies an incentive to engage in the expensive and risky business of creating new intellectual property.

The creation of intellectual property is a central endeavor in high-technology industries, and the management of intellectual property rights has moved to center stage in many of these companies. Developing strategies to protect and enforce intellectual property rights can be an important aspect of competitive advantage. For many companies, this amounts to making sure that their patents and copyrights are respected. It is not uncommon, therefore, to see high-technology companies bringing lawsuits against their competitors for patent infringement. In general, companies often use such lawsuits not only to sanction those they suspect of violating the company's intellectual property rights, but also to signal to potential violators that the company will aggressively defend its property. Legal action alone suffices to protect intellectual property in many industries, but in others, such as software, the low costs of illegally copying and distributing intellectual property call for more creative strategies to manage intellectual property rights.

Digitalization and Piracy Rates

Protecting intellectual property has become more complicated in the past few decades because of **digitalization,** that is, the rendering of creative output in digital form. This can be done for music recordings, films, books, newspapers, magazines, and computer software. Digitalization has dramatically lowered the cost of copying and distributing digitalized intellectual property or digital media. As we have seen, the marginal cost of making one more copy of a software program is very low, and the same is true for any other intellectual property rendered in digital form. Moreover, digital media can be distributed at a very low cost (again, almost zero), for example, by distributing over the Internet. Reflecting on this, one commentator has described the Internet as a "giant out-of-control copying machine."[11] The low marginal costs of copying and distributing digital media have made it very easy to sell illegal copies of such property. In turn, this has helped to produce a high level of piracy (in this context, **piracy** refers to the theft of intellectual property).

In the software industry, estimates suggest that in 2000, some 37 percent of all software used around the world was pirated, costing software companies close to $12 billion in lost revenues. The piracy rate ranged from 94 percent in China to 24 percent in the United States. As a region, Asia had the highest piracy rate at 51 percent and North America had the lowest piracy rate at 25 percent. The piracy rate in Western Europe was 34 percent. Although North America had the lowest rate of software piracy, because of the size of the market, the loss to companies was still huge, amounting to almost $3 billion.[12] The problem of piracy is also endemic in the music industry. The International Federation of the Phonographic Industry estimates that in 2000, some 36 percent of all CDs around the globe were illegally produced and sold, costing the music recording industry some $4.1 billion in lost revenues.[13]

The scale of this problem is so large that simply resorting to legal tactics to enforce intellectual property rights has amounted to nothing more than a partial solution to the piracy problem. Many companies now build sophisticated encryption software into their digital products, which can make it more difficult for pirates to copy digital media and thereby raise the costs of stealing. But the pirates too are sophisticated and often seem to be able to find their way around encryption software. This raises the question of whether there are additional strategies that can be adopted to manage digital rights, and thereby limit piracy.

Strategies for Managing Digital Rights

One strategy is simply to recognize that while the low costs of copying and distributing digital media make some piracy inevitable, the same attributes can be used to the company's advantage. The basic strategy here represents yet another variation of the basic razor and razor blades principle: give something away for free in order to boost the sales of a complementary product. A familiar example concerns Adobe Acrobat Reader, the software program for reading documents formatted by Adobe Acrobat (i.e., PDF formatted documents). Adobe developed Adobe Acrobat to allow people to format documents in a manner that resembled a high-quality printed page and to display and distribute these documents over the Web. Moreover, Adobe documents are formatted in a read-only format, meaning that they cannot be altered by individuals nor can parts of those documents be copied and pasted to other documents. Its strategy has been to give away Adobe Acrobat Reader for free and then make money by selling its Acrobat software for formatting documents. The strategy has worked extremely well. Anyone can download a copy of Acrobat Reader from Adobe's web site. Because the marginal costs of copying and distributing this software over the Web are extremely low, the process is almost costless for both Adobe and its customers. The result is that the Acrobat Reader has diffused very rapidly and is now the dominant format for viewing high-quality documents distributed and downloaded over the Web. As the installed base of Acrobat Readers has grown, sales of Adobe Acrobat software have soared as more and more organizations and individuals realize that formatting their digital documents in Acrobat format makes sense.

Another strategy is to take advantage of the low costs of copying and distributing digital media to drive down the costs of purchasing those media, thereby reducing the incentive that consumers have to steal. When coupled with encryption software that makes piracy more difficult and vigorous legal actions to enforcement of intellectual property regulations, this can slow the piracy rate and generate incremental revenues that cost little to produce.

Several music companies are now experimenting with variants of this strategy. Roxio, a manufacturer of software for copying, or "burning," music onto CDs, has begun to partner with several music labels to develop just such a strategy.[14] In 2001, Roxio's Easy CD Creator and Toast software accounted for 70 percent of the CD burning software sold. The software is now preloaded onto most new personal computers. However, Roxio's sales growth has been hampered by opposition from music labels, which argue that Roxio's software is promoting music piracy and hurting CD sales. In response, Roxio has persuaded several music companies to start experimenting with a service that allows users to burn music onto CDs. In January 2002, Pressplay, a service backed by Sony, Universal Music, and EMI, began to allow users to download songs digitally and burn them onto CDs. Users pay $25 a month to burn twenty songs, although they can burn only two tracks from a single artist each month. This business model allows subscribers to customize a CD, which is what many do anyway when pirating CDs by burning them. However, in theory, the service saves customers money because they do not have to purchase the original CDs. Pressplay and Roxio hope that the strategy will reduce piracy rates, while generating incremental revenues that cost very little to produce due to the extremely low marginal costs of copying and distributing music in this manner.

Capturing First-Mover Advantages

In high-technology industries, companies often compete by striving to be the first to develop revolutionary new products, that is, to be a **first mover.** By definition, the first mover with regard to a revolutionary product is in a monopoly position. If the new product satisfies unmet consumer needs and demand is high, the first mover can capture significant revenues and profits. Such revenues and profits signal to potential rivals that there is money to be made by imitating the first mover. As illustrated in Figure 7.4, in the absence of strong barriers to imitation, this implies that imitators will rush into the market created by the first mover, competing away the first mover's monopoly profits and leaving all participants in the market with a much lower level of returns.

Despite imitation, some first movers have the ability to capitalize on and reap substantial **first-mover advantages**—the advantages of pioneering new technologies and products that lead to an enduring competitive advantage. Intel introduced the world's first microprocessor in 1971 and today still dominates the microprocessor

FIGURE 7.4

The Impact of Imitation on Profits of a First Mover

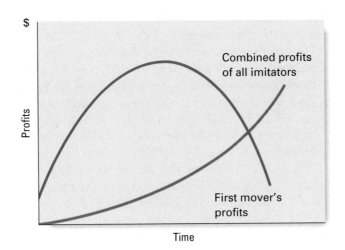

segment of the semiconductor industry. Xerox introduced the world's first photocopier and for a long time enjoyed a leading position in the industry. Cisco introduced the first Internet protocol network router in 1986 and still dominates the market for that equipment today. Some first movers can reap substantial advantages from their pioneering activities that lead to an enduring competitive advantage. They can, in other words, limit or slow the rate of imitation.

But there are plenty of counterexamples suggesting that first-mover advantages might not be easy to capture and, in fact, that there might be **first mover disadvantages**—the competitive *disadvantages* associated with being first. For example, Apple Computer was the first company to introduce a hand-held computer, the Apple Newton, but the product failed; a second mover, Palm, succeeded where Apple had failed. In the market for commercial jet aircraft, DeHavilland was first to market with the Comet, but it was the second mover, Boeing, with its 707 jetliner, that went on to dominate the market.

Clearly being a first mover does not by itself guarantee success. As we shall see, the difference between innovating companies that capture first-mover advantages and those that fall victim to first-mover disadvantages in part turns on the strategy that the first mover pursues. Before considering the strategy issue, however, we need to take a closer look at the nature of first-mover advantages and disadvantages.[15]

First-Mover Advantages

There are five main sources of first-mover advantages.[16] First, the first mover has an opportunity to *exploit network effects* and positive feedback loops, locking consumers into its technology. In the VCR industry, Sony could have exploited network effects by licensing its technology, but instead the company ceded its first-mover advantage to the second mover, Matsushita.

Second, the first mover may be able to establish significant *brand loyalty,* which is expensive for later entrants to break down. Indeed, if the company is successful in this endeavor, its name may become closely associated with the entire class of products, including those produced by rivals. People still talk of "Xeroxing" when they are going to make a photocopy or "FedExing" when they are going to send a package by overnight mail.

Third, the first mover may be able to ramp up sales volume ahead of rivals and thus reap cost advantages associated with the realization of *scale economies and learning effects* (see Chapter 4). Once the first mover has these cost advantages, it can respond to new entrants by cutting prices in order to hold on to its market share and still earn significant profits.

Fourth, the first mover may be able to create *switching costs* for its customers that subsequently make it difficult for rivals to enter the market and take customers away from the first mover. Wireless service providers, for example, will give new customers a "free" wireless phone, but customers must sign a contract agreeing to pay for the phone if they terminate the service contract within a specified time period, such as a year. Because the real cost of a wireless phone may run $100 to $200, this represents a significant switching cost that later entrants have to overcome.

Finally, the first mover may be able to *accumulate valuable knowledge* related to customer needs, distribution channels, product technology, process technology, and so on. This accumulated knowledge gives it a knowledge advantage that later entrants might find difficult or expensive to match. Sharp, for example, was the first mover in the commercial manufacture of active matrix liquid crystal displays used in laptop computers. The process for manufacturing these displays is very difficult, with a high reject rate for flawed displays. Sharp has accumulated such an advantage with regard to production processes that it has been very difficult for later entrants to match it on product quality, and thus costs.

First-Mover Disadvantages Balanced against these first-mover advantages are a number of disadvantages. First, the first mover has to bear significant *pioneering costs* that later entrants do not. The first mover has to pioneer the technology, develop distribution channels, and educate customers about the nature of the product. All of this can be expensive and time-consuming. Later entrants, by way of contrast, might be able to *free-ride* on the first mover's investments in pioneering the market and customer education.

Related to this, first movers are more prone to *make mistakes* because there are so many uncertainties in a new market. Later entrants may be able to learn from the mistakes made by first movers, improve on the product or the way in which it is sold, and come to market with a superior offering that captures significant market share from the first mover. For example, one of the reasons that the Apple Newton failed was that the handwriting software in the hand-held computer failed to recognize human handwriting. The second mover in this market, Palm, learned from Apple's error. When it introduced the PalmPilot, it used software that recognized letters written in a particular way, Graffiti, and then persuaded customers to learn this method of inputting data into the hand-held computer.

Third, first movers run the risk of *building the wrong resources and capabilities* because they are focusing on a customer set that is not going to be characteristic of the mass market. This is the *crossing the chasm* problem that we discussed in the previous chapter. You will recall that the customers in the early market—those we categorized as innovators and early adopters—have different characteristics from the first wave of the mass market, the early majority. The first mover runs the risk of gearing its resources and capabilities to the needs of innovators and early adopters and not being able to switch when the early majority enters the market. As a result, first movers run a greater risk of plunging into the chasm that separates the early market from the mass market.

Finally, the first mover may invest in *inferior or obsolete technology*. This can happen when its product innovation is based on underlying technology that is advancing rapidly. By basing its product on an early version of the technology, it may lock itself into something that rapidly becomes obsolete. In contrast, later entrants may be able to leapfrog the first mover and introduce products that are based on later versions of the underlying technology. This happened in France during the 1980s when, at the urging of the government, France Telecom introduced the world's first consumer online service, Minitel. France Telecom distributed crude terminals to consumers for free, which they could hook up to their phone line and use to browse phone directories. Other simple services were soon added, and before long the French could carry out online shopping, banking, travel, weather, and news—all years before the Web was invented. The problem was that by the standards of the Web, Minitel was very crude and inflexible, and France Telecom, as the first mover, suffered. The French were very slow to adopt personal computers and then the Internet primarily because Minitel had such a presence. As late as 1998, only a fifth of French households had a computer, compared with two-fifths in the United States, and only 2 percent of households were connected to the Internet compared to over 30 percent in the United States. As the result of a government decision, France Telecom, and indeed an entire nation, was slow to adopt a revolutionary new online medium, the Web, because they were the first to invest in a more primitive version of the technology.[17]

Strategies for Exploiting First-Mover Advantages

The task facing a first mover is how to exploit its lead in order to capitalize on first-mover advantages and build a sustainable long-term competitive advantage while simultaneously reducing the risks associated with first mover disadvantages, There are three basic strategies available: (1) develop and market the innovation itself, (2) develop and market the innovation jointly with other companies through a strategic alliance or joint venture, and (3) license the innovation to others and let them develop the market.

The optimal choice of strategy depends on the answers to three questions:

1. Does the innovating company have the *complementary assets* to exploit its innovation and capture first-mover advantages?

2. How difficult is it for imitators to copy the company's innovation? In other words, what is the *height of barriers to imitation?*

3. Are there *capable competitors* that could rapidly imitate the innovation?

Complementary Assets. **Complementary assets** are the assets required to exploit a new innovation and gain a competitive advantage.[18] Among the most important complementary assets are competitive manufacturing facilities capable of handling rapid growth in customer demand while maintaining high product quality. State-of-the-art manufacturing facilities enable the first mover to move quickly down the experience curve without encountering production bottlenecks or problems with the quality of the product. The inability to satisfy demand because of these problems, however, creates the opportunity for imitators to enter the marketplace. For example, in 1998, Immunex was the first company to introduce a revolutionary new biological treatment for rheumatoid arthritis. Sales for this product, Enbrel, ramped up very rapidly, hitting $750 million in 2001. However, Immunex had not invested in sufficient manufacturing capacity. In mid-2000, it announced that it lacked the capacity to satisfy demand and that bringing additional capacity on line would take at least two years. This manufacturing bottleneck gave the second mover in the market, Johnson & Johnson, the opportunity to expand demand for its product rapidly, which by early 2002 was outselling Enbrel. Immunex's first-mover advantage had been partly eroded because it lacked an important complementary asset, the manufacturing capability required to satisfy demand.

Complementary assets also include marketing know-how, an adequate sales force, access to distribution systems, and an after-sales service and support network. All of these assets can help an innovator build brand loyalty and help the innovator achieve market penetration more rapidly.[19] In turn, the resulting increases in volume facilitate more rapid movement down the experience curve and the attainment of a sustainable cost-based advantage due to scale economies and learning effects. One of the reasons that EMI, the first mover in the market for CT scanners, ultimately lost out to established medical equipment companies, such as GE Medical Systems, was that it lacked the marketing know-how, sales force, and distribution systems required to compete effectively in the world's largest market for medical equipment, the United States.

Developing complementary assets can be very expensive, and companies often need large infusions of capital for this purpose. That is the reason first movers often lose out to late movers that are large, successful companies, often established in other industries, with the resources to develop a presence in the new industry quickly. Microsoft and 3M exemplify companies that can move quickly to capitalize on the opportunities when other companies open up new product markets, such as compact discs or floppy disks. For example, although Netscape pioneered the market for Internet browsers with the Netscape Navigator, Microsoft's Internet Explorer ultimately dominated the market for Internet browsers.

Height of Barriers to Imitation. Recall from Chapter 3 that **barriers to imitation** are factors that prevent rivals from imitating a company's distinctive competencies and innovations. Although ultimately any innovation can be copied, the higher the barriers are, the longer it takes for rivals to imitate, and the more time the first mover has to build an enduring competitive advantage.

Barriers to imitation give an innovator time to establish a competitive advantage and build more enduring barriers to entry in the newly created market. Patents, for example, are among the most widely used barriers to imitation. By protecting its photocopier technology with a thicket of patents, Xerox was able to delay any significant imitation of its product for seventeen years. However, patents are often easy to "invent around." For example, one study found that this happened to 60 percent of patented innovations within four years.[20] If patent protection is weak, a company might try to slow imitation by developing new products and processes in secret. The most famous example of this approach is Coca-Cola, which has kept the formula for Coke a secret for generations. But Coca-Cola's success in this regard is an exception. A study of 100 companies has estimated that proprietary information about a company's decision to develop a major new product or process is known to its rivals within about twelve to eighteen months of the original development decision.[21]

Capable Competitors. **Capable competitors** are companies that can move quickly to imitate the pioneering company. Competitors' capability to imitate a pioneer's innovation depends primarily on two factors: (1) R&D skills and (2) access to complementary assets. In general, the greater the number of capable competitors with access to the R&D skills and complementary assets needed to imitate an innovation, the more rapid imitation is likely to be.

In this context, R&D skills refer to the ability of rivals to reverse-engineer an innovation in order to find out how it works and quickly develop a comparable product. As an example, consider the CT scanner. GE bought one of the first CT scanners produced by EMI, and its technical experts reverse-engineered it. Despite the product's technological complexity, GE developed its own version, which allowed it to imitate EMI quickly and ultimately to replace EMI as the major supplier of CT scanners.

With regard to complementary assets, the access that rivals have to marketing, sales know-how, or manufacturing capabilities is one of the key determinants of the rate of imitation. If would-be imitators lack critical complementary assets, not only do they have to imitate the innovation, they may also have to imitate the innovator's complementary assets. This is expensive, as AT&T discovered when it tried to enter the personal computer business in 1984. AT&T lacked the marketing assets (sales force and distribution systems) necessary to support personal computer products. The lack of these assets and the time it takes to build them partly explain why four years after it entered the market, AT&T had lost $2.5 billion and still had not emerged as a viable contender. It subsequently pulled out of this business.

Three Innovation Strategies. The way in which these three factors—complementary assets, height of barriers to imitation, and the capability of competitors—influence the choice of innovation strategy is summarized in Table 7.1. The competitive strategy of *developing and marketing the innovation alone* makes most sense when (1) the innovator has the complementary assets necessary to develop the innovation, (2) the barriers to imitating a new innovation are high, and (3) the number of capable competitors is limited. Complementary assets allow rapid development and promotion of the innovation. High barriers to imitation buy the innovator time to establish a competitive advantage and build enduring barriers to entry through brand loyalty or experience-based cost advantages. The fewer the capable competitors there are, the less likely it is that any one of them will succeed in circumventing barriers to imitation and quickly imitating the innovation.

The competitive strategy of *developing and marketing the innovation jointly with other companies through a strategic alliance or joint venture* makes most sense when (1) the innovator lacks complementary assets, (2) barriers to imitation are high, and (3) there are several capable competitors. In such circumstances, it makes sense to enter into an alliance with a company that already has the complementary assets—in other words, with a capable competitor. Theoretically, such an alliance should prove to be mutually beneficial, and each partner can share in high profits that neither could earn on its own. Moreover, such a strategy has the benefit of co-opting a potential rival. For example, had EMI teamed up with a capable competitor to develop the market for CT scanners, such as GE Medical Systems, instead of going it alone, the company might not only have been able to build a more enduring competitive advantage, it would also have co-opted a potentially powerful rival into its camp.

TABLE 7.1

Strategies for Profiting from Innovation

Strategy	Does the Innovator Have the Required Complementary Assets?	Likely Height of Barriers to Imitation	Number of Capable Competitors
Going it alone	Yes	High	Very few
Entering into an alliance	No	High	Moderate number
License the innovation	No	Low	Many

The third strategy, *licensing,* makes most sense when (1) the innovating company lacks the complementary assets, (2) barriers to imitation are low, and (3) there are many capable competitors. The combination of low barriers to imitation and many capable competitors makes rapid imitation almost certain. The innovator's lack of complementary assets further suggests that an imitator will soon capture the innovator's competitive advantage. Given these factors, because rapid diffusion of the innovator's technology through imitation is inevitable, the innovator can at least share in some of the benefits of this diffusion by licensing out its technology.[22] Moreover, by setting a relatively modest licensing fee, the innovator may be able to reduce the incentive that potential rivals have to develop their own competing, and possibly superior technology. This seems to have been the strategy Dolby adopted to get its technology established as the standard for noise reduction in the music and film businesses (see Strategy in Action 7.2).

Technological Paradigm Shifts

Technological paradigm shifts occur when new technologies come along that revolutionize the structure of the industry, dramatically alter the nature of competition, and require companies to adopt new strategies in order to survive. A good example of a paradigm shift that is currently unfolding is the shift from chemical to digital photography (another example of *digitalization*). For over half a century, the large incumbent enterprises in the photographic industry such as Kodak and Fuji film have generated most of their revenues from selling and processing film using traditional silver halide technology. The rise of digital photography is a huge threat to their business models. Digital cameras do not use film, the mainstay of Kodak's and Fuji's business. Moreover, these cameras are more like specialized computers than conventional cameras and are thus based on scientific knowledge that Kodak and Fuji have little knowledge of. Although both Kodak and Fuji are investing heavily in the development of digital cameras, they are facing intense competition from companies such as Sony, Canon, and Hewlett Packard, which have developed their own digital cameras, from software developers such as Adobe and Microsoft, which make the software for manipulating digital images, and from printer companies such as Hewlett Packard and Canon, which are making the printers that consumers can use to print out their own high-quality pictures at home. As digital substitution gathers speed in the photography industry, it is not clear that the traditional incumbents will be able to survive this shift; the new competitors might well rise to dominance in the new market.

If Kodak and Fuji do decline, they will not be the first large incumbents to be felled by a technological paradigm shift in their industry. In the early 1980s, the computer industry was revolutionized by the arrival of personal computer technology, which gave rise to client-server networks that replaced traditional mainframe and minicomputers for many business uses. Many incumbent companies in the mainframe era, such as Wang, Control Data, and DEC, ultimately did not survive, and even IBM went through a decade of wrenching changes and large losses before it reinvented itself as a provider of e-business solutions. In their place, new entrants such as Microsoft, Intel, Dell, and Compaq rose to dominance in this new computer industry.

Examples such as these raise four questions:

1. When do paradigm shifts occur, and how do they unfold?

2. Why do so many incumbents go into decline following a paradigm shift?

3. What strategies can incumbents adopt in order to increase the probability that they will survive a paradigm shift and emerge the other side of the market abyss created by the arrival of new technology as a profitable enterprise?

4. What strategies can new entrants into a market adopt in order to profit from a paradigm shift?

We shall answer each of these questions in the remainder of this chapter.

Paradigm Shifts and the Decline of Established Companies

Paradigm shifts appear to be more likely to occur in an industry when one, or both, of the following conditions are in place.[23] First, the established technology in the industry is mature and approaching or at its "natural limit," and second, a new "disruptive technology" has entered the marketplace and is taking root in niches that are poorly served by incumbent companies using the established technology.

The Natural Limits to Technology. Richard Foster has formalized the relationship between the performance of a technology and time in terms of what he calls the technology S-curve (see Figure 7.5).[24] This curve shows the relationship over time of *cumulative* investments in R&D and the performance (or functionality) of a given technology. Early in its evolution, R&D investments in a new technology tend to yield rapid improvements in performance as basic engineering problems are solved. After a time, diminishing returns to cumulative R&D begin to set in, the rate of improvement in performance slows, and the technology starts to approach its natural limit, where further advances are not possible. For example, one can argue that there was more improvement in the first fifty years of the commercial aerospace business following the pioneering flight by the Wright Brothers than there has been in the second fifty years. Indeed, the world's largest commercial jet aircraft, the Boeing 747, is based on a 1960s design, as is the world's fastest commercial jet aircraft, the Concorde. In commercial aerospace, therefore, we are now in the region of diminishing returns and may be approaching the natural limit to improvements in the technology of commercial aerospace.

Similarly, it can be argued that we are approaching the natural limit to technology in the performance of silicon-based semiconductor chips. Over the past two decades, the performance of semiconductor chips has been increased dramatically by packing ever more transistors onto a single small silicon chip. This process has helped to increase the power of computers, lower their cost, and shrink their size. But we are starting to approach limits to the ability to shrink the width of lines on a chip and therefore pack ever more transistors onto a single chip. The limit is imposed by the natural laws of physics. Light waves are used to help etch lines onto a chip, and one cannot etch a line that is smaller than the wavelength of light being used. Semiconductor companies are already using light with very small wavelengths, such as extreme ultraviolet, to etch lines onto a chip, but there are limits to how far this

FIGURE 7.5

The Technology
S-Curve

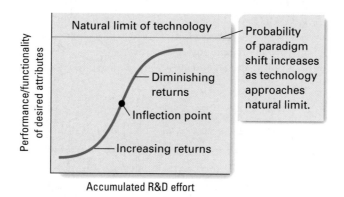

technology can be pushed, and many believe that we will reach those limits within the decade. Does this mean that our ability to make smaller, faster, cheaper computers is coming to an end? Probably not. It is more likely that we will find another technology to replace silicon-based computing and enable us to continue building smaller, faster, cheaper computers. In fact, several exotic competing technologies are already being developed that may replace silicon-based computing. These include self-organizing molecular computers, three-dimensional microprocessor technology, quantum computing technology, and using DNA to perform computations.[25]

What does all of this have to do with paradigm shifts? According to Foster, when a technology approaches its natural limit, research attention turns to possible alternative technologies, and sooner or later one of those alternatives might be commercialized and replace the established technology. That is, the probability that a paradigm shift will occur increases. Thus, sometime in the next decade or two, another paradigm shift might shake the very foundations of the computer industry as exotic computing technology replaces silicon-based computing. If history is any guide, if and when this happens, many of the incumbents in today's computer industry will go into decline, and new enterprises will rise to dominance.

Foster pushes this point a little further, noting that initially, the contenders for the replacement technology are not as effective as the established technology in producing the attributes and features that consumers demand in a product. For example, in the early years of the twentieth century, automobiles were just starting to be produced. They were valued for their ability to move people from place to place, but so was the horse and cart (the established technology). When automobiles originally appeared, the horse and cart was still quite a bit better than the automobile at doing this (see Figure 7.6). After all, the first cars were slow, noisy, and prone to breakdown. Moreover, they needed a network of paved roads and gas stations to be really useful, and that network didn't exist, so for most applications, the horse and cart was still the preferred mode of transportation—to say nothing of the fact that it was cheaper.

However, this comparison ignored the fact that in the early twentieth century, automobile technology was at the very start of its S-curve and was about to experience dramatic improvements in performance as major engineering problems were solved (and those paved roads and gas stations were built). In contrast, after 3,000 years of continuous improvement and refinement, the horse and cart was almost definitely at the end of its technological S-curve. The result was that the rapidly improv-

FIGURE 7.6

Established and Successor Technologies

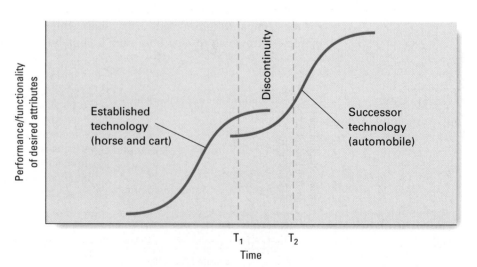

ing automobile soon replaced the horse and cart as the preferred mode of transportation. At time T_1 in Figure 7.6, the horse and cart was still superior to the automobile. By time T_2, the automobile had surpassed the horse and cart.

Foster notes that because the successor technology is initially less efficient than the established technology, established companies and their customers often make the mistake of dismissing it, only to be taken off-guard by its rapid performance improvement. A final point here is that often there is not one potential successor technologies but a swarm of potential successor technologies, only one of which might ultimately rise to the fore (see Figure 7.7). When this is the case, established companies are put at a disadvantage. Even if they recognize that a paradigm shift is imminent, they may not have the resources to invest in all the potential replacement technologies. If they invest in the wrong one, something that is easy to do given the uncertainty that surrounds the entire process, they may be locked out of subsequent development.

Disruptive Technology. Clayton Christensen has built on Foster's insights and his own research to develop a theory of disruptive technology that has become very influential in high-technology circles.[26] Christensen uses the term **disruptive technology** to refer to a new technology that gets its start away from the mainstream of a market and then, as its functionality improves over time, invades the main market. Such technologies are disruptive because they revolutionize industry structure and competition, often causing the decline of established companies. They cause a technological paradigm shift.

Christensen's greatest insight is that established companies are often aware of the new technology but do not invest in it because they listen to their customers, and their customers do not want it. Of course, this arises because the new technology is early in its development, and thus only at the beginning of the S-curve for that technology. Once the performance of the new technology improves, customers *do* want it, but by this time it is new entrants, as opposed to established companies, that have accumulated the knowledge required to bring the new technology into the mass market. Christensen supports his view by several detailed historical case studies, one of which is summarized in Strategy in Action 7.4.

FIGURE 7.7

Swarm of Successor
Technologies

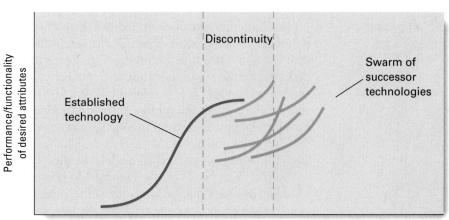

Strategy in Action

7.4

Disruptive Technology in Mechanical Excavators

Excavators are used to dig out foundations for large buildings, trenches to lay large pipes for sewers and the like, and foundations and trenches for residential construction and farm work. Prior to the 1940s, the dominant technology used to manipulate the bucket on a mechanical excavator was based on a system of cables and pulleys. Although these mechanical systems could lift large buckets of earth, the excavators themselves were quite large, cumbersome, and expensive. Thus, they were rarely used to dig small trenches for house foundations, irrigation ditches for farmers, and the like. In most cases, these small trenches were dug by hand.

In the 1940s, a new technology made its appearance: hydraulics. In theory, hydraulic systems had certain advantages over the established cable and pulley systems. Most important, their energy efficiency was higher: for a given bucket size, a smaller engine would be required using a hydraulic system. However, the initial hydraulic systems also had drawbacks. The seals on hydraulic cylinders were prone to leak under high pressure, effectively limiting the size of bucket that could be lifted using hydraulics. Notwithstanding this drawback, when hydraulics first appeared, many of the incumbent firms in the mechanical excavation industry took the technology seriously enough to ask their primary customers whether they would be interested in products based on hydraulics. Since the primary customers of incumbents needed excavators with large buckets to dig out the foundations for buildings and large trenches, their reply was negative. For

this customer set, the hydraulic systems of the 1940s were not reliable or powerful enough. Consequently, after consulting with their customers, these established companies in the industry made the strategic decision not to invest in hydraulics. Instead, they continued to produce excavation equipment based on the dominant cable and pulley technology.

It was left to a number of new entrants, which included J. I. Case, John Deere, J. C. Bamford, and Caterpillar, to pioneer hydraulic excavation equipment. Because of the limits on bucket size imposed by the seal problem, these companies initially focused on a poorly served niche in the market that could make use of small buckets: residential contractors and farmers. Over time, these new entrants were able to solve the engineering problems associated with weak hydraulic seals, and as they did this, they manufactured excavators with larger buckets. Ultimately, they invaded the market niches served by the old-line companies: general contractors that dug the foundations for large buildings, sewers, and so on. At this point, Case, Deere, Caterpillar, and their kin rose to dominance in the industry, while the majority of established companies from the prior era lost share. Of the thirty or so manufacturers of cable-actuated equipment in the United States in the late 1930s, only four survived to the 1950s.

Source: M. Christensen, *The Innovator's Dilemma* (Boston: Harvard Business School Press, 1997).

In addition to listening too closely to their customers, Christensen also identifies a number of other factors that make it very difficult for established companies to adopt a new disruptive technology. He notes that many established companies declined to invest in new disruptive technologies because initially they served such small market niches that it seemed unlikely that they would have an impact on the company's revenues and profits. As the new technology started to improve in functionality and invade the main market, their investment was often hindered by the fact that exploiting the new technology required a new business model totally different from the company's established model, and thus very difficult to implement.

Both of these points can be illustrated by reference to one more example: the rise of online discount stockbrokers during the 1990s such as Ameritrade and E*Trade, which made use of a new technology, the Internet, to allow individual investors to trade stocks for a very low commission fee, whereas full-service stockbrokers, such as

Merrill Lynch, where orders had to be placed through a stockbroker who earned a commission for performing the transaction, did not. (This story is told in more detail in the *Closing Case* in Chapter 5.)

Christensen also notes that a new network of suppliers and distributors typically grows up around the new entrants. Not only do established companies initially ignore disruptive technology, so do their suppliers and distributors. This creates an opportunity for new suppliers and distributors to enter the market to serve the new entrants. As the new entrants grow, so does the associated network. Ultimately, Christensen suggests, the new entrants and their network may replace not only established enterprises, but also the entire network of suppliers and distributors associated with established companies. Taken to its logical extreme, this view suggests that disruptive technologies may result in the demise of the entire network of enterprises associated with established companies in an industry.

The established companies in an industry that is being rocked by a technological paradigm shift often have to cope with internal inertia forces that limit their ability to adapt, but the new entrants do not and thereby have an advantage. They do not have to deal with an established and conservative customer set and an obsolete business model. Instead, they can focus on optimizing the new technology, improving its performance, and riding the wave of disruptive technology into new market segments until they invade the main market and challenge the established companies, by which time they may be well equipped to beat them.

Strategic Implications for Established Companies

Although Christensen has uncovered an important tendency, it is by no means written in stone that all established companies are doomed to fail when faced with disruptive technologies, as we have seen with IBM and Merrill Lynch. Established companies must meet the challenges created by the emergence of disruptive technologies.

First, having access to the knowledge about how disruptive technologies can revolutionize markets is itself a valuable strategic asset. Many of the established companies that Christensen examined failed because they took a myopic view of the new technology and asked their customers the wrong question. Instead of asking, "Are you interested in this new technology?" they should have recognized that the new technology was likely to improve rapidly over time and instead have asked, "Would you be interested in this new technology if it improves its functionality over time?" If they had done this, they may have made very different strategic decisions.

Second, it is clearly important for established enterprises to invest in newly emerging technologies that may ultimately become disruptive technologies. Companies have to hedge their bets about new technology. As we have noted, at any time, there may be a swarm of emerging technologies, any one of which might ultimately become a disruptive technology. Large, established companies that are generating significant cash flows can and often should establish and fund central R&D operations to invest in and develop such technologies. In addition, they may wish to acquire newly emerging companies that are pioneering potentially disruptive technologies or enter into alliances with them to develop the technology jointly. The strategy of acquiring companies that are developing potentially disruptive technology is one that Cisco Systems, a dominant provider of Internet network equipment, is famous for pursuing. At the heart of this strategy must be a recognition on the part of the incumbent enterprise that it is better for the company to develop disruptive technology and then cannibalize its established sales base than to have that sales base taken away by new entrants.

However, Christensen makes the very important point that even when established companies do undertake R&D investments in potentially disruptive technologies, they often fail to commercialize those technologies because of internal forces that suppress change. For example, managers in the parts of the business that are currently generating the most cash may claim that they need the greatest R&D investment to maintain their market position and may lobby top management to delay investment in a new technology. Early on in the S-curve, when it is very unclear what the long-term prospects of a new technology may be, this can be a powerful argument. The consequence, however, may be that the company fails to build a competence in the new technology and will suffer accordingly.

In addition, Christensen argues that the commercialization of new disruptive technology often requires a radically different value chain with a completely different cost structure—a new business model. For example, it may require a different manufacturing system, a different distribution system, and different pricing options and involve very different gross margins and operating margins. Christensen argues that it is almost impossible for two distinct business models to coexist within the same organization. When they try to do that, almost inevitably the established business model will suffocate the business model associated with the disruptive technology.

The solution to this problem is to separate out the disruptive technology and place it in its own autonomous operating division. For example, during the early 1980s Hewlett Packard (HP) built a very successful laser jet printer business. Then along came ink jet technology. Some in the company believed that ink jet printers would cannibalize sales of laser jets and consequently argued that HP should not produce ink jets. Fortunately for HP, senior management at the time saw ink jet technology for what it was: a potential disruptive technology. Far from not investing in it, they allocated significant R&D funds toward its commercialization. Furthermore, when the technology was ready for market introduction, they established an autonomous ink jet division at a different geographic location with its own manufacturing, marketing, and distribution activities. They accepted that the ink jet division might take sales away from the laser jet division and decided that it was better to have an HP division cannibalize the sales of another HP division than have those sales cannibalized by another company. Happily for HP, it turns out that ink jets cannibalize sales of laser jets only on the margin and that both have profitable market niches. This felicitous outcome, however, does not detract from the message of the story: if your company is developing a potentially disruptive technology, the chances of success will be enhanced if it is placed in a stand-alone product division and given its own mandate.

Strategic Implications for New Entrants

This stream of work also holds implications for new entrants. The new entrants, or attackers, have several advantages over established enterprises. Pressures to continue the existing out-of-date business model do not hamstring new entrants, which do not have to worry about product cannibalization issues. They do not have to worry about their established customer base or relationships with established suppliers and distributors. Instead, they can focus all their energies on the opportunities offered by the new disruptive technology, ride the S-curve of technology improvement, and grow rapidly with the market for that technology. This does not mean that the new entrants have no problems to solve. They may be constrained by a lack of capital or have to manage the organizational problems associated with rapid growth; most important, they may need to find a way to take their technology from a small out-of-the-way niche into the mass market.

Perhaps one of the most important issues facing new entrants is the choice of whether to partner with an established company or go it alone in their attempt to develop and profit from a new disruptive technology. Although a new entrant may enjoy all of the advantages of the attacker, it may lack the resources required to exploit them fully. In such a case, it might want to consider forming a strategic alliance with a larger, established company to gain access to those resources. The main issues here are the same as those that we discussed earlier when examining the three strategies that companies can pursue to capture first-mover advantages: go it alone, enter into a strategic alliance, or license its technology.

Summary of Chapter

1. Technical standards are important in many high-tech industries: they guarantee compatibility, reduce confusion in the minds of customers, allow for mass production and lower costs, and reduce the risks associated with supplying complementary products.

2. Network effects and positive feedback loops often determine which standard comes to dominate a market.

3. Owning a standard can be a source of sustained competitive advantage.

4. Establishing a proprietary standard as the industry standard may require the company to win a format war against a competing and incompatible standard. Strategies for doing this include producing complementary products, leveraging killer applications, aggressive pricing and marketing, licensing the technology, and cooperating with competitors.

5. Many high-tech products are characterized by high fixed costs of development but very low or zero marginal costs of producing one extra unit of output. These cost economics create a presumption in favor of strategies that emphasize aggressive pricing to increase volume and drive down average total costs.

6. Many digital products suffer from very high piracy rates due to the low marginal costs of copying and distributing such products. Piracy can be reduced by the appropriate combination of strategy, encryption software, and vigorous defense of intellectual property rights.

7. It is very important for a first mover to develop a strategy to capitalize on first-mover advantages. A company can choose from three strategies: develop and market the technology itself, to do so jointly with another company, and license the technology to existing companies. The choice depends on the complementary assets required to capture a first-mover advantage, the height of barriers to imitation, and the capability of competitors.

8. Technological paradigm shifts occur when new technologies come along that revolutionize the structure of the industry, dramatically alter the nature of competition, and require companies to adopt new strategies in order to survive.

9. Technological paradigm shifts are more likely to occur when progress in improving the established technology is slowing due to diminishing returns and a new disruptive technology is taking root in a market niche.

10. Established companies can deal with paradigm shifts by hedging their bets with regard to technology or setting up a stand-alone division to exploit the technology.

Discussion Questions

1. What is different about high-tech industries? Were all industries once high tech?

2. Why are standards so important in many high-tech industries? What are the competitive implications of this?

3. You work for a small company that has the leading position in an embryonic market. Your boss believes that the company's future is assured because it has a 60 percent share of the market, the lowest cost structure in the industry, and the most reliable and highest-valued product. Write a memo to him outlining why his assumptions might be incorrect.

4. You are working for a small company that has developed an operating system for PCs that is faster and more stable than Microsoft's Windows operating system. What strategies might the company pursue to unseat Windows and establish its new operating system as the dominant technical standard in the industry?

5. You are a manager for a major music record label. Last year, music sales declined by 10 percent, primarily due to very high piracy rates for CDs. Your boss has asked you to develop a strategy for reducing piracy rates. What would you suggest that the company do?

Practicing Strategic Management

SMALL-GROUP EXERCISE: BURNING DVDs

Break up into groups of three to five people, and appoint one group member as a spokesperson who will communicate your findings to the class.

You are a group of managers and software engineers at a small start-up that has developed software that enables customers with PCs to copy films from one DVD to another (i.e., to "burn" DVDs).

1. How do you think that the market for this software is likely to develop? What factors might inhibit adoption of software?
2. Can you think of a strategy that your company might pursue in combination with film studios that will enable your company to increase revenues and the film companies to reduce piracy rates?

ARTICLE FILE 7

Find an example of an industry that has undergone a technological paradigm shift in recent years. What happened to the established companies as that paradigm shift unfolded?

STRATEGIC MANAGEMENT PROJECT: MODULE 7

This module requires you to analyze the industry environment in which your company is based and determine if it is vulnerable to a technological paradigm shift. With the information you have at your disposal, answer the following questions:

1. What is the dominant product technology used in the industry in which your company is based?
2. Are technical standards important in your industry? If so, what are they?
3. What are the attributes of the majority of customers purchasing the product of your company (for example, early adopters, early majority, late majority)? What does this tell you about the strategic issues that the company is likely to face in the future?
4. Did the dominant technology in your industry diffuse rapidly or slowly? What drove the speed of diffusion?
5. Where is the dominant technology in your industry on its S-curve? Are alternative competing technologies being developed that might give rise to a paradigm shift in your industry?
6. Are intellectual property rights important to your company? If so, what strategies is it adopting to protect those rights? Is it doing enough?

EXPLORING THE WEB
Visiting Kodak

Visit the web site of Kodak (**http://www.kodak.com**), and search it to find out what Kodak is doing in the area of digital photography. Use this information to answer the following questions:

1. How important do you think digital photography is in Kodak's total revenues?
2. How is this likely to change over the next decade?
3. Where is digital photography on the S-curve? Where is traditional photography? What are the implications of this comparison for Kodak?
4. Identify Kodak's competitors in (a) its traditional film business and (b) the digital photography business. What are the implications of the change in the set of competitors confronting Kodak?
5. How does the switch from traditional to digital photography change the economics of the photography business?
6. Do you think that Kodak is pursuing the correct strategies to deal with digital substitution? What do you think is the long-term outlook for Kodak's business if it continues pursuing its current strategies? Do you think the company should make some changes? If so, what?

General Task: Search the Web for information that allows you to assess the current state of competition in the market for hand-held computers such as those produced by Palm, Handspring, and Compaq. Use that information to perform an analysis of the market in the United States. Answer the following questions:

1. What is the leading standard for operating systems in this market?
2. How did this standard emerge to become the market leader?
3. How secure is this standard? Could it be supplanted by another standard over the next few years?

Closing Case

The Evolution of IBM

IBM is in many ways a remarkable organization. Founded in 1911 from the merger of two companies, the early IBM sold mechanical clocks, scales, and punch-card tabulating equipment. By 2001, it was the largest technology company on the planet with earnings of $7.7 billion on revenues of $86 billion, almost twice as much as any other technology company. In its ninety-year history, IBM has survived several paradigm shifts in technology that led to the decline and bankruptcy of many of its peers.

During the 1930s, IBM was a leader in the production of mechanical tabulators using punch-card technology. When this technology was ultimately replaced by electronic calculators and computers, many manufacturers of mechanical tabulating equipment went the way of the dinosaur. IBM, however, had begun to build capabilities in electronics during the 1930s. In 1933, it acquired a producer of electric typewriters. This led to the 1935 introduction of IBM's first electric typewriter, a technology that was to transform the typewriter industry where most incumbent enterprises sold mechanical typewriters. More important, the acquisition gave IBM access to knowledge of electronics, which it ultimately put to use elsewhere in the company. In 1947, IBM introduced its first "electronic multiplier," a calculator with electronic, as opposed to mechanical, working elements. More significant, IBM's electronic knowledge underlay its introduction in 1952 of its first production computer, the IBM 701.

In the ensuing decades, IBM rode the wave of disruptive technology. Its revolutionary System 360 computer, introduced in 1964, began to replace mechanical and simple electronic systems for performing scientific and business calculations. Its System 370 computer, introduced in 1970, solidified this trend. By the mid-1980s, IBM had emerged as the largest manufacturer of mainframe computers in the world and at the time had the dominant computing technology, with a virtual lock on the market. But by this time, a new technology was taking root that was to threaten IBM's very survival: the personal computer.

Personal computer technology was developed in the mid-1970s by a number of small start-up enterprises, including MITS and Apple. In 1980, William Lowe, the lab director at IBM's Entry Level Systems (ELS) unit in Boca Raton, Florida, pushed IBM management to give him authorization to try and develop a personal computer. Top management was initially reluctant. Its two previous attempts to introduce a PC had ended in total failure. Lowe ultimately got permission to produce a PC but with an almost unrealistic deadline of one year to complete the job. He recruited another IBM insider, Don Estridge, to head the project team. Estridge was soon persuaded that the only way to meet the deadline was for IBM to purchase off-the-shelf components, such as an Intel microprocessor and a Microsoft operating system, and to adopt an open systems design, where technical specifications were published. This would allow developers to write software applications that would run on the PC. Strategically, this approach represented a radical departure for IBM, which had tended to make the majority of its own components and software in-house and had adopted a closed systems approach. The countercultural strategy was possible only because the ELS unit was outside IBM's business mainstream, geographically separated from the company's center of operations, staffed by a maverick group of engineers and managers, and protected from IBM's bureaucracy by its CEO, Frank Cary.

Introduced in August 1981, the IBM PC was a dramatic success. However, the use of open systems architecture and off-the-shelf components soon gave rise to a thriving industry of companies that made IBM-compatible machines, or clones, such as Compaq Computer. By the mid-1980s, these clone makers were starting to eat into IBM's market share. Moreover, PC architecture based on an Intel microprocessor and Microsoft operating system went on to revolutionize the computer industry. In many companies, client-server systems based on PC technology replaced mainframe and midrange computers. As this occurred, sales of IBM mainframes slumped, and by 1993 IBM was awash in red ink. It lost $8 billion on shrinking sales as the PC technology it had given birth to cannibalized its profitable mainframe computers. Many observers were already writing IBM's obituary.

At this juncture, Lou Gerstner became CEO. A former management consultant and CEO of the tobacco company R. J. Reynolds with no computer industry experience, most observers thought that Gerstner, who knew little about computing technology, was poorly equipped to be IBM's CEO. However, Gerstner soon realized that IBM's computer business was rapidly becoming commoditized. Having given up control over microprocessor technology to Intel and software to Microsoft, IBM had no proprietary advantage. His strategy was to take IBM out of the commoditization game by emphasizing its service business. He believed that if IBM could solve the information technology problems of large corporations, the company would win big sales with recurring sales revenues spread out over years and margins that were a lot better than those IBM could get by competing only at the product level.

Not only has this strategy been very successful, it has given IBM a way to exploit the latest disruptive technology, the Internet. As Internet-centric computing has grown in importance, IBM has reinvented itself as a dominant provider of e-business solutions and services. Now if a company wishes to establish an intranet or use the Internet to execute business transactions, IBM is one of the vendors it turns to first. Although IBM still produces and sells its own computer hardware, it will now recommend the hardware of other companies if it suits the clients' needs better. It has become an e-business solutions company, ideally positioning itself to profit from the spread of web-based technology into every nook and cranny of the modern business corporation.

Case Discussion Questions

1. How many paradigm shifts has IBM survived in its history?

2. Describe how IBM was able to survive each of these paradigm shifts.

3. What does the history of IBM tell you about the strategies that incumbent companies must pursue to survive paradigm shifts?

4. In many ways, the IBM PC launched the personal computer into the mass market. How was a large incumbent enterprise able to develop what was a revolutionary product?

5. With the benefit of hindsight, could IBM have done anything different in the development of the IBM PC that would have not allowed control over the dominant standard in the market to be captured by Microsoft and Intel?

Sources: D. Kirkpatrick, "The Future of IBM," *Fortune,* February 18, 2002, pp. 60–68. P. Freiberger and M. Swaine, *Fire in the Valley* (New York: McGraw-Hill, 2000). "Follow That," *Economist,* February 2, 2002, p. 64. History of IBM from www.ibm.com.

Strategy in the Global Environment

8

Opening Case

MTV Has to Sing a New Song as It Expands Globally

MTV Networks has become something of a symbol of globalization. Established in 1981, the U.S.-based music TV station has been expanding outside its North American base since 1987, when it opened MTV Europe. Now owned by media conglomerate Viacom, MTV Networks, which includes siblings Nickelodeon and VH1, the music station for the baby boomer set, generates over $1 billion in operating profit per year on annual revenues of $3 billion. Since 1987, MTV has become the most ubiquitous cable programmer in the world. By 2001, the network had 29 channels, or distinct feeds, that reached some 330 million households in 140 countries. Although the United States still leads with 70 million households, the most rapid growth is elsewhere, particularly in Asia, where nearly two-thirds of the region's 3 billion people are under thirty-five years old, the middle class is expanding fast, and TV ownership is spreading rapidly.

Despite its success, MTV's global expansion got off to a weak start. In 1987, it piped a single feed across Europe almost entirely composed of American programming with English-speaking veejays. Naively, the network's U.S. managers thought that Europeans would flock to the American programming. But while viewers in Europe shared a common interest in a handful of global super-stars, who at the time included Madonna and Michael Jackson, their tastes turned out to be surprisingly local. What was popular in Germany might not be popular in Britain, and many staples of the American music scene left Europeans cold. MTV suffered as a result. Soon local copycat stations were springing up in Europe that focused on the music scene in individual countries and took view-ers and advertisers away from MTV. As explained by Tom Freston, chairman of MTV Networks, "We were going for the most shallow layer of what united viewers and brought them together. It didn't go over too well."

In 1995, MTV changed its strategy and broke Europe into eight regional feeds: one for the United Kingdom and Ireland; another for Germany, Austria, and Switzerland; one for Scandinavia; one for Italy; one for France; one for Spain; one for Holland; and a feed for the other European nations, including Belgium and Greece. The network adopted the same localization strategy elsewhere in the world. For example, in Asia, it has an English-Hindi chan-nel for India, separate Mandarin feeds for China and Tai-wan, a Korean feed for South Korea, a Bahasa language feed for Indonesia, and a Japanese feed for Japan. Digital and satellite technology have made the localization of programming cheaper and easier. MTV Networks can now beam half a dozen feeds of one satellite transponder.

Although MTV Networks exercises creative control over these different feeds and all of the channels have the same familiar frenetic look and feel of MTV in the United States, an increasing share of the programming and content is local. When MTV opens a local station now, it begins with expatriates from elsewhere in the world to do a "gene transfer" of company culture and operating principles. But once these are established, the network switches over to local employees, and the expa-triates move on. The idea is to produce programming that matches the tastes of the local population. Although as much as 60 percent of the programming still origi-nates in the United States, with staples such as *The Real World* having equivalents in different countries, an increasing share of programming is local in conception. In Italy, *MTV Kitchen* combines cooking with a music

countdown. *Erotica* airs in Brazil and features a panel of youngsters discussing sex. The Indian channel produces twenty-one home-grown shows hosted by local veejays who speak "Hinglish," a city-bred breed of Hindi and English. Hit shows include *MTV Cricket in Control,* appropriate for a land where cricket is a national obses-sion; *MTV Housefull,* which hones in on Hindi film stars (India has the biggest film industry outside of Holly-wood); and *MTV Bakra,* which is modeled on *Candid Camera.*

The same local variation is evident in the music videos aired by the different feeds. Although some music stars still have global appeal, 70 percent of the video con-tent in most markets is now local. Indeed, in a direct countertrend to the notion that popular culture is becoming more global and homogeneous, William Roedy, president of MTV's international networks, observes, "People root for the home team, both culturally and musically. Local repertoire is a worldwide trend. There are fewer global megastars." Moreover, when music tastes do transcend borders, MTV has found that it is often in ways that would have been difficult to predict. Currently, Japanese pop music is all the range in Taiwan, and soul and hip-hop are big in Korea.

This localization push has reaped big benefits for MTV. It has helped MTV capture viewers back from local imitators. In India, ratings increased by more than 700 percent between 1996, when the localization push began, and 2000. In turn, localization helps MTV to capture more of those all-important advertising revenues, even from other multinationals such as Coca-Cola, whose own advertising budgets are often locally determined. In Europe, MTV's advertising revenues increased by 50 per-cent between 1995 and 2000. While the total market for pan-European advertising is valued at just $200 million, the total market for local advertising across Europe is a much bigger pie, valued at $12 billion. MTV now gets 70 percent of its European advertising revenue from local spots, up from 15 percent in 1995. Similar trends are evi-dent elsewhere in the world.

Sources: B. Pulley and A. Tanzer, "Sumner's Gemstone," *Forbes,* Feb-ruary 21, 2000, pp. 107–111. K. Hoffman, "Youth TV's Old Hand Prepares for the Digital Challenge," *Financial Times,* February 18, 2000, p. 8. Presentation by Sumner M. Redstone, chairman and CEO, Viacom, delivered to Salomon Smith Barney Eleventh Annual Global Entertainment and Media Telecommunications Conference, Scottsdale, Arizona, January 8, 2001, archived at www.viacom.com.

Overview

As MTV found when it began to expand globally, it had to change its *business model* and develop a strategy of customizing its product to different national markets. It could not offer a standardized MTV channel worldwide.

This chapter outlines the global strategies that companies can pursue to gain a competitive advantage in the global marketplace and discusses the advantages and disadvantages of each. It also explores two related strategic issues: (1) how managers decide which foreign markets to enter, when to enter them, and on what scale and (2) what kind of vehicle or means a company should use to expand globally and enter a foreign country. Once a company has entered a foreign market, it becomes a **multi-national company,** that is, a company that does business in two or more national markets. The vehicles that companies can employ to enter foreign markets and become multinationals include exporting, licensing, setting up a joint venture with a foreign company, and setting up a wholly owned subsidiary. The chapter closes with a discussion of the benefits and costs of entering into strategic alliances with other global companies.

By the time you have completed this chapter, you will have a good understanding of the various strategic issues that companies face when they decide to expand their operations abroad to achieve competitive advantage and superior profitability.

Increasing Profitability Through Global Expansion

Expanding globally allows companies to increase their profitability in ways not available to purely domestic enterprises. As we shall see, by producing goods and services in other countries, companies may be able to lower their cost structure or better differentiate their final product offering. In addition, a company may be able to increase its sales volume more rapidly and thus reap the cost advantages that flow from greater economies of scale.

Location Economies

Chapter 2 discussed how countries differ from each other along a number of dimensions, including differences in the cost and quality of factors of production. These differences imply that some locations are more suited than others for producing certain goods and services.[1] **Location economies** are the economic benefits that arise from performing a value creation activity in the optimal location for that activity, wherever in the world that might be (transportation costs and trade barriers permitting). Locating a value creation activity in the optimal location for that activity can have one of two effects: (1) it can lower the costs of value creation, helping the company achieve a low-cost position, or (2) it can enable a company to differentiate its product offering, which gives it the option of charging a premium price or keeping price low and using differentiation as a means of increasing sales volume. Thus, efforts to realize location economies are consistent with the business-level strategies of low cost and differentiation. In theory, a company that realizes location economies by dispersing each of its value creation activities to the optimal location for that activity should have a competitive advantage over a company that bases all of its value creation activities at a single location. It should be able to differentiate its product offering better and lower its cost structure more than its single-location competitor. In a world where competitive pressures are increasing, such a strategy may well become an imperative for survival.

For an example of location economies, consider Swan Optical, a U.S. manufacturer and distributor of eyewear. With sales revenues only in the $20 to $30 million range, Swan is hardly a giant, yet it manufactures its eyewear in low-cost factories in Hong Kong and China that it jointly owns with a Hong Kong–based partner. Swan also has a minority stake in eyewear design houses in Japan, France, and Italy. Thus, even small companies can disperse their value creation activities around the world to take advantage of the favorable skill base and cost structure found in other countries. Investments in Hong Kong and then China have helped Swan to lower its cost structure, and investments in Japan, France, and Italy have helped it to produce differentiated designer eyewear for which it can charge a premium price.[2]

For an example of a large company, consider GM's Pontiac Le Mans.[3] Marketed and sold primarily in the United States, the car was designed in Germany; key components were manufactured in Japan, Taiwan, and Singapore; the assembly operation was performed in South Korea; and the advertising strategy was formulated in Great Britain. The car was designed in Germany because GM believed the designers in its German subsidiary were the most capable of producing a car design that added value. Components were manufactured in Japan, Taiwan, and Singapore because favorable factor conditions there—relatively low-cost skilled labor—gave these locations a comparative advantage in the production of components. The car was assembled in South Korea because GM believed that the costs of assembly would be at a minimum there because of low labor costs. Finally, the advertising strategy was formulated in Great Britain because GM believed a particular advertising agency there had a distinct competency to produce an advertising campaign that would help differentiate and sell the car. The result of this kind of strategic thinking is clear: managers must create a global web of value chain activities in which each activity is located in the country where value added through differentiation can be maximized or where the costs of value creation are minimized.

Some Caveats. Introducing transportation costs and trade barriers complicates this picture somewhat. New Zealand might have a comparative advantage for low-cost car assembly operations, but high transportation costs make it an uneconomical location from which to serve global markets. Factoring transportation costs and trade barriers into the cost equation helps explain why many U.S. companies have been shifting their production from Asia to Mexico. Mexico has three distinct advantages over many Asian countries as a location for value creation activities: low labor costs; Mexico's proximity to the large U.S. market, which reduces transportation costs; and the North American Free Trade Agreement (NAFTA), which has removed many trade barriers between Mexico, the United States, and Canada, increasing Mexico's attractiveness as a production site for the North American market. Thus, although the relative costs of value creation are important, transportation costs and trade barriers also must be considered in location decisions.

Another caveat concerns the importance of assessing political and economic risks when making location decisions. Even if a country looks very attractive as a production location when measured against cost or differentiation criteria, if its government is unstable or totalitarian, companies are usually well advised not to base production there. Similarly, if a particular national government appears to be pursuing inappropriate social or economic policies, this might be another reason for not basing production in that location, even if other factors look favorable.

The Experience Curve

As you recall from Chapter 4, the experience curve refers to the systematic decrease in production costs that has been observed to occur over the life of a product. Learning effects and economies of scale underlie the experience curve, and moving down the experience curve allows a company to lower its cost structure and achieve a cost advantage in relation to its competitors.

Many of the underlying sources of experience-based cost economies are found at the level of individual plants. Thus, the key to riding down the experience curve as rapidly as possible is to increase the accumulated volume *produced by a plant* as quickly as possible. Because global markets are larger than domestic markets, companies that produce for a global market from one or a handful of locations are likely to build up accumulated volume faster than companies that focus primarily on serving their home market or on producing for multiple markets from many different production locations. Thus, serving a global market from one or a few plants is consistent with moving down the experience curve and establishing a low-cost position.

Another point to bear in mind is that the cost advantages of serving the world market from one or a few plants will be greater if those plants are based in the country or countries that are optimal for performing that value creation activity. Such a strategy will enable a company to realize cost economies from experience curve effects at the plant level and from location economies *simultaneously*. For an example of a company that excelled in doing just this, consider the history of Matsushita, which makes electronic products under the Panasonic and JVC labels.

In the 1970s, Matsushita, along with competitors Sony and Philips, was in a race to develop a commercially viable VCR. As discussed in Chapter 7, although Matsushita initially lagged behind both Philips and Sony, its strategy to get its VHS format accepted as the global industry standard ultimately allowed it to reap enormous experience curve cost economies. To ensure that it could accommodate the huge increase in worldwide demand for its VCRs once its format was accepted, Matsushita increased its VCR production capacity from 205,000 units in 1977 to 6.8 million units by 1984. Its strategy was to serve the world market from only a handful of large factories, and it took advantage of the highly skilled, low-cost Japanese labor. As a result, Matsushita was able to realize significant learning effects and economies of scale. This allowed it to reduce the prices of its VCRs by 50 percent within five years of selling its first one, a cost advantage that allowed it to become the world's largest VCR producer by 1983 with 45 percent of world sales.[4]

Today companies like Intel are the masters of this kind of strategy. Because the costs of building a state-of-the-art facility to manufacture microprocessors are easily in excess of $1 billion, to make this investment pay Intel *must* pursue experience curve effects—serving world markets from a few plants to maximize the cost economies that derive from scale and learning effects.

Transferring Distinctive Competencies

Distinctive competencies, introduced in Chapter 3, are the firm-specific resources and capabilities that allow a company to achieve superior efficiency, quality, innovation, or responsiveness to customers and thus gain a competitive advantage. Such strengths typically find their expression in new and improved goods and services that other companies find difficult to match or imitate. Thus, distinctive competencies form the bedrock of a company's competitive advantage. They enable a company to lower its cost structure or perform value creation activities in ways that lead to differentiation, premium pricing, and increased demand. For example, Toyota's distinctive competencies allow it to produce high-quality, well-designed cars at a lower delivered cost than any other company in the world.[5]

For such companies, global expansion is a way of further exploiting the value creation potential of their distinctive competencies. Companies with valuable distinctive competencies can often realize enormous returns by using those competencies and selling the products that result from them in overseas markets where indigenous competitors lack similar competencies and products. The *Opening Case* described how MTV has been able to build a vibrant global business by leveraging its competencies in the programming and delivery of music and related content and applying those skills to various national markets where local competitors lack equivalent skills. The network's success has raised the value that viewers ascribe to MTV and, by extension, the value that advertisers ascribe to an advertising slot on an MTV channel. In turn, this has enabled MTV to command a higher price for advertising slots than competitors. Another example is detailed in Strategy in Action 8.1, which describes how McDonald's has leveraged its distinctive competence in running fast food restaurants to overseas markets where indigenous competitors either did not exist or lacked similar skills.

Strategy in Action 8.1

McDonald's Is Here, There, and Everywhere

Established in 1955, by the early 1980s McDonald's faced a problem: after three decades of rapid growth, the U.S. fast food market was beginning to show signs of market saturation. McDonald's response to the slowdown was to expand rapidly abroad. In 1980, 28 percent of the chain's new restaurant openings were abroad; in 1986, the figure was 40 percent, in 1990, it was close to 60 percent; and in 2000, it was almost 90 percent. Since the early 1980s, the company's overseas revenues and profits have grown at 22 percent annually. By the end of 2000, McDonald's had 28,707 restaurants in 120 countries outside the United States, which generated $21 billion, or 53 percent of the company's $40 billion in revenues.

McDonald's shows no signs of slowing down. Management notes that there is still only one McDonald's restaurant for every 500,000 people in the overseas countries that it currently does business in, which compares to one McDonald's restaurant for every 25,000 people in the United States. Moreover, the company currently serves less than 1 percent of the world's population. Thus, the company's strategy is for this overseas expansion to continue at a rapid rate. In Europe, it opened more than 500 new restaurants in 1999 and in 2000, while the figure for Asia was around 600. A major expansion plan is for Latin America, where the company plans to invest $2 billion over the next few years.

McDonald's enters an overseas country only after careful preparation. In what is a fairly typical pattern, before McDonald's opened its first Polish restaurant in 1992, it spent eighteen months establishing essential contacts and getting to know the local culture. Locations, real estate, construction, supply, personnel, legal, and government relations were all worked out in advance. In June 1992, a team of fifty employees from the United States, Russia, Germany, and Britain went to Poland to help with the opening of the first four restaurants there. By mid-1994, all of these employees except one had returned to their home countries. They were no longer needed because Polish nationals had been trained to run an efficient McDonald's operation.

Indeed, another key to the company's global expansion strategy is the export of the business model that spurred its growth in the United States. McDonald's success was built on a formula of close relations with suppliers, nationwide marketing might, tight control over store-level operating procedures, and a franchising system that encourages entrepreneurial individual franchisees. Although this system has worked well in the United States, some modifications must be made in other countries. One of the company's biggest challenges had been to infuse each store with the same culture and standardized operating procedures that have been the hallmark of its success in the United States. To aid in this task, in many countries McDonald's has enlisted the help of large partners through joint venture arrangements. The partners play a key role in learning and transplanting the organization's values to local employees. Overseas partners have also played a key role in helping McDonald's adapt its marketing methods and menu to local conditions. Although U.S.-style fast food remains the staple fare on the menu, local products have been added. In Brazil, for example, McDonald's sells a soft drink made from the guarana, an Amazonian berry. Patrons of McDonald's in Malaysia, Singapore, and Thailand savor milkshakes flavored with durian, a fruit considered an aphrodisiac by the locals. In Arab countries, McDonald's restaurants maintain *halal* menus, which signify compliance with Islamic laws on food preparation, especially beef. In 1995, McDonald's opened the first kosher restaurant in suburban Jerusalem which does not serve dairy products. And in India, the big Mac is made with lamb and called the Maharaja Mac.

McDonald's biggest problem has been to replicate its U.S. supply chain in other countries. U.S. suppliers are fiercely loyal to McDonald's; they must be, because their fortunes are closely linked to those of McDonald's. McDonald's maintains rigorous specifications for all the raw ingredients it uses—the key to its consistency and quality control. Outside the United States, however, McDonald's has found suppliers far less willing to make the investments required to meet its specifications. In Great Britain, for example, McDonald's experienced quality problems with two local bakeries supplying hamburger buns, so it built its own bakery to supply its stores there. In a more extreme case, when McDonald's decided to open a store in Russia, it found that local suppliers lacked the capability to produce goods of the quality it required. The company was forced to integrate vertically through the local food industry on a heroic scale, importing potato seeds and bull semen and indirectly managing dairy farms, cattle ranches, and vegetable plots. It also had to construct the world's largest food-processing plant, at a cost of $40 million. The restaurant itself cost only $4.5 million.

Now that it has a successful overseas operation, McDonald's is experiencing benefits that go beyond the immediate financial ones. Increasingly, it is finding that its overseas franchisees are a source of valuable new ideas. The Dutch operation created a prefabricated modular store that can be moved over a weekend and is now widely used to set up temporary restaurants at big outdoor events. The Swedes came up with an enhanced meat freezer that is now used companywide. And the small satellite stores and low-overhead mini-McDonald's that are now appearing in hospitals and sports arenas in the United States originated in Singapore.

Sources: Kathleen Deveny, et al., "McWorld?" *Business Week,* October 13, 1986, pp. 78–86. "Slow Food," *Economist,* February 3, 1990, p. 64. Harlan S, Byrne. "Welcome to McWorld," *Barron's,* August 29, 1994, pp. 25–28. Andrew E. Serwer, "McDonald's Conquers the World," *Fortune,* October 17, 1994, pp. 103–116.

Leveraging the Skills of Global Subsidiaries

Initially, many multinational companies develop valuable competencies at home and then leverage them overseas. However, it is becoming increasingly apparent that for more mature multinationals that have already established a network of subsidiary operations in foreign markets, the development of valuable competencies can just as well take place in foreign subsidiaries.[6] Indeed, competencies can be created anywhere within a multinational's global network of operations, wherever people have the opportunity and incentive to try new ways of doing things. The competencies that help to lower the costs of production or to enhance perceived value and support higher product pricing are not the monopoly of the corporate center.

For the managers of a multinational company, this phenomenon creates important new challenges. First, they must recognize that the corporate center does not hold a monopoly on the creation of valuable competencies and have the humility to recognize that valuable skills can arise anywhere within the company's global network. Second, they must establish an incentive system that encourages local employees to engage in the business of acquiring new competencies. This is not as easy as it sounds. Creating new competencies is risky because not all new resources and capabilities add value. For every valuable idea created by a McDonald's subsidiary in an overseas country, there may be several failures. The management of the multinational must put incentives in place that encourage employees to take the necessary risks. They must reward people for successes and not sanction them unnecessarily for taking risks that did not pan out. Third, they must have processes in place for identifying when valuable new competencies have been created in a subsidiary, and, finally, they need to act as a facilitator, helping to transfer valuable competencies within the company. For example, after employees in Singapore distinguished themselves by finding ways to reduce production costs through better product design, Hewlett Packard decentralized the authority for the design and production of many of its leading-edge ink jet printers to its operation in Singapore (see Strategy in Action 8.2).

Strategy in Action   8.2

Hewlett Packard in Singapore

In the late 1960s, Hewlett Packard was looking around Asia for a low-cost location to produce electronic components that were to be manufactured using labor-intensive processes. It eventually settled on Singapore, opening its first factory there in 1970. Although Singapore did not have the lowest labor costs in the region, costs were low relative to North America, plus the Singapore location had several important benefits that could not be found at many other locations in Asia. The education level of the local work force was high; English was widely spoken; the government seemed stable and committed to economic development; and the city-state had one of the better-developed infrastructures in the region, including good communications and transportation networks and a rapidly developing industrial and commercial base. HP also extracted favorable terms from the Singapore government with regard to taxes, tariffs, and subsidies.

Initially, the plant manufactured only basic components. The combination of low labor costs and a favorable tax regime helped to make this plant profitable early. In 1973, HP transferred the manufacture of one of its basic hand-held calculators from the United States to Singapore in order to reduce manufacturing costs, which the Singapore factory was quickly able to do. Increasingly confident in the capability of the Singapore factory to handle entire products as opposed to just components, HP's management transferred other products to Singapore over the next few years, including keyboards, solid-state displays, and integrated circuits. However, all of these products were still designed, developed, and initially produced in the United States.

The plant's status shifted in the early 1980s when HP embarked on a worldwide campaign to boost product quality and reduce costs. HP transferred the production of its HP41C hand-held calculator to Singapore. The managers at the Singapore plant were given the goal of substantially reducing manufacturing costs. They argued that this could be achieved only if they were allowed to redesign the product so it could be manufactured at a lower overall cost. HP's central management agreed, and

twenty engineers from the Singapore facility were transferred to the United States for one year to learn how to design application-specific integrated circuits. They took this expertise back to Singapore and set about redesigning the HP41C.

The results were a huge success. By redesigning the product, the Singapore engineers reduced manufacturing costs for the HP41C by 50 percent. Using this newly acquired capability for product design, the Singapore facility then set about redesigning other products it produced. HP's corporate managers were so impressed with the progress made at the factory that they transferred production of the entire calculator line to Singapore in 1983. This was followed by the partial transfer of ink jet production to Singapore in 1984 and keyboard production in 1986. In all cases, the facility redesigned the products and often reduced unit manufacturing costs by more than 30 percent. The initial development and design of all these products, however, still occurred in the United States.

In the late 1980s and early 1990s, the Singapore plant started to take on added responsibilities, particularly in the ink jet printer business. In 1990, it was given the job of redesigning an HP ink jet printer for the Japanese market. Although the initial product redesign was a market failure, the managers at Singapore pushed to be allowed to try again, and in 1991 they were given the job of redesigning HP's DeskJet 505 printer for the Japanese market. This time the redesigned product was a success, garnering significant sales in Japan. Emboldened by this success, the plant has continued to take on additional design responsibilities. Today, it is viewed as a lead plant within HP's global network, with primary responsibility not just for manufacturing but also for the development and design of a family of small ink jet printers targeted at the Asian market.

Sources: K. Ferdows, "Making the Most of Foreign Factories," *Harvard Business Review* (March–April 1997): 73–88. "Hewlett-Packard: Singapore," Harvard Business School Case #694-035 (1996).

Pressures for Cost Reductions and Local Responsiveness

Companies that compete in the global marketplace typically face two types of competitive pressures: *pressures for cost reductions* and *pressures to be locally responsive* (see Figure 8.1).[7] These competitive pressures place conflicting demands on a company. Responding to pressures for cost reductions requires that a company try to minimize its unit costs. To attain this goal, it may have to base its productive activities at the most favorable low-cost location, wherever in the world that might be. It may also have to offer a standardized product to the global marketplace in order to ride down the experience curve as quickly as possible. On the other hand, responding to pressures to be locally responsive requires that a company differentiate its product offering and marketing strategy from country to country in an effort to accommodate the diverse demands arising from national differences in consumer tastes and preferences, business practices, distribution channels, competitive conditions, and government policies. Because differentiation across countries can involve significant duplication and a lack of product standardization, it may raise costs.

While some companies, such as Company A in Figure 8.1, face high pressures for cost reductions and low pressures for local responsiveness, and others, such as Company B, face low pressures for cost reductions and high pressures for local responsiveness, many companies are in the position of Company C. They face high pressures for *both* cost reductions and local responsiveness. Dealing with these conflicting and contradictory pressures is a difficult strategic challenge, primarily because being locally responsive tends to raise costs.

Pressures for Cost Reductions

Increasingly, multinational companies must cope with pressures for cost reductions, which can be particularly intense in industries producing commodity-type products, where meaningful differentiation on nonprice factors is difficult and price is the main competitive weapon. Products that serve universal needs tend to fall into this category. Universal needs exist when the tastes and preferences of consumers in different nations are similar, if not identical. This obviously applies to conventional

FIGURE 8.1

Pressures for Cost Reductions and Local Responsiveness

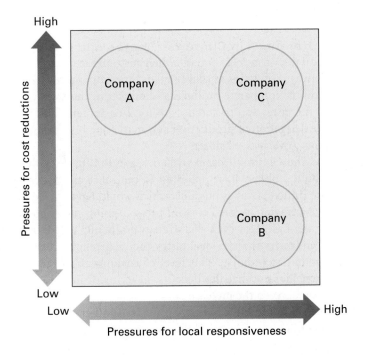

commodity products such as bulk chemicals, petroleum, steel, and sugar. It also tends to be true for many industrial and consumer products—for instance, hand-held calculators, semiconductor chips, and personal computers. Pressures for cost reductions are also intense in industries where major competitors are based in low-cost locations, where there is persistent excess capacity, and where consumers are powerful and face low switching costs. Many commentators have also argued that the liberalization of the world trade and investment environment has generally increased cost pressures by facilitating greater international competition.[8] For example, taking advantage of low barriers to direct investment, Wal-Mart is rapidly expanding globally using its cost-leadership strategy to penetrate new national markets. Its business model is threatening rivals at home and abroad.

Consider the history of the global tire industry, where pressures for cost reductions have been intense in recent years. Tires are essentially a commodity product for which differentiation is difficult and price is the main competitive weapon. The major buyers of tires, automobile companies, are powerful and face low switching costs, so they have been playing tire companies off against each other in an attempt to get lower prices. Moreover, a decline in global demand for automobiles in the early 1990s created serious excess capacity in the tire industry, with as much as 25 percent of world capacity standing idle. The result was a worldwide price war, with almost all tire companies suffering heavy losses in the early 1990s. In response to the cost pressures, most tire companies rationalized their operations in a way consistent with the attainment of a low-cost position. They moved production to low-cost facilities and offered globally standardized products in an attempt to realize experience curve economies.[9]

Pressures for Local Responsiveness

Pressures for local responsiveness arise from differences in consumer tastes and preferences, infrastructure and traditional practices, distribution channels, and host government demands. Recall that responding to pressures to be locally responsive requires that a company differentiate its products and marketing strategy from country to country to accommodate these factors, all of which tends to raise a company's cost structure.

Differences in Customer Tastes and Preferences.

Strong pressures for local responsiveness emerge when customer tastes and preferences differ significantly between countries, as they may for historic or cultural reasons. In such cases, a multinational company's products and marketing message have to be customized to appeal to the tastes and preferences of local customers. This typically creates pressures for the delegation of production and marketing responsibilities and functions to a company's overseas subsidiaries.

The *Opening Case* provided a good example. Other things being equal, MTV would probably have preferred to centralize as much programming and content in the United States as possible, which would have allowed it to realize scale economies by leveraging its fixed costs of programming and content development over a global viewer base. However, this strategy essentially failed. Instead, MTV has found that it needs to respond to local tastes and preferences, customizing its programming and content accordingly. This level of customization raises MTV's costs, but it is clear from the case that the benefits, in terms of increased viewers and advertising revenues, exceed the increased costs.

The automobile industry provides another example. In the 1980s and early 1990s, there was a trend toward the creation of "world cars." The idea was that global companies such as General Motors, Ford, and Toyota would be able to sell the same basic vehicle the world over, sourcing it from centralized production locations. If successful, the strategy would have enabled automobile companies to reap significant gains from global scale economies. However, this strategy has frequently run aground on the hard rocks of consumer reality. The fact is that consumers in different automobile markets do seem to have different tastes and preferences, and therefore they require different types of vehicles. There is a strong demand among North American consumers for pickup trucks, particularly in the South and West. In contrast, in European countries, pickup trucks are considered utility vehicles and are purchased primarily by firms rather than individuals.

As a counterpoint, some commentators have argued that customer demands for local customization are on the decline worldwide.[10] According to this argument, modern communications and transport technologies have created the conditions for a convergence of the tastes and preferences of customers from different nations. The result is the emergence of enormous global markets for standardized consumer products. The worldwide acceptance of McDonald's hamburgers, Coca-Cola, Gap clothes, Nokia cell phones, and Sony television sets, all of which are sold globally as standardized products, are often cited as evidence of the increasing homogeneity of the global marketplace.

This argument, however, has been characterized as extreme by others. For example, Christopher Bartlett and Sumantra Ghoshal have observed that in the consumer electronics industry, buyers reacted to an overdose of standardized global products by showing a renewed preference for products that are differentiated to local conditions.[11]

Differences in Infrastructure and Traditional Practices. Pressures for local responsiveness arise from differences in infrastructure or traditional practices among countries, creating a need to customize products accordingly. Fulfilling this need may require the delegation of manufacturing and production functions to foreign subsidiaries. For example, in North America, consumer electrical systems are based on 110 volts, whereas in some European countries, 240-volt systems are standard. Thus, domestic electrical appliances have to be customized to take this difference in infrastructure into account. Traditional practices also often vary across nations. For example, in Britain, people drive on the left-hand side of the road, creating a demand for right-hand-drive cars, whereas in France (and the rest of Europe), people drive on the right-hand side of the road and therefore want left-hand-drive cars. Obviously, automobiles have to be customized to take this difference in traditional practices into account.

Although many of the country differences in infrastructure are rooted in history, some are quite recent. For example, in the wireless telecommunications industry, different technical standards are found in different parts of the world. A technical standard known as GSM is common in Europe, and an alternative standard, CDMA, is more common in the United States and parts of Asia. The significance of these different standards is that equipment designed for GSM will not work on a CDMA network, and vice versa. Thus, companies such as Nokia, Motorola, and Ericsson, which manufacture wireless handsets and infrastructure such as switches, need to customize their product offering according to the technical standard prevailing in a given country.

Differences in Distribution Channels. A company's marketing strategies may have to be responsive to differences in distribution channels among countries, which may necessitate the delegation of marketing functions to national subsidiaries. In the pharmaceutical industry, for example, the British and Japanese distribution system is radically different from the U.S. system. British and Japanese doctors will not accept or respond favorably to a U.S.-style high-pressure sales force. Thus, pharmaceutical companies have to adopt different marketing practices in Britain and Japan compared with the United States—soft sell versus hard sell.

Host Government Demands. Economic and political demands imposed by host country governments may require local responsiveness. For example, the politics of health care around the world require that pharmaceutical companies manufacture in multiple locations. Pharmaceutical companies are subject to local clinical testing, registration procedures, and pricing restrictions, all of which make it necessary that the manufacturing and marketing of a drug should meet local requirements. Moreover, because governments and government agencies control a significant proportion of the health care budget in most countries, they are in a powerful position to demand a high level of local responsiveness.

More generally, threats of protectionism, economic nationalism, and local content rules (which require that a certain percentage of a product should be manufactured locally) dictate that international businesses manufacture locally. As an example, consider Bombardier, the Canadian-based manufacturer of railcars, aircraft, jet boats, and snowmobiles. Bombardier has twelve railcar factories across Europe. Critics of the company argue that the resulting duplication of manufacturing facilities leads to high costs and helps explain why Bombardier makes lower profit margins on its railcar operations than on its other business lines. In reply, managers at Bombardier argue that in Europe, informal rules with regard to local content favor people who use local workers. To sell railcars in Germany, they claim, you must manufacture in Germany. The same goes for Belgium, Austria, and France. To try and address its cost structure in Europe, Bombardier has centralized its engineering and purchasing functions, but it has no plans to centralize manufacturing.[12]

Choosing a Global Strategy

Pressures for local responsiveness imply that it may not be possible for a firm to realize the full benefits from experience curve and location economies. For example, it may not be possible to serve the global marketplace from a single low-cost location, producing a globally standardized product, and marketing it worldwide to achieve experience curve cost economies. In practice, the need to customize the product offering to local conditions may work against the implementation of such a strategy. For example, automobile firms have found that Japanese, American, and European consumers demand different kinds of cars, and this necessitates producing products that are customized for local markets. In response, firms like Honda, Ford, and Toyota are pursuing a strategy of establishing top-to-bottom design and production facilities in each of these regions so that they can better serve local demands. Although such customization brings benefits, it also limits the ability of a firm to realize significant experience curve cost economies and location economies.

In addition, pressures for local responsiveness imply that it may not be possible to leverage skills and products associated with a firm's distinctive competencies wholesale from one nation to another. Concessions often have to be made to local conditions. Despite being depicted as "poster boy" for the proliferation of standardized global products, even McDonald's has found that it has to customize its product offerings (i.e., its menu) in order to account for national differences in tastes and preferences.

Given the need to balance the cost and differentiation (value) sides of a company's business model, how do differences in the strength of pressures for cost reductions versus those for local responsiveness affect the choice of a company's strategy? Companies make a choice among four strategies to enter and compete in the global market: an international strategy, a multidomestic strategy, a global strategy, and a transnational strategy.[13] The appropriateness of each strategy varies given the extent of pressures for cost reductions and local responsiveness. Figure 8.2 illustrates the conditions under which each of these strategies is most appropriate.

International Strategy

Companies that pursue an **international strategy** try to create value by transferring valuable competencies and products to foreign markets where indigenous competitors lack those competencies and products. Most international companies have created value by transferring differentiated product offerings developed at home to foreign markets. Accordingly, they tend to centralize product development functions (for instance, R&D) at home. However, they also tend to establish manufacturing and marketing functions in each major country in which they do business. Although they may undertake some local customization of product offering and marketing strategy, this tends to be rather limited in scope. Ultimately, in most international companies, the head office retains tight control over marketing and product strategy.

International firms include Toys "R" Us, McDonald's, IBM, Kellogg, Procter & Gamble, Wal-Mart, and Microsoft. Microsoft, for example, develops the core architecture underlying its products at its Redmond campus in Washington State and also writes the bulk of the computer code there. However, it does allow national subsidiaries to develop their own marketing and distribution strategy and to customize aspects of the product to account for such basic local differences as language and

FIGURE 8.2

Four Basic Strategies

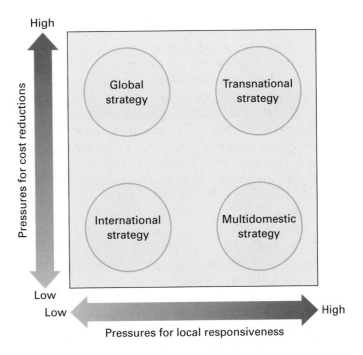

alphabet. For another example, see Strategy in Action 8.3, which profiles IKEA, the Swedish retailer. IKEA has traditionally pursued an international strategy, transferring the business model it developed in Sweden wholesale into other markets. However, this strategy did not work for IKEA once it started to open stores in the United States.

An international strategy makes sense if a company has a valuable competence that indigenous competitors in foreign markets lack and if it faces relatively weak pressures for local responsiveness and cost reductions (as is so with Microsoft). In such circumstances, an international strategy can be very profitable. However, when pressures for local responsiveness are high, companies pursuing this strategy lose out to those that place a greater emphasis on customizing the product offering and market strategy to local conditions. IKEA experienced this problem in the United States and subsequently shifted its strategy to accommodate local differences in tastes and preferences (see Strategy in Action 8.3). Similarly, when MTV originally expanded into Europe, it pursued an international strategy, but as we saw from the *Opening Case,* this strategy failed, given the high need for local responsiveness. In addition, because of duplication of manufacturing facilities, companies that pursue an international strategy tend to suffer from high operating costs. This makes the strategy inappropriate in manufacturing industries where cost pressures are high.

Multidomestic Strategy

Companies pursuing a **multidomestic strategy** develop a business model that allows them to achieve maximum local responsiveness. Because cost considerations often take a back seat to this, few companies are able to pursue this strategy in the intense competitive conditions of the 2000s, and it is mostly a thing of the past.

The key distinguishing feature of multidomestic companies is that they extensively customize both their product offering and their marketing strategy to match different national conditions. Consistent with this, they also have a tendency to establish a complete set of value creation activities, including production, marketing, and R&D, in each major national market in which they do business. As a consequence, they are generally unable to realize value from experience curve effects and location economies. Accordingly, many multidomestic firms have a high cost structure. They also tend to do a poor job of leveraging distinctive competencies within the firm.

A multidomestic strategy makes most sense when there are high pressures for local responsiveness and low pressures for cost reductions. The high cost structure associated with the duplication of production facilities makes this strategy inappropriate in industries where cost pressures are intense. Another weakness of this strategy is that many multidomestic companies have developed into decentralized federations in which each national subsidiary functions in a largely autonomous manner. Consequently, after a time, they begin to lose the ability to transfer the skills and products derived from distinctive competencies to their various national subsidiaries around the world. In a famous case that illustrates the problems this can cause, the failure of Philips NV to establish its V2000 VCR format as the dominant design in the VCR industry during the late 1970s, as opposed to Matsushita's VHS format, was due to the refusal of its U.S. subsidiary company to adopt the V2000 format. Instead, the subsidiary bought VCRs produced by Matsushita and put its own label on them, directly hurting Philips's attempts to establish its V2000 product as the global standard for VCRs.

Global Strategy

Companies that pursue a **global strategy** focus on increasing profitability by reaping the cost reductions that come from experience curve effects and location economies; that is, their business model is based on pursuing a low-cost strategy on a global scale.

Strategy in Action   8.3

IKEA's Swedish Ways

Established in the 1940s in Sweden by Ingvar Kamprad, IKEA has grown rapidly in recent years to become one of the world's largest retailers of home furnishings. In its initial push to expand globally, IKEA largely ignored the retailing rule that international success involves tailoring product lines closely to national tastes and preferences. Instead, it stuck with the vision articulated by founder Kamprad that the company should sell a basic product range that is "typically Swedish" wherever it ventures in the world. The company also remained primarily production oriented; the Swedish management and design group decided what it was going to sell and then presented it to the worldwide public, often with very little research as to what the public actually wanted. Moreover, the company emphasized its Swedish roots in its international advertising, even going as far as to insist on a Swedish blue and gold color scheme for its stores.

Despite breaking some key rules of international retailing, the formula of selling Swedish-designed products in the same manner everywhere seemed to work. Between 1974 and 2000, IKEA expanded from a company with 10 stores, only one of them outside Scandinavia, and annual revenues of $210 million to a group with 159 stores in 30 countries and sales of $8.6 billion. In 2000, only 8 percent of its sales were generated in Sweden. Of the balance, 21.6 percent of sales came from Germany, 49.5 percent from the rest of Europe, and 16 percent from North America. IKEA is now beginning to expand in Asia, which generated 3 percent of total sales in 2000.

The foundation of IKEA's success has been to offer customers good value for money. Its approach starts with a global network of suppliers, which now numbers 1,960 firms in 53 countries. An IKEA supplier gains long-term contracts, technical advice, and leased equipment from the company. In return, IKEA demands an exclusive contract and low prices. Its designers work closely with suppliers to build savings into the products from the outset by designing products that can be produced at a low cost. IKEA displays its enormous range of more than 10,000 products in cheap out-of-town stores. It sells most of its furniture as knocked-down kits for customers to take home and assemble themselves. The firm reaps huge economies of scale from the size of each store and the big production runs made possible by selling the same products all over the world. This strategy allows it to match its rivals on quality, while undercutting them by up to 30 percent on price and still maintaining a healthy after-tax return on sales of around 7 percent.

This strategy worked well until 1985, when IKEA decided to enter the North American market. Between 1985 and 1996, it opened six stores in North America, but unlike the company's experience across Europe, the stores did not quickly become profitable. Indeed, as early as 1990, it was clear that IKEA's North American operations were in trouble. Part of the problem was an adverse movement in exchange rates. In 1985, the exchange rate was $1 per 8.6 Swedish krona; by 1990, it was $1 per 5.8 krona. At this exchange rate, many products imported from Sweden did not look inexpensive to American consumers.

But there was more to IKEA's problems than adverse movements in exchange rates. IKEA's unapologetically Swedish products, which had sold so well across Europe, jarred with American tastes and sometimes physiques. Swedish beds were narrow and measured in centimeters. IKEA did not sell the matching bedroom suites that Americans like. Its kitchen cupboards were too narrow for the large dinner plates needed for pizza. Its glasses were too small for a nation that added ice to everything. The drawers in IKEA's bedroom chests were too shallow for American consumers, who tend to store sweaters in them. And the company made the mistake of selling European-sized curtains that did not fit American windows. As one senior IKEA manager joked later, "American's just wouldn't lower their ceilings to fit our curtains."

By 1991, the company's top management came to the realization that if it was going to succeed in North America, it would have to customize its product offering to North American tastes. The company set about redesigning its product range. The drawers on bedroom chests were designed to be two inches deeper, and sales immediately increased by 30 to 40 percent. IKEA now sells American-style king- and queen-sized beds, measured in inches, and it sells them as part of complete bedroom suites. It has redesigned its entire range of kitchen furniture and kitchenware to appeal to American tastes better. The company has also boosted the amount of products being sourced locally from 15 percent in 1990 to 45 percent in 1997, which makes it far less vulnerable to adverse movements in exchange rates. By 2000, about one-third of IKEA's total product offerings were designed exclusively for the U.S. market.

This break with IKEA's traditional strategy seems to be paying off. Between 1990 and 1994, IKEA's North American sales tripled to $480 million, and they nearly doubled again to around $900 million in 1997 and reached $1.38 billion in 2000. The company claims that it has been making a profit in North America since early 1993, although it does not release precise figures and does admit that its profit rate is lower in America than Europe. Still, the company is pushing ahead with plans for expansion in North America, including a goal of opening 15 new stores between 2000 and 2005, which will bring its total North American stores to 35.

Sources: "Furnishing the World," *Economist*, November 19, 1994, pp. 79–80. H. Carnegy, "Struggle to Save the Soul of IKEA," *Financial Times*, March 27, 1995, p. 12. J. Flynn and L. Bongiorno, "IKEA's New Game Plan," *Business Week*, October 6, 1997, pp. 99–102. IKEA's web site, www.ikea.com.

The production, marketing, and R&D activities of companies pursuing a global strategy are concentrated in a few favorable locations. Companies pursuing a global strategy try not to customize their product offering and marketing strategy to local conditions because customization, which involves shorter production runs and the duplication of functions, raises costs. Instead, they prefer to market a standardized product worldwide so that they can reap the maximum benefits from the economies of scale that underlie the experience curve. They also tend to use their cost advantage to support aggressive pricing in world markets.

This strategy makes most sense when there are strong pressures for cost reductions and demand for local responsiveness is minimal. Increasingly, these conditions prevail in many industrial goods industries. In the semiconductor industry, for example, global standards have emerged, creating enormous demands for standardized global products. Accordingly, companies such as Intel, Texas Instruments, and Motorola all pursue a global strategy. Similarly, Dell Computer pursues a global strategy and sells standardized products around the world (see the *Running Case* later in this chapter).

These conditions are not found in many consumer goods markets, where demands for local responsiveness remain high, as in the markets for automobiles and processed food products. The strategy is inappropriate when demands for local responsiveness are high.

Transnational Strategy

The strategies we have just looked at all have downsides. The multidomestic strategy is rarely profitable today. An international strategy can increase costs and put a company under threat if low-cost competitors emerge. A global strategy can give a company a low-cost advantage, but the strategy may not work if customers do not appreciate and value globally standardized products and instead turn to the more customized or differentiated products of rivals.

What strategy can a company pursue, then, to avoid these problems? This is one of the most complex questions that large global companies are grappling with today. Companies like Ford, Sony, and IBM have been trying for decades to come up with the "perfect" strategy that will give them a competitive advantage in the global arena. Ford has changed strategy repeatedly to try to raise its profitability; so far, it has not succeeded, announcing huge losses in 2001 from failed global ventures. Although the perfect strategy will be specific to each company and must be aligned to its particular business model, some researchers do offer guidelines for companies seeking to maximize their profitability in the global marketplace.

Two of these researchers, Christopher Bartlett and Sumantra Ghoshal, argue that in today's global environment, competitive conditions are so intense that to survive, companies must essentially do all they can to respond to pressures for cost reductions and local responsiveness. They must *simultaneously* exploit experience-based cost economies and location economies, transfer distinctive competencies within the company, and pay attention to pressures for local responsiveness.[14] Moreover, Bartlett and Ghoshal note that in the modern multinational enterprise, distinctive competencies do not reside just in the home country but can develop in any of the company's worldwide operations. Thus, they maintain that the flow of skills and product offerings should not be all one way, from home company to foreign subsidiary, as in the case of companies pursuing an international strategy. Rather, the flow should also be from foreign subsidiary to home country and from foreign subsidiary to foreign subsidiary, a process Bartlett and Ghoshal refer to as *global learning*. They use the term **transnational strategy** to describe the strategy of simultaneously seeking to lower costs, be locally responsive, and transfer competencies in a way that is consistent with global learning.

In essence, companies that pursue a transnational strategy are trying to develop a business model that simultaneously achieves low-cost and differentiation advantages. As attractive as this may sound, the strategy is not an easy one to pursue, as the failure of companies like Ford and ABB (one of the world's largest engineering conglomerates), which did try to pursue one, suggests. Pressures for local responsiveness and cost reductions place conflicting demands on a company; local responsiveness raises costs and makes cost reductions difficult to achieve. How, then, can a company effectively pursue a transnational strategy?

Some clues can be derived from the case of Caterpillar. The need to compete with low-cost competitors such as Komatsu of Japan forced Caterpillar to look for greater cost economies. However, variations in construction practices and government regulations across countries mean that Caterpillar also has to be responsive to local demands. Therefore, as illustrated in Figure 8.3, Caterpillar confronts significant pressures for cost reductions and for local responsiveness.

To deal with cost pressures, Caterpillar redesigned its products to use many identical components and invested in a few large-scale component manufacturing

FIGURE 8.3

Cost Pressures and Pressures for Local Responsiveness Facing Caterpillar

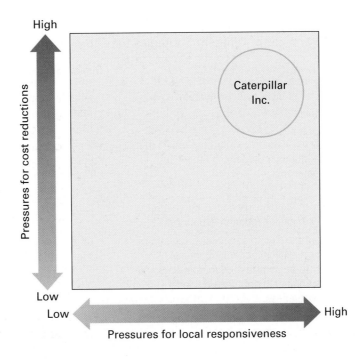

facilities, sited at favorable locations, to fill global demand and realize scale economies. At the same time the company augments the centralized manufacturing of components with assembly plants in each of its major global markets. At these plants, Caterpillar adds local product features, tailoring the finished product to local needs. Thus, Caterpillar is able to realize many of the benefits of global manufacturing while reacting to pressures for local responsiveness by differentiating its product among national markets.[15] Caterpillar started to pursue this strategy in 1979 and by 1997 had succeeded in doubling output per employee, significantly reducing its overall cost structure in the process. Meanwhile, Komatsu and Hitachi, which are still wedded to a Japan-centric global strategy, have seen their cost advantages evaporate and have been steadily losing market share to Caterpillar.

One might also argue that MTV Networks shifted from an international to a transnational strategy in the 1990s (see the *Opening Case*). Rather than creating everything in the United States, MTV now tries to strike a balance between the need to maintain uniformity in operating principles and the "frenetic look" of MTV programming across its global operations and the need to customize programming and content to local tastes and preferences.

Changing a company's business model to build an organization capable of supporting a transnational strategy is a complex and challenging task. Indeed, some would say it is too complex, because the strategy implementation problems of creating a viable organizational structure and control systems to manage this strategy are immense. Thus, a company might be better off focusing on tailoring or adjusting an international or global strategy to its particular needs by working on its business model to achieve the gains from both low cost and differentiation. After all, today, every business model is a matter of balancing pressures to lower a company's cost structure against pressures to provide customers with valuable differentiated products. Recognizing these caveats, the potential advantages and disadvantages of each of these four strategies are summarized in Table 8.1.

TABLE 8.1

The Advantages and Disadvantages of Different Strategies for Competing Globally

Strategy	Advantages	Disadvantages
International	• Transfer of distinctive competencies to foreign markets	• Lack of local responsiveness • Inability to realize location economies • Failure to exploit experience-curve effects
Multidomestic	• Ability to customize product offerings and marketing in accordance with local responsiveness	• Inability to realize location economies • Failure to exploit experience-curve effects • Failure to transfer distinctive competencies to foreign markets
Global	• Ability to exploit experience-curve effects • Ability to exploit location economies	• Lack of local responsiveness
Transnational	• Ability to exploit experience-curve effects • Ability to exploit location economies • Ability to customize product offerings and marketing in accordance with local responsiveness • Reaping benefits of global learning	• Difficulties in implementation because of organizational problems

Basic Entry Decisions

A company contemplating foreign expansion must make three basic decisions: which overseas markets to enter, when to enter those markets, and on what scale.

Which Overseas Markets to Enter

There are over 200 nation-states in the world, and they do not all hold out the same profit potential for a company contemplating foreign expansion. The choice of foreign markets must be made on an assessment of their long-run profit potential. The attractiveness of a country as a potential market for an international business depends on balancing the benefits, costs, and risks associated with doing business in that country. The long-run economic benefits of doing business in a country are a function of factors such as the size of a market (in terms of demographics), the existing wealth (purchasing power) of consumers in that market, and the likely future wealth of consumers. Some markets are very large when measured by numbers of consumers (e.g., China and India), but low living standards may imply limited purchasing power and therefore a relatively small market when measured in economic terms. The costs and risks associated with doing business in a foreign country are typically lower in economically advanced and politically stable democratic nations and greater in less developed and politically unstable nations.

By performing benefit-cost-risk calculations, a company can come up with a ranking of countries in terms of their attractiveness and long-run profit potential.[16] Obviously, preference is given to entering markets that rank highly. For an example, consider the case of the American financial services company Merrill Lynch, whose situation is profiled in Strategy in Action 8.4. During the past decade, Merrill Lynch greatly expanded its operations in the United Kingdom, Canada, and Japan. All three of these countries have a large pool of private savings and exhibit relatively low political and economic risks, so it makes sense that they would be attractive to Merrill Lynch. By offering its financial service products, such as mutual funds and investment advice, Merrill Lynch should be able to capture a large enough proportion of the private savings pool in each country to justify its investment in setting up business there. Of the three countries, Japan is probably the riskiest given the fragile state of its financial system, still suffering from a serious bad debt problem. However, the large size of the Japanese market and the fact that its government seems to be embarking on significant reform explains why Merrill has been attracted to this nation.

One other factor of importance is the value that a company's business model can create in a foreign market. This depends on the suitability of its business model to that market and the nature of indigenous competition.[17] Most important, if the company can offer a product that has not been widely available in that market and satisfies an unmet need, the value of that product to consumers is likely to be much greater than if the company simply offers the same type of product that indigenous competitors and other foreign entrants are already offering. Greater value translates into an ability to charge higher prices or build up unit sales volume more rapidly (or both). Again, on this count, Japan is clearly very attractive to Merrill Lynch.

Timing of Entry

Once a set of attractive national markets has been identified, it is important to consider the timing of entry: *early* (before other overseas companies) or *late* (after other international businesses have already established themselves in the market).

Several first-mover advantages are frequently associated with entering a market early.[18] One advantage is the ability to preempt rivals and capture demand by establishing a strong brand name. A second is the ability to build up demand, sales revenue, and market share in that country and ride down the experience curve ahead of

Strategy in Action

Merrill Lynch in Japan

Merrill Lynch, the U.S.-based financial services institution, is an investment banking titan. It is the world's largest underwriter of debt and equity and the third largest mergers and acquisitions adviser behind Morgan Stanley and Goldman Sachs. As one might expect, its investment banking operations have long had a global reach. The company has a dominant presence not only in New York but also in London and Tokyo. However, until recently, Merrill's international presence was limited to the investment banking side of its business. In contrast, its private client business, which offers banking, financial advice, and stock brokerage services to individuals, has historically been concentrated in the United States. This is now changing rapidly. In 1995, Merrill purchased Smith New Court, the largest stock brokerage firm in Britain and in 1997 acquired Mercury Asset Management, the U.K.'s leading manager of mutual funds. Then in 1998 Merrill acquired Midland Walwyn, Canada's last major independent stock brokerage firm. The company's boldest moves, however, have probably been in Japan.

Merrill started to establish a private client business in Japan in the 1980s but met with limited success. At the time, it was the first foreign firm to enter Japan's private client investment market, and it had great difficulty in attracting employee talent and customers away from Japan's big four stock brokerage firms, which traditionally had monopolized the Japanese market. Moreover, restrictive regulations made it almost impossible for Merrill to offer its Japanese private clients the range of services it offered clients in the United States. For example, foreign exchange regulations meant that it was very difficult for Merrill to sell non-Japanese stocks, bonds, and mutual funds to Japanese investors. In 1993, Merrill admitted defeat, closed down its six retail branches in Kobe and Kyoto, and withdrew from the private client market in Japan.

Over the next few years, however, things started to change. In the mid-1990s, Japan embarked on a wide-ranging deregulation of its financial services industry. Among other things, this led to the removal of many of the restrictions that had made it so difficult for Merrill to do business in Japan. For example, the relaxation of foreign exchange controls meant that by 1998, it was possible for Japanese citizens to purchase foreign stocks, bonds, and mutual funds. Meanwhile, Japan's big four stock brokerage firms continued to struggle with serious

financial problems, the result of the 1991 crash of that country's stock market. In November 1997, in what was a dramatic shock to many Japanese, one of these firms, Yamaichi Securities, declared that it was bankrupt: it had $2.2 billion in accumulated "hidden losses" and would shut its doors. Recognizing the country's financial system was strained and in need of fresh capital, know-how, and the stimulus of greater competition, the Japanese government signaled that it would adopt a much more relaxed attitude to foreign entry into its financial services industry. This attitude underlay Japan's wholehearted endorsement of a 1997 deal brokered by the World Trade Organization (WTO) to liberalize global financial services. Among other things, the WTO deal made it much easier for foreign firms to sell financial service products to Japanese investors.

By 1997, it had become clear to Merrill Lynch that the climate in Japan had changed significantly. The big attraction of the market was still the same: the financial assets owned by Japanese households are huge, amounting to a staggering 1,220 trillion yen in late 1997, with only 3 percent invested in mutual funds (most are invested in low-yielding bank accounts and government bonds). However, attitudes were changing, and it looked as if it would be much easier to do business in Japan.

Accordingly, in mid-1997, Merrill started to consider reentering the Japanese private client market. Initially, it considered a joint venture with Sanwa Bank to sell Merrill's mutual fund products to Japanese consumers through Sanwa's 400 retail branches. The proposed alliance had the advantage of allowing Merrill to leverage Sanwa's existing distribution system rather than having to build a distribution system of its own from scratch. However, in the long run, the strategy would not have given Merrill the presence that it felt it needed to build a solid financial services business in Japan. Merrill's executives reasoned that it was important for them to make a major commitment to the Japanese market in order to establish its brand name as a premier provider of investment products and financial advice to individuals. This would enable the company to entrench itself as a major player before other foreign institutions entered the market—and before Japan's own stock brokerages rose to the challenge. At the same time, given their prior experience in Japan, Merrill's executives were hesitant to go down this road because of the huge costs and risks.

The problem of how best to enter the Japanese market was solved by the bankruptcy of Yamaichi Securities. Suddenly Yamaichi's nationwide network of offices and 7,000 employees were up for grabs. In late December 1997, Merrill announced that it would hire some 2,000 of Yamaichi's employees and acquire up to 50 of Yamaichi's branch offices. The deal, enthusiastically endorsed by the Japanese government, significantly lowered Merrill's costs of establishing a retail network in Japan. Merrill's goal for the new subsidiary was to have $20 billion under management by 2000 and break even by 2001. The company got off to a quick start. In February 1998, Merrill launched its first mutual fund in Japan and saw the value of its assets swell to $1 billion by April. By the beginning of 2001, Merrill Lynch announced that it had $26 billion under management in Japan, giving the company a significant head start over other foreign financial service

institutions in building a private client network in Japan. However, unfortunately for Merrill, Japan's economy weakened significantly in 2001 and it now seems unlikely that Merrill will break even on its Japanese investment until 2003. Still, Merrill's belief is that when the Japanese economy recovers and other foreign institutions enter, it will already have a commanding presence in Japan that will be difficult to challenge.

Sources: "Japan's Big Bang. Enter Merrill," *Economist,* January 3, 1998, p. 72. J. P. Donlon, "Merrill Cinch," *Chief Executive* (March 1998): 28–32. D. Holley, "Merrill Lynch to Open 31 Offices Throughout Japan," *Los Angeles Times,* February 13, 1998, p. D1. A. Rowley, "Merrill Thunders into Japan," *Banker* (March 1998): 6. Staff Reporter. "Hard Times: Foreign Brokers in Japan," *The Economist,* February 23rd, 2002, pp. 78–79. Merrill Lynch's web site, www.ml.com.

future rivals. Both factors give the early entrant a cost advantage over later entrants, which may enable it to respond to later entry by cutting prices below those of later entrants and drive them out of the market. A third advantage is the ability of early entrants to create switching costs that tie customers into their products or services. Such switching costs make it difficult for later entrants to win business.

The case of Merrill Lynch illustrates these ideas. By entering the private client market in Japan early, Merrill hoped to establish a brand name that later entrants would find difficult to match. Moreover, by entering early with a valuable product offering, Merrill hoped to build up its sales volume rapidly, which will enable it to realize scale economies from establishing a network of Japanese branches. In addition, as Merrill trains its Japanese staff, their productivity should rise, due to learning economies, which again translates into lower costs. Thus, Merrill should be able to ride down the experience curve and achieve a lower cost structure than later entrants.

Finally, Merrill's business model is based on establishing close relationships between its financial advisers (i.e., stockbrokers) and private clients. Merrill's financial advisers are taught to get to know the needs of their clients and help manage their finances more effectively. Once these relationships are established, people rarely change. In other words, due to switching costs, they are unlikely to shift their business to later entrants. This effect is likely to be particularly strong in a country like Japan, where long-term relationships have traditionally been very important in business and social settings. For all of these reasons, Merrill Lynch may be able to capture first-mover advantages that will enable it to enjoy a strong competitive position in Japan for years to come.

There can also be first-mover disadvantages associated with entering a foreign market before other global companies.[19] These disadvantages are associated with *pioneering costs*, which an early entrant has to bear that a later entrant can avoid. Pioneering costs arise when the business system in a foreign country is so different from that in a company's home market that a company has to devote considerable effort, time, and expense to learning the rules of the game. Pioneering costs also include the costs of business failure if the company, due to its ignorance of the overseas environment, makes major strategic mistakes. There is a liability associated with being a global company that is one of the first to enter a national market.[20] Research evidence suggests that the probability of survival increases if an international business enters a national market *after* several other overseas companies have already done so.[21] The late entrant, it would appear, benefits by observing and learning from the mistakes made by early entrants.

Pioneering costs also include the costs of promoting and establishing a product offering, including the costs of educating customers. These costs can be particularly significant when the product being promoted is one that local customers are unfamiliar with. In many ways, Merrill Lynch will have to bear such pioneering costs in Japan. Most Japanese are not familiar with the type of investment products and services that it intends to sell, so Merrill will have to invest significant resources in customer education. In contrast, later entrants may be able to free-ride on an early entrant's investments in learning and customer education by watching how the early entrant proceeded in the market, avoiding costly mistakes made by the early entrant, and exploiting the market potential created by the early entrant's investments in customer education.

Scale of Entry and Strategic Commitments

The final issue that a company needs to consider when contemplating market entry is the scale of entry. Entering a market on a large scale involves the commitment of significant resources to that venture. Not all companies have the resources necessary to enter on a large scale, and even some large companies prefer to enter overseas markets on a small scale and then build their presence slowly over time as they become more familiar with the market. The original entry by Merrill Lynch into the private client market in Japan was on a small scale, involving only a handful of branches. In contrast, Merrill's reentry into the Japanese market in 1997 was on a significant scale.

The consequences of entering on a significant scale are associated with the value of the resulting strategic commitments.[22] A *strategic commitment* is a decision that has a long-term impact and is difficult to reverse. Deciding to enter a foreign market on a significant scale is a major strategic commitment. Strategic commitments, such as large-scale market entry, can have an important influence on the nature of competition in a market. For example, by entering Japan's private client business on a significant scale, Merrill has signaled its commitment to the market. This will have several effects. On the positive side, it will make it easier for Merrill to attract clients. The scale of entry gives potential clients reason for believing that Merrill will remain in the market for the long run. It may also give other overseas institutions considering entry into Japan's market pause for thought, since now they will have to compete not only against Japan's indigenous institutions but also against an aggressive and successful U.S. institution. On the negative side, the move may wake up Japan's financial institutions and elicit a vigorous competitive response from them. Moreover, by committing itself heavily to Japan, Merrill may have fewer resources available to support expansion in other desirable markets. In other words, Merrill's commitment to Japan limits its strategic flexibility.

As this example suggests, significant strategic commitments are neither unambiguously good nor bad. Rather, they tend to change the competitive playing field and unleash a number of changes, some of which may be desirable and some of which will not. It is therefore important for a company to think through the implications of large-scale entry into a market and act accordingly. Of particular relevance is trying to identify how actual and potential competitors might react to large-scale entry into a market. It is also important to bear in mind a connection between large-scale entry and first-mover advantages. Specifically, the large-scale entrant is more likely than the small-scale entrant to be able to capture first-mover advantages associated with demand preemption, scale economies, and switching costs.

Balanced against the value and risks of the commitments associated with large-scale entry are the benefits of entering on a small scale. Small-scale entry has the advantage of allowing a company to learn about a foreign market while simultaneously limiting the company's exposure to that market. In this sense, small-scale entry can be seen as a way of gathering more information about a foreign market before deciding whether to enter on a significant scale and how best to enter that market. In other words, by giving the company time to collect information, small-scale entry reduces the risks associated with a subsequent large-scale entry. On the other hand, the lack of commitment associated with small-scale entry may make it more difficult for the small-scale entrant to build market share and capture first-mover or early-mover advantages. The risk-averse company that enters a foreign market on a small scale may limit its potential losses, but it may also lose the chance to capture first-mover advantages.

The Choice of Entry Mode

The issue of when and how to enter a new national market raises the question of how to determine the best mode or vehicle for such entry. There are five main choices of entry mode: exporting, licensing, franchising, entering into a joint venture with a host country company, and setting up a wholly owned subsidiary in the host country. Each entry mode has its advantages and disadvantages, and managers must weigh these carefully when deciding which mode to use.[23]

Exporting

Most manufacturing companies begin their global expansion as exporters and only later switch to one of the other modes for serving a foreign market. Exporting has two distinct advantages: it avoids the costs of establishing manufacturing operations in the host country, which are often substantial, and it may be consistent with realizing experience curve cost economies and location economies. By manufacturing the product in a centralized location and then exporting it to other national markets, the company may be able to realize substantial scale economies from its global sales volume. That is how Sony came to dominate the global television market, how Matsushita came to dominate the VCR market, and how many Japanese auto companies originally made inroads into the U.S. auto market.

There are also a number of drawbacks to exporting. First, exporting from the company's home base may not be appropriate if there are lower-cost locations for manufacturing the product abroad (that is, if the company can realize location economies by moving production elsewhere). Thus, particularly in the case of a company pursuing a global or transnational strategy, it may pay to manufacture in a location where conditions are most favorable from a value creation perspective and then export from that location to the rest of the globe. This is not so much an argument against exporting as an argument against exporting from the company's home country. For example, many U.S. electronics companies have moved some of their manufacturing to Asia because low-cost but highly skilled labor is available there. They export from that location to the rest of the globe, including the United States.

Another drawback is that high transport costs can make exporting uneconomical, particularly in the case of bulk products. One way of getting around this problem is to manufacture bulk products on a regional basis, realizing some economies from large-scale production while limiting transport costs. Many multinational chemical companies manufacture their products on a regional basis, serving several countries in a region from one facility.

Tariff barriers, too, can make exporting uneconomical, and a government's threat to impose tariff barriers can make the strategy very risky. Indeed, the implicit threat from the U.S. Congress to impose tariffs on Japanese cars imported into the United States led directly to the decision by many Japanese auto companies to set up manufacturing plants in the United States.

Finally, a common practice among companies that are just beginning to export also poses risks. A company may delegate marketing activities in each country in which it does business to a local agent, but there is no guarantee that the agent will act in the company's best interest. Often foreign agents also carry the products of competing companies and thus have divided loyalties. Consequently, they may not do as good a job as the company would if it managed marketing itself. One way to solve this problem is to set up a wholly owned subsidiary in the host country to handle local marketing. In this way, the company can reap the cost advantages that arise from manufacturing the product in a single location and exercise tight control over marketing strategy in the host country.

Licensing   International licensing is an arrangement whereby a foreign licensee buys the rights to produce a company's product in the licensee's country for a negotiated fee (normally, royalty payments on the number of units sold). The licensee then puts up most of the capital necessary to get the overseas operation going.[24] The advantage of licensing is that the company does not have to bear the development costs and risks associated with opening up a foreign market. Licensing therefore can be a very attractive option for companies that lack the capital to develop operations overseas. It can also be an attractive option for companies that are unwilling to commit substantial financial resources to an unfamiliar or politically volatile foreign market where political risks are particularly high.

Licensing has three serious drawbacks, however. First, it does not give a company the tight control over manufacturing, marketing, and strategic functions in foreign countries that it needs to have in order to realize experience curve cost economies and location economies—as companies pursuing both global and transnational strategies try to do. Typically, each licensee sets up its own manufacturing operations. Hence, the company stands little chance of realizing experience curve cost economies and location economies by manufacturing its product in a centralized location. When these economies are likely to be important, licensing may not be the best way of expanding overseas.

Second, competing in a global marketplace may make it necessary for a company to coordinate strategic moves across countries so that the profits earned in one country can be used to support competitive attacks in another. Licensing, by its very nature, severely limits a company's ability to coordinate strategy in this way. A licensee is unlikely to let a multinational company take its profits (beyond those due in the form of royalty payments) and use them to support an entirely different licensee operating in another country.

A third problem with licensing is the risk associated with licensing technological know-how to foreign companies. For many multinational companies, technological know-how forms the basis of their competitive advantage, and they would want to maintain control over the use to which it is put. By licensing its technology, a company can quickly lose control over it. RCA, for instance, once licensed its color television technology to a number of Japanese companies. The Japanese companies quickly assimilated RCA's technology and then used it to enter the U.S. market. Now the Japanese have a bigger share of the U.S. market than the RCA brand does.

There are ways of reducing this risk. One way is by entering into a cross-licensing agreement with a foreign firm. Under **a cross-licensing agreement,** a firm might license some valuable intangible property to a foreign partner, and in addition to a royalty payment, also request that the foreign partner license some of its valuable know-how to the firm. Such agreements are reckoned to reduce the risks associated with licensing technological know-how, since the licensee realizes that if it violates the spirit of a licensing contract (by using the knowledge obtained to compete directly with the licensor), the licensor can do the same to it. Put differently, cross-licensing agreements enable firms to hold each other hostage, which thereby reduces the probability that they will behave opportunistically toward each other.[25] Such cross-licensing agreements are increasingly common in high-technology industries. For example, the U.S. biotechnology firm Amgen has licensed one of its key drugs, Nuprogene, to Kirin, the Japanese pharmaceutical company. The license gives Kirin the right to sell Nuprogene in Japan. In return, Amgen receives a royalty payment, and through a licensing agreement it gained the right to sell certain of Kirin's products in the United States.

Franchising   In many respects, franchising is similar to licensing, although franchising tends to involve longer-term commitments than licensing. **Franchising** is basically a specialized form of licensing in which the franchiser not only sells intangible property to the franchisee (normally a trademark), but also insists that the franchisee agree to abide by strict rules as to how it does business. The franchiser will also often assist the franchisee to run the business on an ongoing basis. As with licensing, the franchiser typically receives a royalty payment, which amounts to some percentage of the franchisee revenues.

Whereas licensing is a strategy pursued primarily by manufacturing companies, franchising, which resembles it in some respects, is a strategy employed chiefly by service companies. McDonald's provides a good example of a firm that has grown by using a franchising strategy. McDonald's has set down strict rules as to how franchisees should operate a restaurant. These rules extend to control over the menu, cooking methods, staffing policies, and restaurant design and location. McDonald's also organizes the supply chain for its franchisees and provides management training and financial assistance.[26]

The advantages of franchising are similar to those of licensing. Specifically, the franchiser does not have to bear the development costs and risks of opening up a foreign market on its own, for the franchisee typically assumes those costs and risks. Thus, using a franchising strategy, a service company can build up a global presence quickly and at a low cost.

The disadvantages are less pronounced than in the case of licensing. Because franchising is a strategy used by service companies, a franchiser does not have to consider the need to coordinate manufacturing in order to achieve experience curve effects and location economies. Nevertheless, franchising may inhibit a company's ability to achieve global strategic coordination.

A more significant disadvantage of franchising is the lack of quality control. The foundation of franchising arrangements is the notion that the company's brand name conveys a message to consumers about the quality of the company's product. Thus, a traveler booking into a Hilton International hotel in Hong Kong can reasonably expect the same quality of room, food, and service as she would receive in New York; the Hilton brand name is a guarantee of the consistency of product quality. However, foreign franchisees may not be as concerned about quality as they should be, and poor quality may mean not only lost sales in the foreign market but also a decline in the company's worldwide reputation. For example, if the traveler has a bad experience at the Hilton in Hong Kong, she may never go to another Hilton hotel and steer her colleagues away as well. The geographic distance separating it from its foreign franchisees and the sheer number of individual franchisees—tens of thousands in the case of McDonald's—can make it difficult for the franchiser to detect poor quality. Consequently, quality problems may persist.

To reduce this problem, a company can set up a subsidiary in each country or region in which it is expanding. The subsidiary, which might be wholly owned by the company or a joint venture with a foreign company, then assumes the rights and obligations to establish franchisees throughout that particular country or region. The combination of proximity and the limited number of independent franchisees that have to be monitored reduces the quality control problem. Besides, since the subsidiary is at least partly owned by the company, the company can place its own managers in the subsidiary to ensure the kind of quality monitoring it wants. This organizational arrangement has proved very popular in practice. It has been used by McDonald's, KFC, and Hilton Hotels Corp. to expand their international operations, to name just three examples.

Joint Ventures

Establishing a joint venture with a foreign company has long been a favored mode for entering a new market. One of the most famous long-term joint ventures is the Fuji-Xerox joint venture to produce photocopiers for the Japanese market. The most typical form of joint venture is a fifty-fifty venture, in which each party takes a 50 percent ownership stake and operating control is shared by a team of managers from both parent companies. Some companies have sought joint ventures in which they have a majority shareholding (for example, a 51 percent to 49 percent ownership split), which permits tighter control by the dominant partner.[27]

Joint ventures have a number of advantages. First, a company may feel that it can benefit from a local partner's knowledge of a host country's competitive conditions, culture, language, political systems, and business systems. Second, when the development costs and risks of opening up a foreign market are high, a company might gain by sharing these costs and risks with a local partner. Third, in some countries, political considerations make joint ventures the only feasible entry mode.[28] For example, historically many U.S. companies found it much easier to get permission to set up operations in Japan if they went in with a Japanese partner than if they tried to enter on their own. This is why Xerox originally teamed up with Fuji to sell photocopiers in Japan.

Despite these advantages, joint ventures can be difficult to establish and run because of two main drawbacks. First, as in the case of licensing, a company that enters into a joint venture risks losing control over its technology to its venture partner. To minimize this risk, it can seek a majority ownership stake in the joint venture, for as the dominant partner it would be able to exercise greater control over its technology. The trouble with this strategy is that it may be difficult to find a foreign partner willing to accept a minority ownership position.

The second disadvantage is that a joint venture does not give a company the tight control over its subsidiaries that it might need in order to realize experience curve effects or location economies—as both global and transnational companies try to do—or to engage in coordinated global attacks against its global rivals. Consider the entry of Texas Instruments (TI) into the Japanese semiconductor market. When TI established semiconductor facilities in Japan, part of its objective was to limit Japanese manufacturers' market share and the amount of cash available to them to invade TI's global market. In other words, TI was engaging in global strategic coordination. To implement this strategy, TI's Japanese subsidiary had to be prepared to take instructions from the TI corporate headquarters regarding competitive strategy. The strategy also required that the Japanese subsidiary be run at a loss if necessary. Clearly, a Japanese joint venture partner would have been unlikely to accept such conditions since they would have meant a negative return on investment. Thus, in order to implement this strategy, TI set up a wholly owned subsidiary in Japan instead of entering this market through a joint venture.

Wholly Owned Subsidiaries

A **wholly owned subsidiary** is one in which the parent company owns 100 percent of the subsidiary's stock. To establish a wholly owned subsidiary in a foreign market, a company can either set up a completely new operation in that country or acquire an established host country company and use it to promote its products in the host market (as Merrill Lynch did when it acquired various assets of Yamaichi Securities; see Strategy in Action 8.3).

Setting up a wholly owned subsidiary offers three advantages. First, when a company's competitive advantage is based on its control of a technological competency, a wholly owned subsidiary will normally be the preferred entry mode, since it reduces the company's risk of losing this control. Consequently, many high-tech companies prefer wholly owned subsidiaries to joint ventures or licensing arrangements. Wholly owned subsidiaries tend to be the favored entry mode in the semiconductor, computer, electronics, and pharmaceutical industries. Second, a wholly owned subsidiary gives a company the kind of tight control over operations in different countries that it needs if it is going to engage in global strategic coordination—taking profits from one country to support competitive attacks in another.

Third, a wholly owned subsidiary may be the best choice if a company wants to realize location economies and experience curve effects. When pressures on costs are intense, it may pay a company to configure its value chain in such a way that value added at each stage is maximized. Thus, a national subsidiary may specialize in manufacturing only part of the product line or certain components of the end product, exchanging parts and products with other subsidiaries in the company's global system. Establishing such a global production system requires a high degree of control over the operations of national affiliates. Different national operations have to be prepared to accept centrally determined decisions as to how they should produce, how much they should produce, and how their output should be priced for transfer between operations. A wholly owned subsidiary would have to comply with these mandates, whereas licensees or joint venture partners would most likely shun such a subservient role. This is one reason that Dell Computer has used wholly owned subsidiaries as its vehicle for expanding its global business (see the *Running Case* for Dell's global strategy).

On the other hand, establishing a wholly owned subsidiary is generally the most costly method of serving a foreign market. The parent company must bear all the costs and risks of setting up overseas operations—in contrast to joint ventures, where the costs and risks are shared, or licensing, where the licensee bears most of the costs and risks. But the risks of learning to do business in a new culture diminish if the company acquires an established host country enterprise. Acquisitions, though, raise a whole set of additional problems, such as trying to marry divergent corporate cultures, and these problems may more than offset the benefits. (The problems associated with acquisitions are discussed in Chapter 10.)

Choosing Among Entry Modes   The advantages and disadvantages of the various entry modes are summarized in Table 8.2. Inevitably, there are trade-offs in choosing one entry mode over another. For example, when considering entry into an unfamiliar country with a track record of nationalizing foreign-owned enterprises, a company might favor a joint venture

---

Running Case

Dell's Global Business

For more than a decade, Dell Computer has been expanding outside its U.S. base. In 2001, it generated revenues of $5.59 billion from Europe and $1.80 billion from the Asia-Pacific region. Although this level of sales is still small compared to the $17.88 billion it logged in North America, growth is now more rapid overseas, particularly in Asia. Dell's strategic goal is to be the low-cost player in the global industry. It does not alter its business model from country to country, but instead uses the same direct selling model and supply chain management process that have been the cornerstone of its success in North America. Dell is thus pursuing a global strategy.

Dell's basic approach to overseas expansion has been to serve foreign markets from a handful of regional manufacturing facilities, each established as a wholly owned subsidiary. To support its global business, it operates manufacturing facilities in and around Austin, Texas; Eldorado do Sul, Brazil; Nashville, Tennessee; Limerick, Ireland; Penang, Malaysia; and Xiamen, China. The plants in Austin and Tennessee serve North America, Eldorado do Sul serves South America, and Penang serves all of Asia-Pacific except China and Hong Kong, which are served from Xiamen. Europe is served from the Limerick facility.

Each of these manufacturing plants is large enough to attain significant scale economies, helping to underpin Dell's quest to be the low-cost player in the global industry. When demand in a region starts to get big enough, Dell considers opening up a second plant. It has two plants in Limerick. Its plant in Xiamen, China, was established to accommodate rapid demand growth in that country. Currently, one of Dell's fastest-growing Asian markets is India, and to accommodate demand there, it is looking at the possibility of establishing an Indian manufacturing operation.

Each plant uses exactly the same supply chain management processes that have made Dell famous. Taking advantage of its Internet-based supply chain management software, Dell schedules production of every line in every factory around the world every two hours. Every factory in the world is run with no more than six hours of inventory on hand, including work in progress. To serve Dell's global factories, many of its largest suppliers have also located facilities close to Dell's manufacturing plants so that they can better meet the company's demand for just-in-time inventory.

Dell has set up customer service centers at each of these plants to handle phone and online orders and to provide technical assistance. Each center serves an entire region, which Dell has found to be more efficient than locating a customer service center in each country where the company does business. Although online orders as a percentage of the total are lower outside the United States, they are growing rapidly. In Asia, for example, more than 40 percent of orders are now made online, up from 20 percent a few years ago.

For all of the similarities, however, Dell's customer mix is different overseas. In Asia, for example, Dell is seen primarily as a supplier of PCs and servers to businesses. It does not have the large consumer business that it has in the United States. However, this may be about to change. In 2001, Dell opened an overseas product development center in Beijing, China. Set up as a wholly owned subsidiary, the center has been charged with creating products geared toward the low end of the Chinese market. Apparently, even low-end PCs designed in the United States are too sophisticated and powerful for many Chinese consumers.

Sources: Dell Computer Corporation, 2001 Form 10K. K. James, "What Slowdown? Dell Asia-Pac's Going Great Guns," *Business Times,* January 15, 2001, p. 1. F. Balfour, "Penang's Secret," *Business Week,* November 6, 2000, p. 50.

TABLE 8.2

The Advantages and Disadvantages of Different Entry Modes

Entry Mode	Advantages	Disadvantages
Exporting	• Ability to realize location and experience-curve economies	• High transport costs • Trade barriers • Problems with local marketing agents
Licensing	• Low development costs and risks	• Inability to realize location and experience-curve economies • Inability to engage in global strategic coordination • Lack of control over technology
Franchising	• Low development costs and risks	• Inability to engage in global strategic coordination • Lack of control over quality
Joint ventures	• Access to local partner's knowledge • Shared development costs and risks • Political dependency	• Inability to engage in global strategic coordination • Inability to realize location and experience-curve economies • Lack of control over technology
Wholly owned subsidiaries	• Protection of technology • Ability to engage in global strategic coordination • Ability to realize location and experience-curve economies	• High costs and risks

with a local enterprise. Its rationale might be that the local partner will help it establish operations in an unfamiliar environment and speak out against nationalization should the possibility arise. But if the company's distinctive competency is based on proprietary technology, entering into a joint venture might mean risking loss of control over that technology to the joint venture partner, which would make this strategy unattractive. Despite such hazards, some generalizations can be offered about the optimal choice of entry mode.

Distinctive Competencies and Entry Mode. When companies expand internationally to earn greater returns from their distinctive competencies, transferring the skills and products derived from their competencies to foreign markets where indigenous competitors lack those skills, the companies are pursuing an international strategy. The optimal entry mode for such companies depends to some degree on the nature of their distinctive competency. In particular, we need to distinguish between companies with a distinctive competency in technological know-how and those with a distinctive competency in management know-how.

If a company's competitive advantage—its distinctive competency—derives from its control of proprietary *technological know-how,* licensing and joint venture arrangements should be avoided if possible in order to minimize the risk of losing control of that technology. Thus, if a high-tech company is considering setting up operations in a foreign country in order to profit from a distinctive competency in technological know-how, it should probably do so through a wholly owned subsidiary.

However, this rule should not be viewed as a hard and fast one. For instance, a licensing or joint venture arrangement might be structured in such a way as to reduce the risks that a company's technological know-how will be expropriated by licensees or joint venture partners. We consider this kind of arrangement in more detail later in the chapter when we discuss the issue of structuring strategic alliances. To take another exception to the rule, a company may perceive its technological advantage as being only transitory and expect rapid imitation of its core technology by competitors. In this situation, the company might want to license its technology as quickly as possible to foreign companies in order to gain global acceptance of its technology before imitation occurs.[29] Such a strategy has some advantages. By licensing its technology to competitors, the company may deter them from developing their own, possibly superior, technology. It also may be able to establish its technology as the dominant design in the industry (as Matsushita did with its VHS format for VCRs), ensuring a steady stream of royalty payments. Such situations apart, however, the attractions of licensing are probably outweighed by the risks of losing control of technology, and therefore licensing should be avoided.

The competitive advantage of many service companies, such as McDonald's or Hilton Hotels, is based on *management know-how*. For such companies, the risk of losing control of their management skills to franchisees or joint venture partners is not that great. The reason is that the valuable asset of such companies is their brand name, and brand names are generally well protected by international laws pertaining to trademarks. Given this fact, many of the issues that arise in the case of technological know-how do not arise in the case of management know-how. As a result, many service companies favor a combination of franchising and subsidiaries to control franchisees within a particular country or region. The subsidiary may be wholly owned or a joint venture. In most cases, however, service companies have found that entering into a joint venture with a local partner in order to set up a controlling subsidiary in a country or region works best because a joint venture is often politically more acceptable and brings a degree of local knowledge to the subsidiary.

Pressures for Cost Reduction and Entry Mode. The greater the pressures for cost reductions are, the more likely it is that a company will want to pursue some combination of exporting and wholly owned subsidiaries. By manufacturing in the locations where factor conditions are optimal and then exporting to the rest of the world, a company may be able to realize substantial location economies and experience curve effects. The company might then want to export the finished product to marketing subsidiaries based in various countries. Typically, these subsidiaries would be wholly owned and have the responsibility for overseeing distribution in a particular country. Setting up wholly owned marketing subsidiaries is preferable to a joint venture arrangement or using a foreign marketing agent because it gives the company the tight control over marketing that might be required to coordinate a globally dispersed value chain. In addition, tight control over a local operation enables the company to use the profits generated in one market to improve its competitive position in another market. Hence companies pursuing global or transnational strategies prefer to establish wholly owned subsidiaries.

Global Strategic Alliances

Global strategic alliances are cooperative agreements between companies from different countries that are actual or potential competitors. Strategic alliances run the range from formal joint ventures, in which two or more companies have an equity stake, to short-term contractual agreements, in which two companies may agree to cooperate on a particular problem (such as developing a new product).

Advantages of Strategic Alliances

Companies enter into strategic alliances with competitors to achieve a number of strategic objectives.[30] First, strategic alliances may be a way of *facilitating entry into a foreign market*. For example, Motorola initially found it very difficult to gain access to the Japanese cellular telephone market. In the mid-1980s, it complained loudly about formal and informal Japanese trade barriers. The turning point for Motorola came in 1987, when it formed its alliance with Toshiba to build microprocessors. As part of the deal, Toshiba provided Motorola with marketing help, including some of its best managers. This aided Motorola in the political game of winning government approval to enter the Japanese market and obtaining allocations of radio frequencies for its mobile communications systems. Since then, Motorola has played down the importance of Japan's informal trade barriers. Although privately the company still admits they exist, with Toshiba's help Motorola has become skilled at getting around them.[31]

Second, many companies enter into strategic alliances to share the *fixed costs and associated risks* that arise from the development of new products or processes. Motorola's alliance with Toshiba was partly motivated by a desire to share the high fixed costs associated with setting up an operation to manufacture microprocessors. The microprocessor business is so capital intensive (it cost Motorola and Toshiba close to $1 billion to set up their facility) that few companies can afford the costs and risks of going it alone.

Third, many alliances can be seen as a way of bringing together *complementary skills and assets* that neither company could easily develop on its own. For example, in 1990, AT&T struck a deal with NEC Corp. of Japan to trade technological skills. Under the agreement, AT&T transferred some of its computer-aided design technology to NEC. In return, NEC gave AT&T access to the technology underlying NEC advanced logic computer chips. Such equitable trading of distinctive competencies seems to underlie many of the most successful strategic alliances.

Finally, it may make sense to enter into an alliance if it helps the company *set technological standards for its industry* and if those standards benefit the company. For example, in 1992, the Dutch electronics company Philips entered into an alliance with its global competitor, Matsushita, to manufacture and market the digital compact cassette (DDC) system pioneered by Philips. Linking up with Matsushita would help Philips establish the DCC system as a new technological standard in the recording and customer electronics industries. The issue is an important one because Sony was developing a competing technology that it hoped to establish as the new technical standard. Thus, Philips saw the alliance with Matsushita as a tactic for winning the standard race, for it ties a potential major competitor into its standard.

Disadvantages of Strategic Alliances

The various advantages can be very significant. Nevertheless, some commentators have criticized strategic alliances on the grounds that they give competitors a low-cost route to gain new technology and market access.[32] For example, Robert Reich and Eric Mankin have argued that strategic alliances between U.S. and Japanese companies are part of an implicit Japanese strategy to keep higher-paying, higher-value-added jobs in Japan while gaining the project engineering and production process skills that underlie the competitive success of many U.S. companies.[33] They have viewed Japanese success in the machine tool and semiconductor industries as largely built on U.S. technology acquired through various strategic alliances. And they have asserted that increasingly, U.S. managers are aiding the Japanese in achieving their goals by entering into alliances that channel new inventions to Japan and provide a U.S. sales and distribution network for the resulting products. Although such deals may generate short-term profits, in the long run, according to Reich and Mankin, the result is to "hollow out" U.S. companies, leaving them with no competitive advantage in the global marketplace.

Reich and Mankin have a point: alliances do have risks. Unless it is careful, a company can give away more than it gets in return. Nevertheless, there are so many examples of apparently successful alliances between companies, including alliances between U.S. and Japanese companies, that Reich and Mankin's position seems more than a little extreme. It is difficult to see how the Motorola-Toshiba alliance or the long-standing alliance between Fuji Film and Xerox to manufacture photocopiers (Fuji-Xerox) fit their thesis. In all of these cases, both partners seemed to have gained from the alliance. Because Reich and Mankin undoubtedly do have a point, the question becomes, *Why do some alliances benefit the company, whereas in others, it can end up giving away technology and market access and get very little in return?* The next section provides an answer to this question.

Making Strategic Alliances Work

The failure rate for international strategic alliances is quite high. For example, one study of forty-nine international strategic alliances found that two-thirds run into serious managerial and financial troubles within two years of their formation, and that although many of these problems are ultimately solved, 33 percent are ultimately rated as failures by the parties involved.[34] The success of an alliance seems to be a function of three main factors: partner selection, alliance structure, and the manner in which the alliance is managed.

Partner Selection

One of the keys to making a strategic alliance work is to select the right kind of partner. A good partner has three principal characteristics. First, a good partner helps the company achieve strategic goals such as achieving market access, sharing the costs and risks of new-product development, or gaining access to critical core competencies. In other words, the partner must have capabilities that the company lacks and that it values. Second, a good partner shares the firm's vision for the purpose of the alliance. If two companies approach an alliance with radically different agendas, the chances are great that the relationship will not be harmonious and will end in divorce. This seems to have been the case with the alliance between GM and Daewoo. GM's agenda was to use Daewoo as a source of cheap labor to produce cars for the Korean and U.S. markets, whereas Daewoo wanted to use GM's know-how and distribution systems to increase its own business not just in Korea and the United States but also in Europe. Different perceptions over the strategic role of the venture ultimately contributed to the dissolution of the alliance.

Third, a good partner is unlikely to try to exploit the alliance opportunistically for its own ends—that is, to expropriate the company's technological know-how while giving away little in return. In this respect, firms with reputations for fair play to maintain probably make the best partners. For example, IBM is involved in so many strategic alliances that it would not pay the company to trample roughshod over individual alliance partners. Such actions would tarnish IBM's hard-won reputation of being a good partner and would make it more difficult for IBM to attract alliance partners in the future. Similarly, their reputations make it less likely that Japanese companies such as Sony, Toshiba, and Fuji, which have histories of alliances with non-Japanese firms, would opportunistically exploit an alliance partner.

To select a partner with these three characteristics, a company needs to conduct some comprehensive research on potential alliance candidates. To increase the probability of selecting a good partner, the company should collect as much pertinent publicly available information about potential allies as possible; collect data from informed third parties, including companies that have had alliances with the potential partners, investment bankers who have had dealings with them, and some of their former employees; and get to know potential partners as well as possible before committing to an alliance. This last step should include face-to-face meetings between senior managers (and perhaps middle-level managers) to ensure that the chemistry is right.

Alliance Structure

Having selected a partner, the alliance should be structured so that the company's risk of giving too much away to the partner is reduced to an acceptable level. Figure 8.4 depicts the four safeguards against opportunism by alliance partners that we discuss here. (**Opportunism** includes the "theft" of technology or markets that Reich and Mankin describe.) First, alliances can be designed to make it difficult (if not impossible) to transfer technology not meant to be transferred. Specifically, the design, development, manufacture, and service of a product manufactured by an alliance can be structured so as to "wall off" sensitive technologies to prevent their leakage to the other participant. In the alliance between General Electric and Snecma to build commercial aircraft engines, for example, GE reduced the risk of "excess transfer" by walling off certain sections of the production process. The modularization effectively cut off the transfer of what GE regarded as key competitive technology while permitting Snecma access to final assembly. Similarly, in the alliance between Boeing and the Japanese to build the 767, Boeing walled off research, design, and marketing functions considered central to its competitive position, while allowing the Japanese to share in production technology. Boeing also walled off new technologies not required for 767 production.[35]

Second, contractual safeguards can be written into an alliance agreement to guard against the risk of opportunism by a partner. For example, TRW has three strategic alliances with large Japanese auto component suppliers to produce seat belts, engine valves, and steering gears for sale to Japanese-owned auto assembly plants in the United States. TRW has clauses in each of its alliance contracts that bar the Japanese firms from competing with TRW to supply U.S.-owned auto companies with component parts. By doing this, TRW protects itself against the possibility that the Japanese companies are entering into the alliances merely as a means of gaining access to the North American market to compete with TRW in its home market.

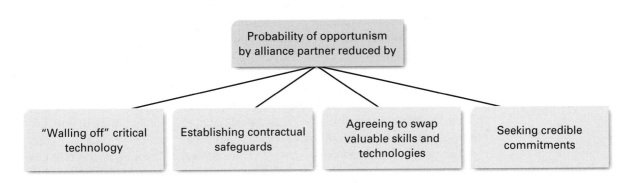

FIGURE 8.4

Structuring Alliances to Reduce Opportunism

Third, both parties to an alliance can agree in advance to swap skills and technologies, thereby ensuring a chance for equitable gain. Cross-licensing agreements are one way to achieve this goal. For example, in the alliance between Motorola and Toshiba, Motorola has licensed some of its microprocessor technology to Toshiba, and in return Toshiba has licensed some of its memory chip technology to Motorola.

Fourth, the risk of opportunism by an alliance partner can be reduced if the firm extracts a significant credible commitment from its partner in advance. The long-term alliance between Xerox and Fuji to build photocopiers for the Asian market perhaps best illustrates this. Rather than enter into an informal agreement or some kind of licensing arrangement (which Fuji Photo initially wanted), Xerox insisted that Fuji invest in a fifty-fifty joint venture to serve Japan and East Asia. This venture constituted such a significant investment in people, equipment, and facilities that Fuji Photo was committed from the outset to making the alliance work in order to earn a return on its investment. By agreeing to the joint venture, Fuji essentially made a credible commitment to the alliance. Given this, Xerox felt secure in transferring its photocopier technology to Fuji.[36]

Managing the Alliance

Once a partner has been selected and an appropriate alliance structure agreed on, the task facing the company is to maximize the benefits from the alliance. One important ingredient of success appears to be sensitivity to cultural differences. Differences in management style can often be attributed to cultural differences. Managers need to make allowances for such differences when dealing with their partner.

In addition, managing an alliance successfully means building interpersonal relationships among managers from the different companies, a lesson that can be drawn from the successful strategic alliance between Ford and Mazda to jointly develop cars for the global auto industry. This partnership resulted in the development of such best-selling cars as the Ford Explorer and the Mazda Navajo. Ford and Mazda have set up a framework of meetings within which managers from Ford and Mazda not only discuss matters pertaining to the alliance but also have sufficient non-work-time to allow them to get to know each other better. The resulting personal friendships can help build trust and facilitate harmonious relations between the two companies.[37] Moreover, personal relationships can create an informal management network between the companies, and this network can then be used to help solve problems that arise in more formal contexts, such as joint committee meetings between personnel from both firms.

A major factor determining how much a company gains from an alliance is its ability to learn from alliance partners. Gary Hamel, Yves Doz, and C. K. Prahalad reached this conclusion after a five-year study of fifteen strategic alliances between major multinationals. They focused on a number of alliances between Japanese companies and Western (European or American) partners. In every case in which a Japanese company emerged from an alliance stronger than its Western partner, the Japanese company had made a greater effort to learn. Indeed, few Western companies seemed to want to learn from their Japanese partners. They tended to regard the alliance purely as a cost-sharing or risk-sharing device rather than as an opportunity to learn how a potential competitor does business.[38]

For an example of an alliance in which there was a clear learning asymmetry, consider the agreement between General Motors and Toyota Motor Corp. to build the Chevrolet Nova. This alliance is structured as a formal joint venture, New United Motor Manufacturing, in which both parties have a 50 percent equity stake. The venture owns an auto plant in Fremont, California. According to one of the Japanese managers, Toyota achieved most of its objectives from the alliance: "We learned about U.S. supply and transportation. And we got the confidence to manage U.S. workers." All that knowledge was then quickly transferred to Georgetown, Kentucky, where Toyota opened a plant of its own in 1988. By contrast, although General Motors got a new product, the Chevrolet Nova, some GM managers complained that their new knowledge was never put to good use inside GM. They say that they should have been kept together as a team to educate GM's engineers and workers about the Japanese system. Instead, they were dispersed to different GM subsidiaries.[39]

When entering an alliance, a company must take some measures to ensure that it learns from its alliance partner and then puts that knowledge to good use within its own organization. One suggested approach is to educate all operating employees about the partner's strengths and weaknesses and make clear to them how acquiring particular skills will bolster their company's competitive position. For such learning to be of value, the knowledge acquired from an alliance has to be diffused throughout the organization—as did not happen at GM. To spread this knowledge, the managers involved in an alliance should be used as a resource in familiarizing others within the company about the skills of an alliance partner.

Summary of Chapter

1. For some companies, international expansion represents a way of earning greater returns by transferring the skills and product offerings derived from their distinctive competencies to markets where indigenous competitors lack those skills.

2. Because of national differences, it pays a company to base each value creation activity it performs at the location where factor conditions are most conducive to the performance of that activity. This strategy is known as focusing on the attainment of location economies.

3. By building sales volume more rapidly, international expansion can assist a company in the process of moving down the experience curve.

4. The best strategy for a company to pursue may depend on the kind of pressures it must cope with: pressures for cost reductions or for local responsiveness. Pressures for cost reductions are greatest in industries producing commodity-type products, where price is the main competitive weapon. Pressures for local responsiveness arise from differences in consumer tastes and preferences, as well as from national infrastructure and traditional practices, distribution channels, and host government demands.

5. Companies pursuing an international strategy transfer the skills and products derived from distinctive competencies to foreign markets, while undertaking some limited local customization.

6. Companies pursuing a multidomestic strategy customize their product offering, marketing strategy, and business strategy to national conditions.

7. Companies pursuing a global strategy focus on reaping the cost reductions that come from experience curve effects and location economies.

8. Many industries are now so competitive that companies must adopt a transnational strategy. This involves a simultaneous focus on reducing costs, transferring skills and products, and local responsiveness. Implementing such a strategy may not be easy.

9. The most attractive foreign markets tend to be found in politically stable developed and developing nations that have free market systems and where there is not a dramatic upsurge in either inflation rates or private sector debt.

10. Several advantages are associated with entering a national market early, before other international businesses have established themselves. These advantages must be balanced against the pioneering costs that early entrants often have to bear, including the greater risk of business failure.

11. Large-scale entry into a national market constitutes a major strategic commitment that is likely to change the nature of competition in that market and limit the entrant's future strategic flexibility. The firm needs to think through the implications of such commitments before embarking on a large-scale entry. Although making major strategic commitments can yield many benefits, there are also risks associated with such a strategy.

12. There are five different ways of entering a foreign market: exporting, licensing, franchising, entering into a joint venture, and setting up a wholly owned subsidiary. The optimal choice among entry modes depends on the company's strategy.

13. Strategic alliances are cooperative agreements between actual or potential competitors. The advantages of alliances are that they facilitate entry into foreign markets, enable partners to share the fixed costs and risks associated with new products and processes, facilitate the transfer of complementary skills between companies, and help companies establish technical standards.

14. The drawbacks of a strategic alliance are that the company risks giving away technological know-how and market access to its alliance partner while getting very little in return.

15. The disadvantages associated with alliances can be reduced if the company selects partners carefully, paying close attention to reputation, and structures the alliance so as to avoid unintended transfers of know-how.

Discussion Questions

1. Plot the position of the following companies on Figure 8.1: Procter & Gamble, IBM, Coca-Cola, Dow Chemicals, AOL, and McDonald's. In each case, justify your answer.

2. Are the following global industries or multidomestic industries: bulk chemicals, pharmaceuticals, branded food products, moviemaking, television manufacture, personal computers, airline travel, and Internet online services such as AOL and MSN?

3. Discuss how the need for control over foreign operations varies with the strategy and distinctive competencies of a company. What are the implications of this relationship for the choice of entry mode?

4. Licensing proprietary technology to foreign competitors is the best way to give up a company's competitive advantage. Discuss.

5. What kind of companies stand to gain the most from entering into strategic alliances with potential competitors? Why?

Practicing Strategic Management

SMALL-GROUP EXERCISE: DEVELOPING A GLOBAL STRATEGY

Break into groups of three to five people, and appoint one group member as a spokesperson who will communicate your findings to the class. You work for a company in the soft drink industry that has developed a line of carbonated fruit-based drinks. You have already established a significant presence in your home market, and now you are planning the global strategy development of the company in the soft drink industry. You need to decide the following:

1. What overall strategy to pursue: a global strategy, multidomestic strategy, international strategy, or transnational strategy

2. Which markets to enter first

3. What entry strategy to pursue (e.g., franchising, joint venture, wholly owned subsidiary)

   What information do you need in order to make this kind of decision? On the basis of what you do know, what strategy would you recommend?

ARTICLE FILE 8

Find an example of a multinational company that in recent years has switched its strategy from a multidomestic, international, or global strategy to a transnational strategy.

Identify why the company made the switch and any problems that the company may be encountering while it tries to change its strategic orientation.

STRATEGIC MANAGEMENT PROJECT: MODULE 8

This module requires you to identify how your company might profit from global expansion, the strategy that your company should pursue globally, and the entry mode that it might favor. With the information you have at your disposal, answer the questions regarding the following two situations:

Your company is already doing business in other countries

1. Is your company creating value or lowering the costs of value creation by realizing location economies, transferring distinctive competencies abroad, or realizing cost economies from the experience curve? If not, does it have the potential to?

2. How responsive is your company to differences among nations? Does it vary its product and marketing message from country to country? Should it?

3. What are the cost pressures and pressures for local responsiveness in the industry in which your company is based?

4. What strategy is your company pursuing to compete globally? In your opinion, is this the correct strategy, given cost pressures and pressures for local responsiveness?

5. What major foreign market does your company serve, and what mode has it used to enter this market? Why is your company active in these markets and not others? What are the advantages and disadvantages of using this mode? Might another mode be preferable?

Your company is not yet doing business in other countries

1. What potential does your company have to add value to its products or lower the costs of value creation by expanding internationally?

2. On the international level, what are the cost pressures and pressures for local responsiveness in the industry in which your company is based? What implications do these pressures have for the strategy that your company might pursue if it chose to expand globally?

3. What foreign market might your company enter, and what entry mode should it use to enter this market? Justify your answer.

EXPLORING THE WEB
Visiting IBM

IBM stands for International Business Machines. Using the significant resources located at IBM's corporate web site (**www.ibm.com**), including annual reports and company history, explain what the "International" means in IBM. Specifically, how many countries is IBM active in? How does IBM create value by expanding into foreign markets? What entry mode does IBM adopt in most markets? Can you find any exceptions to this? How would you characterize IBM's strategy for competing in the global marketplace? Is IBM pursuing a transnational, global, international, or multidomestic strategy?

General Task: Search the Web for a company site where there is a good description of that company's international operations. On the basis of this information, try to establish how the company enters foreign markets and what overall strategy it is pursuing (global, international, multidomestic, transnational).

Closing Case

Global Strategy at General Motors

In many respects, General Motors is one of the oldest multinational corporations in the world. Founded in 1908, it established its first international operations in the 1920s. GM is now the world's largest industrial corporation and full-line automobile manufacturer with annual revenues of over $100 billion. The company sells 8 million vehicles per year, 3.2 million of them produced and marketed outside its North American base. In 1997, GM had a 31 percent share of the North American market and an 8.9 percent share of the market in the rest of the world.

Historically, the bulk of GM's foreign operations have been concentrated in Western Europe. Local brand names such as Opel, Vauxhall, Saab, and Holden helped the company to sell 1.7 million vehicles in 1997 and gain an 11.3 percent market share, second only to that of Ford. Although GM has long had a presence in Latin America and Asia, until recently sales there accounted for only a relatively small fraction of the company's total international business. However, GM's plans call for this to change rapidly over the next few years. Sensing that Asia, Latin America, and Eastern Europe may be the automobile industry's growth markets early in this century, GM has embarked on ambitious plans to invest $2.2 billion in

four new manufacturing facilities in Argentina, Poland, China, and Thailand. One of the most significant things about this expansion is that it is going hand in hand with a sea change in GM's philosophy toward the management of its international operations.

Traditionally, GM saw the developing world as a dumping ground for obsolete technology and outdated models. Just a few years ago, for example, GM's Brazilian factories were churning out U.S.-designed Chevy Chevettes that hadn't been produced in North America for years. GM's Detroit-based executives saw this as a way of trying to squeeze the maximum cash flow from the company's investments in aging technology. GM managers in the developing world, however, took it as an indication that the center did not view developing world operations as being of great significance. This feeling was exacerbated by the fact that most operations in the developing world were instructed to carry out manufacturing and marketing plans formulated in the company's Detroit headquarters rather than being trusted to develop their own.

In contrast, GM's European operations were traditionally managed on an arm's-length basis, with the company's national operations often being allowed to design their own cars and manufacturing facilities and formulate their own marketing strategies. This regional and national autonomy did allow GM's European operations to produce vehicles that were closely tailored to the needs of local customers. However, it also led to the costly duplication of effort in design and manufacturing operations and to a failure to share valuable technology, skills, and practices across different national subsidiaries. Thus, while General Motors exerted tight control over its operations in the developing world, its control over operations in Europe was perhaps too lax. The result was a company whose international operations lacked overall strategic coherence.

Now GM is trying to change this. It is switching from its Detroit-centric view of the world to a philosophy that centers of excellence may reside anywhere in the company's global operations. The company is consciously trying to tap these centers of excellence to provide its global operations with the very latest technology. The four new manufacturing plants being constructed in the developing world are an embodiment of this new approach. Each is identical, each incorporates state-of-the art technology, and each has been designed not by Americans but by a team of Brazilian and German engineers. By building identical plants, GM should be able to mimic Toyota, whose plants are so much alike that a change in a car in Japan can be quickly replicated around the world. The plants are modeled after GM's Eisenach facility in Germany, which is managed by the company's Opel subsidiary. It was at the Eisenach plant that GM figured out how to implement the lean production system pioneered by Toyota. The plant is now the most efficient auto manufacturing operation in Europe and the best within GM, with a productivity rate at least twice that of most North American assembly operations. When completed, each of these new plants will produce state-of-the-art vehicles for local consumption.

In order to realize scale economies, GM is also trying to design and build vehicles that share a common global platform. Engineering teams located in Germany, Detroit, South America, and Australia are designing these common vehicle platforms. The idea is that local plants will be allowed to customize certain features of these vehicles to match the tastes and preferences of local customers. At the same time, adhering to a common global platform will enable the company to spread its costs of designing a car over greater volume and realize scale economies in the manufacture of shared components, both of which should help it lower its overall cost structure. The first fruits of this effort include the 1998 Cadillac Seville, which was designed to be sold in more than forty countries. GM's family of front-wheel-drive minivans was also designed around a common platform that will allow the vehicles to be produced in multiple locations around the globe, as was the 1998 Opel Astra, GM's best-selling car in Europe.

Despite making bold moves in the direction of greater global integration, numerous problems can still be seen on GM's horizon. Compared to Ford, Toyota, or the new Mercedes-Chrysler combination, GM still suffers from high costs, low perceived quality, and a profusion of brands. Moreover, while its aggressive move into emerging markets may be based on the reasonable assumption that demand will grow strong in these areas, other automobile companies are also expanding their production facilities in the same markets, raising the specter of global excess capacity and price wars. Finally, and perhaps most significant, there are those within GM who argue that the push toward "global cars" is misconceived. In particular, the German-based engineering staff at Opel's Russelsheim design facility, which takes the lead on design of many key global models, has voiced concerns that distinctively European engineering features they deem essential to a car's local success may be left by the wayside in a drive to devise what they see as blander "global" cars.

Case Discussion Questions

1. How would you characterize the strategy that GM pursued prior to 1997 in the (a) developing world and (b) Europe?

2. What do you think were the likely competitive effects of the pre-1997 strategy?

3. How would you characterize the strategy that GM has been pursuing since 1997? How should this strategy affect GM's ability to create value in the global automobile market?

Sources: R. Blumenstein, "GM Is Building Plants in Developing Nations to Woo New Markets," *Wall Street Journal,* August 4, 1997, p. A1. Haig Simonian, "GM Hopes to Turn Corner with New Astra," *Financial Times,* November 29, 1997, p. 15. D. Howes, "GM, Ford Play for Keeps Abroad," *Detroit News,* March 8, 1998, p. D1.

Corporate Strategy: Horizontal Integration, Vertical Integration, and Strategic Outsourcing

9

Opening Case

The Rise of WorldCom

In 1983, WorldCom was a small reseller of long-distance telephone service. By 2001, the company generated sales of $40 billion, making it the second largest provider of telecommunications services in the industry, behind AT&T. WorldCom entered 2001 as the number two provider of long-distance phone service in the United States, with 19 percent of the market, the largest single carrier of Internet data in the country, with an estimated 37 percent of the market, and a dazzling array of strategic assets, including a 300,000-mile fiber-optic network that was global in its reach.

WorldCom was very much the creation of its swaggering cowboy CEO, Bernie Ebbers, whose strategy for growth was quite simple: acquire competitors. An apparently savvy deal-maker, over seventeen years Ebbers acquired some sixty other telecommunication service providers, capping off the spree with the acquisition of MCI Communications, which at the time was larger than WorldCom and the number two long-distance telephone company in the nation. Ebbers's deal making was financed by a combination of World-Com stock and debt. As long as the stock continued to rise—and it increased by a staggering 7,000 percent during the 1990s—WorldCom could use its "currency" to buy other companies in the industry. In addition, World-Com borrowed large amounts of money from the debt markets, some $30 billion by late 2001. The debt markets proved only too willing to lend to WorldCom given the company's glittering growth prospects.

Driving the buying spree were two strategic objectives that were central to WorldCom's business model: (1) the desire to reap scale economies in order to drive down costs and (2) the desire to capture and retain customers by bundling together telecommunications services, such as long-distance service and Internet access, and selling them under a single contract. Ebbers reasoned that the scale economies would come from assembling a nationwide and international network to transmit data and voice traffic. The costs of assembling such a network are primarily fixed and include the costs of laying fiber-optic networks and installing switches. Once the network has been built, the costs of sending additional traffic down the network are virtually zero. This gives the company with the largest volume of traffic a huge cost advantage, because it can spread the fixed costs of building and maintaining its network over a very large volume, driving down the average costs of serving each customer. In addition, Ebbers believed that customers would want only one telecommunications service provider, and one bill, for all services they used, including long-distance and local phone service, Internet access, and wireless phone service. By assembling a company that could provide all of those services to consumers in a single bundle with a single bill, Ebbers believed that WorldCom would have a competitive advantage in the marketplace that would help it to increase volume more rapidly than rivals and thus better realize potential scale economies.

WorldCom grew through acquisition, as opposed to organically, because it was quicker to grow this way and cheaper to use a mix of WorldCom's high-flying stock and long-term debt to buy competitors than to build the network entirely on its own. Moreover, when WorldCom made an acquisition, it applied a fairly standard formula: cut the overhead, eliminate any duplication, and drive the traffic of the acquired customers through WorldCom's network to realize scale economies.

The strategy seemed to work well until 2000, when WorldCom made a bid to acquire Sprint for $115 billion. Sprint was the number three long-distance company in the United States with 8 percent of the market, operated

the second largest data network in the country with 16 percent of the market, and was one of the largest providers of wireless service in the United States. The acquisition made perfect strategic sense. It would enable WorldCom to reap additional scale economies and bundle wireless service with its long-distance and Internet access service. Unfortunately for WorldCom, antitrust authorities in both the United States and the European Union thought that it would also give WorldCom substantial monopoly power, and both indicated that they would oppose the acquisition. The U.S. Justice Department claimed that the acquisition would create an unacceptable level of concentration in the long-distance phone business, with AT&T and WorldCom controlling 80 percent of the market after the acquisition. The Department of Justice also claimed that the acquisition would result in the monopolization of high-speed Internet data lines, creating a company that controlled 53 percent of Internet traffic, giving the expanded WorldCom the ability to discriminate against rivals and "irrevocably tip the market" toward a monopoly outcome.

In mid-2000, WorldCom announced that in the face of opposition from antitrust authorities, it would abandon the acquisition. This proved to be a turning point in the company's fortunes. During the next two years the company's stock plummeted from over $50 a share to under $1. A number of factors contributed to the implosion in the stock price. First, a price war erupted in the long-distance telephone service business. A combination of slowing growth and the entry of new competitors, particularly the Baby Bells that had been allowed by the 1996 Telecommunications Act to start offering-long distance telephone service, conspired to drive down prices for long-distance service. Second, in the data area, many of WorldCom's largest customers were other telecommunications providers, particularly new companies that had entered the market in the aftermath of 1996 act. By mid-2001, many of these companies were in trouble. They had taken on too much debt to build out their own networks ahead of demand and now were unable to generate the cash flow to meet their debt obligations. As they crumbled into bankruptcy, WorldCom lost business that it had counted on to generate its own growth and service its debt commitments. It also started to lose customers who had come with the acquisition of other carriers, such as MCI, and complained that the quality of customer service had declined markedly under WorldCom.

The net result was that by 2002, WorldCom was looking at declining revenues and steep losses, a far cry from the double-digit earnings growth it had been predicting eighteen months earlier. Suddenly the company was struggling to generate the cash flow required to service its debt commitments. Moreover, a May 2002 financial audit ordered by WorldCom's board of directors discovered that the company had understated expenses by $3 billion during 2001 and inflated its income by $1.4 billion in the quarter ending March 31st, 2002. This revelation led to the resignation of several senior executives, including CEO Bernie Ebbers. The news of possible accounting fraud, taken together with WorldCom's sudden losses, led rating agencies to downgrade WorldCom's debt. This pushed up the interest rate on that debt, making it more expensive for WorldCom to serve. The company was now caught in a vice—on one side, due to unexpectedly poor business conditions its cash flow was plunging, and on the other, the price of serving its debt was surging. In July 2002, WorldCom bowed to the inevitable and declared bankruptcy. Bernie Ebbers' grand strategic vision lay in ruins.

Sources: S. N. Mehta, "Can Bernie Bounce Back?" *Fortune,* January 22, 2001. S. N. Mehta, "WorldCom's Bad Trip," *Fortune,* March 4, 2002. R. Blumenstein, J. R. Wilke, N. Harris, and D. Solomon, "Called Off?" *Wall Street Journal,* June 28, 2000, p. A1.

Overview

This chapter is the first of two that deal with the issue of corporate-level strategy. The principal concerns of corporate-level strategy are to identify the businesses in which a company should participate, the value creation activities it should perform in those businesses, and the best means for expanding or contracting in different businesses, including mergers, acquisitions, and spin-offs. As with all other strategies, the goal is to maximize the long-run profitability of the company. The focus of this chapter is on three corporate-level strategies: horizontal integration, vertical integration, and strategic outsourcing. In the next chapter, we look at a fourth corporate-level strategy, diversification, and discuss the different means that companies use to execute their corporate-level strategy, such as mergers and acquisitions.

Horizontal integration is the process of acquiring or merging with industry competitors in an effort to achieve the competitive advantages that come with large scale and scope. An **acquisition** occurs when one company uses its capital resources—such as stock, debt, or cash—to purchase the other, and a **merger** is an agreement between equals to pool their operations and create a new entity. The corporate strategy that WorldCom pursued between 1983 and 2001 is an example of horizontal integration. WorldCom acquired over sixty companies over this period in an effort to become one of the largest players in the telecommunications service industry. Although it stayed within the bounds of a single industry, its strategy was to enter different *businesses* within that industry: long-distance service, Internet access, and wireless service. Its goal was to reduce costs by realizing economies of scale and scope and increase its value to customers by bundling together different services, which would give the company more pricing options. The ultimate goal was to execute the business model that CEO Bernie Ebbers had mapped out for the company, thereby boosting WorldCom's profitability (return on invested capital). The story of WorldCom also illustrates some of the risks associated with this strategy.

By **vertical integration,** a company expands its operations either *backward* into an industry that produces inputs for the company's products or *forward* into an industry that uses or distributes the company's products. Traditionally, IBM has been a very vertically integrated corporation. It integrated backward into the disc drive industry to produce the disc drives that go into its computer hardware systems and forward into the computer consulting services industry.

Strategic outsourcing involves separating out some of a company's value creation activities *within a business* and letting them be performed by an independent entity or spinning off the part of the company that performs that activity as an independent entity. In early 2002, for example, IBM announced that it would no longer make personal computers, although it would continue to design and sell personal computers with the IBM brand name. Instead, it entered into an agreement with a contract manufacturer, Sanmina-SCI, under which Sanmina would manufacture all of IBM's PCs. As part of the agreement, IBM sold its PC manufacturing operations in the United States and Scotland to Sanmina for about $200 million. In taking this action, IBM's managers had decided that a value creation activity that was long an integral part of the company's PC business, manufacturing, could be performed more efficiently by a contract manufacturer. IBM would benefit from the lower prices it paid for PCs that it resold under its own brand name, boosting the company's profitability.

Throughout the chapter and the next, we repeatedly stress that to succeed, corporate-level strategies should increase profitability. To understand what this means, we have to go back to the concepts of profitability and the value chain, introduced in Chapter 3. To increase profitability, a corporate strategy should enable a company, or one or more of its business units, to perform one or more of the value-creation functions at a lower cost, or perform one or more of the value-creation functions in a way that allows for differentiation and gives a company pricing options. In addition, corporate-level strategy will boost profitability if it helps the company to manage industry rivalry better by reducing the threat of damaging price competition. Thus, a company's *corporate* strategy should help in the process of establishing a sustainable competitive advantage *at the business level,* and of course, it is that competitive advantage that leads to higher profitability. There is, therefore, a very important link between corporate-level strategy and competitive advantage and profitability at the business level.

By the end of the chapter, you should have a good understanding of how managers can use horizontal integration, vertical integration, and strategic outsourcing to execute their business model and boost their profitability and what the drawbacks associated with each strategy are.

Horizontal Integration

Horizontal integration has been a popular corporate strategy for a decade or so. In industry after industry, there have been numerous mergers and acquisitions. For example, in the automobile industry, Chrysler merged with Daimler Benz to create DaimlerChrysler; in the aerospace industry, Boeing merged with McDonald Douglass to create the world's largest aerospace company; in the pharmaceutical industry, Pfizer acquired Warner Lambert to become the largest pharmaceutical firm; in the financial services industry, Citicorp and Travelers merged to create Citigroup, the world's largest financial services company; and in the computer hardware industry, Compaq acquired Digital Equipment and then itself was acquired by Hewlett Packard. The most recent wave of mergers and acquisitions peaked in 2000, when U.S. firms spent some $1.6 trillion on 11,000 mergers and acquisitions, up from $300 billion in 1991. Although not all of these acquisitions and mergers involved horizontal integration (some entailed vertical integration or diversification), the vast majority appear to have been.[1] Moreover, many of these mergers and acquisitions were cross-border affairs as companies raced to acquire foreign companies in the same industry. In 2000, companies from all nations spent around $1.1 trillion on 7,900 cross-border mergers and acquisitions, over 70 percent of them horizontal mergers and acquisitions.[2] In 2001, the number and value of both domestic and international mergers and acquisitions fell by 20 to 30 percent, although the figure remained high by historic standards.

The net result of this wave of mergers and acquisitions has been to increase the level of concentration in a wide range of industries. Consolidated oligopolies have been replacing more fragmented industry structures. For example, twenty years ago, cable television was dominated by a patchwork of thousands of small, family-owned businesses, but by 2002, three companies controlled nearly two-thirds of the market. In 1990, the three big publishers of college textbooks accounted for 35 percent of the market; by 2002, they accounted for 62 percent. In 1996, there were eight Baby Bells offering regional telephone service in the United States; by 2002, there were four. In the manufacture of basic DRAM semiconductor chips, due to mergers and acquisitions the four largest firms accounted for 83 percent of the global market in early 2002, up from 45 percent in 1995.[3] Why is this happening? An answer can be found by looking at the economic benefits of horizontal integration.

Benefits of Horizontal Integration

Horizontal integration is a way of trying to increase the profitability of a company by (1) reducing costs, (2) increasing the value of the company's product offering through differentiation, (3) managing rivalry within the industry to reduce the risk of price warfare, and (4) increasing bargaining power over suppliers and buyers.

Reducing Costs. Horizontal integration is often seen as a way to capture the cost advantages associated with *economies of scale.* This was one of the motives behind WorldCom's acquisitions during the 1990s (see the *Opening Case*). Such a motive can be very important in industries that have a high fixed-cost structure. In these industries, large size allows companies to spread their fixed costs over a large volume, thereby driving down the average unit cost. As noted in the *Opening Case,* the fixed costs of building a telecommunications network are very high, and to make that investment pay, the company needs a large volume of customers. Thus, WorldCom often acquired other telecommunications companies in order to get their customers, who would then be switched to WorldCom's network, driving up its utilization and driving down the unit cost of serving each customer on the network. Similarly, mergers and acquisition in the pharmaceutical industry have in part been driven by a desire to realize scale economies. The fixed costs of building a nationwide pharmaceutical sales force are very high, and pharmaceutical companies need a good portfolio of products to use that sales force fully. Thus, Pfizer acquired Warner Lambert in part because it would give its sales force more products to talk about and sell when they visited physicians, thereby increasing sales force productivity and lowering costs.

In addition to scale economies, cost savings may also be had by *reducing duplication* between two companies, for example, by eliminating two sets of corporate head offices, duplicate sales forces, and so on. Thus, as part of the justification for acquiring rival computer maker Compaq, Hewlett Packard claimed that the acquisition would save the combined company $2.5 billion in annual expenses by eliminating redundant functions (see the *Running Case*).

Increasing Value. The value of a company's product offerings may be increased if horizontal integration allows the company to offer a wider range of products that can be bundled together. **Product bundling** entails offering a bundle of products to a customer and charging a single price. Because they have to pay only once and deal with one company for a set of products they may need, customers place a higher value on the bundle product offering. In other words, bundling is a source of *differential* advantage. WorldCom was pursuing this strategy. One goal of CEO Bernie Ebbers was to be able to offer customers a single provider and a single bill for a range of telecommunications services. One of the famous illustrations of the value of bundling concerns Microsoft Office, which is a bundle of different software programs, including a word processor, spreadsheet, and presentation program. In the early 1990s, Microsoft was number two or three in each of these product categories behind companies such as WordPerfect (which led in the word processing category), Lotus (which had the best-selling spreadsheet), and Harvard Graphics (which had the best-selling presentation software). By offering all three programs in a single package, Microsoft presented consumers with a superior value proposition, and its product bundle quickly gained market share, ultimately accounting for more than 90 percent of all sales of word processors, spreadsheets, and presentation software.

A variation on the bundling theme is providing a "total solution." Becoming a total solution provider is an important rationale for horizontal integration in the computer sector, where companies have tried to increase the value of their offerings by being able to provide all of the hardware and services needs of corporate customers (for an example, see the *Running Case* in this chapter). The argument is that this saves customers money (because they do not have to deal with several suppliers) and helps ensure that different parts of a customer's information technology system all work together. Both increase the value of the company's offering in the eyes of customers and enable the total solution provider to gain market share.

Another way of trying to increase value is to cross-sell. With **cross selling,** a company tries to leverage its relationship with its customers by acquiring additional product categories that can be sold to them. This has been a very popular strategy in the financial services industry and has driven significant horizontal integration. Here, the basic idea has been a belief that customers would prefer to purchase all of their financial service products from a single provider: their checking account, mortgage loans, insurance policies, and investment services in a sort of *financial services supermarket.* A big part of the rationale behind the creation of Citigroup from the merger of Citicorp and Travelers was to create a company that could sell insurance products directly to banking customers and banking services to insurance customers. The increase in value here comes from the idea that customers will prefer to do business with a single provider of such service and thus place a higher value on purchasing from a company that can provide such services.

Managing Industry Rivalry. Horizontal integration can help a company to manage industry rivalry in two ways. First, acquiring or merging with a competitor may be required in order to *eliminate excess capacity* in an industry. As discussed in Chapter 6, the need to use excess capacity often triggers price wars. By taking excess capacity out of an industry, horizontal integration can create a more manageable environment in which prices might stabilize or even increase.

In addition, by reducing the number of players in an industry, horizontal integration might make it easier to implement *tacit price coordination* between rivals (recall that tacit coordination refers to coordination reached without communication, and explicit communication to fix prices being illegal; see Chapter 6). As a general rule, the larger the number of players in an industry, the more difficult it is to establish pricing conventions, such as price leadership by a dominant firm, that reduce the possibility that a price war will erupt. By concentrating the industry and creating an oligopoly, horizontal integration can make tacit coordination between rivals easier to establish.

Both of these motives seem to have been behind the acquisition of Compaq by Hewlett Packard in 2002. The personal computer industry was suffering from significant excess capacity and a serious price war, triggered by Dell Computer's desire to gain market share. By acquiring Compaq, Hewlett Packard hoped to be able to remove excess capacity in the industry, and by reducing the number of large players, the company hoped to be able to impose some pricing discipline in the industry (see the *Running Case* for details).

Increasing Bargaining Power. A final important motive for horizontal integration is that it may help the company gain bargaining power over suppliers or buyers and thus increase the company's profitability at their expense. By consolidating the industry through horizontal industry, a company can account for more of a supplier's business and use this fact as leverage to bargain down the price it pays to

Running Case

Beating Dell: Why Hewlett Packard Wanted to Acquire Compaq

On September 4, 2001, Hewlett Packard's CEO, Carly Fiorina, shocked the business world by announcing that rival computer maker Compaq had agreed to be acquired by HP. The acquisition announcement came at the end of a year in which slumping demand and strong competition from Dell Computer had buffeted both companies. The merged company would have annual revenues of about $87.4 billion, putting it in the same league as IBM, from a range of products that span printers, personal computers, servers, storage, and information technology services. With the exception of printers, where HP is the clear market leader, there was significant product overlap between HP and Compaq.

To justify the acquisition, Fiorina claimed that it would yield a number of benefits. First, there would be significant cost savings. Some $2.5 billion a year would be taken out of annual expenses by eliminating redundant administrative functions and cutting 15,000 employees. By combining the personal computer businesses of HP and Compaq, Fiorina argued that the new HP would leapfrog Dell to seize the number one position in the PC business with a 21 percent share of the market. The expanded volume would enable HP to capture significant scale economies and thus compete more efficiently with Dell. The same would be true in the computer server and storage businesses, areas where Dell was gaining share. Here too the new HP would take the number one spot, with a 27 percent share of the market in servers and a 26 percent of the market in storage systems. Critics, however, were quick to point out that Dell's competitive advantage was based on its direct selling model and the efficient management of its supply chain, areas where both HP and Compaq lagged Dell. Economies of scale are all very well, they argued, but unless the new HP

could sell computers and servers the way Dell does and manage its supply chain efficiently, the new HP might just give Dell a bigger target to aim at.

In addition to the cost advantages of the merger, Fiorina argued that the acquisition would give the new HP a critical mass in the service area, where it lagged leaders IBM and EDS significantly. By being able to offer customers a total solution to their information technology needs, both hardware *and* services, Fiorina argued that HP could gain back market share among corporate customers from commodity box providers such as Dell and reap the benefits associated with the higher margin service business. Here too, though, critics were quick to perceive flaws. They argued that HP would still be a minnow in the information technology services area, with under 3 percent of the market share, well behind IBM and EDS. Moreover, they noted, Dell's success suggested that building a service business was not necessarily consistent with maximizing profitability.

The proposed acquisition turned into a long-running corporate saga when Walter Hewlett, son of one of the company's founders and an HP board member, came out and publicly opposed the deal, stating that it lacked strategic rationale. A proxy battle between backers of Fiorina and Hewlett ensued. A shareholder vote on March 20, 2002, gave Fiorina's plan a slim majority and in May 2002 the merger was formally completed. Meanwhile, Dell continued to gain share in the critical PC, server, and storage areas.

Sources: P. Burrows and A. Park, "Compaq and HP: What's an Investor to Do?" *Business Week,* March 18, 2002, pp. 62–64. "Carly v Walter," *Economist,* January 26, 2002. "Sheltering from the Storm," *Economist,* September 8, 2001.

suppliers for inputs, thereby lowering the company's costs. Similarly, through consolidation, a company can control a greater percentage of industry output, making buyers more dependent on the company for product. Other things being equal, the company gains power to raise prices and earn more profits, primarily because customers have less choice.

The better ability to raise prices to consumers or bargain down the price paid for inputs is known as **market power** or monopoly power. For an example of how the process of consolidation through horizontal integration can play out, see Strategy in Action 9.1, which looks at the way in which health care providers in eastern Massachusetts have pursued horizontal integration in order to gain bargaining power, and hence market power, over insurance providers.

Drawbacks and Limits of Horizontal Integration

Although horizontal integration has clear benefits, there are also several drawbacks and limitations associated with the strategy. One problem concerns the numerous pitfalls associated with mergers and acquisitions, which are the vehicles by which a horizontal integration strategy is executed. The pitfalls are a topic that we shall discuss in depth in Chapter 10. For now, the important point to note is that a wealth of data suggests that the majority of mergers and acquisitions *do not* create value and that many actually destroy value.[4] For example, a recent study by KPMG, a large accounting and management consulting company, looked at 700 large acquisitions between 1996 and 1998 and found that although some 30 percent of these created value for the acquiring company, 31 percent destroyed value, and the remainder had little impact.[5] Many of these acquisitions were made to execute a strategy of horizontal integration. The implication is that *implementing* a horizontal integration strategy is not easy.

As we shall see in Chapter 10, mergers and acquisitions often fail to produce the anticipated gains for a number of reasons: problems associated with merging very different company cultures, high management turnover in the acquired company when the acquisition was a hostile one, a tendency on the part of managers to underestimate the expenses associated with rationalizing operations to eliminate duplicate assets and realize scale economies, and a tendency of managers to overestimate the benefits to be had from a merger or acquisition and for an acquiring company to overpay for the assets of the acquired company. WorldCom, for example, may well have overpaid for the assets of long-distance telephone provider MCI when it acquired the company in 1999 (see the *Opening Case*). Since the acquisition, the price for long-distance service in the United States has fallen by over 30 percent, and revenues from this business have begun to decline. Similarly, much of the opposition to the merger between Hewlett Packard and Compaq was based on the belief that Carly Fiorina was glossing over the difficulties and costs associated with merging the operations of these two companies and eliminating duplicate operations and products (see the *Running Case*).

Another limitation of a horizontal integration strategy is that it can bring the company into conflict with the government agency responsible for enforcing antitrust law. Antitrust authorities are concerned about the potential for abuse of market power. They believe that in general, more competition (that is, more choice) is better for consumers than less competition. They worry that large companies that dominate their industry may be in a position to use their market power to raise prices to consumers above the level that would exist in more competitive situations. They also believe that dominant enterprises can use their market power to crush potential competitors by, for example, using their financial resources to cut prices selectively

Strategy in Action

Horizontal Integration in Health Care

9.1

In the United States, health maintenance organizations (HMO) have become a powerful force in the health care sector. HMOs are health insurance companies that people choose for their health care coverage. Often companies contract with HMOs on behalf of their employees for health insurance coverage. The HMOs then "supply" patients to health care providers. Thus, the HMOs can be viewed as the suppliers of the critical input—patients—to health care providers. In turn, the revenues of health care providers are dependent on the number of patients who pass through their system. Clearly, it is in the interests of HMOs to bargain down the price they must pay health care providers for coverage. They have gained bargaining power through horizontal integration, merging with each other until they have gotten large enough to control a large volume of patients. But now there are signs that this strategy is backfiring, for the health care providers are also resorting to horizontal integration.

For an example of how this process is being played out, consider how the relationship between HMOs and hospitals has evolved in eastern Massachusetts over the past decade. In the early 1990s, three big HMOs controlled 75 percent of the market for health insurance in eastern Massachusetts. In contrast, there were thirty-four separate hospital networks in the region. Thus, the insurance providers were consolidated, while the health care providers were fragmented, giving the insurance providers considerable bargaining power. The HMOs used their bargaining power to demand deep discounts from health care providers. If a hospital wouldn't offer discounts to an HMO, the HMO would threaten to remove it from its list of providers. Because losing all of those potential patients would severely damage the revenues that a hospital could earn, the hospitals had little chance but to comply with the request.

This began to change in 1994 when two of the most prestigious hospitals in the region, Massachusetts General and Brigham & Women's Hospital, merged with each other to form Partners HealthCare System. Since then, Partners has continued to pursue the strategy, acquiring other hospitals in order to gain power over HMOs. By 2002, it had seven hospitals and some 5,000 doctors in its system. Other regional hospitals pursued a similar strategy, and the number of independent hospital networks in the region fell from thirty-four in 1994 to twelve by 2002.

In 2000, Partners started to exercise its strengthened bargaining power by demanding that HMOs accept a fee increase for services offered by Partners hospitals. One of the biggest HMOs, Tufts, refused to accept the increase and informed nearly 200,000 of its 900,000 subscribers that they would no longer be able to use Partners hospitals or physicians affiliated with Partners. The uproar among subscribers was enormous. So many employers threatened to pull out of the HMO and switch to another if the policy was not changed that Tufts quickly realized it had little choice but to change its policy, and accept the fee increase. Tufts went back to Partners and agreed to a 30 percent fee increase over three years. Clearly, bargaining power in the system had shifted away from the HMOs and toward the hospital networks. However, in 2001, the Massachusetts attorney general received so many complaints from employers about rising health care premiums that he launched an investigation into market power and anticompetitive behavior among health care providers in eastern Massachusetts, although he has stated that he is not focusing on Partners.

Sources: Y. J. Dreazen, G. Ip, and N. Kulish, "Why the Sudden Rise in the Urge to Merge and Create Oligopolies?" *Wall Street Journal,* February 25, 2002, p. A1. L. Kowalczyk, "A Matter of Style," *Boston Globe,* February 22, 2002, p. C1.

whenever new competitors enter a market or market segment, forcing them out of business, and then raising prices again once the threat has been eliminated. Because of these concerns, any merger or acquisition that is perceived by the antitrust authorities as creating too much consolidation and the *potential* for future abuse of market power may be blocked. This is what happened when WorldCom tried to acquire Sprint. The Justice Department was concerned that the proposed acquisition would reduce the number of major long-distance providers in the United States from three to two, creating in their view an unacceptable level of market concentration and lack of competition. WorldCom was obliged to drop the acquisition bid.

In sum, horizontal integration can be a very attractive strategy for a company to pursue but clearly is not without risks and drawbacks. Horizontal integration can be a valid strategy for consolidating an industry and realizing all of the associated gains, but many acquisitions and mergers fail to realize the hoped-for gains, primarily because they are expensive and postacquisition integration may be problematic. Moreover, there are clearly limits to the degree to which a company can pursue this strategy, for sooner or later it will bring the company into direct conflict with the antitrust authorities.

Vertical Integration

Vertical integration means that a company is expanding its operations either *backward* into an industry that produces inputs for the company's products or *forward* into an industry that uses or distributes the company's products. A steel company that supplies its iron ore needs from company-owned iron ore mines exemplifies backward integration. A personal computer maker that sells its PCs through company-owned retail outlets illustrates forward integration. For example, in 2001, Apple Computer entered the retail industry when it decided to set up a chain of Apple Stores to sell its computers.

Figure 9.1 illustrates four *main* stages in a typical raw-material-to-consumer production chain. For a company based in the assembly stage, backward integration means moving into component parts manufacturing and raw material production. Forward integration means moves into distribution. At each stage in the chain, *value is added* to the product. This means that a company at that stage takes the product produced in the previous stage and transforms it in some way so that it is worth more to a company at the next stage in the chain and, ultimately, to the end user. It is important to note that each stage is in a separate industry, or industries, and that within each industry there is also a value chain that encompasses the basic value creation activities we discussed in Chapter 3 of R&D, production, marketing, and customer service. In other words, we can think of a value chain that runs *across* industries, and embedded within that are the value chains *within* each industry.

As an example of the value-added concept, consider the production chain in the personal computer industry, illustrated in Figure 9.2. Here, the raw materials companies include the manufacture of specialty ceramics, chemicals, and metal, such as Kyocera of Japan, which manufactures the ceramic substrate for semiconductors. These companies sell their output to the manufacturers of component products, such as Intel and Micron Technology, which transform the ceramics, chemicals, and metals

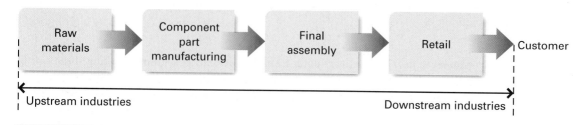

FIGURE 9.1

Stages in the Raw Material to Consumer Value Chain

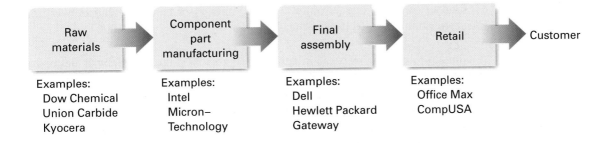

Raw materials	Component part manufacturing	Final assembly	Retail	Customer
Examples: Dow Chemical Union Carbide Kyocera	Examples: Intel Micron– Technology	Examples: Dell Hewlett Packard Gateway	Examples: Office Max CompUSA	

FIGURE 9.2

The Raw Material to Consumer Value Chain in the Personal Computer Industry

they purchase into computer components such as microprocessors, disk drives, and memory chips. In the process, they *add value* to the raw materials they purchase. These components are then sold to assembly companies such as Gateway, Apple, Dell, and Hewlett Packard, which take these components and transform them into personal computers—that is, *add value* to the components they purchase. Many of the completed personal computers are then sold to distributors such as OfficeMax and CompUSA or value-added resellers that sell them to final customers. (Recall that Dell sells direct, while both Apple and Gateway have established some retail stores to sell their products.) The distributors also *add value* to the product by making it accessible to customers and by providing service and support. Thus, companies add value at each stage in the raw-materials-to-consumer chain. Viewed in this way, vertical integration presents companies with a choice about which industries in the raw-material-to-consumer chain to compete in.

Finally, note that besides forward and backward integration, it is also possible to distinguish between **full integration** and **taper integration** (see Figure 9.3).[6] A company achieves full integration when it produces all of a particular input needed for its processes or disposes of all of its output through its own operations. Taper integration occurs when a company buys from independent suppliers in addition to company-owned suppliers or disposes of its output through independent outlets in

FIGURE 9.3

Full and Taper Integration

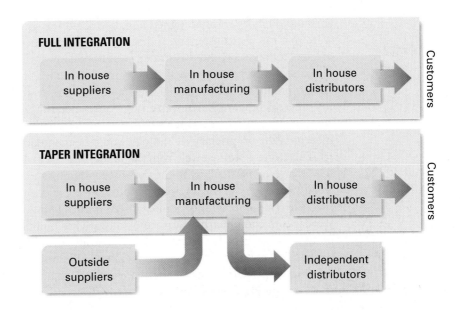

FULL INTEGRATION

In house suppliers → In house manufacturing → In house distributors → Customers

TAPER INTEGRATION

In house suppliers → In house manufacturing → In house distributors → Customers

Outside suppliers →

→ Independent distributors

addition to company-owned outlets. The advantages of taper integration over full integration are discussed later in the chapter.

Increasing Profitability Through Vertical Integration

A company pursuing vertical integration is normally motivated by a desire to strengthen the competitive position of its original, or core, business.[7] There are four main arguments for pursuing a vertical integration strategy. Vertical integration (1) enables the company to build barriers to new competition, (2) facilitates investments in efficiency-enhancing specialized assets, (3) protects product quality, and (4) results in improved scheduling.

Building Barriers to Entry. By vertically integrating backward to gain control over the source of critical inputs or vertically integrating forward to gain control over distribution channels, a company can build barriers to new entry into its industry. To the extent that this strategy is effective, it limits competition in the company's industry, thereby enabling the company to charge a higher price and make greater profits than it could otherwise.[8] To grasp this argument, consider a famous example of this strategy from the 1930s.

At that time, commercial smelting of aluminum was pioneered by companies like Alcoa and Alcan. Aluminum is derived from smelting bauxite. Bauxite is a common mineral, but the percentage of aluminum in it is usually so low that it is not economical to mine and smelt. During the 1930s, only one large-scale deposit of bauxite had been discovered where the percentage of aluminum in the mineral made smelting economical. This deposit was on the Caribbean island of Jamaica. Alcoa and Alcan vertically integrated backward and acquired ownership over this deposit, thereby creating a barrier to entry into the aluminum industry. Potential competitors were deterred from entry because they could not get access to high-grade bauxite. Alcoa and Alcan owned it all. Those that did enter the industry found themselves at a cost disadvantage because they had to use lower-grade bauxite. This situation persisted until the 1950s, when new high-grade deposits were discovered in Australia and Indonesia.

During the 1970s and 1980s, a similar strategy was pursued by vertically integrated companies in the computer sector such as IBM and Digital Equipment. These companies manufactured the main components of computers such as microprocessors and memory chips, designed and assembled the computers, produced the software that ran the computers, and sold the final product directly to end users. The original rationale behind this strategy was that many of the key components and software used in computers contained proprietary elements. These companies reasoned that by producing the proprietary technology in-house, they could limit rivals' access to it, thereby building barriers to entry. Thus, when IBM introduced its PS/2 personal computer system in the mid-1980s, it announced that certain component parts incorporating proprietary technology would be manufactured in-house by IBM.

This strategy worked well from the 1960s until the early 1980s, but it has been failing since then, particularly in the personal computer industry. During the 1990s, the worst performers in the computer industry were precisely the companies that pursued the vertical integration strategy: IBM and Digital Equipment. The shift to open standards in computer hardware and software has nullified the advantages for computer companies of being extensively vertically integrated. In addition, companies such as Dell and Compaq found that they could quickly reverse-engineer and duplicate the proprietary components that companies such as IBM placed in their personal computers, effectively circumventing this barrier to entry.

Facilitating Investments in Specialized Assets. A specialized asset is one that is designed to perform a specific task and whose value is significantly reduced in its next best use.[9] It may be a piece of equipment that has specialized uses or the know-how or skills that an individual or company has acquired through training and experience. Companies (and individuals) invest in specialized assets because these assets allow them to *lower the costs* of value creation or to *differentiate* their product offering from that of competitors better, thereby facilitating premium pricing. A company might invest in specialized equipment because that enables it to lower its manufacturing costs, or it might invest in developing highly specialized technological knowledge because doing so lets it develop better-quality products than its rivals. Thus, specialization can be the basis for achieving a competitive advantage at the business level.

Here we will look at why a company may find it very difficult to persuade other companies in *adjacent* stages in the raw-material-to-consumer production chain to undertake investments in specialized assets. To realize the economic gains associated with such investments, the company may have to integrate vertically into such adjacent stages and make the investments itself. As an illustration, imagine that Ford has developed a new high-performance, high-quality, and uniquely designed fuel injection system that will increase fuel efficiency and thereby help differentiate Ford's cars from those of its rivals. In other words, it will give Ford a competitive advantage. Ford has to decide whether to make the system in-house (vertical integration) or contract out manufacturing to an independent supplier (outsourcing). Manufacturing these systems requires substantial investments in equipment that can be used for only this purpose. Because of its unique design, the equipment cannot be used to manufacture any other type of fuel injection system for Ford or any other automaker. Thus, the investment in this equipment constitutes an investment in specialized assets.

First consider this situation from the perspective of an independent supplier that Ford has asked to make this investment. The supplier might reason that once it has made the investment, it will become dependent on Ford for business *since Ford is the only possible customer for the output of this equipment.* The supplier perceives this as putting Ford in a strong bargaining position and worries that Ford might use this position to squeeze down prices for the carburetors that it makes. Given this risk, the supplier declines to make the investment in specialized equipment.

Now consider Ford's position. Ford might reason that if it contracts out production of these systems to an independent supplier, it might become too dependent on that supplier for a vital input. Because specialized equipment is required to produce the fuel injection systems, Ford cannot easily switch its orders to other suppliers that lack the equipment. Ford perceives this as increasing the bargaining power of the supplier and worries that the supplier might use its bargaining strength to demand higher prices.

The situation of *mutual dependence* that would be created by the investment in specialized assets makes Ford hesitant to contract out and makes any potential suppliers hesitant to undertake the investments. The real problem here is a lack of trust. Neither Ford nor the supplier completely trusts the other to play fair in this situation. The lack of trust arises from the **risk of holdup,** that is, of being taken advantage of by a trading partner after the investment in specialized assets has been made.[10] Because of this risk, Ford might reason that the only safe way to get the new fuel injection systems is to manufacture them itself.

To generalize from this example, when achieving a competitive advantage requires one company to make investments in specialized assets in order to trade with another, the risk of holdup may serve as a deterrent and the investment may not take place. Consequently, the potential for higher profitability from specialization would be lost. To prevent such loss, companies vertically integrate into adjacent stages in the value chain. Historically, this consideration has driven automobile companies to vertically integrate backward into the production of component parts, steel companies to vertically integrate backward into the production of iron, computer companies to vertically integrate backward into chip production, and aluminum companies to vertically integrate backward into bauxite mining. The rationale underlying vertical integration in the aluminum industry is explored in greater detail in Strategy in Action 9.2.

Protecting Product Quality. By protecting product quality, vertical integration enables a company to become a *differentiated* player in its core business, which, as we saw in Chapter 5, gives the company more pricing options. The banana industry illustrates this situation. Historically, a problem facing food companies that import bananas was the variable quality of delivered bananas, which often arrived on

Strategy in Action   9.2

Specialized Assets and Vertical Integration in the Aluminum Industry

The metal content and chemical composition of bauxite ore, used to produce aluminum, vary from deposit to deposit, so each type of ore requires a specialized refinery—that is, the refinery must be designed for a particular type of ore. Running one type of bauxite through a refinery designed for another type reportedly increases production costs by 20 percent to 100 percent. Thus, the value of an investment in a specialized aluminum refinery, and the cost of the output produced by that refinery, depends on receiving the right kind of bauxite ore.

Imagine that an aluminum company has to decide whether to invest in an aluminum refinery designed to refine a certain type of ore. Assume further that this ore is produced only by a bauxite company at a single bauxite mine. Using a different type of ore would raise production costs by 50 percent. Therefore, the value of the aluminum company's investment is dependent on the price it must pay the bauxite company for this bauxite. Recognizing this, once the aluminum company has made the investment in a new refinery, what is to stop the bauxite company from raising bauxite prices? Nothing. Once it has made the investment, the aluminum company is locked into its relationship with its bauxite supplier. The bauxite company can increase prices secure in the knowledge that as long as the increase in the total production

costs of the aluminum company is less than 50 percent, the aluminum company will continue to buy from it. Thus, once the aluminum company has made the investment, the bauxite company can hold up the aluminum company.

How can the aluminum company reduce the risk of holdup? The answer is by purchasing the bauxite company. If the aluminum company can purchase the bauxite company or that company's bauxite mine, it need no longer fear that bauxite prices will be increased after the investment in an aluminum refinery has been made. In other words, it makes economic sense for the aluminum company contemplating the investment to engage in vertical integration. Vertical integration, by eliminating the risk of holdup, makes the specialized investment worthwhile. In practice, it has been argued that these kinds of considerations have driven aluminum companies to pursue vertical integration to such a degree that, according to one study, 91 percent of the total volume of bauxite is transferred within vertically integrated aluminum companies.

Source: J-F. Hennart, "Upstream Vertical Integration in the Aluminum and Tin Industries," *Journal of Economic Behavior and Organization* 9 (1988): 281–299.

the shelves of American stores either too ripe or not ripe enough. To correct this problem, major U.S. food companies such as General Foods have integrated backward to gain control over supply sources. Consequently, they have been able to distribute bananas of a standard quality at the optimal time for consumption. Knowing they can rely on the quality of these brands, consumers are willing to pay more for them. Thus, by vertically integrating backward into plantation ownership, the banana companies have built consumer confidence, which enables them to charge a premium price for their product.

The same kind of considerations can result in forward integration. Ownership of retail outlets may be necessary if the required standards of after-sales service for complex products are to be maintained. For example, in the 1920s, Kodak owned retail outlets for distributing photographic equipment. The company felt that few established retail outlets had the skills necessary to sell and service its photographic equipment. By the 1930s, Kodak decided that it no longer needed to own its retail outlets because other retailers had begun to provide satisfactory distribution and service for Kodak products. It then withdrew from retailing.

Improved Scheduling. It is sometimes argued that strategic advantages arise from the easier planning, coordination, and scheduling of adjacent processes made possible in vertically integrated organizations.[11] Such advantages can be particularly important to companies trying to realize the benefits of just-in-time inventory systems, discussed in detail in Chapter 4. For example, in the 1920s, Ford profited from the tight coordination and scheduling that is possible with backward vertical integration. Ford integrated backward into steel foundries, iron ore shipping, and iron ore mining. Deliveries at Ford were coordinated to such an extent that iron ore unloaded at Ford's steel foundries on the Great Lakes was turned into engine blocks within twenty-four hours. Thus, Ford substantially lowered its cost structure by eliminating the need to hold excessive inventories.

The improved scheduling that vertical integration makes feasible may also enable a company to respond better to sudden changes in demand conditions or to get its product into the marketplace faster. A situation in the microprocessor industry of the early 1990s illustrates this point. Demand for microprocessors was at an all-time high, and most microprocessor manufacturing plants were operating at full capacity. At that time, several microprocessor companies that specialized in chip design but contracted out manufacturing found themselves at a strategic disadvantage. For example, in 1991 Chips & Technologies succeeded in designing a clone of Intel's 386 microprocessor. Chips & Technologies sent its clone design to Texas Instruments (TI) to be manufactured, only to find that it had to wait fourteen weeks until TI could schedule time to manufacture that item. In that short span, prices for 386 microprocessors fell from $112 to $50. By the time TI produced the 386 clone for Chips & Technologies, the company had missed the best part of the market. Had Chips & Technologies been vertically integrated into manufacturing, this loss would not have occurred.[12]

Arguments Against Vertical Integration	Vertical integration has its disadvantages. Most important among them are (1) cost disadvantages, (2) disadvantages that arise when technology is changing fast, and (3) disadvantages that arise when demand is unpredictable. These disadvantages imply that the benefits of vertical integration are not always as substantial as they might seem initially and that far from increasing profitability, vertical integration can actually reduce it.

Cost Disadvantages. Although vertical integration is often undertaken to gain a production cost advantage, it can raise costs if a company becomes committed to purchasing inputs from company-owned suppliers when low-cost external sources of supply exist. For example, during the early 1990s, General Motors made 68 percent of the component parts for its vehicles in-house, more than any other major automaker (at Chrysler, the figure was 30 percent, and at Toyota 28 percent). That vertical integration has caused GM to be the highest-cost producer among the world's major car companies. In 1992, it was paying $34.60 an hour in United Auto Workers wages and benefits to its employees at company-owned suppliers for work that rivals could get done by independent nonunionized suppliers at half these rates.[13] Thus, vertical integration can be a disadvantage when a company's own sources of supply have higher operating costs than those of independent suppliers.

Company-owned suppliers might have high operating costs compared with independent suppliers because those suppliers know that they can always sell their output to other parts of the company. Not having to compete for orders lessens the *incentive* to minimize operating costs. Indeed, the managers of the supply operation may be tempted to pass on any cost increases to other parts of the company in the form of higher transfer prices rather than looking for ways to lower those costs. Thus, the lack of incentive to reduce costs can raise operating costs and reduce profitability. The problem may be less serious when the company pursues taper, rather than full, integration, because the need to compete with independent suppliers can produce a downward pressure on the cost structure of company-owned suppliers.

Technological Change. When technology is changing fast, vertical integration poses the hazard of tying a company to an obsolescent technology.[14] Consider a radio manufacturer that in the 1950s integrated backward and acquired a manufacturer of vacuum tubes. When transistors replaced vacuum tubes as a major component in radios in the 1960s, this company found itself tied to a technologically obsolescent business. Switching to transistors would have meant writing off its investment in vacuum tubes. Therefore, the company was reluctant to change and instead continued to use vacuum tubes in its radios while its nonintegrated competitors were rapidly switching to the new technology. Because it kept making an outdated product, the company rapidly lost market share. Thus, vertical integration can inhibit a company's ability to change its suppliers or its distribution systems to match the requirements of changing technology.

Demand Unpredictablility. Vertical integration can also be risky in unstable or unpredictable demand conditions. When demand is stable, higher degrees of vertical integration might be managed with relative ease. Stable demand allows better scheduling and coordination of production flows among different activities. When demand conditions are unstable or unpredictable, achieving close coordination among vertically integrated activities may be difficult.

The problem is to balance capacity among process stages. For example, an auto manufacturer might vertically integrate backward to acquire a supplier of carburetors that has a capacity exactly matching the auto manufacturer's needs. However, if demand for autos subsequently falls, the automaker will find itself locked into a business running below capacity. Clearly, this would be uneconomical. The auto manufacturer could avoid this situation by continuing to buy carburetors on the open market rather than making them itself. If demand conditions are unpredictable, taper integration might be somewhat less risky than full integration. When a company obtains only part of its total input requirements from company-owned suppliers, it can keep its in-house suppliers running at full capacity in times of low demand by ordering exclusively from them.

Bureaucratic Costs and the Limits of Vertical Integration

Although vertical integration can create value, it may also result in substantial bureaucratic costs caused by a lack of incentive on the part of company-owned suppliers to reduce their operating costs, a possible lack of strategic flexibility in times of changing technology, or uncertain demand. In this context, **bureaucratic costs** are the cost increases that arise in large, complex organizations due to managerial inefficiencies, such as the incentive problems that arise in vertically integrated enterprises. Bureaucratic costs place a limit on the amount of vertical integration that can be profitably pursued: it makes sense for a company to integrate vertically only if the potential of the strategy for increasing profitability is not swamped by the bureaucratic costs associated with expanding the boundaries of the organization to incorporate additional upstream or downstream activities.

Commonsense reasoning suggests that not all vertical integration opportunities have the same potential for increasing profitability. Although vertical integration may initially have a favorable impact, the benefits from additional integration into areas more distant from a company's core business are likely to become increasingly marginal. The more marginal the economic value created by vertical integration move, the more likely it is that the bureaucratic costs associated with expanding the boundaries of the organization into new activities will outweigh the value created and captures by the company. Once this occurs, a limit to profitable vertical integration has been reached.[15]

However, it is worth bearing in mind that the pursuit of taper integration rather than full integration may decrease the bureaucratic costs of vertical integration. This occurs because taper integration creates an incentive for in-house suppliers to reduce their operating costs and increases the company's ability to respond to changing demand conditions. Hence, it reduces some of the organizational inefficiencies that raise bureaucratic costs.

Alternatives to Vertical Integration: Cooperative Relationships

Is it possible to reap the benefits of vertical integration without having to bear the same level of bureaucratic costs? Can the benefits associated with vertical integration be captured while letting other companies perform upstream and downstream activities? The answer seems to be a qualified yes. Under certain circumstances, companies can realize the gains associated with vertical integration without having to bear the bureaucratic costs if they enter into long-term cooperative relationships with their trading partners. Such long term-relationships are typically referred to as strategic alliances. However, companies will generally be unable to realize the gains associated with vertical integration if they enter into short-term contracts with their trading partners. To see why this is so, we first discuss the problems associated with short-term contracts. Then we look at strategic alliances and long-term contracts as an alternative to vertical integration and discuss how companies can build enduring long-term relationships with their trading partners.

Short-Term Contracts and Competitive Bidding

Many companies use short-term contracts, which last for a year or less, to structure the purchasing of their inputs or the sale of their outputs. A classic example is the automobile company that uses a **competitive bidding strategy** to negotiate the price for a particular part produced by component suppliers. For example, General Motors often solicits bids from a number of suppliers for producing a component part and awards a one-year contract to the supplier submitting the lowest bid. At the end of the year, the contract is put out for competitive bid again. There is no guarantee that the company that won the contract one year will hold on to it the next.

The benefit of this strategy is that it forces suppliers to keep down their prices. But GM's lack of long-term commitment to individual suppliers may make them very hesitant to undertake the type of investments in specialized assets that may be needed to improve the design or quality of component parts or to improve scheduling between GM and its suppliers. Indeed, with no guarantee that it would remain a GM supplier the following year, the supplier may refuse to undertake investments in specialized assets. GM then may have to vertically integrate backward in order to realize the gains associated with specialization.

In other words, the strategy of short-term contracting and competitive bidding, *because it signals a lack of long-term commitment to its suppliers on the part of a company,* will make it very difficult for that company to realize the gains associated with vertical integration. This is not a problem when there is minimal need for close cooperation between the company and its suppliers to facilitate investments in specialized assets, improve scheduling, or improve product quality. In such cases, competitive bidding may be optimal. However, when this need is significant, considerations arise. A competitive bidding strategy can be a serious drawback.

Interestingly enough, there are indications that in the past, GM placed itself at a competitive disadvantage by adopting a competitive bidding stance with regard to its suppliers. In 1992, the company instructed its parts suppliers to cut their prices by 10 percent, regardless of prior pricing agreements. In effect, GM tore up existing contracts and tried to force through its policy by threatening to weed out suppliers that did not agree to the price reduction. Although such action may yield short-term benefits for companies, there is a long-term cost: the loss of trust and the hostility created between the company and its suppliers. According to press reports, several suppliers claimed that they cut back on research for future GM parts. They also indicated that they would first impart new ideas to Chrysler (now DaimlerChrysler) or Ford, both of which took a more cooperative approach to forging long-term relationships with suppliers.[16]

Strategic
Alliances and
Long-Term
Contracting

Long-term contracts are long-term cooperative relationships between two companies, often referred to in the popular press as **strategic alliances.** Typically, one company agrees to supply the other, and the other company agrees to continue purchasing from that supplier; both make a commitment to jointly seek ways of lowering the costs or raising the quality of inputs into the downstream company's value creation process. A stable long-term relationship lets the participating companies share the value that might be created by vertical integration while avoiding many of the bureaucratic costs linked with ownership of an adjacent stage in the raw-material-to-consumer production chain. Thus, long-term contracts can substitute for vertical integration.

Consider the cooperative relationships that many Japanese auto companies have with their component-parts suppliers (the *keiretsu* system), which exemplify successful long-term contracting. These relationships often go back decades. Together, the auto companies and their suppliers work out ways to increase value-added—for instance, by implementing just-in-time inventory systems or cooperating on component-parts designs to improve quality and lower assembly costs. As part of this process, the suppliers make substantial investments in specialized assets in order to serve the needs of the auto companies better. Thus, the Japanese automakers have been able to capture many of the benefits of vertical integration without having to bear the associated bureaucratic costs. The component-parts suppliers also benefit from these relationships, for they grow with the company they supply and share in its success.[17]

In contrast to their Japanese counterparts, U.S. auto companies historically tended to pursue formal vertical integration.[18] According to several studies, the increased bureaucratic costs of managing extensive vertical integration helped place GM and Ford at a disadvantage relative to their Japanese competition.[19] Moreover, when U.S. auto companies decided not to integrate vertically, they did not necessarily enter into cooperative long-term relationships with independent component suppliers. Instead, they tended to use their powerful position to pursue an aggressive competitive bidding strategy, playing off component suppliers against each other.[20] This mindset now seems to be changing. For details on how DaimlerChrysler has attempted to build long-term cooperative relationships with suppliers, see Strategy in Action 9.3.

Building Long-Term Cooperative Relationships

The interesting question raised by the preceding section is how a company can achieve a stable long-term strategic alliance with another, given the lack of trust and the fear of holdup that arises when one company has to invest in specialized assets in order to trade with another. How have companies like Toyota managed to develop such enduring relationships with their suppliers?

Companies can take some specific steps to ensure that a long-term cooperative relationship can work and to lessen the chances of a partner's reneging on an agreement. One of those steps is for the company making investments in specialized assets to demand a hostage from its partner. Another is to establish a credible commitment on both sides to build a trusting long-term relationship.[21]

Hostage Taking. Hostage taking is essentially a means of guaranteeing that a partner will keep its side of the bargain. The cooperative relationship between Boeing and Northrop illustrates this type of situation. Northrop is a major subcontractor for Boeing's commercial airline division, providing many component parts for the 747 and 767 aircraft. To serve Boeing's special needs, Northrop has had to make substantial investments in specialized assets. In theory, because of the sunk costs associated with such investments, Northrop is dependent on Boeing, and Boeing is in a position to renege on previous agreements and use the threat to switch orders to other suppliers as a way of driving down prices. However, in practice, Boeing is unlikely to do so since the company is also a major supplier to Northrop's defense division, providing many parts for the Stealth bomber. Boeing has had to make substantial investments in specialized assets in order to serve Northrop's needs. Thus, the companies are *mutually dependent.* Boeing is unlikely to renege on any pricing agreements with Northrop because it knows that Northrop could respond in kind. Each company holds a hostage that can be used as insurance against the other company's unilateral reneging on prior pricing agreements.

Credible Commitments. A credible commitment is a believable commitment to support the development of a long-term relationship between companies. To understand the concept of credibility in this context, consider the following relationship between General Electric and IBM. GE is one of the major suppliers of advanced semiconductor chips to IBM, and many of the chips are customized to IBM's requirements. To meet IBM's specific needs, GE has had to make substantial investments in

Strategy in Action   9.3

DaimlerChrysler's U.S. *Keiretsu*

Like many other long-established companies, Chrysler (now DaimlerChrysler) for most of its history managed suppliers through a competitive bidding process: suppliers were selected on the basis of their ability to supply components at the lowest possible cost to Chrysler. A supplier's track record on performance and quality was relatively unimportant in this process. Contracts were renegotiated every two years, with little or no commitment from Chrysler to continuing to do business with a particular supplier. As a result, the typical relationship between Chrysler and its suppliers was characterized by mutual distrust, suspicion, and a reluctance on the part of suppliers to invest too much in their relationship with Chrysler.

Since the early 1990s, Chrysler has systematically reorganized its dealings with suppliers in an attempt to build stable long-term relationships. The aim of this new approach has been to try and get suppliers to help Chrysler in the process of developing new products and improving its production processes. To encourage suppliers to cooperate and make investments specific to Chrysler's needs, the company has moved sharply away from its old adversarial approach. The average contract with suppliers has been lengthened from two years to over four and a half years. Furthermore, Chrysler has given 90 percent of its suppliers oral commitments that business will be extended for at least the life of a model, if not beyond that. The company has also committed itself to share with suppliers the benefits of any process improvements they might suggest. The basic thinking behind offering suppliers such credible commitments is to align incentives between Chrysler and its suppliers—to create a sense of shared destiny—that encourage mutual cooperation to increase the size of the financial pie available to both.

By 1996 the fruits of this new approach were beginning to appear. By involving suppliers early on in product development and giving them greater responsibility for design and manufacturing, DaimlerChrysler was able to compress its product development cycle and take a lot of cost out of the product development effort. Daimler-Chrysler's U.S. operation also reduced the time it took to develop a new vehicle from 234 weeks during the mid-1980s to about 160 weeks by 1996. The total cost of developing a new vehicle also fell by 20 percent to 40 percent, depending on the model. With development costs in the automobile industry running at between $1 and $2 billion, that translates into a huge financial saving. Many of these savings were the direct result of engineering improvements suggested by suppliers or of improved coordination between the company and suppliers in the design process. To facilitate this process, the number of resident engineers from suppliers who work side by side with Daimler-Chrysler engineers in cross-company design teams increased from 30 in 1989 to more than 300 by 1996.

In 1990, Chrysler began implementing a program known internally as the supplier cost reduction effort (SCORE), which focuses on cooperation between Daimler-Chrysler and suppliers to identify opportunities for process improvements. In its first two years of operation, SCORE generated 875 ideas from suppliers that were worth $170.8 million in annual savings to suppliers. In 1994, suppliers submitted 3,786 ideas that produced $504 million in annual savings. By December 1995, Chrysler had implemented 5,300 ideas that have generated more than $1.7 billion in annual savings. One supplier alone, Magna International, submitted 214 proposals; Chrysler adopted 129 of them for a total cost saving of $75.5 million. Many of the ideas themselves have a relatively small financial impact; for example, a Magna suggestion to change the type of decorative wood grain used on minivans saved $0.5 million per year. But the cumulative impact of thousands of such ideas has had a significant impact on DaimlerChrysler's bottom line.

Source: J. H. Dyer, "How Chrysler Created an American Keiretsu," *Harvard Business Review* (July–August 1996): 42–56.

specialized assets that have little other value. As a consequence, GE is dependent on IBM and faces a risk that IBM will take advantage of this dependence to demand lower prices. Theoretically, IBM could back up its demand with the threat to switch to another supplier. However, GE reduced this risk by having IBM enter into a contractual agreement that committed IBM to purchase chips from GE for a ten-year period. In addition, IBM agreed to share in the costs of developing the customized chips, thereby reducing GE's investments in specialized assets. Thus, by publicly committing itself to a long-term contract and putting some money into the development of the customized chips, IBM has essentially made a *credible commitment* to continue purchasing those chips from GE.

Maintaining Market Discipline. A company that has entered into a long-term relationship can become too dependent on an inefficient partner. Because it does not have to compete with other organizations in the marketplace for the company's business, the partner may lack the incentive to be cost-efficient. Consequently, a company entering into a cooperative long-term relationship must be able to apply some kind of market discipline to its partner.

The company holds two strong cards. First, even long-term contracts are periodically renegotiated, generally every four to five years. Thus, a partner knows that if it fails to live up to its commitments, the company may refuse to renew the contract. Second, some companies engaged in long-term relationships with suppliers use a **parallel sourcing policy**—that is, they enter into a long-term contract with two suppliers for the same part (as is the practice at Toyota, for example).[22] This arrangement gives the company a hedge against a defiant partner, for each supplier knows that if it fails to comply with the agreement, the company can switch all its business to the other. This threat is rarely made explicit, because that would be against the spirit of building a cooperative long-term relationship. But the mere awareness of parallel sourcing serves to inject an element of market discipline into the relationship, signaling to suppliers that if the need arises, they can be replaced at short notice.

The growing importance of just-in-time inventory systems as a way of reducing costs and enhancing quality is increasing the pressure on companies to enter into long-term agreements in a wide range of industries. These agreements thus might become much more popular in the future. However, when such agreements cannot be reached, formal vertical integration may be called for.

Strategic Outsourcing

Strategic outsourcing involves separating out some of a company's value creation activities within a business and letting them be performed by a specialist in that activity (the specialist focuses on just this one activity). In other words, strategic outsourcing is concerned with reducing the boundaries of the company and focusing on *fewer* value creation functions. The activity to be outsourced may encompass an entire function, such as the manufacturing function, or it may entail an activity embedded within a function. For example, many companies outsource management of their pension systems, while keeping other human resource function activities within the company.

There has been a clear move among many enterprises to outsource activities designated as noncore or nonstrategic.[23] One survey found that some 54 percent of the companies polled had outsourced manufacturing processes or services in the past three years.[24] Another survey estimates that some 56 percent of all global product manufacturing is outsourced to manufacturing specialists.[25] Many high-technology companies, for example, outsource much, if not all, of their manufacturing activity to contract manufacturers, which specialize in the manufacturing function. Cisco, which is in the router and switch business, does not actually manufacture routers and switches. Rather, they are made by contract manufacturers such as Flextronics and

Jabil Circuit. What Cisco does is design the routers and switches, sell the routers and switches, and coordinate the supply chain to match demand for routers and switches with the supply of routers and switches (see Strategy in Action 9.4). Palm does not actually make the hand-held computers sold under the Palm brand name; they are made in Mexico by Solectron. It is not just high-technology companies that outsource manufacturing. Nike does not actually make running shoes and The Gap does not make jeans; they are made under contract at low-cost locations (on the other hand, Levi's still makes jeans, which may be a competitive disadvantage).

Nor is strategic outsourcing confined to manufacturing; many other activities are also outsourced. Microsoft has long outsourced its entire customer technical support operation to an independent company, as does Dell Computer. A few years ago, BP Amoco outsourced the bulk of its human resource functions to Exult, a San Antonio company, in a five-year deal worth $600 million. At the time, this was the largest deal of its kind, but a couple of years later, Exult won a $1.1 billion contract to handle personnel matters for all of Bank of America's 150,000 employees for a decade. In early 2002, American Express outsourced its entire information technology function to IBM in a seven-year deal worth $4 billion.[26] The Gartner Group, a market research company, estimates the information technology outsourcing market in North America was worth $101 billion in 2000 and will grow to $160 billion by 2005.[27]

Companies engage in strategic outsourcing because they believe they can better execute their business model by doing so and thus increase their profitability. The process of strategic outsourcing typically begins with a company's identifying the value creation activities that form the basis of its competitive advantage (its distinctive competencies). The idea is to keep performing these activities within the company. The remaining activities are then reviewed to see whether they can be performed more effectively and efficiently by independent companies that specialize in that activity—that is, by companies that can perform those activities at a lower cost or perform them in a way that leads to better differentiation. If they can, these activities are outsourced to those specialists. A possible result is illustrated in Figure 9.4, which shows the primary value creation activities and boundaries of a company before and after outsourcing. In this example, the company decided to outsource its production and customer service functions, leaving just R&D and marketing and sales within the company.

Once outsourcing has been executed, the relationships between the company and specialists are then often structured as long-term contractual relationships with rich information sharing between the company and the specialist organization to which it has contracted the activity. The term **virtual corporation** has been coined to describe companies that have pursued extensive strategic outsourcing.[28]

Benefits of Outsourcing

The trend toward strategic outsourcing is being driven by a realization that outsourcing can *lower the cost structure* of a company and help it to *differentiate* its product offerings in the marketplace better, thereby strengthening its business model and boosting its profitability.[29] In addition, strategic outsourcing of noncore activities helps the company to focus management attention on those activities that are most important for its long term competitive position: its distinctive competencies.

Reducing Costs Through Outsourcing. Outsourcing an activity will reduce costs when the price that must be paid to a specialist company to perform that activity is less than what it would cost the company to perform that activity internally. Specialists may be able to perform an activity at a lower cost because they are able to

Strategy in Action   9.4

Cisco's $2 Billion Blunder

During the late 1990s, Cisco Systems became famous for the way it focused on a few core activities while outsourcing the remainder to specialists. Cisco was known as the hardware maker that didn't make hardware. It dominated the market for Internet protocol (IP) routers and switches, critical components of IP networks, but these products were actually made by a number of contract manufacturers, while Cisco focused its efforts on just three main activities: product innovation, marketing and selling (primarily through Cisco's web site), and managing the supply chain. Cisco claimed that this strategy allowed it to focus on core competencies, while getting out of capital-intensive manufacturing activities, thereby reducing the company's need for capital resources and boosting its return on invested capital. Moreover, Cisco boasted that under its outsourcing strategy, it did not have to deal with the hassle and expense of maintaining inventory. Inventory was maintained at the contract manufacturer, which shipped finished products directly to customers.

Cisco's supply chain was structured like a four-tier pyramid, with Cisco at the pinnacle. The contract manufacturers responsible for final assembly of Cisco's products formed the second tier of the pyramid. These manufacturers were fed by a third tier that supplied components such as processor chips and optical gear. The third-tier companies drew on an even larger base of suppliers of commodity inputs. According to Cisco CEO John Chambers, the system was very responsive to shifts in demand, with Cisco immediately communicating orders it received through its web site back down the supply chain, allowing contract manufacturers and component producers to optimize their production schedules in real time. This dramatically reduced inventory in the supply chain, which reduced Cisco's working capital requirements (since the company did not have to finance extensive inventories) and further boosted the company's return on invested capital.

In May 2001, however, it became apparent that Cisco's vaunted outsourcing strategy had not been working as well as touted. The company announced that it would take a $2.2 billion charge against earnings to write down the value of inventory in the supply chain that had been ordered but could not be used. The problem was that demand for routers and switches had collapsed, but Cisco's systems had not detected this until it was too late.

How did this happen? Why did a system that has been praised for being very responsive to shifts in demand fail to detect a major shift in demand?

As it turns out, there was a flaw in the way in which Cisco managed its supply chain. During the boom years of the late 1990s and 2000, demand for routers and switches rocketed as a large number of companies from established and new telecommunications companies and dot-coms invested in IP networks. These customers could not get products from Cisco quickly enough, so by 2000 they were starting to double- and triple-book from Cisco and its competitors, knowing that they would ultimately make purchases from just one company. Cisco, however, did not detect this. As far as it knew, it couldn't produce products fast enough. Moreover, the problem was amplified as orders moved down the supply chain. Suppose Cisco ordered 10,000 units of a particular router. Each of the contract manufacturers would compete to fill the entire order, and to gain an edge they often tried to lock up supplies of scarce components. If three contract manufacturers were competing to build 10,000 routers, it would look like sudden demand for 30,000 machines, so component makers too would increase their output. But the demand signals were grossly misleading. They reflected double booking by Cisco's customers and, on top of that, double booking by the contract manufacturers. The result was a huge surge in inventory that far outstripped underlying demand. When the telecommunications and dot-com bubble burst in early 2001 and demand from these customers slumped, Cisco was left with a supply chain that was bloated with inventory that was no longer needed.

To reduce the risk of this problem occurring again, Cisco is reconfiguring the way it manages its supply chain. It has created a central Internet-based repository of information, known as eHub, that *all* participants in the supply chain can access. Now, if contract manufacturers get an order for 10,000 routers and all turn around and place orders for 10,000 chips each (for a total of 30,000) to try to tie up scarce components, the chip makers can access eHub and see that the true order is for just 10,000 routers, not 30,000, and plan accordingly.

Sources: S. N. Mehta, "Cisco Fractures Its Own Fairy Tale," *Fortune,* May 14, 2001, pp. 104–112. P. Kaihla, "Inside Cisco's $2 Billion Blunder," *Business 2.0* (March 2002). www.business2.com.

FIGURE 9.4

Strategic Outsourcing of Primary Value Creation Functions

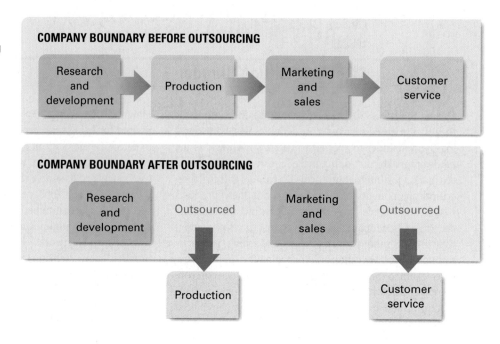

COMPANY BOUNDARY BEFORE OUTSOURCING

Research and development → Production → Marketing and sales → Customer service

COMPANY BOUNDARY AFTER OUTSOURCING

Research and development   Outsourced   Marketing and sales   Outsourced

Production   Customer service

realize scale economies or other efficiencies that are not available to the company. For example, performing basic personnel activities, such as managing pay and benefit systems, requires significant investments in information technology infrastructure (i.e., computers and software). Purchasing this technology represents a considerable fixed cost, but the average cost of performing a personnel transaction can be driven down if a large volume of transactions is handled by the infrastructure. By aggregating the demand from many different companies, vendors that specialize in this activity, such as Exult and Paycheck, can attain huge economies of scale that a company could not hope to achieve by itself. Some of these cost savings can then be passed on to clients in the form of lower prices, while still leaving the specialist with a decent return. A similar dynamic is at work in the contract manufacturing business, where manufacturing specialists like Solectron, Flextronics, and Jabil Circuit bear significant fixed costs to build efficient scale manufacturing facilities, but then are able to spread those fixed costs over a huge volume, driving down unit costs, by building equipment for a number of companies.

In addition to the gains from scale economies, the greater acceleration in *cumulative* volume handled by specialists means that they are likely to realize the cost savings associated with learning effects much more rapidly than the company that performs an activity just for itself (see Chapter 4 for a review of learning effects). For example, because a company like Flextronics is manufacturing similar products for several different companies, it is able to build up *cumulative* volume more rapidly, and thus learn how to manage and operate the manufacturing process more rapidly than any of its clients could. Thus, the specialists realize learning-based gains in employee and management productivity, which drives down their cost structure, allowing them to charge their customers a lower price for the activity than what it would cost the customer itself to perform that activity. In essence, the specialists gain distinctive competencies in the activity that they specialize in, which increases the benefit of outsourcing that activity for a company where the activity is not core.

The specialist may also be able to perform an activity at a lower cost than the company because the specialist is based in a low-cost location. Nike, for example, outsources the manufacture of its running shoe to companies based in China because the lower wage rate in China, for what is a very labor-intensive activity, means that the specialist will have a much lower cost than if Nike performed the same activity itself in the United States. In theory, Nike could set up its own operation in China to manufacture running shoes, but that would limit its ability to switch its production to another location later if costs in China start to rise and the costs of making running shoes can be further reduced by sourcing them from, say, India. So for Nike and many other apparel companies, the efficient choice is to outsource the manufacturing activity, because it gains both lower costs and the opportunity to switch to another more favorable location should the cost equation change.

Differentiation Through Outsourcing. A company may also be able to differentiate its final product offering better by outsourcing certain noncore activities to specialists. For this to occur, the *quality* of the activity performed by the specialists must be greater than if that same activity was performed by the company. On the reliability *dimension* of quality, for example, a specialist may be able to achieve a lower error rate in performing an activity, precisely because it focuses on that activity and has accumulated competencies in total quality management for that activity. Again, this is one advantage claimed for contract manufacturers. Companies like Flextronics have adopted Six Sigma methodologies (see Chapter 4) and driven down the defect rate associated with manufacturing a product. This means they can provide more reliable products to their clients, which in turn can differentiate their products on the basis of superior quality measured by reliability.

Companies can also outsource other differentiating activities to specialists. For example, the excellence of Dell Computer's customer service and maintenance is a differentiating factor. A customer that has a problem with a product purchased from Dell can call customer service and get excellent help over the phone. If it turns out that there is a defective part in the computer, a maintenance person will be dispatched and replace the part within twenty-four hours. The excellence of this service clearly differentiates Dell and helps to guarantee repeat purchases, but what most customers do not realize is that those activities are *not* performed by Dell: they are performed by the employees of specialist organizations. In the same manner, automobile companies outsource part of their vehicle design activities to specialist organizations that focus on this activity and have earned a reputation for design excellence.

Focus Through Outsourcing. A final advantage of strategic outsourcing is that it removes distractions and allows the management of the company to focus both their attention and company resources on performing those activities that are most important for value creation and competitive advantage. Other things being equal, this focus allows companies to enhance their competencies in their chosen areas. Cisco, for example, has developed competencies in product design, marketing and sales, and supply chain management. But Cisco does not physically make the routers and switches it designs and sells; it does not even touch them, for they are delivered straight from the contract manufacturer's factory to customers (see Strategy in Action 9.4). Of course, what really occurs here is that by focusing on just those activities that are essential for competitive advantage, companies like Cisco are better able to build competencies in those activities, and thus drive down the costs of performing those activities, and better differentiate their ultimate product offering.

Identifying and Managing the Risks of Outsourcing

Although outsourcing noncore activities can have considerable benefits, there are also significant risks associated with it—risks associated with holdup, the loss of direct control over the scheduling of activities, and a loss of important information when an activity is outsourced—that must be balanced against the benefits of outsourcing before deciding whether to outsource a particular activity. By taking the appropriate steps, these risks can be reduced.

Holdup. In the context of an outsourcing agreement, **holdup** refers to the risk that a company can become too dependent on the provider of an outsourced activity, and the provider can use that fact to raise prices beyond some previously agreed-on rate. We have already examined the problem of holdup in the discussion of vertical integration. As in the case of alternatives to vertical integration, the risk of holdup can be reduced by outsourcing from several suppliers and pursuing *a parallel sourcing* policy, as Cisco does (see Strategy in Action 9.4). Moreover, when a number of rivals are competing with each other to provide an outsourced activity and that activity can be performed well by any one of those companies, the threat that a contract will not be renewed in the future is normally sufficient to keep the chosen provider from trying to exercise bargaining power and hold up the company. For example, although IBM enters into long-term contracts to provide information technology services to a wide range of companies, it would be highly unlikely to try to raise prices after the contract has been signed because it knows full well that such action would reduce its chance of getting the contract renewed in the future. Moreover, the fact that IBM has many strong competitors in the information technology services business, such as EDS and Computer Sciences, gives it a very strong incentive to deliver significant value to its client and not to practice holdup.

Scheduling of Activities. The risks associated with loss of control with scheduling are clearly illustrated by the experience Cisco faced in 2001, which we reviewed in Strategy in Action 9.4. The essence of the problem is that if the company is not careful, the signals sent down a supply chain can be distorted by practices such as double booking when supplies of inputs are in short supply. This is a potential problem for any enterprise that has to manage demand and a long supply chain, and it is exacerbated when activities once considered core, such as manufacturing, are outsourced to a number of competing specialists. In times of strong demand, the specialists might try to capture a greater share of orders from the company by making sure that they have access to critical components needed in the manufacture the product, so they book orders for more components than they need. This creates a problem when the component suppliers to the specialists have no way of seeing the true demand from the company at the top of the supply chain, and they may produce excess inventory.

Loss of Information. A company that is not careful can lose important competitive information when it outsources an activity. For example, many computer hardware and software companies have outsourced their customer technical support function to specialists. Although this makes good sense from a cost and differentiation perspective, it may also mean that a critical point of contact with the customer, and a source of important feedback, is lost. Customer complaints can be a useful piece of information and a valuable input into future product design, but if those complaints are not clearly communicated to the company by the specialists performing the technical support activity, the company can lose that data. Again, this is not an argument against outsourcing. Rather, it is an argument for making sure that there is good communication flow between the outsourcing specialist and the company. At Dell, for example, a great deal of attention is paid to making sure that the specialist responsible for providing technical support and on-site maintenance collects and communicates all relevant data regarding product failures and other problems to Dell, so that Dell can design better products.

Summary of Chapter

1. A corporate strategy should enable a company, or one or more of its business units, to perform one or more of the value creation functions at a lower cost or in a way that allows for differentiation and a premium price.

2. Horizontal integration can be understood as a way of trying to increase the profitability of a company by (a) reducing costs, (b) increasing the value of the company's product offering through differentiation, (c) managing rivalry within the industry to reduce the risk of price warfare, and (d) increasing bargaining power over suppliers and buyers.

3. There are two drawbacks associated with horizontal integration: the numerous pitfalls associated with mergers and acquisitions and that the strategy can bring a company into direct conflict with the antitrust authorities.

4. Vertical integration can enable a company to achieve a competitive advantage by helping build barriers to entry, facilitating investments in specialized assets, protecting product quality, and helping to improve scheduling between adjacent stages in the value chain.

5. The disadvantages of vertical integration include cost disadvantages if a company's internal source of supply is a high-cost one and lack of flexibility when technology is changing fast or demand is uncertain.

6. Entering into a long-term contract can enable a company to realize many of the benefits associated with vertical integration without having to bear the same level of bureaucratic costs. However, to avoid the risks associated with becoming too dependent on its partner, it needs to seek a credible commitment from its partner or establish a mutual hostage-taking situation.

7. The strategic outsourcing of noncore value creation activities may allow a company to lower its costs, better differentiate its product offering, and make better use of scarce resources, while also enabling it to respond rapidly to changing market conditions. However, strategic outsourcing may have a detrimental effect if the company outsources important value creation activities or becomes too dependent on key suppliers of those activities.

Discussion Questions

1. Why was it profitable for General Motors and Ford to integrate backward into component-parts manufacturing in the past, and why are both companies now trying to buy more of their parts from outside?

2. Under what conditions might horizontal integration be inconsistent with the goal of maximizing profitability?

3. What value creation activities should a company outsource to independent suppliers? What are the risks involved in outsourcing these activities?

4. What steps would you recommend that a company take in order to build long-term cooperative relationships with its suppliers that are mutually beneficial?

Practicing Strategic Management

SMALL-GROUP EXERCISE: COMPARING VERTICAL INTEGRATION STRATEGIES

Break up into small groups of three to five people, and appoint one group member as a spokesperson who will communicate your findings to the class when called on to do so by the instructor. Then read the following description of the activities of Seagate Technologies and Quantum Corporation, both of which manufacture computer disk drives. On the basis of this description, outline the pros and cons of a vertical integration strategy? Which strategy do you think makes most sense in the context of the computer disk drive industry?

Quantum Corporation and Seagate Technologies are major producers of disk drives for personal computers and workstations. The disk drive industry is characterized by sharp fluctuations in the level of demand, intense price competition, rapid technological change, and product life cycles of no more than twelve to eighteen months. In recent years, Quantum and Seagate have pursued very different vertical integration strategies.

Seagate is a vertically integrated manufacturer of disk drives, both designing and manufacturing the bulk of its own disk drives. Quantum specializes in design, while outsourcing most of its manufacturing to a number of independent suppliers including, most importantly, Matsushita Kotobuki Electronics (MKE) of Japan. Quantum makes only its newest and most expensive products in-house. Once a new drive is perfected and ready for large-scale manufacturing, Quantum turns over manufacturing to MKE. MKE and Quantum have cemented their partnership over eight years. At each stage in designing a new product, Quantum's engineers send the newest drawings to a production team at MKE. MKE examines the drawings and is constantly proposing changes that make new disk drives easier to manufacture. When the product is ready for manufacture, eight to ten Quantum engineers travel to MKE's plant in Japan for at least a month to work on production ramp-up.

ARTICLE FILE 9

Find an example of a company whose vertical integration or diversification strategy appears to have dissipated rather than created value. Identify why this has been the case and what the company should do to rectify the situation.

STRATEGIC MANAGEMENT PROJECT: MODULE 9

This module requires you to assess the vertical integration and diversification strategy being pursued by your company. With the information you have at your disposal, answer the questions and perform the tasks listed:

1. Has your company ever pursued a horizontal integration strategy? What was the strategic reason for pursuing this strategy?
2. How vertically integrated is your company? If your company does have vertically integrated operations, is it pursuing a strategy of taper or full integration?
3. Assess the potential for your company to create value through vertical integration. In reaching your assessment, also consider the bureaucratic costs of managing vertical integration.
4. On the basis of your assessment in question 3, do you think your company should (a) outsource some operations that are currently performed in-house or (b) bring some operations in-house that are currently outsourced? Justify your recommendations.
5. Is your company involved in any long-term cooperative relationships with suppliers or buyers? If so, how are these relationships structured? Do you think that these relationships add value to the company? Why?
6. Is there any potential for your company to enter into (additional) long-term cooperative relationships with suppliers or buyers? If so, how might these relationships be structured?

EXPLORING THE WEB
Visiting Motorola

Visit Motorola's web site (**http://www.motorola.com**), and review its various business activities. Using this information, answer the following questions:

1. To what extent is Motorola vertically integrated?
2. Does vertical integration help Motorola establish a competitive advantage, or does it put the company at a competitive disadvantage?

General Task: Search the Web for an example of a company that has pursued a strategic outsourcing strategy. Describe that strategy, and assess whether the strategy has increased the profitability of the company?

Closing Case

AOL Time Warner: Horizontal and Vertical Integration

On January 11, 2001, one of the premier companies of the Internet era, AOL, merged with one of the dominant old media companies, Time Warner, to create AOL Time Warner. Founded in 1923, Time Warner had a vast array of magazine, TV broadcasting, film, music, and cable service properties. These include *Time* and *Life* magazines,

Warner's film and music properties, CNN, TNT, and HBO, and cable systems that serve 20 percent of the United States. AOL, founded only fifteen years ago, has just 20 percent of the revenue and 15 percent of the employees of Time Warner. However, most observers commented that in this "marriage of equals," it was the upstart that was in effect acquiring the older company. The merger had elements of both horizontal and vertical integration. Both were media companies active in content creation, and both had substantial interests in the distribution of content. AOL distributed its content and that of its media partners over the Internet, while Time Warner distributed some of its TV programming content over its cable TV system.

AOL believed that the merger would at a stroke help solve one of the company's biggest problems: how to offer high-speed Internet service to its 22 million subscribers. As many Internet users have found out, downloading graphics-intensive web content over telephone lines using 56k modems can be a very slow process, to say nothing of the wait required to download streaming video data. If the Internet is to fulfill its potential, the speed of Internet connections (the bandwidth) must be increased. There are three ways of increasing bandwidth: offering direct subscriber line service over existing telephone lines, offering Internet service via a satellite as with Direct TV, and making use of the existing cable TV infrastructure to allow consumers to access the Internet over cable systems. Of the three, upgrading cable TV infrastructure to allow it to facilitate access to the Internet seems to offer the most promise. With the addition of a cable modem, computer users would be able to cruise the Internet at speeds 1,000 times faster than that offered by conventional modems. In turn, this would allow for the streaming of high-resolution digital video and audio data. Until this merger was announced, AOL had little access to cable TV providers, many of which, like AT&T, had signed exclusive deals with AOL's competitors, such as Microsoft's MSN. The merger, it was argued, would give AOL access to Time Warner's cable TV system, with its 13 million subscribers. AOL could then offer these customers high-speed access to the Internet over Time Warner's cable TV systems. In effect, the merger allowed AOL to integrate forward into the distribution of its content.

A second benefit claimed for the merger is that AOL would be able to offer Time Warner's rich array of content to its subscribers, thereby enhancing the value of its service. AOL has always seen itself as a media company offering compelling content to its customers. If content is indeed king on the Internet, the combination of AOL's web savvy and Time Warner's magazine and broadcasting properties opens up the potential for delivering a wide range of innovative content over the Internet to AOL's subscriber base. In addition to existing Time Warner services, such as CNN.com, these might include an ability to access TNT's vast film library on demand (assuming a cable modem), archived CNN news clips, web versions of *Time* magazine, and a whole range of web properties that have yet to be imagined.

Before the merger was completed, however, a difficult antitrust issue had to be resolved. Regulators harbored fears that the new AOL would deny competing providers of Internet service, such as Earthlink, Juno, and Microsoft's MSN service, access to its cable TV subscribers. To guard against this, officials at the Federal Trade Commission (FTC) required that AOL Time Warner not only commit to opening up Time Warner's cable system to competing providers, but also sign a deal with a competing provider as a precondition for approval of the merger. The reason that the FTC gave for taking this hard-line stance is that its commissioners did not want the new AOL to offer its service first, before opening up the Time Warner cable system to competing providers. On November 20, 2000, Time Warner announced that it had struck a deal with Earthlink, which would allow this provider to offer Internet service to Time Warner's cable customers. The deal seemed to satisfy the concerns of the FTC, and the merger was approved.

Case Discussion Questions

1. What aspects of the AOL Time Warner merger can be considered horizontal integration? What can be considered vertical integration?

2. What are the benefits associated with this merger? How might it boost the profitability of the combined unit? Can you see any risks here?

3. Why do you think the FTC was concerned about the competitive implications of the merger? Were the FTC's concerns reasonable?

Sources: C. Yang et al., "Welcome to the 21st Century," *Business Week,* January 24, 2000, pp. 36–38. M. Peers, N. Wingfield, and L. Landro, "AOL, Time Warner, Leap Borders to Plan a Mammoth Merger," *Wall Street Journal,* January 11, 2000, p. A1. M. Peters and A. Petersen, "Time Warner Reaches Out to Earthlink," *Wall Street Journal,* November 21, 2000, p. A3.

Corporate Strategy—Diversification, Acquisitions, and Internal New Ventures

10

Opening Case

Tyco International

Tyco International has been one of the great growth stories of the past decade. Under the leadership of Dennis Kozlowski, who became CEO in 1992, Tyco's sales expanded from $3.1 billion in 1992 to $38 billion in 2001, when it earned some $5.12 billion in after-tax profits. Much of this growth was driven by acquisitions that took Tyco into a diverse range of businesses, including medical supplies, security equipment, electronic components, plastics, financial services, and telecommunications. Between 1996 and 2001, Tyco spent some $45 billion in cash (much of it raised from debt offerings) and stock to purchase more than 100 companies. With the acquisitions fueling growth, Tyco's earnings expanded by 35 percent each year between 1996 and 2001.

326

Tyco's success has been attributed to the consistent application of a business model that comprises a number of elements. First, although the company is diversified, it seeks to attain a critical mass in the industries in which it competes. Through acquisitions, it has become one of the largest providers of security systems, basic medical supplies, and electronic components in the United States. Indeed, it sees itself as using acquisitions to consolidate fragmented industries and attain economies of scale, which give it a cost-based advantage over smaller rivals. Second, the company *never* makes hostile acquisitions, which would be too expensive and could result in bad feelings among the managers of an acquired company. Third, Tyco deliberately seeks out companies that make basic products that have a strong market franchise but have been underperforming relative to their peers in recent years. Tyco's management believes that this indicates there is substantial room for improvement. Once it identifies a potential target, Tyco approaches management to see if they are interested in backing a sale of the company. If they express interest in supporting an acquisition, Tyco sends in teams of independent auditors to carefully go through the books of the target and identify the potential for improving performance. If the target company has potential, Tyco makes a formal bid. As a precondition of the bid, the top managers of the target company normally agree to step down (with a substantial severance package). Tyco typically replaces them with up-and-coming managers two or three layers below.

Once an acquisition has been completed, Tyco sets to work improving the performance of the acquired unit. Typically excess capacity is shut down, corporate overhead slashed, unprofitable product lines sold off or discontinued, plants and sales forces merged with those of similar operations within Tyco to attain scale economies, and head count reduced. For example, in 1999, Tyco acquired AMP, the world's largest manufacturer of electronic components, for $12 billion in Tyco stock. Within months, Tyco had identified close to $1 billion in cost savings that could be implemented by 2002 by closing unprofitable plants and reducing the work force by 8,000. On average, Tyco finds cost savings in an acquisition that amount to about 11 percent of the target company's revenues.

In addition to taking excess costs out of a newly acquired company, the employees of the acquired unit are given incentives to boost profitability. No bonuses are paid to anyone at Tyco unless annual net income growth exceeds 10 percent. However, bonuses quickly ramp up for each increment above that minimum and are unlimited for senior managers. In the best years, senior managers receive bonuses that are multiples of their salaries, super-visors at the plant level can receive cash or stock options worth as much as 40 percent of their salary, and hourly factor workers receive two to three weeks of extra pay.

Tyco's corporate structure is also very lean. There are only seventy employees at the head office, most of whom focus on tax and legal issues. Kozlowski ran operations on an arm's-length basis. Performance goals for the coming year are set by negotiation between top management and the management of operating units. Once targets are set, the policy is one of management by exception, with operating managers being given considerable autonomy so long as they hit or exceed their targets.

Despite Tyco's impressive track record, the stock price underperformed the general market during much of 1998–2001. The stock was given a "diversification discount" by investors, who were put off by the complexity of Tyco's financial accounts and the lack of transparency with regard to the profitability of individual operations. In 1999, Tyco was the target of criticism by analysts who accused the company of inappropriate accounting methods. However, a subsequent investigation by the Securities and Exchange Commission gave Tyco's accounting practices a clean bill of health. Despite this, the criticisms persisted, and in late 2001 the company came under renewed attack from critics who argued that it had systematically inflated its profitability to make its performance look better than it actually was. According to the critics, the management at several companies Tyco acquired all artificially depressed the profitability of their companies in the final months before the deals were completed. This was done by taking numerous charges, slowing sales, and pushing up expenses. Consequently, Tyco's operating results were "spring-loaded" for a quarter or two after the acquisition closed as sales and profit margins suddenly expanded. They also argued that the debt that Tyco had taken on to finance some of its acquisitions, which by early 2002 totaled some $23 billion, left the company excessively leveraged and potentially vulnerable should cash flow projections fall short.

Tyco dismissed the charges of accounting tricks and pointed out that it would generate over $4 billion in free cash flow during 2002, more than enough to cover all of its short-term debt commitments. Nevertheless, the attacks persisted, and the stock price slid to under $20 by May 2002. To try to halt the slide, Kozlowski floated a number of ideas, including splitting up the company into four independent units and selling off its plastics and financial services unit, then using the proceeds to pay down the company's debt. However, with none of these ideas seeming to help the stock price, Kozlowski ultimately stated that he would continue to run the company as a diversified entity and focus on generating cash flow to pay down the company's debt load. Tyco would sell off some of its acquired businesses, but only if it could get a decent price for them, and it would use the proceeds to pay down debt. Whatever the ultimate outcome, it seems clear that after a decade of success, investors had turned sour on Tyco's business model, recognizing, belatedly perhaps, that Tyco's growth had been bought at the price of accumulating tremendous debt.

To complicate matters, in June 2002 Kozlowski resigned after being charged with tax evasion. He was replaced by John Fort, Tyco's CEO between 1982 and 1992. One of Fort's first actions was to complete a spin-off of CIT Group, Tyco's finance arm, for $4.6 billion, significantly less than the $11 billion Tyco had paid to acquire CIT in 2000. With this cash in hand, however, Tyco appeared to have enough funds to service its debt commitments through until November 2003, and with the company continuing to generate positive cash flow, its survival seemed more certain.

Sources: J. R. Laing, "Tyco's Titan," *Barron's*, April 12, 1999, pp. 27–32. M. Maremont, "How Is Tyco Accounting for Cash Flow?" *Wall Street Journal*, March 5, 2002, p. C1. J. R. Laing, "Doubting Tyco," *Barron's*, January 28, 2002, pp. 19–20. Staff Reporter, "Tyco's Troubles," *Economist*, June 8th, 2002, p. 71.

Overview

This chapter continues with the theme of corporate-level strategy than we discussed in Chapter 9. It begins with a detailed look at the strategy of **diversification,** which is the process of adding new businesses to the company that are distinct from its established operations. A **diversified company** is thus one that is involved in two or more distinct businesses. After reviewing diversification, we turn to the different vehicles, or means, that companies use to execute a diversification strategy and establish new business areas. The basic choice here is among internal new ventures, acquisitions, and joint ventures. **Internal new venturing** is about starting a new business from scratch, **acquisitions** involve buying an existing business, and **joint ventures** typically establish a new business with the assistance of a partner. The chapter closes with a look at **restructuring,** which is the process of reducing the scope of the company's diversified operations by exiting from business areas. By the end of this chapter you will have a good grasp of the pros and cons of different diversification strategies, and of the relative merits of the different vehicles that can be used to execute a diversification strategy.

Expanding Beyond a Single Industry

The role of management in corporate-level strategy is to identify which industries a company should compete in to maximize its long-run profitability. For many companies, profitable growth and expansion often entails concentrating on a single industry or market. For example, McDonald's focuses on the global fast food restaurant business and Wal-Mart on global discount retailing.

One advantage of staying inside the industry is that it allows a company to focus its total managerial, financial, technological, and functional resources and capabilities on competing successfully in just one area. This is important in fast-growing and fast-changing industries, where demands on the company's resources and capabilities are likely to be substantial, but where the long-term profits that flow from establishing a competitive advantage are also likely to be very significant.

A second advantage of staying inside a single industry is that a company stays focused on what it knows and does best.[1] By doing so, it does not make the mistake of entering new industries where its existing resources and capabilities add little value or where it confronts a whole new set of competitive industry forces that present unanticipated threats. Both Sears and Coca-Cola, like many other companies, have committed this strategic error. Coca-Cola once decided to expand into the movie business, acquiring Columbia Pictures. It also acquired a large wine-producing business. Similarly, Sears, the clothing seller, once decided to become a one-stop shopping place and bought Allstate Insurance, Coldwell Banker (a real estate company), and Dean Witter (a financial services enterprise). Both Coca-Cola and Sears found that they not only lacked the competencies needed to compete successfully in their new industries but had not foreseen the different kinds of competitive forces that existed in these industries. They came to the conclusion that entry into these industries dissipated, rather than created, value and lowered their profitability, and they ultimately sold off the businesses they had acquired, at a loss.

As the previous chapter discussed, companies that stay inside one industry can pursue both horizontal integration and outsourcing to strengthen their competitive position. They can also pursue vertical integration and enter industries at adjacent stages of the value chain to strengthen their position in their core business. However, with all of these strategies, a company's fortunes are still mostly tied to the profitability of its original industry, which can be dangerous if that industry goes into decline. Moreover, companies that concentrate on just one industry may be missing out on opportunities to create value and increase their profitability by leveraging their resources and capabilities to other activities. There is compelling evidence to suggest that companies that rest on their laurels and do not engage in constant learning and force themselves to stretch can lose out to agile new competitors that come along with superior business models.[2] For these reasons, many argue that companies must leverage their resources and capabilities across market segments and industries if they are to survive and prosper.

A Company as a Portfolio of Distinctive Competencies

Gary Hamel and C. K. Prahalad have developed a model that can help managers assess how and when they should expand beyond their current market segments or industry. According to these authors, a fruitful approach to identifying the different product and market opportunities is to reconceptualize the company as a portfolio of distinctive competencies, as opposed to a portfolio of products, and then consider how those competencies might be leveraged to create business opportunities in new industries.[3] Recall from Chapter 4 that a distinctive competency is a value-creating company-specific resource or capability. For example, Canon, the Japanese company best known for its cameras and photocopiers, has distinctive competencies in precision mechanics, fine optics, microelectronics, and electronic imaging.

Hamel and Prahalad maintain that the identification of *current* distinctive competencies constitutes the first step for a company that is engaged in the process of deciding which diversification opportunities to pursue. Once a company has identified its competencies, Hamel and Prahalad advocate using a matrix similar to that illustrated in Figure 10.1 to establish an agenda for building and leveraging competencies to create new businesses. This matrix distinguishes between existing and new competencies, and between the existing industries in which a company participates and new industries. Each quadrant in the matrix has a title, the strategic implications of which are discussed in the text that follows.

Fill-in-the-Blanks. The lower-left quadrant of Figure 10.1 represents the company's existing portfolio of competencies and products. In the 1900s, for example, Canon had distinctive competencies in precision mechanics, fine optics, and microelectronics and was active in two basic industries: cameras and photocopiers. It used the competencies in precision mechanics and fine optics to produce basic mechanical cameras. These two competencies plus an additional competence in

Nor con quiz

FIGURE 10.1

Establishing a
Competency Agenda

Source: Reprinted by
permission of Harvard
Business School Press. From
*Competing for the Future:
Breakthrough Strategies for
Seizing Control of Your Industry
and Creating the Markets of
Tomorrow* by Gary Hamel and
C. K. Prahalad, Boston, MA.
Copyright © 1994 by Gary
Hamel and C. K. Prahalad. All
rights reserved.

Industry

	Existing	New
New (Competence)	**Premier plus 10** What new competencies will we need to build to protect and extend our franchise in current industries?	**Mega-opportunities** What new competencies will we need to build to participate in the most exciting industries of the future?
Existing (Competence)	**Fill in the blanks** What is the opportunity to improve our position in existing industries and better leverage our existing competencies?	**White spaces** What new products or services could we create by creatively redeploying or recombining our current competencies?

microelectronics were required to produce plain paper copiers. The term "fill-in-the-blanks" refers to the opportunity to improve the company's competitive position in existing industries by transferring existing competencies. Canon was able to improve the position of its camera business by transferring microelectronics skills from its copier business to support the development of cameras with electronic features, such as auto-focus capabilities.

Premier Plus 10. The upper-left quadrant in Figure 10.1 is referred to as *premier plus 10.* The wording is meant to suggest another important question: What new distinctive competencies must be built today to ensure that the company remains a *premier* provider of its existing products in *ten* years? Canon decided that in order to maintain a competitive edge in its copier business, it was going to have to build a new competence in electronic imaging (which refers to the ability to capture and store images in a digital format, as opposed to using more traditional chemical-based photographic processes). This new competence has subsequently helped it to extend its product range to include laser copiers, color copiers, and digital cameras.

White Spaces. The lower-right quadrant of Figure 10.1 is referred to as *white spaces* because the issue to be addressed is how best to fill the "white space" by creatively redeploying or recombining current distinctive competencies to enter new industries. Canon has been able to recombine its established competencies in precision mechanics, fine optics, and its recently acquired competence in electronic imaging to produce fax machines and laser jet printers, thereby entering the fax and printer industries. In other words, it has leveraged its competencies to exploit diversification opportunities.

Mega-Opportunities. Opportunities represented by the upper-right quadrant of Figure 10.1 do not overlap with the company's current industries or its current competencies. Rather, they imply entry into new industries where the company currently has none of the competencies required to succeed. Nevertheless, a company may choose to pursue such opportunities if they are seen to be particularly attractive, significant, or relevant to its existing business opportunities. For example, in 1979,

Monsanto was primarily a manufacturer of chemicals, including fertilizers. However, the company saw enormous opportunities in the emerging biotechnology industry. Senior research scientists felt that it might be possible to produce genetically engineered crop seeds that would produce their own "organic" pesticides. In that year, the company embarked on a massive investment that ultimately amounted to several hundred million dollars to build a world-class competence in biotechnology. This investment was funded by cash flows generated from Monsanto's operations in the chemical industry. The investment began to bear fruit in the mid-1990s when Monsanto introduced a series of genetically engineered crop seeds including Bollgard, a cotton seed that is resistant against many common pests, including the bollworm, and Roundup-resistant soybean seeds (Roundup is a herbicide produced by Monsanto).[4]

The Multibusiness Model

A focus on using or recombining existing competencies or building new competencies to enter new market segments and industries helps managers to think strategically about how industry boundaries might change over time and how this will affect their current business models. By thinking about how to transfer and leverage competencies across industries, Prahalad and Hamel's model can help managers to avoid the strategic mistake of entering new markets where their business model will fail to give them a competitive advantage, as both Coca-Cola and Sears did.

Once a decision has been reached to expand beyond one industry and enter others, a company confronts the need to construct its business model at two levels. First, it has to develop a business model for each industry in which it competes. Sometimes it may be able to take the core set of strategies employed in a business model developed in one industry and implant them in a business unit in a new industry. For example, General Electric has developed a business model that involves selling a piece of expensive capital equipment at a low price and then making significant profits from providing ongoing services for that equipment. Thus, it makes jet engines that it sells to airlines at a low price, and it bundles this sale with a contract to service those engines over their twenty-five-year life span. GE makes substantial profits not from the initial sale of the engines, which are priced at cost, but from the ongoing service contract (this is an example of the razor and razor blades strategy discussed in Chapter 7). Although this model was developed originally by its jet engine business, GE has applied it to several other businesses, including medical imaging, where it sells complex medical equipment to hospitals at cost and then makes profits from the service contracts bundled with the sale of equipment. In other cases, however, the company may have to develop an entirely distinct business model for different industries. Again, in the case of GE, the business model used in its jet engine and medical equipment businesses is not appropriate for its broadcasting business (NBC), where the profit comes primarily from advertising revenues.

In addition to developing a business model for each industry in which it competes, a diversified company has to develop a higher-level *multibusiness model* that justifies entry into different industries in terms of the way it will increase the company's profitability. From a distinctive competency perspective, a multibusiness model would explain how and why transferring and leveraging distinctive competencies across industries will increase a company's return on invested capital. A multibusiness model would also explain how a company is seeking to create value through its choice of corporate-level strategies. For example, Tyco's *multibusiness model* was based on strategies that included using acquisitions to consolidate fragmented industries, acquiring companies that were underperforming their peers, never making hostile acquisitions, identifying the potential for cost savings prior to the acquisition, moving rapidly to realize those cost savings after the acquisition had been completed, and making sure that the employees of acquired companies were given incentives to develop distinctive competencies to boost profitability.

Increasing Profitability Through Diversification

Diversification is the process of adding new businesses to the company that are distinct from its established operations. A diversified or multibusiness company is thus one that is involved in two or more distinct industries. To approach this issue, it is useful to restate the proposition put forward in the last chapter: To increase profitability, a diversification strategy should enable a company or one or more of its business units to (1) perform one or more of the value creation functions at a lower cost, (2) perform one or more of the value creation functions in a way that allows for differentiation and gives a company pricing options, or (3) help the company to manage industry rivalry better.

The managers of most companies first consider diversification when they are generating **free cash flow,** which is cash *in excess* of that required to fund investments in the company's existing business and to meet any debt commitments.[5] Put differently, free cash flow is cash in excess of that which can be profitably reinvested in an existing business. Thus, in the *Opening Case,* it was noted that Tyco was predicted to generate $4 billion of *free cash flow* in 2002, this being cash *in excess* of that required to fund all profitable investments in its existing businesses and to meet its short-term debt commitments. *Cash* is simply *capital* by another name. When a company is generating free cash flow, the question managers must tackle is whether to return that capital to shareholders in the form of higher dividend payouts or invest it in diversification. Technically, any free cash flow belongs to the company's owners—its shareholders. For diversification to make sense, the return on investing free cash flow in pursuit of diversification opportunities (the return on invested capital, ROIC) *must* exceed the return that stockholders could get by investing that capital in a diversified portfolio of stocks and bonds. If this were not the case, it would be in the best interests of shareholders for the company to return any excess cash to them through higher dividends rather than pursue a diversification strategy. Thus, a diversification strategy is not consistent with maximizing returns to shareholders unless management can create significant value by pursuing it and thereby generating a positive return on any capital invested in diversification that exceeds the return shareholders could gain by investing the same capital in a portfolio of stocks and bonds. The managers of a diversified company can boost profitability in five main ways: (1) transferring competencies among existing business, (2) leveraging competencies to create new businesses, (3) sharing resources to realize economies of scope, (4) using diversification as a means of managing rivalry in one or more industries, and (5) exploiting general organizational competencies that enhance the performance of all business units within a diversified company.

Transferring Competencies

Transferring competencies involves taking a distinctive competence developed in one industry and applying it to an *existing* business in another industry. For example, Philip Morris developed distinctive competencies in product development, consumer marketing, and brand positioning that took it to a leadership position in the tobacco industry. It then acquired Miller Brewing, at the time a relatively small player in the brewing industry. Philip Morris subsequently transferred some of its very best marketing people to Miller Brewing, where they applied the skills acquired at Philip Morris to Miller's lackluster brewing business (see Figure 10.2). The result was the creation of Miller Light, the first light beer, and a marketing campaign that helped to push Miller from number six to number two in the brewing industry in terms of market share.

Companies that base their diversification strategy on transferring competencies tend to acquire businesses *related* to their existing activities by one or more value creation functions—for example, manufacturing, marketing, materials management, or R&D. For example, Miller Brewing was related to Philip Morris's tobacco business by marketing commonalities; both beer and tobacco are mass market consumer goods where brand positioning, advertising, and product development skills are important. In general, such competency transfers can lower the costs of value creation in one or more of a company's diversified businesses or enable one or more of its diversified businesses to undertake their value creation functions in a way that leads to differentiation and gives that business unit pricing options.

For such a strategy to work, the competencies being transferred must involve activities that are important for establishing a competitive advantage. All too often companies assume that any commonality is sufficient for creating value. General Motors's acquisition of Hughes Aircraft, made simply because autos and auto manufacturing were going electronic and Hughes was an electronics concern, demonstrates the folly of overestimating the commonalities among businesses. The acquisition failed to realize any of the anticipated gains for GM, whose competitive position did not improve, and GM subsequently sold off Hughes.

Leveraging Competencies

Leveraging competencies involves taking a distinctive competency developed by a business in one industry and using it to create a *new* business in a different industry. The central idea here is that a distinctive competency that is the source of competitive advantage in one industry might also be applied to create a differentiation- or cost-based competitive advantage for a new business in a different industry. For example, Canon used its distinctive competencies in precision mechanics, fine optics, and electronic imaging to produce laser jet printers, which for Canon was a new business in a new industry. Its competitive advantage in laser printers came from the fact that its competencies enabled it to produce high-quality (differentiated) printers that could be manufactured at a low cost.

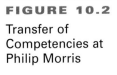

FIGURE 10.2

Transfer of Competencies at Philip Morris

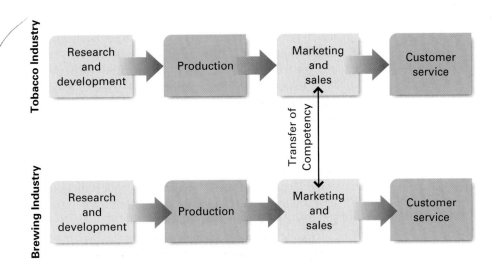

The difference between leveraging competencies and transferring competencies is that in the case of leveraging competencies, an entirely *new* business is being created, whereas transferring competencies involves a transfer between *existing* businesses. Although the distinction may seem subtle, it is actually very important, because different managerial processes are involved. Companies that leverage competencies to establish new business tend to be technology-based enterprises that use their R&D competencies to create new business opportunities in diverse industries. In contrast, companies that transfer competencies typically enter new industries by acquiring established businesses. They then transfer competencies to the acquired businesses in order to enhance their profitability, as Philip Morris did with Miller Brewing.

A number of companies have based their diversification strategy on leveraging competencies and applying them to the creation of new businesses in different industries. Microsoft has leveraged its skills in software development and marketing to create two new businesses, its online network MSN and the X-Box video game business. It is important to emphasize that Microsoft's management decided to invest in these businesses, rather than return the free cash flow generated from its operating system and application software businesses to shareholders in the form of higher dividend payouts, primarily because they believed that the return on invested capital they could earn from those investments exceeded the return that Microsoft shareholders could reasonably be expected to earn by investing that same capital in a diversified portfolio of stocks and bonds. In other words, Microsoft's management believes that the company's diversification strategy is in the best interests of shareholders because they think that the company's competencies will enable it to attain a competitive advantage in the video game and online industries.

Another company that is famous for its ability to leverage competencies and create *new* businesses in diverse industries is 3M, which among other things leveraged its skills in adhesives to create new business opportunities (see Strategy in Action 10.1). From the humble beginning as a manufacturer of sandpaper, 3M has become one of the most diversified corporations in the United States. Most of this diversification was the result not of acquisitions but of the organic creation of new businesses.

Sharing Resources: Economies of Scope

When two or more business units in different industries share resources such as manufacturing facilities, distribution channels, advertising campaigns, or R&D costs, they may be able to realize **economies of scope:** the cost reductions associated with sharing resources across businesses.[6] These cost reductions have two major sources. First, companies that can share resources across businesses have to invest proportionately less in the shared resource than companies that cannot share. For example, Procter & Gamble makes both disposable diapers and paper towels, paper-based products valued for their ability to absorb liquid without disintegrating. Because both products need the same attribute—absorbency—Procter & Gamble can share the R&D costs associated with producing an absorbent paper-based product across the two businesses. Similarly, because both products are sold to the same customer set (supermarkets), it can use the same sales force to sell both products (see Figure 10.3). In contrast, competitors that make just paper towels or just disposable diapers cannot achieve the same economies and have to invest proportionately more in both R&D and maintaining a sales force. The net result is that other things being equal, P&G will have lower expenses and earn a higher return on invested capital than companies that lack the ability to share resources.

Second, resource sharing across businesses may enable a company to use the shared resource more intensively, thereby realizing *economies of scale* (i.e., economies

Strategy in Action   10.1

Diversification at 3M: Leveraging Technology

3M is a 100-year-old industrial colossus that in 2001 generated revenues of $16 billion and profits of $1.4 billion from a portfolio of more than 50,000 individual products ranging from sandpaper and sticky tape to medical devices, office supplies, and electronic components. The company has consistently created new businesses by leveraging its scientific knowledge to find new applications for its proprietary technology. Today the company is composed of more than forty discrete business units grouped into six major sectors: transportation, health care, industrial, consumer and office, electro and communications, and specialty materials. The company has consistently generated 30 percent of sales from products introduced within the prior five years and currently is operating with the goal of producing 40 percent of sales from products introduced within the previous four years. The goal is to attain revenues of $20 billion by 2004, some $8 billion of it expected to come from products that were not launched in 1999, many in new businesses that did not exist in any strategic plan.

The process of leveraging technology to create new businesses at 3M can be illustrated by the following quotation from William Coyne, head of R&D at 3M: "It began with sandpaper: mineral and glue on a substrate. After years as an abrasives company, it created a tape business. A researcher left off the mineral, and adapted the glue and substrate to create the first sticky tape. After creating many varieties of sticky tape—consumer, electrical, medical—researchers created the world's first audio and videotapes. In their search to create better tape backings, other researchers happened on multilayer films that, surprise, have remarkable light management qualities. This multiplayer film technology is being used in brightness enhancement films, which are incorporated in the displays of virtually all laptops and palm computers."

How does 3M do it? First, the company is a science-based enterprise with a strong tradition of innovation

and risk taking. Risk taking is encouraged, and failure is not punished but seen as a natural part of the process of creating new products and business. Second, 3M's management is relentlessly focused on the company's customers and the problems they face. Many of 3M's products have come from helping customers to solve difficult problems. Third, managers set stretch goals that require the company to create new products and businesses at a rapid pace (e.g., the current goal that 40 percent of sales should come from products introduced within the last four years). Fourth, employees are given considerable autonomy to pursue their own ideas. An employee can spend 15 percent of his or her time working on a project of his or her own choosing without management approval. Many products have resulted from this autonomy, including the ubiquitous Post-it notes. Fifth, while products belong to business units and it is business units that are responsible for the profits they generate and are rewarded for maximizing profitability, the technologies belong to everyone within the company. Anyone at 3M is free to try to develop new applications for a technology developed within a business unit; they do not have to belong to that unit. Sixth, there are mechanisms for sharing technological knowledge within 3M so that opportunities can be identified, such as conferences where researchers from different business units are brought together to share the results of their work. And finally, 3M uses numerous mechanisms to recognize and reward those who develop new technologies, products, and businesses, including peer-nominated award programs, a corporate hall of fame, and of course, monetary rewards.

Sources: W. E. Coyne, "How 3M Innovates for Long-Term Growth," *Research Technology Management* (March–April 2001): 21–24. 3M's 2001 10K form.

of scale are a source of economies of scope). For example, one of the motives behind the 1998 merger of Citicorp and Travelers to form Citigroup was that the merger would allow Travelers to sell its insurance products and financial services through Citicorp's retail banking network. The merger allows the expanded group to better use an existing asset—its retail-banking network—thereby realizing economies of scale. Because economies of scale lower the cost structure of one or more businesses, the net result is to increase the profitability of the diversified company.

FIGURE 10.3

Sharing Resources at
Procter & Gamble

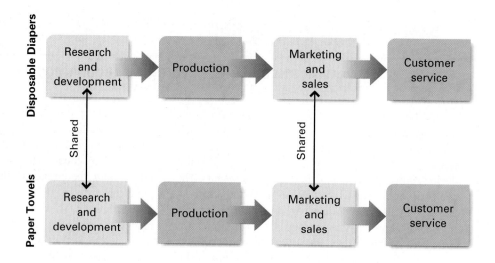

Diversification to attain economies of scope is possible only when there are significant commonalities between one or more of the value creation functions of a company's existing and new activities. Moreover, managers need to be aware that the bureaucratic costs of coordination necessary to achieve economies of scope within a company often outweigh the value that can be created by such a strategy.[7] Consequently, the strategy should be pursued only when sharing is likely to generate a *significant* competitive advantage in one or more of a company's business units.

Managing Rivalry: Multipoint Competition

Sometimes a company benefits by diversifying into an industry in order to hold a competitor in check that has either entered its industry or has the potential to do so. For example, if an aggressive enterprise based in another industry enters a company's market and tries to gain share by cutting prices, the company can respond in kind and diversify into the aggressor's home industry and also cut prices. In this way, the company sends a signal: "If you attack me, I'll respond in kind and make things tough for you." (This is an example of the strategy of tit-for-tat discussed in Chapter 5 under the heading of game theory.) The hope is that such a move will cause the aggressor to pull back from its attack, moderating rivalry in the company's home industry and allowing for higher prices and profits. Of course, for this to stick and the tit-for-tat strategy to have its desired effect, the company would then need to pull back from its competitive attack in the aggressor's home market.

An example of diversification to keep a potential competitor in check occurred in the late 1990s when Microsoft awoke to the fact that Sony might emerge as a rival. Although Sony was in a different industry (consumer electronics as opposed to software), Microsoft realized that the Sony PlayStation was in essence nothing more than a specialized computer and, moreover, one that did not use a Microsoft operating system. Microsoft's fear was that Sony might use the PlayStation II, which came equipped with web browsing potential, as a "Trojan horse" to gain control of web browsing and computing from the living room, ultimately taking customers away from PCs with Microsoft operating systems. The desire to keep Sony's ambitions in check was another part of the rationale for Microsoft's diversification into the video game industry with the launch of the X-Box.

There are other diversified companies that compete against each other in several different industries. Microsoft and Sony now compete directly against each other in the video game industry and the wireless handset industry. Canon and Kodak compete against each other in photocopiers and digital cameras. Unilever and Procter & Gamble compete against each other in laundry detergents, personal care products, and packaged foods. When companies compete against each other in different industries, we refer to it as **multipoint competition.** Companies that are engaged in multipoint competition might be better able to manage rivalry by signaling that competitive attacks in one industry will be met by retaliatory attacks in another industry. If successful, such signaling might lead to *mutual forbearance,* and thus less intense rivalry and higher profit in each industry where a company competes. It follows that the desire to manage rivalry better through multipoint competition might be a motive for diversification that increases profitability.

Exploiting General Organizational Competencies

By **general organizational competencies,** we mean competencies that transcend individual functions or businesses and reside at the corporate level in the multibusiness enterprise, typically in the skills of the company's top managers. These competencies help each business unit within the corporation to perform at a higher level than would be the case were they independent companies in their own right.[8] Such general organizational competencies can take on several forms, which include (1) entrepreneurial capabilities, (2) capabilities in developing effective organizational structures and control systems, and (3) superior strategic capabilities. The important point to recognize is that although any diversified company can develop these capabilities, few do because the required managerial skills are rare and difficult to develop and implement.

Entrepreneurial Capabilities. Some companies have a long history of developing new businesses internally; examples include 3M (see Strategy in Action 10.1), Hewlett Packard, IBM, Canon, Sony, and Matsushita.[9] They do this because they have management systems backed by an organization culture that stimulates managers to act entrepreneurially. The consequence is that these companies generate profitable new businesses at a much higher rate than most other enterprises, and their diversification is a result of this. We will highlight some of the systems required to generate profitable new businesses later in this chapter when we discuss internal new ventures. For now, note that the management systems of the company must (1) encourage managers to take risks, (2) give them the time and resources to pursue novel ideas, (3) not punish managers for taking risks that fail, but also (4) make sure that the company does not waste resources on too many risky ventures that have a low probability of generating a decent return on investment. Obviously, a difficult organizational balancing act is required here, for the company has to simultaneously encourage risk taking while limiting the amount of risk being undertaken.

Companies with entrepreneurial capabilities are able to achieve this balancing act. 3M's corporate goal of generating 40 percent of revenues from products introduced within the past four years focuses the organization's intention of the importance of developing new products and businesses. The company's famous 15 percent rule gives employees the time to pursue novel ideas. The company's long-standing commitment to helping customers solve problems helps ensure that ideas for new businesses are customer focused. The company's celebration of employees who created new businesses helps to reinforce the norm of entrepreneurship and risk taking. Similarly, there is a norm that failure should not be punished but viewed as a learning experience.

Effective Organization Structure and Controls. The organization structure and controls of a diversified company provide the context within which the managers of business units run. Effective organizational structure and controls can create a set of incentives that strongly encourage business unit (divisional) managers to maximize the efficiency and effectiveness of their units, which will increase the company's return on invested capital. We shall look closely at what constitutes effective organization structure and controls in the following chapters. For now, note that an examination of diversified corporations that are successful at boosting profitability through effective organization structure and controls suggests that a number of features are common across such companies.[10] First, the different business units of the company tend to be placed into self-contained divisions. Second, these divisions tend to be managed by senior executives in a decentralized fashion. Rather than get involved in the day-to-day operations of such divisions, they set challenging financial goals for each division, probe the general managers of each division about their strategy for attaining these goals, monitor divisional performance, and hold the general managers accountable for that performance. Third, these internal monitoring and control mechanisms are linked with progressive incentive pay systems that reward divisional personnel for attaining or surpassing performance goals. Although this sounds like a relatively easy strategy to pursue, in practice it seems to require very good senior executives to pull it off—that is, senior executives with superior strategic capabilities.

Superior Strategic Capabilities. For diversification to increase profitability, a company's top managers must have superior strategic capabilities. These capabilities give top managers the intangible governance skills that allow them to manage the different business units within the organization in a way that allows them to perform at a higher level than they would do if they were independent companies in their own right.[11] Simply put, in the context of a diversified company, governance skills determine how effective top managers are at managing business units and the managers who control those units. The business of top management in the diversified company is to manage the managers of business units. This is not an easy thing to do well; governance skills are a rare and valuable capability. However, certain senior executives seem to have developed a skill for managing businesses and pushing the heads of those business units to achieve superior performance. Examples include Jack Welch at General Electric, Bill Gates and Steve Ballmer at Microsoft, and, despite Tyco's recent troubles and his own personal shortcomings, Dennis Kozlowski (see the *Opening Case*).

A flair for entrepreneurship is often found in top managers who have developed superior strategic capabilities or governance skills. As important, if not more so, is the ability to recognize ways to enhance the performance of individual managers, functions, and business units. Jack Welch, for example, was a master in improving the skills of his managers across the board in GE. He created organization-wide management development programs focusing on change management and created procedures to make middle managers question top management actions. At the functional and business levels, he instituted many of the techniques discussed in Chapter 4 to promote superior efficiency and quality, such as the Six Sigma quality improvement methodology, and he pushed hard to make sure that business unit managers used these techniques to improve the efficiency of the operations under their control.

An especially important governance skill in the diversified company is the ability to diagnose the real source of performance problems in an underperforming business unit and take the appropriate steps to fix those problems, whether through pushing the top managers of the unit to take certain strategic actions or replacing top managers with individuals better able to fix the problems. Top managers who have such governance skills tend to be very good at probing business unit managers for information and helping them to think through strategic problems.

Related to this skill, an important way in which a diversified company can increase its profitability is by recognizing inefficient and poorly managed companies, acquiring them, and then restructuring them to improve their performance. The acquired company does not have to be in the same industry as the acquiring company for the strategy to work; thus, the strategy often leads to diversification. Improvements in the performance of the acquired company can come from a number of sources. First, the acquiring company usually replaces the top managers of the acquired company with a more aggressive management team. Second, the new managers of the acquired business are encouraged to sell off any unproductive assets, such as executive jets and elaborate corporate headquarters, and to reduce staffing levels. Third, the new management team is encouraged to intervene in the operations of the acquired business to seek out ways to improve the unit's efficiency, quality, innovativeness, and customer responsiveness. Fourth, to motivate the new management team and other employees of the acquired unit to undertake such actions, increases in their pay are typically linked to increases in the performance of the acquired unit. In addition, the acquiring company often establishes performance goals for the acquired company that cannot be met without significant improvements in operating efficiency. It also makes the new top management aware that failure to achieve performance improvements consistent with these goals within a given amount of time will probably result in their being replaced.

Thus, the system of rewards and sanctions established by the acquiring company gives the new managers of the acquired unit strong incentives to look for ways of improving the performance of the unit under their charge. The strategy of acquiring and restructuring underperforming companies was in fact what Tyco International pursued for most of the 1990s, apparently with considerable success, until Tyco's senior managers erred by getting too ambitious, acquiring too many companies in too short a space of time, and taking on too much debt (see the *Opening Case*). From time to time, General Electric also pursued a similar strategy under the leadership of Jack Welch, again with some success.

Types of Diversification

The two main types of diversification are related diversification and unrelated diversification.[12] **Related diversification** is diversification into a new business activity in a different industry that is *related* to a company's existing business activity, or activities, by commonalities between one or more components of each activity's value chain. Normally, these linkages are based on manufacturing, marketing, or technological commonalities. The diversification of Philip Morris into the brewing industry with the acquisition of Miller Brewing is an example of related diversification because there are marketing commonalities between the brewing and tobacco businesses: both are mass market consumer product businesses in which competitive success depends on brand-positioning skills. 3M is another example of a company that has long pursued a strategy of related diversification. In 3M's case, the commonality is in the development of core technology, which is then applied to a wide range of business areas. Another example of related diversification is given in Strategy in Action 10.2, which looks at Intel's recent diversification into the communications chip business.

Strategy in Action   10.2

Related Diversification at Intel

Although Intel has had a small presence in the communications chip business since the 1980s, for a long time it languished as the company focused all of its attention and resources on the booming business of making microprocessors for personal computers. According to managers at Intel, "feeding the processor monster" consumed all of the company's financial resources. Although Intel was generating high profits and significant positive cash flows, it took the strategic decision to reinvest those cash flows in the design of new generations of its highly successful X86 microprocessor architecture and in large-scale (and expensive) fabrication facilities to manufacture microprocessors in very high volumes. The decision seemed logical: Intel had the dominant position in the microprocessor market, its primary customers (personal computer makers) were growing by leaps and bounds, and demand for its microprocessors was soaring. Indeed, had Intel not made these investments, it may have opened the door to competitors in the microprocessor business, such as AMD.

All this changed at a contentious strategy meeting of Intel's top executives in September 1996. Intel's executives came away from that meeting with two important insights. First, the personal computer industry would approach market saturation in several developed markets by the early 2000s. This meant that the growth in demand for Intel's microprocessors would slow. Therefore, Intel needed to find a new growth driver. Second, the executives decided that with the advent of the Internet, "communications was going to be the driver for everything in the future, that all computing was connected computing, and that connectivity had as important and strategic a role to play as the microprocessor did." Moreover, it was clear that demand for products of the communications industry such as communications network gear, which needed advanced communications chips, was accelerating rapidly.

Intel's executives decided that they could probably boost the company's return on invested capital by diverting some cash flow away from the microprocessor industry and use it to build a strong position in the rapidly growing communications chip industry. This was seen as a different industry because the product technology was different, the production technology was different, the customers were different, and the competitors were different. Intel believed, however, that because the communi-

cations chip industry was closely related to the microprocessor industry, Intel could attain a competitive advantage by transferring its leading-edge technology, honed in the microprocessor industry, and manufacturing and marketing capabilities to the communications chip business.

Once the decision was made to enter the communications chip industry on a significant scale, Intel had to decide how best to execute the strategy. The company's managers decided that the only way they could get big enough fast enough to gain scale economies and establish a sustainable competitive advantage in this booming market was for the company to buy the required technology, fabrication facilities, and sales forces. It could then improve the performance of the acquired businesses by transferring its competencies to them. So Intel went on an acquisition binge. Between January 1997 and June 2001, it made eighteen major acquisitions of companies in the communications chip industry for a combined total of $8 billion. These acquisitions include the purchase of the communications chip business of Digital Equipment Corporation for $625 million, Level One Communications (which made high-speed networking and telecommunications chips) for $2.4 billion, DSP (a maker of chip sets for cell phones) for $1.6 billion, and Giga A/S of Denmark (a maker of optical networking chips) for $1.25 billion.

As a result of these acquisitions, by mid-2001 Intel became the fourth largest global company in the communications chip industry, behind only Lucent, Motorola, and Texas Instruments, with revenues of $2.5 billion. Unfortunately, Intel and all these other companies were hard hit by the slump in global demand for telecommunications equipment that began in 2000 and continued through 2001–2002. As of mid-2002, Intel was losing money in its communications chip business, and revenues were declining. In contrast, although revenues in its microprocessor business had also slipped by 20 percent, it was still making strong profits in that area. Only time will tell whether Intel's diversification move will have been a profitable use of the company's financial resources or an ill-timed entry into a difficult business where the company has no competitive advantage.

Sources: R. Arensman, "Intel's Second Try," *Electronic Business* (March 2001): 62–70. Intel 10K Report, 2001.

Companies that pursue a strategy of related diversification can increase profitability in all of the ways we have just discussed. In contrast, **unrelated diversification** is based on entry into industries that have *no* obvious connection to any of a company's value chain activities in its present industry (or industries). Companies pursuing a strategy of unrelated diversification lack the ability to transfer or leverage competencies and to realize economies of scope. Indeed, most companies that pursue a strategy of unrelated diversification focus on increasing profitability by exploiting general organizational competencies. This was certainly the prime rationale for Tyco's diversification strategy during the 1990s, much of which was unrelated diversification. Kozlowski's focus was on increasing Tyco's profitability by establishing an effective organization structure and set of controls at Tyco, and then acquiring and restructuring businesses that he thought were not performing to their full potential. These acquired businesses were in a wide range of industries with no obvious value chain connection, for example, plastics, security systems, and telecommunications, and medical supplies.

In short, Kozlowski's *multibusiness model* for Tyco, like that of all other companies that pursue an unrelated diversification strategy, was *founded on exploiting the gains from general organizational competencies in order to increase the profitability of the constituent businesses of the corporation.* By contrast, the *multibusiness model* for companies pursuing a strategy of related diversification is first and foremost to *achieve the gains from transferring and leveraging competencies and from sharing resources.* In addition, although both related and unrelated diversification might be associated in theory with managing rivalry through multipoint competition, as a practical matter, related diversified companies are far more likely to encounter each other in different industries than unrelated companies are. So this benefit too is more likely to be attained by companies pursuing a related diversification strategy than those pursuing an unrelated diversification strategy.

The Limits of Diversification

One issue a company must confront is whether to pursue related or unrelated diversification. Because related diversification can boost profitability in more ways than unrelated diversification can, this might lead one to believe that related diversification should be the preferred strategy. In addition, related diversification is sometimes perceived as involving fewer risks because the company is moving into industries about which top management usually has some knowledge. Probably because of these considerations, most diversified companies display a preference for related diversification.[13] However, research suggests that the average related company is at best only marginally more profitable than the average unrelated company.[14]

A large number of academic studies support the conclusion that *extensive* diversification tends to depress rather than improve company profitability.[15] For example, in a study that looked at the diversification of thirty-three major U.S. corporations over thirty-five years, Michael Porter observed that the track record of corporate diversification has been poor.[16] Porter found that most of the companies had divested many more diversified acquisitions than they had kept. He and others have concluded that the corporate diversification strategies pursued by most companies can dissipate value instead of creating it.[17]

Why is related diversification only marginally more profitable than unrelated, and why and how can diversification dissipate rather than create value? On the other hand, why are there many examples of individual companies that have performed spectacularly well using a strategy of related diversification? Two reasons are considered in the next sections: the bureaucratic costs of diversification and the possibility that many companies diversify for the wrong reasons.

Bureaucratic Costs and Diversification Strategy

Although diversification can create value for a company, it can end up doing just the opposite. One reason for the failure of diversification to achieve its aims is that often the *bureaucratic costs* of diversification exceed the value created by the strategy. You will recall from the Chapter 9 that **bureaucratic costs** are the cost increases that arise in large, complex organizations due to managerial inefficiencies. The level of bureaucratic costs in a diversified organization is a function of two factors: (1) the number of businesses in a company's portfolio and (2) the extent of coordination required among the different businesses of the company in order to realize value from a diversification strategy.

Number of Businesses. The greater the number of businesses there are in a company's portfolio, the more difficult it is for corporate management to remain informed about the complexities of each business. Management simply does not have the time to process all the information needed to assess the strategic plan of each business unit objectively. This problem began to occur at General Electric in the 1970s. As then CEO Reg Jones commented,

> I tried to review each plan in great detail. This effort took untold hours and placed a tremendous burden on the corporate executive office. After a while I began to realize that no matter how hard we would work, we could not achieve the necessary in-depth understanding of the 40-odd business unit plans.[18]

The information overload in extensively diversified companies may lead corporate-level management to base important resource allocation decisions on only the most superficial analysis of each business unit's competitive position. For example, a promising business unit may be starved of investment funds, while other business units receive far more cash than they can profitably reinvest in their operations. Furthermore, the lack of familiarity with operating affairs on the part of corporate-level management increases the chances that business-level managers might deceive corporate-level managers. For instance, business unit managers might blame poor performance on difficult competitive conditions, even when it is the consequence of poor management. Thus, information overload can result in substantial inefficiencies within extensively diversified companies that cancel out the value created by diversification. These inefficiencies include the suboptimal allocation of cash resources within the company and a failure by corporate management to encourage and reward aggressive profit-seeking behavior by business unit managers.

The inefficiencies arising from information overload can be viewed as one component of the bureaucratic costs of extensive diversification. Of course, these costs can be reduced to manageable proportions if a company limits the scope of its diversification. Indeed, a desire to decrease these costs lay behind the 1980s and 1990s divestments and strategic concentration strategies of highly diversified conglomerates created in the 1960s and 1970s, such as Esmark Corporation, General Electric, ITT, Textron, Tenneco, and United Technologies. For example, under the leadership of Jack Welch, GE switched its emphasis from forty main business units to sixteen contained within three clearly defined sectors.

Coordination Among Businesses. The coordination required to realize value from transferring competencies and sharing resources to realize economies of scope can also be a source of bureaucratic costs. In particular, the transfer of competencies and the achievement of economies of scope demand close coordination among business units. It is the bureaucratic mechanisms needed for this coordination that give rise to bureaucratic costs. (We discuss the mechanisms for achieving coordination in Chapter 12.)

A more serious matter is that substantial bureaucratic costs can result from a firm's inability to identify the unique profit contribution of a business unit that is sharing resources with another unit in an attempt to realize economies of scope. Consider a company that has two business units: one producing household products (such as liquid soap and laundry detergent) and the other producing packaged food products. The products of both units are sold through supermarkets. In order to lower the costs of value creation, the parent company decides to pool the marketing and sales functions of each business unit. Pooling allows the business units to share the costs of a sales force (one sales force can sell the products of both divisions) and gain cost economies from using the same physical distribution system. The organizational structure required to achieve this might be similar to that illustrated in Figure 10.4. The company is organized into three divisions: a household products division, a food products division, and a marketing division.

Although such an arrangement may create value, it can also give rise to substantial control problems and hence bureaucratic costs. For example, if the performance of the household products business begins to slip, identifying who is to be held accountable—the management of the household products division or of the marketing division—may prove difficult. Indeed, each may blame the other for poor performance. The management of the household products division might blame the marketing policies of the marketing division, and the management of the marketing division might blame the poor quality and high costs of products produced by the household products division. Although this kind of problem can be resolved if corporate management directly audits the affairs of both divisions, this effort is costly in terms of the time and the effort that corporate management must expend.

Now imagine the situation within a company that is trying to create value by sharing marketing, manufacturing, and R&D resources across ten businesses rather than just two. Clearly, the accountability problem could become far more severe in such a company. Indeed, the problem might become so acute that the effort in trying to tie down accountability might create serious information overload for corporate management. When this occurs, corporate management effectively loses control of the company. If accountability cannot be sorted out, the consequences may include

FIGURE 10.4

Coordination Among Related Business Units

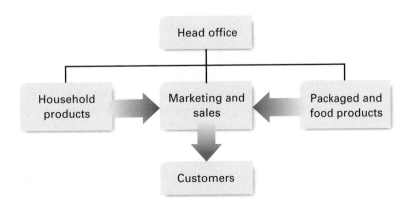

poor resource allocation decisions, a generally high level of organizational slack, and an inability by corporate management to encourage and reward aggressive profit-seeking behavior by business unit managers. All these inefficiencies can be considered part of the bureaucratic costs of diversification to realize economies of scope.

Limits of Diversification. Thus, although diversification can create value for a company, it inevitably involves bureaucratic costs. As is the case with vertical integration, the existence of bureaucratic costs places a limit on the amount of diversification that can profitably be pursued. It makes sense for a company to diversify only as long as the value created by such a strategy exceeds the bureaucratic costs associated with expanding the boundaries of the organization to incorporate additional business activities.

Remember that the greater the number of business units within a company and the greater the need for coordination among those business units, the larger the bureaucratic costs are likely to be. Hence, a company that has twenty businesses, all of them trying to share resources, incurs much larger bureaucratic costs than a company that has ten businesses, none of them trying to share resources. The implications of this relationship are quite straightforward. Specifically, the greater the number of businesses already in a company's portfolio and the greater the need for coordination among those businesses, the more probable it is that the value created by a diversification move will be outweighed by the resulting increase in bureaucratic costs. Once this occurs, a profitable limit to the diversified scope of the enterprise will be reached. However, many companies continue to diversify past this limit, and their performance declines. To solve this problem, a company must reduce the scope of the enterprise through divestments.

Related or Unrelated Diversification? A related diversified company has more opportunities for boosting profitability than an unrelated company, and because of this, managers might think that related diversification should be the preferred strategy. But we also noted that research suggests that the average related company is no more profitable than the average unrelated company.[19] This presents us with a puzzle: If related diversification is associated with more benefits than unrelated diversification, why isn't the strategy consistently more profitable?

The answer has to do with bureaucratic costs and the limits to diversification. As we have seen, bureaucratic costs arise from (1) the number of businesses in a company's portfolio and (2) the extent of coordination required among the different businesses in order to realize value from a diversification strategy. An unrelated company does not have to achieve coordination between business units, and so it has to cope only with the bureaucratic costs that arise from the number of businesses in its portfolio. In contrast, a related diversified company has to achieve coordination among business units if it is to realize the value that comes from skill transfers and resource sharing. Consequently, it has to cope with the bureaucratic costs that arise from *both* the number of business units in its portfolio *and* from coordination among business units. Thus, although it is true that related diversified companies can create value in more ways than unrelated companies, they have to bear higher bureaucratic costs in order to do so. These higher costs may cancel out the higher benefits, making the strategy no more profitable than one of unrelated diversification.

How, then, is a company to choose between these strategies? The choice depends on a comparison of the relative value-added and the bureaucratic costs associated with each strategy. In making this comparison, note that the opportunities for creating value from related (and closely related) diversification are a function of the extent of commonalities between the skills required to compete in the company's core business and the skills required to compete in other industries. Some companies' skills are so specialized that they have few applications outside the core businesses. For example, since the commonalities between steel making and other industrial or commercial operations are few, most steel companies have diversified into unrelated industries (USX into oil and gas). When companies have more generalized skills, they can find many more related diversification opportunities outside the core business. Examples include chemical companies (such as Dow Chemical and Du Pont) and electrical engineering companies. Consequently, the opportunities available to them to create value from related diversification are much greater.

Thus, it pays a firm to concentrate on related diversification when (1) the company's core competencies are applicable to a wide variety of industrial and commercial situations and (2) the bureaucratic costs of implementation do not exceed the value that can be created through resource sharing or transferring competencies. The second condition is likely to hold only for companies that are moderately diversified. At high levels of related diversification, the bureaucratic costs of additional diversification are likely to outweigh the value created by that diversification, and the strategy may become unprofitable.

By the same logic, it may pay a company to concentrate on unrelated diversification when (1) its core functional skills are highly specialized and have few applications outside the company's core business; (2) its top management possess superior strategic capabilities and are able to manage businesses effectively and acquire and restructure poorly run businesses; and (3) the bureaucratic costs of implementation do not exceed the value that can be created by pursuing a restructuring strategy. However, the third condition is *unlikely* to hold for companies that are highly diversified. Thus, no matter whether a company pursues a related or an unrelated diversification strategy, the existence of bureaucratic costs suggests the very real limits to the profitable diversification of the company.

Diversification That Dissipates Value

Another reason so much diversification fails to create value is that many companies diversify for the wrong reasons. This is particularly true of diversification to pool risks or achieve greater growth, both of which are often given by company managers as reasons for diversification.

Consider diversification to pool risks. The benefits of risk pooling are said to come from merging imperfectly correlated income streams to create a more stable income stream. An example of risk pooling might be the diversification by U.S. Steel into the oil and gas industry in an attempt to offset the adverse effects of cyclical downturns in the steel industry. According to advocates of risk pooling, the more stable income stream reduces the risk of bankruptcy and is in the best interests of the company's stockholders.

This simple argument ignores two facts. First, stockholders can easily eliminate the risks inherent in holding an individual stock by diversifying their own portfolios, and they can do so at a much lower cost than the company can. Thus, far from being in the best interests of stockholders, attempts to pool risks through diversification represent an unproductive use of resources. Second, research on this topic suggests that corporate diversification is not a very effective way to pool risks.[20] The business cycles of different industries are not easy to predict and in any case tend to be less important in terms of their impact on profits than a general economic downturn, which hits all industries simultaneously.

Now consider diversification to achieve greater growth. Such diversification is not a coherent strategy because growth on its own does not create value. Growth should be the *byproduct,* not the objective, of a diversification strategy. However, companies sometimes diversify for reasons of growth alone rather than to gain any well-thought-out strategic advantage. The problems that Tyco encountered in 2002 may well be the result of the fact that by the late 1990s, the company's top managers lost sight of the need for diversification to increase profitability and instead became enamored with the pursuit of growth for its own sake. It was unclear to many observers how some of their later acquisitions would add value to Tyco or how Tyco would generate sufficient performance improvements to cover the cost of the acquisition and generate a decent return on invested capital. Moreover, to maintain its growth rate, Tyco had to make ever larger acquisitions (the bigger Tyco became, the larger each subsequent acquisition had to be to add significantly to the company's growth rate). It took on so much debt during the later stages of its expansion phase when it was acquiring large enterprises for billions of dollars at a time that it effectively hamstrung the company with a huge debt burden that would absorb much of the company's free cash flow for years to come.

Entry Strategy: Internal New Ventures

There are three vehicles that companies use to execute corporate-level strategies: internal new ventures, acquisitions, and joint ventures. In this section we look at pros and cons of using internal new ventures. In subsequent sections we look at acquisitions and joint ventures.

The Attractions of Internal New Venturing

Internal new venturing is typically used to execute corporate-level strategies when a company possesses a set of valuable competencies (resources and capabilities) in its existing businesses that can be leveraged or recombined to enter the new business area. As a rule, science-based companies that use their technology to create market opportunities in related business areas tend to favor internal new venturing as an entry strategy. That is, companies pursuing related or closely related diversification often use internal new venturing. Du Pont, for example, has created whole new markets with products such as cellophane, nylon, Freon, and Teflon—all internally generated innovations. 3M has a near-legendary knack for shaping new markets from internally generated ideas (see Strategy in Action 10.1). Similarly, Hewlett Packard moved into computers and peripherals by creating internal new ventures.

Even if it lacks the competencies required to compete in a new business area, a company may pursue an internal venturing strategy when it is entering a newly emerging or embryonic industry with no established players that possess the competencies required to compete in that industry. In this situation, the option of acquiring an established enterprise that possesses those competencies is ruled out, and the company may have no choice but to enter through an internal new venture. This was the position that Monsanto found itself in back in 1979 when it contemplated entering the biotechnology field to produce herbicide and pest-resistant crop seeds. The biotechnology field was young at that time, and there were no incumbent companies focused on applying biotechnology to agricultural products. Accordingly, Monsanto established an internal new venture to enter the field, even though at the time it lacked the required competencies. Indeed, Monsanto's whole venturing strategy was built around the notion that it needed to build competencies ahead of other potential competitors, thereby gaining a strong competitive lead in this newly emerging field.

Pitfalls of New Ventures

Despite the popularity of the internal new-venture strategy, its failure is reportedly high. The evidence on the failure rate of new products indicates the scope of the problem, because most internal new ventures are associated with new-product offerings. According to the evidence, somewhere between 33 and 60 percent of all new products that reach the marketplace do not generate an adequate economic return.[21] Three reasons are often given to explain the relatively high failure rate of internal new ventures: (1) market entry on too small a scale, (2) poor commercialization of the new-venture product, and (3) poor corporate management of the venture process.[22]

Scale of Entry. Research suggests that *on average,* large-scale entry into a new business is often a critical precondition of new-venture success. Although in the short run, large-scale entry means significant development costs and substantial losses, in the long run (which can be as long as five to twelve years, depending on the industry), it brings greater returns than small-scale entry.[23] The reasons include the ability of large-scale entrants to more rapidly realize scale economies, build brand loyalty, and gain access to distribution channels, all of which increase the probability of a new venture's succeeding. In contrast, small-scale entrants may find themselves handicapped by high costs due to a lack of scale economies and a lack of market presence that limits their ability to build brand loyalties and gain access to distribution channels. These scale effects are probably particularly significant when a company is entering an established industry with incumbent companies that possess scale economies, brand loyalties, and access to distribution channels, and the new entrant often has to match these in order to succeed.

Figure 10.5 plots the relationships among scale of entry and profitability over time for successful small-scale and large-scale ventures. The figure shows that successful small-scale entry incurs lower initial losses, but in the long run large-scale entry generates greater returns. However, perhaps because of the costs of large-scale entry and the potential losses if the venture fails, many companies prefer a small-scale entry strategy. Acting on this preference can be a mistake, for the company fails to build up the market share necessary for long-term success.

Commercialization. Many internal new ventures are high-technology operations. To be commercially successful, science-based innovations must be developed with market requirements in mind. Many internal new ventures fail when a company ignores the basic needs of the market. A company can become blinded by the

FIGURE 10.5

Scale of Entry, Profitability, and Cash Flow

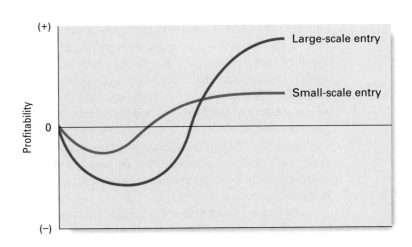

technological possibilities of a new product and fail to analyze market opportunities properly.[24] Thus, a new venture may fail because of a lack of commercialization or because it is marketing a technology for which there is no demand.

For example, consider the desktop computer marketed by NeXT, the company started by the founder of Apple, Steven Jobs. The NeXT system failed to gain market share because the computer incorporated an array of expensive technologies that consumers simply did not want, such as optical disk drives and hi-fidelity sound. The optical disk drives, in particular, turned off customers because they made it tough to switch work from a PC with a floppy drive to a NeXT machine with an optical drive. In other words, NeXT failed because its founder was so dazzled by leading-edge technology that he ignored customer needs.

Poor Implementation. Managing the new-venture process raises difficult organizational issues.[25] Although we deal with the specifics of implementation in later chapters, we must note some of the most common mistakes here.[26] The shotgun approach of supporting many different internal new-venture projects can be a major error, for it places great demands on a company's cash flow and can result in the best ventures being starved of the cash they need for success.

Another common mistake is failure by corporate management to set the strategic context within which new-venture projects should be developed. Simply taking a team of research scientists and allowing them to do research in their favorite field may produce novel results, but these results may have little strategic or commercial value. It is necessary to be very clear about the strategic objectives of the venture and to understand how the venture will seek to establish a competitive advantage.

Failure to anticipate the time and costs involved in the new-venture process constitutes a further mistake. Many companies have unrealistic expectations regarding the time frame. Reportedly, some companies operate with a philosophy of killing new businesses if they do not turn a profit by the end of the third year, clearly an unrealistic view, given the evidence that it can take five to twelve years before a venture generates substantial profits.

Guidelines for Successful Internal New Venturing

To avoid the pitfalls, a company should adopt a structured approach to managing internal new venturing. New venturing typically begins with R&D: *exploratory research* aimed at advancing basic science and technology (the "R" in R&D) and *development research* aimed at finding and refining the commercial applications for a technology (the "D" in R&D). Companies with a strong track record of internal new venturing often excel in both kinds of R&D: they help to advance the basic science, and then they find commercial applications for the science.[27] To advance the basic science, it is important for companies to (1) have strong links with universities, where much of the basic scientific knowledge underlying new technologies is discovered, and (2) to make sure that some basic research funding is left entirely in the hands of research personnel who are given the opportunity to pursue "blue-sky" projects that might ultimately yield unexpected and commercially valuable technologies and products. For example, 3M has close links with a number of universities, including the University of Minnesota in its hometown, and will fund basic research at those universities. 3M also allows (indeed encourages) its researchers to spend 15 percent of their time on projects of their own choosing, a good proportion of which are basic research projects.

However, if the pursuit of basic research (the "R" in R&D) is all that a company does well, it will probably generate very few successful commercial ventures. To translate good science into good products, it is critically important that a good chunk of R&D funding be directed toward commercial ventures. Companies can take a number of steps to make sure that this is the case. First, many companies with large, central research labs place a good proportion of the funding for central research in the hands of business unit managers, who presumably will fund only research projects that promise a commercial payoff (at the same time, some funds must be left for blue-sky projects). Second, to make effective use of its R&D capacity, a company's top managers must spell out key strategic objectives and then communicate them to its scientists and engineers. Much research should be made relevant to strategic goals.[28] For example, one of the biggest research projects at Microsoft Research has long been natural language recognition software, precisely because a central strategic objective of the company has been to make computers easy to use, and researchers reason that if computers can understand spoken language, then commands can be input by voice rather than through a keyboard, and this will make computers easier to use.

To increase the probability of commercial success, a company should foster close links between R&D and marketing personnel, for this is the best way to ensure that research projects address the needs of the market. The company should also foster close links between R&D and manufacturing personnel to ensure that the company has the capability to manufacture any proposed new products. Many companies successfully integrate different functions by setting up project teams, with representatives of the various functional areas, to oversee the development of new products. For example, Hewlett Packard's success in introducing new products in the personal computer industry has been linked to its use of project teams that oversee the development of a new product from its inception to its market introduction.

Another advantage of such teams is that they can significantly reduce the time to develop a new product. While R&D personnel are working on the design, manufacturing personnel can be setting up facilities, and marketing personnel can be developing its plans. Because of such integration, Compaq (now acquired by Hewlett Packard) needed only six months to take the first portable personal computer from an idea on the drawing board to a marketable product.

To use resources to the best effect, a company must also devise a selection process for choosing only the ventures that demonstrate the greatest probability of commercial success. Picking future winners is a tricky business, since by definition new ventures have an uncertain future. One study found the uncertainty surrounding new ventures to be so great that it usually took a company four to five years after launching the venture to reasonably estimate the venture's future profitability.[29] Nevertheless, a selection process is necessary if a company is to avoid spreading its resources too thinly over too many projects.

Once a project has been selected, management needs to monitor the progress of the venture closely. Evidence suggests that the most important criterion for evaluating a venture during its first four to five years is market share growth rather than cash flow or profitability. In the long run, the most successful ventures are those that increase their market share rapidly, for this gives them the volume required to gain scale economies and learning effects, which lead to superior profitability. A company should have clearly defined market share objectives for an internal new venture and decide to retain or kill it in its early years on the basis of its ability to achieve market share goals. Only in the medium term should profitability and cash flow begin to take on greater importance.

The association of large-scale entry with greater long-term profitability suggests that a company can increase the probability of success for an internal new venture by thinking big. This means constructing efficient-scale manufacturing facilities ahead of demand, making large marketing expenditures to build a market presence and brand loyalty, and a commitment by corporate management to accept initial losses as long as market share is expanding.

Entry Strategy: Acquisitions

As we saw in Chapter 9, acquisitions are the main vehicle that companies use to execute a horizontal integration strategy. In addition, acquisitions are an important part of vertical integration and diversification strategies. In the *Opening Case,* we saw how Tyco used acquisitions to grow the company tenfold in ten years. Similarly, between 1997 and 2001, Intel made some eighteen acquisitions valued at around $8 billion in order to execute its strategic decision to diversify into the communications chip business (see Strategy in Action 10.2). Companies rely on acquisitions because they have many advantages over internal new venturing. But as we first noted in Chapter 9, many acquisitions also fail to generate profitable returns for the acquiring company, so there are clearly considerable risks associated with acquisitions. Here we look at the benefits and risks of using acquisitions to execute a corporate-level strategy.

Attractions of Acquisitions

In the case of horizontal integration, acquisitions are the method of executing the strategy. With regard to diversification (or vertical integration), companies often use acquisition to enter a business area that is new to them when they lack important competencies (resources and capabilities) required to compete in that area, but can purchase an incumbent company that has those competencies at a reasonable price. Companies also have a preference for acquisitions when they feel the need to move fast. Building a new business through internal venturing can be a relatively slow process. In contrast, acquisition is a much quicker way to establish a significant market presence and generate profitability. A company can purchase a market leader with a strong position overnight rather than spend years building up a market leadership position through internal development. Thus, when speed is important, acquisition is the favored entry mode. Intel, for example, used acquisitions to build its communications chip business because it sensed that the market was developing very quickly, and it would take too long to develop all of the required competencies internally, so it acquired them by purchasing other companies (see Strategy in Action 10.2).

Acquisitions are also often perceived to be somewhat less risky than internal new ventures, primarily because there is a perception that they involve less uncertainty. Due to the nature of internal new ventures, large uncertainties are associated with projecting future profitability, revenues, and cash flows. In contrast, when a company makes an acquisition, it is acquiring known profitability, known revenues, and known market share, all of which reduce uncertainty. An acquisition allows a company to buy an established business with a track record, and for this reason, many companies favor acquisitions.

Finally, acquisitions may be the preferred entry mode when the industry to be entered is well established and incumbent enterprises enjoy significant protection from barriers to entry. As you recall from Chapter 2, barriers to entry arise from factors associated with product differentiation (brand loyalty), absolute cost advantages, and economies of scale. When such barriers are substantial, a company finds entering an industry through internal new venturing difficult. To enter, a company may have to construct an efficient manufacturing plant, undertake massive advertising to break down established brand loyalties, and quickly build up distribution outlets—all goals that are hard to achieve and likely to involve substantial expenditures. In contrast, by acquiring an established enterprise, a company can circumvent most entry barriers. It can purchase a market leader, which already benefits from substantial scale economies and brand loyalty. Thus the greater the barriers to entry are, the more likely it is that acquisitions will be the favored entry mode. (We should note here that the attractiveness of an acquisition is predicated on the assumption that an incumbent company can be acquired for less than it would cost to enter the same industry by an internal new venture. As we shall see in the next section, the validity of this assumption is often questionable.)

Acquisition Pitfalls   For the reasons just noted, acquisitions have long been a popular vehicle for executing corporate-level strategies. However, despite this popularity, there is ample evidence that many acquisitions fail to add value for the acquiring company and, indeed, often end up dissipating value. For example, a study by Mercer Management Consulting looked at 150 acquisitions worth more than $500 million each that were undertaken between January 1990 and July 1995.[30] The Mercer study concluded that 50 percent of these acquisitions ended up eroding, or substantially eroding, shareholder value, and another 33 percent created only marginal returns. Only 17 percent of these acquisitions were judged to be successful. Similarly, a study by KPMG, an accounting and management consulting company, looked at 700 large acquisitions between 1996 and 1998 and found that although some 30 percent of these actually created value for the acquiring company, 31 percent destroyed value, and the remainder had little impact.[31]

More generally, a wealth of evidence from academic research suggests that many acquisitions fail to realize their anticipated benefits.[32] In a major study of the postacquisition performance of acquired companies, David Ravenscraft and Mike Scherer concluded that the profitability and market shares of acquired companies often declined after acquisition.[33] They also noted that a smaller but substantial subset of acquired companies experienced traumatic difficulties, which ultimately led to their being sold off by the acquiring company. In other words, Ravenscraft and Scherer's evidence, like that presented by McKinsey & Company, suggests that many acquisitions destroy rather than create value.

Many acquisitions apparently fail to create value for four major reasons: (1) companies often experience difficulties when trying to integrate divergent corporate cultures, (2) companies overestimate the potential economic benefits from an acquisition, (3) acquisitions tend to be very expensive, and (4) companies often do not adequately screen their acquisition targets.

Postacquisition Integration. Having made an acquisition, the acquiring company has to integrate the acquired business into its own organizational structure. Integration can entail the adoption of common management and financial control systems, the joining together of operations from the acquired and the acquiring company, or the establishment of linkages to share information and personnel. Many unexpected problems can occur when integration is attempted. Often they stem from differences in corporate cultures. After an acquisition, many acquired companies experience high management turnover, possibly because their employees do not like the acquiring company's way of operating.[34] Research evidence suggests that the loss of management talent and expertise, to say nothing of the damage from constant tension between the businesses, can materially harm the performance of the acquired unit.[35] For an example of what can occur, see Strategy in Action 10.3, which examines the high management turnover at Boston Co. after it was acquired by Mellon Bank.

Strategy in Action 10.3

Postacquisition Problems at Mellon Bank

In the early 1990s, Frank Cahouet, the CEO of Philadelphia-based Mellon Bank, conceived of a corporate strategy that would reduce the vulnerability of Mellon's earnings to changes in interest rates. Cahouet's solution was to diversify into financial services to gain access to a steady flow of fee-based income from money management operations. As part of this strategy, in 1993 Mellon acquired Boston Co. for $1.45 billion. Boston is a high-profile money management company that manages investments for major institutional clients, such as state and corporate pension funds. In 1994, Mellon followed up its Boston acquisition with the acquisition of mutual fund provider Dreyfus Corp., for $1.7 billion. As a result, by 1995 almost half of Mellon's income was generated from fee-based financial services.

In 1995, Mellon hit some serious bumps on the road in its attempt to become a money market powerhouse. Problems at Boston Co. began to surface soon after the Mellon acquisition. From the start, there was a clear clash of cultures. At Mellon, many managers arrive at their mundane offices by 7 A.M. and put in twelve-hour days for modest pay by banking industry standards. They are also accustomed to a firm management hierarchy that is carefully controlled by Frank Cahouet, whose management style emphasized cost containment and frugality. Boston Co. managers also put in twelve-hour days, but they expected considerable autonomy, flexible work schedules, high pay, ample perks, and large performance bonuses. In most years, the top twenty executives at Boston earned between $750,000 and $1 million each. Mellon executives who visited the Boston Co. unit were dumb-struck by the country club atmosphere and opulence they saw. In its move to streamline Boston, Mellon insisted that Boston cut expenses and introduced new regulations for restricting travel, entertainment, and perks.

Things started to go wrong in October 1993 when the Wisconsin state pension fund complained to Mellon of lower returns on a portfolio run by Boston Co. In November, Mellon liquidated the portfolio, taking a $130 million charge against earnings. Mellon also fired the responsible portfolio manager, claiming that this manager was making "unauthorized trades." At Boston Co., however, many managers saw Mellon's action as violating guarantees of operating autonomy that it had given Boston at the time of the acquisition. They blamed Mellon for prematurely liquidating a portfolio whose strategy, they claimed, Mellon executives had approved and that, moreover, could still prove a winner if interest rates fell (which they subsequently did).

Infuriated by Mellon's interference in the running of Boston Co., in March seven managers at Boston Co.'s asset management unit, including the unit's CEO, Desmond Heathwood, proposed a management buyout to Mellon. This unit was one of the gems in Boston's crown, with over $26 billion in assets under management. Heathwood had been openly disdainful of Mellon's bankers, believing that they were out of their league in the investment business. In April, Mellon rejected the buyout proposal, and Heathwood promptly left to start his own investment management company. A few days later, Mellon asked employees at Boston to sign employment contracts that limited their ability to leave and work for Heathwood's competing business. Thirteen senior employees refused to sign and quit to join Heathwood's new money management operation.

The defection of Heathwood and his colleagues was followed by a series of high-profile client defections. The Arizona State Retirement System, for example, pulled $1 billion out of Mellon and transferred it to Heathwood's firm, and the Fresno County Retirement System transferred $400 million in assets over to Heathwood. As one client stated, "We have a relationship with the Boston Co. that goes back over 30 years, and the people who worked on the account are the people who left—so we left too."

Reflecting on the episode, Frank Cahouet noted, "We've clearly been hurt. . . . But this episode is very manageable. We are not going to lose out momentum." Others were not so sure. In this incident, they saw yet another example of how difficult it can be to merge two divergent corporate cultures and how the management turnover that results from such attempts can deal a serious blow to any attempt to create value out of an acquisition.

Sources: M. Murray and J. Rebello, "Mellon Bank Corp: One Big Unhappy Family," *Wall Street Journal,* April 28, 1995, pp. B1, B4. K. Holland, "A Bank Eat Bank World—with Indigestion," *Business Week,* October 30, 1995, p. 130.

Overestimating Economic Benefits. Even when companies achieve integration, they often overestimate the potential for creating value by joining together different businesses. They overestimate the strategic advantages that can be derived from the acquisition and thus pay more for the target company than it is probably worth. Richard Roll has attributed this tendency to hubris on the part of top management. According to Roll, top managers typically overestimate their ability to create value from an acquisition, primarily because rising to the top of a corporation has given them an exaggerated sense of their own capabilities.[36]

Coca-Cola's acquisition of a number of medium-sized wine-making companies illustrates the situation of a company that overestimates the economic benefits from an acquisition. Reasoning that a beverage is a beverage, Coca-Cola wanted to use its distinctive competence in marketing to dominate the U.S. wine industry. But after buying three wine companies and enduring seven years of marginal profits, Coca-Cola finally conceded that wine and soft drinks are very different products, with different kinds of appeal, pricing systems, and distribution networks. It subsequently sold the wine operations to Joseph E. Seagram & Sons for $210 million—the price it had paid for the purchases and a substantial loss when adjusted for inflation.[37]

The Expense of Acquisitions. Acquisition of companies whose stock is publicly traded tends to be very expensive. One reason is that shareholders of the acquired company are unlikely to sell out unless they are paid a significant premium over the current market value of the stock. Another is that the management of the target company is not likely to agree to an acquisition unless there is a substantial premium over the current market value. In general, premiums tend to run 30 to 50 percent over the market value prior to a takeover bid. This implies that if the prior market value was an accurate reflection of the future profit potential of a company, the acquiring company must be able to increase the value of the target company after the acquisition by at least the same amount to make the acquisition pay, a tall order.

Moreover, the price of acquisition targets can get bid up in the acquisition process. This is likely to occur in the case of contested bids, where two or more companies simultaneously bid for control of a single target company. In addition, when there is a lot of acquisition activity in an industry or sector, the price of *potential* target companies can get bid up by investors who are speculating that a bid will be made at some point, which further increases the cost of making an acquisition. This happened in the telecommunications sector between 1996 and 2000. There was a common perception at the time that demand for telecommunications equipment was accelerating rapidly. To make sure they could meet the needs of customers who were demanding leading-edge equipment, many of the larger telecommunications equipment suppliers went on acquisition binges. JDS Uniphase, Cisco Systems, Nortel, Corning, and Lucent all raced each other to buy up smaller telecommunications equipment suppliers that were developing promising technology. The result was that stock prices for such companies got bid up by investors who speculated that the companies they invested in would get bought out at a premium. In the end, the process got totally out of hand, with companies that had very few tangible assets being acquired for huge sums of money. When the telecommunications boom turned to bust, many of the acquiring companies found that they had overpaid for their acquisitions, which generated few revenues and even fewer profits, and they had to take large accounting write-downs. In 2001, Nortel Networks wrote down $12.3 billion in goodwill on its balance sheet to reflect a reduction in the value of the assets it had acquired during the boom. Another telecom equipment supplier, Corning, wrote down $4.8 billion, and JDS Uniphase wrote down a staggering $40 billion. Strategy in Action 10.4 provides the details.

Related to the high costs of acquisition is the debt that companies often take on to finance them. Many of the most aggressive acquirers of the 1990s, for example, took on large amounts of debt to finance their acquisitions. Tyco International used a mix of cash and its own stock to pay for its acquisitions. Although some of the cash it used came from internally generated funds, much of it came from issuing bonds (i.e., by adding debt). As a result, by decade's end, Tyco had $23 billion in debt on its balance sheet. The debt could easily have been financed had the economy continued to grow during 2000–2001, but a slowdown in economic activity made it difficult for

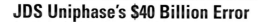

Strategy in Action   10.4

JDS Uniphase's $40 Billion Error

In 1999, it looked as if JDS Uniphase had the perfect storm at its back and was riding a wave of new orders for the optical gear that it made for telecommunications networks to financial nirvana. Only one problem seemed to stand in the way of the company's achieving this glittering future: it could not ramp up capacity fast enough. To meet the wall of orders before it and expand its portfolio of product offerings, JDS Uniphase decided to acquire any and all competitors it could get its hands on. The decision was made easy by the high price of JDS's own stock, which had soared to $150, valuing the company at almost $220 billion. To many, the valuation seemed excessive given that in June 2000, the company had revenues of $1.43 billion and was losing money. Nevertheless, JDS decided to use its own richly valued stock as "cheap currency" to finance its acquisitions.

Between November 1999 and July 2000, JDS made three acquisitions for $58.6 billion, including the $41 billion acquisition of SDL, a company with a book value of only $2 billion (SDL made voice, data, and Internet transmission technologies). The difference between SDL's book value of $2 billion and the purchase price of $41 billion was entered in JDS's balance sheet as "goodwill." **Goodwill** reflects the premium a company pays over and above the value of a target company's identifiable or tangible assets—in other words, it represents intangible assets such as technological knowledge, customer relationships, and brand loyalty.

By early 2001, it was becoming clear that JDS's acquisition strategy would not have a short-term payoff. Demand for telecommunications equipment had suddenly imploded, and JDS was confronted with revenues

that were estimated to hit $1.1 billion in the year ending June 2002, down from $3.2 billion a year earlier. The clear implication was that JDS had overpaid for its acquisitions. The recently acquired SDL unit, for example, was generating revenues of a few hundred million, losing money, and faced with a shrinking order book. It was now hard to construct any scenario under which SDL was worth $41 billion, or even $2 billion for that matter. On July 26, 2001, JDS announced that it would write down the value of goodwill on its balance sheet, taking a $44.8 billion noncash charge against earnings to do so. In the aftermath of the write-down, some analysts and several managers at JDS claimed that in a sense, it did not matter. After all, they said, no "real" money had been lost. JDS had not taken on any debt to finance its acquisitions; it had simply used its overvalued currency (high-priced stock) to buy assets that would have a tangible value going forward once the market for telecommunications equipment improved. Indeed, after the write-down, JDS had no debt at all and $440 million in cash on its balance sheet. Others questioned this logic, pointing out that the claim that there was no "real money" involved would seem absurd to long-term stockholders, who had seen the value of their stock decline from its high of over $150 to under $6 a share by April 2002. Real stockholder value had been destroyed because JDS had massively overpaid for its acquisitions during the telecom feeding frenzy.

Sources: C. Sewell, "When Boom Goes to Bust," *Telephony,* October 22, 2001, pp. 38–44. B. Ojo, "Wall Street, SEC Question Write Downs," *EBN,* July 23, 2001, p. G1. JDS Uniphase, 2001 10K Report.

Tyco to increase its own profits fast enough to generate the cash flow required to meet its debt obligations. Tyco was by no means the worst offender in this area. For example, George Pacific took on $12 billion in debt to spend $17 billion on acquiring other pulp and paper makers during the 1990s in an attempt to execute a horizontal integration strategy. By early 2002, with the economy weak and paper and pulp prices plunging, several analysts questioned whether George Pacific would be able to meet its debt obligations.[38]

Inadequate Preacquisition Screening. After researching acquisitions made by twenty different companies, a study by Philippe Haspeslagh and David Jemison came to the conclusion that one reason for acquisitions failure is management's inadequate attention to preacquisition screening.[39] They found that many companies decide to acquire other firms without thoroughly analyzing the potential benefits and costs. After the acquisition has been completed, many acquiring companies discover that instead of buying a well-run business, they have purchased a troubled organization.

That was the experience of the fast-growing insurance provider Conseco when it acquired Green Tree Financial Corp for $7.6 billion in 1998. Green Tree, the largest subprime and mobile home lender in the United States, specialized in lending money to low-income households. It charged high interest rates on its loans, which had a high risk of default. Green Tree was also highly leveraged, with a lot of debt on its balance sheet. At the time of the deal, Conseco's CEO, Stephen Hilbert, hailed the acquisition as "the deal of a lifetime," but to some observers, the margin for error seemed small. The skeptics were proved right in March 2000, when Hilbert announced that Conseco would take a $350 million charge against earnings to reflect significantly higher-than-expected loan losses. In other words, Green Tree's customers were defaulting on their loans at a high rate. The stock price plummeted, and Hilbert was forced to resign. Ultimately, Green Tree's loan portfolio was sold off for $1.5 billion, a substantial loss for Conseco.[40] In retrospect, it seems clear that Conseco did not adequately audit the financial statements and operations of Green Tree prior to completing the acquisition. If it had, it may well have discovered that Green Tree's customers were defaulting on their loans at a very rapid rate.

Guidelines for Successful Acquisition

To avoid pitfalls and make successful acquisitions, companies need to take a structured approach with four main components: (1) target identification and preacquisition screening, (2) bidding strategy, (3) integration, and (4) learning from experience.[41]

Identification and Screening. Thorough preacquisition screening increases a company's knowledge about potential takeover targets, leads to a more realistic assessment of the problems involved in executing an acquisition and integrating the new business into the company's organizational structure, and lessens the risk of purchasing a potential problem business. The screening should begin with a detailed assessment of the strategic rationale for making the acquisition and identification of the kind of enterprise that would make an ideal acquisition candidate.

Next, the company should scan a target population of potential acquisition candidates, evaluating each according to a detailed set of criteria, focusing on (1) financial position, (2) product market position, (3) competitive environment, (4) management capabilities, and (5) corporate culture. Such an evaluation should enable the company to identify the strengths and weaknesses of each candidate, the extent of potential economies of scope between the acquiring and the acquired companies, potential integration problems, and the compatibility of the corporate cultures of the acquiring and the acquired companies.

The company should then reduce the list of candidates to the most favored ones and evaluate them further. At this stage, it should sound out third parties, such as investment bankers, whose opinions may be important and who may be able to give valuable insights about the efficiency of target companies. The company that leads the list after this process should be the acquisition target.

After a target has been identified, there is still much that can be done before finalizing a deal. Tyco International, for example, routinely sent in a team of independent accountants to audit the books of an acquisition target to make sure that there were no skeletons in the accounting closet (see the *Opening Case*). This kind of detailed internal auditing of the books can be done only when the proposed acquisition is a friendly one in which the management team and board of the target company agree to the acquisition. If the bid is hostile, with the management team and board of the target company opposing the takeover bid, it is unlikely that the acquiring company will get the kind of access that it needs to do thorough due diligence. This is one reason that Tyco made only friendly acquisitions.

Bidding Strategy. The objective of bidding strategy is to reduce the price that a company must pay for an acquisition candidate. Probably the most effective thing that an acquirer can do is make only friendly takeover bids. In a hostile bid, the price of the target company often gets bid up by speculators who expect that the offer price will be raised by the acquirer, or that another company, sometimes called a *white knight,* might come in with a counteroffer more favorable to the management of the target company. It is this kind of reasoning that led Tyco International to eschew hostile takeover bids and make only friendly acquisitions.

Another essential element of a good bidding strategy is timing. For example, Hanson PLC, one of the most successful takeover machines of the 1980s, always looked for essentially sound businesses that were suffering from short-term problems due to cyclical industry factors or problems localized in one division. Such companies are typically undervalued by the stock market and thus can be picked up without payment of the standard 40 or 50 percent premium over current stock prices. With good timing, a company can make a bargain purchase. Tyco International also seemed to follow this practice, buying essentially sound businesses that were underperforming their peers due to short-term problems.

Integration. Despite good screening and bidding, an acquisition will fail unless positive steps are taken to integrate the acquired company into the organizational structure of the acquiring one quickly. Integration should center on the source of the potential strategic advantages of the acquisition—for instance, opportunities to share marketing, manufacturing, procurement, R&D, financial, or management resources. Integration should also be accompanied by steps to eliminate any duplication of facilities or functions. In addition, any unwanted activities of the acquired company should be sold. Finally, if the different business activities are closely related, they will require a high degree of integration. Again, it is clear from the *Opening Case* that Tyco International moved rapidly to integrate acquired units into its organization. Steps were taken immediately after an acquisition was completed to close or sell off duplicate or unwanted facilities and lay off excess employees. Tyco's incentive systems and internal financial controls were also introduced immediately after an acquisition closed. The reason Tyco was able to move so fast was that most of the groundwork was down *before* the acquisition closed.

Learning from Experience. There is quite a bit of evidence that although on average, most acquisitions fail to create value for the acquiring company, some repeat acquirers get very good at the process and generate significant value from acquisitions.[42] Tyco is an example of a repeat acquirer, as is General Electric. Although both have had their share of problems (and Tyco's are obviously serious), historically they do seem to have been able to make astute acquisitions. One reason may have been that they learned from their experience and developed a "playbook" of how to execute an acquisition. In Tyco's case, this playbook included not making hostile acquisitions, detailed auditing of the accounts of the target company, acquiring companies that would help Tyco achieve critical mass in an industry, moving quickly to realize cost savings after an acquisition, promoting managers one or two layers down to lead the newly acquired entity, and introducing profit-based incentive pay systems in the acquired unit.

Nevertheless, experience alone does not guarantee success.[43] It is important for managers to learn from their experience with acquisitions, performing postacquisition audits of the overall process to review what worked, what did not, and how things might be improved the next time.

Entry Strategy: Joint Ventures

Although joint ventures are not as widely used as acquisitions and internal new ventures for establishing new business activities, in certain circumstances they make a good deal of sense. A company may prefer internal new venturing to acquisition as an entry strategy into new business areas, yet hesitate to commit itself to an internal new venture because of the risks and costs of building a new operation up from the ground floor. Such a situation is most likely to occur when a company sees the possibility of establishing a new business in an embryonic or growth industry but the risks and costs associated with the project are more than it is willing to assume on its own. In these circumstances, the company may decide to enter into a joint venture with another company and use the joint venture as a vehicle for entering the new business area. Such an arrangement enables the company to share the substantial risks and costs posed by the new project. In addition, a joint venture makes sense when a company can increase the probability of successfully establishing a new business by joining forces with another company. For a company that has some of the skills and assets necessary to establish a successful new venture, teaming up with another company that has *complementary* skills and assets may increase the probability of success.

Consider the joint venture between United Technologies and Dow Chemical to build plastic-based composite parts for the aerospace industry. United Technologies was already involved in the aerospace industry (it built Sikorsky helicopters), and Dow Chemical had skills in the development and manufacture of plastic-based composites. The alliance called for United Technologies to contribute its advanced aerospace skills and for Dow to contribute its skills in developing and manufacturing plastic-based composites to a joint venture in which each company would have a 50 percent equity stake. The joint venture was to undertake the task of developing, manufacturing, and marketing a new line of plastic-based composite parts for the aerospace industry. Through the venture, both companies would become involved in new activities. They would, in short, be able to realize some of the benefits associated with related diversification without having to merge activities formally or bear the costs and risks of developing the new products on their own.

There are three main drawbacks to joint venture arrangements. First, a joint venture allows a company to share the risks and costs of developing a new business, but it also requires the sharing of profits if the new business succeeds. Second, the venture partners must share control. If the partners have different business philosophies, time horizons, or investment preferences, substantial problems can arise. Conflicts over how to run the joint venture can tear it apart and result in business failure. Third, a company that enters into a joint venture always runs the risk of giving critical know-how away to its joint venture partner, which might use that know-how to compete directly with the company in the future. For example, having gained access to Dow's expertise in plastic-based composites, United Technologies might dissolve the alliance and produce these materials on its own. However, such risk can be minimized if Dow gets a *credible commitment* from United Technologies. By entering into a formal joint venture rather than a more loosely structured alliance, United Technologies has given such a commitment because it has had to invest substantial amounts of capital. Thus if United Technologies tried to produce plastic-based composites on its own, it would essentially be competing against itself.

In sum, although joint ventures often have a distinct advantage over internal new venturing as a means of establishing a new business operation, they also have certain drawbacks. When deciding whether to go it alone or cooperate with another company in a joint venture, strategic managers need to assess the pros and cons of the alternatives carefully.

Restructuring

So far we have focused on strategies for expanding the scope of a company and entering into new business areas. We turn now to their opposite: strategies for reducing the scope of the company by *exiting* business areas. Reducing the scope of a company through restructuring has become an increasingly popular strategy, particularly among the companies that diversified their activities during the 1980s and 1990s. In most cases, companies that are engaged in restructuring are divesting themselves of diversified activities in order to concentrate on fewer businesses.[44] For example, in 1996 AT&T spun off its telecommunications equipment business (Lucent), and after acquiring two large cable TV companies in the late 1990s, AT&T sold its cable unit off to rival cable TV provider Comcast for $72 billion in 2002.

The first question that must be asked is why so many companies are restructuring at this time. After answering it, we examine the strategies that companies adopt for exiting from business areas. Then we discuss the various turnaround strategies that companies employ to revitalize their core business area.

Why Restructure?

A prime reason that extensively diversified companies restructure is that in recent years, the stock market has assigned a diversification discount to the stock of such enterprises.[45] The **diversification discount** refers to the empirical fact that the stock of highly diversified companies is often assigned a lower valuation relative to their earnings than the stock of less diversified enterprises. Investors apparently see highly diversified companies as less attractive investments than more focused enterprises. There are two reasons for this. First, investors are often put off by the complexity and lack of transparency in the consolidated financial statements of highly diversified enterprises, which do not give them a good picture of how the individual parts of the company are performing. In other words, they perceive the company as being a riskier investment than more focused companies, precisely because their financial statements are difficult to interpret. In such cases, restructuring tends to be an attempt to boost the returns to shareholders by splitting up the company into a number of parts.

A second reason for the diversification discount is that many investors have learned from experience that managers often have a tendency to pursue too much diversification, or diversify for the wrong reasons, such as the pursuit of growth for its own sake, rather than the pursuit of greater profitability.[46] We discussed this phenomenon earlier in the chapter. Suffice it to say that some senior managers have a tendency to expand the scope of their company beyond that point where the bureaucratic costs of managing extensive diversification exceed the additional value that can be created, and the performance of the company begins to decline. Restructuring in such cases is often a response to declining financial performance.

Restructuring can also be a response to failed acquisitions. This is true whether the acquisitions were made to support a horizontal integration, vertical integration, or diversification strategy. We noted earlier in the chapter that many acquisitions fail to deliver the anticipated gains. When this is the case, management often responds by cutting losses and exiting from the acquired business. Since there was a merger and acquisition boom between 1996 and 2000, if history is any guide we would expect to see this followed by a wave of restructurings as companies exit from businesses acquired during the boom, as indeed seems to be occurring.

A final factor of some importance in restructuring trends is that innovations in management processes and strategy have diminished the advantages of vertical integration or diversification. In response, companies have reduced the scope of their activities through restructuring and divestments. For example, ten years ago, there was little understanding of how long-term cooperative relationships between a company and its suppliers could be a viable alternative to vertical integration. Most companies considered only two alternatives for managing the supply chain: vertical integration or competitive bidding. As we noted in Chapter 9, however, if the conditions are right, a third alternative for managing the supply chain, *long-term contracting,* can be a superior strategy to both vertical integration and competitive bidding. Like vertical integration, long-term contracting facilitates investments in specialization. But unlike vertical integration, it does not involve high bureaucratic costs or dispense with market discipline. As this strategic innovation has spread throughout the business world, the relative advantages of vertical integration have declined.

Exit Strategies   Companies can choose from three main strategies for exiting business areas: divestment, harvest, and liquidation. You have already encountered all three in Chapter 6, where we discussed strategies for competing in declining industries. We review them briefly here.

Divestment. Of the three main strategies, divestment is usually favored. It represents the best way for a company to recoup as much of its initial investment in a business unit as possible. The idea is to sell the business unit to the highest bidder. Three types of buyers are independent investors, other companies, and the management of the unit to be divested. Selling off a business unit to independent investors, normally referred to as a **spinoff,** makes good sense when the unit to be sold is profitable and the stock market has an appetite for new stock issues (which is normal during market upswings but *not* during market downswings). Thus, for example, in 1992 the timber products company Weyerhaeuser successfully spun off its Paragon Trade

Brands to independent investors. Investors snapped up the stock of the new issue, which makes "own label" disposable diapers for supermarket chains and is highly profitable. Spinoffs do not work if the unit to be spun off is unprofitable and unattractive to independent investors or if the stock market is slumping and unresponsive to new issues.

Selling off a unit to another company is a strategy frequently pursued when a unit can be sold to a company in the same line of business as the unit. In such cases, the purchaser is often prepared to pay a considerable amount of money for the opportunity to substantially increase the size of its business virtually overnight.

Selling off a unit to its management is normally referred to as a **management buyout (MBO):** the unit is sold to its management, which often finances the purchase through the sale of high-yield bonds to investors. The bond issue is normally arranged by a buyout specialist, which along with management will typically hold a sizable proportion of the shares in the MBO. MBOs often take place when financially troubled units have only two other options: a harvest strategy or liquidation.

An MBO can be very risky for the management team, since its members may have to sign personal guarantees to back up the bond issue and may lose everything if the MBO ultimately fails. If the management team succeeds in turning around the troubled unit, its reward can be a significant increase in personal wealth. Thus, an MBO strategy can be characterized as a *high risk–high return* strategy for the management team. Faced with the possible liquidation of their business unit, many management teams are willing to take the risk. However, the viability of this option depends not only on a willing management team, but also on there being enough buyers of high yield–high risk bonds—so-called junk bonds—to be able to finance the MBO. In recent years, the general slump in the junk bond market has made the MBO strategy a more difficult one for companies to follow.

Harvest and Liquidation. A harvest or liquidation strategy is generally considered inferior to a divestment strategy because the company can probably best recoup its investment in a business unit by divestment. Second, a harvest strategy means halting investment in a unit in order to maximize short- to medium-term cash flow from that unit before liquidating it. Although this strategy seems fine in theory, it is often a poor one to apply in practice. Once it becomes apparent that the unit is pursuing a harvest strategy, the morale of the unit's employees, as well as the confidence of the unit's customers and suppliers in its continuing operation, can sink quickly. If this occurs, as it often does, the rapid decline in the unit's revenues can make the strategy untenable. Finally, a liquidation strategy is the least attractive of all to pursue since it requires the company to write off its investment in a business unit, often at a considerable cost. For a poorly performing business unit where a selloff or spinoff is unlikely and where an MBO cannot be arranged, it may be the only viable alternative.

Summary of Chapter

1. Managers often first consider diversification when their company is generating free cash flow, which are financial resources in excess of those necessary to maintain a competitive advantage in the company's original, or core, business.

2. A diversified company can create value by (a) transferring competencies among existing businesses, (b) leveraging competencies to create new businesses, (c) sharing resources to realize economies of scope, (d) using diversification as a means of managing rivalry in one or more industries, and (e) exploiting general organizational competencies that enhance the

performance of all business units within a diversified company. The bureaucratic costs of diversification are a function of the number of independent business units within the company and the extent of coordination between those business units.

3. Diversification motivated by a desire to pool risks or achieve greater growth is often associated with the dissipation of value.

4. There are three vehicles that companies use to enter new business areas: internal ventures, acquisition, and joint ventures.

5. Internal new venturing is typically employed as an entry strategy when a company has a set of valuable competencies in its existing businesses that can be leveraged or recombined to enter the new business area.

6. Many internal ventures fail because of entry on too small a scale, poor commercialization, and poor corporate management of the internal venture process. Guarding against failure involves a structured approach toward project selection and management, integration of R&D and marketing to improve commercialization of a venture idea, and entry on a significant scale.

7. Acquisitions are often favored as an entry strategy when the company lacks important competencies (resources and capabilities) required to compete in an area, but it can purchase an incumbent company that has those competencies and do so at a reasonable price. Acquisitions also tend to be favored when the barriers to entry into the target industry are high and the company is unwilling to accept the time frame, development costs, and risks of internal new venturing.

8. Many acquisitions fail because of poor postacquisition integration, overestimation of the value that can be created from an acquisition, the high cost of acquisition, and poor preacquisition screening. Guarding against acquisition failure requires structured screening, good bidding strategies, positive attempts to integrate the acquired company into the organization of the acquiring one, and learning from experience.

9. Joint ventures may be the preferred entry strategy when (a) the risks and costs associated with setting up a new business unit are more than the company is willing to assume on its own and (b) the company can increase the probability of successfully establishing a new business by teaming up with another company that has skills and assets complementing its own.

10. Restructuring is often a response to (a) excessive diversification, (b) failed acquisitions, and (c) innovations in management process that have reduced the advantages of vertical integration and diversification.

11. Exit strategies include divestment, harvest, and liquidation. The choice of exit strategy is governed by the characteristics of the relevant business unit.

Discussion Questions

1. When is a company likely to choose related diversification and when unrelated diversification? Discuss with reference to an electronics manufacturer and an ocean shipping company.

2. Under what circumstances might it be best to enter a new business area by acquisition, and under what circumstances might internal new venturing be the preferred entry mode?

3. Imagine that IBM has decided to diversify into the cellular telecommunication provider business. What entry strategy would you recommend the company pursue? Why?

4. Look at Honeywell's portfolio of businesses (described in Honeywell's 10K statements, which can be accessed on the web at **www.honeywell.com**). How many different industries is Honeywell involved in? Would you describe Honeywell as a related or unrelated diversification company? How do you think that Honeywell's diversification strategy increases profitability?

Practicing Strategic Management

SMALL-GROUP EXERCISE: DUN & BRADSTREET

Break into small groups of three to five people, and appoint one group member as a spokesperson who will communicate your findings to the class when called on to do so by the instructor. Then read the following news release from Dun & Bradstreet. On the basis of this information, identify the strategic rationale for the split and evaluate how the

split might affect the performance three successor companies. If you were a stockholder in the old Dun & Bradstreet Corporation, would you approve of this split? Why?

Dun & Bradstreet CEO Robert E. Weissman today announced a sweeping strategy that will transform the 155-year-old business information giant into three publicly traded, global corporations. "This important action is designed to increase shareholder value by unlocking D&B's substantial underlying franchise strengths," said Weissman.

Building on preeminent Dun & Bradstreet businesses, the reorganization establishes three independent companies focused on high-growth information markets; financial information services; and consumer-product market research.

"Since the 1800s, D&B has grown by effectively managing a portfolio of businesses and gaining economies of scale," stated Weissman. "But the velocity of change in information markets has dramatically altered the rules of business survival. Today, market focus and speed are the primary drivers of competitive advantage. This plan is our blueprint for success in the 21st century," said Weissman.

The plan, approved today at a special meeting of D&B's board of directors, calls for D&B to create three separate companies by spinning off two of its businesses to shareholders. "D&B is the leader in business information," said Weissman. "By freeing our companies to tightly focus on our core vertical markets, we can more rapidly leverage this leadership position into emerging growth areas."

The three new companies are:

- Cognizant Corporation, a new high-growth company, including IMS International, the leading global supplier of marketing information to the pharmaceutical and healthcare industries; Nielsen Media Research, the leader in audience measurement for electronic media; and Gartner Group, the premier provider of advisory services to high-tech users, vendors and suppliers, in which Cognizant will hold a majority interest.
- The Dun & Bradstreet Corporation, consisting of Dun & Bradstreet Information Services, the world's largest source of business-to-business marketing and commercial-credit information; Moody's Investors Service, a global leader in rating debt; and Reuben H. Donnelley, a premier provider of Yellow Pages marketing and publishing.
- A. C. Nielsen, the global leader in marketing information for the fast-moving consumer packaged goods industry.

"These three separate companies will tailor their strategies to the unique demands of their markets, determining investments, capital structures and policies that will strengthen their respective global capabilities. This plan also clarifies D&B from an investor's perspective by grouping the businesses into three logical investment categories, each with distinct risk/reward profiles," said Weissman.

The Dun & Bradstreet Corporation is the world's largest marketer of information, software and services for business decision-making, with worldwide revenue of $4.9 billion in 1994.

ARTICLE FILE 10

Find an example of a company that has made an acquisition that apparently failed to create any value. Identify and critically evaluate the rationale that top management used to justify the acquisition when it was made. Explain why the acquisition subsequently failed.

STRATEGIC MANAGEMENT PROJECT: MODULE 10

This module requires you to assess your company's use of acquisitions, internal new ventures, and joint ventures as strategies for entering a new business area or as attempts to restructure its portfolio of businesses.

A. If your company has entered a new business area during the past decade

1. Pick one new business area that your company has entered during the past ten years.
2. Identify the rationale for entering this business area.
3. Identify the strategy used to enter this business area.
4. Evaluate the rationale for using this particular entry strategy. Do you think that this was the best entry strategy to use? Justify your answer.
5. Do you think that the addition of this business area to the company has added or dissipated value? Again, justify your answer.

B. If your company has restructured its business during the past decade

1. Identify the rationale for pursuing a restructuring strategy.
2. Pick one business area that your company has exited from during the past ten years.
3. Identify the strategy used to exit from this particular business area. Do you think that this was the best exit strategy to use? Justify your answer.
4. In general, do you think that exiting from this business area has been in the company's best interest?

EXPLORING THE WEB
Visiting General Electric

Visit the web site of General Electric Company of the United States (**www.ge.com**). Using the information contained on that web site, answer the following questions.

1. Review GE's portfolio of major businesses. Does this portfolio make sense from a value creation perspective? Why?
2. What (if any) changes would you make to GE's portfolio of businesses? Why would you make these changes?
3. What (if any) core competencies do you think are held in common by one or more of GE's major business units? Is there any evidence that GE creates new businesses by leveraging its core competencies?

General Task: By searching through information sources on the Web, find an example of a company that has recently restructured its portfolio of businesses. Identify and evaluate the strategic rationale behind this restructuring to determine whether it makes sense.

Closing Case

The Changing Boundaries of AT&T, 1995–2002

On September 20, 1995, AT&T, the world's largest telecommunications company with annual revenues of $75 billion, announced that it would split itself into three independent companies. The largest of these, which was to retain the AT&T name, would manage the company's long-distance, international, and wireless telecommunications businesses. The new AT&T would retain its position as the largest provider of telecommunications service in the world, with 1995 revenues in excess of $50 billion. Second in size of the new companies was to be the network equipment business. Renamed Lucent Technologies, this business generated 1995 revenues of $21 billion and ranked as the third largest provider of telecommunication network equipment in the world after Germany's Alcatel and Motorola of the United States. The smallest of the new companies was AT&T's Global Information Solutions business, a manufacturer of computer systems with annual revenues of $9 billion. Global Information Solutions was built around NCR, a computer company that AT&T had acquired in 1991 for $7.5 billion.

The decision to break up AT&T into three parts was the result of a number of factors that came to a head in the mid-1990s. First was the impending deregulation of the U.S. telecommunications industry. After deregulation (which occurred in 1996), local and long-distance telephone companies would be free to enter each other's markets. AT&T would face more competition in its core long-distance business as the Regional Bell Operating Companies (RBOCs) tried to enter this market. At the same time, AT&T would be able to enter the local phone businesses and compete directly against the RBOCs. Second was the privatization of state-owned telephone companies around the world and the deregulation of many foreign telephone markets. These developments created enormous opportunities for AT&T, which for the first time saw the possibility of building a truly global telephone network by forming alliances with newly privatized telephone companies, and by entering foreign markets. Third was rapid change in the telecommunications business as new technologies, such as wireless communications and the Internet, created significant opportunities and threats for AT&T. Faced with such changes in its operating environment, AT&T's management decided that they needed to focus all their energies and resources on the company's core telecommunications business, unencumbered by the distractions presented by the network equipment and computer businesses.

There was also an understanding on the part of AT&T's management that the performance of the computer and network equipment businesses had suffered as a result of its association with AT&T. The equipment business was trying to sell products to companies that competed directly against AT&T, such as MCI and Sprint, or would compete against AT&T after deregulation, such as the RBOCs. These potential customers were increasingly reluctant to purchase equipment from a supplier that was also a competitor. For example, just before the breakup was announced, Motorola beat AT&T to an $800 million order for wireless telecommunications equipment from GTE. GTE had long been one of AT&T's largest equipment customers, but now it faced the threat of competing against AT&T in the local phone business. Freed from its association with AT&T, the network equipment business would have a greater chance of capturing business from other telephone service providers.

As for the computer business, this was forecast to lose around $1 billion in 1995. Although AT&T had always had some significant computer skills—after all, many network equipment products, such as digital switches, are essentially specialized computers—it had never been able to establish a profitable computer operation. During the 1980s, it had lost billions of dollars trying to establish a presence in the personal computer market through an internal new venture. Moreover, its 1991 acquisition of NCR, an attempt to strengthen this venture, turned out to be a disaster, partly because the computer market shifted away from the kind of customized equipment provided by NCR, and partly because there was a clash between the management cultures of the two companies that led to high management turnover in the acquired unit. Many now felt that AT&T's deep pockets had kept the computer operation in markets that it should have exited years ago, such as the personal computer market. They believed that an independent computer operation might be more responsive to market demands and would not be burdened by the clashing cultural heritage of AT&T and NCR.

Having completed its exit from the equipment and computer businesses, in 1999 AT&T purchased two large providers of cable TV: TCI and Media One. The theory behind the acquisitions was that AT&T would be able to use cable to offer local phone service to its customers, in addition to long-distance service, and just as important, to avoid paying access fees to local phone companies (the

RBOCs). Prior to the acquisitions, AT&T had no direct access to its customers and had to use the phone lines of local phone companies to *originate* and *terminate* calls for its long-distance customers. AT&T had to pay the local phone companies a *termination fee* for every phone call routed through their lines. The termination fee amounted to about 35 percent of the cost of every phone call made through AT&T's network. AT&T's hope was that it could use coaxial cable to originate and terminate calls to residential customers, thereby avoiding the termination fee and saving substantial costs.

The cable strategy did not work out as planned. After making the acquisition, AT&T discovered that it would cost billions of dollars to upgrade the cable TV systems so that they could also handle phone calls. Moreover, AT&T took on $56 billion in debt to finance the acquisitions of TCI and Media One. With billions more needing to be spent before it could offer phone service over cable, AT&T concluded that it would be years before it could generate sufficient income from these assets to cover the costs of serving existing and additional debt, so the CEO decided to cut the company's losses and sell the cable TV assets to the highest bidder. That turned out to be Comcast, another cable TV company, which paid AT&T $72 billion for these assets.

Case Discussion Questions

1. What changes in AT&T's operating environment triggered its 1995 decision to break the company up into three entities?

2. How might the breakup create value for shareholders?

3. Does the 1995 breakup imply that AT&T's pre-1995 strategic vision was seriously flawed?

4. Was the strategic rationale for acquiring TCI and Media One sound? If so, why did AT&T reverse course and sell off its cable assets in 2002? How might AT&T have handled this whole episode differently?

Sources: T. Jackson, "Giant Bows to Colossal Pressure," *Financial Times,* September 22, 1995, p. 13. "AT&T's Three Way Split," *Economist,* September 23, 1995, pp. 51–52. "Fatal Attraction," *Economist,* March 23, 1996, pp. 73–74. A. Ramirez, "Opportunity and New Risk for a Spinoff," *New York Times,* September 22, 1995, pp. C1, C4. J. Krause, "The Last AT&T Story," *Telephony,* February 4, 2002, pp. 32–40. "Comcast Hangs in to Win Auction for AT&T Cable," *Mergers and Acquisitions* (February 2002): 10–11.

Corporate Performance, Governance, and Business Ethics

11

Opening Case

The Fall of Enron

In early December 2001, the Enron Corporation filed for Chapter 11 bankruptcy protection. Enron, which started off as a natural gas pipeline operator and independent power producer, had emerged during the late 1990s as the principal player in the rapidly expanding market for energy trading. At its height in 2000, the company had boasted revenues of $101 billion, a stock market capitalization of $63 billion, and a chairman, Kenneth Lay, who was a high-profile confidant of then President-elect George W. Bush. The company was leveraging its expertise in energy trading to other market opportunities, including trading in paper, metals, water, and telecommunication capacity (or broadband). Enron believed that it could exploit the power of the Internet to create online markets in almost anything. The media loved the company. In 2000, *Fortune* magazine voted Enron "the most innovative company of the year." The *Economist* wrote that Enron "has created what may be the most successful Internet venture of any company in any industry anywhere."

A few months after these words were written, Enron had ceased to exist as a functioning entity. On its last trading day, the stock stood at 61 cents per share, down from a high of $90 just a year earlier. Numbered among the stockholders who had seen their Enron holdings implode in value were many Enron employees, who had been obliged by company policies to hold Enron stock in their retirement accounts.

What made the collapse of Enron so disturbing was not just the size of the failure, but the manner in which the company unraveled. What bought Enron down so rapidly was an accumulation of more than $27 billion in off-balance-sheet debt held by partnerships hidden from the view of most investors, employees, and regulators. These partnerships were set up to exploit Enron's forays into ever more exotic online trading ventures, such as water and bandwidth trading. The partnerships were controlled by Enron managers but not owned by Enron, so the debt did not appear on Enron's balance sheets and thus did not affect the company's credit rating and borrowing costs. The partnerships were financed with debt raised from institutional investors. Using the company's high-flying stock as collateral, Enron guaranteed that debt. It often transferred its own assets to the partnerships, registering the transfer as revenues.

The partnerships were the brainchild of Enron's chief financial officer, Andrew Fastow, who used the partnership as a way of making Enron's balance sheet and earnings look stronger than they really were. Fastow also personally profited from the partnerships, many of which he controlled, reportedly making over $30 million from them. The partnership strategy, however, was very risky. If the aggressive investments the partnerships were making did not pan out, Enron, as the guarantor of partnership debt, would be on the hook. Moreover, if Enron's stock fell too far, guarantees backed by stock would have be replaced by cash, which would require Enron to raise more debt.

The first cracks in Enron's facade started to appear in August 2001 when the CEO, Jeffrey Skilling, suddenly and unexpectedly resigned, citing "personal reasons." Skilling had sold some $17.5 million of Enron stock in the months before he quit. Chairman Kenneth Lay, himself the former CEO, stepped back into the CEO position and reassured investors, spooked by Skilling's sudden departure. Then in October 2001, Enron recorded a third-quarter loss of $618 million and announced that it was reducing shareholder equity by $1.2 billion, primarily because of losses accumulated at partnerships. Enron's

stock, which had lost half its value since December 2000, suddenly plummeted. This created a death spiral in which Enron had to raise debt to guarantee debt accumulated at partnerships, a spiral that quickly led to bankruptcy.

When the existence of the partnerships was revealed, the financial community was stunned: there had been scarcely a reference to any of them in Enron's audited financial statements. By implication, investors were ignorant of the tremendous risks associated with the partnership strategy. It was difficult to escape the conclusion that Enron's management had deliberately played down the existence of the partnerships in order to mislead the financial markets about the true state of the company. Questions were also asked about Enron's auditor, Arthur Andersen. Why had it not drawn attention to the partnerships? Surely as auditor, it must have known about them? Why had Andersen apparently agreed with the tactic of keeping these partnerships hidden from public view? Was it to protect a lucrative financial relationship with an important client? Enron paid Andersen some $52 million in 2000—$25 million for auditing and $27 million for consulting services. The questions about Andersen's role became even sharper when it was revealed that the Andersen partner responsible for the Enron audit had instructed his staff to shred documents relating to the audit. Was Andersen trying to hide what it had known about the true financial state of the company?

The voices of critics grew louder when it was discovered that in August 2001, a midlevel Enron official, Sherron Watkins, had sent a memo to Kenneth Lay outlining the risks associated with the partnership strategy. Watkins warned Lay that Enron could implode in a wave of accounting scandals. Lay apparently expressed concern but continued to present a bullish face to the outside world and appears to have done nothing to rein in the CFO, Fastow. Lay moved to replace Fastow only on October 24, two days after the Securities and Exchange Commission announced that it had started an investigation into Enron's accounting practices. Worse still, throughout 2001, Enron's senior managers continued to sell millions of dollars of their own holdings in Enron's stock, while many employees were limited or prohibited from selling the Enron stock they held in their retirement accounts. Did the managers know something that they kept hidden from their own employees?

In the aftermath of Enron's collapse, the U.S. Congress announced that it would investigate allegations of financial misdealings at the company. Called before a House Committee, Lay and Fastow took the Fifth, while Skilling claimed ignorance of the details of the partnership dealings. Was the law broken? It looks that way. In August 2002, one senior Enron executive had pleaded guilty to money laundering and conspiracy charges, and agreed to cooperate with the government in bringing possible charges against other executives, including former CFO Fastow, whom the Justice Department named as an "unindicted co-conspirator in the fraud case." What seems clear is that billions of dollars in shareholder value evaporated and thousands of employees lost their jobs, while senior managers enriched themselves, because those same managers pursued very risky and highly leveraged strategies that were deliberately concealed from public view. Worse, this seems to have occurred with the blessing of the very people who were meant to expose the truth about a company's financial position to the public: the company's auditors, in this case Arthur Andersen.

Sources: "Why Honesty Is the Best Policy," *Economist,* March 9, 2002. "The Amazing Disintegrating Firm—Enron," *Economist,* December 8, 2001. Wendy Zellner et al., "The Fall of Enron," *Business Week,* December 17, 2001, pp. 30–40. Ken Brown et al., "Paper Trail: Andersen Fires Partner It Says Led Shredding of Enron Documents," *Wall Street Journal,* January 16, 2002, p. A1. Johnathan Weil, "Justice Department finds Building a Case Against Lay Tough," *Wall Street Journal,* August 26, 2002, p. A3.

Overview

The collapse of Enron raises troubling questions about corporate performance, corporate governance, and business ethics. It is now clear that at the very least, several senior managers at Enron behaved in an unethical manner, deliberately misleading shareholders and employees about the true state of the company's performance. It would seem that they did this to continue to meet the high financial performance expectations that they themselves had established for the company. By setting and then meeting these expectations, they hoped that Enron's stock price would continue to skyrocket, giving them the opportunity to exercise stock options for substantial personal gain. It is hard to escape the conclusion that senior managers at Enron deliberately misstated the true financial state of the company to enrich themselves. The losers in this process were key stakeholders in Enron: the company's stockholders, creditors, and employees.

Increasingly, the corporate scandals at companies like Enron and Arthur Andersen and the huge across-the-board decline in stock prices that occurred in 2001–2002 have the public asking, "What is happening in the world of business today?" Why is it that people like Ken Lay at Enron and Bernie Ebbers at WorldCom can take hundreds of millions in dollars out of their companies through their stock options, yet their shareholders have lost hundreds of billions of dollars in the value of their stock either directly or through their pension plans? Moreover, many thousands of hardworking Enron and WorldCom managers and employees have lost their jobs, and customers have received poorer-quality goods and services (customer complaints at WorldCom are increasing, and Enron is being investigated for its role in artificially manipulating the supply of electricity to California homes, which boosted its profits but contributed to the rolling blackouts experienced in California in 2001.)

This chapter examines the many important factors and issues that may prevent a company's strategies from being implemented in ways that raise corporate performance and lead to superior profitability. This chapter is concerned with how to ensure that managers implement strategies that are in the long-run interests of key stakeholders of the company, such as stockholders and employees. Corporate governance and business ethics are tools that can be put in place to make sure the interests of stakeholders are recognized and incorporated into the strategy-making process.

By the end of this chapter, you will understand why managers, when formulating and implementing strategies aimed at establishing a sustainable competitive advantage and superior profitability, should choose those that are legal and ethical and balance the claims of all its stakeholder groups.

The Causes of Poor Performance

Most of this book has been focused on what managers should do to maximize the long-run profitability of their company. The reality, however, is that many companies find it very difficult to earn a rate of return that exceeds their cost of capital—in other words, they are not very profitable. For example, in the air express industry, the cost of capital has been estimated at 12 percent (the cost of capital is the return that stockholders and bond holders expect on their investment of capital in the company). Between 1996 and 2001, UPS's average return on invested capital (ROIC) was 17.9 percent, Federal Express earned an average of 10.8 percent and Airborne Express 8 percent.[1] The implication is that neither Federal Express nor Airborne generated a return that exceeded their cost of capital. They were not good investments. This situation is not uncommon. In most industries, there are companies that are unable to generate a return on invested capital that exceeds their cost of capital and therefore are not performing up to the expectations of investors.

Sometimes poor performance is temporary, caused primarily by short-term declines in demand for an industry's product due to recessionary conditions; once demand recovers, so does company profitability. However, for other companies, poor performance is a persistent problem. Kmart, for example, has underperformed Wal-Mart for years and now is in Chapter 11 bankruptcy proceedings. DaimlerChrysler has been underperforming its primary rivals in the global automobile industry for several years.

Six causes of persistent poor performance stand out in most case studies of persistent poor performance:[2]

- Poor management
- A high cost structure
- A lack of adequate differentiation
- Overexpansion
- Structural shifts in demand and new competitors
- Organization inertia

Normally several, if not all, of these factors are present in a decline. For example, IBM's poor financial performance in the early 1990s was brought on by structural shifts in demand away from mainframe computers and toward client-server networks based on PCs, compounded by the emergence of powerful new competitors such as Compaq and Dell. IBM's slow response to these problems was due to poor senior management and organizational inertia.

Poor Management

Poor management covers a multitude of sins, ranging from sheer incompetence to neglect of core businesses and an insufficient number of good managers. One-person rule is not necessarily a bad thing, but it often seems to be at the root of poor management. One study found that the presence of a dominant and autocratic chief executive with a passion for empire-building strategies often characterizes many failing companies.[3] Another study of eighty-one turnaround situations found that in thirty-six cases, troubled companies suffered from an autocratic manager who tried to do it all and, in the face of complexity and change, could not.[4] In a review of the empirical studies of turnaround situations, Richard Hoffman identified a number of other management defects commonly found in poorly performing companies.[5] These included a lack of balanced expertise at the top (e.g., too many engineers), a lack of strong middle management, a failure to provide for orderly management succession by a departing CEO (which may result in an internal succession battle), and a failure by the board of directors to monitor management's strategic decisions adequately.

As we shall see later in the chapter, poor management also includes executives who pursue strategies designed to enrich themselves at the expense of stockholders, employees, and other stakeholders. Such strategic actions often depress the overall profitability of the company. In theory, the board of directors exists to hire, evaluate, and, if necessary, replace, the senior management of the company, and particularly the CEO. As such, the board should be in a position to make sure that such a situation does not occur. However, as we will see later in the chapter when we return to this issue and consider it in depth, many boards do not do their jobs.

High Cost Structure

A high cost structure will make it difficult for a company to earn a decent return on its invested capital. The two main causes of a high cost structure are low labor productivity and low capital productivity. Low labor productivity may stem from union-imposed restrictive working practices (as in the case of the auto and steel industries), management's failure to invest in labor-saving technologies or technologies that can boost the productivity of employees (such as information technology), and an organization that does not create incentives for employees to work productively. Low capital productivity can be due to failure to fully use the fixed assets of a company, such as its property, plant, and equipment. For example, a failure to use production capacity fully because of low market share can result in an inability to attain economies of scale and high unit costs. Low capital productivity can also be due to a failure to minimize working capital, by, for example, holding too much inventory.

Low employee and capital productivity can often be traced to deeper problems within an organization, such as inadequate financial controls. The most common aspect of inadequate financial controls is a failure to assign profit responsibility to key decision makers within the organization. A lack of accountability for the financial consequences of their actions can encourage middle-level managers to employ excess staff and spend resources beyond what is necessary for maximum efficiency. In such cases, bureaucracy may balloon and costs spiral out of control. In addition, a lack of adequate financial controls can lead managers to waste capital resources in unproductive investments. Just how this problem might be avoided is another topic that we return to later in the chapter.

Inadequate Differentiation

A lack of adequate differentiation can make it difficult for a company to earn a decent return on its invested capital. Inadequate differentiation has a number of sources, including poor product quality and a lack of compelling product attributes, such as superior features, performance, and styling. It means that a company will lack the ability to charge a premium price for its goods and services or the ability to hold prices low and use its superior differentiation as a tool for increasing sales volume and attaining scale economies. Either way, the net effect is to lower the profitability of the enterprise below what it might otherwise have been.

Inadequate differentiation can often be traced to deeper problems in the organization. For example, a failure to establish and properly manage cross-functional product development teams (see Chapter 4 for details) may mean that the company's product development efforts fall short, and its products lack the differential features and functions of those produced by competitors. Similarly, a failure to implement quality improvement processes, such as the Six Sigma quality improvement methodology discussed in Chapter 4, may result in poor product quality and, consequently, a negative perception of the company's products in the minds of consumers.

Overexpansion The empire-building strategies of autocratic CEOs often involve rapid expansion and extensive diversification. Later in this chapter, we examine why a CEO might pursue empire-building strategies. For now, note that much of this diversification tends to be poorly conceived and adds little value to a company. As pointed out in Chapter 9, the consequences of too much diversification include loss of control and declining profitability. Moreover, companies that expand rapidly tend to do so by taking on large amounts of debt. This can subsequently place a huge financial burden on the company if economic conditions deteriorate and the company is no longer able to generate the cash flows required to service its debt payments.

Something like this happened to Tyco International, the acquisitive conglomerate profiled in the *Opening Case* to Chapter 10. Tyco expanded during the economic boom years of the 1990s, in part by using borrowed money (debt raised through bond issues) to finance ever larger acquisitions. As long as the economy remained strong, Tyco was able to generate the free cash flow required to service its debt commitments. However, as the economy weakened in 2000–2001, Tyco found itself struggling to generate the required cash flows and had to start selling off some of its previously acquired businesses, often at a considerable discount to their original purchase price, in order to raise the necessary cash. A similar problem beset WorldCom, profiled in the *Opening Case* to Chapter 9.

Structural Shifts in Demand and New Competitors A **structural shift** in demand is one that is permanent, as opposed to a temporary cyclical shift due to short-term macroeconomic conditions. Structural shifts in demand can be brought about by major changes in technology, economic or political conditions, and social and cultural norms. Although such changes can open up market opportunities for new competitors, they also revolutionize industry structure and threaten the existence of many established enterprises, necessitating restructuring. For example, changing social habits have lead to a structural decline in consumption of breakfast cereal in the United States (people are substituting bagels and muffins for cereal). The result is that the profitability of major cereal companies such as Kellogg's has come under pressure in the face of declining revenue. In many cases, structural shifts in demand are difficult to anticipate, but once they occur, they can cause major problems for established companies. IBM's troubles in the early 1990s were in part due to a structural shift in demand away from mainframe computers and toward client server networks.

New competitors often go hand in hand with structural shifts in demand, particularly when the shift is caused by the arrival of a new technology. New competitors riding the wave of a new disruptive technology can revolutionize competition in an industry, making it very difficult for established enterprises to survive, a topic that we discussed in depth in Chapter 7.

Organizational Inertia On their own, the emergence of powerful new competition and a structural shift in demand might not be enough to cause declining performance. What is also required is an organization that is slow to respond to such environmental changes. **Organizational inertia,** the inability of an organization to adapt in a timely manner to new circumstances, stands out as a major reason that companies are often so slow to respond to new competitive conditions.

Organizational inertia is complex and has a number of underlying causes.[6] One source is the existing distribution of power and influence within an organization.[7] The power and influence that individual managers enjoy is in part a function of their role in the organization hierarchy, as defined by structural position. By definition, most substantive changes in an organization require a change in structure and, by extension, a change in the internal distribution of power and influence. Some individuals will see their power and influence increase as a result of organization change, and some will see the converse. In general, managers whose power and influence is reduced as a consequence of organization change can be expected to resist it, primarily by arguing that the change might not work. To the extent that they are successful, this constitutes a source of organization inertia that might slow or stop change.

Another source of organization inertia is the existing culture of an organization, as expressed in norms and value systems. Value systems in particular reflect deeply held beliefs, and they can be very hard to change. If the formal and informal socialization mechanisms within an organization have been emphasizing a consistent set of values for a prolonged period of time, and if hiring, promotion, and incentive systems have all reinforced these values, then suddenly announcing that those values are no longer appropriate and need to be changed can quite naturally produce resistance and dissonance among the employees of an organization.

Organization inertia might also derive from preconceptions about the appropriate business model that is held in the heads of senior managers. The Icarus paradox explored in Chapter 3 notes the tendency of companies to continue to rely on the skills and capabilities that made them successful even when those capabilities do not match the new competitive environment.[8] When a particular business model has worked well in the past, managers might have difficulties accepting that it is no longer appropriate. Such cognitive myopia can result in an inability to accept the need for change until serious problems have already developed.

Strategic Change: Improving Performance

Improving the profitability of a company suffering from persistently low profitability usually involves a substantial turnaround in the way a company operates and the strategies it pursues. There is no standard model of how a company should respond to a decline in its profitability. Indeed, there can be no such model because every situation is unique. However, in most successful turnaround situations, a number of common features are present: changing the leadership, changing the strategy of the company, and changing the organization so that it can better implement the new strategy.

Changing the Leadership

Because the old leadership bears the stigma of failure, new leadership is an essential element of most turnaround situations. Often the new leader is from outside the company. For example, as the first step in implementing a turnaround, IBM replaced CEO John Akers with outsider Lou Gerstner. New leadership from outside may be necessary because the existing managers have been socialized into the long-established ways of operating within the company and might find it very difficult to see how things might be done differently. To resolve a crisis, the new leader should be able to make difficult decisions, motivate lower-level managers, listen to the views of others, and delegate power when appropriate.

Changing the Strategy

In many cases, poor profitability reflects a failed strategy that has left the company saddled with high costs, inadequate differentiation, and, perhaps, too many unprofitable lines of business. It follows that changing the strategy of the company is often a central ingredient of a successful turnaround. For a single-business enterprise, redefining strategic focus involves a reevaluation of the company's business-level strategy. A failed cost leader, for example, may reorient toward a more focused or differentiated strategy. For a diversified company, redefining strategic focus means identifying the businesses in the portfolio that have the best long-term profit and growth prospects and concentrating investment there.

Having redefined its strategic focus, a company should divest as many unwanted assets as it can find buyers for and liquidate whatever remains. It is important not to confuse unwanted assets with unprofitable assets. Assets that no longer fit in with the redefined strategic focus of the company may be very profitable. Their sale can bring the company much-needed cash, which it can invest in improving the operations that remain.

Improving the profitability of the operations that remain after asset sales and closures takes a number of steps to improve efficiency, quality, innovation, and customer responsiveness. (We discuss many of the functional-level strategies that companies can pursue to achieve these ends in Chapter 5, so you may want to review that chapter.) Note, though, that improving profitability typically involves one or more of the following: (1) laying off excess employees, (2) investing in productivity-enhancing equipment, (3) assigning profit responsibility to individuals and subunits within the company, by a change of organizational structure if necessary, (4) tightening financial controls, (5) cutting back on marginal products, (6) reengineering business process to cut costs and boost productivity, and (7) introducing total quality management processes.

Finally, a somewhat surprising but quite common turnaround strategy is to make acquisitions, primarily to strengthen the competitive position of a company's remaining core operations. For example, Champion International Corporation used to be a very diversified company, manufacturing a wide range of paper and wood products. After years of declining performance, Champion in the mid-1980s decided to focus on its profitable newsprint and magazine paper business. The company divested many of its other paper and wood products businesses, but at the same time it paid $1.8 billion for St. Regis Corp., one of the country's largest manufacturers of newsprint and magazine paper.

Changing the Organization

Changing leadership and strategy are by themselves not enough to improve the profitability of a poorly performing company. The organization itself must also be changed so that the company can better implement its strategy. The basic principles for successful organization change can be summarized as follows: (1) unfreeze the organization through shock therapy, (2) move the organization to a new state through change in the strategy and structure, and (3) refreeze the organization in its new state.

Unfreezing the Organization.

Due to inertia forces, incremental change is often no change at all. Those whose power is threatened by a change effort can too easily resist incremental change. This leads to the big bang theory of change, which maintains that effective change requires taking bold action early on to "unfreeze" the established culture of an organization and change the distribution of power and influence. Shock therapy to unfreeze the organization might include closing down plants deemed uneconomic or planning and then announcing a dramatic structural reorganization. It is also important to realize that change will not take place unless senior managers are themselves committed to it. Senior managers must be able to articulate the need for change clearly so that employees understand both why it is being pursued and the benefits that will flow from successful change. Senior managers must also be willing to practice what they preach and take the necessary bold steps. If employees see senior managers preaching the need for change but not changing their own behavior or making substantive changes in the organization, they will soon loose faith in the change effort, which will flounder.

Movement. Once an organization has been unfrozen, it must be moved to its new state. Movement requires taking action, including closing down operations; reorganizing the structure; reassigning responsibilities; changing control, incentive, and reward systems; redesigning processes; and letting people go who are seen as an impediment to change. In other words, movement requires a substantial change in the form of a company's strategy and structure so that it matches the desired new strategic posture of the organization. For movement to be successful, it must be done with sufficient speed. Involving employees in the change effort is an excellent way to get them to appreciate and buy into the needs for change and to help with rapid movement. For example, a company might delegate substantial responsibility for designing operating processes to lower-level employees. If enough of their recommendations are then acted on, the employees will see the consequences of their efforts and consequently buy into the notion that change is really taking place.

Refreezing the Organization. Refreezing the organization takes longer. It may require that a new culture be established while the old one is being dismantled. Thus, refreezing requires that employees be socialized into the new way of doing things. Companies often use management education programs to achieve this effect. At General Electric, where long-time CEO Jack Welch instituted a major change in the culture of the company, management education programs were used to communicate new values to organization members. On its own, however, management education programs are not enough. Hiring policies must be changed to reflect the new realities, with an emphasis on hiring individuals whose own values are consistent with that of the new culture the firm is trying to build. Similarly, control and incentive systems must be consistent with the new realities of the organization, or change will never take hold. Equally important, senior management must recognize that changing culture takes a long time. Any let-up in the pressure to change may allow the old culture to reemerge as employees fall back into familiar ways of acting. The communication task facing senior managers therefore is a long-term endeavor that requires managers to be relentless and persistent in their pursuit of change. One of the striking features of Jack Welch's two-decade-long tenure at GE, for example, is that he never stopped pushing his change agenda. It was a consistent theme of his tenure. He was always thinking up new programs and initiatives to keep pushing the culture of the organization along the desired trajectory.

In sum, the successful turnaround of a persistently unprofitable organization requires new leadership, new strategy, and an extensive and ongoing effort to change the organization of the company so that it is aligned with the new strategic objectives. Successfully executing such an effort is perhaps one of the most difficult endeavors in management. However, there are some dramatic examples of companies and management teams that have been successful, including the team that ran IBM under Lou Gerstner and American Express under Harvey Golub. In both cases, these managers led teams that pushed through revolutionary changes in the strategy and organization of the respective companies, transforming them from failing enterprises into successful corporations once again.

Many companies have tried repeatedly to turn themselves around and failed. They either end up going bankrupt or being acquired by competitors for their remaining valuable assets. The big losers in such a process are the stakeholders of the company. In the next section, we look at how managers can reduce the probability of declining corporate performance by taking the interests of stakeholders into account when formulating and implementing strategies.

Stakeholders and Corporate Performance

A company's **stakeholders** are individuals or groups with an interest, claim, or stake in the company, in what it does, and in how well it performs.[9] They include stockholders, creditors, employees, customers, the communities in which the company does business, and the general public. Stakeholders can be divided into internal stakeholders and external stakeholders (see Figure 11.1). **Internal stakeholders** are stockholders and employees, including executive officers, other managers, and board members. **External stakeholders** are all other individuals and groups that have some claim on the company. Typically, this group comprises customers, suppliers, creditors (including banks and bondholders), governments, unions, local communities, and the general public.

All stakeholders are in an exchange relationship with the company. Each of the stakeholder groups listed in Figure 11.1 supplies the organization with important resources (or contributions), and in exchange each expects its interests to be satisfied (by inducements).[10] Stockholders provide the enterprise with risk capital and in exchange expect management to try to maximize the return on their investment. Creditors, and particularly bondholders, also provide the company with capital, and they expect that the interest due to them will be paid on time and in full. Employees provide labor and skills and in exchange expect commensurate income, job satisfaction, job security, and good working conditions. Customers provide a company with its revenues and in exchange want high-quality, reliable products that represent value for money. Suppliers provide a company with inputs and in exchange seek revenues and dependable buyers. Governments provide a company with rules and regulations that govern business practice and maintain fair competition and in exchange want companies that adhere to these rules. Unions help to provide a company with productive employees and in exchange they want benefits for their members in proportion to their contributions to the company. Local communities provide companies with local infrastructure and in exchange want companies that are responsible citizens. The general public provides companies with national infrastructure and in exchange seeks some assurance that the quality of life will be improved as a result of the company's existence.

FIGURE 11.1

Stakeholders and the Enterprise

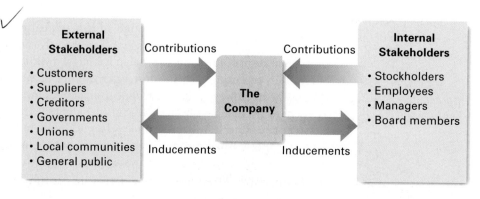

A company must take these claims into account when formulating its strategies, or else stakeholders may withdraw their support. For example, stockholders may sell their shares, bondholders demand higher interest payments on new bonds, employees leave their jobs, and customers buy elsewhere. Suppliers may seek more dependable buyers. Unions may engage in disruptive labor disputes. Government may take civil or criminal action against the company and its top officers, imposing fines and in some cases jail terms. Communities may oppose the company's attempts to locate its facilities in their area, and the general public may form pressure groups, demanding action against companies that impair the quality of life. Any of these reactions can have a damaging impact on an enterprise. A detailed example is given in Strategy in Action 11.1, which looks at how Bill Agee, the former CEO of Morrison Knudson, lost his job because the strategies he pursued failed to satisfy the interests of two important stakeholder groups: the company's employees and its stockholders.

Strategy in Action 11.1

Bill Agee at Morrison Knudsen

Bill Agee made his name as a whiz kid who became the chief financial officer of paper maker Boise Cascade during the 1970s while he was in his early thirties. He left Boise Cascade after the company was forced to write down its profits by $250 million due to earlier overstatements of the value of timberland sales. At the time, the write-downs were the largest in corporate history, but this did not stop Agee from being appointed CEO of defense contractor Bendix in 1976 when he was only thirty-eight years old. At Bendix, Agee became involved in a famous corporate soap opera that began when he promoted a young manager, Mary Cunningham, to a senior post, over the heads of many other more experienced executives. At the time, many felt the promotion occurred because the two were romantically involved. Both denied this, but in 1982 Agee divorced his wife and married Cunningham, who by this time had left Bendix.

In 1988, Agee became CEO of Idaho-based Morrison Knudson (MK), a seventy-five-year-old construction company that had made its name as the prime contractor on a number of large western construction projects, including the Hoover Dam and the Trans Alaska pipeline. By the time Agee joined the company, MK was perceived as a venerable institution that wasn't quite living up to its performance potential. Agee's strategy for improving performance was to sell off certain of MK's assets and invest the proceeds in the securities of other companies. At the same time, he pushed MK to pursue large construction projects aggressively and to develop its rail car manufacturing business. At one time, the rail car manufacturing business had been a major success story at MK, but it had fallen on hard times, unable to hold its own in the face of aggressive competition.

On the surface, MK appeared to be prospering under Agee's leadership. In 1993, MK earned $35.8 million, and Agee proclaimed it a "banner year" and a "watershed period" for the company's drive into railroad and mass transit industries. Underneath the surface, however, things were unraveling for Bill Agee. For one thing, 62 percent of MK's profits in 1993 came from Agee's financial plays in securities trading and capital gains on asset sales. Strip out these one-time gains, and it was clear that the operating performance of MK was poor. A prime reason seems to have been Agee's insistence that in order to win new business, MK should be the low bidder on large contracts. For instance, when MK bid on a contract to build eighty transit cars for the Bay Area Rapid Transit District (BART) in Oakland, California, Agee knocked down the bid to $142 million. According to one insider, the result was that "we were looking at a $14 million loss on the contract the day we won it." In the second quarter of 1994, MK announced a $40.5 million loss after taking a $59.4 million charge for underbidding various transit car contracts. Similarly, in the third quarter of 1994, MK took a $9.2 million charge against profits for underbidding on a $100 million contract to rebuild locomotives for Southern Pacific.

To compound matters, there had been significant employee opposition to Agee's leadership. An anonymous letter sent to MK's board in November 1994 by a group of

MK executives calling themselves the MK Committee for Excellence leveled a whole slew of charges at Agee. Right off, they claimed, Agee irked subordinates by removing the portrait of MK's founder from the headquarters and replacing it with a near life-sized portrait of him and his wife, Mary Cunningham, paid for by the company. Agee further estranged insiders by quietly moving the CEO's office to his Pebble Beach estate in California and by scoffing at the company's engineering-oriented culture. Several old-hand MK engineering executives, who had top reputations in their field, were fired, usually after crossing swords with Agee over his policies.

There was also the matter of Agee's pay and perks. At $2.4 million, Agee's 1993 compensation was equal to 6.8 percent of MK's net income, more than any other CEO of a company with earnings in that range, according to a *Forbes* magazine list. According to insiders, MK paid $4 million a year for a corporate jet for Agee, equal to 13 percent of the company's general and administrative budget. The company also paid for landscaping services at Agee's Pebble Beach estate.

Things came to a head on February 1, 1995, when MK's board announced that the company would record a large loss for 1994. The board also announced that Agee would be stepping down as CEO, although initial indications were that he would stay on as chairman of the board. Preliminary figures suggested that MK would have to take a $179.6 million pretax charge in its 1994 fourth quarter, which would result in a net loss of $141 million for the quarter. At the same time, Standard & Poor's downgraded MK's long-term debt to junk bond rating, signaling that a significant risk of default existed.

The announcement gave rise to a blizzard of shareholder lawsuits and criticism, not only of Agee, but also of MK's board for acting so slowly. Many commentators wondered why it took a huge loss and an anonymous letter from MK employees to prod the board into action. Privately, several board members, most of whom were appointees and long-time friends of Agee, indicated that they were led astray by Agee, who repeatedly urged them not to worry about poor results. Still, many felt that the audit committee of the board of directors had not done a good job of vetting MK's financial accounts under Agee's leadership. Stung by this criticism, the growing evidence of financial mismanagement under Agee's leadership, and the downgrade of MK's debt by Standard & Poor's, the board reversed its earlier position and decided to strip Agee of all posts at MK.

The shareholder lawsuits were settled in September 1995. Under the agreement, MK was to pay out $63 million in cash and stock to shareholders. The settlement also required the company to strengthen its board by adding seven new directors over the next two years. As part of the settlement, Agee agreed to relinquish rights to about $3 million in severance pay and to a cut in his MK pension from $303,000 a year for life to $99,750 a year for life.

Sources: J. E. Rigdon and J. S. Lubin, "Why Morrison Board Fired Agee," *Wall Street Journal,* February 13, 1995, p. B1. C. McCoy. "Worst Five and One Year Performer: Morrison Knudson," *Wall Street Journal,* February 29, 1996, p. R2. "Morrison Knudson Settles Most Shareholder Lawsuits," *Wall Street Journal,* September 21, 1995, p. B8. J. E. Rigdon, "William Agee to Leave Morrison Knudson," *Wall Street Journal,* February 2, 1995, p. B1.

Stakeholder Impact Analysis

A company cannot always satisfy the claims of all stakeholders. The goals of different groups may conflict, and in practice few organizations have the resources to manage all stakeholders.[11] For example, union claims for higher wages can conflict with consumer demands for reasonable prices and stockholder demands for acceptable returns. Often the company must make choices. To do so, it must identify the most important stakeholders and give highest priority to pursuing strategies that satisfy their needs. Stakeholder impact analysis can provide such identification. Typically, stakeholder impact analysis follows these steps:

1. Identify stakeholders.

2. Identify stakeholders' interests and concerns.

3. As a result, identify what claims stakeholders are likely to make on the organization.

4. Identify the stakeholders who are most important from the organization's perspective.

5. Identify the resulting strategic challenges.[12]

Such an analysis enables a company to identify the stakeholders most critical to its survival and to make sure that the satisfaction of their needs is paramount. Most companies that have gone through this process quickly come to the conclusion that three stakeholder groups must be satisfied above all others if a company is to survive and prosper: customers, employees, and stockholders. Bill Agee, for example, lost his position because he failed to satisfy the demands of stockholders for a good return on their investment and the demands of employees for income, job satisfaction, job security, and good working conditions. More generally, companies that fail to satisfy the needs of its customers soon see their revenues fall and ultimately go out of business. Interestingly, Agee probably was satisfying the needs of customers since he was insisting on low prices; however, at the prices Agee was requiring, Morrison Knudsen could not possibly have been profitable.

The Unique Role of Stockholders

A company's stockholders are usually put in a different class from other stakeholder groups, and for good reason. Stockholders are legal owners and the providers of risk capital, a major source of the capital resources that allow a company to operate its business. The capital that stockholders provide to a company is seen as **risk capital** because there is no guarantee that stockholders will ever recoup their investment and or earn a decent return.

Recent history demonstrates all too clearly the nature of risk capital. Many investors who bought shares in companies that went public during the late 1990s and early 2000s through an initial public offering (IPO) subsequently saw the value of their holdings decline to zero, or something close to it. For example, in early 2000, Oniva.com, a provider of an online business-to-business marketplace aimed at small businesses, went public. On the first day of trading, the shares hit $25. They fell steadily afterward, and two years later, having lost 99 percent of their value, they were trading at $0.25, effectively wiping out the investment many made in the company. Of course, there are also some spectacular successes: investors who purchased shares of Dell, Microsoft, or Intel at their IPO have done extraordinarily well. But this is the nature of risk capital: the variance of returns is very high. To reward stockholders for providing the company with risk capital, management is obligated to pursue strategies that maximize the returns that stockholders get from their investment in the company's stock.

Over the past decade, maximizing returns to stockholders has taken on added importance as more and more employees have themselves become stockholders in the company for which they work through an employee stock ownership plan (ESOP). At Wal-Mart, for example, all employees who have served for more than one year are eligible for the company's ESOP. Under an ESOP, employees are given the opportunity to purchase stock in their company, sometimes at a discount to the market value of the stock. The company may also contribute to a certain proportion of the purchase price. By making employees stockholders, ESOPs tend to increase the already strong emphasis on maximizing returns to stockholders, for this now helps to satisfy two key stakeholder groups: stockholders and employees.

Profitability and Stakeholder Claims

Because of the unique position assigned to stockholders, managers normally seek to pursue strategies that maximize the returns that stockholders receive from holding shares in the company. As we noted in Chapter 1, stockholders receive a return on their investment in a company's stock in two ways: from dividend payments and from capital appreciation in the market value of a share (that is, by increases in stock market prices). The best way for managers to generate the funds for future dividend payments and to keep the stock price appreciating is for them to pursue strategies that maximize the company's long-run return on invested capital (ROIC).[13] As we saw in Chapter 3, ROIC is an excellent measure of the profitability of a company. It tells managers how efficiently they are using the capital resources of the company (including the risk capital provided by stockholders) to generate profits. A company that is generating a positive ROIC is covering all of its ongoing expenses and has money left over, which is then added to shareholders' equity, thereby increasing the value of a company, and thus the value of a share of stock in the company. Thus, maximizing long-run ROIC is the route to maximizing returns to stockholders.

In addition to maximizing returns to stockholders, boosting a company's profitability, as measured by its ROIC, is also consistent with satisfying the claims of several other key stakeholder groups. The more profitable a company is, the higher are the salaries that it can pay to productive employees, and the greater is the ability of the company to afford other benefits, such as health insurance coverage, all of which help to satisfy that stakeholder group. In addition, companies with a high level of profitability have no problem meeting their debt commitments, which provides creditors, including bondholders, with a measure of security. More profitable companies are also better able to undertake philanthropic investments, which can help to satisfy some of the claims that local communities and the general public place on a company. Pursuing strategies that maximize the long-run ROIC of the company is therefore generally consistent with satisfying the claims of various stakeholder groups.

There is an important cause-and-effect relationship here. It is pursuing strategies to maximize profitability that helps a company to better satisfy the demands that several stakeholder groups place on it, not the other way around. The company that overpays its employees in the current period, for example, may have very happy employees for a short while, but such action will raise the company's cost structure and limit its ability to attain a competitive advantage in the marketplace, thereby depressing its long-run profitability and hurting its ability to award future pay increases. As far as employees are concerned, the way many companies deal with this situation is to make future pay increases contingent on improvements in labor productivity. If labor productivity goes up, labor costs as a percentage of revenues will fall, profitability will rise, and the company can afford to pay its employees more and offer greater benefits.

The basic cause-and-effect relationship is summarized in Figure 11.2. This shows that strategies to increase long-run ROIC will, if successfully executed, lead to higher ROIC, which increases the ability of the company to satisfy key stakeholders. In turn, satisfied stakeholders are more likely to support the company: happy employees will work hard, satisfied customers will continue to buy the company's products, satisfied stockholders will support secondary stock offerings allowing the company to raise additional risk capital, and content bondholders will be more likely to purchase additional bonds at favorable interest rates—all of which can lead to higher long-term profitability.

Of course, not all stakeholder groups want the company to maximize its long-run ROIC. Suppliers are more comfortable about selling goods and services to profitable companies, because they can be assured that the company will have the funds to pay for those products. Similarly, customers may be more willing to purchase from profitable companies, because they can be assured that those companies will be around in the long run to provide after-sales services and support. But neither suppliers nor customers want the company to maximize its ROIC *at their expense.* Rather, they

FIGURE 11.2

Relationship Between
ROIC, Stakeholder
Satisfaction, and
Stakeholder Support

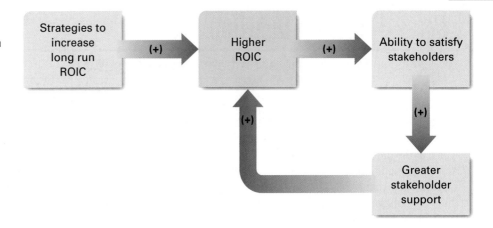

would like to capture some of these profits from the company in the form of higher
prices for their goods and services (in the case of suppliers) or lower prices for the
products they purchase from the company (in the case of customers). Thus, the company is in a bargaining relationship with some of its stakeholders, which was a phenomenon we discussed in Chapter 2.

Moreover, despite the argument that maximizing long-run ROIC is the best way
to satisfy the claims of several key stakeholder groups, it should also be noted that a
company has the obligation to do so within the limits set by the law and in a manner
consistent with societal expectations. The unfettered pursuit of profit can lead to
behaviors that are outlawed by government regulations, opposed by important public constituencies, or are simply unethical. Governments have enacted a wide range of
regulations to govern business behavior, including antitrust laws, environmental
laws, and laws pertaining to health and safety in the workplace. It is incumbent on
managers to make sure that the company is in compliance with these laws when pursuing strategies.

Both illegal and unethical behavior seemed to have occurred at Enron. More generally, there is plenty of evidence that managers can be tempted to cross the line
between the legal and illegal in their pursuit of greater profitability. The chief executive of Archer Daniels Midland, for example, was sent to jail after an FBI investigation
revealed that the company had systematically tried to fix the price for lysine by col-
luding with other manufacturers in the global marketplace. In another example of
price fixing, the seventy-six-year-old chairman of Sotheby's auction house was
recently sentenced to a jail term and the former CEO to house arrest for fixing prices
with rival auction house Christie's over a six-year period (see Strategy in Action 11.2).

Finally, it has been consistently emphasized that the goal of management should
be to maximize *long-run* ROIC. This emphasis reflects two facts. First, investors,
employees, and customers are generally interested only in companies that are going
to be around for the long run. Employees, for example, are more likely to work for
enterprises that can promise longer-term job security. Second, as noted in Chapter 1,
maximizing short-run ROIC may not be consistent with maximizing long-run
ROIC. A company can boost its ROIC in the current year by sharply curtailing capital investments. However, if such investments are required to maintain the long-run
competitive position of the company, the result of reduced investment over several
years may be a loss of competitive position and declining ROIC. Indeed, in more
extreme cases, a focus on maximizing current ROIC can lead to actions that are
entirely inappropriate and jeopardize the long-run survival of the company. This

Strategy in Action   11.2

Price Fixing at Sotheby's and Christie's

Sotheby's and Christie's are the two largest fine art auction houses in the world. In the mid-1990s, the two companies controlled 90 percent of fine art auction market, which at the time was worth some $4 billion a year. Traditionally, auction houses make their profit by the commission they charge on auction sales. In good times, these commissions can range as high as 10 percent on some items, but in the early 1990s, the auction business was in a slump, with the supply of art for auction drying up. With Sotheby's and Christie's desperate for works of art, sellers played the two houses off against each other, driving commissions down to 2 percent or even lower.

To try to control this situation, Sotheby's CEO, Dede Brooks, met with her opposite number at Christie's, Christopher Davidge, in a series of clandestine meetings held in car parking lots that began in 1993. Brooks claims that she was acting on behalf of her boss, Alfred Taubman, the chairman and controlling shareholder of Sotheby's. According to Brooks, Taubman had agreed with the chairman of Christie's, Anthony Tennant, to work together in the weak auction market and limit price competition. In their meetings, Brooks and Davidge agreed to a fixed and nonnegotiable commission structure. Based on a sliding scale, the commission structure would range from 10 percent on a $100,000 item to 2 percent on a $5 million item. In effect, Brooks and Davidge were agreeing to eliminate price competition between them, thereby guaranteeing both auction houses higher

profits. The price-fixing agreement started in 1993 and continued unabated for six years until federal investigators uncovered the arrangement and brought charges against Sotheby's and Christie's.

With the deal out in the open, lawyers filed several class action lawsuits on behalf of sellers who had been defrauded by Sotheby's and Christie's. Ultimately, some 100,000 sellers signed on to the class action lawsuits, which the auction houses settled with a $512 million payment. The auction houses also pleaded guilty to price fixing and paid $45 million in fines to U.S. antitrust authorities. As for the key players, the chairman of Christie's, as a British subject, was able to avoid prosecution in the United States (price fixing is not an offense for which someone can be extradited). Christie's CEO, Davidge, struck a deal with prosecutors and in return for amnesty handed over incriminating documents to the authorities. Brooks also cooperated with federal prosecutors and avoided jail (in April 2002 she was sentenced to three years' probation, six months' home detention, 1,000 hours of community service, and a $350,000 fine). Taubman, ultimately isolated by all his former co-conspirators, was sentenced to a year in jail and fined $7.5 million.

Sources: S. Tully, "A House Divided," *Fortune,* December 18, 2000, pp. 264–275. J. Chaffin, "Sotheby's Ex CEO Spared Jail Sentence," *Financial Times,* April 30, 2002, p. 10. T. Thorncroft, "A Courtroom Battle of the Vanities," *Financial Times,* November 3, 2001, p. 3.

seems to have occurred at Enron, where an obsession with maximizing current profitability led some managers to engage in risky (and fraudulent) actions that ultimately led to the collapse of the company. This rather begs the question of why managers would behave in such risky behavior. Agency theory provides an answer and an explanation for what went on at Enron and other companies.

Agency Theory

Agency theory looks at the problems that can arise in a business relationship when one person delegates decision making authority to another. Agency theory offers a way of understanding why managers do not always act in the best interests of stakeholders.[14] Although agency theory was originally formulated to capture the relationship between management and stockholders, the basic principles have also been extended to cover the relationship with other key stakeholders, such as employees, as well as between different layers of management within a corporation.[15] Although the focus of attention in this section is on the relationship between senior management and stockholders, it should not be forgotten that some of the same language can be applied to the relationship between other stakeholders and top managers and between top management and lower levels of management.

Principal-Agent Relationships

The basic propositions of agency theory are relatively straightforward. First, an **agency relationship** is held to arise whenever one party delegates decision-making authority or control over resources to another. The **principal** is the person delegating authority, and the **agent** is the person to whom authority is delegated. The relationship between stockholders and senior managers is the classic example of an agency relationship. Stockholders, who are the *principals,* provide the company with risk capital, but they delegate control over that capital to senior managers, and particularly the CEO, who as their *agent* is expected to use that capital in a manner that is consistent with the best interests of stockholders. As we have seen, this means using that capital to maximize the company's long-run ROIC.

The agency relationship continues on down within the company. For example, in the large, complex multibusiness company, top managers cannot possibly make all important decisions, so they delegate some decision-making authority and control over capital resources to business unit (divisional) managers. Thus, just as senior managers such as the CEO are the *agents* of stockholders, business unit managers are the *agents* of the CEO (and in this context, the CEO is the *principal*). The CEO entrusts business unit managers to use the resources over which they have control in the most effective manner so that they maximize the ROIC of their units, which helps the CEO to make sure that he or she maximizes the ROIC of the entire company, thereby discharging agency obligation to stockholders. More generally, whenever managers delegate authority to managers below them in the hierarchy and give them the right to control resources, an agency relation is established.

The Agency Problem

The essence of the **agency problem** is that agents and principals may have different goals, and consequently, agents may pursue goals that are not in the best interests of their principals. Agents may be able to do this because there is an **information asymmetry** between the principal and the agent; agents almost always have more information about the resources they are managing than the principal does. Unscrupulous agents can take advantage of any information asymmetry to mislead principals and maximize their own interests at the expense of principals.

In the case of stockholders, the information asymmetry arises because they delegate decision-making authority to the CEO, their agent, who by virtue of his or her position inside the company is likely to know far more than stockholders do about the company's operations. Indeed, there may be certain information about the company that the CEO is unwilling to share with stockholders because it would also help competitors. In such a case, withholding some information from stockholders may be in their best interests. More generally, the CEO, involved in the day-to-day running of the company, is bound to have an information advantage over stockholders, just as the CEO's subordinates may well have an information advantage over the CEO with regard to the resources under their control.

The information asymmetry between principals and agents is not necessarily a bad thing, but it can make it difficult for principals to measure how well an agent is performing, and thus hold the agent accountable for how well he or she is using the entrusted resources. There is a certain amount of performance ambiguity inherent in the relationship between a principal and agent: principals cannot know for sure if the agent is acting in his or her best interests. They cannot know for sure if the agent is using the resources to which he or she has been entrusted as effectively and efficiently as possible. To an extent, principals have to *trust* the agent to do the right thing.

Of course, this trust is not blind: principals do put mechanisms in place whose purpose is to monitor agents, evaluate their performance, and if necessary, take corrective action. As we shall see shortly, the board of directors is one such mechanism, for in part the board exists to monitor and evaluate senior managers on behalf of stockholders. Other mechanisms serve a similar purpose. In the United States, the requirement that publicly owned companies regularly file detailed financial statements with the Securities and Exchange Commission (SEC) that are in accordance with generally agreed accounting principles (GAAP) exists to give stockholders consistent and detailed information about how well management is using the capital to which they have been entrusted. Similarly, internal control systems within a company are there to help the CEO make sure that subordinates are using the resources to which they have been entrusted as efficiently and effectively as possible.

Despite the existence of governance mechanisms and comprehensive measurement and control systems, a degree of information asymmetry will always remain between principals and agents, and there is always an element of trust involved in the relationship. Unfortunately, not all agents are worthy of this trust, and a minority will deliberately mislead principals for personal gain. The interests of principals and agents are not always the same; they diverge, and some agents may take advantage of information asymmetries to maximize their own interests at the expense of principals.

For example, some authors have argued that like many other people, senior managers are motivated by desires for status, power, job security, and income.[16] By virtue of their position within the company, certain managers, such as the CEO, can use their authority and control over corporate funds to satisfy these desires at the cost of returns to stockholders. CEOs might use their position to invest corporate funds in various perks that enhance their status—executive jets, lavish offices, and expense-paid trips to exotic locations—rather than investing those funds in ways that increase stockholder returns. Economists have termed such behavior *on-the-job consumption*.[17] Bill Agee provides us with an example of a CEO who appeared to engage in excessive on-the-job consumption (see Strategy in Action 11.1).

Besides engaging in on-the-job-consumption, CEOs, along with other senior managers, might satisfy their desires for greater income by using their influence or control over the board of directors to get the compensation committee of the board to grant such pay increases. Critics of U.S. industry claim that extraordinary pay has now become an endemic problem and that senior managers are enriching themselves at the expense of stockholders and other employees. They point out that CEO pay has been increasing far more rapidly than the pay of average workers, primarily due to very liberal stock option grants that enable a CEO to earn huge pay bonuses in a rising stock market, even if the company underperforms the market and competitors.[18] In 1950, when *Business Week* started its annual survey of CEO pay, the highest-paid executive was General Motors CEO Charles Wilson, whose $652,156 pay packet translates into $4.4 million in inflation-adjusted dollars in 2001. In contrast, the highest-paid executive in *Business Week*'s 2001 survey, Larry Ellison, the CEO of Oracle Corporation, earned $706.1 million, primarily from exercising stock options.[19] In 1980, the average CEO earned 42 times what the average blue collar-worker earned. By 1990, this figure had increased to 85 times. Today, the average CEO earns more than 400 times the pay of the average blue collar worker.[20]

What rankles critics is the size of some CEO pay packages and their apparent lack of relationship to company performance.[21] In 1998, for example, Disney CEO Michael Eisner earned $575 million, mostly in the form of stock options, despite the fact that Disney did not do particularly well that year and the stock price fell 10 percent. Similarly, Larry Ellison's $706.1 million pay packet came in a year when Oracle's stock price plunged. Another big gainer in 2001, Jozef Straus, earned $150 million from stock options in a year when the company he serves as CEO, JDS Uniphase, recorded a $50 billion loss related to the writing down of goodwill for companies acquired at premium prices during the booming 1990s. Critics feel that the size of these pay awards was out of all proportion to the achievement of the CEOs.[22] If so, this represents a clear example of the agency problem.

A further concern is that in trying to satisfy a desire for status, security, power, and income, a CEO might engage in *empire building,* buying many new businesses in an attempt to increase the size of the company through diversification.[23] Although such growth may do little to enhance the company's profitability, and thus stockholder returns, it increases the size of the empire under the CEO's control and, by extension, the CEO's status, power, security, and income (there is a strong relationship between company size and CEO pay). To quote Carl Icahn, a famous financier:

> Make no mistake, a strongly knit corporate aristocracy exists in America. The top man, what's more, usually finds expanding his power more important than rewarding owners [stockholders]. When Mobil and USX had excess cash, did they enrich shareholders? Of course not. They bought Marcor and Marathon— disastrous investments, but major increases in the size of the manor.[24]

Thus, instead of maximizing stockholder returns, in an example of the agency problem, some senior managers may trade long-run profitability for greater company growth by buying new businesses. Figure 11.3 graphs profitability against the rate of growth in company revenues. A company that does not grow is probably missing out on some profitable opportunities.[25] A moderate revenue growth rate of G^* allows a company to maximize profitability, generating a return of Π^*. Thus, a growth rate of G_0 in Figure 11.3 is not consistent with maximizing profitability ($\Pi_1 < \Pi^*$). However, attaining growth in excess of G_1 requires diversification into areas that the company knows little about. Consequently, it can be achieved only by sacrificing

FIGURE 11.3

The Tradeoff Between Profitability and Revenue Growth Rates

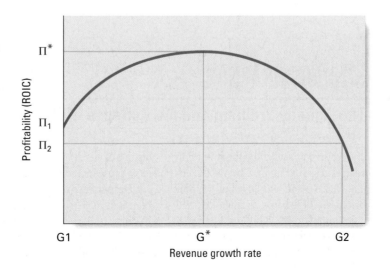

profitability (that is, past G_1, the investment required to finance further growth does not produce an adequate return and the company's profitability declines). Yet G_2 may be the growth rate favored by an empire-building CEO, for it will increase his or her power, status, and income. At this growth rate, profits are equal only to Π_2. Because $\Pi^* > \Pi_2$, a company growing at this rate is clearly not maximizing its profitability or the wealth of its stockholders. However, a growth rate of G_2 may be consistent with attaining managerial goals of power, status, and income.

For an example of this kind of excessive growth, consider once more the example of Tyco International, the subject of the *Opening Case* in Chapter 10. Whatever the motivation of the CEO, with hindsight it is clear that Tyco grew too fast, paid too much for its acquisitions, and took on too much debt to finance those acquisitions. Tyco's revenue growth rate was impressive, but the resulting debt burden hurt the company's profitability and stock price.

The agency problem is not confined to the relationship between senior managers and stockholders. It can also bedevil the relationship between the CEO and subordinates and between them and their subordinates. A subordinate might use control over information to distort the true performance of the unit under his control in order to enhance his pay, increase his job security, or make sure that his unit gets more than its fair share of company resources.[26] In the Enron case, the former CEO, Jeffrey Skilling, has claimed that he was ignorant of the dealings of his CFO, Andrew Fastow, who used the creation of off-balance-sheet partnerships to net some $30 million. If true, this implies that Fastow deliberately misled his boss in order to profit for himself, and as such this would be an excellent example of the agency problem between a top manager and subordinate within a company. One of the most dramatic examples of an agency problem within a company during the last decade is given in Strategy in Action 11.3. This looks at how a rogue trader, Nick Leeson, took advantage of his superiors' ignorance to take extreme risks in an attempt to maximize his own personal wealth and ended up bankrupting his employer, Barings Bank.

Confronted with the possibility of the agency problem, the challenge for principals is to (1) shape the behavior of agents so that they act in accordance with the goals set by principles, (2) reduce the information asymmetry between agents and principles, and (3) develop mechanisms for removing agents who do not act in accordance with the goals of principles. Principals try to deal with these challenges through a series of governance mechanisms.

Strategy in Action   11.3

The Agency Problem and the Collapse of Barings Bank

In February 1995, the world was shaken by the revelation that unauthorized derivatives trading by a twenty-seven-year-old Englishman, Nick Leeson, employed at the Singapore Office of Britain's oldest bank, Barings Plc, had amassed losses that amounted to $1.33 billion. The debacle resulted in the collapse of Barings and its purchase, for one pound sterling, by a Dutch bank, ING. So ended the

history of a 233-year-old bank whose clients at the time of its collapse included Queen Elizabeth II of England.

Despite his youth, Leeson had been a highly successful trader for Barings in Asia and was viewed as the senior Barings trader in Singapore. In September 1994, he started to speculate on the volatility of Japan's Nikkei 255 stock index. His motives were to maximize the size of his bonus, which could have easily run into seven figures had his strategy been successful, and solidify his position as a major trader. His strategy involved simultaneously writing uncovered put and call options on Nikkei 255 futures. This procedure will make money for the option writer provided that the market stays within a relatively narrow trading range. When Leeson began his trades, the Nikkei was trading at around 19,000. Leeson's strategy made Barings money so long as the Nikkei stayed between 18,500 and 19,500. Once the Nikkei went outside this range, Barings started to lose large amounts of money: about $70 million for every 1 percent move above or below these limits. The loss was exacerbated by Leeson's aggressive use of leverage: he was writing the options using borrowed money.

At first, the strategy worked. Leeson may have earned as much as $150 million for Barings from this strategy by the end of 1994. However, the strategy started to fall apart when the Kobe earthquake struck on January 17, 1995. Following the earthquake, the Nikkei fell below 18,500. In an attempt to push the market back above 18,500, Leeson purchased Nikkei futures, again using borrowed money, and increasing the size of his bet. It didn't work. Leeson's position deteriorated further on January 23 when the Nikkei fell 1,000 points to under 17,800. Increasingly desperate, Leeson responded to the crisis by borrowing more money to continue purchasing Nikkei futures in what was to prove to be a futile attempt to prop up the Nikkei index. By late February 1995, Barings had accumulated index positions that effectively amounted to a $7 billion highly leveraged bet that the Nikkei index would recover—a bet that was wrong.

Leeson's actions did not go unnoticed by other traders in Singapore or executives at Barings Bank in London. However, Barings executives and other traders were under the impression that Leeson was acting on behalf of a major client—perhaps a big hedge fund. No one could conceive that the positions belonged to Barings. As for the cash required to purchase Nikkei futures, apparently much of this came from an account for a fictitious client that Leeson had set up as early as 1992. Into this account went some of Barings's own cash, along with all of the proceeds of Leeson's option sales, and some fictitious profits from falsified arbitrage deals. He then used this fictitious account to pay the costs of borrowing money to finance his trading positions. When the account was exhausted, Leeson turned to Barings in London, saying that he was executing trades on behalf of a major client who would settle up in a few days. Barings proved willing to send more money to their star trader in Singapore.

Bolstered by the arrival of additional funds from London, Leeson kept up the charade until February 23 when the cash flowing out to cover borrowing costs exceeded Barings's preset limits. With the Nikkei continuing to decline, Leeson realized that he could no longer carry on with the game. He hurriedly faxed a letter to Barings in London tendering his resignation, adding that he was sorry for the trouble he had caused, and along with his wife boarded a plane out of Singapore. The next day, shocked Barings executives informed the Bank of England that they were technically bankrupt. The liabilities from Leeson's trades already exceeded $800 million and were growing by the hour as the Nikkei index continued to tumble.

The collapse of Barings had much to do with a lack of internal management controls, which allowed Leeson to speculate on a massive scale using borrowed money. Leeson was able to get away with this because of the poor monitoring of his activities by Barings's senior managers in England. In July 1995, the Bank of England issued a report on the collapse of Barings. According to the bank, "Significant amounts were regularly remitted to BFS without any clear understanding on the part of Barings' management on whose behalf these monies were to be applied, and without any real demur." The Bank of England's report also cited a number of senior managers at Barings for failing to apply proper controls.

Leeson was later tracked down, arrested in Malaysia, and ultimately sentenced to a four-year jail term for fraud. In an interview he gave to the BBC from his jail cell, Leeson gave more insight into the collapse of Barings. Leeson said that he got away with his trading for so long because of the failure of key executives at Barings's London headquarters to understand the business he was engaged in and to look more closely into his activities: "The first day that I asked for funding there should have been massive alarm bells ringing. But senior people in London that were arranging these payments didn't understand the basic administration of futures and options. . . . They wanted to believe in the profits being reported, and therefore they weren't willing to question."

In a spectacular example of the agency problem, Leeson exploited the information asymmetry that existed between himself and senior managers to pursue his own interests, placing risky bets on the Nikkei stock market index that could have netted Leeson millions but in the event plunged Barings into bankruptcy and sent Leeson to jail.

Sources: N. Bray and G. Whitney, "Barings Collapse Tied to Wide Cast," *Wall Street Journal,* July 19, 1995, p. A5. T. Shale, "Why Barings Was Doomed," *Euromoney* (March 1995): 38–41. "A Fallen Star," *Economist,* March 4, 1995, pp. 19–21.

Governance Mechanisms

Governance mechanisms are mechanisms that principals put in place to align incentives between principals and agents and to monitor and control agents. The purpose of governance mechanisms is to reduce the scope and frequency of the agency problem: to help ensure that agents act in a manner that is consistent with the best interests of their principals. In this section, the primary focus is on the governance mechanisms that exist to align the interests of senior managers (as agents) with their principals, stockholders. It should not be forgotten, however, that governance mechanisms also exist to align the interests of business unit managers with those of their superiors, and so on down within the organization.

Here we look at four main types of governance mechanisms for aligning stockholder and management interests: the board of directors, stock-based compensation, financial statements, and the takeover constraint. The section closes with a discussion of governance mechanism within a company to align the interest of senior and lower-level managers.

The Board of Directors

The board of directors is the centerpiece of the corporate governance system in the United States and the United Kingdom. Board members are directly elected by stockholders, and under corporate law they represent the stockholders' interests in the company. Hence, the board can be held legally accountable for the company's actions. Its position at the apex of decision making within the company allows it to monitor corporate strategy decisions and ensure that they are consistent with stockholder interests. If the board's sense is that corporate strategies are not in the best interest of stockholders, it can apply sanctions, such as voting against management nominations to the board of directors or submitting its own nominees. In addition, the board has the legal authority to hire, fire, and compensate corporate employees, including, most importantly, the CEO.[27] The board is also responsible for making sure that audited financial statements of the company present a true picture of its financial situation. Thus, the board exists to reduce the information asymmetry between stockholders and managers and to monitor and control management actions on behalf of stockholders.

The typical board of directors is composed of a mix of inside and outside directors. *Inside directors* are senior employees of the company, such as the CEO. They are required on the board because they have valuable information about the company's activities. Without such information, the board cannot adequately perform its monitoring function. But because insiders are full-time employees of the company, their interests tend to be aligned with those of management. Hence, outside directors are needed to bring objectivity to the monitoring and evaluation processes. *Outside directors* are not full-time employees of the company. Many of them are full-time professional directors who hold positions on the boards of several companies. The need to maintain a reputation as competent outside directors gives them an incentive to perform their tasks as objectively and effectively as possible.[28]

There is little doubt that many boards perform their assigned functions admirably. For example, one factor that led to the dismissal of Morrison Knudsen's CEO, Bill Agee, was that his strategies lost the support of the board (see Strategy in Action 11.1). Similarly, when the board of Sotheby's discovered that the company had been engaged in price fixing with Christie's, board members moved quickly to oust both the CEO and the chairman of the company (see Strategy in Action 11.2). But not all boards perform as well as they should. The board of Enron signed off on that company's audited financial statements, which were later shown to be grossly misleading.

Critics of the existing governance system charge that inside directors often dominate the outsiders on the board. Insiders can use their position within the management hierarchy to exercise control over what kind of company-specific information the board receives. Consequently, they can present information in a way that puts them in a favorable light. In addition, insiders have the advantage of intimate knowledge of the company's operations and because of their superior knowledge and control over information are sources of power, they may be better positioned than outsiders to influence boardroom decision making. The board may become the captive of insiders and merely rubber-stamp management decisions instead of guarding stockholder interests.

Some observers contend that many boards are dominated by the company CEO, particularly when the CEO is also the chairman of the board.[29] To support this view, they point out that both inside and outside directors are often the personal nominees of the CEO. The typical inside director is subordinate to the CEO in the company's hierarchy and therefore unlikely to criticize the boss. Because outside directors are frequently the CEO's nominees as well, they can hardly be expected to evaluate the CEO objectively. Thus, the loyalty of the board may be biased toward the CEO, not the stockholders. Moreover, a CEO who is also chairman of the board may be able to control the agenda of board discussions in such a manner as to deflect any criticisms of his or her leadership. This was a problem in the case of Bill Agee: he was both CEO and chairman of the board at Morrison Knudsen.

Today, there are clear signs that many corporate boards are moving away from merely rubber-stamping top management decisions and are beginning to play a much more active role in corporate governance. One catalyst has been an increase in the number of lawsuits filed by stockholders against board members. The trend started in the 1980s when a Delaware court ruled that the directors of Trans Union Corporation had been too quick to accept a takeover bid. The court held the directors personally liable for the difference between the offer they accepted and the price the company might have fetched in a sale. The directors then agreed to make up the $23.5 million difference. Since that ruling, a number of major lawsuits have been filed by stockholders against board members. Among them are suits directed against board members at Holly Farms, Northrop Corp., Lincoln Savings & Loan, Lotus Development Corp., and RJR Nabisco.[30]

Another catalyst has been the growing willingness of some institutional investors, such as the managers of large pension funds or index-linked mutual funds, to use their stockholding in a company, and the voting power it gives them, to gain seats on the board of directors, pressure managers to adopt policies that improve the performance of the company's stock, and pressure the board to replace the CEOs of poorly performing companies. For example, in the mid-1990s, officials of New York City's five major pension funds stated that they would nominate three candidates for seats on the board of Ethyl Corp., a maker of petroleum additives that has performed poorly in recent years. Their objective was to use these board seats to push management harder to improve the performance of Ethyl and, hence, the value of their stock in Ethyl. The pension funds were ultimately successful in getting their nominees on Ethyl's board.[31]

Spurred on by the threat of legal action and pressures from powerful institutional shareholders, an increasing number of boards have started to assert their independence from company management in general and from corporate CEOs in particular. Since the mid-1990s, boards of directors have engineered the removal or resignation of CEOs at a number of major companies, including American Express,

Compaq Computer, Digital Equipment, General Motors, IBM, and Sunbeam. Another trend of some significance is the increasing tendency for outside directors to be made chairs of the board. By the late 1990s, according to estimates from the National Association of Corporate Directors, 40 to 50 percent of big companies had an outside director as chair, up from less than half that figure in 1990.[32] Such appointments limit the ability of corporate insiders, and particularly of the CEO, to exercise control over the board. It is notable that the removal of Robert Stempel as the CEO of General Motors in the late 1990s followed the appointment of an outside director, John Smale, as chairman of the GM board. Still, when all is said and done, it must be recognized that boards of directors do not work as well as they should, and other mechanisms are need to align the interests of stockholders and managers.

Stock-Based Compensation

According to agency theory, one of the best ways to reduce the scope of the agency problem is for principals to establish incentives for agents to behave in their best interest through pay-for-performance systems. In the case of stockholders and top managers, stockholders can encourage top managers to pursue strategies that maximize a company's long-run ROIC, and thus the gains from holding its stock, by linking the pay of those managers to the performance of the stock price.

The most common pay-for-performance system has been to give managers stock options: the right to buy the company's shares at a predetermined (strike) price at some point in the future, usually within ten years of the grant date. Typically, the strike price is the price that the stock was trading at when the option was originally granted. The idea behind stock options is to motivate managers to adopt strategies that increase the share price of the company, for in doing so they will also increase the value of their own stock options.

Many top managers often earn huge bonuses from exercising stock options that were granted several years previously. While not denying that these options do motivate managers to improve company performance, critics claim that they are often too generous. A particular cause for concern is that stock options are often granted at such low strike prices that the CEO can hardly fail to make a significant amount of money by exercising them, even if the company underperforms the stock market by a significant margin.

Other critics, including the famous investor Warren Buffett, complain that huge stock option grants increase the outstanding number of shares in a company and therefore dilute the equity of stockholders; accordingly, they should be shown in company accounts as an expense against profits. However, under current accounting regulations, stock options, unlike wages and salaries, are not expensed. Buffett has noted that when his investment company, Berkshire Hathaway, "acquires an option issuing company, we promptly substitute a cash compensation plan having an economic value equivalent to that of the previous option plan. The acquiree's true compensation cost is therefore brought out of the closet and charged, as it should be, against earnings."[33] Buffett's point is that stock options are accounted for incorrectly in company financial statements. Table 11.1 details the amount that reported profits would have been reduced during the 1996–2000 period for several high-profile companies if stock options had been accounted for as an expense and deducted from profits. As can be seen, the impact would have been to depress profits severely at some of these companies, and by extension, ROIC.

Several academic studies suggest that stock-based compensation schemes for executives, such as stock options, can align management and stockholder interests. For instance, one study found that managers were more likely to consider the effects

TABLE 11.1

How Options Skew the Bottom Line

Company	Reduction in Net Profit If Options Had Been Expensed
AOL Time Warner	75 percent
Viacom	66 percent
NVIDIA	40 percent
MedImmune	31 percent
Lucent	30 percent
Pharmacia	28 percent
Cisco Systems	26 percent
Boise Cascade	17 percent

Source: D. Henry and M. Conlin, "Too Much of a Good Incentive?" *Business Week*, March 4, 2002, pp. 38–39.

of their acquisition decisions on stockholder returns if they themselves were significant shareholders.[34] According to another study, managers who were significant stockholders were less likely to pursue strategies that would maximize the size of the company rather than its profitability.[35] More generally, it is difficult to argue with the proposition that the chance to get rich from exercising stock options is the primary reason for the fourteen-hour days and six-day work weeks that many employees of fast-growing companies put in.

In summary, in theory, stock options and other stock-based compensation methods are a good idea; in practice, they have been abused. To limit the abuse, Alan Greenspan, chairman of the U.S. Federal Reserve, has joined Warren Buffett in arguing that accounting rules should be changed to treat options as an expense that must be charged against profits. Some companies have taken matters into their own hands even without a change in accounting rules. Microsoft, for example, routinely issues two sets of financial accounts: one in which options are expensed and one in which they are not. Boeing issues one set of accounts in which options are counted as an expense. The aerospace company has also gone an important step further in an effort to align management and stockholder interests, issuing what it calls "performance share" units that are convertible into common stock only if its stock appreciates at least 10 percent annually for five years. Similarly, Unilever has created a system in which stock options do not vest unless the company achieves total shareholder returns over a rolling three-year period that are above the median for the group of twenty peer companies, including Coca-Cola, Nestlé, and Procter & Gamble. What all of these companies are trying to do in their own way is to limit the free ride that many holders of stock options enjoyed during the boom of the 1990s, while continuing to maintain a focus on aligning management and stockholder interests through stock-based compensation schemes.[36]

Financial Statements and Auditors

Publicly trading companies in the United States are required to file quarterly and annual reports with the SEC that are prepared according to GAAP. The purpose of this requirement is to give consistent, detailed, and accurate information about how efficiently and effectively the agents of stockholders, the managers, are running the company. To make sure that managers do not misrepresent this financial information, the SEC also requires that the accounts be audited by an independent and accredited accounting firm. Similar regulations exist in most other developed nations. If the system works as intended, stockholders can have a lot of faith that the information contained in financial statements accurately reflects the state of affairs at a company. Among other things, such information can enable a stockholder to calculate the profitability (ROIC) of a company in which she invests and to compare its ROIC against that of competitors.

Unfortunately, in the United States at least, this system has not been working as intended. Although the vast majority of companies do file accurate information in their financial statements and although most auditors do a good job of reviewing that information, there is substantial evidence that a minority of companies have abused the system, aided in part by the compliance of auditors. This was clearly an issue at Enron, where the CFO and others misrepresented the true financial state of the company to investors by creating off-balance-sheet partnerships that hid the true state of Enron's indebtedness from public view. Enron's auditor, Arthur Andersen, also apparently went along with this deception in direct violation of its fiduciary duty.

There have been numerous examples in recent years of managers' gaming financial statements to present a distorted picture of their company's finances to investors. The typical motive has been to inflate the earnings or revenues of a company, thereby generating investor enthusiasm and propelling the stock price higher, which gives managers an opportunity to cash in stock option grants for huge personal gain, obviously at the expense of stockholders who have been mislead by the reports. Another alleged example of such behavior is given in Strategy in Action 11.4, which discusses how top managers at Computer Associates may have managed that company's financial statements in order to present a rosy picture and cash in very lucrative stock awards.

The gaming of financial statements by companies such as Enron and allegedly Computer Associates raises serious questions about the accuracy of the information contained in audited financial statements. First, it would appear that GAAPs are loose enough that unscrupulous managers can manipulate them to their advantage, at the expense of other stakeholder groups. Clearly, there may be need for reform here to tighten up regulations. For example, the regulation that allows companies to accumulate debt off balance sheet in special-purpose entities is clearly open to abuse, as the Enron debacle proves, and should be changed. Stockholders, bondholders, and employees have a right to know how indebted the company is, and managers have an obligation to report this, not hide debt in a special-purpose entity.

Second, the auditors are apparently not always doing their job. An explanation can be found in the conflict of interest that many auditing companies face, for in addition to an auditing business, many big accounting firms also have a lucrative consulting business with the very companies whose accounts they are required to audit in an impartial fashion. The desire to continue to cash in on lucrative consulting contracts, some claim, is why auditors may turn a blind eye to questionable accounting practices at a company. Again, fixing this problem may require reform, and in particular, the separation of auditing and consulting businesses into different companies.

Finally, the proliferation of accounting problems raises questions once more about how well boards of directors are discharging their fiduciary duty to stockholders. It is the board that appoints the auditors and is meant to ensure that the auditors are thorough. The problem is that many boards are still dominated by insiders, and when that is the case, the independence of the board can be questioned. Clearly, fix-

Strategy in Action   11.4

Did Computer Associates Inflate Revenues to Enrich Managers?

Computer Associates is one of the world's largest software companies. During the 1990s, its stock price appreciated at a rapid rate, driven in large part by surging revenues and a commensurate rise in profits. Because its revenues were growing more rapidly than those of rivals during the late 1990s, investors assumed that the company was gaining market share and that high profitability would follow, so they bid up the price of the company's stock. The senior managers of Computer Associates were major beneficiaries of this process.

Under a generous incentive program given to the company's three top managers by the board of directors—Charles Wang, then CEO and chairman of the board, Sanjay Kumar, the chief operating officer, and Russell Artzt, the chief technology officer—if the stock price stayed above $53.13 for sixty days, they would receive a special incentive stock award amounting to some 20 million shares. In May 1998, Kumar announced that Computer Associates had "record" revenues and earnings for the quarter. The stock price surged over the $53.13 trigger and stayed there long enough for all three to receive the special incentive stock award, then valued at $1.1 billion.

In late July 1998, after all three had received the award, Kumar announced that the effect of Asian economic turmoil and the year 2000 bug "leads us to believe that our revenue and earnings growth will slow over the next few quarters." The stock price promptly fell from the high 50s to under $40 a share. What followed was a series of class action lawsuits, undertaken on behalf of stockholders, that claimed that management had misled stockholders to enrich themselves. As a result of the lawsuits, the three were compelled to give back some of their gains, and the size of the award was reduced to 4.5 million shares. Wang stepped down as CEO, although he retained his position as chairman of the board, and Kumar became the CEO.

This was not the end of matters, however, for Computer Associates had attracted the attention of both the Justice Department and the SEC, which launched a joint investigation into the company's accounting practices. By 2002, they were reportedly focusing on a little-noticed action the company had taken in May 2000 to reduce its revenues by 10 percent, or $1.76 billion, below what it had previously reported for the three fiscal years that ended March 2000. The downward revisions, detailed in the company's 10K filings with the SEC, retroactively took hundreds of millions of dollars away from the top line in the fourteen months preceding the May 1998 stock award to senior managers, including some $513 million for the year ending March 1998. According to the company, earnings were unaffected by the revision because the lost revenue was offset by a commensurate downward revision of expenses. The downward revision reportedly came at the urging of auditor KPMG, which replaced Ernst & Young as the company's accountant in June 1999.

While the investigation was still ongoing in mid-2002, the implication that some observers were drawing was that Computer Associates deliberately overstated its revenues in the period prior to May 1998 to enrich the three top managers. The losers in this process were stockholders who purchased shares at the inflated price and longer-term shareholders who saw the value of their holdings diluted by the stock awarded to Wang, Kumar, and Artzt. In a statement issued after a report of the ongoing investigation was published in the *Wall Street Journal,* Computer Associates stated that it changed how it classified revenue and expenses at the advice of its auditors. "We continue to believe CA has acted appropriately," the company said. "This change in presentation had no impact on reported earnings, earnings per share, or cash flows."

Sources: J. Guidera, "Probe of Computer Associates Centers on Firm's Revenues," *Wall Street Journal,* May 20, 2002, pp. A3, 15. Ronna Abramson, "Computer Associates Probe Focus on 1998, 1999 Revenue," *The Street.Com,* May 20, 2002.

ing this problem requires the establishment of boards that are dominated by outside members and where the chairman of the board is not a company insider.

The government took some tentative steps toward reforming the corporate governance system in the United States in July 2002 when President Bush signed into law a measure that set up a new oversight board for accounting firms, required CEOs and CFOs to endorse their company's financial statements, and barred companies from hiring the same accounting firm for auditing and consulting services. However, many critics felt that this legislation did not go far enough and that it should have contained other elements, such as a requirement that stock options be treated as an expense. Others complained that the problem was not a lack of legislation, but that existing legislation had not been enforced aggressively enough by the Justice Department. To be fair though, by mid-2002 it was clear that the Justice Department was moving aggressively to bring criminal fraud charges against some of the key figures in corporate accounting scandals.

The Takeover Constraint

Given the imperfections in corporate governance mechanisms, it is clear that the agency problem may still exist at some companies. However, stockholders still have some residual power, for they can always sell their shares. If they start doing so in large numbers, the price of the company's shares will decline. If the share price falls far enough, the company might be worth less on the stock market than the book value of its assets. At this point, it may become an attractive acquisition target and runs the risk of being purchased by another enterprise, against the wishes of the target company's management.

The risk of being acquired by another company is known as the **takeover constraint.** The takeover constraint limits the extent to which managers can pursue strategies and take actions that put their own interests above those of stockholders. If they ignore stockholder interests and the company is acquired, senior managers typically lose their independence and probably their jobs as well. So the threat of takeover can constrain management action and limit the worst excesses of the agency problem.

During the 1980s and early 1990s, the threat of takeover was often enforced by **corporate raiders:** individuals or corporations that buy up large blocks of shares in companies that they think are pursuing strategies inconsistent with maximizing stockholder wealth. Corporate raiders argue that if these underperforming companies pursued different strategies, they could create more wealth for stockholders. Raiders buy stock in a company either to take over the business and run it more efficiently, or to precipitate a change in the top management, replacing the existing team with one more likely to maximize stockholder returns. Raiders are motivated not by altruism but by gain. If they succeed in their takeover bid, they can institute strategies that create value for stockholders, including themselves. Even if a takeover bid fails, raiders can still earn millions, for their stockholdings will typically be bought out by the defending company for a hefty premium. Called **greenmail,** this source of gain stirred much controversy and debate about its benefits. While some claim that the threat posed by raiders has had a salutary effect on enterprise performance by pushing corporate management to run their companies better, others claim there is little evidence of this.[37]

Although the incidence of hostile takeover bids has fallen off significantly since the early 1990s, this should not be taken to imply that the takeover constraint is no longer operating. Unique circumstances exist in the early 2000s that have made it more difficult to execute hostile takeovers. The boom years of the 1990s left many corporations with excessive debt (corporate America entered the new century with record levels of debt on its balance sheets), which limits the ability of companies to finance acquisitions, particularly hostile acquisitions, which are often particularly expensive. In addition, the market valuations of many companies got so out of line with underlying fundamentals during the stock market bubble of the 1990s that even after a substantial fall in certain segments of the stock market, such as the technology sector, valuations are still high relative to historic norms, making the hostile acquisition of even poorly run and unprofitable companies expensive. However, takeovers tend to go in cycles, and it seems likely that once excesses are worked out of the stock market and worked off corporate balance sheets, the takeover constraint will begin to reassert itself. It should be remembered that the takeover constraint is the governance mechanism of last resort and is often invoked only when other governance mechanisms have failed.

Governance Mechanisms Inside a Company

So far this section has focused on the governance mechanisms designed to reduce the agency problem that potentially exists between stockholders and managers. Agency relationships also exist within a company, and the agency problem can thus arise *between* levels of management. In this section, we explore how the agency problem can be reduced within a company by using two complementary governance mechanisms to align the incentives and behavior of employees with those of upper-level management: strategic control systems and incentive systems.

Strategic Control Systems. Strategic control systems are the primary governance mechanisms established within a company to reduce the scope of the agency problem between levels of management. These systems are the formal target setting, measurement, and feedback systems that allow managers to evaluate whether a company is executing the strategies necessary to maximize its long-run ROIC and, in particular, whether the company is achieving superior efficiency, quality, innovation, and customer responsiveness. They are discussed in more detail in subsequent chapters.

The purpose of strategic control systems is to (1) establish standards and targets against which performance can be measured, (2) create systems for measuring and monitoring performance on a regular basis, (3) compare actual performance against the established targets, and (4) evaluate results and take corrective action if necessary. In governance terms, their purpose is to make sure that lower-level managers, as the agents of top managers, are acting in a way that is consistent with top managers' goals, which should be to maximize the wealth of stockholders, subject to legal and ethical constraints.

One increasingly influential model that guides managers through the process of creating the right kind of strategic control systems to enhance organizational performance is the balanced scorecard model.[38] According to the **balanced scorecard model,** traditionally managers have primarily used financial measures of performance such as return on invested capital to measure and evaluate organizational performance. Financial information is extremely important, but it is not enough by itself. If managers are to obtain a true picture of organizational performance, financial information must be supplemented with performance measures that indicate how well an organization has been achieving the four building blocks of competitive advantage: efficiency, quality, innovation, and responsiveness to customers. This is so because financial results simply inform strategic managers about the results of decisions they have *already taken;* the other measures balance this picture of performance by informing managers about how accurately the organization has in place the building blocks that drive *future performance.*[39]

One version of the way the balanced scorecard operates is presented in Figure 11.4. Based on an organization's mission and goals, strategic managers develop a set of strategies to build competitive advantage to achieve these goals. They then establish an organizational structure to use resources to obtain a competitive advantage.[40] To evaluate how well the strategy and structure are working, managers develop specific

FIGURE 11.4

A Balanced Scorecard
Approach

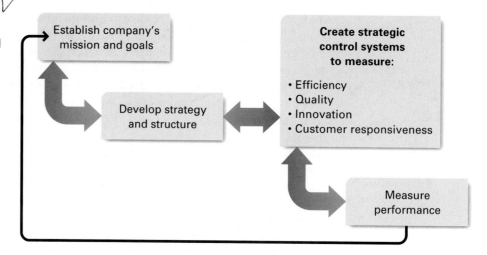

performance measures that assess how well the four building blocks of competitive advantage are being achieved:

■ *Efficiency* can be measured by the level of production costs, the productivity of labor (such as the employee hours needed to make a product), the productivity of capital (such as revenues per dollar invested in property, plant, and equipment), and the cost of raw materials.

■ *Quality* can be measured by the number of rejects, the number of defective products returned from customers, and the level of product reliability over time.

■ *Innovation* can be measured by the number of new products introduced, the percentage of revenues generated from new products in a defined period, the time taken to develop the next generation of new products versus the competition, and the productivity of R&D (i.e., how much R&D spending is required to produce a successful product).

■ *Responsiveness to customers* can be measured by the number of repeat customers, customer defection rates, level of on-time delivery to customers, and level of customer service.

As Kaplan and Norton, the developers of this approach suggest, "Think of the balanced scorecard as the dials and indicators in an airplane cockpit. For the complex task of navigating and flying an airplane, pilots need detailed information about many aspects of the flight. They need information on fuel, air speed, altitude, learning, destination, and other indicators that summarize the current and predicted environment. Reliance on one instrument can be fatal. Similarly, the complexity of managing an organization today requires that managers be able to view performance in several areas simultaneously."[41]

The way in which managers' ability to build a competitive advantage translates into organizational performance is then measured using financial measures such as the return on invested capital, the return on sales, and the capital turnover ratio (see Chapter 3). Based on an evaluation of the complete set of measures in the balanced scorecard, strategic managers are in a good position to reevaluate the company's mission and goals and take corrective action to rectify problems, limit the agency problem, or exploit new opportunities by changing the organization's strategy and structure—which is the purpose of strategic control.

Employee Incentives. Control systems alone may not be sufficient to align incentives between stockholders, senior management, and the rest of the organization. To help do this, positive incentive systems are often put into place to motivate employees to work toward goals that are central to maximizing long-run ROIC. As already noted, employee stock ownership plans (ESOP) are one form of positive incentive, as are stock option grants. In the 1990s, ESOPs and stock ownership grants got pushed down deep within many organizations. At Microsoft, for example, all full-time employees receive stock options, and the amount of options they receive is determined by their performance evaluation in the prior year. In addition, all full-time employees are eligible to enroll in the company's ESOP. The logic behind such systems is straightforward: recognizing that the stock price, and therefore their own wealth, is dependent on the profitability of the company, employees will work toward maximizing profitability.

In addition to stock-based compensation systems, employee compensation can also be tied to goals that are linked to the attainment of superior efficiency, quality, innovation, and customer responsiveness. For example, the bonus pay of a manufacturing employee might depend on attaining quality and productivity targets, which if reached will lower the costs of the company, increase customer satisfaction, and boost the ROIC. Similarly, the bonus pay of a salesperson might be dependent on surpassing sales targets, and of an R&D employee on the success of new products she had a hand in developing.

Ethics and Strategy

The Enron story reviewed in the *Opening Case,* along with several other examples considered in this chapter, all underline the need for managers to behave in an ethical manner when making strategic decisions. From a management perspective, an **ethical decision** is one that reasonable or typical stakeholders would find acceptable because it aids stakeholders, the organization, or society. By contrast, an **unethical decision** is a decision a manager would prefer to disguise or hide from other people because it enables a company or a particular individual to gain at the expense of society or other stakeholders. There seems to be little question, for example, that by disguising the true state of the company to important stakeholders, such as stockholders, bondholders, and employees, some senior managers at Enron were able to push the value of the company's stock higher than would otherwise have been the case, enabling those same managers to profit from the sale of Enron stock they owned. This section looks at the issue of ethics and strategy and identifies some guiding principles that can help managers to make strategic decisions that are ethical.

The Purpose of Business Ethics

The purpose of business ethics is not so much to teach the difference between right and wrong as to give people the tools for dealing with moral complexity—tools that they use to identify and think through the moral implications of strategic decisions.[42] Most of us already have a good sense of what is right and wrong. The problem, however, is that although most managers rigorously adhere to such moral principles in their private life, some fail to apply them in their professional life, occasionally with disastrous consequences.

The sorry history of Manville Corporation illustrates such failure. Two decades ago, Manville (then Johns Manville) was solid enough to be included among the giants of U.S. industry. By 1989, 80 percent of the equity of Manville was owned by a trust representing people who had sued the company for liability in connection with one of its principal former products, asbestos. More than forty years ago, information began to reach the medical department of Johns Manville—and through it the company's managers—suggesting that inhalation of asbestos particles was a major cause of asbestosis, a fatal lung disease. Manville's managers suppressed the research. Moreover, as a matter of company policy, they apparently decided to conceal the information from affected employees, and the company's medical staff collaborated in the cover-up. Somehow, managers at Manville persuaded themselves that it was more important to cover up the situation than to take steps to improve working conditions and find safer ways to handle asbestos. They calculated that the cost of improving working conditions was greater than the cost of health insurance to cover those who became ill, and so the best "economic" decision was to conceal information from employees.[43]

The key to understanding the Manville story is the realization that the men and women at Manville who participated in the cover-up were not amoral monsters but just ordinary people. Most of them would probably never dream of breaking the law or of physically harming anyone. And yet they consciously made a decision that led directly to great human suffering and death. What seemed to have occurred was that the decision to suppress information was considered on purely economic grounds. Its moral dimension was ignored. Somehow the managers were able to convince themselves that they were engaged in making a rational business decision that should be subjected to an economic cost-benefit analysis. Ethical considerations never entered into this calculation. Such behavior is possible only in an environment where business decisions are viewed as having no ethical component. But as the Manville example shows, business decisions *do* have an ethical component.

The task of business ethics, therefore, is to make two central points: (1) business decisions have an ethical component and (2) managers must weigh the ethical implications of strategic decisions before choosing a course of action. Had managers at Manville been trained to think through the ethical implications of their decision, it is unlikely that they would have chosen the same course of action.

Shaping the Ethical Climate of an Organization

To foster awareness that strategic decisions have an ethical dimension, a company must establish an organizational climate that emphasizes the importance of ethics. This requires at least three steps. First, top managers have to use their leadership position to incorporate an ethical dimension into the values they stress. At Hewlett Packard, for example, Bill Hewlett and David Packard, the company's founders, propagated a set of values known as the HP Way. These values, which shape the way business is conducted both within and by the corporation, have an important ethical component. Among other things, they stress the need for confidence in and respect for people, open communication, and concern for the individual employee. Had these values been operational at Manville, they would have helped managers there avoid their catastrophic mistake.

Second, ethical values must be incorporated into the company's mission statement. Third—and this is most important—ethical values must be acted on. Top managers have to implement hiring, firing, and incentive systems that explicitly recognize the importance of adhering to ethical values in strategic decision making. At Hewlett Packard, for example, it has been said that although it is difficult for employees to lose their job (because of the concern for individual employees), nothing gets an employee fired more quickly than violating the ethical norms of the company as articulated in the HP Way.[44] In contrast, although Enron did have a code of ethics that explicitly incorporated ethical values into the company's mission statement, it is very clear that several of the senior managers did not act on those values, and in fact took actions that were directly counter to them.

Thinking Through Ethical Problems

Besides establishing the right kind of ethical climate in an organization, managers must be able to think through the ethical implications of strategic decisions in a systematic way. Philosophers have debated for centuries about the specific criteria that should be used to determine whether decisions are ethical or unethical. Three models of what determines whether a decision is ethical—the *utilitarian, moral rights,* and *justice* models—are summarized in Table 11.2. In theory, each model offers a different and complementary way of determining whether a decision or behavior is ethical, and all three models should be used to sort out the ethics of a particular course of action. Ethical issues, however, are seldom clear-cut, and the interests of different stakeholders often conflict, so it is frequently extremely difficult for a decision maker to use these models to ascertain the most ethical course of action. For this reason,

TABLE 11.2

Comparing Utilitarian, Moral Rights, and Justice

Model	Managerial Implications	Problems for Managers
Utilitarian model: An ethical decision is one that produces the greatest good for the greatest number of people.	Managers should compare and contrast alternative courses of action based on the benefits and costs of these alternatives for different organizational stakeholder groups. They should choose the course of action that provides the most benefits to stakeholders. For example, managers should locate a new manufacturing plant at the place that will most benefit its stakeholders.	How do managers decide on the relative importance of each stakeholder group? How are managers to measure the benefits and harms to each stakeholder group precisely? For example, how do managers choose among the interests of stockholders, workers, and customers?
Moral rights model: An ethical decision is one that best maintains and protects the fundamental rights and privileges of the people affected by it. For example, ethical decisions protect people's rights to freedom, life and safety, privacy, free speech, and freedom of conscience.	Managers should compare and contrast alternative courses of action based on the effect of these alternatives on stakeholders' rights. They should choose the course of action that best protects stakeholders' rights. For example, decisions that would involve significant harm to the safety or health of employees or customers are unethical.	If a decision will protect the rights of some stakeholders and hurt the rights of others, how do managers choose which stakeholder rights to protect? For example, in deciding whether it is ethical to snoop on an employee, does an employee's right to privacy outweigh an organization's right to protect its property or the safety of other employees?
Justice model: An ethical decision is one that distributes benefits and harm among stakeholders in a fair, equitable, or impartial way.	Managers should compare and contrast alternative courses of action based on the degree to which the action will promote a fair distribution of outcomes. For example, employees who are similar in their level of skill, performance, or responsibility should receive the same kind of pay. The allocation of outcomes should not be based on arbitrary differences such as gender, race, or religion.	Managers must learn not to discriminate among people because of observable differences in their appearance or behavior. Managers must also learn how to use fair procedures to determine how to distribute outcomes to organizational members. For example, managers must not give people they like bigger raises than they give to people they do not like or bend the rules to help their favorites.

many experts on ethics propose a practical guide to determine whether a decision or behavior is ethical.[45] A decision is probably acceptable on ethical grounds if a manager can answer yes to each of these questions:

1. Does my decision fall within the accepted values or standards that typically apply in the organizational environment?

2. Am I willing to see the decision communicated to all stakeholders affected by it—for example, by having it reported in newspapers or on television?

3. Would the people with whom I have a significant personal relationship, such as family members, friends, or even managers in other organizations, approve of the decision?

To think through ethical problems, several authors have recommended a four-step process.[46] In Step 1, managers must identify which stakeholders the decision would affect and in what ways. Most important, they need to determine whether the proposed decision would violate the rights of any stakeholders. The term **rights** refers to the fundamental entitlements of a stakeholder. For example, we might argue that the right to information about health risks in the workplace is a fundamental entitlement of employees. It is an entitlement that Manville ignored.

Step 2 involves judging the ethics of the proposed strategic decision given the information gained in Step 1. This judgment should be guided by various moral principles that should not be violated. The principles might be those articulated in a corporate mission statement or other company documents (such as Hewlett Packard's HP Way). In addition, certain moral principles that we have adopted as members of society—for instance, the prohibition on stealing—should not be violated. The judgment at this stage will also be guided by the decision rule that is chosen to assess the proposed strategic decision. Although long-run profit maximization is rightly the decision rule that most companies stress, it should be applied subject to the constraint that no moral principles are violated.

Step 3, establishing moral intent, means that the company must resolve to place moral concerns ahead of other concerns in cases where either the rights of stakeholders or key moral principles have been violated. At this stage, input from top management might be particularly valuable. Without the encouragement of top managers, middle-level managers might tend to place the narrow economic interests of the company before the interests of stakeholders. They might do so in the (usually erroneous) belief that top managers favor such an approach. Step 4 requires the company to engage in ethical behavior.

Summary of Chapter

1. The causes of persistently poor company performance include poor management, a high cost structure, inadequate differentiation, extensive diversification, structural shifts in demand, the emergence of powerful new competitors, and organization inertia.

2. Instituting a successful turnaround strategy requires new leadership, a change of strategy, and a change in organization.

3. Stakeholders are individuals or groups that have an interest, claim, or stake in the company, in what it does, and in how well it performs.

4. Stakeholders are in an exchange relationship with the company. They supply the organization with important resources (or contributions) and in exchange expect its interests to be satisfied (by inducements).

5. A company cannot always satisfy the claims of all stakeholders. The goals of different groups may conflict. The company must identify the most important

stakeholders and give highest priority to pursuing strategies that satisfy their needs.

6. A company's stockholders are its legal owners and the providers of risk capital, a major source of the capital resources that allow a company to operate its business. As such, they have a unique role among stakeholder groups.

7. Maximizing long-run ROIC is the route to maximizing returns to stockholders, and it is also consistent with satisfying the claims of several other key stakeholder groups.

8. Although maximizing long-run ROIC is the best way to satisfy the claims of several key stakeholder groups, a company has the obligation to do so within the limits set by the law and in a manner consistent with societal expectations.

9. An agency relationship is held to arise whenever one party delegates decision-making authority or control over resources to another.

10. The essence of the agency problem is that the interests of principals and agents are not always the same, and some agents may take advantage of information asymmetries to maximize their own interests at the expense of principals.

11. A number of governance mechanisms serve to limit the agency problem. These include the board of direc-

tors, stock-based compensation schemes, and the threat of a takeover.

12. Many strategic decisions have an ethical dimension. Any action by a company inevitably has an impact on the welfare of its stakeholders.

13. The purpose of business ethics is not so much to teach the difference between right and wrong, but to give people the tools for dealing with moral complexity–for identifying and thinking through the moral implications of strategic decisions.

Discussion Questions

1. How prevalent was the agency problem in corporate America during the late 1990s?

2. Who benefited the most from the late 1990s boom in initial public offerings of Internet companies: investors (stockholders) in those companies, managers, or investment bankers?

3. Why is maximizing return on invested capital consistent with maximizing returns to stockholders?

4. How might a company configure its strategy-making processes to reduce the probability that managers will pursue their own self-interest, at the expense of stockholders?

5. Should stock options be treated as an expense? If they were, what impact would this have on a company?

Practicing Strategic Management

SMALL-GROUP EXERCISE: EVALUATING STAKEHOLDER CLAIMS

Break up into groups of three to five people, and appoint one group member as a spokesperson who will communicate your findings to the class when called on by the instructor. Discuss the following:

1. Identify the key stakeholders of your educational institution. What claims do they place on the institution?

2. Strategically, how is the institution responding to those claims? Do you think the institution is pursuing the correct strategies in view of these claims? What might it do differently, if anything?

3. Prioritize the stakeholders in order of their importance for the survival and health of the institution. Do the claims of different stakeholder groups conflict with each other? If claims conflict, whose should be tackled first?

ARTICLE FILE 11

Find an example of a company that ran into trouble because it failed to take into account the rights of one of its stakeholder groups when making an important strategic decision.

STRATEGIC MANAGEMENT PROJECT: MODULE 11

This module deals with the relationships your company has with its major stakeholder groups. With the information you have at your disposal, perform the tasks and answer the questions that follow:

1. Identify the main stakeholder groups in your company. What claims do they place on the company? How is the company trying to satisfy those claims?

2. Evaluate the performance of the CEO of your company from the perspective of (a) stockholders, (b) employees, (c) customers, and (d) suppliers. What does this evaluation tell you about the ability of the

CEO and the priorities that he or she is committed to?

3. Try to establish whether the governance mechanisms that operate in your company do a good job of aligning the interests of top managers with those of stockholders.

4. Pick a major strategic decision made by your company in recent years, and try to think through the ethical implications of that decision. In the light of your review, do you think that the company acted correctly?

EXPLORING THE WEB
Visiting Merck

Visit the web site of Merck, the world's largest pharmaceutical company (**www.merck.com/overview/philosophy. html**), and read the mission statement posted there. Then answer the following questions:

1. Evaluate this mission statement in the light of the material contained in this chapter. Does the mission

clearly state what Merck's basic strategic goal is? Do the values listed here provide a good guideline for managerial action at Merck? Do those values recognize stakeholder claims?

2. Follow the hypertext link "benefits humanity." Read the section on corporate responsibility. How does Merck attempt to balance the goals of providing stockholders with an adequate rate of return on their investment, while at the same time developing medicines that benefit humanity and that can be acquired by people in need at an affordable price? Do you think that Merck does a good job of balancing these goals?

General Task: Using the Web, find an example of a company where there was overt conflict between principals and agents over the future strategic direction of the organization.

Closing Case

Chainsaw Al Gets the Ax

In July 1996, Sunbeam, a troubled maker of small appliances, announced that it had hired Al Dunlap as its chief executive officer. Sunbeam's stock jumped 50 percent on the news to $18 5/8 as investors eagerly anticipated the gains that the legendary "Chainsaw Al" would bring to Sunbeam. Dunlap's reputation was built on a highly successful career as a turnaround specialist. Before joining Sunbeam, he had engineered a tough turnaround at Scott Paper. There he had laid off 31 percent of the workforce, including 70 percent of all upper-level managers. The stock market valuation of Scott tripled during his tenure. After only eighteen months at Scott, Dunlap walked away with $100 million in salary, bonus, stock gains, and perks, a richly deserved reward, he claimed, given the gains that he engineered in the stock of Scott Paper. Now investors hoped that he would work the same magic at Sunbeam.

Upon arrival at Sunbeam, Dunlap quickly fired seven of Sunbeam's top executives. Then he spent three months formulating his strategy, which he unveiled at an analyst meeting in November 1996. It was classic Dunlap: Sunbeam's workforce would be cut in half to just 6,000, eighteen of the company's twenty-six factories would be closed, four divisions would be disposed of, and the num-

ber of products Sunbeam offered would be reduced by 81 percent to 1,500. These measures were projected to produce annual savings of $225 million. Dunlap also laid out ambitious growth goals for Sunbeam, including doubling revenues to $2 billion (after divestitures), raising operating profit margins to 20 percent from 2.5 percent, launching at least thirty new products a year, and increasing international sales to $600 million. "Our growth mission," he proclaimed, "is to become the dominant and most profitable small household appliance and outdoor cooking company in North America, with a leading share of Latin American and Asian Pacific markets."

Right from the start, there were questions about the feasibility of this strategy. Several securities analysts that followed Sunbeam wondered how the company could possibly increase revenues given the depth of the cuts in employment and products, particularly since the North American market for small appliances was experiencing no growth. Nevertheless, Sunbeam's initial results seemed to suggest that Dunlap could pull off this trick. Revenues grew by 18 percent in 1997, while operating margins income rose to $109.4 million and the stock price surged to around $50 a share. It looked as if Dunlap was about to prove once again that tough guys finish first.

However, under the surface were problems. To increase revenues, Dunlap was urging Sunbeam's managers to engage in a "bill and hold" strategy with retailers. Under this arrangement, Sunbeam's products were purchased at large discounts and then held at third-party warehouses for delivery later. In effect, Dunlap was shifting sales from future periods into the current period. Although the approach was not illegal, the ethics of the approach were certainly questionable. Later, Dunlap defended the practice, claiming that it was an effort to extend the selling season and better meet surges in demand. Sunbeam's auditors, Arthur Andersen, also insisted that the practice met accounting standards.

In early March 1998, Dunlap announced that Sunbeam would acquire three companies, including Coleman, the manufacturer of outdoor camping stoves. The stock market responded enthusiastically, and the stock hit an all-time high of $53. Some critics wondered, however, if this implied that Sunbeam could not hit its growth goals from internally generated sales. Shortly afterward, Dunlap announced that the company would book a first-quarter loss of $44.6 million. Dunlap blamed the loss on underlings who had offered "stupid, low-margin deals" and insisted that it would "never happen again." To drive home his point, he fired a number of senior managers who, he claimed, were responsible for the "stupid, low-margin deals," including Donald Uzzi, Sunbeam's well-regarded executive vice president for worldwide consumer products. Around the same time, Dunlap announced that he would cut 5,100 more jobs at the acquired companies and at Sunbeam.

Dunlap's layoff announcement did not stop the fall in Sunbeam's stock price, which had been declining ever since the announcement of a first-quarter loss and now stood under $20. The decline in the stock price accelerated in late May 1998, when the highly regarded financial newspaper *Barron's* published a scathing analysis of Sunbeam. In the article, *Barron's* alleged that Dunlap had employed $120 million of artificial profit boosters in 1997, without which Sunbeam would have recorded a loss.

Dunlap was so concerned about the *Barron's* article that he called a special meeting of the company's board of directors on June 9, 1998. The board had been supportive of Dunlap to this point, and he could count several long-time friends among its number. What began as a straightforward meeting rebutting the *Barron's* article took a strange turn when one director asked Sunbeam's chief financial officer, Russ Kersh, if the company would make its next quarter's numbers. Kersh admitted that they were "challenging." At this point, Dunlap asked all of the outside advisers to step out and then told the board that he and the CFO would resign unless they got the right level of support from the board. "I have all of the necessary documents in my briefcase," Dunlap was reported to have said and then stormed out of the room.

Over the next few days, the board members started to dig deeper. One director placed a call to several top executives. He quickly discovered that many had lost confidence in Dunlap, whom they characterized as abusive and unethical. He was also disturbed to hear that not only would Sunbeam miss its growth goals in the coming quarter, but that revenues would probably come in $60 million *below* the $290 million recorded in the same quarter a year earlier.

Armed with this information, the board convened a second meeting on June 13. At that meeting, the directors all agreed that Dunlap had to go. Most of the directors were friends of Dunlap, but they felt betrayed by him, misled about the company's financial condition, its second-quarter earnings, and its yearly numbers. That day they placed a call to Dunlap and told him that he had been dismissed. Three days later, the board also fired Russ Kersh, the CFO. Commenting on Dunlap's demise, the CEO of a competitor to Sunbeam stated that Dunlap "is the logical extreme of an executive who has no values, no loyalty, no honor, no ethics. And yet he was held up as a corporate god in our culture. It greatly bothers me." A former plant manager whom Dunlap had fired remarked, "I guess the house of cards came tumbling down. When you reduce your workforce by 50 percent, you lose your ability to manage. You can survive like that for months, not years." Following the announcement that Dunlap had been fired, Sunbeam stock fell to under $8 a share, lower than it had been before Dunlap joined the company.

Case Discussion Questions

1. In whose best interests was Al Dunlap acting? Do you think he was honestly trying to discharge his obligation to key stakeholder groups, such as stockholders, employees, and customers?

2. Do you think the Sunbeam board exercised its fiduciary duty? What does this tell you about how boards can work?

3. In retrospect, what might Al Dunlap have done differently to engineer a turnaround at Sunbeam?

Sources: John Byrne, "How Al Dunlap Self-Destructed," *Business Week,* July 6, 1998, p. 58. G. DeGeorge, "Al Dunlap Revs Up His Chainsaw," *Business Week,* November 25, 1996, p. 37. "Exit Bad Guy," *Economist,* June 20, 1998, p. 70. Ellen Pollock and Martha Brannigan, "Mixed Grill: The Sunbeam Shuffle," *Wall Street Journal,* August 19, 1998, p. A1.

Implementing Strategy in Companies That Compete in a Single Industry

Opening Case

Strategy Implementation at Dell Computer

Dell Computer, was one of the fastest-growing companies of the 1990s, and its stock price increased at the rate of 100 percent a year, delighting its stockholders. Achieving this high return was a constant challenge for Michael Dell, and one of his biggest battles has been to manage and change Dell's organizational structure, control systems, and culture as his company grew.

Dell was nineteen when, in 1984, he took $1,000 and spent it on the computer parts he assembled himself into PCs that he then sold over the phone. Increasing demand for his PCs meant that within a few weeks, he needed to hire people to help him, and soon he found himself supervising three employees who worked together around a six-foot table to assemble computers while two more employees took orders over the phone.

By 1993, Dell employed 4,500 workers and was hiring over a hundred new workers each week just to keep pace with the demand for the computers. When he found himself working eighteen-hour days managing the company, he realized that he could not lead the company single-handedly. The company's growth had to be managed, and he knew that he had to recruit and hire strategic managers who had experience in managing different functional areas, such as marketing, finance, and manufacturing. He recruited executives from IBM and Compaq and with their help created a functional structure, one in which employees are grouped by the common skills they have or tasks they perform, for example, sales or manufacturing, to organize the value chain activities necessary to deliver his PCs to customers. As a part of this organizing process, Dell's structure also became taller, with more levels in the management hierarchy, to ensure he and his managers had sufficient control over the different activities of his growing business. Dell delegated authority to control Dell's functional value chain activities to his managers, which gave him the time he needed to perform his entrepreneurial task of finding new opportunities for the company.

Dell's functional structure worked well, and under its new management team, the company's growth continued to soar. By 1993, the company had sales of over $2 billion, twice as much as in 1992. Moreover, Dell's new structure had given functional managers the control they needed to squeeze out costs, and Dell had become the lowest-cost PC maker. Analysts also reported that Dell had developed a lean organizational culture, meaning that employees had developed norms and values that emphasized the importance of working hard to help each other find innovative new ways of making products to keep costs low and increase their reliability. Indeed, with the fewest customer complaints, Dell rose to the top of the customer satisfaction rankings for PC makers; its employees became known for the excellent customer service they give to PC buyers experiencing problems with setting up their computers.

Michael Dell realized that new and different kinds of problems were arising. Dell was now selling huge numbers of computers to different kinds of customers, for example, home, business, and educational customers and the different branches of government. Because customers now demanded computers with very different features or different amounts of computing power, its product line broadened rapidly. It started to become more difficult for employees to meet the needs of these different kinds of customers efficiently because each employee needed information about all product features or all of Dell's thousands of different sales offers across its product range.

In 1995, Dell moved to change his company to a market structure and created separate divisions, each geared to the needs of the different groups of customers—a consumer division, business division, and so on. In each division, teams of employees specialize in servicing the needs of one of these customer groups. This move to a more complex structure also allowed each division to develop a unique subculture that suited its tasks, and employees were able to obtain in-depth knowledge about the needs of their market that helped them to respond better to their customers' needs. So successful was this change in structure and culture that by 1999, Dell's revenues were over $30 billion, and its profits were in excess of $2.5 billion, a staggering increase from 1984.

Dell has continued to alter his company's structure to respond to the changing nature of its customers' needs and because its own distinctive competencies have increased over time. For example, Dell realized he could leverage his company's strengths in materials management, manufacturing, and Internet sales over a wider range of computer hardware products. So he decided to begin assembling servers, workstations, and storage devices to compete with IBM, Sun, and Compaq. The increasing importance of the Internet led him to split the market divisions into thirty-five smaller subunits that focus on more specialized groups of customers, and they all conduct the majority of their business over the Internet. Today, for example, Dell can offer large and small companies and private buyers a complete range of computers, workstations, and storage devices that can be customized to their needs.

To help coordinate its growing activities, Dell is increasingly making use of its corporate intranet and using information technology (IT) to standardize activities across divisions to integrate across functions. Dell's hierarchy is shrinking as managers are increasingly delegating everyday decision making to employees who have access, through IT, to the information they need to provide excellent customer service. To help reduce costs, it has also outsourced some of its customer service activities. As a result of these moves, Dell's workforce has become even more committed to sustaining its low-cost advantage, and its cost-conscious culture has become an important source of competitive advantage that is the envy of its competitors.

Sources: G. McWilliams, "Dell Looks for Ways to Rekindle the Fire It Had as an Upstart," *Wall Street Journal,* August 31, 2000, pp. A.1, A.8. "Dell Hopes to Lead Firm out of Desert," *Houston Chronicle,* September, 3, 2000, p. 4D. **www.dell.com,** 2002.

Overview

As the story of Dell suggests, this chapter examines how managers can best implement their strategies to achieve a competitive advantage and superior performance. A well-thought-out business model becomes profitable to pursue only if it can be implemented successfully. In practice, strategy implementation is a difficult and challenging task and a never-ending task. Managers cannot just create an organizing framework for a company's value chain activities and then assume it will keep working efficiently and effectively, just as they cannot select strategies and assume that these strategies will work as intended in the future when the environment is changing.

First, the main elements of strategy implementation and the way they work together to create an organizing framework for a company's people and activities are considered. Second, each of these elements—structure, control systems, and culture—is analyzed in detail. Third, the way strategic managers can use structure, control, and culture at the functional level to pursue functional-level strategies that create and build distinctive competencies is examined. The analysis then goes up to the industry level and the many different issues facing managers in implementing strategy to gain a competitive advantage in a single industry are addressed. The next chapter takes up where this one leaves off and examines strategy implementation across industries and across countries—that is, implementing corporate and global strategy.

By the end of this chapter and the next, you will understand the dynamics of strategy implementation and why the fortunes of a company often rest on its managers' abilities to design and manage its structure, control systems, and culture.

Implementing Strategy Through Organizational Structure, Control, and Culture

Strategy implementation refers to how a company should create, use, and combine organizational structure, control systems, and culture to pursue strategies that lead to a competitive advantage and superior performance. **Organizational structure** assigns employees to specific value creation tasks and roles and specifies how these tasks and roles are to be linked together in a way that increases efficiency, quality, innovation, and responsiveness to customers—the building blocks of competitive advantage. The purpose of organizational structure is to *coordinate and integrate* the efforts of employees at all levels—corporate, business, and functional—and across a company's functions and business units so that they work together in the way that will allow it to achieve the specific set of strategies in its business model.

Organizational structure does not by itself provide the set of incentives through which people can be *motivated* to make it work. Hence, there is a need for control systems. The purpose of a **control system** is to provide managers with (1) a set of incentives to motivate employees to work toward increasing efficiency, quality, innovation, and responsiveness to customers and (2) specific feedback on how well an organization and its members are performing and building competitive advantage so that managers can constantly take action to strengthen a company's business model. Structure provides an organization with a skeleton; control gives it the muscles, sinews, nerves, and sensations that allow managers to regulate and govern its activities.

Organizational culture, the third element of strategy implementation, is the specific collection of values, norms, beliefs, and attitudes shared by people and groups in an organization and that control the way they interact with each other and with stakeholders outside the organization.[1] As discussed in detail following, top managers can influence how and which beliefs and values develop in an organization, and values and beliefs are a third important determinant of how organizational members will work toward achieving organizational goals.[2] If organizational control has an impact on how a particular kind of organizational structure will work, so organizational culture determines how both structure and control will work in practice.

Figure 12.1 sums up the argument so far. Organizational structure, control, and culture are the means by which an organization motivates, coordinates, and "incentivizes" its members to work toward achieving the building blocks of competitive advantage. Top managers who wish to find out why it takes a long time for people to make decisions in a company, why there is a lack of cooperation between sales and manufacturing, or why product innovations are few and far between need to understand how the design of a company's structure and control system and the values and norms in its culture affect the way its employees are coordinated and motivated and rewarded by working together. *Organizational structure, control, and culture shape the way people behave, their values and attitudes, and determine how they will implement an organization's business model and strategies.*[3] On the basis of such an analysis, top managers can devise a plan to restructure or change their company's structure, control systems, and culture to improve coordination and motivation. Effective strategy implementation allows a company to obtain a competitive advantage and achieve above-average profitability.

Building Blocks of Organizational Structure

After formulating a company's business model and strategies, managers must make designing organizational structure its next priority. The value creation activities of organizational members are meaningless unless some type of structure is used to assign them to tasks and connect the activities of different people and functions.[4] Three basic choices are involved when managers design an organization's structure:

1. How best to group tasks into functions and group functions into business units or divisions to create distinctive competencies and pursue a particular strategy

2. How to allocate authority and responsibility to these functions and divisions

3. How to increase the level of coordination or integration between functions and divisions as a structure evolves and becomes more complex

The basic issues are discussed next and then taken up again when appropriate choices of structure at the different levels of strategy are considered.

FIGURE 12.1

Implementing Strategy

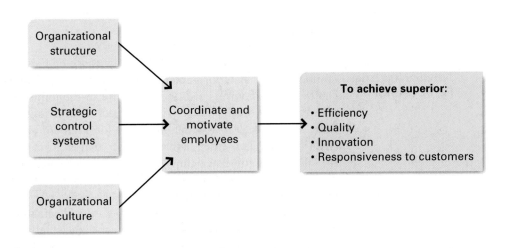

Grouping Tasks, Functions, and Divisions

Because, to a large degree, an organization's tasks are a function of its strategy, the dominant view is that companies choose a form of structure to match their organizational strategy. Perhaps the first person to address this issue formally was the Harvard business historian, Alfred D. Chandler.[5] After studying the organizational problems experienced in large U.S. corporations such as Du Pont and GM as they grew in the early decades of the twentieth century, Chandler reached two conclusions: (1) that in principle, organizational structure follows the range and variety of tasks that the organization chooses to pursue and (2) that U.S. companies' structures change as their strategy changes in a predictable way over time.[6] In general, this means that most companies first group people and tasks into functions, and functions into divisions.[7]

A *function* is a collection of people who work together and perform the same types of tasks or hold similar positions in an organization.[8] For example, the salespeople in a car dealership belong to the sales function. Together, car sales, car repair, car parts, and accounting are the set of functions that allow a car dealership to sell and maintain cars.

As organizations grow and produce a wider range of products, the amount and complexity of the handoffs or transfers between people, functions, and subunits necessary to create a product and deliver it to the customer increase. Recall from previous chapters that the communications and measurement problems surrounding transfers or handoffs are a major source of **bureaucratic costs,** the information distortion problems that increase the costs of negotiating, monitoring, and enforcing the exchanges necessary to add value to a product as it flows along a company's value chain to the final customer.[9]

The reasons that bureaucratic costs increase as companies pursue more complex strategies is discussed in detail following. For now, it is important to note that managers group tasks into functions and, when necessary, group functions into business units or divisions to reduce transaction costs. For example, as Dell Computer started to produce different kinds of products, it created separate divisions, each with its own marketing, sales, and accounting functions. A *division* is a group of functions created to allow an organization to better produce and dispose of its goods and services to customers. In developing an organizational structure, managers must decide how to group an organization's activities by function and division in a way that achieves organizational goals effectively, such as happened at Dell.[10]

Top managers can choose from among many kinds of structure to group their activities, with the choice made on the basis of its ability to meet the needs of their strategies best.

Allocating Authority and Responsibility

As organizations grow and produce a wider range of goods and services, the size and number of their functions and divisions increase. The number of handoffs or transfers between employees also increases, and to economize on transaction costs and effectively coordinate the activities of people, functions, and divisions, managers must develop a clear and unambiguous **hierarchy of authority:** an organization's chain of command—the relative authority that each manager has—extending from the CEO at the top down through the middle managers and first-line managers, to the nonmanagerial employees who actually make goods or provide services.[11] Every manager, at every level of the hierarchy, supervises one or more subordinates. The term **span of control** refers to the number of subordinates who report directly to a manager. When managers know exactly what their authority and responsibility is, information distortion problems are kept to a minimum, and handoffs and transfers can be negotiated and monitored in a way that economize on bureaucratic costs. For example, managers are less likely to risk invading another manager's turf and thus avoid the costly fights and conflicts that will inevitably result.

Tall and Flat Organizations. Companies choose the number of hierarchical levels they need on the basis of their strategy and the functional tasks necessary to achieve it.[12] As an organization grows in size or complexity (normally measured by the number of its employees, functions, and divisions), its hierarchy of authority normally lengthens, making the organizational structure taller. A tall organization has many levels of authority relative to company size; a flat organization has fewer levels relative to company size (see Figure 12.2). As a hierarchy becomes taller, problems that make the organization's structure less flexible and slow managers' response to changes in the organizational environment may result. It is vital that managers understand how these problems arise so they know how to change a company's structure to respond to them.

First, communication problems may arise. When an organization has many levels in the hierarchy, it can take a long time for the decisions and orders of upper-level managers to reach managers further down in the hierarchy, and it can take a long time for top managers to learn how well their decisions worked out. Feeling out of touch, top managers may want to verify that lower-level managers are following orders and may require written confirmation from them. Middle managers, who know they will be held strictly accountable for their actions, start devoting more time to the process of making decisions in order to improve their chances of being right. They might even try to avoid responsibility by making top managers decide what actions to take.

A second communication problem that can result is the distortion of commands and orders as they are transmitted up and down the hierarchy, which causes managers at different levels to interpret what is happening differently. Distortion of orders and messages can be accidental, occurring because different managers interpret messages from their own narrow functional perspectives. Or it can be intentional,

FIGURE 12.2

Tall and Flat Structures

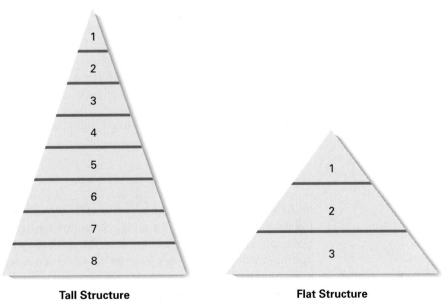

Tall Structure
(8 levels)

Flat Structure
(3 levels)

occurring because managers low in the hierarchy decide to interpret information to increase their own personal advantage.

A third problem with tall hierarchies is that they usually indicate that an organization is employing many managers, and managers are expensive. Managerial salaries, benefits, offices, and secretaries are a huge expense for organizations. Large companies such as IBM and General Motors pay their managers billions of dollars a year. In the 2000s, hundreds of thousands of middle managers were laid off as dot-coms collapsed and high-tech companies like Hewlett Packard and Lucent attempted to reduce costs by restructuring and downsizing their workforces.

The Minimum Chain of Command. To ward off the problems that result when an organization becomes too tall and employs too many managers, top managers need to ascertain whether they are employing the right number of top, middle, and first-line managers and see whether they can redesign their hierarchies to reduce the number of managers. Top managers might well follow a basic organizing principle: the principle of the minimum chain of command states that a company should choose the hierarchy with the *fewest* levels of authority necessary to use organizational resources efficiently and effectively.

Effective managers constantly scrutinize their hierarchies to see whether the number of levels can be reduced—for example, by eliminating one level and giving the responsibilities of managers at that level to managers above and empowering employees below. This practice has become increasingly common in the United States as companies that are battling low-cost foreign competitors search for new ways to reduce costs. One manager who is constantly trying to empower employees and keep the hierarchy flat is Colleen C. Barrett, the number-two executive of Southwest Airlines.[13] Barrett, the highest-ranking woman in the airline industry, is well known for continually reaffirming Southwest's message that employees should feel free to go above and beyond their prescribed roles to provide better customer service. Her central message is that Southwest values and trusts its employees, who are empowered to take responsibility. Southwest employees are encouraged not to look to their superiors for guidance but rather to take responsibility to find ways to do the job better themselves. As a result, Southwest keeps the number of its middle managers to a minimum.

When companies become too tall and the chain of command too long, strategic managers tend to lose control over the hierarchy, which means that they lose control over their strategies. Disaster often follows because a tall organizational structure decreases, rather than promotes, motivation and coordination between employees, and functions and bureaucratic costs escalate as a result. One important way to overcome such problems, at least partially, and to lessen bureaucratic costs is to decentralize authority—that is, vest authority in the hierarchy's lower levels as well as at the top.

Centralization or Decentralization? Authority is centralized when managers at the upper levels of a company's hierarchy retain the authority to make the most important decisions. When authority is decentralized, it is delegated to divisions, functions, and employees at lower levels in the company. By delegating authority in this fashion, managers can economize on bureaucratic costs and avoid communication and coordination problems because information does not have to be constantly sent to the top of the organization for decisions to be made. There are three advantages to decentralization.

First, when strategic managers delegate operational decision-making responsibility to middle and first-level managers, they reduce information overload, enabling strategic managers to spend more time developing competitive strategy. Second, when managers in the bottom layers of the company become responsible for adapting strategy to suit local conditions, their motivation and accountability increase. The result is that decentralization promotes flexibility and reduces bureaucratic costs because lower-level managers are authorized to make on-the-spot decisions; handoffs are not needed. The third advantage is that when lower-level employees are given the right to make important decisions, fewer managers are needed to oversee their activities and tell them what to do. Consider some of the advantages set out in Strategy in Action 12.1 that Union Pacific experienced after it decentralized its operations.

If decentralization is so effective, why don't all companies decentralize decision making and avoid the problems of tall hierarchies? The answer is that centralization has its advantages too. Centralized decision making allows easier coordination of the organizational activities needed to pursue a company's strategy. If managers at all levels can make their own decisions, overall planning becomes extremely difficult, and the company may lose control of its decision making.

Centralization also means that decisions fit broad organization objectives. When its branch operations were getting out of hand, for example, Merrill Lynch increased centralization by installing more information systems to give corporate managers greater control over branch activities. Similarly, Hewlett Packard centralized R&D responsibility at the corporate level to provide a more directed corporate strategy. Furthermore, in times of crisis, centralization of authority permits strong leadership

Strategy in Action 12.1

Union Pacific Decentralizes to Increase Customer Responsiveness

Union Pacific, one of the biggest rail freight carriers in the United States, was experiencing a crisis in the late 1990s. The U.S. economic boom was causing a record increase in the amount of freight that the railroad had to transport, but at the same time, the railroad was experiencing record delays in moving the freight. Union Pacific's customers were irate and complaining bitterly about the problem, and the delays were costing the company millions of dollars in penalty payments—$150 million annually.

The problem stemmed from Union Pacific's very centralized management approach, devised in its attempt to cut costs. All scheduling and route planning was handled centrally at its headquarters office in the attempt to promote operating efficiency. The job of regional managers was largely to ensure the smooth flow of freight through their regions. Now, recognizing that efficiency had to be

balanced by the need to be responsive to customers, Union Pacific's CEO, Dick Davidson, announced a sweeping reorganization to the company's customers. Henceforth, regional managers were to be given the authority to make operational decisions at the level at which it was most important: field operations. Regional managers could now alter scheduling and routing to accommodate customer requests even if this raised costs. The goal of the organization was now to "return to excellent performance by simplifying our processes and becoming easier to deal with." In making this decision, the company was following the lead of its competitors, most of which had already moved to decentralize their operations, recognizing its many advantages.

Sources: "Union Pacific to Reorganize," *cnnfn.com*, August 20, 1998, p. 20. **www.unionpacific.com,** press release, 1998.

because authority is focused on one person or group. This focus allows for speedy decision making and a concerted response by the whole organization. How to choose the right level of centralization for a particular strategy is discussed later.

Integration and Integrating Mechanisms

Much coordination takes place between people, functions, and divisions through the hierarchy of authority. Often, however, as a structure becomes complex, this is not enough, and top managers need to use various **integrating mechanisms** to increase communication and coordination among functions and divisions. The greater the complexity of an organization's structure, the greater is the need for coordination among people, functions, and divisions to make the organizational structure work efficiently.[14] Three kinds of integrating mechanisms that illustrate the kinds of issues involved are discussed next.[15] Once again, the issue is that these mechanisms are employed to economize on the information distortion problems that commonly arise when managing the handoffs or transfers between the ideas and activities of different people, functions, and divisions.

Direct Contact. Direct contact among managers creates a context within which managers from different functions or divisions can work together to solve mutual problems. However, several problems are associated with establishing contact among managers in different functions or divisions. Managers from different functions may have different views about what must be done to achieve organizational goals. But if the managers have equal authority (as functional managers typically do), the only manager who can tell them what to do is the CEO. If functional managers cannot reach agreement, no mechanism exists to resolve the conflict apart from the authority of the boss. In fact, one sign of a poorly performing organizational structure is the number of problems sent up the hierarchy for top managers to solve. The need to solve everyday conflicts and solve handoff or transfer problems raises bureaucratic costs. To reduce such conflicts and solve transfer problems, top managers use more complex integrating mechanisms to increase coordination among functions and divisions.

Liaison Roles. Managers can increase coordination among functions and divisions by establishing liaison roles. When the volume of contacts between two functions increases, one way to improve coordination is to give one manager in each function or division the responsibility for coordinating with the other. These managers may meet daily, weekly, monthly, or as needed to solve handoff issues and transfer problems. The responsibility for coordination is part of the liaison's full-time job, and usually an informal relationship forms between the people involved, greatly easing strains between functions. Furthermore, liaison roles provide a way of transmitting information across an organization, which is important in large organizations whose employees may know no one outside their immediate function or division.

Teams. When more than two functions or divisions share many common problems, direct contact and liaison roles may not provide sufficient coordination. In these cases, a more complex integrating mechanism, the **team,** may be appropriate. One manager from each relevant function or division is assigned to a team that meets to solve a specific mutual problem; members are responsible for reporting back to their subunits on the issues addressed and the solutions recommended. Teams are increasingly being used at all organizational levels.

Strategic Control Systems

Strategic managers choose the organizational strategies and structure they hope will allow the organization to use its resources most effectively to pursue its business model and create value and profit. Then they create **strategic control systems,** tools that allow them to monitor and evaluate whether, in fact, their strategy and structure are working as intended, how they could be improved, and how they should be changed if they are not working.

Strategic control is not just about monitoring how well an organization and its members are performing currently or about how well the firm is using its existing resources. It is also about how to create the incentives to keep employees motivated and focused on the important problems that may confront an organization in the future so that they work together to find solutions that can help an organization perform better over time.[16] To understand the vital importance of strategic control, consider how it helps managers to obtain superior efficiency, quality, innovation, and responsiveness to customers, the four basic building blocks of competitive advantage:

■ *Control and efficiency.* To determine how *efficiently* they are using organizational resources, managers must be able to measure accurately how many units of inputs (raw materials, human resources, and so on) are being used to produce a unit of output. They must also be able to measure the number of units of outputs (goods and services) they produce. A control system contains the measures or yardsticks that allow managers to assess how efficiently they are producing goods and services. Moreover, if managers experiment with changing the way they produce goods and services to find a more efficient way of producing them, these measures tell managers how successful they have been. Without a control system in place, managers have no idea how well their organizations are performing and how they can make it perform better, something that is becoming increasingly important in today's highly competitive environment.[17]

■ *Control and quality.* Today, competition often revolves around increasing the *quality* of goods and services. In the car industry, for example, within each price range, cars compete against one another in terms of their features, design, and reliability. So whether a customer buys a Ford Taurus, a GM Cavalier, a Chrysler Intrepid, a Toyota Camry, or a Honda Accord depends significantly on the quality of each company's product. Strategic control is important in determining the quality of goods and services because it gives managers feedback on product quality. If managers consistently measure the number of customers' complaints and the number of new cars returned for repairs, they have a good indication of how much quality they have built into their product.

■ *Control and innovation.* Strategic control can help to raise the level of *innovation* in an organization. Successful innovation takes place when managers create an organizational setting in which employees feel empowered to be creative and authority is decentralized to employees so that they feel free to experiment and take risks. Deciding on the appropriate control systems to encourage risk taking is an important management challenge, and, as discussed later in the chapter, an organization's culture becomes important in this regard.

■ *Control and responsiveness to customers.* Finally, strategic managers can help make their organizations more *responsive to customers* if they develop a control system that allows them to evaluate how well employees with customer contact are performing their jobs. Monitoring employees' behavior can help managers find ways to help increase employees' performance level, perhaps by revealing areas in which skills training can help employees or by finding new procedures that allow employees to perform their jobs better. When employees know their behaviors are being monitored, they may have more incentive to be helpful and consistent in the way they act toward customers.

Strategic control systems are the formal target-setting, measurement, and feedback systems that allow strategic managers to evaluate whether a company is achieving superior efficiency, quality, innovation, and customer responsiveness and implementing its strategy successfully. An effective control system should have three characteristics. It should be *flexible* enough to allow managers to respond as necessary to unexpected events; it should provide *accurate information,* giving a true picture of organizational performance; and it should supply managers with the information in a *timely manner* because making decisions on the basis of outdated information is a recipe for failure.[18] As Figure 12.3 shows, designing an effective strategic control system requires four steps:

Step 1: *Establish the standards and targets against which performance is to be evaluated.* General performance standards often derive from the goal of achieving superior efficiency, quality, innovation, or customer responsiveness. Specific performance targets are derived from the strategy pursued by the company. For example, if a company is pursuing a low-cost strategy, then reducing costs by 7 percent a year might be a target. If the company is a service organization such as Wal-Mart or McDonald's, its standards might include time targets for serving customers or guidelines for food quality.

Step 2: *Create the measuring and monitoring systems that indicate whether the standards and targets are being reached.* The company establishes procedures for assessing whether work goals at all levels in the organization are being achieved. In some cases, measuring performance is fairly straightforward. For example, managers can measure quite easily how many customers their employees serve by counting the number of receipts from the cash register. In many cases, however, measuring performance is a difficult task because the organization is engaged in many complex activities. How can managers judge how well their R&D department is doing when it may take five years for products to be developed? How can they measure the company's performance when the company is entering new

FIGURE 12.3

Steps in Designing an Effective Control System

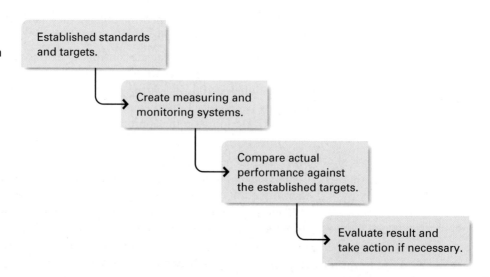

Established standards and targets.

Create measuring and monitoring systems.

Compare actual performance against the established targets.

Evaluate result and take action if necessary.

markets and serving new customers? How can they evaluate how well divisions are integrating? The answer is that managers need to use the various types of control systems discussed below.

Step 3: *Compare actual performance against the established targets.* Managers evaluate whether and to what extent performance deviates from the standards and targets developed in Step 1. If performance is higher, management may decide that it has set the standards too low and may raise them for the next time period. If performance is too low, managers must decide whether to take remedial action. This decision is easy when the reasons for poor performance can be identified—for instance, high labor costs. More often, however, the reasons for poor performance are hard to uncover. They may stem from involved external factors, such as a recession. Alternatively, the cause may be internal. For instance, the R&D laboratory may have underestimated the problems it would encounter or the extra costs of doing unforeseen research. For any form of action, however, Step 4 is necessary.

Step 4: *Initiate corrective action when it is decided that the standards and targets are not being achieved.* Corrective action may mean changing any aspect of strategy or structure discussed in this book. For example, managers may invest more resources in improving R&D, or diversify, or even decide to change their organizational structure.

Levels of Strategic Control

Strategic control systems are developed to measure performance at four levels in a company: corporate, divisional, functional, and individual. Managers at all levels must develop the most appropriate set of measures to evaluate corporate-, business-, and functional-level performance. As the balanced scorecard approach discussed in Chapter 11 suggests, these measures should be tied as closely as possibly to the goals of achieving superior efficiency, quality, innovativeness, and responsiveness to customers. Care must be taken, however, to ensure that the standards used at each level do not cause problems at the other levels—for example, that a division's attempts to improve performance do not conflict with corporate performance. Furthermore, controls at each level should provide the basis on which managers at the levels below can select their control systems. Figure 12.4 illustrates these links.

Types of Strategic Control System

In Chapter 11, the balanced scorecard approach was discussed as a way of ensuring that managers complement the use of ROIC with other kinds of strategic controls to ensure they are pursuing strategies that maximize long-run performance. Here we consider three more types of control system: *personal control, output control, and behavior control.*

Personal Control. **Personal control** is the desire to shape and influence the behavior of a person in a *face-to-face interaction* in the pursuit of a company's goals. The most obvious kind of personal control is direct supervision from a manager further up in the hierarchy. The personal approach is useful because managers can question and probe subordinates about problems or new issues they are facing to get a better understanding of the situation, as well as to ensure that subordinates are performing their work effectively and not hiding any information that could cause problems down the line. Personal control also can come from a group of peers, such as occurs when people work in teams. Once again, personal control at the group level means that there is more possibility for learning to occur and competencies to develop, as well as greater opportunities to prevent free-riding or shirking.

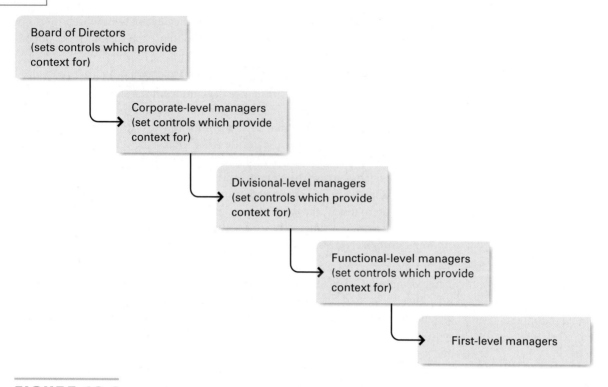

FIGURE 12.4

Levels of Organizational Control

Output Control. Output control is a system in which strategic managers estimate or forecast appropriate performance goals for each division, department, and employee and then measure actual performance relative to these goals. Often a company's reward system is linked to performance on these goals, so output control also provides an incentive structure for motivating employees at all levels in the organization. Goals keep managers informed about how well their strategies are creating a competitive advantage and building the distinctive competencies that lead to future success. Goals exist at all levels in an organization.

Divisional goals state corporate managers' expectations for each division concerning performance on such dimensions as efficiency, quality, innovation, and responsiveness to customers. Generally, corporate managers set challenging divisional goals to encourage divisional managers to create more effective strategies and structures in the future. At Dell, for example, each division is given a clear performance goal to achieve, and divisional managers are given considerable autonomy in formulating a strategy to meet this goal.

Output control at the functional and individual levels is a continuation of control at the divisional level. Divisional managers set goals for functional managers that will allow the division to achieve its goals. As at the divisional level, functional goals are established to encourage development of competencies that provide the company with a competitive advantage. The four building blocks of competitive advantage act as the goals against which functional performance is evaluated. In the sales function, for example, goals related to efficiency (such as cost of sales), quality (such as number of returns), and customer responsiveness (such as the time needed to respond to customer needs) can be established for the whole function.

Finally, functional managers establish goals that individual employees are expected to achieve to allow the function to achieve its goals. Sales personnel, for example, can be given specific goals (related to functional goals) that they are required to achieve. Functions and individuals are then evaluated on the basis of achieving or not achieving their goals, and in sales, compensation is commonly pegged to achievement. The achievement of these goals is a sign that the company's strategy is working and meeting organizational objectives.

The inappropriate use of output control can promote conflict among divisions. In general, setting across-the-board output targets, such as return on investment targets, for divisions can lead to destructive results if divisions single-mindedly try to maximize divisional profits at the expense of corporate objectives. Moreover, to reach output targets, divisions may start to distort the numbers and engage in strategic manipulation of the figures to make their divisions look good.[19]

Behavior Control. **Behavior control** is control through the establishment of a comprehensive system of rules and procedures to direct the actions or behavior of divisions, functions, and individuals.[20] The intention of using behavior controls is not to specify the goals but to standardize the way of reaching them. Rules standardize behavior and make outcomes predictable. If employees follow the rules, then actions are performed and decisions handled the same way time and time again. The result is predictability and accuracy, the aim of all control systems. The main kind of behavior controls are operating budgets, standardization, and rules and procedures.

Once managers at each level have been given a goal to achieve, operating budgets that regulate how managers and workers are to attain those goals are established. An **operating budget** is a blueprint that states how managers intend to use organizational resources to achieve organizational goals most efficiently. Most commonly, managers at one level allocate to managers at a lower level a specific amount of resources to use to produce goods and services. Once they have been given a budget, managers must decide how they will allocate certain amounts of money for different organizational activities. These lower-level managers are then evaluated on the basis of their ability to stay inside the budget and make the best use of it. For example, managers at GE's washing machine division might have a budget of $50 million to develop and sell a new line of washing machines; they have to decide how much money to allocate to R&D, engineering, sales, and so on so that the division generates the most revenue and hence makes the biggest profit. Most commonly, large companies treat each division as a stand-alone profit center, and corporate managers evaluate each division's performance by its relative contribution to corporate profitability, something discussed in detail in the next chapter.

Standardization refers to the degree to which a company specifies how decisions are to be made so that employees' behavior becomes predictable.[21] In practice, there are three things an organization can standardize: *inputs, conversion activities,* and *outputs.*

When managers standardize, they screen *inputs* according to preestablished criteria or standards that determine which inputs to allow into the organization. If employees are the input in question, for example, then one way of standardizing them is to specify which qualities and skills they must possess and then to select only applicants who possess them. If the inputs in question are raw materials or component parts, the same considerations apply. The Japanese are renowned for the high quality and precise tolerances they demand from component parts to minimize problems with the product at the manufacturing stage. Just-in-time inventory systems also help standardize the flow of inputs.

The aim of standardizing *conversion activities* is to program work activities so that they are done the same way time and time again. The goal is predictability. Behavior controls, such as rules and procedures, are among the chief means by which companies can standardize throughputs. Fast-food restaurants such as McDonald's and Burger King standardize all aspects of their restaurant operations; the result is consistent fast food.

The goal of standardizing *outputs* is to specify what the performance characteristics of the final product or service should be—the dimensions or tolerances the product should conform to, for example. To ensure that their products are standardized, companies apply quality control and use various criteria to measure this standardization. One criterion might be the number of goods returned from customers or the number of customers' complaints. On production lines, periodic sampling of products can indicate whether they are meeting performance characteristics.

As with other kinds of controls, the use of behavior control is accompanied by potential pitfalls that must be managed if the organization is to avoid strategic problems. Top management must be careful to monitor and evaluate the usefulness of behavior controls over time. Rules constrain people and lead to standardized, predictable behavior. However, rules are always easier to establish than to get rid of, and over time the number of rules an organization uses tends to increase. As new developments lead to additional rules, often the old rules are not discarded, and the company becomes overly bureaucratized. Consequently, the organization and the people in it become inflexible and are slow to react to changing or unusual circumstances. Such inflexibility can reduce a company's competitive advantage by lowering the pace of innovation and reducing its responsiveness to customers.

Using Information Technology

Information technology is playing an increasing role in strategy implementation at all organizational levels. In fact, it is making it much easier for organizations to cost-effectively develop output and behavior controls that give strategic managers much more and much better information to monitor the many aspects of their strategies and to respond appropriately. IT, which provides a way of standardizing behavior through the use of a consistent, often cross-functional software platform, is a form of behavior control. IT is also a form of output control because when all employees or functions use the same software platform to provide up-to-date information on their activities, this codifies and standardizes organizational knowledge and makes it easier to monitor progress toward strategic objectives. IT is also a form of integrating mechanism because it provides people at all levels in the hierarchy and across all functions with more of the information and knowledge they need to perform their roles effectively. For example, today functional-level employees are able to access information easily from other functions using cross-functional software systems that keep them all informed about changes in product design, engineering, manufacturing schedules, and marketing plans that will have an impact on their activities. In this sense, IT overlays the structure of tasks and roles that is normally regarded as the "real" organizational structure. The many ways in which IT affects strategy implementation is discussed in the different sections of this and the next chapter. Strategy in Action 12.2 illustrates one way in which IT can help managers monitor and coordinate the effectiveness with which their strategies are being put into action.

Strategy in Action   12.2

Control at Cypress Semiconductor

In the fast-moving semiconductor business, a premium is placed on organizational adaptability. At Cypress Semiconductor, CEO T. J. Rodgers was facing a problem: How to control his growing 1,500-employee organization without developing a bureaucratic management hierarchy. Rodgers believed that a tall hierarchy hinders the ability of an organization to adapt to changing conditions. He was committed to maintaining a flat and decentralized organizational structure with a minimum of management layers. At the same time, he needed to control his employees to ensure that they perform in a manner consistent with company goals.

The solution that Rodgers adopted was to implement a computer-based information system through which he can manage what every employee and team is doing in decentralized organization. Each employee maintains a list of ten to fifteen goals, such as "Meet with marketing for new product launch" or "Make sure to check with customer X." Noted next to each goal is when it was agreed on, when it is due to be finished, and whether it has been finished. All of this information is stored on a central computer. Rodgers claims that he can review the goals of all 1,500 employees in about four hours, and he does so each week. How is this possible? He manages by exception, looking only for employees who are falling behind. He then calls them—not to scold but to ask whether there is anything he can do to help them get the job done. It takes only about half an hour each week for employees to review and update their lists. This system allows Rodgers to exercise control over his organization without resorting to the expensive layers of a management hierarchy.

Sources: **www.cypress.com,** press release, 1998. B. Dumaine, "The Bureaucracy Busters," *Fortune,* June 17, 1991, p. 46.

Strategic Reward Systems

Organizations strive to control employees' behavior by linking reward systems to their control systems.[22] Based on its strategy (low cost or differentiation, for example), strategic managers must decide which behaviors to reward. They then create a control system to measure these behaviors and link the reward structure to them. Determining how to relate rewards to performance is a crucial strategic decision because it determines the incentive structure that affects the way managers and employees at all levels in the organization behave. As Chapter 11 points out, top managers can be encouraged to work in the shareholders' interests by being rewarded with stock options linked to the company's long-term performance. Furthermore, companies such as Kodak and GM require managers to buy company stock. When managers are made shareholders, they are more motivated to pursue long-term rather than short-term goals. Similarly, in designing a pay system for salespeople, the choice is whether to motivate them through straight salary or salary plus a bonus based on how much they sell. Neiman Marcus, the luxury retailer, pays employees a straight salary because it wants to encourage high-quality service but discourage a hard-sell approach. Thus, there are no incentives based on quantity sold. On the other hand, the pay system for rewarding car salespeople encourages high-pressure selling; it typically contains a large bonus for the number and price of cars sold.

Organizational Culture

The third element that goes into successful strategy implementation is managing *organizational culture,* the specific collection of values and norms shared by people and groups in an organization.[23] Organizational values are beliefs and ideas about what kinds of goals members of an organization *should* pursue and about the appropriate kinds or standards of behavior organizational members *should* use to achieve these goals. Bill Gates is a CEO who is famous for the set of organizational values that he emphasizes: entrepreneurship, ownership, creativity, honesty, frankness, and open communication. By stressing entrepreneurship and ownership, he strives to make Microsoft behave less like a big bureaucracy and more like a collection of smaller and very adaptive companies. Gates has emphasized giving lower-level managers considerable decision-making autonomy and encouraged them to take risks—that is, to be more like entrepreneurs and less like corporate bureaucrats. The stress he places on values such as honesty, frankness, and open communication is a reflection of his belief that an open internal dialogue is necessary for successful operations at Microsoft.[24]

From organizational values develop organizational norms, guidelines, or expectations that *prescribe* appropriate kinds of behavior by employees in particular situations and control the behavior of organizational members toward one another. The norms of behavior for software programmers at Microsoft include working long hours and weekends, wearing whatever clothing is comfortable (but never a suit and tie), consuming junk food, and communicating with other employees by email and the company's state-of-the-art intranet.

Organizational culture functions as a kind of control in that strategic managers can influence the kind of values and norms that develop in an organization—values and norms that specify appropriate and inappropriate behaviors and that shape and influence the way its members behave.[25] Strategic managers such as Gates deliberately cultivate values that tell their subordinates they should perform their roles in innovative, creative ways. They establish and support norms dictating that to be innovative and entrepreneurial, employees should feel free to experiment even if there is a significant chance of failure.

Other managers might cultivate values that say employees should always be conservative and cautious in their dealings with others, consult with their superiors before they make important decisions, and record their actions in writing so they can be held accountable for what happens. Managers of organizations such as chemical and oil companies, financial institutions, and insurance companies—any organization in which caution is needed—may encourage a conservative, cautious approach to making decisions.[26] In a bank or mutual fund, for example, the risk of losing investors' money makes a cautious approach to investing highly appropriate. Thus, we might expect that managers of different kinds of organizations will deliberately try to cultivate and develop the organizational values and norms that are best suited to their strategy and structure.

Organizational socialization is the term used to describe how people learn organizational culture. Through socialization, people internalize and learn the norms and values of the culture so that they *become* organizational members.[27] Control through culture is so powerful because once these values have been internalized, they become part of the individual's values, and the individual follows organizational values without thinking about them.[28] Often the values and norms of an organization's culture are transmitted to its members through the stories, myths, and language that people in the organization use, as well as by other means. This chapter's *Closing Case,* for example, discusses many of the stories and myths about Sam Walton and about how frugal he was (he used to drive a thirty-year-old pickup truck, for example, and lived in a very modest home) to reinforce Wal-Mart's low-cost strategy and frugal approach.

Culture and Strategic Leadership

Organizational culture is created by the strategic leadership provided by an organization's founder and top managers. The organization's founder is particularly important in determining culture because the founder imprints his or her values and management style on the organization. Walt Disney's conservative influence on the company he established continued until well after his death, for example. Managers were afraid to experiment with new forms of entertainment because they were afraid "Walt Disney wouldn't like it." It took the installation of a new management team under Michael Eisner to turn around the company's fortunes and allow it to deal with the realities of the new entertainment industry.

The leadership style established by the founder is transmitted to the company's managers, and as the company grows, it typically attracts new managers and employees who share the same values. Moreover, members of the organization typically recruit and select only those who share their values. Thus, a company's culture becomes more and more distinct as its members become more similar. The virtue of these shared values and common culture is that it *increases integration and improves coordination among organizational members.* For example, the common language that typically emerges in an organization because people share the same beliefs and values facilitates cooperation among managers. Similarly, rules and procedures and direct supervision are less important when shared norms and values control behavior and motivate employees. When organizational members buy into cultural norms and values, this bonds them to the organization and increases their commitment to find new ways to help it succeed. That is, employees are more likely to commit themselves to organizational goals and work actively to develop new skills and competencies to help achieve those goals. Strategy in Action 12.3 profiles how Ray Kroc built a strong culture at McDonald's.

Strategic leadership also affects organizational culture through the way managers design organizational structure, that is, the way they delegate authority and divide up task relationships. Michael Dell, for example, has tried to keep his company as flat as possible and has decentralized authority to lower-level managers and employees who are charged with striving to get "as close to the customer" as they can. As a result, he has created a cost-conscious customer service culture at Dell in which employees strive to provide high-quality customer service. Thus, the way an organization designs its structure affects the cultural norms and values that develop within the organization. Managers need to be aware of this fact when implementing their strategies.

Traits of Strong and Adaptive Corporate Cultures

Few environments are stable for any prolonged period of time. If an organization is to survive, managers must take actions that enable it to adapt to environmental changes. If they do not take such action, they may find themselves faced with declining demand for their products.

One way that managers can try is to create an **adaptive culture,** one that is innovative and encourages and rewards initiative taking by middle- and lower-level managers.[29] Managers in organizations with adaptive cultures are able to introduce changes in the way the organization operates, including changes in its strategy and structure that allow it to adapt to changes in the external environment. Organizations with adaptive cultures are more likely to survive in a changing environment and indeed should have higher performance than organizations with inert cultures.

Several scholars in the field have tried to uncover the common traits that strong and adaptive corporate cultures share and to find out whether there is a particular set of values that dominates adaptive cultures that is missing from weak or inert ones.

Strategy in Action   12.3

How Ray Kroc Established McDonald's Culture

In the restaurant business, maintaining product quality is all-important because the quality of the food, the service, and the restaurant premises vary with the chefs and waiters as they come and go. If a customer gets a bad meal, poor service, or dirty silverware, not only may that customer be lost but also other potential customers too, as negative comments travel by word of mouth. In this context, consider the problem Ray Kroc, the man who pioneered McDonald's growth, faced when McDonald's franchises began to open by the thousands throughout the United States. Kroc developed a sophisticated control system that specified every detail of how each McDonald's restaurant was to be operated and managed in order to create an organizational culture.

First, Kroc developed a comprehensive system of rules and procedures for franchise owners and employees to follow in running each restaurant. The most effective way to perform tasks from cooking burgers to cleaning tables was worked out in advance, written down in rule books, and then taught to each McDonald's manager and employee through a formal training process. Prospective franchise owners had to attend "Hamburger University," the company's training center in Chicago, where in an intensive, month-long program they learned all aspects of a McDonald's operation. They were expected to train their workforce and make sure that employees understood operating procedures thoroughly. Kroc's goal in establishing this system of rules and procedures was to build a common culture so that customers would always find the same level of quality in food and service. If customers always get what they expect from a restaurant, the restaurant has developed superior customer responsiveness.

Kroc also developed the McDonald's franchise system to help the company control its structure as it grew. He believed that a manager who is also a franchise owner (and thus receives a large share of the profits) is more motivated to buy into a company's culture than a manager paid on a straight salary. Thus, the McDonald's reward and incentive system allowed it to keep control over its operating structure as it expanded. Moreover, McDonald's was very selective in selling to its franchisees; they had to be people with the skills and capabilities that Kroc believed McDonald's managers should have.

Within each restaurant, franchise owners were instructed to pay particular attention to training their employees and instilling in them McDonald's concepts of efficiency, quality, and customer service. Shared norms, values, and an organizational culture also helped McDonald's standardize employees' behavior so that customers would know how they would be treated in a McDonald's restaurant. Moreover, McDonald's includes customers in its culture: customers bus their own tables, and it also shows concern for customers' needs by building playgrounds, offering Happy Meals, and organizing birthday parties for children. In creating its family-oriented culture, McDonald's ensures future customer loyalty because satisfied children are likely to become loyal adult customers.

An early but still influential attempt is T. J. Peters and R. H. Waterman's account of the values and norms characteristic of successful organizations and their cultures.[30] They argue that adaptive organizations show three common value sets. First, successful companies have values promoting a *bias for action.* The emphasis is on autonomy and entrepreneurship, and employees are encouraged to take risks—for example, to create new products—even though there is no assurance that these products will be winners. Managers are closely involved in the day-to-day operations of the company and do not simply make strategic decisions isolated in some ivory tower, and employees have a hands-on, value-driven approach.

The second set of values stems from the *nature of the organization's mission.* The company must stick with what it does best and develop a business model focused on its mission. A company can easily get sidetracked into pursuing activities outside its area of expertise just because they seem to promise a quick return. Management should cultivate values so that a company sticks to its knitting, which means strengthening its business model. A company must also establish close relationships with customers as a way of improving its competitive position. After all, who knows more about a company's performance than those who use its products or services? By emphasizing customer-oriented values, organizations are able to learn customers' needs and improve their ability to develop products and services that customers' desire. All of these management values are strongly represented in companies such as McDonald's, Wal-Mart, and Toyota, which are sure of their mission and take constant steps to maintain it.

The third set of values bears on *how to operate the organization.* A company should try to establish an organizational design that will motivate employees to do their best. Inherent in this set of values is the belief that productivity is obtained through people and that respect for the individual is the primary means by which a company can create the right atmosphere for productive behavior. An emphasis on entrepreneurship and respect for the employee leads to the establishment of a structure that gives employees the latitude to make decisions and motivates them to succeed. Because a simple structure and a lean staff best fit this situation, the organization should be designed with only the number of managers and hierarchical levels that are necessary to get the job done. The organization should also be sufficiently decentralized to permit employees' participation but centralized enough for management to make sure that the company pursues its strategic mission and that cultural values are followed.

In summary, these three main sets of values are at the heart of an organization's culture, and management transmits and maintains them through strategic leadership. Strategy implementation continues as managers build strategic control systems that help perpetuate a strong adaptive culture, further the development of distinctive competencies, and provide employees with the incentives to act in ways that build a company's competitive advantage. Finally, organizational structure contributes to the implementation process by providing the framework of tasks and roles that reduces transaction difficulties and allows employees to think and behave in ways that allow a company to achieve superior performance.

Building Distinctive Competencies at the Functional Level

Now that the main elements of strategy implementation have been outlined, the issue of creating the structure, control systems, and culture to put a company's strategies into action can be addressed. The first level of strategy to examine is the functional level because, as Chapter 3 discussed, a company's competitive advantage depends on its ability to use and develop distinctive competencies. Recall that an important aspect of *strategic intent* is the obsession that strategic managers have for building organizational resources and capabilities that will allow them to outperform their competitors; it means managers "focusing the organization's attention on the essence of winning, motivating people by communicating the value of the target, leaving room for individual and team contributions, sustaining enthusiasm . . . and using intent consistently to guide resource allocation."[31] Considering the three elements of strategy implementation in turn, what is the best way for managers to group people and tasks to build competencies? The answer for most companies is to group them by function and create a functional structure.

Grouping by Function: Functional Structure

On the quest to deliver a final product to the customer, two related value chain pressures mount. First, the range of value chain activities that must be performed expands, and it quickly becomes clear, as in Dell's case, that the expertise needed to perform them effectively is lacking. For example, it becomes apparent that the services of a professional accountant or a production manager or a marketing expert are needed to take control of specialized tasks. Second, it becomes clear that no one person can successfully perform more than one value chain activity without becoming overloaded. The company's founder, for instance, who may have been performing many value chain activities, realizes that he or she can no longer simultaneously make and sell the product. As most entrepreneurs discover, they have to decide how to group new employees to perform the various value chain activities most efficiently. Most choose the functional structure.

Functional structures group people on the basis of their common expertise and experience or because they use the same resources.[32] For example, engineers are grouped in a function because they perform the same tasks and use the same skills or equipment. Figure 12.5 shows a typical functional structure. Each of the rectangles represents a different functional specialization—R&D, sales and marketing, manufacturing, and so on—and each function concentrates on its own specialized task.

Functional structures have several advantages. First, if people who perform similar tasks are grouped together, they can learn from one another and become more specialized and productive at what they do. This can create capabilities and competencies in each function. Second, they can monitor each other to make sure that all are performing their tasks effectively and not shirking their responsibilities. As a result, the work process becomes more efficient, reducing manufacturing costs and increasing operational flexibility. A third important advantage of functional structures is that they give managers greater control of organizational activities. As already noted, many difficulties arise when the number of levels in the hierarchy increases. If people are grouped into different functions, each with their own managers, then *several different hierarchies are created,* and the company can avoid becoming too tall. There will be one hierarchy in manufacturing, for example, and another in accounting and finance. Managing the business is much easier when different groups specialize in different organizational tasks and are managed separately.

The Role of Strategic Control

Behind the concept of strategic intent is a vision of strategic control as a system that sets ambitious goals and targets for all managers and employees and then develops performance measures that *stretch and encourage managers and employees* to excel in their quest to raise performance. A functional structure promotes this goal because it promotes the ability of managers and employees to monitor and make constant improvements to operating procedures. It also allows for organizational learning,

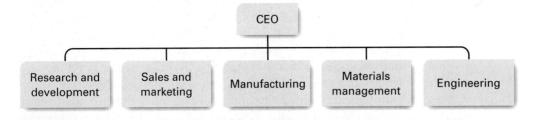

FIGURE 12.5

Functional Structure

since managers, working closely with subordinates, can mentor them and help their technical development further.

Grouping by function also makes it easier to apply output control. Measurement criteria can be developed to suit the needs of each function to encourage members to stretch themselves. Each function knows how well it is contributing to overall performance, and indeed the part it plays in contributing to reductions in cost of good sold or gross margin. Managers can look closely to see if they are following the principle of the minimum chain of command and whether they need middle managers or perhaps could substitute this with control by **management by objectives,** a system in which employees are encouraged to help set their own goals so that managers, like Cypress's Rodgers, manage by exception, intervening only when they sense something is not going right. Given this increase in control, a functional structure also makes it possible to institute an effective strategic reward system in which pay can be closely linked to performance and managers can accurately assess the value of each person's contributions.

Developing Culture at the Functional Level	Often functional structures offer the easiest way for managers to build a cohesive culture. Consider Hewlett Packard (HP), a major provider of IT and computer infrastructure and services. Established in the 1940s, HP's culture is an outgrowth of the strong personal beliefs of the company's founders, Bill Hewlett and Dave Packard. Bill and Dave, as they were known within the company, created HP's culture in a formal statement of HP's basic values to serve everyone who had a stake in the company with integrity and fairness, including customers, suppliers, employees, stockholders, and society in general. They helped establish these values and build HP's culture by hiring like-minded people and letting these values guide their own actions as managers. Thus, the values developed by HP's founders helped guide managerial action at HP. In turn, the commitment to employees that this action signaled has helped foster a productive workforce that is willing to go to great lengths to help the company succeed. The result has been superior company performance over time.

In order to see how the different components of the strategy implementation process work together to implement functional strategy, consider how it works in three functions: manufacturing, R&D, and sales.

Manufacturing. In manufacturing, functional strategy usually centers on improving efficiency, quality, and responsiveness to customers. A company must create an organizational setting in which managers can learn how to economize on costs. In implementing functional strategies in a manufacturing setting, many companies today follow the lead of Japanese companies such as Toyota and Sony, which developed strong capabilities and competencies in manufacturing by operating total quality management (TQM) and flexible manufacturing systems (see Chapter 4).

With TQM, the inputs and involvement of all employees in the decision-making process are necessary to improve production efficiency and quality. Thus, it becomes necessary to decentralize authority to motivate employees to improve the production process. In TQM, work teams are created, and workers are given the responsibility and authority to discover and implement improved work procedures. Managers assume the role of coach and facilitator, and team members jointly take on the supervisory burdens. Work teams are often given the responsibility to control and discipline their own members and even to decide who should work in their team. Frequently, work teams develop strong norms and values, and work group culture becomes an important means of control; this type of control matches the new decentralized team approach. Quality control circles are created to exchange information and suggestions about problems and work procedures. A bonus system or employee stock ownership plan (ESOP) is frequently established to motivate workers and to allow them to share in the increased value that TQM often produces.

Nevertheless, to move down the experience curve quickly, most companies still exercise tight control over work activities and create behavior and output controls that standardize the manufacturing process. For example, human inputs are standardized through the recruitment and training of skilled personnel, the work process is programmed, often by computers, and quality control is used to make sure that outputs are being produced correctly. In addition, managers use output controls such as operating budgets to monitor costs and quality continuously. The extensive use of output controls and the continuous measurement of efficiency and quality ensure that the work team's activities meet the goals set for the function by management. Efficiency and quality increase as new and improved work rules and procedures are developed to raise the level of standardization. The aim is to find the match between structure and control and a TQM approach, so that manufacturing develops the distinctive competency that leads to superior efficiency and quality. However, control systems need to be chosen carefully, as the experience of Gateway, described in Strategy in Action 12.4, suggests.

R&D. The functional strategy for an R&D department is to develop a distinctive competency in innovation and technology that results in products that fit customers' needs. Consequently, the R&D department's structure, control, and culture should provide the coordination necessary for scientists and engineers to bring products quickly to market. Moreover, these systems should motivate R&D scientists to develop innovative products or processes.

In practice, R&D departments typically have a flat, decentralized structure that gives their members the freedom and autonomy to be innovative. Scientists and engineers are also grouped into teams because their performance can typically be judged only over the long term (it may take several years for a project to be completed). Consequently, extensive supervision by managers and the use of behavior control is a waste of managerial time and effort.[33] By letting teams manage their own transfer and handoff issues rather than using managers and the hierarchy of authority to coordinate work activities, managers implement R&D strategy in a way that avoids the information distortion problems that cause bureaucratic costs. Strategic managers take advantage of scientists' ability to work jointly to solve problems and to enhance each other's performance. In small teams too, the professional values and norms that highly trained employees bring to the situation promote coordination. A culture for innovation frequently emerges to control employees' behavior, as has occurred at Motorola and Intel, where the race to be first energizes the R&D teams. To create an innovative culture and speed product development, Intel uses a team structure in its R&D function. Intel has six teams that work on the next generation of chips so that each team's innovations can be put together to make the final product and ensure a state-of-the-art product. It also has six teams working simultaneously on the subsequent generation of chips and six teams working on the generation of chips to follow that one. In other words, to sustain its leading-edge technology, the company has created healthy competition between teams in which its scientists and engineers battle to be the one that produces the innovations that will allow Intel to control the technology of tomorrow.[34]

Strategy in Action   12.4

Gateway's New Rules Backfire

In 2001, Gateway, the personal computer maker, saw its customer satisfaction rating plummet as it dropped from third to fifth in consumer satisfaction among personal computer makers. This drop caused Gateway's managers considerable anxiety because they use this measure of customer satisfaction as an important indicator of their company's ongoing performance. A drop is very serious to a computer maker because the volume of its online sales depends on how easy it is for customers to put their mail order computer together when it reaches their homes and how easy it is for them to get advice and good service when they encounter a software or hardware problem. Customer satisfaction ratings also directly affect a company's profits, and as Gateway's computer shipments slipped by over 11 percent in 2001 compared to 2000, it began to lose money.

Gateway randomly surveys its customers thirty days after they receive their computer to inquire about the nature of their buying experience. Mike Ritter, director of Gateway consumer marketing, discovered that the source of customer dissatisfaction was a series of new rules and policies the company had instituted for its customer service reps to follow in its effort to reduce the escalating costs of after-sales service. As Gateway's product line had broadened and many different software and hardware options were made available to customers, so had the complexity of its customer service procedures. Employees had to have a great deal more information at their disposal to solve customer problems. These problems were often made more serious when customers installed other desired software on their computers, which then caused problems with the software already installed on the Gateway machine. As everybody who has installed new software knows, it can take considerable time to iron out the problems and get the new installation to work. This was costing Gateway millions of dollars in employee time spent on solving these problems—hence Gateway's desire to reduce these costs.

Ritter reported to Gateway CEO Ted Waitt that the fifteen rules and procedures that the company had insti-

tuted for its customer service reps to follow, and two rules in particular, were the source of customer dissatisfaction. The first problematic rule concerned the issue of customer-installed software. Gateway had told its service reps to inform customers that if they installed any other software on their machines, this would invalidate Gateway's warranty. This infuriated customers. The second policy was one of rewarding customer support reps on the basis of how quickly they handled customer calls, meaning that the more calls they handled in an hour or day, the higher the bonus they received.

The joint effect of these two rules was that customer reps were now motivated to minimize the length of a service call and in particular were unwilling to help solve customer problems that resulted from installation of "outlawed software" since this took a lot of time. Customers resented this treatment, and the result was the big decline in customer satisfaction. Moreover, customer reps were not happy because they felt they were violating Gateway's cultural values and norms about providing excellent customer service, and Gateway had prided itself on having a strong corporate culture.

Once Gateway's managers realized the source of the problem, they abolished the fifteen rules immediately. Within one month in 2001, the thirty-day survey saw customer satisfaction jump by over 10 percent. In retrospect, Gateway's managers described these new rules and policies as "misguided and stupid." They hope that the company's sales will start to increase and it will regain some market share it lost to Dell and Compaq. However, in July 2001, Gateway announced that it was closing its global computer-making operations and is in a tough race against Dell Computer, which now has over a 25 percent market share compared with less than 10 percent for Gateway. As Gateway's managers discovered, it is necessary to carefully choose and evaluate the rules and policies used to control employees' behavior to prevent unexpected problems from arising.

To spur teams to work effectively, the reward system should be linked to the performance of the team. If scientists, individually or in a team, do not share in the profits a company obtains from its new products or processes, they may have little motivation to contribute wholeheartedly to the team. To prevent the departure of their key employees and encourage high motivation, companies such as Merck, Intel, and Microsoft give their researchers stock options and rewards tied to their individual performance, their team performance, and the company's performance.

Sales. Salespeople work directly with customers, and when they are dispersed in the field, these employees are especially difficult to monitor. The cost-effective way to monitor their behavior and encourage high responsiveness to customers is usually to develop sophisticated output and behavior controls. Output controls, such as specific sales goals or goals for increasing responsiveness to customers, can be easily established and monitored by supervisors. Then output controls can be linked to a bonus reward system to motivate salespeople. Behavior controls, for instance, detailed reports that salespeople file describing their interactions with customers, can also be used to standardize salespeople's behavior and make it easier for supervisors to review their performance.[35]

Usually, few managers are needed to monitor their activities, and a sales director and regional sales managers can oversee even large sales forces because outputs and behavior controls are employed. Frequently, however, and especially when salespeople deal with complex products such as sales of pharmaceutical drugs or even luxury clothing, it becomes important to develop shared employee values and norms about the importance of patient safety or high-quality customer service, and managers spend considerable time training and educating employees to create such norms.

Similar considerations apply to the other functions, such as accounting, finance, engineering, and human resource management. Managers must implement functional strategy through the combination of structure, control, and culture that allows each function to create the competencies that lead to superior efficiency, quality, innovation, and responsiveness to customers. Strategic managers must also develop the incentive systems that motivate and align employees' interests with those of their companies.

Functional Structure and Bureaucratic Costs	No matter how complex their strategies become, most companies always retain a functional orientation because of the many advantages obtained by using a functional structure. Whenever different functions work together, bureaucratic costs inevitably arise because of the information distortions that lead to the communications and measurement problems discussed in Chapter 10. Often these problems arise from the transfers or handoffs across the different functions necessary to deliver the final product to the customer.[36] It is important that strategic managers understand when and how these problems arise because the need to implement more complex business- and corporate-level strategies only makes these information distortion problems worse. Indeed, it is the need to economize on the bureaucratic costs of solving such problems that lead to organizational arrangements that reduce the scope of information distortions. Most commonly, companies superimpose a more complex grouping on their activities to match their business model and strategy in a discriminating way. These more complex groupings are discussed later in the chapter. First, five factors that cancause information distortions—communications, measurement, customer, location, and strategic—are reviewed.

Communications Problems. As separate functional hierarchies evolve, functions can grow more remote from one another, and it becomes increasingly difficult to communicate across functions and to coordinate their activities. This communication problem stems from *differences in goal orientations,* noted in Chapter 11, that occur because the various functions develop distinct outlooks or understandings of the strategic issues facing a company.[37] Often, the different functions' pursuit of different competencies lead them to develop different time or goal orientations, for example. Some, such as manufacturing, have a short time frame and concentrate on achieving short-run goals, such as reducing manufacturing costs. Others, such as R&D, have a long-term point of view; their product development goals may have a time horizon of several years. These factors may cause each function to develop a different view of the strategic issues facing the company. Manufacturing, for example, may see the strategic issue as the need to reduce costs, sales may see it as the need to increase customer responsiveness, and R&D may see it as the need to create new products. These communication and coordination problems between functions increase bureaucratic costs.

Measurement Problems. Often a company's product range widens as it develops new competencies and enters new market segments, as happened to Dell. When this happens, a company may find it difficult to gauge or measure the contribution of a product or a group of products to its overall profitability—as noted in Chapter 10. Consequently, the company may turn out some unprofitable products without realizing it and may also make poor decisions about resource allocation. This means that the company's measurement systems are not complex enough to serve its needs. Dell Computer's explosive growth in the early 1990s, for example, caused it to lose control of its inventory management systems; hence, it could not accurately project supply and demand for the components that go into its personal computers. Problems with its organizational structure plagued Dell, reducing efficiency and quality. As one manager commented, designing its structure to keep pace with its growth was like "building a high performance car while going around the race track."[38] However, Dell succeeded and today enjoys a 10 to 20 percent cost advantage over competitors like Gateway and HP/Compaq.

Customer Problems. As the range and quality of an organization's goods and services increase, often more, and different kinds of, customers are attracted to its products. Servicing the needs of more customer groups and tailoring products to suit new kinds of customers cause increasing handoff problems between functions. It becomes increasingly difficult to coordinate the activities of value chain functions across the growing product range. Also, functions like production, marketing, and sales have little opportunity to differentiate products and increase value for customers by specializing in the needs of particular customer groups. Instead, they are responsible for servicing the complete product range. Thus, the ability to identify and satisfy customer needs may fall short in a functional structure.

Location Problems. Location factors may hamper coordination and control. If a growing company begins producing or selling in many different regional areas, then a functional structure may not be able to provide the flexibility needed for managers to respond to the different customer needs or preferences in the various regions. A functional structure is simply not the right way to handle regional diversity.

Strategic Problems. Sometimes the combined effect of all these factors is that long-term strategic considerations are ignored because managers are preoccupied with solving communication and coordination problems. As a result, a company may lose direction and fail to take advantage of new opportunities while bureaucratic costs escalate.

Experiencing one or more of these problems is a sign that bureaucratic costs are increasing and a company no longer has the correct approach to strategy implementation. Managers must change and adapt the organization's structure, control systems, and culture to economize on bureaucratic costs, strengthen distinctive competencies, and enhance its competitive advantage. These problems indicate that the company has outgrown its structure and managers need to develop a more complex structure that can meet the needs of its competitive strategy. They could also move to reduce some of these problems by adopting the outsourcing option as well. At this point, implementing strategy at the business level comes into focus.

The Outsourcing Option

Rather than move to a more complex, expensive structure, increasingly companies are turning to the outsourcing option and contracting with other companies to perform specific functional tasks for them. Obviously, it does not make sense to outsource activities in which a company has a distinctive competence because this would lessen its competitive advantage. But it does makes sense to outsource and contract with companies to perform such activities when they have a competitive advantage because they *specialize* in a particular value chain activity.

Thus, one way of avoiding the kinds of communication and measurement problems that arise when a company's product line becomes complex is to reduce the number of functional value chain activities it performs. This allows a company to focus on those competencies that are at the heart of its competitive advantage and economize on bureaucratic costs. Today, responsibility for activities such as a company's marketing, pension and health benefits, materials management, and information systems is being increasingly outsourced to companies that often specialize in the needs of a company in a particular industry. More outsourcing options such as using a global network structure are considered in Chapter 13.

Implementing Strategy in a Single Industry

Building capabilities in strategy implementation that allow a company to develop a competitive advantage starts at the functional level. However, to pursue its business-level strategy successfully, managers must find the right combination of structure, control, and culture that *links and combines* the competencies in a company's value chain functions in a way that enhances the ability to differentiate products and economizes on bureaucratic costs. In other words, the need to coordinate and integrate across functions and business units becomes of central importance at the business level. In this section, the strategy implementation issues for a company seeking to implement a successful competitive business-level strategy are considered.

There are two important issues that managers must address in strategy implementation at the business level: one concerns the revenue side of the profit equation and the other the cost side, as Figure 12.6 illustrates. First, effective strategy implementation improves the way in which people and groups choose strategies and make decisions that lead to increasing differentiation, more value for customers, and the opportunity to charge a premium price. Capabilities in managing its structure and culture allow a company to more rapidly and effectively combine its distinctive competencies or transfer or leverage competencies across business units to create new and improved differentiated products, for example.

Second, effective strategy implementation reduces the bureaucratic costs associated with solving the measurement and communications problems that derive from such things as transferring a product in progress between functions or a lack of cooperation between marketing and manufacturing or between business units. A poorly

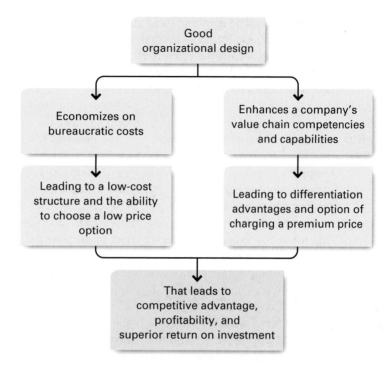

FIGURE 12.6

How Organizational Design Increases Profitability

designed or inappropriate choice of structure or control system or a slow-moving bureaucratic culture (for example, a structure that is too centralized, an incentive system that causes functions to compete and not to cooperate, or a culture whose value and norms have little impact on employees) can cause the motivation, communication, measurement, and coordination problems that lead to high bureaucratic costs.

Effective strategy implementation, which often means the move to a more complex structure, economizes on bureaucratic costs, ultimately lowers a company's cost structure, and can give a company a low-cost advantage that raises profits. A more complex structure will cost more to operate because more highly paid managers will be needed, a more expensive IT system will be required, there may be a need for extra offices or even buildings, and so on. However, these are simply costs of doing business, and a company will happily bear this extra expense provided its new structure leads to increased revenues obtained from differentiating its products to attract more customers and new ways to lower its *overall* cost structure by obtaining scale economies from its expanded operations.

As discussed in Chapter 6, the most successful companies today are those that take great care to manage both the cost and differentiation sides of the profitability equation, although commonly one of these sides dominates their business model, such as Wal-Mart's low-cost approach and Sony's differentiation approach. The issue at the business level is that strategic managers must identify and implement the structure, control, and culture that coordinates and integrates its functions to achieve business-level strategy objectives. Because the focus at the business level is on managing cross-functional relationships, the issue of how to group organizational activities and functions and how to integrate them becomes vitally important.[39] Also, control systems must be selected and a culture managed with the need to coordinate cross-functional activities in mind.

Following, the strategy implementation issues involved in pursuing both a cost-leadership and a differentiation strategy are examined briefly. Then the way these approaches can be combined and an organizational structure chosen to allow companies to pursue business models oriented at (1) managing broad product lines, (2) being responsive to customers; (3) expanding nationally; (4) competing in a fast-changing high tech environment; and (5) focusing on a deep product line are considered.

Implementing a Cost-Leadership Approach

The aim of the cost-leadership strategy is to make the company pursuing it the lowest-cost producer in the market.[40] At the business level, this means reducing costs across *all* functions in the organization, including R&D and sales and marketing. If a company is pursuing a cost-leadership strategy, its R&D efforts probably focus on product and process development rather than on the more expensive product innovation, which carries no guarantee of success. In other words, the company stresses competencies that improve product characteristics or lower the cost of making existing products. Similarly, a company tries to decrease the cost of sales and marketing by offering a standard product to a mass market rather than different products aimed at different market segments, which is also more expensive.[41]

To implement a cost-leadership strategy, the company chooses a combination of structure, control, and culture compatible with the needs of the low-cost strategy. In practice, the functional structure is the most suitable provided that care is used to select the appropriate integrating mechanisms that reduce communications and measurement problems. For example, a TQM program can be effectively implemented when a functional structure is overlaid with cross-functional teams, for now team members can search for ways to improve operating rules and procedures that lower the cost structure or standardize and raise product quality.[42]

A cost-leadership approach also requires that strategic managers continuously monitor the way their structures and control systems are working to find ways to restructure or streamline it so that it operates more effectively. For example, managers need to be alert to ways to use IT to standardize operations and lower costs. To reduce costs further, cost-leadership companies use the cheapest and easiest forms of control available: output controls. For each function, a company adopts output controls that allow it to monitor and evaluate functional performance closely. In the manufacturing function, for example, the company imposes tight controls and stresses meeting budgets based on production, cost, or quality targets.[43] In R&D, too, the emphasis falls on the bottom line, and to demonstrate their contribution to cost savings, R&D teams focus their efforts on improving process technology. Cost-leadership companies are likely to reward employees through generous incentive and bonus plans to encourage high performance. Often their culture is based on values that emphasize the bottom line, such as those of Dell and McDonald's.

Implementing a Differentiation Approach

Effective strategy implementation can improve a company's ability to add value and to differentiate its products. To make its product unique in the eyes of the customer, for example, a differentiated company must design its structure, control, and culture around the *particular source* of its competitive advantage.[44] Specifically, companies implementing a differentiation approach need to design their structures around the source of their distinctive competencies, the differentiated qualities of their product, and the customer groups they serve.

Commonly, in pursuing differentiation, a company starts to produce a wider range of products and serve more market segments, which means it has to customize its products to the needs of different groups of customers. These factors make it more difficult to standardize activities and usually increase the bureaucratic costs associated with managing the handoffs or transfers between functions. Integration becomes much more of a problem; communications, measurement, location, and strategic problems increasingly arise; and the demands on functional managers increase.

To respond to these problems, strategic managers develop more sophisticated control systems, increasingly make use of IT, and focus on developing cultural norms and values that overcome problems associated with differences in functional orientations and focus on cross-functional objectives. The control systems used to match the structure are geared to a company's distinctive competency. For successful differentiation, it is important that the various functions do not pull in different directions; indeed, cooperation among the functions is vital for cross-functional integration. However, when functions work together, output controls become much harder to use. In general, it is much more difficult to measure the performance of people in different functions when they are engaged in cooperative efforts. Consequently, a company must rely more on behavior controls and shared norms and values when pursuing a strategy of differentiation.

That is why companies pursuing a differentiation strategy often have a markedly different kind of culture from those pursuing a low-cost strategy. Because human resources—good scientists, designers, or marketing people—are often the source of differentiation, these organizations have a culture based on professionalism or collegiality, a culture that emphasizes the distinctiveness of the human resource rather than the high pressure of the bottom line.[45] HP, Motorola, and Coca-Cola, all of which emphasize some kind of distinctive competency, exemplify companies with professional cultures.

In practice, the implementation decisions that confront managers who must simultaneously strive to increase the differentiated appeal of their products while being mindful of the need to manage its cost structure are dealt with together as strategic managers move to implement new, more complex kinds of organizational structure. As a company's business model and strategies evolve, strategic managers usually start to *superimpose* a more complex grouping of activities on its functional grouping and move to a new form of structure and control system that allows it to motivate employees better to coordinate its value chain activities.

Although more complex structures cost more to implement and operate than a simple functional structure, managers are willing to bear this extra cost so long as the new structure makes better use of functional competencies, increases its revenues, and lowers its overall cost structure. Recall from Chapter 10 that to economize on bureaucratic costs, organizational arrangements must be matched to the business model and strategy in a *discriminating way*.

Implementing a Broad Product Line—Product Structure

The structure that organizations most commonly adopt to solve the control problems that result from producing many different kinds of products for many different market segments is the *product structure*. The intent behind the change to a product structure is to break up a company's growing product line into a number of smaller, more manageable subunits within an organization to reduce bureaucratic costs due to communication, measurement, and the other problems noted earlier.

An organization that decides to group activities by product first decides how to group its overall product line into product groups or categories so that each product group can be developed, manufactured, distributed, and sold at the lowest cost consistent with permitting the differentiation needed to create value for customers. Each product group is targeted at satisfying the needs of a particular customer group and is managed by its own team of managers who focus their efforts on that group.

Second, to keep costs as low as possible, the decision is made to centralize support value chain functions such as R&D, marketing, sales, and accounting at the top of the organization, and the different product groups share their services. Each support function, in turn, is divided into product-oriented teams of functional specialists who focus on the needs of one particular product group. This arrangement allows each team to specialize and become expert in managing the needs of its product group. However, because all of the R&D teams belong to the same centralized function, they can share knowledge and information with each other that allows them to build their competence over time.

Strategic control systems can now be developed to measure the performance of each product group separately from the others. Thus, the performance of each product group is easy to monitor and evaluate, and corporate managers at the center can move more quickly to intervene if necessary. Also, the strategic reward system can be more closely linked to the performance of each product group, although top managers can still decide to make rewards based on corporate performance an important part of the incentive system. This will encourage the different product groups to share ideas and knowledge and promote the development of a corporate culture, as well as the product group culture that naturally develops inside each product group. A product structure is commonly used by food processors, furniture makers, personal and health products companies and large electronics companies. Strategy in Action 12.5 illustrates and describes how Kodak uses a product structure.

As the figure in Strategy in Action 12.5 shows, each of Kodak's product line uses the services of the central support functions and does not have its own support functions. The expense of creating separate support functions for each product line could be justified only if the needs of the different product lines were so different that *different sets of functional specialists* were required for each group of product. Normally, this happens only when a company enters new industries and markets and its range of product offerings becomes increasingly diverse and unrelated to each other. When this happens, a company requires an even more complex form of structure, a multidivisional structure, which is discussed in Chapter 13.

Increasing Responsiveness to Customer Groups—Market Structure

Suppose the source of competitive advantage in an industry depends on the ability to meet the needs of distinct and important sets of customers or different customer groups. What is the best way of implementing strategy now? Many companies develop a **market structure** that is conceptually quite similar to the product structure except that the focus is on customer groups instead of product groups.

For a company pursuing a strategy based on increasing responsiveness to customers, it is vital that the nature and needs of each different customer group be identified. Then people and functions are grouped by customer or market segment, and a different set of managers becomes responsible for developing the products that each group of customers wants and tailoring or customizing products to the needs of each particular customer group. In other words, to promote superior responsiveness to customers, companies design a structure around their customers and a market structure is adopted. A typical market structure is shown in Figure 12.7.

A market structure brings customer group managers and employees closer to specific groups of customers. These people can then take their detailed knowledge and feed it back to the support functions, which are kept centralized to reduce costs. For example, information about changes in customers' preferences can be quickly fed back to R&D and product design so that a company can protect its competitive advantage by supplying a constant stream of improved products for its installed

Strategy in Action

Kodak's Product Structure

12.5

The Eastman Kodak Company is one of the oldest and best-known companies in the world. The film used in the camera to capture Neil Armstrong's walk on the moon and John F. Kennedy, Jr.'s salute to his father's casket was Kodak film. For decades, Kodak monopolized the global film market, but starting in the 1970s, new low-cost competitors like Fuji began to take market share from Kodak.

To respond to these challenges, Kodak decided to strengthen its core photographic business by bringing out new and improved products, but it had to find a low-cost way to do so because it was already at a cost disadvantage compared to Fuji. Kodak's CEO, Daniel Carp, decided it would be necessary to move to a product structure, shown in the figure.

Carp decided to streamline Kodak's structure by dividing all its products into different product categories, such as consumer photographic products, digital imaging and digital cameras, health imaging products, and commercial imaging products. Each product group is headed by a separate team of managers responsible for managing the value chain functions necessary to develop advanced new products for customers. However, to reduce costs, each product line shares the services of R&D imaging, marketing, sales, accounting, and so on, which remain centralized. In essence, responsibility for strategy making is decentralized to managers inside each product line, but support value chain activities are kept centralized to defray costs and because developments can be quickly spread over and shared by Kodak's different imaging groups. For example, the R&D team that focuses on medical imaging can share discoveries about new methods for digitizing images with the R&D team for commercial products. As a result, Kodak is able to transfer its skills and leverage its competencies across product groups and market segments, and advances in digital imaging technology can be quickly communicated to each group to speed product development. Also, by keeping sales centralized, a single national sales force can sell the complete range of Kodak's imaging products. So far, this grouping of organizational activities by product as well as function has helped Kodak lower its cost structure and overcome many of its old problems of handing off or transferring its knowledge and skills across its many different product lines.

Sources: **www.kodak.com,** 2000. L. Johannes, "Kodak Streamlines Units to Be Nimbler in Digital Age," *Wall Street Journal,* November 3, 2000, p. B.1.

Kodak's Product Structure

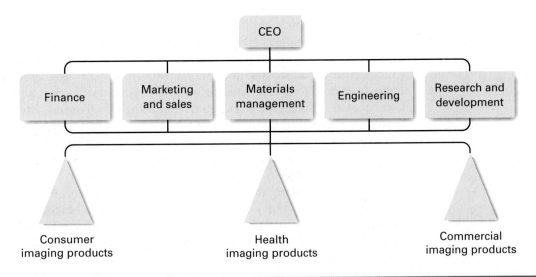

FIGURE 12.7
Market Structure

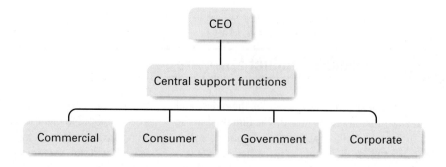

customer base. This is especially important when a company serves well-identified customer groups such as Fortune 500 companies or small businesses. The *Opening Case* describes how Dell uses a market structure to maximize its responsiveness to important customer groups while at the same time keeping its overall cost structure as low as possible.

Expanding Nationally— Geographic Structure

Suppose a company starts to expand nationally through internal expansion or by engaging in horizontal integration and merging with other companies to expand its geographical reach. A company pursuing this competitive approach frequently moves to a **geographic structure** in which geographic regions become the basis for the grouping of organizational activities. A company may divide its manufacturing operations and establish manufacturing plants in different regions of the country, for example. This allows it to be responsive to the needs of regional customers and reduces transportation costs. Similarly, as a service organization such as a store chain or bank expands beyond one geographic area, it may begin to organize sales and marketing activities on a regional level to serve the needs of customers in different regions better.

A geographic structure provides more coordination and control than a functional structure because several regional hierarchies are created to take over the work, just as in a product structure, several product group hierarchies are created. A company such as FedEx clearly needs to operate a geographic structure to fulfill its corporate goal: next-day delivery. Large merchandising organizations, such as Neiman Marcus, Dillard's Department Stores, and Wal-Mart, have also moved to a geographic structure as they started building stores across the country. With this type of structure, different regional clothing needs (for example, sunwear in the South, down coats in the Midwest) can be handled as required. At the same time, because the information systems, purchasing, distribution, and marketing functions remain centralized, they can leverage their skills across all the regions. Thus, in using a geographic structure, a company can achieve economies of scale in buying, distributing, and selling and lower its costs structure while at the same time being more responsive (differentiated) to customer needs.

Neiman Marcus developed a geographic structure similar to the one shown in Figure 12.8 to manage its nationwide chain of stores. In each region, it established a team of regional buyers to respond to the needs of customers in each geographic area, for example, the western, central, eastern, and southern regions. The regional buyers then fed their information to the central buyers at corporate headquarters, who coordinated their demands to obtain purchasing economies and to ensure that Neiman Marcus's high-quality standards, on which its differentiation advantage depends, were maintained nationally.

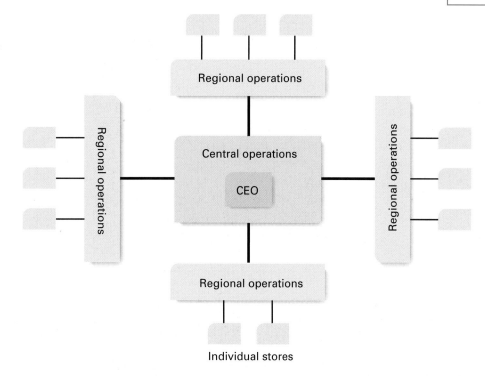

Individual stores

Competing in Fast-Changing, High-Tech Environments— Product-Team and Matrix Structures

The communication and measurement problems that lead to bureaucratic costs escalate quickly when technology is rapidly changing and industry boundaries are blurring. Frequently, competitive success depends on fast mobilization of a company's skills and resources, and managers face complex strategy implementation issues. A new grouping of people and resources becomes necessary, often one that is based on fostering a company's distinctive competencies in R&D, and managers need to make structure, control, and culture choices around the R&D function. At the same time, managers need to ensure that implementation will result in new products that meet customer needs and in a way that is cost-effective and will not result in high-priced products that are so expensive customers will not wish to buy them.

Matrix Structure. To address these problems many companies choose a matrix structure.[46] In a **matrix structure,** value chain activities are grouped in two ways (see Figure 12.9). First, activities are grouped vertically by *function,* so that there is a familiar differentiation of tasks into functions such as engineering, sales and marketing, and R&D. In addition, superimposed on this vertical pattern is a horizontal pattern based on grouping by *product or project* in which people and resources are grouped to meet ongoing product development needs. The result is a complex network of reporting relationships among projects and functions designed to make R&D the focus of attention, as depicted in Figure 12.9.

Matrix structures are flat and decentralized, and employees inside a matrix have two bosses: a *functional boss,* who is the head of a function, and a *product or project boss,* who is responsible for managing the individual projects. Employees work on a project team with specialists from other functions and report to the project boss on project matters and the functional boss on matters relating to functional issues. All employees who work in a project team are called **two-boss employees** and are

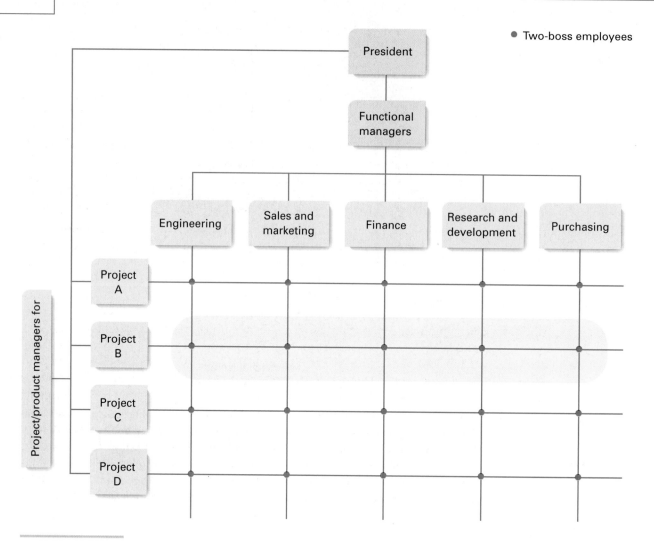

● Two-boss employees

FIGURE 12.9
Matrix Structure

responsible for managing coordination and communication among the functions and projects.

Implementing a matrix structure promotes innovation and speeds product development, for this type of structure permits intensive cross-functional integration. Integrating mechanisms such as teams help transfer knowledge among functions and are designed around the R&D function. Sales, marketing, and production targets are geared to R&D goals; marketing devises advertising programs that focus on technological possibilities, and salespeople are evaluated on their understanding of new-product characteristics and their ability to inform potential customers about them.

Matrix structures were first developed by companies in high-technology industries such as aerospace and electronics; for example, TRW and Hughes. These companies were developing radically new products in uncertain, competitive environments, and speed of product development was the crucial consideration. They needed a structure that could respond to this need, but the functional structure was too inflexible to allow the complex role and task interactions necessary to meet new-product development requirements. Moreover, employees in these companies tend to be highly qualified and professional and perform best in autonomous, flexible working conditions. The matrix structure provides such conditions.

This structure requires a minimum of direct hierarchical control by supervisors. Team members control their own behavior, and participation in project teams allows them to monitor other team members and learn from each other. Furthermore, as the project goes through its different phases, different specialists from various functions are required. For example, at the first stage, the services of R&D specialists may be called for, and then at the next stage, engineers and marketing specialists may be needed to make cost and marketing projections. As the demand for the type of specialist changes, team members can be moved to other projects that require their services. Thus, the matrix structure can make maximum use of employees' skills as existing projects are completed and new ones come into existence. The freedom given by the matrix not only provides the autonomy to motivate employees but also leaves top management free to concentrate on strategic issues, since they do not have to become involved in operating matters. On all these counts, the matrix is an excellent tool for creating the flexibility necessary for quick reactions to competitive conditions.

In terms of strategic control and culture, the development of norms and values based on innovation and product excellence is vital if a matrix structure is to work effectively.[47] The constant movement of employees around the matrix means that time and money are spent establishing new team relationships and getting the project off the ground. The two-boss employee's role, balancing as it does the interests of the project with the function, means that cooperation between people is problematic and communication and conflict between both functions and between function and projects is possible and must be managed. Furthermore, the changing composition of product teams, the ambiguity arising from having two bosses, and the greater difficulty of monitoring and evaluating the work of teams increases the problems of coordinating task activities. A strong and cohesive culture with unifying norms and values can mitigate these problems, as can a strategic reward system based on a group and organizational level reward system.

Product-Team Structure. A major structural innovation in recent years has been the **product-team structure.** Its advantages are similar to those of a matrix structure, but it is much easier and far less costly to operate because of the way people are organized into permanent cross-functional teams, as Figure 12.10 illustrates. In the product-team structure, as in the matrix structure, tasks are divided along product or project lines. However, instead of being assigned only *temporarily* to different projects, as in the matrix structure, functional specialists become part of a *permanent* cross-functional team that focuses on the development of one particular range of products such as luxury cars or computer workstations. As a result, the problems associated with coordinating cross-functional transfers and handoffs are much lower than in a matrix structure, in which tasks and reporting relationships change rapidly. Moreover, cross-functional teams are formed at the beginning of the product development process, so that any difficulties that arise can be ironed out early, before they lead to major redesign problems. When all functions have direct input from the beginning, design costs and subsequent manufacturing costs can be kept low. Moreover, the use of cross-functional teams speeds innovation and customer responsiveness because when authority is decentralized, team decisions can be made more quickly.

A product-team structure groups tasks by product, and each product group is managed by a cross-functional product team that has all the support services

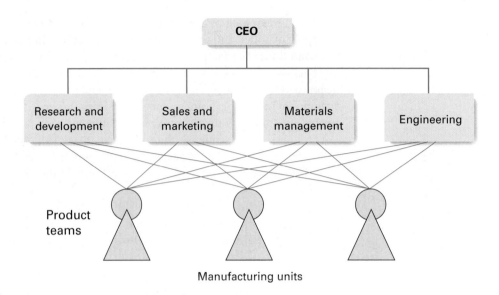

FIGURE 12.10

Product-Team Structure

necessary to bring the product to market. This is why it is different from the product structure, where support functions remain centralized. The role of the product team is to protect and enhance a company's differentiation advantage and at the same time coordinate with manufacturing to lower costs. John Fluke Manufacturing, a leader in electronic testing tools, is a good example of a company that makes use of product teams to speed product development. The company assembles "Phoenix teams," cross-functional groups that are given 100 days and $100,000 to identify a market need and a new product to fill it.[48] So far, these teams have led to the development of two successful new products.

Focusing on a Narrow Product Line

As Chapter 5 discusses, a focus strategy is directed at a particular market or customer segment. A company focuses on a narrow or deep product or range of products aimed at one type of customer or region. This strategy tends to have higher production costs than the other generic strategies because output levels are lower, making it harder to obtain substantial scale economies. As a result, a company using a focus strategy must exercise cost control. On the other hand, because some attribute of its product usually gives such a company its distinctive advantage—possibly its ability to provide customers with high-quality, personalized service—a company using a focus strategy has to develop some form of distinctive competency. For both reasons, the structure and control system adopted by a company following a focus strategy has to be inexpensive to operate but flexible enough to allow a distinctive competency to emerge.

A company using a focus strategy normally adopts a functional structure to meet these needs. This structure is appropriate because it is complex enough to manage the activities necessary to service the needs of a market segment or produce a narrow but deep range of products. At the same time, the handoff problems associated with pursuing a focused strategy are likely to be relatively easy to solve because a company remains small and specialized. Thus, a functional structure can provide all the integration necessary, provided that the focused firm has a strong, adaptive culture,

Strategy in Action   12.6

Restructuring at Lexmark

Lexmark, a printer and typewriter manufacturer, was one of IBM's many divisions, but IBM sold it after years of losses brought on by high operating costs and an inability to produce new products that could compete with Hewlett Packard and Japanese printer makers such as Canon and Epson.

Marvin Mann, an ex-IBM executive, was given the task of finding a way to restructure the company and turn it around. Mann realized at once the need for the company to focus its resources on producing a particular kind of printer to lower its out-of-control cost structure. One of the biggest contributors to its high cost structure was Lexmark's structure and control, so he decided to transform it. Then, he believed, he could begin to focus the company on producing a line of state-of-the-art laser and ink jet office printers.

Like the rest of IBM at that time, Lexmark had developed a tall, centralized structure, and all important decision making was made by top managers. This slowed decision making and made it very difficult to communicate across functions because so many managers at different levels and in different functions had to approve new plans. Moving quickly to change this system, Mann streamlined the company's hierarchy, which meant terminating 50 percent of its managers. This action cut out three levels in the

hierarchy. He then decentralized authority to the managers of each of the company's four product groups and told them to develop their own plans and goals. In addition, to continue the process of decentralization, product managers were instructed to develop cross-functional teams comprising employees from all functions, with the goal of finding new and improved ways of organizing task activities to reduce costs. The teams were to use competitive benchmarking and evaluate their competitors' products in order to establish new performance standards to guide their activities. Finally, as an incentive for employees to work hard at increasing efficiency, innovation, and quality, Mann established a company stock ownership scheme to reward employees for their efforts.

Mann's strategy of restructuring Lexmark to focus on a narrow range of printer was successful. Within two years, the cost of launching new products went down by 50 percent and its new-product development cycle speeded up by 30 percent. In addition, by focusing the company's resources on a narrow range of products, he improved its R&D competence. Lexmark is a technology leader in the laser and ink jet industry. Its stock has performed well, and the company is enjoying considerable success against HP and Japanese competitors.

which is vital to the development of some kind of distinctive competency.[49] Additionally, because such a company's competitive advantage is often based on personalized service, the flexibility of this kind of structure lets the company respond quickly to customers' needs and change its products in response to customers' requests. The way in which Lexmark reorganized itself to focus on the production of office printers, examined in Strategy in Action 12.6, illustrates many of the issues in implementing a focus strategy.

The message of the preceding section is clear. Strategic managers must continually monitor the performance of their organizations as measured by its ability to increase differentiation, lower costs, and increase profitability and move to take action to change the way its people and activities are organized and controlled when managers sense declining performance or, indeed, when managers sense ways to increase performance. Combining and harmonizing structure, control, and culture is a demanding and difficult task but one that is crucial to promoting and sustaining competitive advantage and strengthening a company's business model.

Restructuring and Reengineering

Often, to improve corporate performance, the single business company employs restructuring and reengineering. **Restructuring** a company involves two steps: (1) streamlining the hierarchy of authority and reducing the number of levels in the hierarchy to a minimum and then (2) downsizing the work force by reducing the number of employees to reduce operating costs. When Jack Smith took over as the head of General Motors, for example, GM had more than twenty-two levels in the hierarchy and more than 20,000 corporate managers. Describing his organization as a top-heavy bureaucracy, Smith quickly moved to slash costs and restructure the company. Today, GM has only twelve levels in the hierarchy and half as many corporate managers.

There are many reasons that restructuring becomes necessary and an organization may need to downsize its operations.[50] Sometimes a change in the business environment occurs that could not have been foreseen; perhaps a shift in technology made the company's products obsolete, or a worldwide recession has reduced the demand for its products. Sometimes an organization has excess capacity because customers no longer want the goods and services it provides, perhaps because they are outdated or offer poor value for the money. Sometimes organizations downsize because they have grown too tall and inflexible and bureaucratic costs have become much too high. Sometimes they restructure even when they are in a strong position simply to build and improve their competitive advantage and stay on top.

All too often, however, companies are forced to downsize and lay off employees because they have not monitored the way they operate their basic business processes and have not made the incremental changes to their strategies and structures that allow them to adjust to changing conditions and keep bureaucratic costs under control. Advances in strategic management thinking, such as the development of new models of organizing work activities, or advances in information technology often offer managers the opportunity to implement their strategies in more effective ways.

One way of helping a company operate more effectively is to employ reengineering. **Reengineering** is the "fundamental rethinking and radical redesign of business processes to achieve dramatic improvements in critical, contemporary measures of performance such as cost, quality, service, and speed."[51] As this definition suggests, strategic managers who use reengineering must completely rethink how they organize their value chain activities. Instead of focusing on how a company's *functions* operate, strategic managers make business *processes* the focus of attention.

A **business process** is any activity that is vital to delivering goods and services to customers quickly or that promotes high quality or low costs (such as IT, materials management, or product development) that is not the responsibility of any *one* function but *cuts across functions.* Because reengineering focuses on business processes and not on functions, a company that reengineers always has to adopt a different approach to organizing its activities. Companies that take up reengineering deliberately ignore the existing arrangement of tasks, roles, and work activities. They start the reengineering process with the customer (not the product or service) and ask, "How can we reorganize the way we do our work, our business processes, to provide the best quality and the lowest-cost goods and services to the customer?"

Frequently, when companies ask this question, they realize that there are more effective ways to organize their value chain activities. For example, a business process that encompasses members of ten different functions working sequentially to provide goods and services might be performed by one person or a few people at a fraction of the cost after reengineering. Often individual jobs become increasingly complex, and people are grouped into cross-functional teams as business processes are reengineered to reduce costs and increase quality.

Hallmark Cards, for example, reengineered its card design process with great success. Before the reengineering effort, artists, writers, and editors worked separately in different functions to produce all kinds of cards. After reengineering, these same artists, writers, and editors were put in cross-functional teams, each of which now works on a specific type of card, such as birthday, Christmas, or Mother's Day. The result was that the time it took to bring a new card to market dropped from years to months, and Hallmark's performance increased dramatically.

Reengineering and total quality management (TQM), discussed in Chapter 4, are highly interrelated and complementary. After reengineering has taken place and value chain activities have been altered to speed the product to the final customer, TQM takes over, with its focus on how to continue to improve and refine the new process and find better ways of managing task and role relationships. Successful organizations examine both questions simultaneously and continuously attempt to identify new and better processes for meeting the goals of increased efficiency, quality, and customer responsiveness. Thus, they are always seeking to improve their visions of their desired future state.

Another example of reengineering is the change program that took place at IBM Credit, a wholly owned division of IBM that manages the financing and leasing of IBM computers, particularly mainframes, to IBM's customers. Before reengineering took place, when a financing request arrived at the division's headquarters in Old Greenwich, Connecticut, it went through a five-step approval process that involved the activities of five different functions. First, the IBM salesperson called the credit department, which logged the request and took details about the potential customer. Second, this information was taken to the credit-checking department, where a credit check on the potential customer was made. Third, when the credit check was complete, the request was taken to the contracts department, which wrote the contract. Fourth, from there it went to the pricing department, which determined the actual financial details of the loan, such as the interest rate and the term of the loan. Finally, the whole package of information was assembled by the dispatching department and delivered to the sales representative, who gave it to the customer.

This series of cross-functional activities took an average of seven days to complete, and sales representatives constantly complained that this delay resulted in a low level of customer responsiveness that reduced customer satisfaction. Also, potential customers were tempted to shop around for financing and even to look at competitors' machines. The delay in closing the deal caused uncertainty for all concerned.

The change process began when two senior IBM credit managers reviewed the finance approval process. They found that the time spent by different specialists in the different functions actually processing a loan application was only ninety minutes. The seven-day approval process was caused because of the delay in transmitting information and requests between departments. The managers also came to understand that the activities taking place in each department were not complex; each department had its own computer system containing its own work procedures, but the work done in each department was pretty routine.

Armed with this information, IBM managers realized that the approval process could be reengineered into one overarching process handled by one person with a computer system containing all the necessary information and work procedures to perform the five loan-processing activities. If the application were complex, a team of experts stood ready to help process it, but IBM found that after the reengineering effort, a typical application could be done in four hours rather than the previous seven days. A sales representative could go back to the customer the same day to close the deal, and all the uncertainty surrounding the transaction was removed.

As reengineering consultants Hammer and Champy note, this dramatic performance increase was brought about by a radical change to the process as a whole.[52] Change through reengineering requires managers to go back to the basics and pull apart each step in the work process to identify a better way to coordinate and integrate the activities necessary to provide customers with goods and services. As this example makes clear, the introduction of new IT is an integral aspect of reengineering. IT also allows a company to restructure its hierarchy since it provides more and better-quality information. IT today is an integral part of the strategy implementation process.

Summary of Chapter

1. Implementing a strategy successfully depends on selecting the right combination of organizational structure, control systems, and culture. Companies need to monitor and oversee the strategy implementation process to achieve superior profitability.

2. Effective strategy implementation can increase profitability in two ways. First, it economizes on bureaucratic costs and helps a company lower its cost structure. Second, it enhances the ability of a company's value creation functions to achieve superior efficiency, quality, innovativeness, and customer responsiveness and to obtain the advantages of differentiation.

3. The main issues in designing organization structure are how to group tasks, functions, and divisions; how to allocate authority and responsibility; and how to use integrating mechanisms to improve coordination between functions.

4. Strategic control provides the monitoring and incentive systems necessary to make an organizational structure work as intended and extends corporate governance down to all levels inside the company. The main kinds of strategic control system are output control and bureaucratic control, rewards systems, and control through information technology.

5. Organizational culture is the set of values, norms, beliefs, and attitudes that help to energize and motivate employees and control their behavior. A company's founder and top managers help determine which kinds of values emerge in an organization, and as such they should try to build a strong and adaptive culture to help increase performance over time.

6. At the functional level, each function requires a different combination of structure and control system to achieve its functional objectives.

7. At the business level, structure, control, and culture must be combined in a way that helps them implement their business-level strategy and manage the relationships among all the functions.

8. Cost-leadership and differentiation strategies each require a structure and control system that matches the source of their competitive advantage. Implementing a simultaneous cost-leadership and differentiation strategy is the problem facing many companies today.

9. Other specialized kinds of structures include the product, market, geographic, matrix, and product-team structures. Each has a specialized use and is implemented as a company's strategy warrants.

10. Restructuring and reengineering are two ways of improving the way a company's strategy is implemented.

Discussion Questions

1. What is the relationship of organizational structure, control, and culture? Give some examples of when and under what conditions a mismatch between these components might arise.

2. What kind of structure best describes the way your (a) business school and (b) university operate? Why is the structure appropriate? Would another structure fit better?

3. When would a company choose a matrix structure? What are the problems associated with managing this structure, and why might a product-team structure be preferable?

4. For each of the structures discussed in the chapter, outline the most suitable control systems.

5. What kind of structure, controls, and culture would you would be likely to find in (a) a small manufacturing company, (b) a chain store, (c) a high-tech company, and (d) a Big Four accounting firm?

Practicing Strategic Management

SMALL-GROUP EXERCISE: DECIDING ON AN ORGANIZATIONAL STRUCTURE

Break up into groups of three to five people. You are a group of managers of a major soft drinks company that is going head-to-head with Coca-Cola to increase market share. Your strategy is to increase your product range to offer a soft drink in every segment of the market to attract customers. Currently you have a functional structure. What you are trying to work out now is how best to implement your strategy in order to launch your new products. Should you move to a more complex kind of product structure, and, if so, which one? Alternatively, should you establish new-venture divisions, and spin off each kind of new soft drink into its own company so that it can focus its resources on its market niche? Thinking strategically, to improve your decision making, debate the pros and cons of the possible organizational structures, and decide which structure you will implement.

ARTICLE FILE 12

Find an example of a company that competes in one industry that has recently changed the way it implements its strategy. What changes did it make? Why did it make these changes? What effect did these changes have on the behavior of people and functions?

STRATEGIC MANAGEMENT PROJECT: MODULE 12

This module asks you to identify how your company implements its strategy. For this part of your project, you need to obtain information about your company's structure, control, systems, and culture. This information may be hard to obtain unless you can interview managers directly. But you can make many inferences about the company's structure from the nature of its activities, and if you write to the company, it may provide you with an organizational chart and other information. Also, published information, such as compensation for top management, are available in the company's annual reports or 10K. If your company is well known, magazines such as *Fortune* and *Business Week* frequently report on corporate culture or control issues. Nevertheless, you may be forced to make some bold assumptions to complete this part of the project.

1. How large is the company as measured by the number of its employees? How many levels in the hierarchy does it have from the top to the bottom? Based on these two measures and any other information you may have, would you say your company operates with a relatively tall or a flat structure? Does your company have a centralized or a decentralized approach to decision making?

2. What changes (if any) would you make to the way the company allocates authority and responsibility?

3. Draw an organizational chart showing the main way in which your company groups its activities. Based on this chart, decide what kind of structure (functional, product, or divisional) your company operates with.

4. Why did your company choose this structure? In what ways is it appropriate for its business? In what ways is it not?

5. What kind of integration or integration mechanisms does your company use?

6. What are the main kinds of control systems your company is using? What kinds of behaviors is the organization trying to (a) shape and (b) motivate through the use of these control systems?

7. What role does the top management team play in creating the culture of your organization? Can you identify the characteristic norms and values that describe the way people behave in your organization? How does the design of the organization's structure affect its culture?

8. What are the sources of your company's distinctive competencies? Which functions are most important to it? How does your company design its structure, control, and culture at the *functional level* to enhance its (a) efficiency, (b) quality, (c) innovativeness, (d) and responsiveness to customers?

9. What is your company's business-level strategy? How does it design its structure and control systems to enhance and support its business-level strategy? For example, what steps does it take to further cross-functional integration? Does it have a functional, product, or matrix structure?

10. How does your company's culture support its strategy? Can you determine any ways in which its top management team influences its culture?

11. Based on this analysis, would you say your company is coordinating and motivating its people and subunits effectively? Why or why not? What changes (if any) would you make to the way your company's structure operates? What use could it make of restructuring or reengineering?

EXPLORING THE WEB
Visiting Home Depot

Go to **www.homedepot.com,** and examine corporate information such as the company overview, history, and press releases. Based on this information, what kind of structure, control systems, and culture do you think Home Depot has in place to implement its business model and strategies?

General Task: Search the Web for an example of a company that has been involved in changing the way it implements its strategy. What were its problems? How did it use structure, control, and culture to improve the way it operates?

Closing Case

Sam Walton's Approach to Implementing Wal-Mart's Strategy

Wal-Mart, headquartered in Bentonville, Arkansas, is the largest retailer in the world, with sales of almost $65 billion in 2002. Its success rests on the nature of the strategic control systems that its founder, the late Sam Walton, established for the company. Walton wanted all his managers and workers to have a hands-on approach to their jobs and to be totally committed to Wal-Mart's main goal, which he defined as total customer satisfaction. To motivate his employees, Walton created a strategic control system that gave employees at all levels continuous feedback about their and the company's performance.

First, Walton developed a financial control system that provided managers with day-to-day feedback about the performance of all aspects of the business. Through a sophisticated companywide satellite system, corporate managers at its Bentonville headquarters can evaluate the performance of each store, and even of each department in each store. Information about store profits and the rate of turnover of goods is provided to store managers daily, and store managers in turn communicate this information to Wal-Mart's 625,000 employees (who are called associates). By sharing such information, Walton's method encourages all associates to learn the fundamentals of the retailing business so they can work to improve it.

If any store seems to be underperforming, managers and associates meet to probe the reasons and to find solutions to help raise performance. Wal-Mart's top managers routinely visit stores having problems to lend their expertise, and each month top managers use the company's aircraft to fly to various Wal-Mart stores so they can keep their fingers on the pulse of the business. It is also customary for Wal-Mart's top managers to spend their Saturdays meeting together to discuss the week's financial results and their implications for the future.

Walton insisted on linking performance to rewards. Each manager's individual performance, measured by his or her ability to meet specific goals or output targets, is reflected in pay raises and chances for promotion (promotion to bigger stores in the company's 2,000-store empire and even to corporate headquarters, because Wal-Mart routinely promotes from within the company rather than hires managers from other companies). While top managers receive large stock options linked to the company's performance targets and stock price, even ordinary associates receive stock in the company. An associate who started with Walton in the 1970s would by now have accumulated more than $250,000 in stock because of the appreciation of Wal-Mart's stock over time.

Walton instituted an elaborate system of controls, such as rules and budgets, to shape employees' behavior. Each store performs the same activities in the same way, and all employees receive the same kind of training so they know how to behave toward customers. In this way, Wal-Mart is able to standardize its operations, which leads to major cost savings and allows managers to make storewide changes easily.

Finally, Walton was not content just to use output and behavior controls and monetary rewards to motivate his associates. To involve associates in the business and encourage them to develop work behaviors focused on providing quality customer service, he established strong cultural values and norms for his company. Some norms that associates are expected to follow include the *ten-foot attitude* that developed when Walton, during his visits to the stores, encouraged associates to "promise that whenever you come within 10 feet of a customer you will look him in the eye, greet him, and ask him if you can help him"; the *sundown rule,* which states that employees should strive to answer customers' requests by sundown on the day they receive them; and the *Wal-Mart cheer* ("Give me a *W,* give me an *A,*" and so on), which is used in all its stores.

The strong customer-oriented values that Walton created are exemplified in the stories its members tell one another about the company's concern for its customers. They include stories such as the one about Sheila, who risked her own safety when she jumped in front of a car to prevent a little boy from being struck; about Phyllis, who administered CPR to a customer who had suffered a heart attack in her store; and about Annette, who gave up the Power Ranger she had on layaway for her own son so a customer's son could have his birthday wish. The strong Wal-Mart culture also helps to control and motivate its employees and helps associates to achieve the stringent output and financial targets the company has set for itself.

Case Discussion Questions

1. What were the main elements of the control system that Sam Walton created?

2. In what ways will this control system facilitate Wal-Mart's strategy of global expansion?

Sources: J. Pettet, "Wal-Mart Yesterday and Today," *Discount Merchandiser* (December 1995): 66–67. M. Reid, "Stores of Value," *Economist,* March 4, 1995, pp. ss5–ss7. M. Troy, "The Culture Remains the Constant," *Discount Store News,* June 8, 1998, pp. 95–98. **www.walmart.com.**

Implementing Strategy in Companies That Compete Across Industries and Countries

Opening Case

The "New HP" Gets Up to Speed

In May 2002, the merger between Hewlett Packard and Compaq to form the "new HP" was finally approved, and the two companies moved quickly to combine their skills and resources. The new HP is a leading global multibusiness IT-infrastructure provider, selling a complete range of computer hardware, software and solutions, information services, and imaging and printing products. HP currently serves more than 1 billion customers across 162 countries with 150,000 employees and generated almost $90 billion in 2001. The immediate task facing HP's managers is how to position the company to compete across industries against competitors like IBM, also a multibusiness IT infrastructure provider, and Dell, the leader in the fiercely competitive PC industry.

The justification for the merger to create the new HP would be the new company's ability to combine the former companies' cross-industry product lines and reap the benefits of both cost savings and differentiation. Joining both company's product lines would allow them to streamline the product range, eliminate the duplication of costly functional activities, and achieve billions in cost savings. Combining their joint operations would allow them to transfer, share, and leverage their competencies and achieve the value-creating benefits of increased product differentiation. Where will these gains come from?

First, the new HP is a leader in all the important industries in the computing and IT sector: servers, storage, management software, imaging and printing, personal computers and personal access devices, and so on. In other words, it will be able to provide customers with a *complete range* of totally compatible computing and IT products backed by a services group that will be able to provide the software and expertise to customize these products to the needs of customers. As a result, HP claims its products will provide better flexibility, better interoperability, and the lowest cost of ownership of any company in the industry.

To achieve these benefits, the two companies' many business units have been integrated and reorganized into four major product divisions, with a multidivisional structure selected to integrate the activities of its new four divisions: hardware, software, services, and imaging and printing. Each division will be treated as an independent profit center, and the divisions will be expected to work together to coordinate their new products and activities to make sure they are in keeping with its corporate strategy. The top executives in these divisions will report to Carly Fiorina, HP's CEO. Michael Capellas, the former CEO of Compaq and former HP president, was responsible for HP's global business groups, worldwide sales, supply chain management, and e-commerce operations. Capellas was totally committed to leveraging HP's competencies and capabilities in these areas because most of his time at Compaq was spent dealing with these critical issues.

Indeed, Capellas attributed Compaq's poor performance in the 1990s to a combination of factors that had affected HP as well. First, as it had grown through the 1990s, it had implemented a matrix structure to control its diverse businesses (as had the old HP at one time). Over time, however, the matrix structure resulted in increasingly slow decision making because *geography* rather than *product-line* considerations drove strategy making. The needs of the whole corporation were being ignored as the needs of each geographic business or division took precedence. Capellas scrapped the decentralized matrix structure and replaced it with a multidivisional one based on product line—for example, personal computers or high-end corporate workstations. At the same time, he instituted strict controls: each business was made

a profit center, and each division's managers were given clear sales and profit objectives and the responsibility to achieve those objectives.

Second, Capellas attributed Compaq's problems to its slowness in developing an Internet strategy and reaching out to customers, both corporate and individual. Capellas insisted that each division should integrate its activities and products around the Internet to streamline and integrate its own operations to reduce costs and speed decision making. He championed this idea and created an "Internet culture" at Compaq, and soon employees began to talk only about their division's business model in terms of its relationship to the Internet. Capellas charged a team of corporate managers with establishing a series of Internet teams to speed the development of Internet-based software systems to facilitate direct sales to all types of customers. Moreover, he demanded that these Internet systems be standardized across divisions in order to integrate their activities better and allow them to work together to provide large customers with a complete computer package consisting of mainframes and servers, as well as desktop and portable computers. Third, Capellas recognized how much of a competitive advantage Dell had gained over Compaq by its use of the Internet to facilitate the management of its value chain. He instructed managers to take all of Compaq's supply chain activities online to try to reduce Dell's 10 to 15 percent cost advantage.

Capellas was in charge of accomplishing these same things in the new HP while Fiorina, as CEO, was and is responsible for taking the broad view of HP's multibusiness model and forecasting how changes in IT might shift industry boundaries and affect the company in the future. Formulating HP's global multibusiness strategy will also be one of her major concerns, for the complexity of HP's global operations is staggering. The need to customize products to the needs of different world regions and to work out where to make them to lower HP's cost structure and increase the appeal of its products are major questions the whole of HP's top management is confronting right now.

Sources: M. Hays, "Compaq Maps Future," *Informationweek,* June 17, 1998, p. 14. A. Taylor III, "Compaq Looks Inside for Salvation," *Fortune,* August 16, pp. 124–128. **www.compaq.com,** press release, September 1999. **www.hp.com,** 2002.

Overview   The story of the new HP's efforts to develop a competitive multibusiness model to allow it to combine the old HP and Compaq's competencies to battle competitors like IBM and Dell suggests how complex strategic thinking can become at the corporate level. Companies have to continually examine how to improve the way they implement their multibusiness models to raise their performance.

This chapter takes off where the last one ends and examines how to implement strategy when a company decides to enter and compete in new industries, or countries when it expands globally, and when it chooses means such as merger or outsourcing to strengthen its multibusiness model. The strategy implementation issue remains the same: how to use organizational structure, control, and culture to allow a company to pursue its business model and strategies successfully. Once a company decides to compete across industries and countries, however, it confronts a new set of problems, some of them continuations of problems discussed in Chapter 12 and some of them a direct consequence of the more complex product and market choices it has made and hence which have to be implemented.

By the end of the chapter, you will appreciate the many complex issues and choices confronting managers with the task of managing multibusiness and global companies and the reasons that strategy implementation is an integral part of the process of achieving superior performance.

Managing Corporate Strategy Through The Multidivisional Structure

As Chapter 10 discusses, there are many ways in which corporate-level strategies such as vertical integration or diversification can be used to strengthen a company's competitive position in the industries in which it competes. However, substantial implementation problems arise as well, many of them due to the increasing bureaucratic costs associated with managing a larger collection of companies that operate in different industries. These costs are especially high when a company is seeking to gain the differentiation and low-cost advantages of transferring, sharing, or leveraging its distinctive competencies across industries. For companies pursuing a multibusiness model, the problems and costs of managing the handoffs or transfers between value chain functions across industries to obtain these benefits rise sharply. It is the need to economize on these costs that propels strategic managers to search for improved ways of implementing the corporate-level strategies necessary to pursue a multibusiness model.

As a company begins to enter new industries and produce completely different kinds of products for different markets, such as cars, fast food, and computers, the structures described in Chapter 12, such as the functional and product structure, are not up to the task. They cannot provide sufficient coordination between functions and motivation to employees that implementing a multibusiness model requires. As a result, the control problems (measurement, customer, location, strategic) that give rise to bureaucratic costs rise. Experiencing these problems is a sign that the company has outgrown its structure. Strategic managers need to invest more resources to develop a more complex structure—one that can meet the needs of its multibusiness strategy. The answer for most large, complex companies is to move to a multidivisional structure, design a cross-industry control system, and fashion a corporate culture to reduce these problems and economize on bureaucratic costs.

The multidivisional structure possesses two main innovations over a functional or product structure that allow a company to grow and diversify while reducing the coordination and control problems inherent in entering and competing in new industries. First, in each industry in which a company operates, strategic managers organize the companies in that industry into one or more subunits called *divisions*. Sometimes each division contains a full set of all the value chain functions it needs to pursue its business model; in this case, it is called a *self-contained division*. For example, GE competes in over 150 different industries, and in each industry, all of its divisions are self-sufficient and perform all the value creation functions. Sometimes the divisions inside an industry share value chain functions to obtain cost savings and because this often helps the divisions to benefit from leveraging competencies across divisions, as discussed in detail below. For example, PepsiCo has two major divisions in the soft drinks and snack foods industries; each has its own R&D and manufacturing functions, but they share the marketing and distribution functions to lower operating costs and achieve the gains from differentiation.

Second, the office of *corporate headquarters staff* is created to monitor divisional activities and to exercise financial control over each of the divisions.[1] This staff contains the corporate-level managers who oversee the activities of divisional managers. Hence, the organizational hierarchy is taller in a multidivisional structure than in a product or functional structure. The role of the extra managers is to develop strategic control systems that lower a company's overall cost structure, including finding ways to economize on the costs of controlling the handoffs and transfers between divisions. The extra cost of these corporate managers is more than justified if their actions lead to cost savings elsewhere or revenue-enhancing differentiation that boosts overall return on investment capital (ROIC) of the company.

In the multidivisional structure, day-to-day operations of a division are the responsibility of divisional management; that is, divisional management has *operating responsibility*. The corporate headquarters, which includes top executives as well as their support staff, is responsible for overseeing the company's long-term multibusiness model and for providing guidance for interdivisional projects. These executives have *strategic responsibility*. Such a combination of self-contained divisions with a centralized corporate management provides the extra coordination and control necessary to manage entry into new industries.

Figure 13.1 illustrates a typical multidivisional structure found in a large chemical company such as Du Pont. Although this company might easily have twenty different divisions, only three—the oil, pharmaceuticals, and plastics divisions—are represented here. Each division possesses some combination of the value chain functions it needs to pursue its own business model. Each is also normally treated by the corporate center as a profit center, and strategic control measures such as ROIC are used to monitor and evaluate each division's performance.[2] The use of this kind of output control makes it easier for corporate managers to identify high-performing and underperforming divisions and to take corrective action as necessary.

Because they have been separated into subunits by industry, each division is also able to develop the structure and culture that best suits its particular business model, for example, a product, matrix, or market structure. As a result, implementing a multidivisional structure allows a multibusiness company to take into account the need for each separate division to adopt the structure and control systems necessary to pursue its own business-level strategy effectively.

Figure 13.1 shows that the oil division has a functional structure because it is pursuing a low-cost approach, the pharmaceuticals division has a product-team structure to encourage speedy development of new drugs, and the plastics division has a matrix structure to allow it to quickly develop new kinds of customized plastic products to suit the changing needs of its customers. Sometimes size of operations alone is enough to compel a company to use a multidivisional structure. For example, inside one industry, the car industry, GM operates the whole corporation through a multidivisional structure, and each of its main car brands—Cadillac, Buick, and so on—is organized as separate divisions. Some issues in the way GM has operated its multidivisional structure over time are discussed in Strategy in Action 13.1.

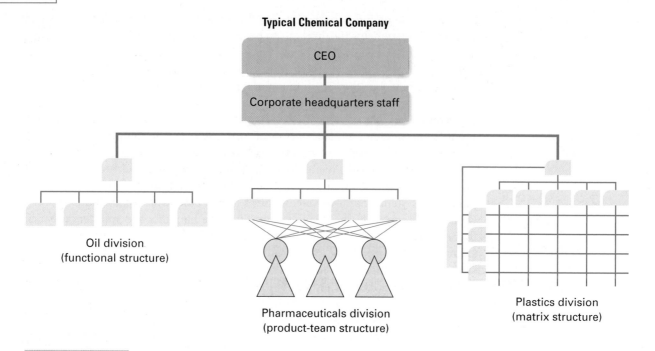

FIGURE 13.1

Multidivisional Structure

As the GM story suggests, operating a multidivisional structure is a *continuing* challenge for managers. Because the multidivisional structure is so widely used, it is necessary to look closely at its advantages and disadvantages.

Advantages of a Multidivisional Structure

When managed effectively at both the corporate and the divisional levels, a multidivisional structure offers several advantages. Together, they can raise corporate profitability to a new peak because they allow the organization to implement the corporate-level strategies necessary to pursue the multibusiness model.

Enhanced Corporate Financial Control. The profitability of different business divisions is clearly visible in the multidivisional structure.[3] Because each division is its own profit center, financial controls can be applied to each business on the basis of profitability criteria such as ROIC. Typically, these controls cover establishing targets, monitoring performance on a regular basis, and selectively intervening when problems arise. Corporate headquarters is also in a better position to allocate corporate financial resources among competing divisions. The visibility of divisional performance means that corporate headquarters can identify the divisions in which investment of funds will yield the greatest long-term ROIC. In a sense, the corporate office is in a position to act as the investor or banker in an internal capital market, channeling funds to high-yield uses.

Enhanced Strategic Control. The multidivisional structure frees corporate managers from business-level responsibilities. Corporate managers have the time and scope for contemplating wider strategic issues and for developing responses to environmental changes, such as quickly changing industry boundaries. The multidivisional

Strategy in Action   13.1

GM's Multidivisional Structure Changes over Time

William C. Durant formed the General Motors Company on September 16, 1908. Into it, he brought about twenty-five different companies. Only four of them—Buick, Chevrolet, Pontiac, and Cadillac—survive as operating divisions today. Originally, each company retained its own operating identity, and the GM organization was simply a holding company, a central office surrounded by twenty-five satellites. When Alfred P. Sloan took over as president of GM in 1923, he inherited this collection of independently managed car companies, which made their own decisions, did their own R&D, and produced their own range of cars.

GM's principal competitor, the Ford Motor Car Company, was organized very differently. From the beginning, Henry Ford had emphasized the advantages of economies of scale and mass production and had designed a mechanistic structure to achieve them. He built a highly centralized hierarchy in which he had complete personal control over decision making. To reduce costs, Ford at first produced only one vehicle, the Model T, and gave enormous attention to finding improved ways of producing it. Because of its organizational design, Ford's company was initially much more profitable than GM. The problem facing Sloan was to compete with Ford not only in terms of product but in financial performance too.

Confronted with Ford's success, Sloan must have been tempted to close several of GM's small operations and concentrate production in a few locations where the company could enjoy the benefits of fewer models and cost savings from economies of scale. For example, he could have adopted a product division structure, created three product divisions to manufacture three kinds of car, and centralized support functions such as marketing, R&D, and engineering to reduce costs. Sloan, however, recognized the importance of the diverse sets of research, design, and marketing skills and competencies present in the small car companies. He realized that there was a great risk of losing this diversity of talent if he combined all these skills into one centrally located research and design department. Moreover, if the same set of support functions, such as engineering and design, worked for all of GM's divisions, there was a danger that all GM cars would begin to look alike. Nevertheless, Sloan also recognized the advantages of centralized control in achieving economies of scale, controlling costs, and providing for the development of a strategic plan for the company as a

whole rather than for each company separately. So he searched for an organizational structure that would allow him to achieve all these objectives simultaneously and found his answer in the multidivisional structure. In 1921, he instituted this change, noting that GM "needs to find a principle for coordination without losing the advantages of decentralization."

Each of GM's different businesses was placed in a self-contained operating division with support services like sales, production, engineering, and finance. Each division became a profit center and was evaluated on its return on investment. Sloan was quite clear about the main advantage of linking decentralization to return on investment: It raised the visibility of each division's performance. And, Sloan observed, it (1) "increases the morale of the organization by placing each operation on its own foundation, . . . assuming its own responsibility and contributing its share to the final result"; (2) "develops statistics correctly reflecting. . .the true measure of efficiency"; and (3) "enables the corporation to direct the placing of additional capital where it will result in the greatest benefit to the corporation as a whole."

Sloan recommended that transactions between divisions be set by a transfer-pricing scheme based on cost plus some predetermined rate of return. However, to avoid protecting a high-cost internal supplier, he also recommended a number of steps involving analysis of the operations of outside competitors to determine the fair price. Sloan established a strong, professional, centralized headquarters management staff to perform such calculations. Corporate management's primary role was to audit divisional performance and plan strategy for the total organization. Divisional managers were to be responsible for all product-related decisions.

In the 1980s, after fierce competition from the Japanese, GM took a hard look at its multidivisional structure. The duplication of R&D and engineering, and the purchasing of inputs by each division independently, was costing the company billions of extra dollars. In 1984, GM's five autonomous car divisions were combined into two groups: Chevrolet and Pontiac would concentrate on small cars and Buick, Oldsmobile, and Cadillac would focus on large cars.

GM hoped that the reorganization would reduce costs and speed product development, but it was a disaster. With control of design and engineering more centralized at the group level, the cars of the different divisions started to look the same. Nobody could tell a Buick from a Cadillac or an Oldsmobile. Sales plummeted. Moreover, the reorganization did not speed decision making. It increased the number of levels in the hierarchy by introducing the group level into the organization. As a result, GM had thirteen levels in its hierarchy; in comparison, Toyota had just five. Once again the company was in trouble. Before the reorganization, it had been too decentralized; now it was too centralized. What to do?

Realizing its mistake, GM moved to return control over product design to the divisions while continuing to centralize functions like engineering and purchasing to realize scale economies. This restructuring has had some success. Cadillac's management moved quickly to establish a new product identity and design new models. However, Oldsmobile never regained its differentiated appeal and the division was disbanded in 2001. Currently, GM is focusing on finding ways to lower its cost structure, which was one of the highest in the industry, and it has been successful. For example, it has reduced the number of cars in its product range and the number of different platforms used to make cars; it has also vertically disintegrated by spinning off high-cost internal suppliers and recentralized the purchasing of component parts using the car industry's B2B network to outsource more of its components. In 2002, it announced that its per unit costs of car making were down almost to the level of Ford and Chrysler, something it had to achieve to boost profitability and remain a major player in the global marketplace.

Sources: A. P. Sloan, *My Years at General Motors* (Garden City, N.Y.: Doubleday, 1946). A. Taylor III, "Can GM Remodel Itself?" *Fortune,* January 13, 1992, pp. 26–34; W. Hampton and J. Norman, "General Motors: What Went Wrong?" *Business Week,* March 16, 1987, pp. 102–110. **www.gm.com,** 2002. The quotations are on pp. 46 and 50 in Sloan, *My Years at General Motors.*

structure also enables corporate headquarters to obtain the proper information to perform long-run strategic and scenario planning for the entire corporation, including decisions about which businesses to expand and which to exit from.

Growth. The multidivisional structure lets the company overcome an organizational limit to its growth. By reducing information overload at the center, corporate managers can consider emerging opportunities for further growth and diversification. Communication problems are reduced because the same set of standardized accounting and financial output controls can be used for all divisions. Also, from a behavior control perspective, corporate managers are able to implement a policy of management by exception, which means that they intervene only when problems arise.

Stronger Pursuit of Internal Efficiency. Within a functional structure, the interdependence of functional departments means that the performance of each *individual* function inside a company cannot be measured by objective criteria. For example, the profitability of the finance function, marketing function, or manufacturing function cannot be assessed in isolation, because they are only part of the whole. This often means that within the functional structure, considerable degrees of organizational slack, that is, the unproductive use of functional resources, can go undetected. For example, the head of the finance function might employ a larger staff than required for efficiency to reduce work pressures inside the department and to bring the manager higher status. In a multidivisional structure, however, the individual efficiency of each autonomous division can be directly observed and measured in terms of the profit it generates. Thus, autonomy makes divisional managers accountable for their own performance; they can have no alibis for poor performance. The corporate office is thus in a better position to identify inefficiencies.

Problems in Implementing a Multidivisional Structure

Although research suggests that large companies that adopt a multidivisional structure outperform those that retain the functional structure, this structure has its disadvantages as well.[4] Good management can eliminate some of them, but others are inherent in the way the structure operates and require constant managerial attention, as the GM example in Strategy in Action 13.1 suggests.

Establishing the Divisional-Corporate Authority Relationship. The authority relationship between corporate headquarters and the divisions must be correctly established. The multidivisional structure introduces a new level in the hierarchy: the corporate level. The problem lies in deciding how much authority and control to delegate to the operating divisions and how much authority to retain at corporate headquarters. This was the problem first noted by Sloan when he implemented the multidivisional structure into GM.[5] What Sloan found was that when headquarters retained too much power and authority, the operating divisions lacked sufficient autonomy to develop the business strategy that might best meet the needs of the division. On the other hand, when too much power was delegated to the divisions, they pursued divisional objectives, with little heed to the needs of the whole corporation. As a result, not all the potential gains from using this structure could be achieved.

Thus, the central issue in managing the multidivisional structure is how much authority should be *centralized* at corporate headquarters and how much should be *decentralized* to the divisions. This issue must be decided by each company in reference to the nature of its business- and corporate-level strategies. There are no easy answers, and as the environment changes or the company alters its strategies over time, the balance between corporate and divisional control will also change, as Strategy in Action 13.2 suggests.

Distortion of Information. If corporate headquarters places too much emphasis on each division's individual profitability—for instance, by setting very high and stringent ROIC targets—divisional managers may choose to distort the information they supply top management and paint a rosy picture of it at the expense of future profitability. Bureaucratic costs now increase as divisions may attempt to make ROIC look better by cutting product development or new investments or marketing expenditures. Although such actions might boost short-run ROIC, they do so at the cost of cutting back on investments and expenditures that may be necessary to maintain the long-term profitability of the company. The problem stems from too tight financial control. GM suffered from this problem in recent years as declining performance prompted divisional managers to try to make their divisions look good to corporate headquarters to secure greater funds for future investment. Managing the corporate-divisional interface requires coping with subtle power issues.

Competition for Resources. The third problem of managing a multidivisional structure is that the divisions themselves may compete for resources, and this rivalry can prevent gains from transferring, sharing, or leveraging distinctive competencies across businesses. For example, the amount of capital for investment that corporate managers have to distribute to the divisions is fixed. Generally, the divisions that can demonstrate the highest ROIC get the lion's share of the money. Because that large share strengthens them in the next time period, the strong divisions grow stronger. Consequently, divisions may actively compete for resources and thereby

Strategy in Action   13.2

Amoco, ARCO, and Burmah Castrol Become Part of BP

As with most other global oil companies, Amoco was engaged in three major activities: oil exploration, refining, and chemicals manufacturing. To manage these activities, it used a three-legged structure and created three independent operating subsidiaries to manage each of its three main activities. Each subsidiary had its own set of managers responsible for overseeing all the many different divisions inside each subsidiary; thus, there was an extra level of control: the subsidiary level. The managers of all three subsidiaries then reported to Amoco's corporate-level managers, who oversaw their activities and made the final decision on what each subsidiary should be doing. Because all important decision making at Amoco was centralized at the top, it often took a long time to make decisions because of the many managerial layers between Amoco's corporate managers and its divisional managers. The slow decision-making process hampered divisional managers' attempts to build a competitive advantage, but this situation was left unattended too during the prosperous oil industry of the 1980s.

By the 1990s, Amoco, like other global oil companies such as Exxon, British Petroleum, and Mobil, had experienced intense pressure to reduce costs because of flat gas prices. To try to boost profits, Amoco laid off more than one-quarter of its workforce, but this did not work. Amoco's managers then took a close look at its structure to see whether there was a way to increase its performance.

Amoco's chairman and CEO, H. Laurence Fuller, decided that a massive reorganization of Amoco's structure was necessary. Fuller eliminated Amoco's three-legged structure completely and removed all the managers at the subsidiary level. The three subsidiaries were divided into seventeen independent divisions according to their industry, and Amoco changed to a multidivisional structure. Henceforth, strategic responsibilities were decentralized to the managers of each division, who were free to choose their own business-level strategy. Each division was evaluated on the basis of its ability to reach certain ROIC targets set by corporate managers, but their own managers determined the way they achieved those targets.

By 1996, it was clear that Fuller's move to a multidivisional structure had worked. Managers were acting more entrepreneurially, and the company was operating more efficiently. However, in the late 1990s, oil industry companies began to consolidate further to make better use of their resources and lower their cost structure. Fuller agreed to merge Amoco with British Petroleum (BP). Because many of both companies' divisions were competing in the same industries, their activities overlapped and duplicated one another, so BP developed a value creation grid and then merged Amoco's seventeen divisions with its own thirty-three divisions. In 2001, BP acquired ARCO for its extensive gas reserves and Burmah Castrol, the well-known fuel oil maker. Once again, it integrated these companies into its existing operations, and from these mergers it strengthened its differentiated position in its major sectors of oil, gas, chemicals, and downstream activities such as retailing. BP also announced that it expected to achieve $5.9 billion in cost savings from these moves.

Sources: C. Soloman, "Amoco to Cut More Jobs and Radically Alter Its Structure," *Wall Street Journal,* July 22, 1995, p. B4. "Shell Reorganizes for Speed and Profit," *Oil and Gas Journal,* December 21, 1998, p. 31.

---

reduce interdivisional coordination. As a result, the potential gains from pursuing a multibusiness model will be lost.

Transfer Pricing. Divisional competition may lead to battles over **transfer pricing,** that is, conflicts over establishing the fair or "competitive" price of a resource or skill developed in one division that is to be transferred and sold to other divisions that require it. As discussed in Chapter 10, one of the origins of the problems of handoffs or transfers between divisions, and thus a major source of bureaucratic costs, is the problem of setting prices for resource transfers to obtain the benefits of the multibusiness models when pursuing a vertical integration or related diversification strategy.

Rivalry among divisions is common in the transfer pricing process because each supplying division has the incentive to set the highest price for its resources or skills to maximize its own revenues and profits. However, purchasing divisions view attempts to charge high prices as undermining their own profitability—hence the problem. Such competition can completely undermine the corporate culture and make a company a battleground. If such battles go unresolved, the benefits of the multibusiness model will not be achieved. Hence, there is a need for the sensitive design of incentive and control systems to make the multidivisional structure work.

Short-Term R&D Focus. If corporate headquarters sets extremely high and rigid ROIC targets, there is a danger that the divisions will cut back on R&D expenditures to improve their financial performance. Although this inflates divisional performance in the short term, it undermines a division's ability to develop new products and leads to a fall in the stream of long-term profits. Hence, corporate headquarters personnel must carefully control their interactions with the divisions to ensure that both the short- and long-term goals of the business are being achieved.

Duplication of Functional Resources. Because each division often possesses its own set of functions, such as finance or R&D, multidivisional structures are expensive to run and manage. R&D is an especially costly activity, and so some companies centralize such functions at the corporate level to serve all divisions. The duplication of specialist services is not a problem if the cost and differentiation gains from having separate specialist functions are substantial. Corporate managers decide whether duplication is financially justified and which services to centralize or decentralize to optimize short- and long-run profitability.

In sum, the advantages of divisional structures must be balanced against problems of implementing them, but an observant, professional management team that is aware of the issues involved can manage these problems. The increasing use of information technology is also making implementation easier and this is discussed after the issue of implementing structure, control, and culture for different kinds of multibusiness models has been addressed.

Structure, Control, Culture, and Corporate- Level Strategy

Once strategic managers select a multidivisional structure, they must then make choices about what kind of integrating mechanisms and control systems to use to make the structure work efficiently. Such choices depend on whether a company chooses to pursue a multibusiness model based on a strategy of unrelated diversification, vertical integration, or related diversification.

As discussed in Chapter 9, many possible differentiation and cost advantages derive from vertical integration. A company can coordinate resource-scheduling decisions among divisions operating in adjacent industries to reduce manufacturing costs and improve quality, for example.[6] This might mean locating a rolling mill next to a steel furnace to save the costs of reheating steel ingots and make it easier to control the quality of the final product. The many benefits from related diversification also come from transferring, sharing, or leveraging functional resources or skills across divisions, such as sharing distribution and sales networks to increase differentiation or lower the overall cost structure. With both strategies, the benefits to the company come from some *exchange of distinctive competencies* among divisions. To secure these benefits, the company must coordinate activities among divisions. Consequently, structure and control must be designed to handle the handoffs or transfers among divisions.

In the case of unrelated diversification, the multibusiness model is based on using capabilities in entrepreneurship, capabilities in managing organizational structure or culture effectively, or strategic capabilities—for example, through the ability to promote a culture that supports entrepreneurial behavior that leads to rapid product development or from restructuring an underperforming company and establishing an efficient internal capital market that allows corporate managers to make superior capital allocation decisions than would be possible using the external capital market. With this strategy, there are no exchanges among divisions, each operates separately and independently, and the exchanges that need to be coordinated take place between divisions and corporate headquarters. Structure and control must therefore be designed to allow each division to operate independently while giving corporate managers easy ability to monitor and to intervene if necessary.

The choice of structure and control mechanisms depends on the degree to which a company using a multidivisional structure needs to control the handoffs and interactions among divisions. The more interdependent the divisions—that is, the more they depend on each other for skills and resources—the greater are the bureaucratic costs associated with obtaining the potential benefits from a particular strategy.[7] Table 13.1 indicates what forms of structure and control companies should adopt to economize on the bureaucratic costs associated with the three corporate strategies.[8] We examine them in detail in the next sections.

Unrelated Diversification. Because there are *no exchanges or linkages* among divisions, unrelated diversification is the easiest and cheapest strategy to manage; it is associated with the lowest level of bureaucratic costs. The main requirement of the structure and control system is that it allows corporate managers to evaluate divisional performance easily and accurately. Thus, companies use a multidivisional

TABLE 13.1

Corporate Strategy and Structure and Control

Corporate Strategy	Appropriate Structure	Need for Integration	Type of Control		
			Financial Control	**Behavior Control**	**Organizational Culture**
Unrelated diversification	Multidivisional	Low (no exchanges between divisions)	Great use (e.g., ROI)	Some use (e.g., budgets)	Little use
Vertical integration	Multidivisional	Medium (scheduling resource transfers)	Great use (e.g., ROI, transfer pricing)	Great use (e.g., standardization, budgets)	Some use (e.g., shared norms and values)
Related diversification	Multidivisional	High (achieving synergies between divisions by integrating roles)	Little use	Great use (e.g., rules, budgets)	Great use (e.g., norms, values, common language)

structure, and each division is evaluated by output controls such as return on invested capital. A company also applies sophisticated accounting controls to obtain information quickly from the divisions so that corporate managers can readily compare divisions on several dimensions. Textron and Dover are good examples of companies that use sophisticated computer networks and accounting controls to manage their structures, which allow them almost daily access to divisional performance.

Divisions usually have considerable autonomy *unless* they fail to reach their ROIC goals. Generally, corporate headquarters will not intervene in the operations of a division unless there are problems. If problems arise, corporate headquarters may step in to take corrective action, perhaps replacing managers or providing additional financial resources, depending on the reason for the problem. If they see no possibility of a turnaround, they may decide to divest the division. The multidivisional structure allows the unrelated company to operate its businesses as a portfolio of investments that can be bought and sold as business conditions change. Often managers in the various divisions do not know one another; they may not even know what other companies are in the corporate portfolio. Hence, the idea of a corporate culture is meaningless.

The use of financial controls to manage a company means that no integration among divisions is necessary. This is why the bureaucratic costs of managing an unrelated company are low. The biggest problem facing corporate personnel is determining capital allocations to the various divisions so that the overall profitability of the portfolio is maximized. They also have to oversee divisional managers and make sure that divisions are achieving ROIC targets. Alco Standard's way of managing its businesses, described in Strategy in Action 13.3, demonstrates how to operate a strategy of unrelated diversification.

Strategy in Action   13.3

Alco Standard Gets It Right

Alco Standard, based in Valley Forge, Pennsylvania, is one of the largest office supply companies in the United States, distributing office and paper supplies and materials through a nationwide network of wholly owned distribution companies. It pursues a highly successful strategy of unrelated diversification. The policy of Alco's top management is that authority and control should be completely decentralized to the managers in each of the company's fifty divisions. Each division is left alone to make its own manufacturing or purchasing decisions even though some potential benefits, in the form of corporate-wide purchasing or marketing, are being lost. Top management pursues this nonintervention policy because it believes that the gains from allowing its managers to act as independent entrepreneurs exceed any potential cost savings that might result from coordinating interdivisional activities. It believes that a decentralized operating system allows a big company to act in a way that is similar to a small company, avoiding the problem of growing bureaucracy and organizational inertia.

At Alco, top management interprets its role as relieving the divisions of administrative chores, such as bookkeeping and accounting, and collecting market information on competitive pricing and products, which allows divisional managers to improve their business-level strategy. Centralizing these information activities reduces each division's cost structure and provides the standardization that lets top management make better decisions about resource allocation. Alco's division heads are regarded as partners in the corporate enterprise and are rewarded through stock options linked to the performance of their divisions. So far, Alco has been very successful with its decentralized operating structure and has achieved a compound growth rate of 19 percent a year.

Vertical Integration. Vertical integration is a more expensive strategy to manage than unrelated diversification because *sequential resource flows* from one division to the next must be coordinated. Once again, the multidivisional structure economizes on the bureaucratic costs associated with achieving such coordination. This structure provides the centralized control necessary for the vertically integrated company to achieve benefits from the control of resource transfers. Corporate personnel assume the responsibility for devising output and behavior controls that solve the problems of transferring resources among divisions; for example, they are involved in solving transfer pricing problems. Also, complex rules and procedures are instituted that specify how exchanges are to be made to solve potential transaction problems. As previously noted, complex resource exchanges can lead to conflict among divisions, and corporate managers must try to minimize divisional conflicts.

Centralizing authority at corporate headquarters must be done with care in vertically related companies. It carries the risk of involving corporate managers in operating issues at the business level to the point at which the divisions lose their autonomy and motivation. These companies must strike the right balance of centralized control at corporate headquarters and decentralized control at the divisional level if it is to implement this strategy successfully.

Because their interests are at stake, divisions need to have input into scheduling and decisions regarding resource transfer. For example, the plastics division in a chemical company has a vital interest in the activities of the oil division, for the quality of the products it gets from the oil division determines the quality of its own products. Divisional integrating mechanisms can bring about direct coordination and information transfers among divisions.[9] To handle communication among divisions, a company sets up teams for the purpose; it can also use **integrating roles,** whereby an experienced senior manager assumes responsibility for managing complex transfers between two or more divisions. The use of integrating roles to coordinate divisions is common in high-tech and chemical companies, for example.

Thus, a strategy of vertical integration is managed through a combination of corporate and divisional controls. As a result, the organizational structure and control systems used for managing this strategy to economize on bureaucratic costs are more complex and more difficult to implement than those used for unrelated diversification. However, as long as the benefits that derive from vertical integration are realized, the extra expense in implementing this strategy can be justified.

Related Diversification. In the case of related diversification, the gains from pursuing this multibusiness model derive from the transfer, sharing, or leveraging of R&D knowledge, industry information, customer bases, and so on across divisions. Also, with this structure, the high level of resource sharing and joint production by divisions makes it hard for corporate managers to measure the performance of each individual division.[10] Thus, bureaucratic costs are substantial. The multidivisional structure helps to economize on these costs because it provides some of the extra coordination and control that is required. However, if a related company is to obtain the potential benefits from using its competencies efficiently and effectively, it has to adopt more complicated forms of integration and control at the divisional level to make the structure work.

First, output control is difficult to use because divisions share resources, so it is not easy to measure the performance of an individual division. Therefore, a company needs to develop a corporate culture that stresses cooperation among divisions and corporate rather than purely divisional goals. Second, corporate managers must establish sophisticated integrating devices to ensure coordination among divisions. Integrating roles and even integrating teams of managers are often essential because they provide the context in which managers from different divisions can meet and develop a common vision of corporate goals. The new HP, for instance, created a high-level integrating team composed of scores of managers to coordinate the merger process.[11]

An organization with a multidivisional structure must have the right mix of incentives and rewards for cooperation if it is to achieve gains from sharing skills and resources among divisions.[12] With unrelated diversification, divisions operate autonomously, and the company can quite easily reward managers on their division's individual performance. With related diversification, however, rewarding divisions is more difficult because they are engaged in so many shared activities and strategic managers must be sensitive and alert to achieve equity in rewards among divisions. The aim always is to design structure and control systems so that they can maximize the benefits from pursuing the strategy while economizing on bureaucratic costs.

The Role of Information Technology

The increasing use of IT is increasing the advantages and reducing the problems associated with implementing a multibusiness model effectively. IT does this because it facilitates output control, behavior control, and integration between divisions and between divisions and corporate headquarters.

On the advantage side, IT provides a common software platform that can make it much less problematic for divisions to share information and knowledge and obtain the benefits from leveraging their competencies. IT also facilitates output and financial control, making it easier for corporate headquarters to monitor divisional performance and decide when to intervene selectively. It also helps corporate managers better use their strategic and implementation skills because they can react more quickly given that they possess higher-quality, more timely information from the use of a sophisticated cross-organizational IT infrastructure.

In a similar fashion, IT makes it easier to manage the problems that occur when implementing a multidivisional structure. Because it provides both corporate and divisional managers with more and better information, it makes it easier for corporate managers to decentralize control to divisional managers and yet react quickly if the need arises. IT can also make it more difficult to distort information and hide bad news because divisional managers must provide standardized information that can be compared across divisions. Finally, IT eases the transfer pricing problem because divisional managers have access to detailed up-to-date information about how much a certain resource or skill would cost to buy in the external marketplace. Thus, a fair transfer price is easier to determine.

The multidivisional structure is ubiquitous for companies operating with a multibusiness model and pursuing corporate-level strategies to increase company profitability. This does not mean that they are easy to implement; however, they necessarily increase profitability, at least in the short run. Companies like HP and Compaq and AOL and Time Warner and Daimler and Chrysler justified their mergers on the basis that their combined operations will allow them to implement a multidivisional structure that will lead to substantial improvements in operational efficiency and an increased ability to innovate a stream of differentiated products.

Yet DaimlerChrysler has been unable to obtain the benefits it foresaw through combining its competencies in high quality with Chrysler's low-cost car making skills. AOL Time Warner's stock plunged in 2002 when the claimed cost savings and profitable new products expected from its merger were slow to appear. The stocks of WorldCom and Tyco profiled in Chapters 9 and 10 have also plunged as investors doubt these companies can in fact implement their multibusiness models to increase the value they can create. Will the new HP fare any better?

Implementing Strategy Across Countries

Global strategy can play a crucial role in strengthening the business model of both single-business and multibusiness companies. Indeed, few large companies that have expanded into new industries have not already expanded globally into new countries. Companies can use four basic strategies as they begin to market their products and establish production facilities abroad:

- A *multidomestic strategy* is oriented toward local responsiveness, and a company decentralizes control to subsidiaries and divisions in each country in which it operates to produce and customize products to local markets.

- An *international strategy* is based on R&D and marketing being centralized at home and all the other value creation functions being decentralized to national units.

- A *global strategy* is oriented toward cost reduction, with all the principal value creation functions centralized at the optimal global location.

- A *transnational strategy* is focused so that it can achieve local responsiveness and cost reduction. Some functions are centralized and others decentralized at the global location best suited to achieving these objectives.

The need to coordinate and integrate global value chain activities increases as a company moves from a multidomestic to an international to a global and then to a transnational strategy. To obtain the benefits of pursuing a transnational strategy, a company must transfer its distinctive competencies to the global location where they can create the most value and establish a global network to coordinate its divisions at home and abroad. The objective of such coordination is to obtain the benefits from transferring or leveraging competencies across a company's global business units. Thus, the bureaucratic costs associated with solving communications and measurement problems that arise in managing handoffs or transfers across countries to pursue a transnational strategy are much higher than those of pursuing the other strategies. The multidomestic strategy does not require coordinating activities on a global level because value creation activities are handled locally, by country or world region. The international and global strategies fit between the other two strategies: although products have to be sold and marketed globally, and hence global product transfers must be managed, there is less need to coordinate skill and resource transfers than for a transnational strategy.

The implication is that as companies change from a multidomestic to an international, global, or transnational strategy, they require a more complex structure, control system, and culture to coordinate the value creation activities associated with implementing that strategy. More complex structures economize on bureaucratic costs. In general, the choice of structure and control systems for managing a global business is a function of three factors:

1. The decision on how to distribute and allocate responsibility and authority between managers at home and abroad so that effective control over a company's global operations is maintained

2. The selection of the organizational structure that groups divisions both at home and abroad in a way that allows the best use of resources and serves the needs of foreign customers most effectively

3. The selection of the right kinds of integration and control mechanisms and organizational culture to make the overall global structure function effectively

Table 13.2 summarizes the appropriate design choices for companies pursuing each of these strategies.

Implementing a Multidomestic Strategy

When a company pursues a multidomestic strategy, it generally operates with a global-area structure (see Figure 13.2). When using this structure, a company duplicates all value creation activities and establishes an overseas division in every country or world area in which it operates. Authority is decentralized to managers in each overseas division, who devise the appropriate strategy for responding to the needs of the local environment. Managers at global headquarters use market and output controls, such as ROIC, growth in market share, and operation costs, to evaluate the performance of overseas divisions. On the basis of such global comparisons, they can make decisions about capital allocation and orchestrate the transfer of new knowledge among divisions.

A company that makes and sells the same products in many different countries often groups its overseas divisions into world regions to simplify the coordination of products across countries. Europe might be one region, the Pacific Rim another, and the Middle East a third. Grouping allows the same set of output and behavior controls to be applied across all divisions inside a region. Thus, global companies can reduce communications and transfer problems because information can be transmitted more easily across countries with broadly similar cultures. For example, consumers' preferences regarding product design and marketing are likely to be more similar among countries in one world region than among countries in different world regions.

TABLE 13.2

Global Strategy/Structure Relationships

	Multidomestic Strategy	International Strategy	Global Strategy	Transnational Strategy
	Low ←	Need for Coordination	→	High
	Low ←	Bureaucratic Costs	→	High
Centralization of Authority	Decentralized to national unit	Core competencies centralized, others decentralized to national units	Centralized at optimal global location	Simultaneously centralized and decentralized
Horizontal Differentiation	Global-area structure	International-division structure	Global product-group structure	Global-matrix structure, matrix in the mind
Need for Complex Integrating Mechanisms	Low	Medium	High	Very High
Organizational Culture	Not important	Quite important	Important	Very important

FIGURE 13.2

Global-Area Structure

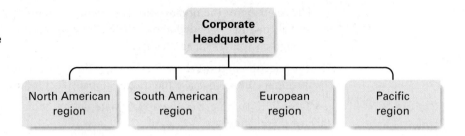

Because the overseas divisions themselves have little or no contact with others in different regions, no integrating mechanisms are needed. Nor does a global organizational culture develop because there are no transfers of skills or resources or transfer of personnel among managers from the various world regions. Historically, car companies such as DaimlerChrysler, GM, and Ford used global-area structures to manage their overseas operations. Ford of Europe, for example, had little or no contact with its U.S. parent; capital was the principal resource exchanged.

One problem with a global-area structure and a multidomestic strategy is that the duplication of specialist activities across countries raises a company's overall cost structure. Moreover, the company is not taking advantage of opportunities to transfer, share, or leverage its competencies and capabilities on a global basis; for example, it cannot apply the low-cost manufacturing expertise that has developed in one world region in another. Thus, multidomestic companies lose the many benefits of operating globally. As Chapter 8 discusses, the popularity of this strategic orientation has decreased.

Implementing International Strategy

A company pursuing an international strategy adopts a different route to global expansion. Normally, the company shifts to this strategy when it decides to sell domestically made products in markets abroad. Until the 1990s, for example, companies such as Mercedes-Benz and Jaguar made no attempt to produce in a foreign market; instead, they distributed and sold their domestically produced cars internationally. Such companies usually just add a *foreign sales organization* to their existing structure and continue to use the same control system. If a company is using a functional structure, this department has to coordinate manufacturing, sales, and R&D activities with the needs of the foreign market. Efforts at customization are minimal. In overseas countries, a company usually establishes a subsidiary to handle local sales and distribution. For example, the Mercedes-Benz overseas subsidiaries allocate dealerships, organize supplies of spare parts, and, of course, sell cars. A system of behavior controls is then established to keep the home office informed of changes in sales, spare parts requirements, and so on.

A company with many different products or businesses operating from a multidivisional structure has the challenging problem of coordinating the flow of different products across different countries. To manage these transfers, many companies create an *international division,* which they add to their existing divisional structure (see Figure 13.3).[13] International operations are managed as a separate divisional business, with managers given the authority and responsibility for coordinating domestic product divisions with overseas markets. The international division also monitors and controls the overseas subsidiaries that market the products and decides how much authority to delegate to managers in these countries.

This arrangement of tasks and roles reduces the transaction of managing handoffs across countries and world regions. However, managers abroad are essentially

FIGURE 13.3

International Division
Structure

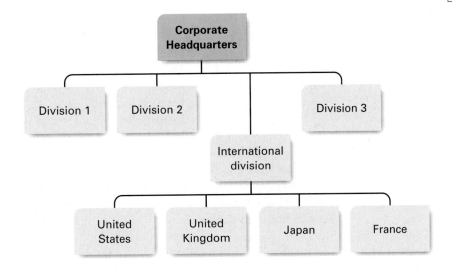

under the control of managers in the international division, and if domestic and overseas managers compete for control of strategy making, conflict and lack of cooperation may result. Many companies such as IBM, Citibank, and DaimlerChrysler have experienced this problem. Very often, significant strategic control has been decentralized to overseas divisions. When cost pressures force corporate managers to reassess their strategy and they decide to intervene, this frequently provokes resistance, much of it due to differences in culture—not just corporate but also country differences.

**Implementing
Global Strategy**

When a company embarks on a global strategy today, it locates its manufacturing and other value chain activities at the global location that will allow it to increase efficiency, quality, and innovation. In doing so, it has to solve the problems of coordinating and integrating its global value chain activities. It has to find a structure that lowers the bureaucratic costs associated with resource transfers between corporate headquarters and its global divisions and provides the centralized control that a global strategy requires. The answer for many companies is a *global product division structure* (see Figure 13.4).

In this structure, a product division headquarters is created to coordinate the activities of its home and overseas operations. Within each division, headquarters

FIGURE 13.4

Global Product-
Division Structure

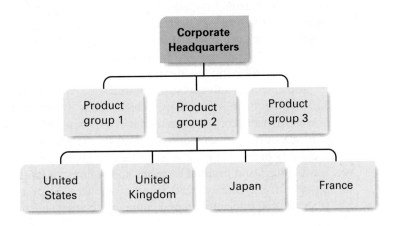

managers decide where to locate the different functions at the optimal global location for performing that activity. For example, Phillips has one division responsible for global R&D, manufacturing, marketing, and sales of its light bulbs, another for medical equipment, and so on. The headquarters of the medical division and its R&D is located in Bothell, Washington, manufacturing is done in Taiwan, and the products are sold by sales subsidiaries in each local market.

The product division structure allows managers to decide how best to pursue a global strategy—for example, to decide which value chain activities, such as manufacturing or product design, should be performed in which country to increase efficiency. Increasingly, U.S. and Japanese companies are moving manufacturing to low-cost countries such as China but establishing product design centers in Europe or the United States to take advantage of foreign skills and capabilities to obtain the benefits from this strategy.

Implementing Transnational Strategy

The main failing of the global product division structure is that although it allows a company to achieve superior efficiency and quality, it is weak when it comes to responsiveness to customers because the focus is still on centralized control to reduce costs. Moreover, this structure makes it difficult for the *different product divisions* to trade information and knowledge and to obtain the benefits from transferring, sharing, and leveraging their competencies. Sometimes the potential gains from sharing product, marketing, or R&D knowledge between product groups are high, but so too are the bureaucratic costs associated with achieving these gains. Is there a structure that can simultaneously economize on these costs and provide the coordination necessary to obtain these benefits?

In the 1990s, many companies implemented a *global matrix structure* to simultaneously lower their global cost structures *and* differentiate their activities through superior innovation and responsiveness to customers globally. Figure 13.5 shows such a structure that might be used by a company such as HP or a large oil and chemical company. On the vertical axis, instead of functions, there are the company's corporate *product groups,* which provide specialist services such as R&D, product design, and marketing information to its overseas divisions, which are often grouped by world region. These might be the petroleum, plastics, pharmaceuticals, or fertilizer product groups. On the horizontal axis are the company's *overseas divisions* in the various countries or world regions in which it operates. Managers at the regional or country level control local operations. Through a system of output and behavior controls, they then report to corporate product group personnel back in the United States and ultimately to the CEO or president; for example, Michael Capellas (before his recent departure from HP) was ultimately responsible for overseeing the way HP's global structure works. The heads of the world regions or country managers are also responsible for working with U.S. product group managers to develop the control and reward systems that will promote the transfer, sharing, or leveraging of competencies that will result in superior performance.

Implementing a matrix structure thus decentralizes control to overseas managers and provides them with considerable flexibility for managing local issues, but can still give product and corporate managers in the United States the centralized control they need to coordinate company activities on a global level. The matrix structure can allow knowledge and experience to be transferred among geographic regions, product divisions, and product divisions and regions. Because it offers many opportunities for face-to-face contact between managers at home and abroad, the matrix facilitates the transmission of a company's norms and values and, hence, the devel-

FIGURE 13.5

Global Matrix
Structure

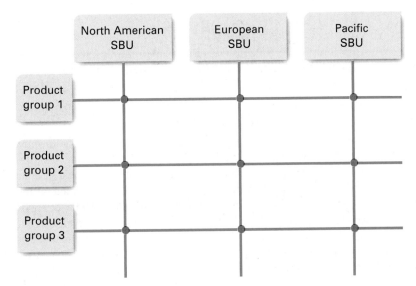

● Individual operating companies

opment of a global corporate culture. This is especially important for a company with far-flung global operations for which lines of communication are longer. Club Med, for instance, uses a matrix to standardize high-quality customer service across its global vacation villages. Nestlé's experience with the global matrix structure is profiled in Strategy in Action 13.4.

Nestlé is not the only company to find the task of integrating and controlling a global matrix structure a difficult task. Some, like ABB, Ford, and Motorola, have dismantled their matrix structures and moved to a simplified global product group approach using IT to integrate across countries. If a matrix is chosen, however, other possible ways of making it work effectively include developing a strong cross-country organizational culture to facilitate communication and coordination among managers. For example, many companies are increasingly transferring managers between their domestic and overseas operations so they can implant the domestic culture in the new location and also learn by studying how their structure and systems work in the foreign country.

Toyota has made great efforts to understand how to manage car plants in overseas locations and how to transplant its culture into those plants. When it decided to enter and make cars in the United States, it first formed a joint venture with GM, and the companies combined their expertise in this car-making venture known as NUMMI. Toyota was responsible for implanting its knowledge of lean production in this plant; all the workers were cross-trained and taught how to monitor and benchmark their own performance and how to work in quality teams to improve it. Toyota then took all its learning from this venture and transferred it to its wholly owned car plant in Spartanburg, Virginia, where it turns out cars with as good a reliability record as those produced in its Japanese plants.

Every Toyota plant is under the control of Japanese managers, however, and managers from Toyota's Japanese headquarters are constantly monitoring its plant's performance and transferring and implanting Toyota's R&D innovations into its next car models. Toyota used a similar implementation strategy when it established car component and assembly operations in south Wales to serve the European Union market. Indeed, it chose south Wales and Virginia as locations for its plants because both

Strategy in Action

13.4

Using IT to Make Nestlé's Global Structure Work

Nestlé, based in Vevey, Switzerland, is the world's biggest food company, with global sales in excess of $50 billion in 2001. The company has been pursuing an ambitious program of global expansion by acquiring many famous companies—for instance, Perrier, the French mineral water producer, and Rowntree Mackintosh, the British candy maker. In the United States, Nestlé bought the giant Carnation Company, Stouffer Foods, Contadina, and Ralston Purina in 2002, which also made it the world's largest pet food maker.

Traditionally, Nestlé pursued a multidomestic strategy and managed its operating companies through a global area structure. In each country, each individual company (such as its Carnation division) was responsible for managing all aspects of its business-level strategy: in other words, companies were free to control their own product development and marketing and to manage all local operations. Nestlé's corporate executives decided acquisitions, expansions, and corporate resource decisions such as capital investment at the Vevey headquarters. Because all important decisions were made centrally, the size of the corporate staff increased dramatically. In the early 1990s, Nestlé realized it had major problems.

Corporate managers had become remote from the difficulties experienced by the operating companies, and the centralized operating structure slowed decision making. Nestlé had trouble responding quickly to the changing environment. Moreover, the company was forfeiting all the possible benefits from sharing and leveraging its distinctive competencies in food product development and marketing between operating companies and world regions. Because each subsidiary was operated separately, corporate executives had no ability to integrate their activities around the world. To raise its performance, Nestlé's managers sought to find a new way of organizing its activities.

Its CEO at the time, Helmut Maucher, started restructuring Nestlé from the top down. He stripped away the power of corporate management by decentralizing authority to the managers of seven global product groups that he created to oversee the company's major product lines (for example, coffee, milk, and candy) on a global level. The role of each global product group was to integrate the activities of the operating companies in their group to transfer and leverage distinctive competencies to

create value. After the change, managers in the candy product group, for instance, began orchestrating the marketing and sale of Rowntree candy products, such as After Eight Mints and Smarties, throughout Europe and the United States, and sales climbed by 60 percent.

Maucher then grouped all operating companies within a country or region into one national or regional subsidiary and created a team of subsidiary managers to link and coordinate the activities of the various companies in that subsidiary. When the different companies or divisions started to share joint purchasing, marketing, and sales activities, major cost savings resulted. In the United States, the subsidiary management team reduced the number of sales officers nationwide from 115 to 22 and decreased the number of suppliers of packaging from 43 to 3.

Finally, Maucher decided to use a matrix structure to integrate the activities of the seven global product groups with the operations of Nestlé's country- or region-based subsidiaries. The goal of this matrix structure is to have the company pursue a transnational strategy, allowing it to obtain the gains from differentiation through global learning and cost reduction. For example, regional subsidiary managers now spend considerable time in Vevey with product division executives, discussing ways of exploiting and sharing the resources of the company on a global basis.

Although the new decentralized matrix structure improved Nestlé's ability to coordinate its structure, by 1998 it was clear that it still was not providing enough integration and coordination. Although more coordination was taking place between product groups *inside* a region such as the United States, little coordination was taking place across regions. Nestlé's top managers searched for ways to improve integration on a global scale. Their conclusion was that more output and behavior control was needed so that different product groups and different regions could learn from and understand what everyone else was doing—for example, what their product development plans were or how each product group handled its global supply chain.

Nestlé's solution was to sign, in June 2000, a $200 million contract with mySAP.com, with an extra $80 million for consulting and maintenance to install a standardized enterprise resource system (ERP) to integrate across *all* its global operations. Top managers hoped this system would give them the information they needed to exert centralized control of its operations that the matrix structure apparently did not provide. In essence, Nestlé began to use mySAP's value chain management software as a *substitute* for the matrix. With this IT, they would no longer need to rely on divisional managers to transfer information but henceforth could obtain it from mySAP's system. They would then be able to intervene at a global level as necessary.

To standardize Nestlé's IT system to ensure global compatibility, top managers decided to invest in a next-generation IT infrastructure and put this out for bid. Both IBM and HP bid for the contract to provide, install, program, and service the new network of computers so that they would work seamlessly with mySAP's software. IBM won this $500 million contract in March 2002 for what is now called Nestlé's "Globe Project" to create uniform business processes and computer systems around the world. Whether Nestlé will obtain the cost savings and differentiation advantages from using IT to integrate its global operations is still unclear. What is clear is that if the new IT works as expected, it will lead many other global companies to bolster their matrix or product group structures and use IT to improve their performance.

Sources: A. Edgecliffe-Johnson, "Nestle and Pillsbury Forge Ice Cream Alliance in U.S.," *Financial Times,* August 20, 1999, p. 2. B. Worthen, "Nestlé's ERP Odyssey," *CIO,* May 15, 2002, pp. 1–5. "Nestle Picks IBM over HP for $500 Million Contract," *Wall Street Journal,* March 7, 2002, p. B. 6. www.nestle.com, 2002.

regions have a strong local culture based on family and tradition that closely parallels Japan's culture. Toyota's managers felt that by choosing a similar local culture, they would have more chance of being able to implement its highly efficient work processes and procedures.

As the examples of Toyota and MTV (see the *Opening Case* in Chapter 8) suggest, companies that form global networks of managers who can move to and work in other countries so they can turn to each other for help are an important aspect of helping a company realize the benefits from its global operations. When managers can hold a "*matrix-in-the-mind,*" that is, learn to think about how they could transfer competencies around the company to create value, they can work to develop an information network that lets a company capitalize globally on the skills and capabilities of its employees.[14] To foster the development of the matrix-in-the-mind concept and promote cooperation, companies are increasingly making use of IT's integrating capability by using online teleconferencing, email, and global intranets among the parts of their global operations. For example, Hitachi coordinates its nineteen Japanese laboratories by means of an online teleconferencing system. Both Microsoft and HP make extensive use of global intranets to integrate their activities, and Nestlé hopes its Globe Project will accomplish the same goal.

These IT integration mechanisms help provide the coordination that is necessary for a global matrix structure to work effectively. However, the enormous number of global transfers and handoffs associated with achieving its benefits means that the bureaucratic costs associated with pursuing a transnational strategy are high. However, the potential gains for a company from using this strategy to share and leverage its competencies and capabilities to achieve superior efficiency, quality, innovation, and responsiveness to customers can easily outweigh these costs, making it a worthwhile strategy to pursue. Indeed, in most global industries today, there is usually one company—a Dell, Toyota, or McDonald's—that has learned how to pursue both a low-cost and a differentiation approach. In the complicated game of global competition, if companies do not at least strive to obtain these goals, they are likely to suffer at the hands of more agile rivals in the future.

Entry Mode and Implementation

As Chapter 10 noted, today many organizations are changing their corporate-level strategies and restructuring their organizations to find new ways to use their resources and capabilities to create value. This section focuses on the implementation issues that arise when companies use the three different modes of entry into new industries: internal new venturing, joint ventures, and mergers and acquisitions.

Internal New Venturing

Chapter 10 discusses how companies can enter new industries by transferring and leveraging their existing resources to create the set of value chain activities necessary to compete effectively in a new industry. Some of the benefits and pitfalls associated with internal new venturing were discussed there. Now we consider how structure, control, and culture can be used to increase the success of the new venturing process.

Most managers today are engaged full time in the effort to develop a competitive advantage in their existing product markets. Money and resources are always scarce, and employees are almost always overburdened, so how can managers create a setting in which employees are to be encouraged to act in ways that allow them to see how their functional competencies or products can be used in other industries?

At the heart of the issue is that corporate managers must treat the internal new-venturing process as a form of entrepreneurship and the people who are to pioneer and lead new ventures as **intrapreneurs,** or inside or internal entrepreneurs. This means that organizational structure, control, and culture must be designed to encourage creativity and give new-venture managers autonomy and freedom to develop and champion new products. At the same time, corporate managers want to make sure that the investment in new markets will be profitable and that a fit does exist between the new industry and the old one so that benefits can in fact be leveraged.[15] HP, for example, has worked hard to provide this balance between autonomy and constraint. To encourage innovation, its founders pioneered the idea of requiring its scientists and engineers to spend 15 percent of their time on projects of their own choosing; at the same time, scientists know that their ideas and the business models they developed to prove the value of their ideas will be scrutinized closely by divisional managers.[16]

3M also has carefully used structure, control, and culture to create a formal organization-wide new-venturing process that is one of the best known for promoting product innovation. 3M's goal is that at least 25 percent of its growth in sales each year should be attributed to new products developed within the past five years. To achieve this challenging goal, 3M has developed an implementation formula to ensure its employees are provided with the freedom and motivation to experiment and take risks.

On the structure side, 3M recognized early on the increasing importance of linking and coordinating the efforts of people in different functions to speed product development. As noted in the previous chapter, people in different functions tend to develop different subunit orientations and to focus their efforts on their own tasks to the exclusion of the needs of other functions. The danger of such tendencies is that each function will develop norms and values that suit its own needs but do little to promote organizational coordination and integration.

To avoid this problem, 3M established a system of cross-functional teams composed of members of product development, process development, marketing, manufacturing, packaging, and other functions to create organization-wide norms and values of innovation. So that all groups have a common focus, the teams work closely with customers; customers' needs become the platform on which the different functions can then apply their skills and capabilities.[17] For example, one of 3M's cross-functional teams worked closely with disposable diaper manufacturers to develop the right kind of sticky tape for their needs. To promote integration in the team and foster cooperative norms and values, each team is headed by a "product champion" who takes the responsibility for building cohesive team relationships and developing a team culture. In addition, one of 3M's senior managers becomes a "management sponsor" whose job is to help the team get resources and provide support when the going gets tough. After all, product development is a highly risky process; many projects do not succeed.

3M is also careful to use integrating mechanisms such as high-level product development committees to screen new ideas. Proven entrepreneurs and experienced managers from the other divisions and from R&D, marketing, sales, and manufacturing serve on this committee to screen the new ideas. New-product champions defend their products and projects before this committee to secure the resources for developing them. (Chapter 4 describes this development funnel.)

On the control side, 3M copied HP and developed a companywide norm that researchers should use 15 percent of their time on their own projects; it was this norm that helps to lead to the development of new products such as Post-it notes. In addition, 3M is careful to establish career ladders for its scientists in order to gain their long-term commitment, and it rewards successful product innovators. For example, it established the "Golden Step" program that gives employees substantial monetary bonuses to honor and reward the launch of successful new products and to develop norms and values that support and reward the sharing of information among scientists and people in different functions.

3M's structure and control systems have created an atmosphere in which employees know it is better to take a chance and risk making a mistake than do nothing at all. Managers understand that their job is to encourage creativity in their employees and teams and to foster a culture of innovation. However, the regular work of the organization goes on side by side with all this intrapreneurial activity.

The other main approach to internal new venturing has been championed by those who believe that the best way to encourage new-product development is to separate this effort from the rest of the organization. To provide new-venture managers with the autonomy to experiment and take risks, the company sets up a **new-venture division,** separate and independent from its other divisions, for the development of a new product. The logic behind this is that if a new-product team works from within a company's existing structure, its members will never have the freedom or autonomy to pursue radical new-product ideas. Away from the day-to-day scrutiny of top managers, new-venture managers will be able to pursue the creation of a new product and develop a new business model as though they were external entrepreneurs.

The new-venture division is controlled in a way that reinforces the entrepreneurial spirit. Thus, output controls are regarded as inappropriate because they can promote short-term thinking and inhibit risk taking. Instead, stock options are often used to reinforce a culture for entrepreneurship. Another issue with output controls is to keep top managers at bay. The thinking is that the up-front R&D costs of new venturing are high and its success uncertain. After spending millions of dollars, corporate managers might become concerned about the new-venture division's performance and might try to introduce tight output controls or strong budgets to increase accountability, measures that hurt the entrepreneurial culture.[18] Corporate managers may believe it is important to institute behavior and output controls that put some limits on freedom of action; otherwise, costly mistakes may be made and resources wasted on frivolous ideas.

Recently, there have been some indications that 3M's internal approach may be superior to the use of external new-venture divisions. This is because it appears that many new-venture divisions have failed to get successful new products to market. And even if they do, usually the new-venture division eventually begins to operate like any other division, and a company's cost structure rises because of the duplication of value chain activities.

Another issue is that scientists are often not the best people to develop successful business models because they lack formal training. Just as many medical doctors are earning MBAs today to understand the many strategic issues confronting their profession, so scientists need to be able to think strategically, and these skills may be lacking in a new-venture division.

HP illustrates many of these issues. Early in its history, HP used the new-venturing approach. As soon as a new self-supporting product was developed in one of HP's operating divisions, a new-venture division was spun off to develop and market the product. In this fashion, HP's goal was to keep its divisions small and entrepreneurial. Soon HP had over twenty-eight different divisions, each with its own value chain functions. At first, the value these divisions created exceeded their operating costs, but then problems emerged because of changing technological and industry conditions. Because they were operated separately, the divisions could not learn from each other, and because they all had separate R&D departments, sales forces, and so on, they began to compete for resources. For example, when one HP scientist pioneered what was to become biotechnology, the managers of other divisions could not see the logic of how it related to HP's existing activities and would not fund it. HP became saddled with high operating costs and missed-product opportunities. To solve the problem, it merged some divisions and brought their technologies and product lines together. It also sold off divisions to other companies to focus its activities and thus make it easier to transfer resources between its divisions.

Joint Venturing

Internal new venturing is an important means by which large, established companies can maintain their momentum and grow from within.[19] One alternative is to form strategic alliances, and even establish a formal joint venture with a company that has a valuable distinctive competency. Often in joint venturing, two or more companies agree to pool specific resources and capabilities that they believe will create more value for both companies and appoint managers from both companies to control the new operation. In this case, no separate entity is set up. Sometimes companies do establish a separate and independent company and agree to establish and share ownership of the new company, possibly with fifty-fifty ownership, or sometimes one company insists on having a 51 percent or more stake to give it the controlling interest. The companies then transfer to the new company whatever resources and capabilities they have agreed on to help it pursue the business model that will promote both companies' interests. This has been Microsoft's favored strategy in recent years as it enters industries with links to computing, such as the communications and entertainment industries. Normally, it takes a 51 percent stake to give it the right to buy out the company and integrate it into Microsoft should it have technology that proves vital to Microsoft's future interests.

Many of the advantages and pitfalls of joint venturing across industries and across cultures are discussed in Chapters 8 and 10. From an implementation perspective, important issues concern the way the venture is structured and controlled and the problems that frequently emerge in managing differences between the cultures of companies in a joint venture.

Allocating authority and responsibility is the first major implementation issue companies have to decide on. Both companies need to be able to monitor the progress of the joint venture so that they can learn from what goes on and benefit the most. One reason that some companies prefer to establish a new company and obtain a 51 percent ownership of it is to solve the problem of which company will have the ultimate authority and control over the new venture. The problem of a company's risking losing control of its core technology or competence when its enters into a strategic alliance was discussed in Chapter 8. The issue is that the future is unknown; it is not clear which company will benefit the most from whatever innovations the new company might develop.[20] Given this problem, steps must be taken up front to address this issue; this is why Microsoft normally insists on 51 percent ownership. Of course, to get the other company to agree to this, it pays a premium price for the other company.

Many companies form a contract to share skills and invest in each other and do not confront the issue of future ownership. Some of these have learned how dangerous this is, not only because their partners may take their learning and then go it alone and because the other party might be acquired by a competitor. For example, Compaq shared its technical knowledge with a company in the computer storage industry to promote joint product development, only to watch helplessly as that company was acquired by Sun Microsystems, which consequently obtained Compaq's knowledge.

The implementation issues are strongly dependent on whether the purpose of the joint venture is to share and develop technology, jointly distribute and market products and brands, or share access to customers. Whether the companies involved are competitors is also an important issue here. Some have claimed that Toyota received more benefit from the GM-Toyota venture discussed earlier because GM did not take Toyota's lean production knowledge and apply it quickly enough in its other divisions, while Toyota did and this put GM at a competitive disadvantage. Sometimes companies in different industries can simply realize joint benefits from collaboration. For example, in 2001, Nestlé and Coca-Cola announced a ten-year joint venture, to be called Beverage Partners Worldwide, through which Coca-Cola will distribute and sell Nestlé's Nestea ice tea, Nescafe, and other brands throughout the globe.[21] Similarly, Starbuck's Frappuccino is distributed by Pepsi. In this kind of joint venture, both companies can gain from sharing and pooling different competencies so that both realize value that would not otherwise be possible. In these cases, issues of ownership are less important, although the issue of allocating responsibility and monitoring performance remains.

Once the ownership issue has been settled, one company appoints the CEO, who is responsible for creating a cohesive top management team from the ranks of managers who have been transferred from the parent companies. The job of the top management team is to develop a successful business model. These managers then need to choose an organizational structure, such as the functional or product-team, that will make the best use of the resources and skills transferred from the parent. The need to provide a framework that combines their activities and integrates across people and functions is of paramount importance. So is the need to build a new company culture that can unite the members of the hitherto different cultures. In essence, solving all the implementation problems discussed in the previous chapter is on top managers' agenda.

Because solving these issues is expensive and time-consuming, it is not surprising that if the stakes are great and the future possibilities unknown, many companies decide that they might be better off by acquiring the other company and integrating it into their operations. Note also that this avoids the duplication of functional activities. If the stakes are less, however, and the future easier to forecast, as in the venture between Coca-Cola and Nestlé, then it makes sense to establish a new entity that can manage the transfers of complementary resources and skills between companies.

Mergers and Acquisitions

Mergers and acquisitions are the third, and most widely used, vehicle that companies can use to enter new industries or countries.[22] How to implement structure, control systems, and culture to manage a new acquisition is important because many acquisitions are unsuccessful. And one of the main reasons acquisitions perform poorly is that many companies do not anticipate the difficulties associated with merging or integrating new companies into their existing operations.[23]

At the level of structure, managers of both the acquiring and acquired companies have to confront the problem of how to establish new lines of authority and responsibility that will allow them to make the best use of both companies' competencies and capabilities. The *Opening Case* on the merger between HP and Compaq illustrates the issues. Before the merger Fiorina, Capellas, and their top management teams spent thousands of hours analyzing the range of both companies' activities, performing a value-chain grid analysis to determine how cost and differentiation advantages might be achieved. Based on this analysis, they merged all their divisions into four main product groups.

Imagine the problems in deciding who would control which group and which operating division and to whom these managers would report to: Fiorina or Capellas? In press releases, the companies' managers were careful to announce that the process of merging divisions was going smoothly and that battles over responsibilities and control of resources were being resolved to counter fears that infighting would prevent the benefits of the merger from being realized. One problem with a mishandled merger is that skilled managers who feel they have been demoted will leave the company, and if many do leave, this also may prevent its benefits from being realized.

Once the issue of lines of authority has been addressed, the issue of how to coordinate and integrate the merged companies to streamline and rationalize its operations to reduce costs and leverage competencies has to be addressed. For large companies, the answer, as for HP, is the multidivisional structure, but important control issues have to be resolved. In general, the more similar or related are the acquired companies' products and markets (a company has made a related acquisition, as in the HP case), the easier the job is of integrating their operations. Providing the acquiring company has an efficient control system, it can be adapted to the new company to standardize the way its activities are monitored and measured. Or managers can work hard to combine the best elements of each company's control systems and cultures or introduce a new IT system.

If managers make unrelated acquisitions, however, and then try to interfere with a company's strategy in an industry they know little about or apply inappropriate structure and controls to manage the new business, then major strategy implementation problems can arise. For example, if managers try to integrate unrelated companies with related ones in the search for some elusive benefits, apply the wrong kinds of controls at the divisional level, or interfere in business-level strategy, corporate performance can suffer as bureaucratic costs skyrocket. These mistakes explain why related acquisitions are sometimes more successful than unrelated ones.[24]

Even in the case of related diversification, the business processes of each company frequently are different, and their computer systems may be incompatible, as in the Nestlé case. The issue facing the merged company is how to use output and behavior controls to standardize business processes and reduce the cost of handing off and transferring resources. While installing the mySAP software, for example, managers in charge of the U.S. effort discovered that each of Nestlé's 150 different U.S. divisions was buying its own supply of the flavoring vanilla from the same set of suppliers. However, the divisions were not sharing information about how they were doing this, and vanilla suppliers, dealing with each Nestlé division separately, tried to charge each division as much as they could, with the result that each division paid a different price for the same input![25] How could this happen? Each division used a different code for its independent purchase, and managers at U.S. headquarters did not have the information to discover this. mySAP's software provides such information.

Finally, even when acquiring a company in a closely related industry, managers must realize that each company has a unique culture, or way of doing things. Such idiosyncrasies must be understood in order to manage the merged company effectively. Indeed, such idiosyncrasies are likely to be especially important when companies from different countries merge. Over time, top managers can change the culture and alter the internal workings of the company, but this is a difficult implementation task. The differences between HP and Compaq are a case in point. HP has a research-oriented culture and prizes its technology and the people who create it. Compaq is a marketing-driven organization and prizes a hands-on, value-driven approach. In June 2002, many analysts were waiting to see how the culture of the combined company would shake out. Would there be a departure of top Compaq managers given that HP is in control of the new company and its culture? Would it be possible to integrate their skills if they have such a different orientation? Where would most of the layoffs that would occur for cost-savings reason be coming from: HP's employees or Compaq's? The way the new HP deals with these issues is vital to determining its future culture.

In sum, managers' capability of managing structure, control, and culture and to integrating and connecting divisions to permit gains from leveraging competencies ultimately determines how well the new merged company will perform.[26] Some authors have argued that this is why the quality or capabilities of management is so important: Do Fiorina, and other HP managers have the skills to integrate the two companies? Analysts attribute Compaq's poor performance in the 1990s to its failure to integrate Digital Equipment's operations into Compaq's after it bought Digital in 1998. Will a similar fate befall HP? As discussed in Chapter 10 managers must have good entrepreneurial, strategic, and implementation capabilities to recognize opportunities for leveraging skills across different divisions to produce a new stream of products that customers want.[27] In 2002, AOL Time Warner, which defended their merger on their ability to accomplish just such a feat, was experiencing major problems because it turned out that customers were reluctant to buy such services as video on demand and online video game playing.

The path to merger and acquisition is fraught with dangers, which is why some companies claim that internal new venturing is the safest path, and it is best to grow organically from within. Yet with industry boundaries blurring and new global competitors emerging, companies often do not have the time to go it alone. How to enter a new industry or country is a complex implementation issue that requires thorough strategic analysis to make the right choice.

IT, the Internet, and Outsourcing

Understanding the many ways in which advances in information systems and technology are having an impact on strategy implementation is an important issue today. By improving the ability of managers to coordinate and control the activities of the organization and helping managers make more effective decisions, computer-based information systems have become an important aspect of strategy implementation. Evidence that capabilities in managing information systems can be a source of competitive advantage is growing; organizations that do not adopt leading-edge information systems are likely to be at a competitive disadvantage.

Information systems include many different varieties of software platforms and databases. These encompass companywide systems designed to manage all of a company's value chain activities provided by companies such as mySAP, PeopleSoft, JD Edwards, and others, to more general-purpose database products targeted toward specific uses, such as the products offered by Oracle, Microsoft, and many others. Information technologies encompass a broad array of communication media and devices that link information systems and people including voicemail, email, voice conferencing, videoconferencing, the Internet, groupware and corporate intranets, cell phones, fax machines, personal digital assistants, and so on. Information systems and information technologies are often inextricably linked and together are normally referred to as IT.[28]

IT and Strategy Implementation

At the level of organizational structure, control, and culture, IT has given strategic managers many new options in implementing their strategies. IT is instrumental in both shaping and integrating resources and capabilities. Moreover, its capabilities can be difficult to imitate since they are present not just in physical information systems but also in the organization-specific IT capabilities that develop inside a company over time. Wal-Mart legally protected what it regards as a core competency in IT by blocking the movement of some of its key programmers to dot-coms like Amazon.com.

Competitive strategy and the ability to pursue a low-cost and differentiation approach depend on a firm's ability to increase efficiency, quality, innovation, and customer responsiveness, and IT has a major impact on these sources of competitive advantage.[29] One advantage of IT is knowledge leveraging that involves sharing and integrating cross-functional expertise through appropriate forms of IT. Benefits include the delivery to customers of new differentiated goods and services. The way in which Citibank implemented an organization-wide IT to increase responsiveness to customers is instructive. In 2000, Citibank set as its goal to be the premier global international financial company. Studying its business model, it was clear that the main customer complaint was the amount of time customers had to wait for a response to their request, so it set out to solve this problem. Teams of managers examined the way Citibank's current IT worked and then redesigned it to empower employees and reduce the handoffs between people and functions. Employees were then given extensive training in operating the new IT system. Citibank has been able to document significant time and cost savings, as well as an increase in the level of personalized service it is able to offer its clients, which has led to a significant increase in the number of global customers.[30]

Indeed, IT has important effects on a company's ability to innovate. It improves the base of knowledge that employees draw on when they engage in problem solving and decision making and provides a mechanism to promote collaboration and information sharing both inside and across functions and business units. However, knowledge or information availability alone will not lead to innovation; it is the ability to use knowledge creatively that is the key to promoting innovation and creating competitive advantage. Prahalad and Hamel, for example, suggest that it is not the absolute level of knowledge a firm possesses that leads to competitive advantage, but the speed or velocity with which it is circulated in the firm.[31] IT transfers knowledge where it can add the highest value to the organization.

The project-based work characteristic of matrix structures provides a vivid example of this process. As a project progresses, the need for particular team members waxes and wanes. Some employees will be part of a project from beginning to end, and others will be asked to participate only at key times when their expertise is required. IT provides managers with the real-time capability to monitor project progress and needs and allocate resources accordingly to increase the value added of each employee. Traditionally, product design has involved sequential processing across functions, with handoffs as each stage of the process is completed (see Chapter 4). This linear process is being replaced by parallel, concurrent engineering made possible through the application of IT, allowing employees to work simultaneously with continual interaction through electronic communication, which can promote innovation.

IT has major effects on other aspects of a company's structure and control systems. The increasing use of IT has been associated with a flattening of the organizational hierarchy and a move toward greater decentralization and increased integration within organizations. By electronically providing managers with high-quality, timely, and relatively complete information, IT has reduced the need for a management hierarchy to coordinate organizational activities. Email systems and the development of organization-wide corporate intranets is breaking down the barriers that have traditionally separated departments and the result has been improved performance.[32] To facilitate the use of IT and to make organizational structure work, however, a company must create a control and incentive structure to motivate people and subunits, as Strategy in Action 13.5 suggests.

Some companies are taking full advantage of IT's ability to help them integrate their activities to simultaneously respond better to customer needs while making the most cost-effective use of their employees' skills by using a virtual organizational structure. The **virtual organization** is composed of people who are linked by computers, faxes, computer-aided design systems, and video teleconferencing and who may rarely, if ever, see one another face to face. People come and go as and when their services are needed, much as in a matrix structure.

Accenture, the global management consulting company, is becoming just such a virtual organization. Consultants are connected by laptops to an organization's **knowledge management system,** its company-specific information system that systematizes the knowledge of its employees and provides them with access to other employees who have the expertise to solve the problems that they encounter as they perform their jobs. The consultants pool their knowledge in a massive internal database they can easily access through computer and the company's intranet. The company's 40,000 consultants often work from their homes, traveling to meet the company's clients throughout the world and only rarely stopping in at one of Accenture's branch offices to meet their superiors and colleagues. CEO George Shaheen says the company's headquarters are wherever he happens to be at the time. (He spends 80 percent of his time traveling.)[33]

Strategy in Action   13.5

Oracle's New Approach to Control

Oracle is the second largest independent software company after Microsoft. Like Bill Gates, Microsoft's chairman, Oracle's cofounder and chairman, Larry Ellison, recognized that his company had a major problem in 1999: it was not using the latest Internet software—software it had developed itself—to control its activities even though its customers were! As a result, Oracle was having a difficult time understanding its customers' needs, and internally it was not experiencing the cost savings that result from implementing its own database and financial control software. Ellison moved quickly to change Oracle's control systems so that they were Internet based.

One of the main advantages of Internet-based control software is that it permits the centralized management of a company's widespread operations. Corporate managers can easily compare and contrast the performance of different divisions spread throughout the globe in real time and can quickly identify problems and take corrective action. However, to his embarrassment, Ellison discovered that Oracle's financial and human resource information was located on over seventy different computing systems across the world. It took a lot of time and effort to track such basic things as the size of the company's workforce and the sales of its leading products. As a result, it took a long time to take corrective action, and many opportunities were being missed.

Recognizing the irony of the situation, Ellison ordered his managers to change the way the company controlled—that is, monitored and evaluated—its activities and to implement its new Internet-based control systems as quickly as possible. His goal was to have all of Oracle's sales, cost, profit, and human resource information systems consolidated in two locations and to make this information available to managers throughout the company instantaneously with one click of a mouse. In addition, he instructed managers to investigate which kinds of activities were being monitored and controlled by people and wherever possible to substitute Internet-based control. For example, previously Oracle had over 300 people responsible for monitoring and managing such tasks as paper-based travel planning and expense report systems. These tasks were automated into software systems and put online, and employees were made responsible for filing their own reports. These 300 people were then transferred into sales and consulting positions. The savings was over $1 billion a year.

By using Internet software-based control systems, Oracle's managers are also able to get closer to their customers. In 1999, Oracle gave all its salespeople new customer relationship management software and instructed them to enter into the system detailed information about customers' purchases, future plans, web orders, and service requests. As a result, headquarters managers can track sales orders easily and if they see problems such as lost sales or multiple service requests can quickly contact customers to solve problems and so build better customer relations.

So amazed has Ellison been at the result of implementing Internet software systems that he has radically rethought Oracle's control systems. He now believes that because of the advances of modern computer information systems, Oracle's employees should be doing only one of three things: building its products, servicing its products, or selling its products. All other activities should be automated by developing new information control systems, and it should be the manager's job to use control only to facilitate one of these three front-line activities.

Source: M. Moeller, "Oracle: Practicing What It Preaches." *Business Week,* August 16, 1999, pp. 1–5.

Strategic Outsourcing and Network Structure   Another major impact of IT on strategy implementation has been its effects on a company's ability to pursue strategic outsourcing to strengthen its business model. As Chapter 9 discusses, the use of strategic outsourcing is increasing rapidly as organizations recognize the many opportunities it offers to promote differentiation, reduce costs, and increase their flexibility. U.S. companies spent $500 billion on outsourcing in 2000, and companies such as EDS, IBM, FedEx, and UPS are major beneficiaries of this increase.

Recall that outsourcing occurs as companies use short- and long-term contracts, joint ventures, and strategic alliances to link or form interorganizational relationships with other companies. IT increases the efficiency of such relationships. For example, it allows for the more efficient movement of raw materials and component parts between a company and its suppliers and distributors. It also promotes the transfer, share, and leveraging of competencies between companies, which can lead to design and engineering improvements that increase differentiation and lower costs.

As a consequence, there has been growing interest in electronic **business-to-business (B2B)** networks in which most or all of the companies in an industry (for example, car makers) use the same software platform to link to each other and establish industry specifications and standards. Then these companies jointly list the quantity and specifications of the inputs they require and invite bids from the thousands of potential suppliers around the world. Suppliers also use the same software platform so electronic bidding, auctions, and transactions are possible between buyers and sellers around the world. The idea is that high-volume standardized transactions can help drive down costs and raise quality at the industry level. The role Li & Fung plays in managing the global supply chain for companies in Southeast Asia is instructive in this regard, as Strategy in Action 13.6 shows.

Cross-company global electronic networks reduce the information costs associated with the search, evaluation, and monitoring of competing suppliers, often making global strategic alliances more attractive than vertical integration. In addition, firms that use electronic networks not only reduce costs; because they increase the pool of potential suppliers, they also reduce the bargaining power of suppliers. Similarly, beyond using IT to link backward with suppliers, companies can use IT to link forward in the value chain to connect its operations with those of customers, something that reduces their costs and creates a disincentive for customers to seek other suppliers.[34]

In order to implement outsourcing effectively, strategic managers must decide what organizational arrangements to adopt. Increasingly, a **network structure**—the set of strategic alliances that an organization creates with suppliers, manufacturers, and distributors to produce and market a product—is becoming the structure of choice to implement outsourcing. An example of a network structure is the series of strategic alliances that Japanese car companies such as Toyota and Honda formed with their suppliers of inputs, such as car axles, gearboxes, and air-conditioning systems. Members of the network work together on a long-term basis to find new ways to reduce costs and increase the quality of their products. Moreover, developing a network structure allows an organization to avoid the high costs of operating a complex organizational structure (the costs of employing many managers, for example). Finally, a network structure allows a company to form strategic alliances with foreign suppliers, which gives managers access to low-cost foreign sources of inputs, keeping costs low. The way Nike uses a global network structure to produce and market its sports, casual, and dress shoes is instructive.

Nike, located in Beaverton, Oregon, is the largest and most profitable sports shoe manufacturer in the world. The key to Nike's success is the network structure that Philip Knight, its founder and CEO, created to allow his company to produce and market shoes. The most successful companies today simultaneously pursue a low-cost and a differentiation strategy. Knight realized this early on and created an organizational structure to allow his company to achieve this goal.

By far, the largest function at Nike's headquarters in Beaverton is the design function, staffed by talented designers who pioneer innovations in sports shoe design

Strategy in Action   13.6

Li & Fung's Global Supply Chain Management

Finding the foreign suppliers that offer the lowest-priced and highest-quality products is an important task facing the managers of global organizations. These suppliers are located in thousands of cities in many countries around the world, so finding them is difficult. Often global companies use the services of foreign intermediaries or brokers, located near these suppliers, to find the one that best meets their input requirements. Li & Fung, now run by brothers Victor and William Fung, is one of these brokers that has helped hundreds of global companies to locate suitable foreign suppliers, especially suppliers in mainland China.

By 2001, managing global companies' supply chains became an even more complicated task. Foreign suppliers were increasingly specializing in just one part of the task of producing a product in their search for ways to reduce costs. For example, in the past, a company such as Target might have negotiated with a foreign supplier to manufacture 1 million units of a shirt at a certain cost per unit. But with specialization, Target might find it can reduce the costs of producing the shirt even further by splitting the operations involved in producing the shirt and having a different foreign supplier, often in different countries, perform each operation. For example, to get the lowest cost per unit, Target might first negotiate with a yarn manufacturer in Vietnam to make the yarn; then ship the yarn to a Chinese supplier to weave it into cloth; and then

to several different factories in Malaysia and the Philippines to cut the cloth and sew the shirts. Another foreign company might take responsibility for packaging and shipping the shirts to wherever in the world they are required. Since a company like Target has thousands of different clothing products under production and these change all the time, the problems of managing such a supply chain to get the full cost savings from global expansion are clear.

This is the opportunity that Li & Fung has capitalized on. Realizing that many global companies do not have the time or expertise to find such specialized low-price suppliers, they moved quickly to provide such a service. Li & Fung employs 3,600 agents who travel across thirty-seven countries to find new suppliers and inspect existing suppliers to find new ways to help their clients, global companies, get lower prices or higher-quality products. Global companies are happy to outsource their supply chain management to Li & Fung because they realize significant cost savings. And although they pay a hefty fee to Li & Fung, they avoid the costs of employing their own agents. As the complexity of supply chain management continues to increase, more and more companies like Li & Fung are appearing.

Source: "Business: Link in the Global Chain," *Economist,* June 2, 2001, pp. 62–63.

such as the air pump and Air Jordans that Nike introduced so successfully. Designers use computer-aided design (CAD) to design their shoes, and all new-product information, including manufacturing instructions, is stored electronically. When the designers have done their work, they relay the blueprints for the new products electronically to a network of suppliers and manufacturers throughout Southeast Asia with which Nike has formed strategic alliances.[35] Instructions for the design of a new sole, for example, may be sent to a supplier in Taiwan, and instructions for the leather uppers to a supplier in Malaysia. These suppliers produce the shoe parts, which are then sent for final assembly to a manufacturer in China with which Nike has established an alliance. From China, these shoes are shipped to distributors throughout the world. Of the 99 million pairs of shoes Nike makes each year, 99 percent are made in Southeast Asia.

There are three main advantages to this network structure for Nike. First, Nike's costs are very low because wages in Southeast Asia are a fraction of what they are in the United States, and this gives Nike a low-cost advantage. Second, Nike is able to respond to changes in sports shoe fashion very quickly. Using its global computer system, it can, literally overnight, change the instructions it gives to each of its suppliers so that within a few weeks, its foreign manufacturers are producing new kinds of shoes.[36] Any alliance partners that fail to perform up to Nike's standards are replaced with new partners, so Nike has great control over its network structure. In fact, the company works closely with its suppliers to take advantage of any new developments in technology that can help it reduce costs and increase quality. Third, the ability to outsource all its manufacturing abroad allows Knight to keep Nike's U.S. structure fluid and flexible. Nike uses a functional structure to organize its activities, and Knight decentralizes control of the design process to teams that are assigned to develop each of the new kinds of sports shoes for which Nike is known.

In conclusion, the implications of IT for strategy implementation are still evolving and will continue to do so as new software and hardware reshape a company's business model and its strategies. IT is changing the nature of value chain activities both inside and between organizations, affecting all four building blocks of competitive advantage: efficiency, quality, innovation, and responsiveness to customers. For the multibusiness company as for the single-business company, the need to be alert to such changes to strengthen its position in its core business has become a vital matter, and the success of companies like Dell and Wal-Mart and the failure of others such as Gateway and Kmart can be traced, in part, to their success in developing the IT capabilities that lead to sustained competitive advantage.

Summary of Chapter

1. At the corporate level, a company must choose the combination of structure, control systems, and culture that will allow it to operate a multibusiness model in a way that will lead to superior profitability.

2. As a company grows and diversifies, it adopts a multidivisional structure. Although this structure costs more to operate than a functional or product structure, it economizes on the bureaucratic costs associated with operating through a functional structure and gives a company the capability to handle its value creation activities more effectively.

3. As companies change their corporate strategies over time, they must change their structure because different strategies are managed in different ways. In particular, the move from unrelated diversification to vertical integration to related diversification increases the bureaucratic costs associated with managing a multibusiness model. Each requires a different combination on structure, control, and culture to economize on those costs.

4. As a company moves from a multidomestic to an international, global, and transnational strategy, it also needs to switch to a more complex structure that allows it to coordinate increasingly complex resource trans-

fers. Similarly, it needs to adopt a more complex integration and control system that facilitates resource sharing and the leverage of competencies around the globe. When the gains are substantial, companies frequently adopt a global matrix structure to share knowledge and expertise or implement control systems and culture to allow them to achieve its advantages.

5. To encourage internal new venturing, companies must design an internal venturing process that gives new-venture managers the autonomy they need to develop new products. Corporate managers need to provide the oversight that keeps new-venture managers motivated and on track.

6. The profitability of mergers and acquisitions depends on the structure and control systems that companies adopt to manage them and the way a company integrates them into its existing businesses.

7. IT is having increasingly important effects on the way multibusiness companies implement their strategies. Not only is it helping improve the efficiency with which the multidivisional structure operates, it also allows for the better control of complex value chain activities. The growth of outsourcing has also been promoted by IT and some companies have developed network structures to coordinate their global value chain activities.

Discussion Questions

1. When would a company decide to change from a functional to a multidivisional structure?
2. If a related company begins to buy unrelated businesses, in what ways should it change its structure or control mechanisms to manage the acquisitions?
3. What prompts a company to change from a global to a transnational strategy, and what new implementation problems arise as it does so?
4. How would you design a structure and control system to encourage entrepreneurship in a large, established corporation?
5. What are the problems associated with implementing a strategy of related diversification through acquisitions?

Practicing Strategic Management

SMALL-GROUP EXERCISE: DECIDING ON AN ORGANIZATIONAL STRUCTURE (Continued)

Break into the same groups used for the Chapter 12 Small Group Exercise. Reread the scenario in the Chapter 12 exercise and recall your group's debate about the appropriate organizational structure for your soft drinks company. Because it is your intention to compete with Coca-Cola for market share worldwide, there should also be a global dimension to your strategy, and you must consider what is the best structure globally as well as domestically. Debate the pros and cons of the types of global structures, and decide which is most appropriate and will best fit with your domestic structure.

ARTICLE FILE 13

Find an example of a company pursuing a multibusiness model that has changed its structure and control systems to manage its strategy better. What were the problems with the way it formerly implemented its strategy? What changes did it make to its structure and control systems? What effects does it expect these changes to have on performance?

STRATEGIC MANAGEMENT PROJECT: MODULE 13

Take the information you collected in the Chapter 12 on strategy implementation, and link it to the multibusiness model. You should collect information to determine if your company competes across industries or countries and also to see what role IT plays in allowing it to implement its business model.

1. Does your company use a multidivisional structure? Why or why not? What crucial implementation problems must your company manage to implement its strategy effectively? For example, what kind of integration mechanisms does it employ?

2. What is your company's corporate-level strategy? How does this affect the way it uses organizational structure, control, and culture?
3. What kind of international strategy does your company pursue? How does it control its global activities? What kind of structure does it use? Why?
4. Can you suggest ways of altering the company's structure or control systems to allow it to create more value? Would this change increase or decrease bureaucratic costs?
5. Does your company have a particular entry mode that it has used to implement its strategy?
6. In what ways does your company use IT to coordinate its value chain activities?
7. Assess how well you think your company has implemented its multibusiness (or business) model.

EXPLORING THE WEB
Visiting Sears

Go to **www.sears.com** and locate information for investors. Study the pattern in the history of Sears's diversification strategy in the 1980s, and look at its press releases. What have been the changes in its multibusiness model over time? How would you characterize its strategy today? What effects on its performance would you expect its recent strategic moves to have? Based on this analysis, how do you think Sears's structure, control systems, and culture have changed over time?

General Task: Search the Web for a multibusiness company that is in the process of modifying or changing the way it implements its strategy. What changes is it making to its structure or control systems? Does IT have a role in the changes? What structure is it moving toward? Why is this structure more appropriate than the old one?

Closing Case

Hughes Aircraft Changes Its Divisional Structure

Hughes Aircraft is one of the large U.S. defense companies battered by the end of the cold war and the decline in the defense budget. Hughes had been accustomed to a protected environment in which lavish government revenues allowed it to develop advanced technology for military uses, such as missiles, satellites, and radar systems. However, by 1990, Hughes was confronted with a major strategic problem. How could it compete in a new environment in which government revenues were scarce? To survive, Hughes had to find a new strategy based on diversifying and developing its technology for nonmilitary uses—and find it fast.

As a first step in changing direction, C. Michael Armstrong, an ex-IBM top manager, was appointed as CEO. In IBM's European division, Armstrong had developed a reputation as someone who could turn around a company and redeploy its resources quickly and effectively; investors hoped he could do so at Hughes. Armstrong began by analyzing the company's strategy and structure. What he found was a firm pursuing a differentiated strategy based on developing advanced technological products. To pursue its differentiated strategy, Hughes had developed a divisional structure to lead its development efforts. It had created seven separate technology divisions, each responsible for a different kind of product—missiles, radar, and so forth. Over time, the organization had become very tall and centralized as each technology division developed its own empire to support its efforts. The primary coordination between divisions took place at the top of the organization, where top divisional managers met regularly with corporate managers to report on and plan future product developments.

Armstrong recognized that this fit between strategy and structure might be appropriate for a company operating in a protected environment in which money was not a problem. However, it was not appropriate for a company facing intense pressure to lower costs and develop products for nonmilitary applications, such as consumer electronics and home satellites. The divisional structure duplicated expensive R&D activities, and no mechanism was in place to promote the sharing of knowledge and expertise among the different divisions. Moreover, there were few incentives for managers to cut costs because scarce resources had not been a problem, and managers had been rewarded mainly for the success of their product development efforts. Armstrong realized that to make

the company more competitive and improve the way it used its skills and resources, he had to find a new operating strategy and structure.

Armstrong began the process of change by focusing the company's strategy on customers and markets, not on technology and products. Henceforth, the needs of customers, not the needs of technology, would be the logic behind the organization of the company's activities. He changed the structure from a divisional one based on technology to one based on the needs of customers. The seven technology divisions were reengineered into five market groups according to the kinds of customers' needs they satisfied. Thus, consumer electronics became one market group, and industrial and commercial applications became another. Then technological expertise was reorganized to serve the needs of each kind of customer.

Continuing his reengineering program, Armstrong slashed the number of levels in the managerial hierarchy, eliminating two levels in order to bring managers closer to the customer. He continued this reengineering effort by decentralizing authority and pushing decision making down into the divisions, so that lower-level managers could better respond to customers' needs. In addition, he reorganized the company's international operations by transferring managers from the United States to foreign countries so that they would be closer to their customers.

To make this new customer-oriented structure work effectively, Armstrong also changed the organization's control systems. He created a system of output controls based on benchmarking competitors' costs to provide managers with standards against which to evaluate their performance and force them to pay attention to costs and quality. He then set up new incentive programs for managers and workers at all levels, linking the programs to achievement of the new targets for efficiency, quality, and responsiveness to customers. Finally, he worked hard with his top management team to establish and promote the norms and values of a customer-oriented organizational culture across the new market divisions. Henceforth, technology would be made to fit the customer, not vice versa.

Armstrong's efforts to engineer a new fit between strategy and structure at Hughes have been spectacularly successful. His top management team has fully bought into the new corporate culture, and divisional managers are adopting new entrepreneurial values based on meeting customers' needs. Some of the company's successes include the launch of its RCA minidisk satellite television system and the development of one of the largest private space-based satellite systems in the world. Its stock price has soared as Hughes uses its leading-edge technology to provide customers with quality products at competitive prices. With its new simultaneous differentiation and low-cost strategy, Hughes is performing well in the new competitive environment.

Case Discussion Questions

1. What problems did Armstrong discover with Hughes's strategy and structure?

2. What steps did he take to reengineer the company?

Source: J. Cole, "New CEO at Hughes Studied Its Managers, Got Them on His Side," *Wall Street Journal,* March 30, 1993, pp. A1, A8.

Notes

Chapter 1

1. There are several different ratios for measuring profitability, such as return on invested capital, return on assets, and return on equity. Although these different measures are highly correlated with each other, finance theorists argue that the return on invested capital is the most accurate measure of profitability. See Tom Copeland, Tim Koller, and Jack Murrin, *Valuation: Measuring and Managing the Value of Companies* (New York: Wiley, 1996).

2. Trying to estimate the relative importance of industry effects and firm strategy on firm profitability has been one of the most important areas of research in the strategy literature during the past decade. See Y. E. Spanos and S. Lioukas, "An Examination of the Causal Logic of Rent Generation," *Strategic Management Journal* 22:10 (October 2001): 907–934; and R. P. Rumelt, "How Much Does Industry Matter?" *Strategic Management Journal* 12 (1991): 167–185. See also A. J. Mauri and M. P. Michaels, "Firm and Industry Effects Within Strategic Management: An Empirical Examination," *Strategic Management Journal* 19 (1998): 211–219.

3. K. R. Andrews, *The Concept of Corporate Strategy* (Homewood, Ill.: Dow Jones Irwin, 1971); H. I. Ansoff, *Corporate Strategy* (New York: McGraw-Hill, 1965); C. W. Hofer and D. Schendel, *Strategy Formulation: Analytical Concepts* (St. Paul, Minn.: West, 1978).

4. **http://www.boeing.com/companyoffices/aboutus/mission/2016_VISION_8.5X11.**

5. **http://www.microsoft.com/mscorp/.**

6. These three questions were first proposed by P. F. Drucker, *Management—Tasks, Responsibilities, Practices* (New York: Harper & Row, 1974), pp. 74–94.

7. Derek F. Abell, *Defining the Business: The Starting Point of Strategic Planning* (Englewood Cliffs, N.J.: Prentice-Hall, 1980).

8. P. A. Kidwell and P. E.Ceruzzi, *Landmarks in Digital Computing* (Washington, D.C.: Smithsonian Institute, 1994).

9. J. C. Collins and J. I. Porras, "Building Your Company's Vision," *Harvard Business Review* (September–October 1996): 65–77.

10. **http://www.nucor.com/.**

11. See J. P. Kotter and J. L. Heskett, *Corporate Culture and Performance* (New York: Free Press, 1992). For similar work, see Collins and Porras, "Building Your Company's Vision."

12. E. Freeman, *Strategic Management: A Stakeholder Approach* (Boston: Pitman Press, 1984).

13. M. D. Richards, *Setting Strategic Goals and Objectives* (St. Paul, Minn.: West, 1986).

14. E. A. Locke, G. P. Latham, and M. Erez, "The Determinants of Goal Commitment," *Academy of Management Review* 13 (1988): 23–39.

15. R. E. Hoskisson, M. A. Hitt, and C. W. L. Hill, "Managerial Incentives and Investment in R&D in Large Multiproduct Firms," *Organization Science* 3 (1993): 325–341.

16. Robert H. Hayes and William J. Abernathy, "Managing Our Way to Economic Decline," *Harvard Business Review* (July–August 1980): 67–77.

17. Andrews, *Concept of Corporate Strategy; Ansoff, Corporate Strategy;* Hofer and Schendel, *Strategy Formulation.*

18. For details, see R. A. Burgelman, "Intraorganizational Ecology of Strategy Making and Organizational Adaptation: Theory and Field Research," *Organization Science* 2 (1991): 239–262; H. Mintzberg, "Patterns in Strategy Formulation," *Management Science* 24 (1978): 934–948; S. L. Hart, "An Integrative Framework for Strategy Making Processes," *Academy of Management Review* 17 (1992): 327–351; and G. Hamel, "Strategy as Revolution," *Harvard Business Review* 74 (July–August 1996): 69–83.

19. This is the premise of those who advocate that chaos theory should be applied to strategic management. See R. Stacey and D. Parker, *Chaos, Management and Economics* (London: Institute for Economic Affairs, 1994). See also H. Courtney, J. Kirkland, and P. Viguerie, "Strategy Under Uncertainty," *Harvard Business Review* 75 (November–December 1997): 66–79.

20. Hart, "Integrative Framework"; Hamel, "Strategy as Revolution."

21. See Burgelman, "Intraorganizational Ecology of Strategy Making and Organizational Adaptation," and Mintzberg, "Patterns in Strategy Formulation."

22. R. A. Burgelman and A. S. Grove, "Strategic Dissonance," *California Management Review* (Winter 1996): 8–28.

23. This story was related to the author by George Rathmann, who at the time was heading up 3M's research activities.

24. Richard T. Pascale, "Perspectives on Strategy: The Real Story Behind Honda's Success," *California Management Review* 26 (1984): 47–72.

25. This viewpoint is strongly emphasized by Burgelman and Grove, "Strategic Dissonance."

26. C. C. Miller and L. B. Cardinal, "Strategic Planning and Firm Performance: A Synthesis of More Than Two Decades of Research," *Academy of Management Journal* 37 (1994): 1649–1665. Also see P. R. Rogers, A. Miller, and W. Q. Judge, "Using Information Processing Theory to Understand Planning/Performance Relationships in the Context of Strategy," *Strategic Management Journal* 20 (1999): 567–577; and P. J. Brews and M. R. Hunt, "Learning to Plan and Planning to Learn," *Strategic Management Journal* 20: 889–913.

27. Courtney, Kirkland, and Viguerie, "Strategy Under Uncertainty."

28. P. J. H. Schoemaker, "Multiple Scenario Development: Its Conceptual and Behavioral Foundation," *Strategic Management Journal* 14 (1993): 193–213.

29. C. Kim and R. Mauborgne, "Procedural Justice, Strategic Decision Making, and the Knowledge Economy," *Strategic Management Journal* 19 (1998): 323–338; W. C. Kim and R. Mauborgne, "Fair Process: Managing in the Knowledge Economy," *Harvard Business Review* 75 (July–August 1997): 65–76.

30. G. Hamel and C. K. Prahalad, *Competing for the Future* (New York: Free Press, 1994).

31. See G. Hamel and C. K. Prahalad, "Strategic Intent," *Harvard Business Review* (May–June 1989): 64.

32. See C. R. Schwenk, "Cognitive Simplification Processes in Strategic Decision Making," *Strategic Management Journal* 5 (1984): 111–128; and K. M. Eisenhardt and M. Zbaracki, "Strategic Decision Making," *Strategic Management Journal* 13 (Special Issue, 1992): 17–37.

33. For a summary of research on strategic leadership, see D. C. Hambrick, "Putting Top Managers Back into the Picture," *Strategic Management Journal* 10 (Special Issue, 1989): 5–15. See also D. Goldman, "What Makes a Leader?" *Harvard Business Review* (November-December 1998): 92–105; H. Mintzberg, "Covert Leadership," *Harvard Business Review*

(November–December 1998): 140–148; and R. S. Tedlow, "What Titans Can Teach Us," *Harvard Business Review* (December 2001): 70–79.

34. N. M. Tichy and D. O. Ulrich, "The Leadership Challenge: A Call for the Transformational Leader," *Sloan Management Review* (Fall 1984): 59–68. F. Westley and H. Mintzberg, "Visionary Leadership and Strategic Management," *Strategic Management Journal* 10 (Special Issue, 1989): 17–32.

35. E. Wrapp, "Good Managers Don't Make Policy Decisions," *Harvard Business Review* (September–October 1967): 91–99.

36. J. Pfeffer, *Managing with Power* (Boston: Harvard Business School Press, 1992).

37. D. Goldman, "What Makes a Leader?" *Harvard Business Review* (November–December 1998): 92–105.

38. H. Simon, *Administrative Behavior* (New York: McGraw-Hill, 1957).

39. The original statement of this phenomenon was made by A. Tversky and D. Kahneman, "Judgment Under Uncertainty: Heuristics and Biases," *Science* 185 (1974): 1124–1131.

40. Schwenk, "Cognitive Simplification Processes," pp. 111–128.

41. B. M. Staw, "The Escalation of Commitment to a Course of Action," *Academy of Management Review* 6 (1981): 577–587.

42. R. Roll, "The Hubris Hypotheses of Corporate Takeovers," *Journal of Business* 59 (1986): 197–216.

43. Irvin L. Janis, *Victims of Groupthink,* 2nd ed. (Boston: Houghton Mifflin, 1982). For an alternative view, see S. R. Fuller and R. J. Aldag, "Organizational Tonypandy: Lessons from a Quarter Century of the Groupthink Phenomenon," *Organizational Behavior and Human Decision Processes* 73 (1998): 163–184.

44. See R. O. Mason, "A Dialectic Approach to Strategic Planning," *Management Science* 13 (1969): 403–414; R. A. Cosier and J. C. Aplin, "A Critical View of Dialectic Inquiry in Strategic Planning," *Strategic Management Journal* 1 (1980): 343-356; and I. I. Mintroff and R. O. Mason, "Structuring III—Structured Policy Issues: Further Explorations in a Methodology for Messy Problems," *Strategic Management Journal* 1 (1980): 331–342.

45. Mason, "A Dialectic Approach," pp. 403–414.

Chapter 2

1. M. E. Porter, *Competitive Strategy* (New York: Free Press, 1980).

2. Charles W. L. Hill has acted as an outside consultant to Tacoma City Light and evaluated the strategy on their behalf.

3. J. E. Bain, *Barriers to New Competition* (Cambridge Mass.: Harvard University Press, 1956). For a review of the modern literature on barriers to entry, see R. J. Gilbert, "Mobility Barriers and the Value of Incumbency," in R. Schmalensee and R. D. Willig, *Handbook of Industrial Organization*, vol. 1 (Amsterdam: North-Holland, 1989).

4. A detailed discussion of switching costs and lock in can be found in C. Shapiro and H. R. Varian, *Information Rules: A Strategic Guide to the Network Economy* (Boston: Harvard Business School Press, 1999).

5. Most of this information on barriers to entry can be found in the industrial organization economics literature. See especially the following works: Bain, *Barriers to New Competition;* M. Mann, "Seller Concentration, Barriers to Entry and Rates of Return in 30 Industries," *Review of Economics and Statistics* 48 (1966): 296–307; W. S. Comanor and T. A. Wilson, "Advertising, Market Structure and Performance," *Review of Economics*

and Statistics 49 (1967): 423–440; Gilbert, "Mobility Barriers"; and K. Cool, L.-H. Roller, and B. Leleux, "The Relative Impact of Actual and Potential Rivalry on Firm Profitability in the Pharmaceutical Industry," *Strategic Management Journal* 20 (1999): 1–14.

6. K. Fiewege, "Wall Street Hot on Airlines Despite 4th-Qtr Losses," Reuters Wire Report, January 15, 2002.

7. For a discussion of tacit agreements, see T. C. Schelling, *The Strategy of Conflict* (Cambridge, Mass.: Harvard University Press, 1960).

8. P. Ghemawat, *Commitment: The Dynamics of Strategy* (Boston: Harvard Business School Press, 1991).

9. A. S. Grove, *Only the Paranoid Survive* (New York: Doubleday, 1996).

10. In standard microeconomic theory, the concept used for assessing the strength of substitutes and complements is the cross elasticity of demand.

11. For details and further references, see Charles W. L. Hill, "Establishing a Standard: Competitive Strategy and Technology Standards in Winner Take All Industries," *Academy of Management Executive* 11 (1997): 7–25; and Shapior and Varian, *Information Rules.*

12. The development of strategic group theory has been a strong theme in the strategy literature. Important contributions include the following: R. E. Caves and Michael E. Porter, "From Entry Barriers to Mobility Barriers," *Quarterly Journal of Economics* (May 1977): 241–262; K. R. Harrigan, "An Application of Clustering for Strategic Group Analysis," *Strategic Management Journal* 6 (1985): 55–73; K. J. Hatten and D. E. Schendel, "Heterogeneity Within an Industry: Firm Conduct in the U.S. Brewing Industry, 1952–71," *Journal of Industrial Economics* 26 (1977): 97–113; Michael E. Porter, "The Structure Within Industries and Companies' Performance," *Review of Economics and Statistics* 61 (1979): 214–227. For more recent work, see K. Cool and D. Schendel, "Performance Differences Among Strategic Group Members," *Strategic Management Journal* 9 (1988): 207–233; C. S. Galbraith, G. B. Merrill, and G. Morgan. "Bilateral Strategic Groups," *Strategic Management Journal* 15 (1994): 613–626; and A. Nair and S. Kotha, "Does Group Membership Matter? Evidence from the Japanese Steel Industry," *Strategic Management Journal* (2001): 221–235.

13. For details on the strategic group structure in the pharmaceutical industry, see K. Cool and I. Dierickx, "Rivalry, Strategic Groups, and Firm Profitability," *Strategic Management Journal* 14 (1993): 47–59.

14. Charles W. Hofer has argued that life cycle considerations may be the most important contingency when formulating business strategy. See Hofer, "Towards a Contingency Theory of Business Strategy," *Academy of Management Journal* 18 (1975): 784–810. There is empirical evidence to support this view. See C. R. Anderson and C. P. Zeithaml, "Stages of the Product Life Cycle, Business Strategy, and Business Performance," *Academy of Management Journal* 27 (1984): 5–24; and D. C. Hambrick and D. Lei, "Towards an Empirical Prioritization of Contingency Variables for Business Strategy," *Academy of Management Journal* 28 (1985): 763–788. Also see G. Miles, C. C. Snow, and M. P. Sharfman, "Industry Variety and Performance," *Strategic Management Journal* 14 (1993): 163–177.

15. The characteristics of declining industries have been summarized by K. R. Harrigan, "Strategy Formulation in Declining Industries," *Academy of Management Review* 5 (1980): 599–604.

16. This perspective is associated with the Austrian school of economics, which goes back to Schumpeter. For a summary of this school and its implications for strategy, see R. Jacobson, "The Austrian School of Strategy," *Academy of Management Review* 17 (1992): 782–807. C. W. L. Hill and D. Deeds, "The Importance of Industry Structure for the Determination of Industry Profitability: A Neo-Austrian Approach," *Journal of Management Studies* 33 (1996): 429–451.

17. "A Tricky Business," *Economist,* June 30, 2001, pp. 55–56

18. D. F. Barnett and R. W. Crandall, *Up from the Ashes* (Washington, D.C.: Brookings Institute, 1986).

19. M. E. Porter, *The Competitive Advantage of Nations* (New York: Free Press, 1990).

20. The term *punctuated equilibrium* is borrowed from evolutionary biology. For a detailed explanation of the concept, see M. L. Tushman, W. H. Newman, and E. Romanelli, "Convergence and Upheaval: Managing the Unsteady Pace of Organizational Evolution," *California Management Review* 29:1 (1985): 29–44; and C. J. G. Gersick, "Revolutionary Change Theories: A Multilevel Exploration of the Punctuated Equilibrium Paradigm," *Academy of Management Review* 16 (1991): 10–36.

21. A. J. Slywotzky, *Value Migration: How to Think Several Moves Ahead of the Competition* (Boston: Harvard Business School Press, 1996).

22. R. D'Avani, *Hypercompetition* (New York: Free Press, 1994).

23. Hill and Deeds, "Importance of Industry Structure."

24. R. P. Rumelt, "How Much Does Industry Matter?" *Strategic Management Journal* 12 (1991): 167–185. See also A. J. Mauri and M. P. Michaels, "Firm and Industry Effects Within Strategic Management: An Empirical Examination," *Strategic Management Journal* 19 (1998): 211–219.

25. See R. Schmalensee, "Inter-Industry Studies of Structure and Performance," in Schmalensee and Willig (eds.), *Handbook of Industrial Organization.* Similar results were found by A. N. McGahan and M. E. Porter, "How Much Does Industry Matter, Really?" *Strategic Management Journal* 18 (1997): 15–30.

26. For example, see K. Cool and D. Schendel, "Strategic Group Formation and Performance: The Case of the U.S. Pharmaceutical Industry, 1932–1992," *Management Science* (September 1987): 1102–1124.

27. See M. Gort and J. Klepper, "Time Paths in the Diffusion of Product Innovations," *Economic Journal* (September 1982): 630–653. Looking at the history of forty-six products, Gort and Klepper found that the length of time before other companies entered the markets created by a few inventive companies declined from an average of 14.4 years for products introduced before 1930 to 4.9 years for those introduced after 1949.

28. The phrase was originally coined by J. Schumpeter, *Capitalism, Socialism and Democracy* (London: Macmillan, 1950), p. 68.

29. M. E. Porter, "Strategy and the Internet," *Harvard Business Review* (March 2001): 62–79.

30. U.S. Dept. of Labor, Bureau of Labor Statistics.

31. *Economist, The Economist Book of Vital World Statistics* (New York: Random House, 1990).

32. For a detailed discussion of the importance of the structure of law as a factor explaining economic change and growth, see D. C. North, Institutions, *Institutional Change and Economic Performance* (Cambridge: Cambridge University Press, 1990).

33. Charles W. L. Hill, *International Business* (New York: McGraw-Hill, 2003).

34. P. Dicken, *Global Shift* (New York: Guilford Press, 1992).

35. I. Metthee, "Playing a Large Part," *Seattle Post Intelligence,* April 9, 1994, p. 13.

36. T. Levitt, "The Globalization of Markets," *Harvard Business Review* (May–June 1983): 92–102.

37. Porter, *Competitive Advantage of Nations.* See also R. Grant, "Porter's Competitive Advantage of Nations: An Assessment," *Strategic Management Journal* 7 (1991): 535–548.

Chapter 3

1. M. Cusumano, *The Japanese Automobile Industry* (Cambridge, Mass.: Harvard University Press, 1989). S. Spear and H. K. Bowen, "Decoding the DNA of the Toyota Production System," *Harvard Business Review* (September–October 1999): 96–108.

2. The material in this section relies on the so-called resource-based view of the company. For summaries of this perspective, see J. B. Barney, "Company Resources and Sustained Competitive Advantage," *Journal of Management* 17 (1991): 99–120; J. T. Mahoney and J. R. Pandian, "The Resource-Based View Within the Conversation of Strategic Management," *Strategic Management Journal* 13 (1992): 63–380; R. Amit and P. J. H. Schoemaker, "Strategic Assets and Organizational Rent," *Strategic Management Journal* 14 (1993): 33–46; and M. A. Peteraf, "The Cornerstones of Competitive Advantage: A Resource-Based View," *Strategic Management Journal* 14 (1993): 179–191. B. Wernerfelt. "A Resource Based View of the Company," *Strategic Management Journal* 15 (1994): 171–180. K. M. Eisenhardt and J. A. Martin, "Dynamic Capabilities: What Are They?" *Strategic Management Journal,* 21 (2000): 1105–1121.

3. For a discussion of organizational capabilities, see R. R. Nelson and S. Winter, *An Evolutionary Theory of Economic Change* (Cambridge, Mass.: Belknap Press, 1982).

4. W. Chan Kim and R. Mauborgne, "Valu Innovation: The Strategic Logic of High Growth," *Harvard Business Review* (January–February 1997): 102–115.

5. The concept of consumer surplus is an important one in economics. For a more detailed exposition, see D. Besanko, D. Dranove, and M. Shanley, *Economics of Strategy* (New York: Wiley, 1996).

6. However, $P = V$ only in the special case when the company has a perfect monopoly and it can charge each customer a unique price that reflects the value of the product to that customer (i.e., where perfect price discrimination is possible). More generally, except in the limiting case of perfect price discrimination, even a monopolist will see most customers capture some of the value of a product in the form of a consumer surplus.

7. This point is central to the work of Michael Porter. See M. E. Porter, *Competitive Advantage* (New York: Free Press, 1985). See also P. Ghemawat, *Commitment: The Dynamic of Strategy* (New York: Free Press, 1991), chap. 4.

8. A. Priddle, "Efficiency by the Numbers," *Ward's Auto World* (July 2001): 57–59. D. C. Smith, "Power Surveys Set Standards for Measuring Quality," *Ward's Auto World* (July 2001): 34–35.

9. Porter, *Competitive Advantage.*

10. Ibid.

11. This approach goes back to the pioneering work by K. Lancaster: *Consumer Demand, a New Approach* (New York: 1971).

12. D. Garvin, "Competing on the Eight Dimensions of Quality," *Harvard Business Review* (November–December 1987): 101–119. P. Kotler. *Marketing Management* (Millennium ed.) (Upper Saddle River, N.J.: Prentice-Hall, 2000).

13. C. K. Prahalad and M. S. Krishnan, "The New Meaning of Quality in the Information Age," *Harvard Business Review* (September–October 1999): 109–118.

14. See D. Garvin, "What Does Product Quality Really Mean," *Sloan Management Review* 26 (Fall 1984): 25–44; P. B. Crosby, *Quality Is Free* (New York: Mentor, 1980); and A. Gabor, *The Man Who Discovered Quality* (New York: Times Books, 1990).

15. M. Cusumano, *The Japanese Automobile Industry* (Cambridge, Mass.: Harvard University Press, 1989). S. Spear and H. K. Bowen, "Decoding the DNA of the Toyota Production System," *Harvard Business Review* (September–October 1999): 96–108.

16. Kim and Mauborgne, "Valu Innovation."

17. G. Stalk and T. M. Hout, *Competing Against Time* (New York: Free Press, 1990).

18. Ibid.

19. Tom Copeland, Tim Koller, and Jack Murrin, *Valuation: Measuring and Managing the Value of Companies* (New York: Wiley, 1996). Also see S. F. Jablonsky and N. P. Barsky, *The Manager's Guide to Financial Statement Analysis* (New York: Wiley, 2001)

20. Copeland, Koller, and Murrin, *Valuation.*

21. This is done as follows. Signifying net profit by π, invested capital by K, and revenues by R, then ROIC = π/K. If we multiply through by revenues, R, this becomes $R \times (\pi/K) = (\pi \times R)/(K \times R)$, which can be rearranged as $\pi/R \times R/K$. π/R is the return on sales and R/K capital turnover.

22. Note that Figure 3.10 is a simplification and ignores some other important items that enter the calculation, such as depreciation/sales (a determinant of ROS) and other assets/sales (a determinant of capital turnover).

23. For examples of how to construct detailed profitability trees, see Copeland, Koller, and Murrin, *Valuation.* Also see Jablonsky and Barsky, *Manager's Guide to Financial Statement Analysis.*

24. This is the nature of the competitive process. For more detail, see C. W. L. Hill and D. Deeds, "The Importance of Industry Structure for the Determination of Company Profitability: A Neo-Austrian Perspective," *Journal of Management Studies,* 33 (1996): 429–451.

25. As with resources and capabilities, so the concept of barriers to imitation is also grounded in the resource-based view of the company. For details, see R. Reed and R. J. DeFillippi, "Causal Ambiguity, Barriers to Imitation, and Sustainable Competitive Advantage," *Academy of Management Review* 15 (1990): 88–102.

26. E. Mansfield, "How Economists See R&D," *Harvard Business Review* (November–December 1981): 98–106.

27. S. L. Berman, J. Down, and C. W. L. Hill, "Tacit Knowledge as a Source of Competitive Advantage in the National Basketball Association," *Academy of Management Journal* (2002): 13–33.

28. P. Ghemawat, *Commitment: The Dynamic of Strategy* (New York: Free Press, 1991).

29. W. M. Cohen and D. A. Levinthal, "Absorptive Capacity: A New Perspective on Learning and Innovation," *Administrative Science Quarterly* 35 (1990): 128–152.

30. M. T. Hannah and J. Freeman, "Structural Inertia and Organizational Change," *American Sociological Review* 49 (1984): 149–164.

31. See "IBM Corporation," Harvard Business School Case #180-034.

32. Ghemawat, *Commitment.*

33. D. Miller, *The Icarus Paradox* (New York: HarperBusiness, 1990).

34. P. M. Senge, *The Fifth Discipline: The Art and Practice of the Learning Organization* (New York: Doubleday, 1990).

35. D. Kearns, "Leadership Through Quality," *Academy of Management Executive* 4 (1990): 86–89.

36. The classic statement of this position was made by A. A. Alchain, "Uncertainty, Evolution, and Economic Theory," *Journal of Political Economy* 84 (1950): 488–500.

Chapter 4

1. G. J. Miller, *Managerial Dilemmas: The Political Economy of Hierarchy* (Cambridge: Cambridge University Press, 1992).

2. H. Luft, J. Bunker, and A. Enthoven, "Should Operations Be Regionalized?" *New England Journal of Medicine* 301 (1979): 1364–1369.

3. G. Hall and S. Howell, "The Experience Curve from an Economist's Perspective," *Strategic Management Journal* 6 (1985): 197–212. M. Lieberman. "The Learning Curve and Pricing in the Chemical Processing Industries," *RAND Journal of Economics* 15 (1984): 213–228.

4. Boston Consulting Group, *Perspectives on Experience* (Boston: Boston Consulting Group, 1972); Hall and Howell, "The Experience Curve," pp. 197–212; W. B. Hirschmann, "Profit from the Learning Curve," *Harvard Business Review* (January–February 1964): 125–139.

5. A. A. Alchian, "Reliability of Progress Curves in Airframe Production," *Econometrica* 31 (1963): 679–693.

6. M. Borrus, L. A. Tyson, and J. Zysman, "Creating Advantage: How Government Policies Create Trade in the Semi-Conductor Industry," in P. R. Krugman (ed.), *Strategic Trade Policy and the New International Economics* (Cambridge, Mass.: MIT Press, 1986). S. Ghoshal and C. A. Bartlett, "Matsushita Electrical Industrial (MEI) in 1987," Harvard Business School Case #388-144 (1988).

7. Abernathy and Wayne, "Limits of the Learning Curve," pp. 109–119.

8. D. F. Barnett and R. W. Crandall, *Up from the Ashes: The Rise of the Steel Minimill in the United States* (Washington, D.C.: Brookings Institute, 1986).

9. See P. Nemetz and L. Fry, "Flexible Manufacturing Organizations: Implications for Strategy Formulation," *Academy of Management Review* 13 (1988): 627–638; N. Greenwood, *Implementing Flexible Manufacturing Systems* (New York: Halstead Press, 1986); and J. P. Womack, D. T. Jones, and D. Roos, *The Machine That Changed the World* (New York: Rawson Associates, 1990). R. Parthasarthy and S. P. Seith, "The Impact of Flexible Automation on Business Strategy and Organizational Structure," *Academy of Management Review* 17 (1992): 86–111.

10. B. J. Pine, *Mass Customization: The New Frontier in Business Competition* (Boston: Harvard Business School Press, 1993). S. Kotha, "Mass Customization: Implementing the Emerging Paradigm for Competitive Advantage," *Strategic Management Journal* 16 (1995): 21–42. J. H. Gilmore and B. J. Pine II, "The Four Faces of Mass Customization," *Harvard Business Review* (January–February 1997): 91–101.

11. "The Celling Out of America," *Economist,* December 17, 1994, pp. 63–64.

12. F. F. Reichheld and W. E. Sasser, "Zero Defections: Quality Comes to Service," *Harvard Business Review* (September–October 1990): 105–111.

13. The example comes from ibid.

14. Ibid.

15. R. Narasimhan and J. R. Carter, "Organization, Communication and Coordination of International Sourcing," *International Marketing Review* 7 (1990): 6–20.

16. H. F. Busch, "Integrated Materials Management," IJDP & MM 18 (1990): 28–39.

17. G. Stalk and T. M. Hout, *Competing Against Time* (New York: Free Press, 1990).

18. See Peter Bamberger and Ilan Meshoulam, *Human Resource Strategy: Formulation, Implementation, and Impact* (Thousand Oaks, Calif.: Sage, 2000). P. M. Wright and S. Snell, "Towards a Unifying Framework for Exploring Fit and Flexibility in Human Resource Management," *Academy of Management Review* 23 (October 1998): 756–772.

19. A. Sorge and M. Warner, "Manpower Training, Manufacturing Organization, and Work Place Relations in Great Britain and West Germany," *British Journal of Industrial Relations* 18 (1980): 318–333. R. Jaikumar, "Postindustrial Manufacturing," *Harvard Business Review* (November–December 1986): 72–83.

20. J. Hoerr, "The Payoff from Teamwork," *Business Week,* July 10, 1989, pp. 56–62.

21. "The Trouble with Teams," *Economist,* January 14, 1995, p. 61.

22. T. C. Powell and A. Dent-Micallef, "Information Technology as Competitive Advantage: The Role of Human, Business, and Technology Resource," *Strategic Management Journal* 18 (1997): 375–405. B. Gates, *Business @ the Speed of Thought* (New York: Warner Books, 1999).

23. "Cisco@speed," *Economist,* June 26, 1999, p. 12. S. Tully, "How Cisco Mastered the Net," *Fortune,* August 17, 1997, pp. 207–210. C. Kano, "The Real King of the Internet," *Fortune,* September 7, 1998, pp. 82–93.

24. Gates, *Business @ the Speed of Thought.*

25. K. J. Stiroh, "Investing in Information Technology: Productivity Payoffs in U.S. Industries," *Current Issues in Economic and Finance* 7 (June 2001): 1–7.

26. See the articles published in the special issue of the *Academy of Management Review on Total Quality Management* 19:3 (1994). The following article provides a good overview of many of the issues involved from an academic perspective: J. W. Dean and D. E. Bowen, "Management Theory and Total Quality," *Academy of Management Review* 19 (1994): 392–418. Also see T. C. Powell, "Total Quality Management as Competitive Advantage," *Strategic Management Journal* 16 (1995): 15–37.

27. For general background information, see "How to Build Quality," *Economist,* September 23, 1989, pp. 91–92; A. Gabor, *The Man Who Discovered Quality* (New York: Penguin, 1990); and P. B. Crosby, *Quality Is Free* (New York: Mentor, 1980).

28. W. E. Deming, "Improvement of Quality and Productivity Through Action by Management," *National Productivity Review* 1 (Winter 1981–1982): 12–22.

29. J. Bowles, "Is American Management Really Committed to Quality?" *Management Review* (April 1992): 42–46.

30. O. Port and G. Smith, "Quality," *Business Week,* November 30, 1992, pp. 66–75. See also "The Straining of Quality," *Economist,* January 14, 1995, pp. 55–56.

31. Bowles, "Is American Management Really Committed to Quality?" pp. 42–46. "The Straining of Quality," pp. 55–56.

32. Gabor, *The Man Who Discovered Quality.*

33. Deming, "Improvement of Quality and Productivity," pp. 12–22.

34. W. E. Deming, *Out of the Crisis* (Cambridge, Mass.: MIT Center for Advanced Engineering Study, 1986).

35. A. Ries and J. Trout, *Positioning: The Battle for Your Mind* (New York: Warner Books, 1982).

36. R. G. Cooper, *Product Leadership* (Reading, Mass.: Perseus Books, 1999).

37. E. Mansfield, "How Economists See R&D," *Harvard Business Review* (November–December 1981): 98–106.

38. Ibid.

39. Booz, Allen, and Hamilton, *New Products Management for the 1980's* (privately published research report, 1982).

40. A. L. Page, "PDMA's New Product Development Practices Survey: Performance and Best Practices" (paper presented at the PDMA Fifteenth Annual International Conference, Boston, October 16, 1991).

41. S. L. Brown and K. M. Eisenhardt, "Product Development: Past Research, Present Findings, and Future Directions," *Academy of Management Review* 20 (1995): 343–378. M. B. Lieberman and D. B. Montgomery, "First Mover Advantages," *Strategic Management Journal* 9 (Special Issue, Summer 1988): 41–58. D. J. Teece, "Profiting from Technological Innovation: Implications for Integration, Collaboration, Licensing and Public Policy," *Research Policy* 15 (1987): 285–305. G. J. Tellis and P. N. Golder, "First to Market, First to Fail?" *Sloan Management Review* (Winter 1996): 65–75.

42. G. Stalk and T. M. Hout, *Competing Against Time* (New York: Free Press, 1990).

43. K. B. Clark and S. C. Wheelwright, *Managing New Product and Process Development* (New York: Free Press, 1993). M. A. Schilling and C. W. L. Hill, "Managing the New Product Development Process," *Academy of Management Executive* 12:3 (August 1998): 67–81.

44. K. B. Clark and S. C. Wheelwright, *Managing New Product and Process Development* (New York: Free Press, 1993).

45. P. Sellers, "Getting Customers to Love You," *Fortune,* March 13, 1989, pp. 38–42.

46. O. Port, "Moving Past the Assembly Line," *Business Week,* (Special Issue, Reinventing America, 1992): 177–180.

47. G. P. Pisano and S. C. Wheelwright, "The New Logic of High Tech R&D," *Harvard Business Review* (September–October 1995): 93–105.

48. K. B. Clark and T. Fujimoto, "The Power of Product Integrity," *Harvard Business Review* (November–December 1990): 107–118. Clark and Wheelwright, *Managing New Product and Process Development.* Brown and Eisenhardt, "Product Development." Stalk and Hout, *Competing Against Time.*

49. C. Christensen, "Quantum Corporation—Business and Product Teams," Harvard Business School Case, #9-692-023.

50. S. Caminiti, "A Mail Order Romance: Lands' End Courts Unseen Customers," *Fortune,* March 13, 1989, pp. 43–44.

51. P. Sellers, "Getting Customers to Love You," *Fortune,* March 13, 1989, pp. 38–42.

52. Caminiti, "A Mail Order Romance: Lands' End Courts Unseen Customers," pp. 43–44.

53. Stalk and Hout, *Competing Against Time.*

Chapter 5

1. Derek F. Abell, *Defining the Business: The Starting Point of Strategic Planning* (Englewood Cliffs, N.J.: Prentice-Hall, 1980), p. 169.

2. R. Kotler, *Marketing Management,* 5th ed. (Englewood Cliffs, N.J.: Prentice-Hall, 1984). M. R. Darby and E. Karni, "Free Competition and the Optimal Amount of Fraud," *Journal of Law and Economics* 16 (1973): 67–86.

3. Abell, *Defining the Business,* p. 8.

4. Michael E. Porter, *Competitive Advantage: Creating and Sustaining Superior Performance* (New York: Free Press, 1985).

5. R. D. Buzzell and F. D. Wiersema, "Successful Share Building Strategies," *Harvard Business Review* (January–February 1981): 135–144. L. W. Phillips, D. R. Chang, and R. D. Buzzell, "Product Quality, Cost Position, and Business Performance: A Test of Some Key Hypotheses," *Journal of Marketing* 47 (1983): 26–43.

6. Michael E. Porter, *Competitive Strategy: Techniques for Analyzing Industries and Competitors* (New York: Free Press, 1980), p. 45.

7. Abell, *Defining the Business*, p. 15.

8. Some of the theoretical underpinnings for this approach can be found in G. R. Jones and J. Butler, "Costs, Revenues, and Business Level Strategy," *Academy of Management Review* 13 (1988): 202–213; and C. W. L. Hill, "Differentiation versus Low Cost or Differentiation and Low Cost: A Contingency Framework," *Academy of Management Review* 13 (1988): 401–412.

9. This section, and material on the business model, draw heavily on C. W. L. Hill and G. R. Jones, "The Dynamics of Business-Level Strategy" (unpublished paper, 2002).

10. Porter, *Competitive Advantage*.

11. Many authors have discussed cost leadership and differentiation as basic competitive approaches—for example, F. Scherer, *Industrial Market Structure and Economic Performance*, 10th ed. (Boston: Houghton Mifflin, 2000). The basic cost-leadership/differentiation dimension has received substantial empirical support; see, for example, D. C. Hambrick, "High Profit Strategies in Mature Capital Goods Industries: A Contingency Approach," *Academy of Management Journal* 26 (1983): 687–707.

12. Porter, *Competitive Advantage*, p. 37.

13. Ibid., pp. 13–14.

14. **www.walmart.com (2002).**

15. D. Miller, "Configurations of Strategy and Structure: Towards a Synthesis," *Strategic Management Journal* 7 (1986): 217–231.

16. Porter, *Competitive Advantage*, pp. 44–46.

17. Charles W. Hofer and D. Schendel, *Strategy Formulation: Analytical Concepts* (St. Paul, Minn.: West, 1978).

18. W. K. Hall, "Survival Strategies in a Hostile Environment," *Harvard Business Review* 58 (1980): 75–85. Hambrick, "High Profit Strategies," pp. 687–707.

19. J. Guyon, "Can the Savoy Cut Costs and Be the Savoy," *Wall Street Journal*, October 25, 1994, p. B1.

20. Porter, *Competitive Strategy*, p. 46.

21. Peter F. Drucker, *The Practice of Management* (New York: Harper, 1954).

22. Porter, *Competitive Advantage*, pp. 44–46.

23. G. Hamel and C. K. Prahalad, *Competing for the Future* (Boston: Harvard Business School Press, 1994), p. 129.

24. The development of strategic group theory has been a strong theme in the strategy literature. Important contributions include R. E. Caves and Michael Porter, "From Entry Barriers to Mobility Barriers," *Quarterly Journal of Economics* (May 1977): 241–262; K. R. Harrigan, "An Application of Clustering for Strategic Group Analysis," *Strategic Management Journal* 6 (1985): 55–73; K. J. Hatten and D. E. Schendel, "Heterogeneity Within an Industry: Company Conduct in the U.S. Brewing Industry, 1952–1971," *Journal of Industrial Economics* 26. pp. 97–113; and Michael E. Porter, "The Structure Within Industries and Companies' Performance," *Review of Economics and Statistics* 61 (1979): 214–227.

25. Hofer and Schendel, *Strategy Formulation*, pp. 102–104.

26. Our discussion of the investment, or posturing, component of business-level strategy draws heavily from ibid., especially Chap. 6.

27. Ibid., pp. 75–77.

28. K. R. Harrigan, "Strategy Formulation in Declining Industries," *Academy of Management Review* 5 (1980): 599–604.

29. Hofer and Schendel, *Strategy Formulation*, pp. 169–172.

30. L. R. Feldman and A. L. Page, "Harvesting: The Misunderstood Market Exit Strategy," *Journal of Business Strategy* 4 (1985): 79–85.

31. C. W. Hofer, "Turnaround Strategies," *Journal of Business Strategy* 1 (1980): 19–31.

32. For a basic introduction to game theory, see A. K. Dixit and B. J. Nalebuff, *Thinking Strategically* (New York: Norton, 1991). Also see A. M. Brandenburger and B. J. Nalebuff, "The Right Game: Using Game Theory to Shape Strategy," *Harvard Business Review* (July–August 1995): 59–71; and D. M. Kreps, *Game Theory and Economic Modeling* (Oxford: Oxford University Press, 1990).

Chapter 6

1. M. Porter, *Competitive Strategy: Techniques for Analyzing Industries and Competitors* (New York: Free Press, 1980), pp. 191–200.

2. S. A. Shane, "Hybrid Organizational Arrangements and Their Implications for Firm Growth and Survival: A Study of New Franchisors," *Academy of Management Journal* 1 (1996): 216–234.

3. Microsoft is often accused of not being an innovator, but the fact is that Gates and Allen wrote the first commercial software program for the first commercially available PC. Microsoft was the first mover in the industry. See P. Freiberger and M. Swaine, *Fire in the Valley* (New York: McGraw-Hill, 2000).

4. J. M. Utterback, *Mastering the Dynamics of Innovation* (Boston: Harvard Business School Press, 1994).

5. G. A. Moore, *Crossing the Chasm* (New York: HarperCollins, 1991), and *Living on the Fault Line* (New York: Harper Business, 2000).

6. Freiberger and Swaine, *Fire in the Valley*.

7. Moore, *Crossing the Chasm*.

8. Utterback, *Mastering the Dynamics of Innovation*.

9. Freiberger and Swaine, *Fire in the Valley*.

10. Everett Rogers, *Diffusion of Innovations* (New York: Free Press, 1995).

11. J. Brander and J. Eaton, "Product Line Rivalry," *American Economic Review* 74 (1985): 323–334.

12. P. Milgrom and J. Roberts, "Predation, Reputation, and Entry Deterrence," *Journal of Economic Theory* 27 (1982): 280–312. See also A. K. Dixit and B. J. Nalbuff, *Thinking Strategically* (New York: Norton, 1991).

13. Porter, *Competitive Strategy*, pp. 76–86.

14. O. Heil and T. S. Robertson, "Towards a Theory of Competitive Market Signaling: A Research Agenda." *Strategic Management Journal* 12 (1991): 403–418.

15. Robert Axelrod, *The Evolution of Cooperation* (New York: Basic Books, 1984).

16. F. Scherer, *Industrial Market Structure and Economic Performance*, 10th ed.(Boston: Houghton Mifflin, 2000), chap. 8.

17. The model differs from Ansoff's model for this reason.

18. H. Igor Ansoff, *Corporate Strategy* (London: Penguin Books, 1984), pp. 97–100.

19. Robert D. Buzzell, Bradley T. Gale, and Ralph G. M. Sultan, "Market Share—A Key to Profitability," *Harvard Business Review* (January–February 1975): 97–103. Robert Jacobson and David A. Aaker, "Is Market Share All That It's Cracked Up to Be?" *Journal of Marketing* 49 (1985): 11–22.

20. Ansoff, *Corporate Strategy,* pp. 98–99.

21. S. L. Brown and K. M. Eisenhardt, "Product Development: Past Research, Present Findings, and Future Directions," *Academy of Management Review* 20 (1995): 343–378.

22. The next section draws heavily on Marvin B. Lieberman, "Strategies for Capacity Expansion," *Sloan Management Review* 8 (1987): 19–27; and Porter, *Competitive Strategy,* pp. 324–338.

23. Jack Willoughby, "The Last Iceman," *Forbes,* July 13, 1987, pp. 183–202.

Chapter 7

1. Bureau of Economic Analysis, *Survey of United States Current Business, 2001.*

2. P. Woodall, "Survey: The New Economy: Untangling E-conomics," *Economist,* September 23, 2000, pp. S5–S7.

3. J. M. Utterback, *Mastering the Dynamics of Innovation* (Boston: Harvard Business School Press, 1994). H. R. Varian, *Information Rules: A Strategic Guide to the Network Economy* (Boston: Harvard Business School Press, 1999).

4. The layout is not universal, although it is widespread. The French, for example, use a different layout.

5. M. Craig, "Dueling DVD Recorder Formats," *Seattle Times,* January 9, 2002, p. C3.

6. For details, see Charles W. L. Hill, "Establishing a Standard: Competitive Strategy and Technology Standards in Winner Take All Industries," *Academy of Management Executive* 11 (1997): 7–25; Shapiro and Varian, *Information Rules;* B. Arthur, "Increasing Returns and the New World of Business," *Harvard Business Review* (July–August 1996): 100–109.

7. See Shapiro and Varian, *Information Rules.* Hill, "Establishing a Standard." M. A. Shilling, "Technological Lockout: An Integrative Model of the Economic and Strategic Factors Driving Technology Success and Failure," *Academy of Management Review* 23:2 (1998): 267–285.

8. Microsoft does not disclose the per unit licensing fee that it gets from original equipment manufacturers.

9. P. M. Romer, "The Origins of Endogenous Growth," *Journal of Economic Perspectives* 8:1 (1994): 3–22.

10. Data from **www.btechnews.com.**

11. Varian, *Information Rules.*

12. Business Software Association, *Sixth Annual Global Software Piracy Study* (May 2001).

13. International Federation of the Phonographic Industry, at **http://www.ifpi.org/.**

14. N. Ridgeway, "Let Them Burn," *Forbes,* March 4, 2002, p. 88.

15. Much of this section is based on Charles W. L. Hill, Michael Heeley, and Jane Sakson, "Strategies for Profiting from Innovation," in *Advances in Global High Technology Management* (Greenwich, Conn.: JAI Press, 1993), 3: 79–95.

16. M. Lieberman and D. Montgomery, "First Mover Advantages," *Strategic Management Journal* 9 (Special Issue, Summer 1988): 41–58.

17. J. Borzo, "Aging Gracefully," *Wall Street Journal,* October 15, 2001, p. R22.

18. The importance of complementary assets was first noted by D. J. Teece. See D. J. Teece, "Profiting from Technological Innovation," in D. J. Teece (ed.), *The Competitive Challenge* (New York: Harper & Row, 1986), pp. 26–54.

19. M. J. Chen and D. C. Hambrick, "Speed, Stealth, and Selective Attack: How Small Firms Differ from Large Firms in Competitive Behavior," *Academy of Management Journal* 38 (1995): 453–482.

20. E. Mansfield, M. Schwartz, and S. Wagner, "Imitation Costs and Patents: An Empirical Study," *Economic Journal* 91 (1981): 907–918.

21. E. Mansfield, "How Rapidly Does New Industrial Technology Leak Out?" *Journal of Industrial Economics* 34 (1985): 217–223.

22. This argument has been made in the game theory literature. See R. Caves, H. Cookell, and P. J. Killing, "The Imperfect Market for Technology Licenses," *Oxford Bulletin of Economics and Statistics* 45 (1983): 249–267; N. T. Gallini, "Deterrence by Market Sharing: A Strategic Incentive for Licensing," *American Economic Review* 74 (1984): 931–941; and C. Shapiro, "Patent Licensing and R&D Rivalry," *American Economic Review* 75 (1985): 25–30.

23. M. Christensen, *The Innovator's Dilemma* (Boston: Harvard Business School Press, 1997). R. N. Foster, *Innovation: The Attackers Advantage* (New York: Summit Books, 1986).

24. Foster, *Innovation.*

25. Ray Kurzweil, *The Age of the Spiritual Machines* (New York: Penguin Books, 1999).

26. See Christensen, *The Innovator's Dilemma,* and C. M. Christensen and M. Overdorf, "Meeting the Challenge of Disruptive Change," *Harvard Business Review* (March–April 2000): 66–77.

Chapter 8

1. M. E. Porter, *The Competitive Advantage of Nations* (New York: Free Press, 1990).

2. C. S. Tranger, "Enter the Mini-Multinational," *Northeast International Business* (March 1989): 13–14.

3. R. B. Reich, *The Work of Nations* (New York: Knopf, 1991).

4. "Matsushita Electrical Industrial in 1987," in C. A. Bartlett and S. Ghoshal (eds.), *Transnational Management* (Homewood, Ill.: Irwin, 1992).

5. J. P. Woomack, D. T. Jones, and D. Roos, *The Machine That Changed the World* (New York: Rawson Associates, 1990).

6. See J. Birkinshaw and N. Hood, "Multinational Subsidiary Evolution: Capability and Charter Change in Foreign Owned Subsidiary Companies," *Academy of Management Review* 23 (October 1998): 773–795. A. K. Gupta and Govindarajan, "Knowledge Flows Within Multinational Corporations," *Strategic Management Journal* 21 (2000): 473–496.

7. C. K. Prahalad and Yves L. Doz, *The Multinational Mission: Balancing Local Demands and Global Vision* (New York: Free Press, 1987). Also see J. Birkinshaw, A. Morrison, and J. Hulland, "Structural and Competitive Determinants of a Global Integration Strategy," *Strategic Management Journal* 16 (1995): 637–655.

8. Prahalad and Doz, *The Multinational Mission.*

9. "The Tire Industry's Costly Obsession with Size," *Economist,* June 8, 1993, pp. 65–66.

10. T. Levitt, "The Globalization of Markets," *Harvard Business Review* (May–June 1983): 92–102.

11. C. A. Bartlett and S. Ghoshal, *Managing Across Borders* (Boston: Harvard Business School Press, 1989).

12. C. J. Chipello, "Local Presence Is Key to European Deals," *Wall Street Journal,* June 30, 1998, p. A15.

13. Bartlett and Ghoshal, *Managing Across Borders.*
14. Ibid.
15. T. Hout, M. E. Porter, and E. Rudden, "How Global Companies Win Out," *Harvard Business Review* (September–October 1982): 98–108.
16. See Charles W. L. Hill, *International Business: Competing in the Global Marketplace* (New York: McGraw-Hill, 2000).
17. This can be reconceptualized as the resource base of the entrant, relative to indigenous competitors. For work that focuses on this issue, see W. C. Bogenr, H. Thomas, and J. McGee, "A Longitudinal Study of the Competitive Positions and Entry Paths of European Firms in the U.S. Pharmaceutical Market," *Strategic Management Journal* 17 (1996): 85–107. D. Collis, "A Resource Based Analysis of Global Competition," *Strategic Management Journal* 12 (1991): 49–68. S. Tallman, "Strategic Management Models and Resource Based Strategies Among MNE's in a Host Market," *Strategic Management Journal* 12 (1991): 69–82.
18. For a discussion of first-mover advantages, see M. Liberman and D. Montgomery, "First Mover Advantages," *Strategic Management Journal* 9 (Special Issue, Summer 1988): 41–58.
19. J. M. Shaver, W. Mitchell, and B. Yeung, "The Effect of Own Company and Other Company Experience on Foreign Direct Investment Survival in the U.S., 1987–92," *Strategic Management Journal* 18 (1997): 811–824.
20. S. Zaheer and E. Mosakowski, "The Dynamics of the Liability of Foreignness: A Global Study of Survival in the Financial Services Industry," *Strategic Management Journal* 18 (1997): 439–464.
21. Shaver, Mitchell, and Yeung, "The Effect of Own Company and Other Company Experience."
22. P. Ghemawat, *Commitment: The Dynamics of Strategy* (New York: Free Press, 1991).
23. This section draws on several studies, including: C. W. L. Hill, P. Hwang, and W. C. Kim, "An Eclectic Theory of the Choice of International Entry Mode," *Strategic Management Journal* 11 (1990): 117–128; C. W. L. Hill and W. C. Kim, "Searching for a Dynamic Theory of the Multinational Company: A Transaction Cost Model," *Strategic Management Journal* 9 (Special Issue on Strategy Content, 1988): 93–104. E. Anderson and H. Gatignon, "Modes of Foreign Entry: A Transaction Cost Analysis and Propositions," *Journal of International Business Studies* 17 (1986): 1–26; F. R. Root, *Entry Strategies for International Markets* (Lexington, Mass.: D. C. Heath, 1980). A. Madhok, "Cost, Value and Foreign Market Entry: The Transaction and the Company," *Strategic Management Journal* 18 (1997): 39–61.
24. F. J. Contractor, "The Role of Licensing in International Strategy," *Columbia Journal of World Business* (Winter 1982): 73–83.
25. O. E. Williamson, *The Economic Institutions of Capitalism* (New York: Free Press, 1985).
26. Andrew E. Serwer, "McDonald's Conquers the World," *Fortune,* October 17, 1994, pp. 103–116.
27. B. Kogut, "Joint Ventures: Theoretical and Empirical Perspectives," *Strategic Management Journal* 9 (1988): 319–332.
28. D. G. Bradley, "Managing Against Expropriation," *Harvard Business Review* (July–August 1977): 78–90.
29. C. W. L. Hill, "Strategies for Exploiting Technological Innovations," *Organization Science* 3 (1992): 428–441.
30. See K. Ohmae, "The Global Logic of Strategic Alliances," *Harvard Business Review* (March–April 1989): 143–154; G. Hamel, Y. L. Doz, and C. K. Prahalad, "Collaborate with Your Competitors and Win!" *Harvard Business Review* (January–February 1989): 133–139; and W. Burgers, C. W. L. Hill, and W. C. Kim, "Alliances in the Global Auto Industry," *Strategic Management Journal* 14 (1993): 419–432. P. Kale, H. Singh, and H. Perlmutter, "Learning and Protection of Proprietary Assets in Strategic Alliances: Building Relational Capital," *Strategic Management Journal* 21 (2000): 217–237.
31. "Asia Beckons," *Economist,* May 30, 1992, pp. 63–64.
32. Kale, Singh, and Perlmutter, "Learning and Protection of Proprietary Assets."
33. R. B. Reich and E. D. Mankin, "Joint Ventures with Japan Give Away Our Future," *Harvard Business Review* (March–April 1986): 78–90.
34. J. Bleeke and D. Ernst, "The Way to Win in Cross-Border Alliances," *Harvard Business Review* (November–December 1991): 127–135.
35. W. Roehl and J. F. Truitt, "Stormy Open Marriages Are Better," *Columbia Journal of World Business* (Summer 1987): 87–95.
36. K. McQuade and B. Gomes-Casseres, "Xerox and Fuji–Xerox," Harvard Business School Case #9-391-156.
37. T. Khanna, R. Gulati, and N. Nohria, "The Dynamics of Learning Alliances: Competition, Cooperation, and Relative Scope," *Strategic Management Journal* 19 (1998): 193–210. Kale, Singh, and Perlmutter, "Learning and Protection of Proprietary Assets."
38. Hamel, Doz, and Prahalad, "Collaborate with Your Competitors and Win!"
39. B. Wysocki, "Cross Border Alliances Become Favorite Way to Crack New Markets," *Wall Street Journal,* March 4, 1990, p. A1.

Chapter 9

1. Y. J. Dreazen, G. Ip, and N. Kulish, "Why the Sudden Rise in the Urge to Merge and Create Oligopolies?" *Wall Street Journal,* February 25, 2002, p. A1.
2. United Nations, *World Investment Report 2001* (New York: United Nations, November 2001).
3. Dreazen, Ip, and Kulish. "Why the Sudden Rise?"
4. For evidence on acquisitions and performance, see R. E. Caves, "Mergers, Takeovers, and Economic Efficiency," *International Journal of Industrial Organization* 7 (1989): 151–174; M. C. Jensen and R. S. Ruback, "The Market for Corporate Control: The Scientific Evidence," *Journal of Financial Economics* 11 (1983): 5–50; R. Roll, "Empirical Evidence on Takeover Activity and Shareholder Wealth," in J. C. Coffee, L. Lowenstein, and S. Rose (eds.), *Knights, Raiders and Targets* (Oxford: Oxford University Press, 1989); and A. Schleifer and R. W. Vishny, "Takeovers in the 60s and 80s: Evidence and Implications," *Strategic Management Journal* 12 (Special Issue, Winter 1991): 51–60. T. H. Brush, "Predicted Changes in Operational Synergy and Post Acquisition Performance of Acquired Businesses," *Strategic Management Journal* 17 (1996): 1–24.
5. "Few Takeovers Pay Off for Big Buyers," *Investors Business Daily,* May 25, 2001, p. 1.
6. K. R. Harrian, "Formulating Vertical Integration Strategies," *Academy of Management Review* 9 (1984): 638–652.
7. This is the essence of Chandler's argument. See Alfred D. Chandler, *Strategy and Structure* (Cambridge, Mass.: MIT Press, 1962). The same argument is also made by Jeffrey Pfeffer and Gerald R. Salancik, *The External Control of Organizations* (New York: Harper & Row, 1978). See also K. R. Harrigan, *Strategic Flexibility* (Lexington, Mass.: Lexington Books, 1985); K. R. Harrigan, "Vertical Integration and Corporate Strategy,"

Academy of Management Journal 28 (1985): 397–425; and F. M. Scherer, *Industrial Market Structure and Economic Performance* (Chicago: Rand McNally, 1981).

8. T. Chipty, "Vertical Integration, Market Foreclosure and Consumer Welfare in the Cable Television Industry," *American Economic Review* 91 (2001): 428–453. D. L. Rubinfeld and H. Singer, "Vertical Foreclosure in Broadband Access?" *Journal of Industrial Economics* 49 (2001): 299–318. This section is based on the transaction cost approach popularized by Oliver E. Williamson, *The Economic Institutions of Capitalism* (New York: Free Press, 1985).

9. Oliver E. Williamson, *The Economic Institutions of Capitalism.* For recent empirical work that uses this framework, see L. Poppo and T. Zenger, "Testing Alternative Theories of the Firm: Transaction Cost, Knowledge Based, and Measurement Explanations for Make or Buy Decisions in Information Services," *Strategic Management Journal* 19 (1998): 853–878.

10. Williamson, *Economic Institutions of Capitalism.*

11. A. D. Chandler, *The Visible Hand* (Cambridge, Mass.: Harvard University Press, 1977).

12. Julia Pitta, "Score One for Vertical Integration," *Forbes,* January 18, 1993, pp. 88–89.

13. Joseph White and Neal Templin, "Harsh Regimen: A Swollen GM Finds It Hard to Stick with Its Crash Diet," *Wall Street Journal,* September 9, 1992, p. A1.

14. Harrigan, *Strategic Flexibility,* pp. 67–87. See also Allan Afuah, "Dynamic Boundaries of the Firm: Are Firms Better Off Being Vertically Integrated in the Face of a Technological Change?" *Academy of Management Journal* 44 (2001): 1121–1228.

15. For a detailed theoretical rationale for this argument, see G. R. Jones and C. W. L. Hill, "A Transaction Cost Analysis of Strategy-Structure Choice," *Strategic Management Journal* 9 (1988): 159–172.

16. Kevin Kelly, Zachary Schiller, and James Treece, "Cut Costs or Else," *Business Week,* March 22, 1993, pp. 28–29.

17. X. Martin, W. Mitchell, and A. Swaminathan, "Recreating and Extending Japanese Automobile Buyer-Supplier Links in North America," *Strategic Management Journal* 16 (1995): 589–619. C. W. L. Hill, "National Institutional Structures, Transaction Cost Economizing, and Competitive Advantage," *Organization Science* 6 (1995): 119–131.

18. Standard & Poor's Industry Survey, Autos–Auto Parts, June 24, 1993.

19. See James Womack, Daniel Jones, and Daniel Roos, *The Machine That Changed the World* (New York: Rawson Associates, 1990). James Richardson, "Parallel Sourcing and Supplier Performance in the Japanese Automobile Industry," *Strategic Management Journal* 14 (1993): 339–350.

20. R. Mudambi and S. Helper, "The Close But Adversarial Model of Supplier Relations in the U.S. Auto Industry," *Strategic Management Journal* 19 (1998): 775–792.

21. Williamson, *Economic Institutions.* See also J. H. Dyer, "Effective Inter-Firm Collaboration: How Firms Minimize Transaction Costs and Maximize Transaction Value," *Strategic Management Journal* 18 (1997): 535–556.

22. Richardson, "Parallel Sourcing."

23. W. H. Davidow and M. S. Malone, *The Virtual Corporation* (New York: Harper & Row, 1992).

24. A. M. Porter, "Outsourcing Gains Popularity," *Purchasing,* March 11, 1999, pp. 22–24.

25. D. Garr, "Inside Outsourcing," *Fortune* 142:1 (2001): 85–92.

26. J. Krane, "American Express Hires IBM for $4 billion," *Columbian,* February 26, 2002, p. E2.

27. J. Vijayan, "The Outsourcing Boom," *Computerworld,* March 18, 2002, pp. 42–43.

28. Davidow and Malone, *The Virtual Corporation.*

29. Ibid. H. W. Chesbrough and D. J. Teece, "When Is Virtual Virtuous? Organizing for Innovation," *Harvard Business Review* (January–February 1996): 65–74. J. B. Quinn, "Strategic Outsourcing: Leveraging Knowledge Capabilities," *Sloan Management Review* (Summer 1999): 9–21.

Chapter 10

1. T. J. Peters and R. H. Waterman, *In Search of Excellence* (New York: Harper & Row, 1982).

2. G. Hamel and C. K. Prahalad, *Competing for the Future* (Boston: Harvard Business School Press, 1994).

3. Ibid.

4. D. Leonard Barton and G. Pisano, "Monsanto's March into Biotechnology," Harvard Business School Case #690-009 (1990). See Monsanto's home page for details of its genetically engineered seed products (**http://www.monsanto.com**).

5. This resource-based view of diversification can be traced to Edith Penrose's seminal book, *The Theory of the Growth of the Firm* (Oxford: Oxford University Press, 1959).

6. D. J. Teece, "Economies of Scope and the Scope of the Enterprise," *Journal of Economic Behavior and Organization* 3 (1980): 223–247. For recent empirical work on this topic, see C. H. St. John and J. S. Harrison, "Manufacturing Based Relatedness, Synergy and Coordination," *Strategic Management Journal* 20 (1999): 129–145.

7. For a detailed discussion, see C. W. L. Hill and R. E. Hoskisson, "Strategy and Structure in the Multiproduct Firm," *Academy of Management Review* 12 (1987): 331–341.

8. See, for example, G. R. Jones and C. W. L. Hill, "A Transaction Cost Analysis of Strategy Structure Choice," *Strategic Management Journal* (1988): 159–172; and Williamson, *Markets and Hierarchies* (New York: Free Press), pp. 132–175.

9. R. Buderi, *Engines of Tomorrow* (New York: Simon & Schuster, 2000).

10. C. W. L. Hill, "The Role of Headquarters in the Multidivisional Firm," in R. Rumelt, D. J. Teece, and D. Schendel, *Fundamental Issues in Strategy Research* (Cambridge, Mass.: Harvard Business School Press, 1994), pp. 297–321.

11. See, for example, Jones and Hill, "A Transaction Cost Analysis." Williamson, *Markets and Hierarchies.* Hill, "The Role of Headquarters in the Multidivisional Firm."

12. The distinction goes back to R. P. Rumelt, *Strategy, Structure and Economic Performance* (Boston: Harvard Business School Press, 1974).

13. For example, see C. W. L. Hill, "Diversified Growth and Competition," *Applied Economics* 17 (1985): 827–847. Rumelt, *Strategy, Structure and Economic Performance.* Jones and Hill, "A Transaction Cost Analysis."

14. See H. K. Christensen and C. A. Montgomery, "Corporate Economic Performance: Diversification Strategy Versus Market Structure," *Strategic Management Journal* 2 (1981): 327–343. Jones and Hill, "A Transaction Cost Analysis." G. Dess, J-F. Hennart, C. W. L. Hill, and A. Gupta, "Research Issues in Strategic Management," *Journal of Management* 21 (1995): 357–392. Hill. "The Role of Headquarters in the Multidivisional Company."

15. For reviews of the evidence, see V. Ramanujam and P. Varadarajan, "Research on Corporate Diversification: A Synthesis," *Strategic Management Journal* 10 (1989): 523–551; Dess, Hennart, Hill, and Gupta, "Research Issues in Strategic Management"; and David C. Hyland and J. David Diltz, "Why Companies Diversify: An Empirical Examination," *Financial Management* 31 (Spring 2002): 51–81.

16. M. E. Porter, "From Competitive Advantage to Corporate Strategy," *Harvard Business Review* (May–June 1987): 43–59.

17. For reviews of the evidence, see Ramanujam and Varadarajan, "Research on Corporate Diversification"; Dess, Hennart, Hill, and Gupta, "Research Issues in Strategic Management"; Hyland and Diltz, "Why Companies Diversify."

18. C. R. Christensen et al., *Business Policy Text and Cases* (Homewood, Ill.: Irwin, 1987), p. 778.

19. See H. K. Christensen and C. A. Montgomery, "Corporate Economic Performance: Diversification Strategy Versus Market Structure," *Strategic Management Journal* 2 (1981): 327–343; Jones and Hill, "A Transaction Cost Analysis"; Dess, Hennart, Hill, and Gupta, "Research Issues in Strategic Management"; Hill, "The Role of Headquarters."

20. For evidence, see C. W. L. Hill, "Conglomerate Performance over the Economic Cycle," *Journal of Industrial Economics* 32 (1983): 197–212; and D. T. C. Mueller, "The Effects of Conglomerate Mergers," *Journal of Banking and Finance* 1 (1977): 315–347.

21. See Booz, Allen, and Hamilton, *New Products Management for the 1980's* (privately published, 1982); A. L. Page, "PDMA's New Product Development Practices Survey: Performance and Best Practices" (presented at the PDMA Fifteenth Annual International Conference, Boston, October 16, 1991); and E. Mansfield, "How Economists See R&D," *Harvard Business Review* (November–December 1981): 98–106.

22. See R. Biggadike, "The Risky Business of Diversification," *Harvard Business Review* (May–June 1979): 103–111. R. A. Burgelman, "A Process Model of Internal Corporate Venturing in the Diversified Major Firm," *Administrative Science Quarterly* 28 (1983): 223–244. Z. Block and I. C. Macmillan, *Corporate Venturing* (Boston: Harvard Business School Press, 1993).

23. Biggadike, "The Risky Business of Diversification." Block and Macmillan, *Corporate Venturing.*

24. Buderi, *Engines of Tomorrow.*

25. I. C. MacMillan and R. George, "Corporate Venturing: Challenges for Senior Managers," *Journal of Business Strategy* 5 (1985): 34–43.

26. See R. A. Burgelman, M. M. Maidique, and S. C. Wheelwright, *Strategic Management of Technology and Innovation* (Chicago: Irwin, 1996), pp. 493–507. Also see Buderi, *Engines of Tomorrow.*

27. Buderi, *Engines of Tomorrow.*

28. See Block and Macmillan, *Corporate Venturing.* Burgelman, Maidique, and Wheelwright, *Strategic Management of Technology and Innovation.*

29. G. Beardsley and E. Mansfield, "A Note on the Accuracy of Industrial Forecasts of the Profitability of New Products and Processes," *Journal of Business* 23 (1978): 127–130.

30. J. Warner, J. Templeman, and R. Horn, "The Case Against Mergers," *Business Week,* October 30, 1995, pp. 122–134.

31. "Few Takeovers Pay Off for Big Buyers," *Investors Business Daily,* May 25, 2001, p. 1.

32. For evidence on acquisitions and performance, see R. E. Caves, "Mergers, Takeovers, and Economic Efficiency," *International Journal of Industrial Organization* 7 (1989): 151–174; M. C. Jensen and R. S. Ruback, "The Market for Corporate Control: The Scientific Evidence," *Journal of Financial Economics* 11 (1983): 5–50; R. Roll, "Empirical Evidence on Takeover Activity and Shareholder Wealth," in J. C. Coffee, L. Lowenstein, and S. Rose (eds.), *Knights, Raiders and Targets* (Oxford: Oxford University Press, 1989); and A. Schleifer and R. W. Vishny, "Takeovers in the 60s and 80s: Evidence and Implications," *Strategic Management Journal* 12 (Special Issue, Winter 1991): 51–60. T. H. Brush, "Predicted Changes in Operational Synergy and Post Acquisition Performance of Acquired Businesses," *Strategic Management Journal* 17 (1996): 1–24. T. Loughran and A. M. Vijh, "Do Long Term Shareholders Benefit from Corporate Acquisitions?" *Journal of Finance* 5 (1997): 1765–1787.

33. D. J. Ravenscraft and F. M. Scherer, *Mergers, Selloffs, and Economic Efficiency* (Washington, D.C.: Brookings Institution, 1987).

34. See J. P. Walsh, "Top Management Turnover Following Mergers and Acquisitions," *Strategic Management Journal* 9 (1988): 173–183.

35. See A. A. Cannella and D. C. Hambrick, "Executive Departure and Acquisition Performance," *Strategic Management Journal* 14 (1993): 137–152.

36. R. Roll, "The Hubris Hypothesis of Corporate Takeovers," *Journal of Business* 59 (1986): 197–216.

37. "Coca-Cola: A Sobering Lesson from Its Journey into Wine," *Business Week,* June 3, 1985, pp. 96–98.

38. D. Foust, "They Shopped—Now They've Dropped," *Business Week,* February 25, 2002, pp. 36–37.

39. P. Haspeslagh and D. Jemison, *Managing Acquisitions* (New York: Free Press, 1991).

40. D. Sparks, "No Money Grows Here," *Business Week,* April 17, 2000, pp. 174–176.

41. For views on this issue, see L. L. Fray, D. H. Gaylin, and J. W. Down, "Successful Acquisition Planning," *Journal of Business Strategy* 5 (1984): 46–55; C. W. L. Hill, "Profile of a Conglomerate Takeover: BTR and Thomas Tilling," *Journal of General Management* 10 (1984): 34–50; D. R. Willensky, "Making It Happen: How to Execute an Acquisition," *Business Horizons* (March–April 1985): 38–45; Haspeslagh and Jemison, *Managing Acquisitions;* and P. L. Anslinger and T. E. Copeland, "Growth Through Acquisition: A Fresh Look," *Harvard Business Review* (January–February 1996): 126–135.

42. M. L. A. Hayward, "When Do Firms Learn from Their Acquisition Experience? Evidence from 1990–1995," *Strategic Management Journal* 23 (2002): 21–39. K. G. Ahuja, "Technological Acquisitions and the Innovation Performance of Acquiring Firms: A Longitudinal Study," *Strategic Management Journal* 23 (2001): 197–220. H. G. Barkema and F. Vermeulen, "International Expansion Through Startup or Acquisition," *Academy of Management Journal* 41 (1998): 7–26.

43. Hayward, "When Do Firms Learn from Their Acquisition Experience?"

44. For a review of the evidence and some contrary empirical evidence, see D. E. Hatfield, J. P. Liebskind, and T. C. Opler, "The Effects of Corporate Restructuring on Aggregate Industry Specialization," *Strategic Management Journal* 17 (1996): 55–72.

45. A. Lamont and C. Polk, "The Diversification Discount: Cash Flows Versus Returns," *Journal of Finance* 56 (October 2001): 1693–1721. R. Raju, H. Servaes, and L. Zingales, "The Cost of

Diversity: The Diversification Discount and Inefficient Investment," *Journal of Finance* 55 (February 2000): 35–80.

46. For example, see Schleifer and Vishny, "Takeovers in the 60s and 80s."

Chapter 11

1. Salomon Smith Barney Research, 2001.

2. See J. Argenti, *Corporate Collapse: Causes and Symptoms* (New York: McGraw-Hill, 1976); R. C. Hoffman, "Strategies for Corporate Turnarounds: What Do We Know About Them?" *Journal of General Management* 14 (1984): 46–66; D. Schendel, G. R. Patton, and J. Riggs, "Corporate Turnaround Strategies: A Study of Profit Decline and Recovery," *Journal of General Management* 2 (1976): 1–22; and S. Siafter, *Corporate Recovery: Successful Turnaround Strategies and Their Implementation* (Harmondsworth, England: Penguin Books, 1984), pp. 25–60.

3. D. B. Bibeault, *Corporate Turnaround* (New York: McGraw-Hill, 1982).

4. Hoffman, "Strategies for Corporate Turnarounds," pp. 46–66.

5. Ibid.

6. M. T. Hannan and J. Freeman, "Structural Inertia and Organizational Change," *American Sociological Review* 49 (1984): 149–164. M. L. Tushman and C. A. O'Reilly, *Winning Through Innovation* (Boston: Harvard Business School Press, 1997).

7. J. Pfeffer, *Managing with Power: Politics and Influence Within Organizations* (Boston: Harvard Business School Press, 1992).

8. D. Miller, *The Icarus Paradox* (New York: Harper Business, 1990).

9. E. Freeman, *Strategic Management: A Stakeholder Approach* (Boston: Pitman Press, 1984).

10. C. W. L. Hill and T. M. Jones, "Stakeholder-Agency Theory," *Journal of Management Studies* 29 (1992): 131–154. J. G. March and H. A. Simon, *Organizations* (New York: Wiley, 1958).

11. Hill and Jones, "Stakeholder-Agency Theory."

12. I. C. Macmillan and P. E. Jones, *Strategy Formulation: Power and Politics* (St. Paul, Minn.: West, 1986).

13. Tom Copeland, Tim Koller, and Jack Murrin, *Valuation: Measuring and Managing the Value of Companies* (New York: Wiley, 1996).

14. M. C. Jensen and W. H. Meckling, "Theory of the Firm: Managerial Behavior, Agency Costs and Ownership Structure," *Journal of Financial Economics* 3 (1976): 305–360. E. F. Fama, "Agency Problems and the Theory of the Firm," *Journal of Political Economy* 88 (1980): 375–390.

15. Hill and Jones, "Stakeholder-Agency Theory."

16. For example, see R. Marris, *The Economic Theory of Managerial Capitalism* (London: Macmillan, 1964), and J. K. Galbraith, *The New Industrial State* (Boston: Houghton Mifflin, 1970).

17. E. F. Fama, "Agency Problems and the Theory of the Firm," *Journal of Political Economy* 88 (1980): 375–390.

18. A. Rappaport, "New Thinking on How to Link Executive Pay with Performance," *Harvard Business Review* (March–April 1999): 91–105.

19. L. Lavelle, F. F. Jespersen, and M. Arndt, "Executive Pay," *Business Week,* April 15, 2002, pp. 80–86.

20. John Byrne et al., "How to Fix Corporate Governance," *Business Week,* May 6, 2002, pp. 69–78.

21. For academic studies that look at the determinants of CEO pay, see M. C. Jensen and K. J. Murphy, "Performance Pay and Top Management Incentives," *Journal of Political Economy* 98 (1990): 225–264. Charles W. L. Hill and Phillip Phan, "CEO Tenure as a Determinant of CEO Pay," *Academy of Management Journal* 34 (1991): 707–717. H. L. Tosi and L. R. Gomez-Mejia, "CEO Compensation Monitoring and Firm Performance," *Academy of Management Journal* 37 (1994): 1002–1016. Joseph F. Porac, James B. Wade, and Timothy G. Pollock, "Industry Categories and the Politics of the Comparable Firm in CEO Compensation," *Administrative Science Quarterly* 44 (1999): 112–144.

22. Ellen Goodman, "CEO Pay Cap: Why Not Try It for Size?" *Houston Chronicle,* April 18, 1999, p. 6.

23. For recent research on this issue, see Peter J. lane, A. A. Cannella, and M. H. Lubatkin, "Agency Problems as Antecedents to Unrelated Mergers and Diversification: Amihud and Lev Reconsidered," *Strategic Management Journal* 19 (1998): 555–578.

24. Carl Icahn, "What Ails Corporate America—and What Should Be Done?" *Business Week,* October 27, 1986, p. 101.

25. E. T. Penrose, *The Theory of the Growth of the Firm* (London: Macmillan, 1958).

26. G. J. Miller, *Managerial Dilemmas: The Political Economy of Hierarchy* (Cambridge: Cambridge University Press, 1992).

27. O. E. Williamson, *The Economic Institutions of Capitalism* (New York: Free Press, 1985).

28. Fama, "Agency Problems and the Theory of the Firm."

29. S. Finkelstein and R. D'Aveni, "CEO Duality as a Double Edged Sword," *Academy of Management Journal* 37 (1994): 1079–1108. B. Ram Baliga and R. C. Moyer, "CEO Duality and Firm Performance," *Strategic Management Journal* 17 (1996): 41–53. M. L. Mace, *Directors: Myth and Reality* (Cambridge, Mass.: Harvard University Press, 1971). S. C. Vance, *Corporate Leadership: Boards of Directors and Strategy* (New York: McGraw-Hill, 1983).

30. Michele Galen, "A Seat on the Board Is Getting Hotter," *Business Week,* July 3, 1989, pp. 72–73.

31. J. S. Lublin. "Irate Shareholders Target Ineffective Board Members," *Wall Street Journal,* November 6, 1995, p. B1.

32. Gilbert Fuchsberg, "Chief Executives See Their Power Shrink," *Wall Street Journal,* March 15, 1993, pp. B1, B3.

33. Quoted in G. Morgenson, "Stock Options Are Not a Free Lunch," *Forbes,* May 18, 1998, pp. 212–217.

34. W. G. Lewellen, C. Eoderer, and A. Rosenfeld, "Merger Decisions and Executive Stock Ownership in Acquiring Firms," *Journal of Accounting and Economics* 7 (1985): 209–231.

35. C. W. L. Hill and S. A. Snell, "External Control, Corporate Strategy, and Firm Performance," *Strategic Management Journal* 9 (1988): 577–590.

36. D. Henry and M. Conlin, "Too Much of a Good Incentive?" *Business Week,* March 4, 2002, pp. 38–39.

37. J. P. Walsh and R. D. Kosnik, "Corporate Raiders and Their Disciplinary Role in the Market for Corporate Control," *Academy of Management Journal* 36 (1993): 671–700.

38. R. S. Kaplan and D. P. Norton, "The Balanced Scorecard—Measures That Drive Performance," *Harvard Business Review* (January–February 1992): 71–79.

39. R. S. Kaplan and D. P. Norton, "Using the Balanced Scorecard as a Strategic Management System," *Harvard Business Review* (January–February 1996): 75–85.

40. R. S. Kaplan and D. P. Norton, "Putting the Balanced Scorecard to Work," *Harvard Business Review* (September–October 1993): 134–147.

41. Kaplan and Norton, "The Balanced Scorecard," p. 72.

42. Robert C. Solomon, *Ethics and Excellence* (New York: Oxford University Press, 1992).

43. Saul W. Gellerman, "Why Good Managers Make Bad Ethical Choices," in Kenneth R. Andrews (ed.), *Ethics in Practice: Managing the Moral Corporation* (Boston: Harvard Business School Press, 1989).

44. Kirk O. Hanson and Manuel Velasquez, "Hewlett-Packard Company: Managing Ethics and Values," in *Business Roundtable, Corporate Ethics: A Prime Business Asset* (February 1988).

45. For example, see R. Edward Freeman and Daniel Gilbert, *Corporate Strategy and the Search for Ethics* (Englewood Cliffs, N.J.: Prentice-Hall, 1988). Thomas Jones, "Ethical Decision Making by Individuals in Organizations," *Academy of Management Review* 16 (1991): 366–395. J. R. Rest, *Moral Development: Advances in Research and Theory* (New York: Praeger, 1986).

46. For example, see Freeman and Gilbert, *Corporate Strategy and the Search for Ethics. Jones,* "Ethical Decision Making by Individuals in Organizations." Rest, *Moral Development.*

Chapter 12

1. L. Smircich, "Concepts of Culture and Organizational Analysis," *Administrative Science Quarterly* 28 (1983): 339–358.

2. G. R. Jones and J. M. George, "The Experience and Evolution of Trust: Implications for Cooperation and Teamwork," *Academy of Management Review* 3 (1998): 531–546.

3. Ibid.

4. J. R. Galbraith, *Designing Complex Organizations* (Reading, Mass.: Addison-Wesley, 1973).

5. Alfred D. Chandler, *Strategy and Structure* (Cambridge, Mass.: MIT Press, 1962).

6. The discussion draws heavily on ibid. and B. R. Scott, *Stages of Corporate Development* (Cambridge, Mass.: Intercollegiate Clearing House, Harvard Business School, 1971).

7. R. L. Daft, *Organizational Theory and Design,* 3rd ed. (St. Paul, Minn.: West, 1986), p. 215.

8. Child, *Organization,* pp. 52–70.

9. G. R. Jones and J. Butler, "Costs, Revenues, and Business Level Strategy," *Academy of Management Review* 13 (1988): 202–213; G. R. Jones and C. W. L. Hill, "Transaction Cost Analysis of Strategy-Structure Choice," *Strategic Management Journal* 9 1988): 159–172.

10. G. R. Jones, *Organizational Theory: Text and Cases* (Englewood Cliffs, N.J.: Prentice-Hall, 2000).

11. P. Blau, "A Formal Theory of Differentiation in Organizations," *American Sociological Review* 35 (1970): 684–695.

12. G. R. Jones, "Organization-Client Transactions and Organizational Governance Structures," *Academy of Management Journal* 30 (1987): 197–218.

13. S. McCartney, "Airline Industry's Top-Ranked Woman Keeps Southwest's Small-Fry Spirit Alive," *Wall Street Journal,* November 30, 1995, p. B.1.

14. P. R. Lawrence and J. Lorsch, *Organization and Environment* (Boston: Division of Research, Harvard Business School, 1967), pp. 50–55.

15. Galbraith, *Designing Complex Organizations,* chap. 1; J. R. Galbraith and R. K. Kazanjian, *Strategy Implementation: Structure System and Process,* 2nd ed. (St. Paul, Minn.: West, 1986), chap. 7.

16. R. Simmons, "Strategic Orientation and Top Management Attention to Control Systems," *Strategic Management Journal* 12 (1991): 49–62.

17. R. Simmons, "How New Top Managers Use Control Systems as Levers of Strategic Renewal," *Strategic Management Journal* 15 (1994): 169–189.

18. W. G. Ouchi, "The Transmission of Control Through Organizational Hierarchy," *Academy of Management Journal* 21 (1978): 173–192; and W. H. Newman, *Constructive Control* (Englewood Cliffs, N.J.: Prentice-Hall, 1975).

19. E. Flamholtz, "Organizational Control Systems as a Managerial Tool," *California Management Review* (Winter 1979): 50–58.

20. O. E. Williamson, *Markets and Hierarchies* (New York: Free Press, 1975); and W. G. Ouchi, "Markets, Bureaucracies, and Clans," *Administrative Science Quarterly* 25 (1980): 129–141.

21. H. Mintzberg, *The Structuring of Organizations* (Englewood Cliffs, N.J.: Prentice-Hall, 1979), pp. 5–9.

22. E. E. Lawler III, *Motivation in Work Organizations* (Monterey, Calif.: Brooks/Cole, 1973); and Galbraith and Kazanjian, *Strategy Implementation,* chap. 6.

23. L. Smircich, "Concepts of Culture and Organizational Analysis," *Administrative Science Quarterly* 28 (1983): 339–358.

24. General Electric, Harvard Business School Case #9-385-315 (1984).

25. Ouchi, "Markets, Bureaucracies, and Clans," p. 130.

26. Jones, *Organizational Theory.*

27. J. Van Maanen and E. H. Schein, "Towards a Theory of Organizational Socialization," in B. M. Staw (ed.), *Research in Organizational Behavior* (Greenwich, Conn.: JAI Press, 1979), pp. 1, 209–264.

28. G. R. Jones, "Socialization Tactics, Self-Efficacy, and Newcomers' Adjustments to Organizations," *Academy of Management Journal* 29 (1986): 262–279.

29. J. P. Kotter and J. L. Heskett, *Corporate Culture and Performance.*

30. T. J. Peters and R. H. Waterman, *In Search of Excellence: Lessons from America's Best-Run Companies* (New York: Harper & Row, 1982).

31. G. Hamel and C. K. Prahalad, "Strategic Intent," *Harvard Business Review* (May–June 1989): 64.

32. Galbraith and Kazanjian, *Strategy Implementation.* Child, *Organization;* R. Duncan, "What Is the Right Organization Structure?" *Organizational Dynamics* (Winter 1979): 59–80.

33. W. G. Ouchi, "The Relationship Between Organizational Structure and Organizational Control," *Administrative Science Quarterly* 22 (1977): 95–113.

34. R. Bunderi, "Intel Researchers Aim to Think Big While Staying Close to Development," *Research-Technology Management* (March–April 1998): 3–4.

35. K. M. Eisenhardt, "Control: Organizational and Economic Approaches," *Management Science* 16 (1985): 134–148.

36. O. E. Williamson, *Markets and Hierarchies: Analysis and Antitrust Implications* (New York: Free Press, 1975).

37. Lawrence and Lorsch, *Organization and Environment.*

38. K. Pope, "Dell Refocuses on Groundwork to Cope with Rocketing Sales," *Wall Street Journal,* June 18, 1993, p. B5.

39. Galbraith, *Designing Complex Organizations.* Lawrence and Lorsch, *Organization and Environment.* D. Miller, "Strategy Making and Structure: Analysis and Implications for Performance," *Academy of Management Journal* 30 (1987): 7–32.

40. Michael E. Porter, *Competitive Strategy: Techniques for Analyzing Industries and Competitors* (New York: Free Press, 1980). D. Miller, "Configurations of Strategy and Structure," *Strategic Management Journal* 7 (1986): 233–249.

41. D. Miller and P. H. Freisen, *Organizations: A Quantum View* (Englewood Cliffs, N.J.: Prentice-Hall, 1984).

42. J. Woodward, *Industrial Organization: Theory and Practice* (London: Oxford University Press, 1965). Lawrence and Lorsch, *Organization and Environment.*

43. R. E. White, "Generic Business Strategies, Organizational Context and Performance: An Empirical Investigation," *Strategic Management Journal* 7 (1986): 217–231.

44. Porter, *Competitive Strategy.* Miller, "Configurations of Strategy and Structure."

45. E. Deal and A. A. Kennedy, *Corporate Cultures* (Reading, Mass.: Addison-Wesley, 1985). "Corporate Culture," *Business Week,* October 27, 1980, pp. 148–160.

46. S. M. Davis and R. R. Lawrence, *Matrix* (Reading, Mass.: Addison-Wesley, 1977). J. R. Galbraith, "Matrix Organization Designs: How to Combine Functional and Project Forms," *Business Horizons* 14 (1971): 29–40.

47. Duncan, "What Is the Right Organizational Structure?" Davis and Lawrence, *Matrix.*

48. B. Saporito, "How to Revive a Fading Firm," *Fortune,* March 22, 1993, p. 80.

49. D. Miller, "Configurations of Strategy and Structure," in R. E. Miles and C. C. Snow (eds.), *Organizational Strategy, Structure, and Process* (New York: McGraw-Hill, 1978).

50. G. D. Bruton, J. K. Keels, and C. L. Shook, "Downsizing the Firm: Answering the Strategic Questions," *Academy of Management Executive* (May 1996): 38–45.

51. M. Hammer and J. Champy, *Reengineering the Corporation* (New York: HarperCollins, 1993).

52. Ibid., p. 39.

Chapter 13

1. Alfred D. Chandler, *Strategy and Structure* (Cambridge, Mass.: MIT Press, 1962). Williamson, *Markets and Hierarchies* (New York: Free Press). L. Wrigley, "Divisional Autonomy and Diversification" (Ph.D. diss., Harvard Business School, 1970).

2. R. P. Rumelt, *Strategy, Structure, and Economic Performance* (Boston: Division of Research, Harvard Business School, 1974). B. R. Scott, *Stages of Corporate Development* (Cambridge, Mass.: Intercollegiate Clearing House, Harvard Business School, 1971). Williamson, *Markets and Hierarchies.*

3. The discussion draws on each of the sources cited in endnotes 20–27 and on G. R. Jones and C. W. L. Hill, "Transaction Cost Analysis of Strategy-Structure Choice," *Strategic Management Journal* 9 (1988): 159–172.

4. H. O. Armour and D. J. Teece, "Organizational Structure and Economic Performance: A Test of the Multidivisional Hypothesis," *Bell Journal of Economics* 9 (1978): 106–122.

5. Alfred Sloan, *My Years at General Motors* (New York: Doubleday, 1983), chap. 3.

6. Jones and Hill, "Transaction Cost Analysis of Strategy."

7. Ibid.

8. R. A. D'Aveni and D. J. Ravenscraft, "Economies of Integration Versus Bureaucracy Costs: Does Vertical Integration Improve Performance?" *Academy of Management Journal* 5 (1994): 1167–1206.

9. Lawrence and Lorsch, *Organization and Environment.* J. R. Galbraith, *Designing Complex Organizations* (Reading, Mass.: Addison-Wesley, 1973). Michael Porter, *Competitive Advantage: Creating and Sustaining Superior Performance* (New York: Free Press, 1985).

10. P. R. Nayyar, "Performance Effects of Information Asymmetry and Economies of Scope in Diversified Service Firm," *Academy of Management Journal* 36 (1993): 28–57.

11. **www.hp.com,** 2002.

12. L. R. Gomez-Mejia, "Structure and Process of Diversification, Compensation Strategy, and Performance," *Strategic Management Journal* 13 (1992): 381–397.

13. J. Stopford and L. Wells, *Managing the Multinational Enterprise* (London: Longman, 1972).

14. C. A. Bartlett and S. Ghoshal, *Managing Across Borders: The Transnational Solution* (Cambridge, Mass.: Harvard Business School, 1991).

15. R. A. Burgelman, "Managing the New Venture Division: Research Findings and the Implications for Strategic Management," *Strategic Management Journal* 6 (1985): 39–54.

16. N. D. Fast, "The Future of Industrial New Venture Departments," *Industrial Marketing Management* 8 (1979): 264–279.

17. G. Imperato, "3M Expert Tells How to Run Meetings That Really Work," *Fast Company,* May 23, 1999, p. 18.

18. Burgelman, "Managing the New Venture Division."

19. R. A. Burgelman, "Corporate Entrepreneurship and Strategic Management: Insights from a Process Study," *Management Science* 29 (1983): 1349–1364.

20. R. Jones, "Towards a Positive Interpretation of Transaction Cost Theory: The Central Role of Entrepreneurship and Trust," in M. Hitt, R. E. Freeman, and J. S. Harrison (eds.), *Handbook of Strategic Management* (London: Blackwell, 2001), pp. 208–228.

21. M. Prendergast, "Is Coke Turning into a Mickey Mouse Outfit," *Wall Street Journal,* March 5, 2001, p. A.22.

22. M. S. Salter and W. A. Weinhold, *Diversification Through Acquisition* (New York: Free Press, 1979).

23. F. T. Paine and D. J. Power, "Merger Strategy: An Examination of Drucker's Five Rules for Successful Acquisitions," *Strategic Management Journal* 5 (1984): 99–110.

24. H. Singh and C. A. Montgomery, "Corporate Acquisitions and Economic Performance," unpublished manuscript, 1984.

25. B. Worthen, "Nestlé's ERP Odyssey," *CIO,* May 15, 2002, pp. 1–5.

26. G. D. Bruton, B. M. Oviatt, and M. A. White, "Performance of Acquisitions of Distressed Firms," *Academy of Management Journal* 4 (1994): 972–989.

27. C. K. Prahalad and R. A. Bettis, "The Dominant Logic: A New Linkage Between Diversity and Performance," *Strategic Management Journal* 7 (1986): 485–501. Porter, *Competitive Strategy.*

28. T. Dewett and G. R. Jones, "The Role of Information Technology in the Organization: A Review, Model, and Assessment," *Journal of Management* 27 (2001): 313–346.

29. Porter, 1996; Prahalad and Hamel, 1990

30. Rucker, 2000.

31. Prahalad and Hamel

32. Ibid.

33. "Andersen's Androids," *Economist,* May 4, 1996, p. 72.

34. Fulk and DeSanctis, 1995.

35. G. S. Capowski, "Designing a Corporate Identity," *Management Review* (June 1993): 37–38.

36. J. Marcia, "Just Doing It," *Distribution* (January 1995): 36–40.

Appendix:
Analyzing a Case Study and Writing a Case Study Analysis

What Is Case Study Analysis?

Case study analysis is an integral part of a course in strategic management. The purpose of a case study is to provide students with experience of the strategic management problems that actual organizations face. A case study presents an account of what happened to a business or industry over a number of years. It chronicles the events that managers had to deal with, such as changes in the competitive environment, and charts the managers' response, which usually involved changing the business- or corporate-level strategy. Cases cover a wide range of issues and problems that managers have had to confront. Some cases are about finding the right business-level strategy to compete in changing conditions. Some are about companies that grew by acquisition, with little concern for the rationale behind their growth, and how growth by acquisition affected their future profitability. Each case is different because each organization is different. The underlying thread in all cases, however, is the use of strategic management techniques to solve business problems.

Cases prove valuable in a strategic management course for several reasons. First, cases provide you, the student, with experience of organizational problems that you probably have not had the opportunity to experience firsthand. In a relatively short period of time, you will have the chance to appreciate and analyze the problems faced by many different companies and to understand how managers tried to deal with them.

Second, cases illustrate the theory and content of strategic management—that is, all the information presented to you in the previous chapters of this book. This information has been collected, discovered, and distilled from the observations, research, and experience of managers and academicians. The meaning and implications of this information are made clearer when they are applied to case studies. The theory and concepts help reveal what is going on in the companies studied and allow you to evaluate the solutions that specific companies adopted to deal with their problems. Consequently, when you analyze cases, you will be like a detective who, with a set of conceptual tools, probes what happened and what or who was responsible and then marshals the evidence that provides the solution. Top managers enjoy the thrill of testing their problem-solving abilities in the real world. It is important to remember that no one knows what the right answer is. All that managers can do is to make the best guess. In fact, managers say repeatedly that they are happy if they are right only half the time in solving strategic problems. Strategic management is an uncertain game, and using cases to see how theory can be put into practice is one way of improving your skills of diagnostic investigation.

Third, case studies provide you with the opportunity to participate in class and to gain experience in presenting your ideas to others. Instructors may sometimes call on students as a group to identify what is going on in a case, and through classroom discussion the issues in and solutions to the case problem will reveal themselves. In such a situation, you will have to organize your views and conclusions so that you can present them to the class. Your classmates may have analyzed the issues differently from you, and they will want you to argue your points before they will accept your conclusions, so be prepared for debate. This mode of discussion is an example of the dialectical approach to decision making set out in Chapter 1. This is how decisions are made in the actual business world.

Instructors also may assign an individual, but more commonly a group, to analyze the case before the whole class. The individual or group probably will be responsible for a thirty- to forty-minute presentation of the case to the class. That presentation must cover the issues posed, the problems facing the company, and a series of recommendations for resolving the problems. The discussion then will be thrown open to the class, and you will have to defend your ideas. Through such discussions and presentations, you will experience how to convey your ideas effectively to others. Remember that a great deal of managers' time is spent in these kinds of situations: presenting their ideas and engaging in discussion with other managers who have their own views about what is going on. Thus, you will experience in the classroom the actual process of strategic management, and this will serve you well in your future career.

If you work in groups to analyze case studies, you also will learn about the group process involved in working as a team. When people work in groups, it is often difficult to schedule time and allocate responsibility for the case analysis. There are always group members who shirk their responsibilities and group members who are so sure of their own ideas that they try to dominate the group's analysis. Most of the strategic management takes place in groups, however, and it is best if you learn about these problems now.

Analyzing a Case Study

The purpose of the case study is to let you apply the concepts of strategic management when you analyze the issues facing a specific company. To analyze a case study, therefore, you must examine closely the issues confronting the company. Most often you will need to read the case several times—once to grasp the overall picture of what is happening to the company and then several times more to discover and grasp the specific problems.

Generally, detailed analysis of a case study should include eight areas:

1. The history, development, and growth of the company over time

2. The identification of the company's internal strengths and weaknesses

3. The nature of the external environment surrounding the company

4. A SWOT analysis

5. The kind of corporate-level strategy that the company is pursuing

6. The nature of the company's business-level strategy

7. The company's structure and control systems and how they match its strategy

8. Recommendations

To analyze a case, you need to apply the concepts taught in this course to each of these areas. Where to look for a review of the concepts you need to use is obvious from the chapter titles. For example, to analyze the company's environment, you would use Chapter 2, on environmental analysis. To help you further, we next offer a summary of the steps you can take to analyze the case material for each of the eight points we just noted:

1. *Analyze the company's history, development, and growth.* A convenient way to investigate how a company's past strategy and structure affect it in the present is to chart the critical incidents in its history—that is, the events that were the most unusual or the most essential for its development into the company it is today. Some of the events have to do with its founding, its initial products, how it makes new-product market decisions, and how it developed and chose functional competencies to pursue. Its entry into new businesses and shifts in its main lines of business are also important milestones to consider.

2. *Identify the company's internal strengths and weaknesses.* Once the historical profile is completed, you can begin the SWOT analysis. Use all the incidents you have charted to develop an account of the company's strengths and weaknesses as they have emerged historically. Examine each of the value creation functions of the company, and identify the functions in which the company is currently strong and currently weak. Some companies might be weak in marketing; some might be strong in research and development. Make lists of these strengths and weaknesses. The SWOT Checklist (Table 1) gives examples of what might go in these lists.

3. *Analyze the external environment.* To identify environmental opportunities and threats, apply all the concepts from Chapter 2 on industry and macroenvironments to analyze the environment the company is confronting. Of particular importance at the industry level are Porter's five forces model and the stage of the life cycle model. Which factors in the macroenvironment will appear salient depends on the specific company being analyzed. Use each factor in turn (for instance, demographic factors) to see whether it is relevant for the company in question.

   Having done this analysis, you will have generated both an analysis of the company's environment and a list of opportunities and threats. The SWOT Checklist table also lists some common environmental opportunities and threats that you may look for, but the list you generate will be specific to your company.

4. *Evaluate the SWOT analysis.* Having identified the company's external opportunities and threats as well as its internal strengths and weaknesses, consider what your findings mean. You need to balance strengths and weaknesses against opportunities and threats. Is the company in an overall strong competitive position? Can it continue to pursue its current business- or corporate-level strategy profitably? What can the company do to turn weaknesses into strengths and threats into opportunities? Can it develop new functional, business, or corporate strategies to accomplish this change? *Never merely generate the SWOT analysis and then put it aside.* Because it provides a succinct summary of the company's condition, a good SWOT analysis is the key to all the analyses that follow. Chapters 3 and 4 provide a wealth of material that can be used to guide your thinking here.

5. *Analyze corporate-level strategy.* To analyze corporate-level strategy, you first need to define the company's mission and goals. Sometimes the mission and goals are

---

TABLE 1

A SWOT Checklist

Potential internal strengths	Potential internal weaknesses
Many product lines?	Obsolete, narrow product lines?
Broad market coverage?	Rising manufacturing costs?
Manufacturing competence?	Decline in R&D innovations?
Good marketing skills?	Poor marketing plan?
Good materials management systems?	Poor material management systems?
R&D skills and leadership?	Loss of customer good will?
Information system competencies?	Inadequate human resources?
Human resource competencies?	Inadequate information systems?
Brand name reputation?	Loss of brand name capital?
Portfolio management skills?	Growth without direction?
Cost of differentiation advantage?	Bad portfolio management?
New-venture management expertise?	Loss of corporate direction?
Appropriate management style?	Infighting among divisions?
Appropriate organizational structure?	Loss of corporate control?
Appropriate control systems?	Inappropriate organizational structure and control systems?
Ability to manage strategic change?	
Well-developed corporate strategy?	High conflict and politics?
Good financial management?	Poor financial management?
Others?	Others?
Potential environmental opportunities	Potential environmental threats
Expand core business(es)?	Attacks on core business(es)?
Exploit new market segments?	Increases in domestic competition?
Widen product range?	Increase in foreign competition?
Extend cost or differentiation advantage?	Change in consumer tastes?
Diversify into new growth businesses?	Fall in barriers to entry?
Expand into foreign markets?	Rise in new or substitute products?
Apply R&D skills in new areas?	Increase in industry rivalry?
Enter new related businesses?	New forms of industry competition?
Vertically integrate forward?	Potential for takeover?
Vertically integrate backward?	Existence of corporate raiders?
Enlarge corporate portfolio?	Increase in regional competition?
Overcome barriers to entry?	Changes in demographic factors?
Reduce rivalry among competitors?	Changes in economic factors?
Make profitable new acquisitions?	Downturn in economy?
Apply brand name capital in new areas?	Rising labor costs?
Seek fast market growth?	Slower market growth?
Others?	Others?

stated explicitly in the case; at other times, you will have to infer them from available information. The information you need to collect to find out the company's corporate strategy includes such factors as its lines of business and the nature of its subsidiaries and acquisitions. It is important to analyze the relationship among the company's businesses. Do they trade or exchange resources? Are there gains to be achieved from synergy? Alternatively, is the company just running a portfolio of investments? This analysis should enable you to define the corporate strategy that the company is pursuing (for example, related or unrelated diversification, or a combination of both) and to conclude whether the company operates in just one core business. Then, using your SWOT analysis, debate the merits of this strategy. Is it appropriate given the environment the company is in? Could a change in corporate strategy provide the company with new opportunities or transform a weakness into a strength? For example, should the company diversify from its core business into new businesses?

Other issues should be considered as well. How and why has the company's strategy changed over time? What is the claimed rationale for any changes? Often, it is a good idea to analyze the company's businesses or products to assess its situation and identify which divisions contribute the most to or detract from its competitive advantage. It is also useful to explore how the company has built its portfolio over time. Did it acquire new businesses, or did it internally venture its own? All of these factors provide clues about the company and indicate ways of improving its future performance.

6. *Analyze business-level strategy.* Once you know the company's corporate-level strategy and have done the SWOT analysis, the next step is to identify the company's business-level strategy. If the company is a single-business company, its business-level strategy is identical to its corporate-level strategy. If the company is in many businesses, each business will have its own business-level strategy. You will need to identify the company's generic competitive strategy—differentiation, low cost, or focus—and its investment strategy, given its relative competitive position and the stage of the life cycle. The company also may market different products using different business-level strategies. For example, it may offer a low-cost product range and a line of differentiated products. Be sure to give a full account of a company's business-level strategy to show how it competes.

Identifying the functional strategies that a company pursues to build competitive advantage through superior efficiency, quality, innovation, and customer responsiveness and to achieve its business-level strategy is very important. The SWOT analysis will have provided you with information on the company's functional competencies. You should investigate its production, marketing, or research and development strategy further to gain a picture of where the company is going. For example, pursuing a low-cost or a differentiation strategy successfully requires very different sets of competencies. Has the company developed the right ones? If it has, how can it exploit them further? Can it pursue both a low-cost and a differentiation strategy simultaneously?

The SWOT analysis is especially important at this point if the industry analysis, particularly Porter's model, has revealed threats to the company from the environment. Can the company deal with these threats? How should it change its business-level strategy to counter them? To evaluate the potential of a company's business-level strategy, you must first perform a thorough SWOT analysis that captures the essence of its problems.

Once you complete this analysis, you will have a full picture of the way the company is operating and be in a position to evaluate the potential of its strategy. Thus, you will be able to make recommendations concerning the pattern of its future actions. However, first you need to consider strategy implementation, or the way the company tries to achieve its strategy.

7. *Analyze structure and control systems.* The aim of this analysis is to identify what structure and control systems the company is using to implement its strategy and to evaluate whether that structure is the appropriate one for the company. As we discuss in Chapters 12 and 13, different corporate and business strategies require

different structures. These chapters provide you with the conceptual tools to determine *the degree of fit between the company's strategy and structure.* For example, does the company have the right level of vertical differentiation (e.g., does it have the appropriate number of levels in the hierarchy or decentralized control?) or horizontal differentiation (does it use a functional structure when it should be using a product structure?)? Similarly, is the company using the right integration or control systems to manage its operations? Are managers being appropriately rewarded? Are the right rewards in place for encouraging cooperation among divisions? These are all issues to consider.

In some cases, there will be little information on these issues, whereas in others there will be a lot. In analyzing each case, you should gear the analysis toward its most salient issues. For example, organizational conflict, power, and politics will be important issues for some companies. Try to analyze why problems in these areas are occurring. Do they occur because of bad strategy formulation or because of bad strategy implementation?

Organizational change is an issue in many cases because the companies are attempting to alter their strategies or structures to solve strategic problems. Thus, as part of the analysis, you might suggest an action plan that the company in question could use to achieve its goals. For example, you might list in a logical sequence the steps the company would need to follow to alter its business-level strategy from differentiation to focus.

8. *Make recommendations.* The quality of your recommendations is a direct result of the thoroughness with which you prepared the case analysis. Recommendations are directed at solving whatever strategic problem the company is facing and increasing its future profitability. Your recommendations should be in line with your analysis; that is, they should follow logically from the previous discussion. For example, your recommendation generally will center on the specific ways of changing functional, business, and corporate strategies and organizational structure and control to improve business performance. The set of recommendations will be specific to each case, and so it is difficult to discuss these recommendations here. Such recommendations might include an increase in spending on specific research and development projects, the divesting of certain businesses, a change from a strategy of unrelated to related diversification, an increase in the level of integration among divisions by using task forces and teams, or a move to a different kind of structure to implement a new business-level strategy. Make sure your recommendations are mutually consistent and written in the form of an action plan. The plan might contain a timetable that sequences the actions for changing the company's strategy and a description of how changes at the corporate level will necessitate changes at the business level and subsequently at the functional level.

After following all these stages, you will have performed a thorough analysis of the case and will be in a position to join in class discussion or present your ideas to the class, depending on the format used by your professor. Remember that you must tailor your analysis to suit the specific issue discussed in your case. In some cases, you might completely omit one of the steps in the analysis because it is not relevant to the situation you are considering. You must be sensitive to the needs of the case and not apply the framework we have discussed in this section blindly. The framework is meant only as a guide, not as an outline.

Writing a Case Study Analysis

Often, as part of your course requirements, you will need to present a written case analysis. This may be an individual or a group report. Whatever the situation, there are certain guidelines to follow in writing a case analysis that will improve the evaluation your work will receive from your instructor. Before we discuss these guidelines and before you use them, make sure that they do not conflict with any directions your instructor has given you.

The structure of your written report is critical. Generally, if you follow the steps for analysis discussed in the previous section, *you already will have a good structure for your written discussion.* All reports begin with an *introduction* to the case. In it, outline briefly what the company does, how it developed historically, what problems it is experiencing, and how you are going to approach the issues in the case write-up. Do this sequentially by writing, for example, "First, we discuss the environment of Company X. . . . Third, we discuss Company X's business-level strategy. . . . Last, we provide recommendations for turning around Company X's business."

In the second part of the case write-up, the *strategic analysis* section, do the SWOT analysis, analyze and discuss the nature and problems of the company's business-level and corporate strategies, and then analyze its structure and control systems. Make sure you use plenty of headings and subheadings to structure your analysis. For example, have separate sections on any important conceptual tool you use. Thus, you might have a section on Porter's five forces model as part of your analysis of the environment. You might offer a separate section on portfolio techniques when analyzing a company's corporate strategy. Tailor the sections and subsections to the specific issues of importance in the case.

In the third part of the case write-up, present your *solutions and recommendations.* Be comprehensive, and make sure they are in line with the previous analysis so that the recommendations fit together and move logically from one to the next. The recommendations section is very revealing because your instructor will have a good idea of how much work you put into the case from the quality of your recommendations.

Following this framework will provide a good structure for most written reports, though it must be shaped to fit the individual case being considered. Some cases are about excellent companies experiencing no problems. In such instances, it is hard to write recommendations. Instead, you can focus on analyzing why the company is doing so well, using that analysis to structure the discussion. Following are some minor suggestions that can help make a good analysis even better:

1. Do not repeat in summary form large pieces of factual information from the case. The instructor has read the case and knows what is going on. Rather, use the information in the case to illustrate your statements, defend your arguments, or make salient points. Beyond the brief introduction to the company, you must avoid being *descriptive;* instead, you must be *analytical.*

2. Make sure the sections and subsections of your discussion flow logically and smoothly from one to the next. That is, try to build on what has gone before so that the analysis of the case study moves toward a climax. This is particularly important for group analysis, because there is a tendency for people in a group to split up the work and say, "I'll do the beginning, you take the middle, and I'll do the end." The result is a choppy, stilted analysis; the parts do not flow from one to the next, and it is obvious to the instructor that no real group work has been done.

3. Avoid grammatical and spelling errors. They make your work look sloppy.

4. In some instances, cases dealing with well-known companies end in 1998 or 1999 because no later information was available when the case was written. If possible, do a search for more information on what has happened to the company in subsequent years.

   Many libraries now have comprehensive web-based electronic data search facilities that offer such sources as *ABI/Inform*, *The Wall Street Journal Index*, the *F&S Index*, and the *Nexis-Lexis* databases. These enable you to identify any article that has been written in the business press on the company of your choice within the past few years. A number of nonelectronic data sources are also useful. For example, *F&S Predicasts* publishes an annual list of articles relating to major companies that appeared in the national and international business press. *S&P Industry Surveys* is a great source for basic industry data, and *Value Line Ratings and Reports* can contain good summaries of a firm's financial position and future prospects. You will also want to collect full financial information on the company. Again, this can be accessed from web-based electronic databases such as the Edgar database, which archives all forms that publicly quoted companies have to file with the Securities and Exchange Commission (SEC; e.g., 10-K filings can be accessed from the SEC's Edgar database). Most SEC forms for public companies can now be accessed from Internet-based financial sites, such as Yahoo's finance site (**http://finance.yahoo.com/**).

5. Sometimes instructors hand out questions for each case to help you in your analysis. Use these as a guide for writing the case analysis. They often illuminate the important issues that have to be covered in the discussion.

   If you follow the guidelines in this section, you should be able to write a thorough and effective evaluation.

Guidelines for the Strategic Management Project

The case study guidelines also can be followed to help you conduct research for the Strategic Management Project Modules at the end of every chapter in this book. In order to answer the questions contained in each module, for example, it is necessary to locate and access articles on your chosen company in the same way that you will update the information on companies highlighted in the case studies. Obviously, however, you need to collect more information on your chosen company because it is *your case*.

The guidelines also can be used to help you write your Strategic Management Project. The experience you develop from analyzing one or more of the companies in the case studies and writing the resulting report should help you improve the analytical skills needed for the Strategic Management Project. Essentially, in your Strategic Management Project, you are writing about and analyzing a company at the same time to show how that company creates value through its strategy and structure.

The Role of Financial Analysis in Case Study Analysis

An important aspect of analyzing a case study and writing a case study analysis is the role and use of financial information. A careful analysis of the company's financial condition immensely improves a case write-up. After all, financial data represent the concrete results of the company's strategy and structure. Although analyzing financial statements can be quite complex, a general idea of a company's financial position can be determined through the use of ratio analysis. Financial performance ratios can be calculated from the balance sheet and income statement. These ratios can be classified into five subgroups: profit ratios, liquidity ratios, activity ratios, leverage ratios, and shareholder-return ratios. These ratios should be compared with the industry average or the company's prior years of performance. It should be noted, however, that deviation from the average is not necessarily bad; it simply warrants further investigation. For example, young companies will have purchased assets at a different price and will likely have a different capital structure than older companies do. In addition to ratio analysis, a company's cash flow position is of critical importance and should be assessed. Cash flow shows how much actual cash a company possesses.

Profit Ratios   Profit ratios measure the efficiency with which the company uses its resources. The more efficient the company, the greater is its profitability. It is useful to compare a company's profitability against that of its major competitors in its industry to determine whether the company is operating more or less efficiently than its rivals. In addition, the change in a company's profit ratios over time tells whether its performance is improving or declining.

A number of different profit ratios can be used, and each of them measures a different aspect of a company's performance. Here, we look at the most commonly used profit ratios.

Return on Invested Capital. This ratio measures the profit earned on the capital invested in the company. It is defined as follows:

$$\text{Return on invested capital (ROIC)} = \frac{\text{Net profit}}{\text{Invested capital}}$$

Net profit is calculated by subtracting the total costs of operating the company away from its total revenues (total revenues − total costs). Total costs are the (1) costs of goods sold, (2) sales, general, and administrative expenses, (3) R&D expenses, and (4) other expenses. Net profit can be calculated before or after taxes, although many financial analysts prefer the before-tax figure. Invested capital is the amount that is invested in the operations of a company, that is, in property, plant, equipment, inventories, and other assets. Invested capital comes from two main sources: interest-bearing debt and shareholders' equity. Interest-bearing debt is money the company borrows from banks and from those who purchase its bonds. Shareholders' equity is the money raised from selling shares to the public, *plus* earnings that have been retained by the company in prior years and are available to fund current investments. ROIC measures the effectiveness with which a company is using the capital funds that it has available for investment. As such, it is recognized to be an excellent measure of the value a company is creating.[1] Remember that a company's ROIC can be decomposed into its constituent parts. Chapter 3 lays out how to do this.

Return on Total Assets (ROA). This ratio measures the profit earned on the employment of assets. It is defined as follows:

$$\text{Return on total assests} = \frac{\text{Net profit}}{\text{Total assets}}$$

Return on Stockholders' Equity (ROE). This ratio measures the percentage of profit earned on common stockholders' investment in the company. It is defined as follows:

[1] Tom Copeland, Tim Koller, and Jack Murrin, *Valuation: Measuring and Managing the Value of Companies* (New York: Wiley, 1996).

$$\text{Return on stockholders' equity} = \frac{\text{Net profit}}{\text{Stockholders' equity}}$$

If a company has no debt, this will be the same as ROIC.

Liquidity Ratios   A company's liquidity is a measure of its ability to meet short-term obligations. An asset is deemed liquid if it can be readily converted into cash. Liquid assets are current assets such as cash, marketable securities, accounts receivable, and so on. Two liquidity ratios are commonly used.

Current Ratio. The current ratio measures the extent to which the claims of short-term creditors are covered by assets that can be quickly converted into cash. Most companies should have a ratio of at least 1, because failure to meet these commitments can lead to bankruptcy. The ratio is defined as follows:

$$\text{Current ratio} = \frac{\text{Current assets}}{\text{Current liabilities}}$$

Quick Ratio. The quick ratio measures a company's ability to pay off the claims of short-term creditors without relying on selling its inventories. This is a valuable measure since in practice the sale of inventories is often difficult. It is defined as follows:

$$\text{Quick ratio} = \frac{\text{Current assets 2 inventory}}{\text{Current liabilities}}$$

Activity Ratios   Activity ratios indicate how effectively a company is managing its assets. Two ratios are particularly useful.

Inventory Turnover. This measures the number of times inventory is turned over. It is useful in determining whether a firm is carrying excess stock in inventory. It is defined as follows:

$$\text{Inventory turnover} = \frac{\text{Cost of goods sold}}{\text{Inventory}}$$

Cost of goods sold is a better measure of turnover than sales because it is the cost of the inventory items. Inventory is taken at the balance sheet date. Some companies choose to compute an average inventory, beginning inventory, and ending inventory, but for simplicity, use the inventory at the balance sheet date.

Days Sales Outstanding (DSO) or Average Collection Period. This ratio is the average time a company has to wait to receive its cash after making a sale. It measures how effective the company's credit, billing, and collection procedures are. It is defined as follows:

$$\text{DSO} = \frac{\text{Accounts receivable}}{\text{Total sales}/360}$$

Accounts receivable is divided by average daily sales. The use of 360 is the standard number of days for most financial analysis.

Leverage Ratios   A company is said to be highly leveraged if it uses more debt than equity, including stock and retained earnings. The balance between debt and equity is called the *capital structure*. The optimal capital structure is determined by the individual company. Debt has a lower cost because creditors take less risk; they know they will get their interest and principal. However, debt can be risky to the firm because if enough profit is not made to cover the interest and principal payments, bankruptcy can result. Three leverage ratios are commonly used.

Debt-to-Assets Ratio. The debt-to-assets ratio is the most direct measure of the extent to which borrowed funds have been used to finance a company's investments. It is defined as follows:

$$\text{Debt-to-assets ratio} = \frac{\text{Total debt}}{\text{Total assets}}$$

Total debt is the sum of a company's current liabilities and its long-term debt, and total assets are the sum of fixed assets and current assets.

Debt-to-Equity Ratio. The debt-to-equity ratio indicates the balance between debt and equity in a company's capital structure. This is perhaps the most widely used measure of a company's leverage. It is defined as follows:

$$\text{Debt-to-equity ratio} = \frac{\text{Total debt}}{\text{Total equity}}$$

Times-Covered Ratio. The times-covered ratio measures the extent to which a company's gross profit covers its annual interest payments. If this ratio declines to less than 1, the company is unable to meet its interest costs and is technically insolvent. The ratio is defined as follows:

$$\text{Times-covered ratio} = \frac{\text{Profit before interest and tax}}{\text{Total interest charges}}$$

Shareholder-Return Ratios   Shareholder-return ratios measure the return that shareholders earn from holding stock in the company. Given the goal of maximizing stockholders' wealth, providing shareholders with an adequate rate of return is a primary objective of most companies. As with profit ratios, it can be helpful to compare a company's shareholder returns against those of similar companies as a yardstick for determining how well the company is satisfying the demands of this particularly important group of organizational constituents. Four ratios are commonly used.

Total Shareholder Returns. Total shareholder returns measure the returns earned by time $t + 1$ on an investment in a company's stock made at time t. (Time t is the time at which the initial investment is made.) Total shareholder returns include both dividend payments and appreciation in the value of the stock (adjusted for stock splits) and are defined as follows:

$$\text{Total shareholder returns} = \frac{\begin{array}{c}\text{Stock price } (t + 1) - \text{stock price } (t) \\ + \text{ sum of annual dividends per share}\end{array}}{\text{Stock price } (t)}$$

If a shareholder invests $2 at time t and at time $t + 1$ the share is worth $3, while the sum of annual dividends for the period t to $t + 1$ has amounted to $0.20, total shareholder returns are equal to $(3 - 2 + 0.2)/2 = 0.6$, which is a 60 percent return on an initial investment of $2 made at time t.

Price-Earnings Ratio. The price-earnings ratio measures the amount investors are willing to pay per dollar of profit. It is defined as follows:

$$\text{Price-earnings ratio} = \frac{\text{Market price per share}}{\text{Earnings per share}}$$

Market-to-Book Value. Market-to-book value measures a company's expected future growth prospects. It is defined as follows:

$$\text{Market-to-book value} = \frac{\text{Market price per share}}{\text{Earnings per share}}$$

Dividend Yield. The dividend yield measures the return to shareholders received in the form of dividends. It is defined as follows:

$$\text{Dividend yield} = \frac{\text{Dividend per share}}{\text{Market price per share}}$$

Market price per share can be calculated for the first of the year, in which case the dividend yield refers to the return on an investment made at the beginning of the year. Alternatively, the average share price over the year may be used. A company must decide how much of its profits to pay to stockholders and how much to reinvest in the company. Companies with strong growth prospects should have a lower dividend payout ratio than mature companies. The rationale is that shareholders can invest the money elsewhere if the company is not growing. The optimal ratio depends on the individual firm, but the key decider is whether the company can produce better returns than the investor can earn elsewhere.

Cash Flow   Cash flow position is cash received minus cash distributed. The net cash flow can be taken from a company's statement of cash flows. Cash flow is important for what it reveals about a company's financing needs. A strong positive cash flow enables a company to fund future investments without having to borrow money from bankers or investors. This is desirable because the company avoids paying out interest or dividends. A weak or negative cash flow means that a company has to turn to external sources to fund future investments. Generally, companies in strong-growth industries often find themselves in a poor cash flow position (because their investment needs are substantial), whereas successful companies based in mature industries generally find themselves in a strong cash flow position.

A company's internally generated cash flow is calculated by adding back its depreciation provision to profits after interest, taxes, and dividend payments. If this figure is insufficient to cover proposed new investments, the company has little choice but to borrow funds to make up the shortfall or to curtail investments. If this figure exceeds proposed new investments, the company can use the excess to build up its liquidity (that is, through investments in financial assets) or repay existing loans ahead of schedule.

Conclusion

When evaluating a case, it is important to be *systematic*. Analyze the case in a logical fashion, beginning with the identification of operating and financial strengths and weaknesses and environmental opportunities and threats. Move on to assess the value of a company's current strategies only when you are fully conversant with the SWOT analysis of the company. Ask yourself whether the company's current strategies make sense given its SWOT analysis. If they do not, what changes need to be made? What are your recommendations? Above all, link any strategic recommendations you may make to the SWOT analysis. State explicitly how the strategies you identify take advantage of the company's strengths to exploit environmental opportunities, how they rectify the company's weaknesses, and how they counter environmental threats. Also, do not forget to outline what needs to be done to implement your recommendations.

Index